LONGMAN STUDENT
ATLAS

AUTHOR Olly Phillipson

CHIEF CONSULTANT Dr Stephen Scoffham

KEY STAGE 4 CONSULTANT Dr David Lambert

EDITORIAL CONSULTANTS Paul Baker, Denise Freeman, Joanne Norcup

PEARSON
Longman

CONTENTS

HOW TO USE THE ATLAS

This atlas has two main purposes: to locate places in the physical world and to explore important issues in geography. To introduce these issues and explain how they relate to a particular region, statistics, graphs, diagrams and photos accompany each map. Much of the data can be compared across different continents so that broader trends can be studied. In addition, a number of topics are explored in greater depth in 'Focus on...' pages, found in each section.

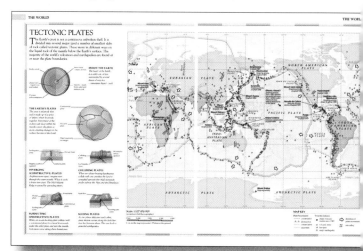

WORLD MAPS

This section contains nine world maps covering key themes such as quality of life, population trends, the world economy, climate and tectonic plates. This section also includes 'Focus on...' pages, which look at major worldwide issues such as HIV/AIDS, climate change and access to fresh water.

Shows the location of the region in relation to the rest of the world

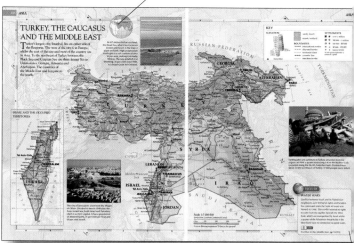

REGIONAL MAPS

Each regional map has a brief introduction to some of the main trends or issues in the region. Photographs illustrate different aspects of the area's physical and human geography.

Regional maps includ a short 'Focus on...' b to highlight an impor issue in the region. T often link to one of th longer 'Focus on...' pa or contain useful web for further research.

Fact box for extra information

A detailed physical map of the continent shows major natural geographic features

CONTINENTAL SECTIONS

Each continental section opens with six main maps: political, physical, climate, population, land use and environment. On each page, tables, graphs, and smaller maps are included to provide more detailed information about the continent.

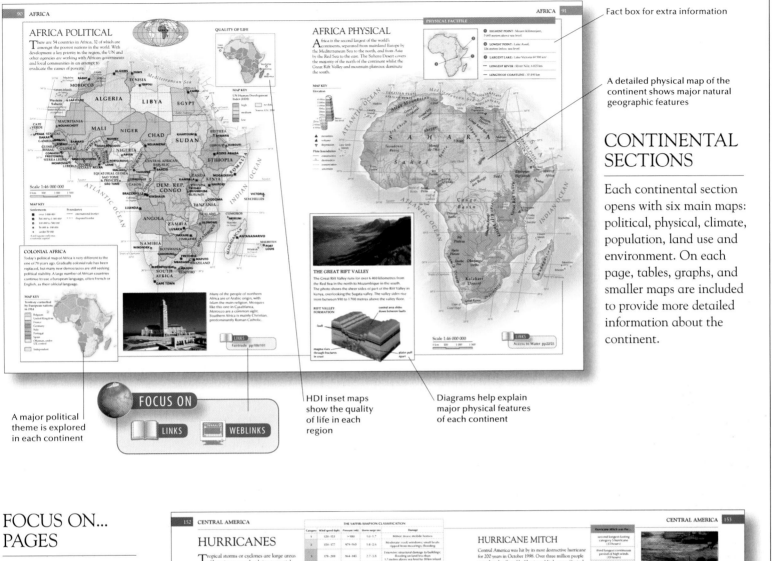

A major political theme is explored in each continent

HDI inset maps show the quality of life in each region

Diagrams help explain major physical features of each continent

FOCUS ON... PAGES

These pages focus on big themes in geography today, starting with an introduction to the issue — for example hurricanes — followed by an in-depth study of that issue in a particular region.

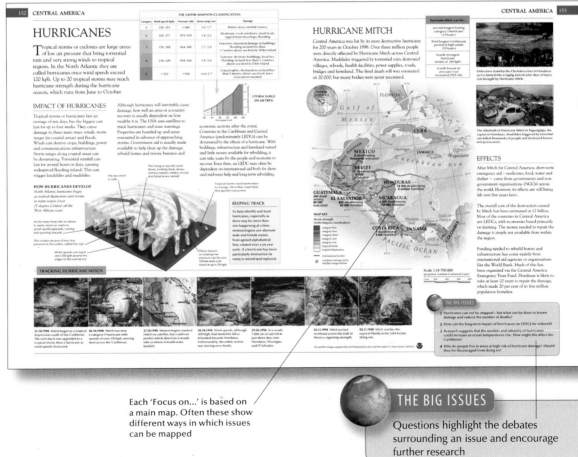

Each 'Focus on...' is based on a main map. Often these show different ways in which issues can be mapped

Questions highlight the debates surrounding an issue and encourage further research

THE EARTH

The Earth is made up of three layers: the core, the mantle and the crust. The crust is made up of many different kinds of rock. The geological processes that create these rocks include the movement of tectonic plates and volcanic eruptions.

When the Earth's plates move, cracks occur. These cracks are known as faults, and some, like the San Andreas fault in the western USA, are clearly visible.

THE EARTH'S STRUCTURE

The layers of the Earth's interior are kept hot by pressure and by heat from radioactive elements. Heat flows from the top of the core through the mantle by convection currents. As the hot magma rises, it slowly cools and sinks back towards the core, producing a conveyor belt movement within the mantle. Some heat also escapes through weak points in the Earth's crust.

Continental crust:
STATE: Solid
DEPTH: 0 – 70 km below surface
TEMPERATURE: less than 1000°C

Plume of hot, upwelling mantle rock carries heat to the surface.

Outer core:
STATE: Liquid
DEPTH: 5 150 km below surface
TEMPERATURE: 3 500 – 4 000°C

Inner core:
STATE: Solid
DEPTH: 6 370 km below surface
TEMPERATURE: 4 000 – 4 700°C

Core-mantle boundary, where the liquid outer core and solid lava mantle layers meet.

WHERE WE LIVE

About 70 per cent of the Earth's surface is submerged beneath vast oceans: the Pacific, Atlantic, Indian, Southern and Arctic oceans. Photographs taken from space show the Earth as a blue planet. They also show the Earth as a slightly flattened ball – a shape known as the geoid. The Earth's rotation makes it bulge slightly at the Equator and flatten a little at the Poles.

About 20 per cent of the Earth's surface is desert. Some, such as Antarctica, are cold, whilst others, such as the Sahara, are hot. A simple definition of a desert is that it is a region where the annual rainfall is less than 250mm.

About half the world's people live in coastal areas. Eight of the most populated areas in the world, such as Tokyo (above), are situated on estuaries or the coast.

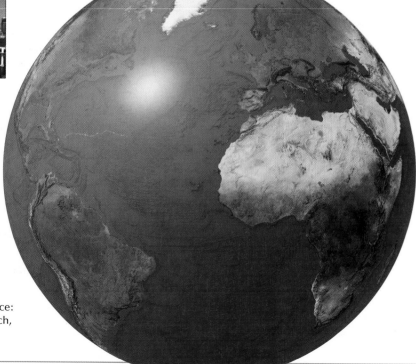

Rainforests such as the Relic Rainforest in Otway, Australia (above), cover just 7 per cent of the Earth's land but form the richest ecosystems on the planet. More plant and animal species are found here than anywhere else on Earth.

The Pacific Ocean contains the deepest places on the Earth's surface: ocean trenches. The deepest trench, Challenger Deep, plunges 11 200 metres beneath sea level.

HEMISPHERES

The Earth is divided along two imaginary lines. One, the Equator, which runs around the Earth at the halfway point between the two poles, divides the globe into the Northern and Southern Hemispheres. The other line, which runs from Prime Meridian (0°) to 180° longitude, creates the Eastern and Western Hemispheres.

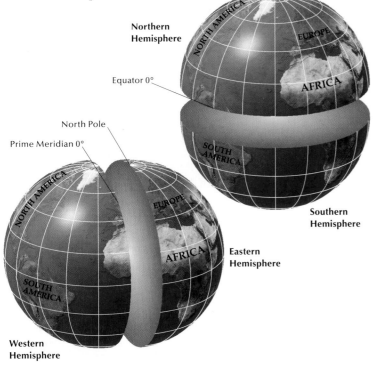

Northern Hemisphere

Equator 0°

North Pole

Prime Meridian 0°

NORTH AMERICA

EUROPE

AFRICA

SOUTH AMERICA

Southern Hemisphere

Eastern Hemisphere

AFRICA

EUROPE

NORTH AMERICA

SOUTH AMERICA

Western Hemisphere

LAND AND WATER

The Earth can also be divided into land and water hemispheres. The water hemisphere is dominated by the Pacific Ocean. From this view, the Earth is almost completely covered by water.

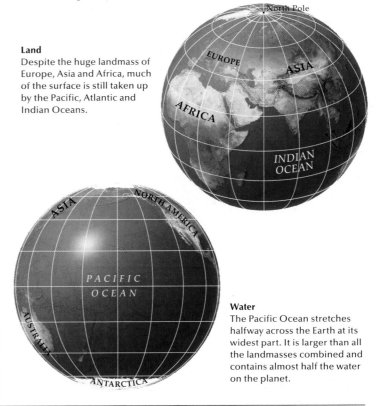

Land
Despite the huge landmass of Europe, Asia and Africa, much of the surface is still taken up by the Pacific, Atlantic and Indian Oceans.

North Pole

EUROPE

ASIA

AFRICA

INDIAN OCEAN

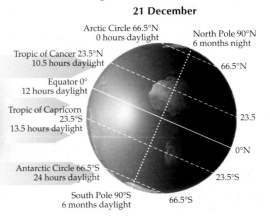

ASIA

NORTH AMERICA

PACIFIC OCEAN

AUSTRALIA

ANTARCTICA

Water
The Pacific Ocean stretches halfway across the Earth at its widest part. It is larger than all the landmasses combined and contains almost half the water on the planet.

SEASONS

As the Earth orbits the sun it spins on another imaginary line – the axis – which runs through the centre of the Earth between the North and South Poles. The axis tilts at an angle of 23.5° to the Earth's orbit. As a result each place moves nearer and then further away from the sun, causing seasonal changes in weather patterns.

Australia, 21 December: In the Southern Hemisphere summer is in December and winter is in June.

UK, 21 December: In winter the Northern Hemisphere tilts away from the sun, receiving less heat and light.

21 June

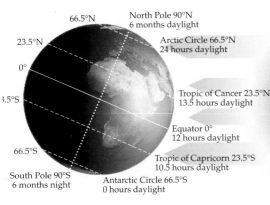

66.5°N

North Pole 90°N
6 months daylight

23.5°N

Arctic Circle 66.5°N
24 hours daylight

0°

3.5°S

Tropic of Cancer 23.5°N
13.5 hours daylight

Equator 0°
12 hours daylight

66.5°S

Tropic of Capricorn 23.5°S
10.5 hours daylight

South Pole 90°S
6 months night

Antarctic Circle 66.5°S
0 hours daylight

21 December

Arctic Circle 66.5°N
0 hours daylight

North Pole 90°N
6 months night

Tropic of Cancer 23.5°N
10.5 hours daylight

66.5°N

Equator 0°
12 hours daylight

Tropic of Capricorn
23.5°S
13.5 hours daylight

23.5

Antarctic Circle 66.5°S
24 hours daylight

0°N

South Pole 90°S
6 months daylight

66.5°S

23.5°S

On 21 June the Northern Hemisphere receives most direct light from the sun and has its longest day.

Places between the tropics are hot all year round. Here, the sun's rays strike the Earth almost vertically, so are more intense. Places near the poles have the coldest climate. At high latitudes the sun's rays hit the Earth at an angle so are less intense.

On 21 December the Southern Hemisphere receives the most direct heat and light.

MAP PROJECTIONS

The only truly accurate map of the whole world is a globe. But a globe is impractical to carry around so cartographers produce flat maps. Changing the globe into a flat map is not simple and there is always some distortion of area, distance or direction.

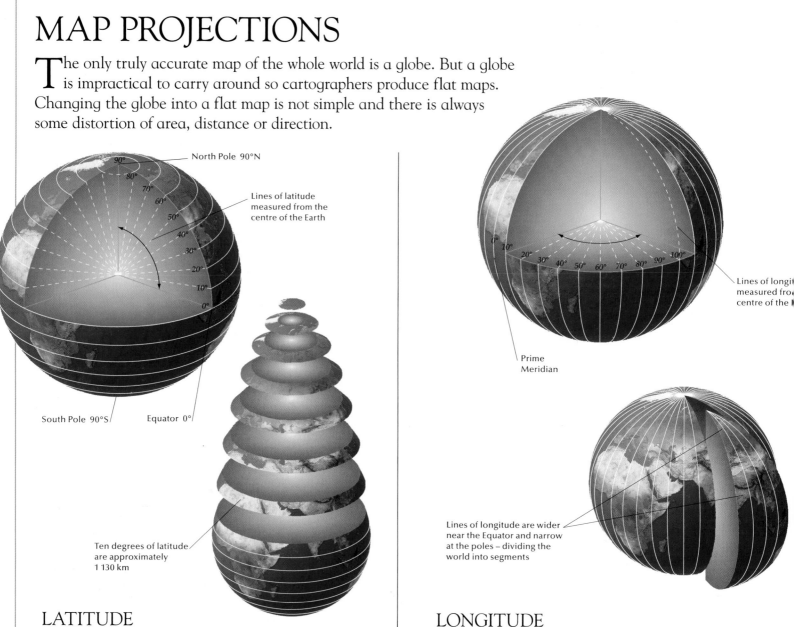

North Pole 90°N

Lines of latitude measured from the centre of the Earth

South Pole 90°S

Equator 0°

Ten degrees of latitude are approximately 1 130 km

Prime Meridian

Lines of longitude measured from the centre of the Earth

Lines of longitude are wider near the Equator and narrow at the poles – dividing the world into segments

LATITUDE

The lines that run east to west around the Earth are called lines of latitude. Latitude is measured in degrees from 0° at the Equator. The poles are at 90° latitude. The degree of latitude indicates how far north or south a place is.

LONGITUDE

The lines that run north to south between the poles are the lines of longitude. The Prime Meridian, which runs through Greenwich, London is numbered 0°. All other lines of longitude are numbered in degrees east or west of the Prime Meridian.

WHERE ON EARTH?

By drawing two sets of imaginary lines – the lines of latitude and longitude – around the Earth a grid can be created. Using this grid any place on Earth can be located by referring to the point where its line of latitude intersects with its line of longitude.

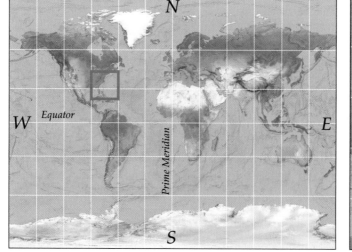

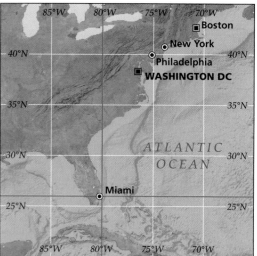

MAKING A FLAT MAP FROM A GLOBE

Cartographers use a technique called projection to show the Earth's curved surface on a flat map. There are a number of different projections, and whilst a distortion in one – either area, distance or direction – can be minimised, another feature will become more distorted. The cartographer must choose which is most suitable for a particular purpose. There are three major types of projection:

Cylindrical projections The surface of the globe is transferred on to a surrounding cylinder. This is then cut down top to bottom and 'rolled out' to give a flat map. The Mercator projection (right) is a good example.

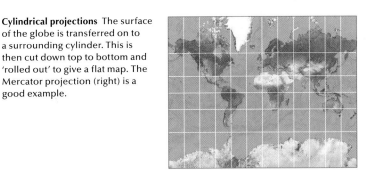

 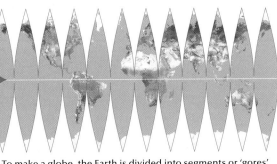

To make a globe, the Earth is divided into segments or 'gores' along lines of Longitude.

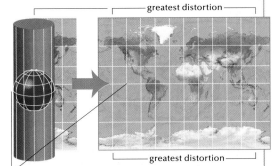

greatest distortion

greatest distortion

scale accurate at Equator

North Pole

accurate scale at central point

greatest distortion

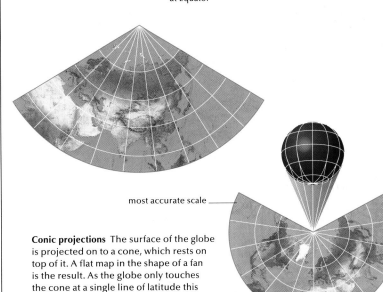

most accurate scale

Azimuthal projections The globe is placed on a flat circle. The circle only touches the globe's surface at one point and the scale is only accurate at this point. Azimuthal projections are good for maps focusing on a hemisphere, continent or the poles. When used to show a larger area great distortion occurs at the edges.

Conic projections The surface of the globe is projected on to a cone, which rests on top of it. A flat map in the shape of a fan is the result. As the globe only touches the cone at a single line of latitude this projection is best used for smaller areas of the world, such as country maps.

PROJECTIONS USED IN THIS ATLAS

The projections used have been chosen carefully to ensure as little distortion occurs as possible. Projections appropriate for maps of world, continental or country scale are quite different.

World maps

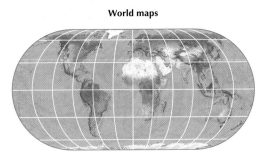

The Eckert VII projection is used for world maps as it shows countries at their correct size relative to one another.

Continents

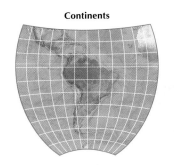

The Lambert Azimuthal Equal Area is used for continental maps. The shape distortion is relatively small and countries retain their correct sizes relative to one another.

Countries

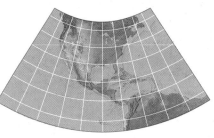

The Lambert Conformal Conic shows countries with the smallest amount of distortion possible. The angles from any point on the map are the same as they would be on the surface of the globe.

ANCIENT AND MODERN

Computers and information from satellites have revolutionised mapping, making the process easier and more accurate, but it is still a skilled and time-consuming process. Information about the world needs to be researched, sorted and checked. The cartographer must make decisions about the function of the map and what information to show to make it as clear as possible.

Accurate large scale maps of the world only started to appear from the 1580s onwards. Before that many maps were highly stylised. The Mappa Mundi (left), is a thirteenth century map of the world. Jerusalem is at the centre of the map, reflecting religious beliefs rather than physical geography.

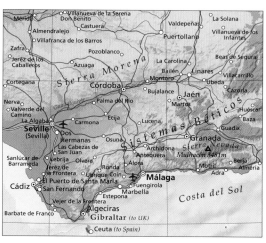

HISTORICAL MAP MAKING

Early maps were a pictorial representation of what the surface of the Earth looked like. Later maps were drawn using survey teams to gather information. They marked out and calculated the height of the land, the position of towns and other geographical features.

NEW TECHNIQUES

Today satellites collect and process detailed information about the Earth's surface. Locations can be verified using GPS (Global Positioning Systems) linked to satellites. Computers are used to combine different sorts of map information. Any computerised map is produced using a GIS (Geographical Information System).

SCHEMATIC MAPS

Schematic maps are highly stylised, simplified diagrams that deliberately distort distance and location in order to make the map more readable. They are often used for public transport or tourist maps.

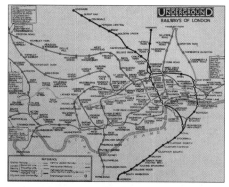

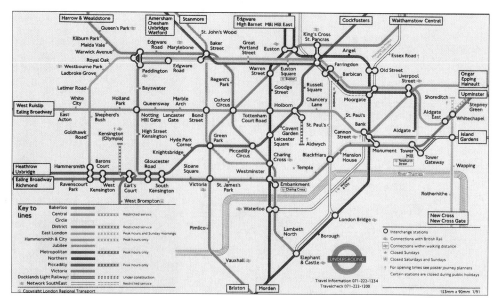

The first maps of the London Underground were produced in the 1860s. Cartographers tried to make them geographically realistic, which meant that the twists and turns of the tunnels were shown. By the 1920s, when the map above was produced, this approach had resulted in a map that was very complex and difficult to use.

In 1933 Henry Beck designed a new Underground map. By straightening the lines and distorting distances and location so that routes followed a basic North South East West orientation, he produced a map that was much simpler and easier to use. Today's map (above) is still based on his original design.

MODERN MAP MAKING

1. Measuring the Earth's surface
The surface is divided into squares, and satellites take measurements of the height of the land in each square. The data collected can then be manipulated on a computer to produce a digital terrain model (DTM).

2. Making a terrain model
A detailed 3-D model can be produced using the data. Computer software can then recreate the effects of the sun shining on to mountains and into valleys so they can be seen much more clearly.

3. Adding detail to the land surface
The height of the land can be shown using bands of colour, or by contour lines, which are applied to the digitally created surface. Colour can also be used to show different kinds of vegetation, such as deserts, forests and grasslands.

4. Adding map detail
Features such as roads, rivers and cities can now be added. They are compiled and scanned digitally into the computer. The information can then be 'draped' on top of the main terrain model to create a map.

SHOWING INFORMATION ON A MAP

A map is a selective diagram of a place. It is the cartographer's job to decide what kind of information to show on a map. They might highlight certain kinds of features – such as roads, rivers and land height. They might also show other features such as sea depth, place names and borders that would be impossible to see either on the ground or in a photograph. The information shown on a map is influenced by a number of factors, most importantly by its scale.

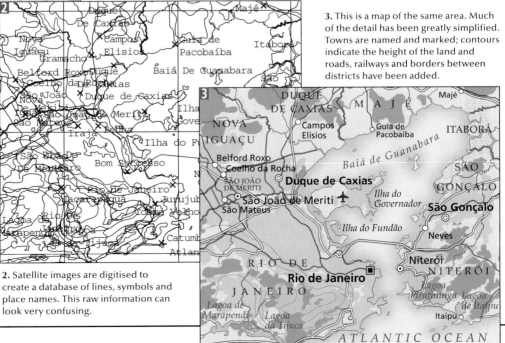

1. This is a satellite photograph of the harbour area of Rio de Janeiro in Brazil. Although you can see the bay and where most of the housing is, it is impossible to see roads or get any sense of the position of places relative to one another.

2. Satellite images are digitised to create a database of lines, symbols and place names. This raw information can look very confusing.

3. This is a map of the same area. Much of the detail has been greatly simplified. Towns are named and marked; contours indicate the height of the land and roads, railways and borders between districts have been added.

HOW TO USE A MAP

A map is a graphic representation of all or part of the Earth's surface. It displays information about the Earth in a visual way, using colours, symbols and styles of print to show different geographical features. In order to read a map and understand all the information that is on it, you will need to use the scale bar and key, which are included on each map in this atlas.

LOCATOR GLOBE

Use the locator globe to find out where a region is in the world.

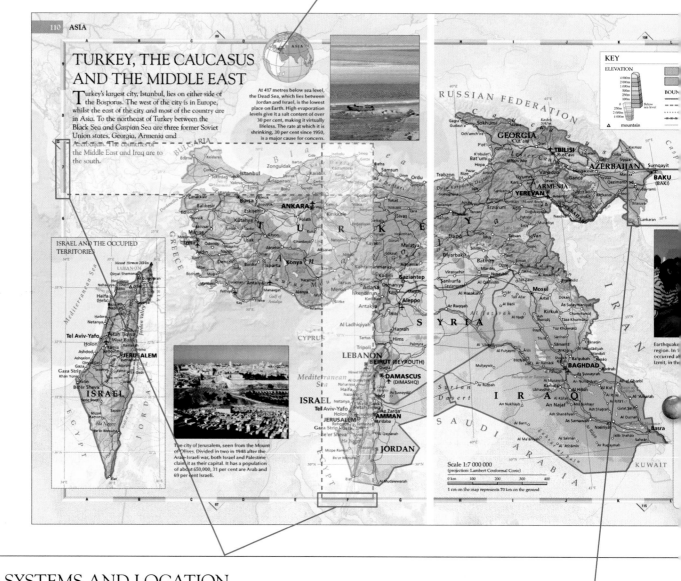

GRID SYSTEMS AND LOCATION

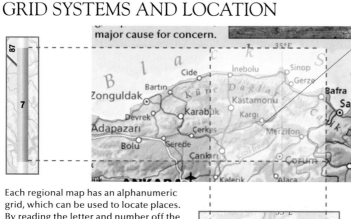

Kargī 110 F7 Turkey *41°9'N 34°32'E*

All the named settlements in this atlas are indexed using their alphanumeric grid reference, for example Kargī in F7. To find a place, first look up its page number, then its grid reference. Settlements are also given a latitude and longitude, which can be used with the map graticule to pinpoint the location.

Each regional map has an alphanumeric grid, which can be used to locate places. By reading the letter and number off the bottom and side of the grid, settlements can quickly be located.

Graticules
The lines of latitude and longitude are known as graticules. They are shown on the map as thin blue lines, with their degree of latitude or longitude given at the edge of the map.

HOW A KEY WORKS

The key gives you information about the physical features represented on the map, but also on human features, such as settlements, roads and political borders.

4 000m
2 000m
1 000m
500m
250m
100m
0
250m   Below
2 000m   sea level
4 000m

All the regional and country maps show the relief of the land. Colours are used to represent different elevations: green is for low-lying land and yellows, browns and greys indicate higher land. Water features like rivers and lakes are also shown.

SETTLEMENTS

■ ⊙ over 1 million

◨ ◎ 500 000 – 1 million

■ ⊙ 100 000 – 500 000

■ ○ 50 000 – 100 000

■ ○ below 50 000

A red square indicates a national capital

Different symbols and styles of font are used to show a settlement's location, size and political status.

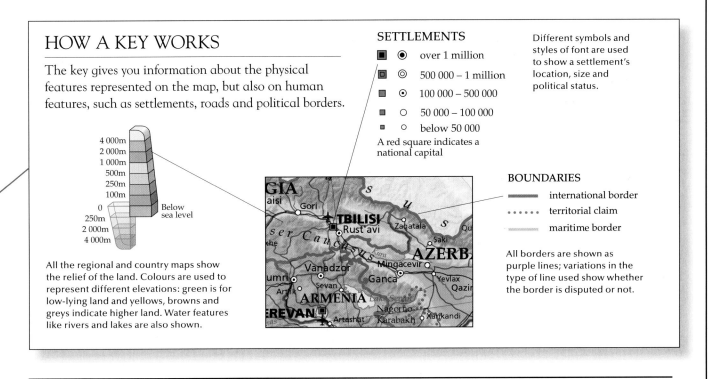

BOUNDARIES

━━━ international border

• • • • • territorial claim

～～～ maritime border

All borders are shown as purple lines; variations in the type of line used show whether the border is disputed or not.

SCALE

To represent an area as a map, it needs to be greatly reduced in size. A map's scale shows by how much the area has been reduced. The smaller the scale, the larger the amount of land that can be shown but the less detail that can be included. Large scale maps show an area in great detail, but only cover a small area.

LONDON 1:21 500 000

This map is drawn to a small scale. It shows the location of the UK in relation to the rest of Europe. Very few features can be seen – only major rivers, relief features and settlements.

LONDON 1:1 000 000

This map is at a much larger scale and shows more detail about London, such as open spaces and the names of larger roads and suburbs.

LONDON 1:5 500 000

At a scale of 1:5 500 000 only southeast England is shown. However, at this scale towns of different sizes can be identified, as well as major roads and smaller rivers.

LONDON 1:12 500

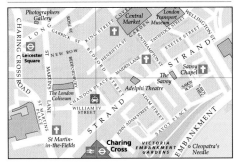

This is a street map of London. At this scale, almost every road is named. Individual buildings, such as tourist attractions and train stations may also be shown.

SCALE BARS

The scale bar shows the ratio between distances on the map and corresponding distances in reality. There are different ways of showing map scales:

Scale 1:1 400 000
(projection: Lambert Conformal Conic)

0 km   20   40   60   80

1 cm on the map represents 14.0 km on the ground

One unit on the map represents 1 400 000 units on the ground.

The line is marked off in units that represent real distances, which are given in kilometres.

This means that 1 cm on the map represents 14.0 km on the ground.

POLITICAL

Today there are almost 200 separate countries in the world. National borders are influenced by physical features such as natural resources and the terrain, and by human factors such as ethnicity, culture, language and religion. Straight-line borders often indicate former colonial rule. Whilst many countries have had the same borders for a long time, others are still disputing theirs.

NEW NATIONS AND THE COUNTRIES THAT PREVIOUSLY ADMINISTERED THEM (1970–2000)

Administration at the time of independence

- Australia
- Aust/NZ/UK
- Czechoslovakia
- Ethiopia
- France
- Indonesia
- Netherlands
- Pakistan
- Portugal
- South Africa
- Spain
- UK
- Germany reunified
- USA
- USSR
- Yugoslavia

MAP KEY

Boundaries

——— international border
----- disputed border
········· territorial claim
✕✕✕ ceasefire line
——— maritime border
- - - - disputed maritime border

Political status

LAOS independent state
Niue *(to NZ)* self-governing dependent territory
Nicobar Islands (to India) non self-governing dependent territory

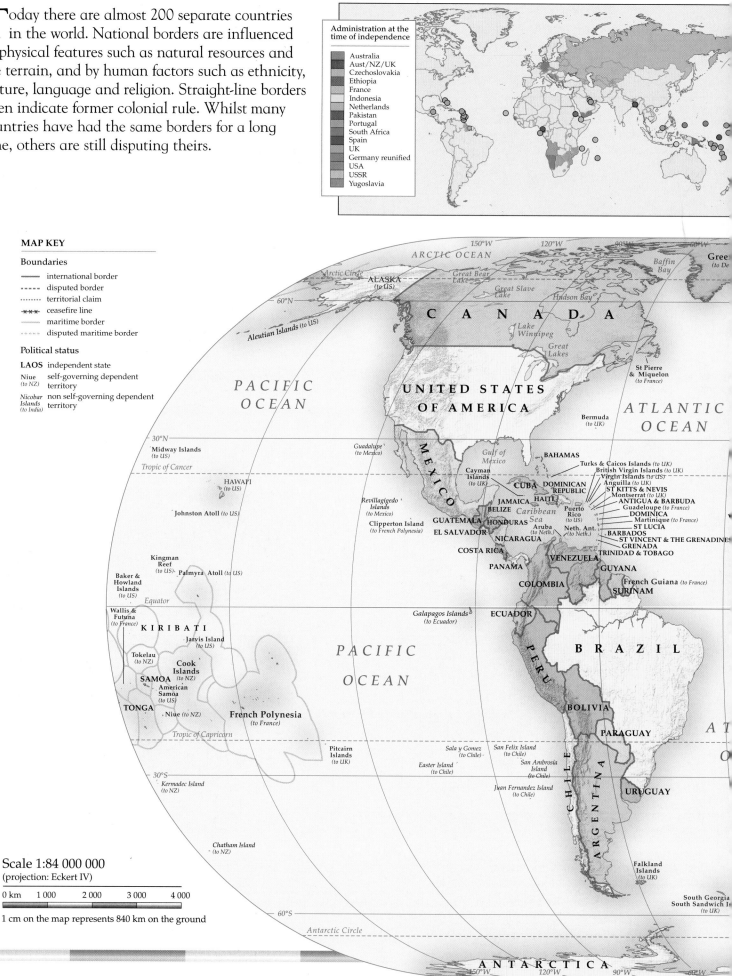

Scale 1:84 000 000
(projection: Eckert IV)

0 km   1 000   2 000   3 000   4 000

1 cm on the map represents 840 km on the ground

POLAND'S SHIFTING BORDERS

1634 By 1634 the borders of Poland had reached their greatest extent. It was the largest country in Europe, with the third largest population.

1772–1795 Between 1772 and 1795 Poland was partitioned between Russia, Prussia and Austria, ending the existence of Poland as a sovereign state.

After the First World War By the end of the First World War the collapse of Russia, Germany and Austria enabled Poland to regain its independence. However, the country was only half the size it had been in 1634.

After the Second World War The Allies moved Poland's borders westwards after the Second World War. It lost a substantial amount of land, as the territories annexed by the Soviet Union in the east were nearly twice the size of the land gained from Germany in the west. Millions of people were displaced as a result of the border changes.

POPULATION

The world's population has trebled over the last 100 years to an estimated 6.4 billion in 2005. However, the rate of increase is now slowing down. In 2004, for the first time ever, as many people lived in towns and cities as in the countryside.

MILLION CITIES

MAP KEY

· city with a population over 1 million

Source: UN, 2004

POPULATION DENSITY BY COUNTRY

Monaco
Vatican City
Malta
Barbados
Bahrain
Maldives
Singapore
Mauritius
Nau

MAP KEY

Population density (people per square km)

- above 500
- 250 to 499
- 100 to 249
- 50 to 99
- 10 to 49
- 1 to 9
- no data

POPULATION DENSITY

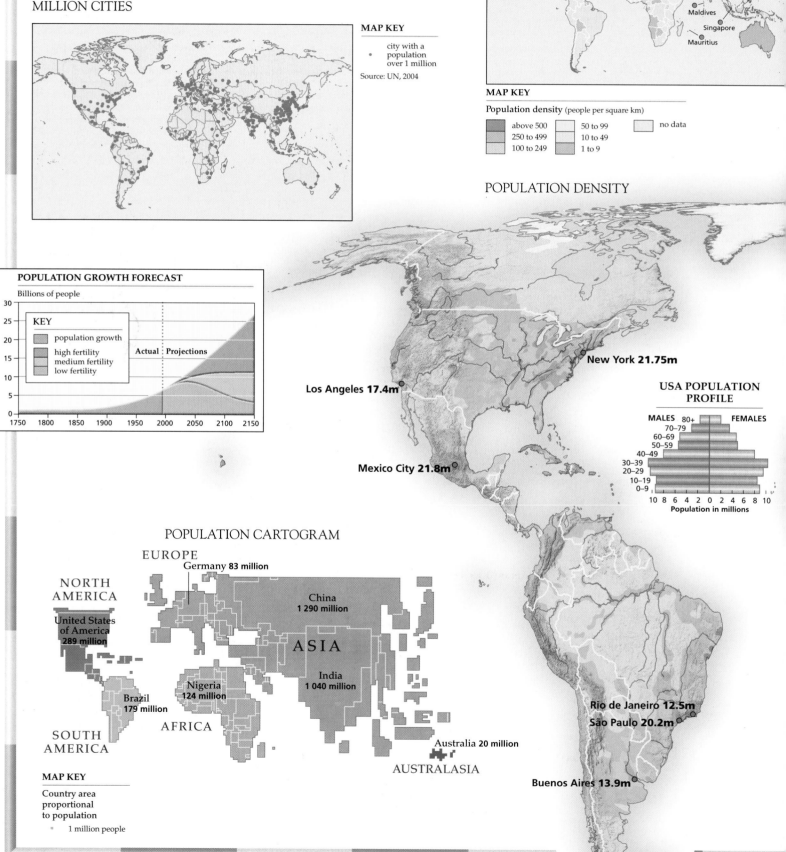

New York **21.75m**

Los Angeles **17.4m**

Mexico City **21.8m**

Rio de Janeiro **12.5m**

São Paulo **20.2m**

Buenos Aires **13.9m**

USA POPULATION PROFILE

MALES   80+   FEMALES
70–79
60–69
50–59
40–49
30–39
20–29
10–19
0–9

10 8 6 4 2 0 2 4 6 8 10
Population in millions

POPULATION GROWTH FORECAST

Billions of people

KEY

- population growth
- high fertility
- medium fertility
- low fertility

Actual : Projections

30
25
20
15
10
5
0
1750 1800 1850 1900 1950 2000 2050 2100 2150

POPULATION CARTOGRAM

EUROPE

Germany 83 million

NORTH AMERICA

United States of America **289 million**

China **1 290 million**

ASIA

India **1 040 million**

Nigeria **124 million**

Brazil **179 million**

AFRICA

SOUTH AMERICA

Australia 20 million

AUSTRALASIA

MAP KEY

Country area proportional to population

· 1 million people

URBANISATION

POPULATION GROWTH

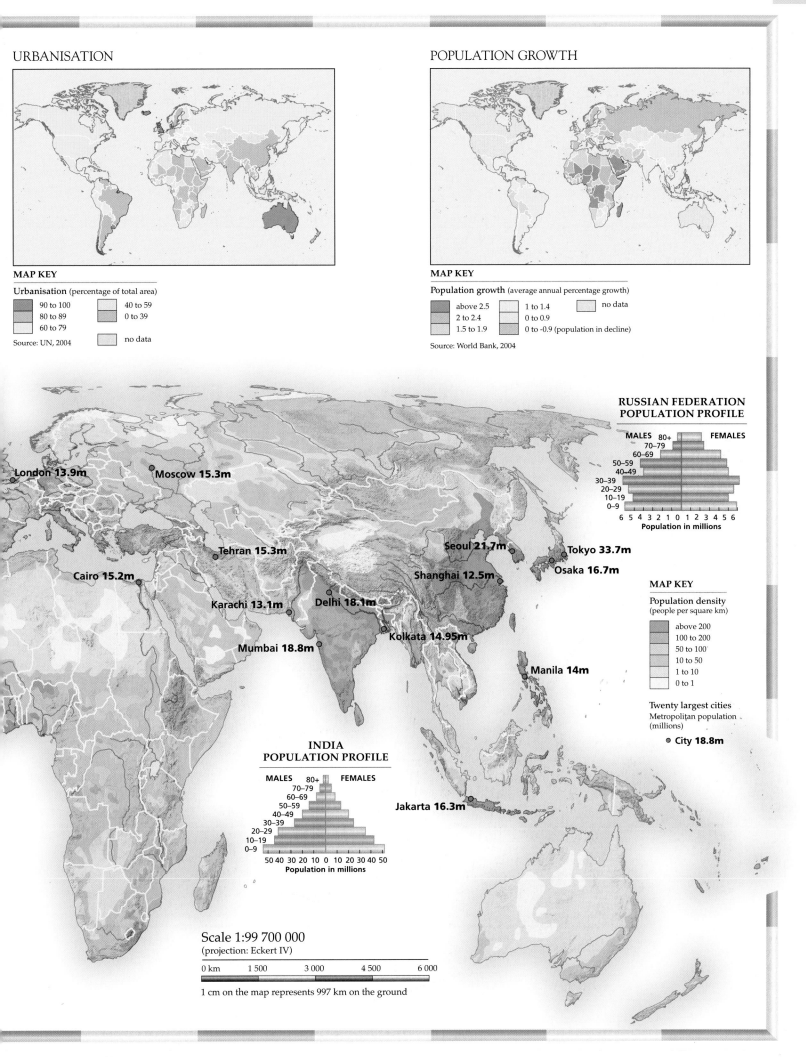

London 13.9m

Moscow 15.3m

Tehran 15.3m

Cairo 15.2m

Karachi 13.1m

Delhi 18.1m

Mumbai 18.8m

Kolkata 14.95m

Seoul 21.7m

Tokyo 33.7m

Osaka 16.7m

Shanghai 12.5m

Manila 14m

Jakarta 16.3m

RUSSIAN FEDERATION POPULATION PROFILE

MALES 80+ FEMALES
70–79
60–69
50–59
40–49
30–39
20–29
10–19
0–9

6 5 4 3 2 1 0 1 2 3 4 5 6
Population in millions

INDIA POPULATION PROFILE

MALES 80+ FEMALES
70–79
60–69
50–59
40–49
30–39
20–29
10–19
0–9

50 40 30 20 10 0 0 10 20 30 40 50
Population in millions

Scale 1:99 700 000
(projection: Eckert IV)

0 km   1 500   3 000   4 500   6 000

1 cm on the map represents 997 km on the ground

HIV/AIDS

One of the most important global health issues today is the HIV/AIDS pandemic. Unrecognised until 1980, by 2004 28 million people had died from AIDS and a further 40 million were thought to be infected with the HIV virus. By 2020 it is estimated that there will be over 60 million more deaths.

USEFUL DEFINITIONS	
Pandemic	A disease which affects whole countries, regions and continents across the world
Epidemic	Widespread and severe outbreak of a disease in an area at a particular time
Virus	An infection or disease caused by an infected particle that multiplies in the cells of the host organism. There are two kinds – DNA and RNA viruses
Retrovirus	RNA (ribonucleic acid) viruses that insert a DNA copy of their genome in the host cell e.g. HIV
DNA	Deoxyribonucleic acid – the genetic base of cells and organisms

WHAT IS HIV/AIDS?

HIV (Human Immunodeficiency Virus) is the retrovirus that causes AIDS (Acquired Immunodeficiency Syndrome). It is a disease that progressively weakens the body's immune system. This can eventually lead to the sufferer having no resistance to even minor infections, which can become life-threatening. It is possible to be HIV positive for many years without becoming ill. The HIV virus is carried in blood, sexual fluids and breast milk, and is passed on when these enter another person's system.

WORLD MAP OF HIV/AIDS INFECTIONS, 2004

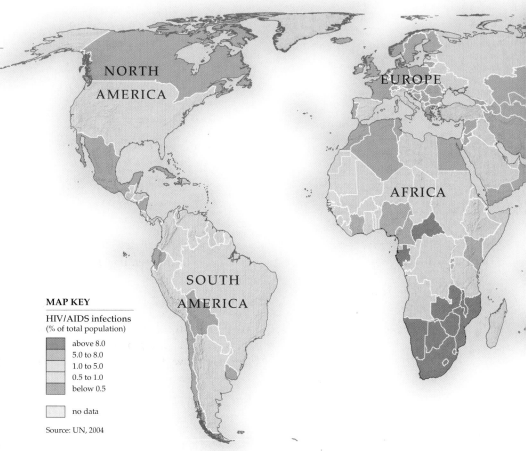

MAP KEY

HIV/AIDS infections
(% of total population)

- above 8.0
- 5.0 to 8.0
- 1.0 to 5.0
- 0.5 to 1.0
- below 0.5

- no data

Source: UN, 2004

HIV INFECTIONS 1980–2002

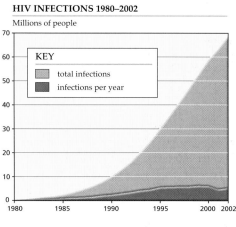

Millions of people

KEY
- total infections
- infections per year

AIDS DEATHS 1980–2002

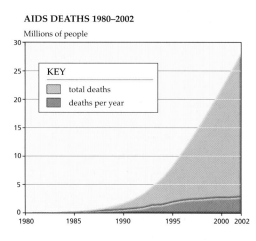

Millions of people

KEY
- total deaths
- deaths per year

HIV/AIDS TODAY

When the HIV virus was first diagnosed it mainly affected intravenous drug users and homosexual men – predominantly in richer MEDCs. However, in the last five years the majority of those infected have been in poorer LEDCs, with heterosexual sex the main cause. Russia, India, China and Sub-Saharan Africa are the countries and regions causing most concern as they are experiencing the fastest growth and spread of HIV/AIDS in the world.

Before 2000, just under 30 000 people were known to be infected with HIV in Russia. This doubled in 2001, mainly amongst young people. About 90 per cent of those infections are thought to be due to drug use. India has the second highest total of HIV infections in the world, with 4.5 million people carrying HIV. Seventy per cent of the population live in rural areas and poor awareness about HIV and lack of access to condoms and HIV testing have been major factors in its spread.

The first HIV cases in China were discovered in 1985 in Yunnan province, but it wasn't until the mid 1990s that it spread outside the region. It is thought that 1.5 million people are now infected, mainly through drug use and heterosexual transmission – although the true figure could be much higher.

[H]IV/AIDS IN SUB-SAHARAN AFRICA

[N]owhere in the world is the impact of HIV/AIDS [gr]eater than in Sub-Saharan Africa, home to 10 [p]er cent of the world's population:

[3] million people in the region became infected in 2002.

[2].2 million adults and children died as a result of HIV/AIDS in 2002 – 75 per cent of the total global [d]eaths from AIDS that year.

[2]5 million people were living with HIV in 2004, an increase of 30 per cent over five years.

[A]verage life expectancy for all Africans has fallen by an average of 15 years as a direct result of HIV/AIDS (see map). By 2010, the populations of Botswana, Mozambique, Lesotho, Swaziland and South Africa will have started to fall as a result of AIDS deaths. The growth rate in Zimbabwe and Namibia will be almost zero.

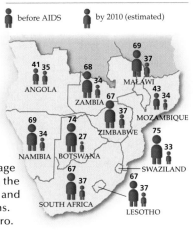

LIFE EXPECTANCY IN YEARS

before AIDS   by 2010 (estimated)

ANGOLA 41 35
ZAMBIA 68 34
MALAWI 69 37
MOZAMBIQUE 67 43 34
ZIMBABWE 74 37
NAMIBIA 69 34
BOTSWANA 27
SWAZILAND 75 33
SOUTH AFRICA 67 37
LESOTHO 67 37

Some advances in treatment have been made, including providing antiretroviral medicines (ARVs). However, less than half a million (7 per cent) of people in LEDCs who need antiretroviral medicines have access to treatment. This is mainly because the cost of these drugs has been very high, certainly for the majority of sufferers in LEDCs. Recently though, a number of the main pharmaceutical companies agreed to license the manufacture of antiretroviral drugs in a number of LEDCs. This should make them available at a fraction of the previous cost.

SIA

AUSTRALASIA
AND OCEANIA

Scale 1:130 600 000
(projection: Eckert IV)

0 km   2 000   4 000   6 000

A woman receiving antiretroviral treatment at a clinic in Cape Town, South Africa. In 2002, for the first time, half of those infected with HIV were women. In Sub-Saharan Africa, where many women are economically dependent on men and have little control over sexual relations or the use of condoms, they are particularly vulnerable.

WIDER IMPACTS

HIV/AIDS has a far wider impact than just on the health of individuals:

- Families are broken up as parents become ill and die. AIDS created 13 million orphans in 2001 – a figure which may rise to 25 million by 2010. Many orphans in LEDCs are looked after by older siblings or are forced to live on the streets.

- In LEDCs, money has to be spent on medicines, rather than on education or basic necessities like food.

- As more workers become ill and die, the economy suffers. In some countries large numbers of health professionals and teachers have died and cannot easily be replaced.

- In southern Africa AIDS may kill 20 per cent of farmers and farm workers by 2020 – a major blow to the economies of several countries.

- The workforce in 38 countries (mostly African) is predicted to decrease by between 5 per cent and 35 per cent by 2020.

GLOBAL RESPONSES TO HIV/AIDS

In 2000, one of the stated millennium goals of the United Nations was to '*halt and begin to reverse the spread of HIV/ AIDS*'. The UN estimated that by 2005 US $10 billion per year would be needed to respond to the AIDS epidemic. By 2004 only about half that had been pledged by donors through the UN system.

Prevention programmes are crucial to halting the spread of HIV/AIDS. Raising awareness is the first step in preventing infection and in countries like Zambia (above) awareness and education programmes have reduced infection rates.

Whilst the availability of cheaper drugs will help those infected, they are not a cure. Greater efforts are needed to reduce HIV infection – and there have already been some successes. The Dominican Republic, Uganda, Thailand and Brazil have all managed to reduce the number of HIV carriers by providing money for both treatment and HIV awareness programmes.

THE BIG ISSUES

1 What are the main ways in which HIV infection is spread?

2 Which parts of the world have been most affected by HIV/AIDS? Why?

3 Why are women especially vulnerable to HIV?

4 Should ARVs be made available to all who need them? How?

5 Apart from health, what are the main impacts of HIV/AIDS?

ECONOMY

Economic development can be assessed by comparing countries' Gross Domestic Product per capita. The relative size of the three main sectors of the economy: primary, secondary and tertiary, also indicate how economically developed a country is. Usually, MEDCs have large tertiary sectors, whilst LEDCs are more reliant on primary industry.

NORTH AMERICA (2000)			
Sector	USA	Mexico	Jamaica
Primary (% of GDP)	1.61	4.17	6.71
Secondary (% of GDP)	24.45	28.01	31.46
Tertiary (% of GDP)	73.94	67.82	61.83

PRIMARY SECTOR

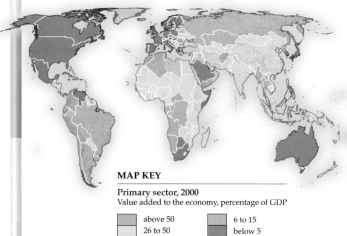

Farming is the world's main primary industry. The majority of those living in LEDCs, like the Guambiano farmers in Colombia (above) rely on some form of subsistence farming to provide for their basic needs.

MAP KEY

Primary sector, 2000
Value added to the economy, percentage of GDP

- above 50
- 26 to 50
- 16 to 25
- 6 to 15
- below 5
- no data

WORLD GDP PER CAPITA

MAP KEY

Gross Domestic Product (GDP) per capita
US dollars

- above 10 000
- 2 500 to 10 000
- 1 200 to 2 500
- 400 to 1 200
- below 400

- no data

SECONDARY SECTOR

The car industry is a major global secondary industry. Production is usually via automated assembly lines, like the Toyota factory in Durban, South Africa, (above).

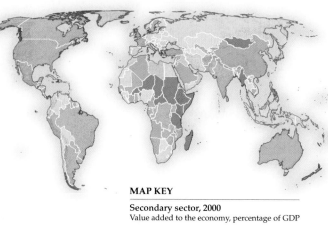

MAP KEY

Secondary sector, 2000
Value added to the economy, percentage of GDP

- above 50
- 40 to 49
- 30 to 39
- 20 to 29
- below 20
- no data

SOUTH AMERICA (2000)			
Sector	Argentina	Brazil	Bolivia
Primary (% of GDP)	5.05	7.22	14.87
Secondary (% of GDP)	28.06	27.88	33.76
Tertiary (% of GDP)	66.88	66.88	51.38

TERTIARY SECTOR

Increasing numbers of people are employed in tertiary or service industries. These include jobs in retailing, such as the Pacific Place shopping complex, Hong Kong.

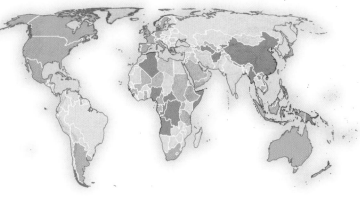

MAP KEY

Tertiary sector, 2000
Value added to the economy, percentage of GDP

- above 65
- 55 to 64
- 45 to 54
- 35 to 44
- below 35
- no data

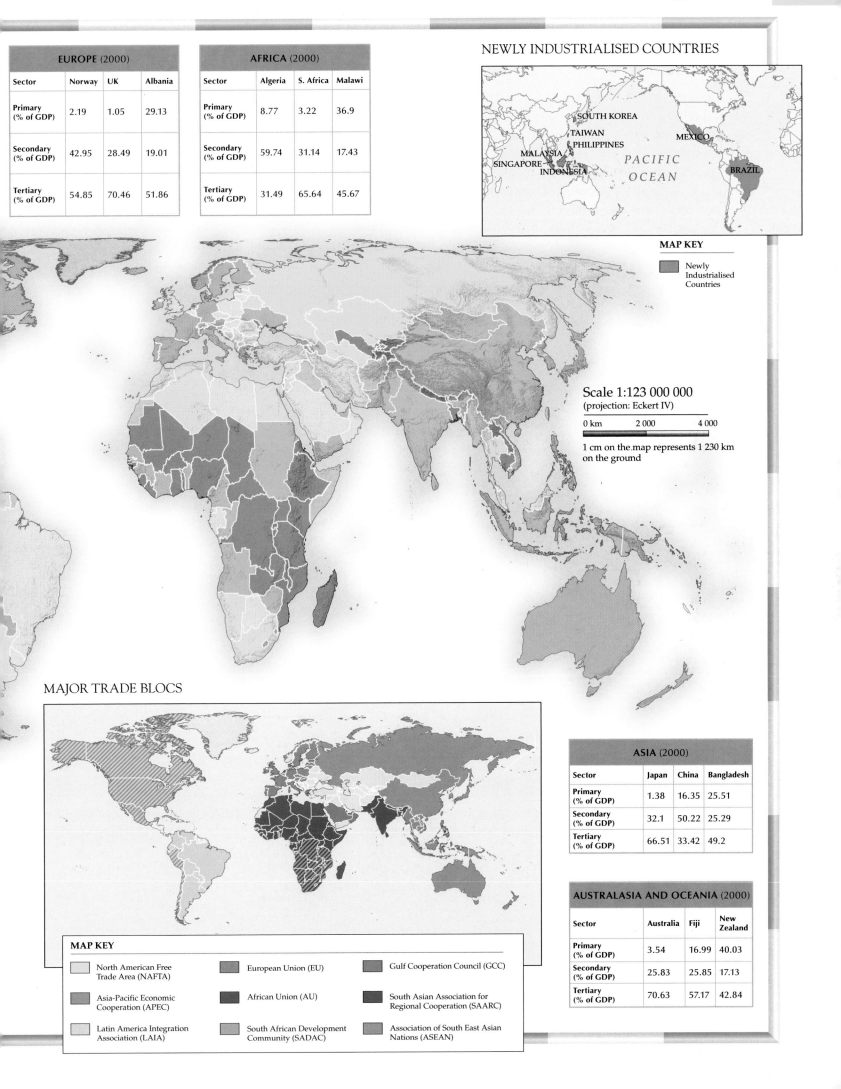

EUROPE (2000)

Sector	Norway	UK	Albania
Primary (% of GDP)	2.19	1.05	29.13
Secondary (% of GDP)	42.95	28.49	19.01
Tertiary (% of GDP)	54.85	70.46	51.86

AFRICA (2000)

Sector	Algeria	S. Africa	Malawi
Primary (% of GDP)	8.77	3.22	36.9
Secondary (% of GDP)	59.74	31.14	17.43
Tertiary (% of GDP)	31.49	65.64	45.67

NEWLY INDUSTRIALISED COUNTRIES

SOUTH KOREA
TAIWAN
PHILIPPINES
MEXICO
MALAYSIA
SINGAPORE
INDONESIA
PACIFIC OCEAN
BRAZIL

MAP KEY

Newly Industrialised Countries

Scale 1:123 000 000
(projection: Eckert IV)

0 km   2 000   4 000

1 cm on the map represents 1 230 km on the ground

MAJOR TRADE BLOCS

MAP KEY

- North American Free Trade Area (NAFTA)
- Asia-Pacific Economic Cooperation (APEC)
- Latin America Integration Association (LAIA)
- European Union (EU)
- African Union (AU)
- South African Development Community (SADAC)
- Gulf Cooperation Council (GCC)
- South Asian Association for Regional Cooperation (SAARC)
- Association of South East Asian Nations (ASEAN)

ASIA (2000)

Sector	Japan	China	Bangladesh
Primary (% of GDP)	1.38	16.35	25.51
Secondary (% of GDP)	32.1	50.22	25.29
Tertiary (% of GDP)	66.51	33.42	49.2

AUSTRALASIA AND OCEANIA (2000)

Sector	Australia	Fiji	New Zealand
Primary (% of GDP)	3.54	16.99	40.03
Secondary (% of GDP)	25.83	25.85	17.13
Tertiary (% of GDP)	70.63	57.17	42.84

QUALITY OF LIFE

The maps here show a range of different development indicators based on data collected annually by the United Nations. The main map shows the Human Development Index for each country, based on data for GDP per capita, life expectancy at birth, education and literacy. Other maps are based on single sets of data, all of which reflect relative levels of development.

WORLD HDI

MAP KEY

UN Human Development Index (HDI)

- high
- medium
- low
- no data

Source: UN, 2004

Scale 1:92 000 000
(projection: Eckert IV)

| 0 km | 1 500 | 3 000 | 4 500 |

1 cm on the map represents 920 km on the ground

NORTH AMERICA (2004)

	USA	Mexico	Jamaica
Infant mortality (deaths per 1 000 births)	7	24	17
Calorie consumption (daily calorie intake per capita)	3 766	3 160	2 705
Literacy (% of total population)	97	92.2	87.9
Life expectancy (at birth in years)	77	74	76

EUROPE (2004)

	Norway	UK	Albania
Infant mortality (deaths per 1 000 births)	4	5	26
Calorie consumption (daily calorie intake per capita)	3 382	3 368	2 900
Literacy (% of total population)	100	99	86.5
Life expectancy (at birth in years)	79	77	74

SOUTH AMERICA (2004)

	Argentina	Brazil	Bolivia
Infant mortality (deaths per 1 000 births)	16	30	56
Calorie consumption (daily calorie intake per capita)	3 171	3 002	2 267
Literacy (% of total population)	97.1	86.4	87.2
Life expectancy (at birth in years)	74	69	64

AFRICA (2004)

	Algeria	S. Africa	Malawi
Infant mortality (deaths per 1 000 births)	39	52	114
Calorie consumption (daily calorie intake per capita)	2 987	2 921	2 168
Literacy (% of total population)	70	86.4	62.7
Life expectancy (at birth in years)	71	46	38

CALORIE CONSUMPTION

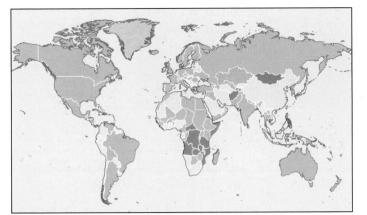

MAP KEY

Daily calorie intake per person

- above 3 000
- 2 500 to 2 999
- 2 500 to 2 499
- below 2 000
- no data

LITERACY

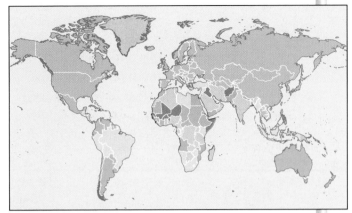

MAP KEY

Literacy (percentage of population)

- 90 to 100
- 80 to 89
- 60 to 79
- 40 to 59
- below 40
- no data

INFANT MORTALITY

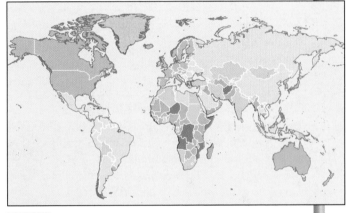

MAP KEY

Deaths per thousand live births

- above 125
- 75 to 124
- 35 to 74
- 15 to 34
- below 15
- no data

LIFE EXPECTANCY

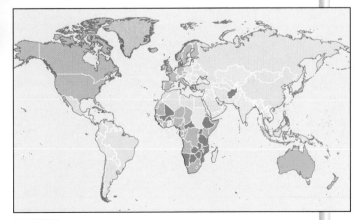

MAP KEY

Life expectancy at birth in years

- above 75
- 65 to 74
- 55 to 64
- 45 to 54
- below 45
- no data

ASIA (2004)	Japan	China	Bangladesh
Infant mortality (deaths per 1 000 births)	4	5	51
Calorie consumption (daily calorie intake per capita)	2 746	2 963	2 187
Literacy (% of total population)	99	86	43.1
Life expectancy (at birth in years)	82	71	62

AUSTRALASIA AND OCEANIA (2004)	Australia	Fiji	New Zealand
Infant mortality (deaths per 1 000 births)	6	17	6
Calorie consumption (daily calorie intake per capita)	3 126	2 789	3 235
Literacy (% of total population)	100	93.7	99
Life expectancy (at birth in years)	79	70	78

ACCESS TO WATER

Water covers 70 per cent of our planet, yet 40 per cent of the world's people experience water shortages – a figure likely to increase rapidly over the next ten years as population growth continues, especially in LEDCs.

In Africa alone, 40 billion hours are used every year to fetch and carry water – mainly by women and children. Having good local supplies, like this well in the Gambia, saves time enabling children to attend school and women to do other, paid work.

THE WORLD'S WATER RESOURCES

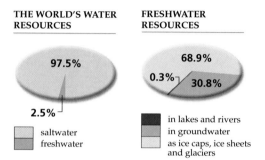

97.5%

2.5%

- saltwater
- freshwater

FRESHWATER RESOURCES

68.9%

0.3%

30.8%

- in lakes and rivers
- in groundwater
- as ice caps, ice sheets and glaciers

AVAILABILITY OF FRESHWATER

One of the main reasons for the shortage of water is that 97.5 per cent of the water that covers the Earth is saltwater, whilst just 2.5 per cent is freshwater. To add to the problem, 70 per cent of freshwater is in the form of ice and snow. The World Health Organization (WHO) estimates that less than 1 per cent of this is available and accessible for human consumption. The freshwater that can be accessed most easily is in rivers and lakes, but 25 per cent of the world has to rely on groundwater or deep aquifers for water supplies.

The distribution of the world's freshwater supply is uneven. Areas with the least water available include most of Africa, the Middle East, Asia and Europe. Those with the most available per person include South America and Oceania.

WATER CONSUMPTION

There are three main uses for freshwater – agriculture, industry and domestic (personal) use. Water use is highest in MEDCs and in countries where industry is growing rapidly.

By far the greatest use of freshwater (over two thirds) is for agriculture. Irrigation is essential for crops to be grown in many regions. In the USA, 49 per cent of freshwater consumption is used by agriculture, with 80 per cent of that for irrigation. In Africa, up to 90 per cent of freshwater used is for agriculture.

By 2025, it is estimated that 17 per cent more freshwater will be needed simply to grow enough food to cope with the estimated increase in population.

Many industrial and manufacturing processes use vast amounts of water and industry accounts for 22 per cent of total freshwater use. Personal or domestic use accounts for 8 per cent of total water consumption. Average demand is about 50 litres per day, but actual use varies considerably. Water use can be as low as 10 litres in LEDCs and as high as 150 litres in countries such as the UK.

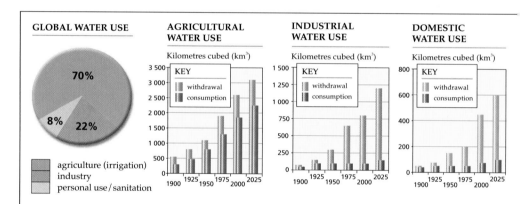

GLOBAL WATER USE

70%

8% 22%

- agriculture (irrigation)
- industry
- personal use / sanitation

AGRICULTURAL WATER USE

Kilometres cubed (km³)

KEY
- withdrawal
- consumption

1900 1925 1950 1975 2000 2025

INDUSTRIAL WATER USE

Kilometres cubed (km³)

KEY
- withdrawal
- consumption

1900 1925 1950 1975 2000 2025

DOMESTIC WATER USE

Kilometres cubed (km³)

KEY
- withdrawal
- consumption

1900 1925 1950 1975 2000 2025

AVAILABILITY OF FRESHWATER

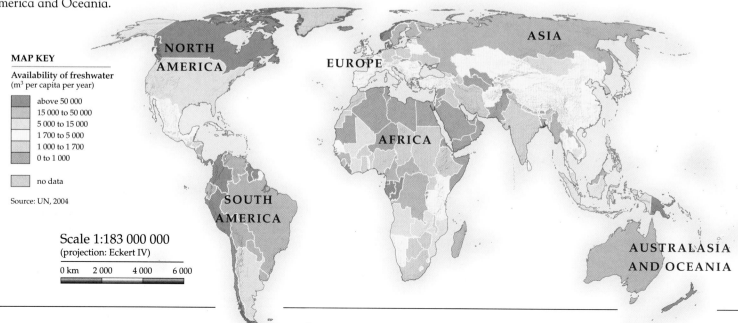

MAP KEY

Availability of freshwater (m³ per capita per year)

- above 50 000
- 15 000 to 50 000
- 5 000 to 15 000
- 1 700 to 5 000
- 1 000 to 1 700
- 0 to 1 000

- no data

Source: UN, 2004

NORTH AMERICA

EUROPE

ASIA

AFRICA

SOUTH AMERICA

AUSTRALASIA AND OCEANIA

Scale 1:183 000 000
(projection: Eckert IV)

0 km   2 000   4 000   6 000

CAUSES OF WATER STRESS

The two maps below show the percentages of available freshwater being used in 1995 and predicted levels for 2025. Countries with high percentages are said to be water stressed.

Causes of water stress:

- rising demand from a growing population and increasing industrialisation;

- the impact of global warming and climate change on water supply;

- conflicts or 'water wars' between countries. Over 300 of the world's largest river basins occupy several countries. As water supplies become scarce, disputes over water extraction and access are likely to increase;

- wastage of water. Up to 45 per cent of freshwater is wasted through leaky pipes, pollution or by simply draining away.

POPULATION WITHOUT ACCESS TO CLEAN WATER

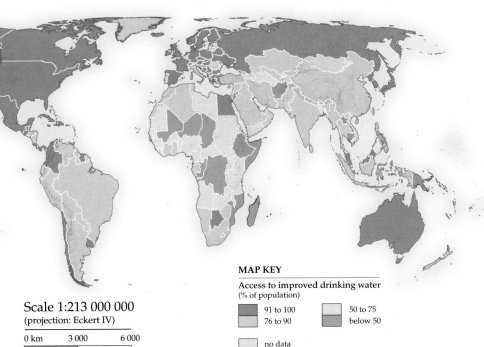

Scale 1:213 000 000
(projection: Eckert IV)

0 km   3 000   6 000

MAP KEY

Access to improved drinking water
(% of population)

- 91 to 100
- 76 to 90
- 50 to 75
- below 50
- no data

Source: UN, 2004

WATER STRESS IN 1995

MAP KEY

Freshwater stress - water withdrawal
(% of total available)

- above 40
- 10 to 20
- 20 to 40
- below 10

Source: UN, 2004

PREDICTED WATER STRESS IN 2025

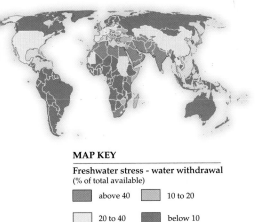

MAP KEY

Freshwater stress - water withdrawal
(% of total available)

- above 40
- 10 to 20
- 20 to 40
- below 10

Source: UN, 2004

ACCESS TO CLEAN WATER

Access to clean, safe water is a basic necessity of life and one of the most important global issues – and will continue to be so as demand increases. It is estimated that 1.4 billion people (20 per cent of the world's population) do not have access to clean water.

It is mainly the poorer LEDCs who have least access. This lack of access is a major barrier to a country's development.

IMPACT ON HEALTH AND QUALITY OF LIFE

'No single measure would do more to reduce disease and save lives in the developing world than bringing safe water and adequate sanitation to all.'

Kofi Annan, UN Secretary General, Millennium Report 2000

Contaminated water is responsible for the cause and spread of 80 per cent of the world's diseases. These include cholera, typhoid and dysentery. Diseases associated with lack of access to safe drinking water, inadequate sanitation and poor hygiene kill 2.2 million people (mainly children) in LEDCs each year. Many of these diseases can be prevented if the water supply is made clean, and others can be treated if there is access to suitable health care and medicines.

ACCESS TO WATER – EQUAL SHARES?

- 2.8 billion people suffer from water shortages – this is expected to rise to 3.8 billion by 2015.

- One flush of a toilet in the UK uses as much water as the average person in an LEDC uses each day for washing, cleaning, cooking and drinking.

- Many urban dwellers in LEDCs without piped water spend as much as 10 per cent of their money on buying water from street vendors or tankers.

- 2.4 billion people (40 per cent) do not have access to adequate sanitation.

- Every 15 seconds a child dies from diseases caused by dirty water or poor sanitation.

THE BIG ISSUES

1 Access to freshwater is uneven. How does this influence development?

2 What are some of the ways freshwater is being used unsustainably?

3 What is water stress? Is it inevitable that it will continue to increase?

4 Where might water wars break out in the future?

PHYSICAL

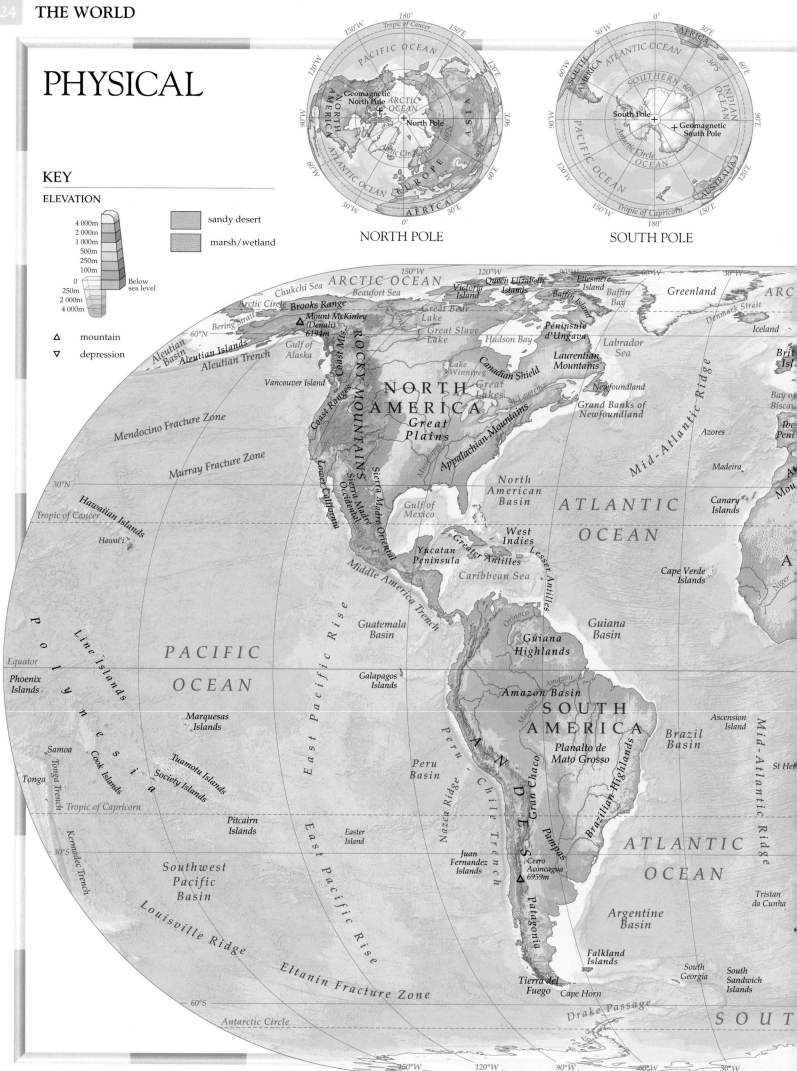

KEY

ELEVATION

4 000m
2 000m
1 000m
500m
250m
100m
0
250m
2 000m
4 000m

Below sea level

sandy desert

marsh/wetland

△ mountain

▽ depression

NORTH POLE

PACIFIC OCEAN
Tropic of Cancer
Geomagnetic North Pole
ARCTIC OCEAN
North Pole
NORTH AMERICA
ASIA
EUROPE
Arctic Circle
ATLANTIC OCEAN
AFRICA

SOUTH POLE

AFRICA
SOUTH AMERICA
ATLANTIC OCEAN
INDIAN OCEAN
SOUTHERN
South Pole
Geomagnetic South Pole
Antarctic Circle
PACIFIC OCEAN
AUSTRALIA
Tropic of Capricorn

ARCTIC OCEAN
Chukchi Sea
Beaufort Sea
Victoria Island
Queen Elizabeth Islands
Ellesmere Island
Baffin Bay
Greenland
ARC
Brooks Range
Great Bear Lake
Baffin Island
Arctic Circle
Mount McKinley (Denali) 6194m
Great Slave Lake
Péninsule d'Ungava
Denmark Strait
Bering Strait
Hudson Bay
Labrador Sea
Iceland
Aleutian Basin
Aleutian Islands
Gulf of Alaska
Coast Mts.
ROCKY MOUNTAINS
Lake Winnipeg
Canadian Shield
Laurentian Mountains
Brit. Isl.
Aleutian Trench
Vancouver Island
Coast Ranges
NORTH AMERICA
Great Lakes
St. Lawrence
Newfoundland
Grand Banks of Newfoundland
Mid-Atlantic Ridge
Bay of Biscay
Mendocino Fracture Zone
Great Plains
Appalachian Mountains
Azores
Ibe. Peni
Murray Fracture Zone
Sierra Madre Occidental
Sierra Madre Oriental
Mississippi
North American Basin
ATLANTIC
Madeira
Mou
30°N
Lower California
Gulf of Mexico
OCEAN
Canary Islands
Hawaiian Islands
Tropic of Cancer
Yucatan Peninsula
Greater Antilles
West Indies
Lesser Antilles
Cape Verde Islands
A
Hawai'i
Caribbean Sea
Middle America Trench
P
o
l
y
n
e
s
i
a
Line Islands
Guatemala Basin
Orinoco
Guiana Basin
Niger
PACIFIC
Galapagos Islands
Guiana Highlands
Equator
East Pacific Rise
Phoenix Islands
OCEAN
Amazon
Marquesas Islands
Amazon Basin
SOUTH AMERICA
Ascension Island
Samoa
Madeira
Brazil Basin
Mid-Atlantic Ridge
Tonga Trench
Cook Islands
Tuamotu Islands
Society Islands
Peru Basin
ANDES
Planalto de Mato Grosso
Brazilian Highlands
St Hel
Tonga
Nazca Ridge
Gran Chaco
Tropic of Capricorn
Pitcairn Islands
Easter Island
Peru-Chile Trench
Pampas
ATLANTIC
Kermadec Trench
Juan Fernandez Islands
Cerro Aconcagua 6959m
OCEAN
Southwest Pacific Basin
Patagonia
Argentine Basin
Tristan da Cunha
East Pacific Rise
Louisville Ridge
Falkland Islands
South Georgia
South Sandwich Islands
Eltanin Fracture Zone
Tierra del Fuego
Cape Horn
Drake Passage
SOUT
Antarctic Circle

PHYSICAL FACTFILE

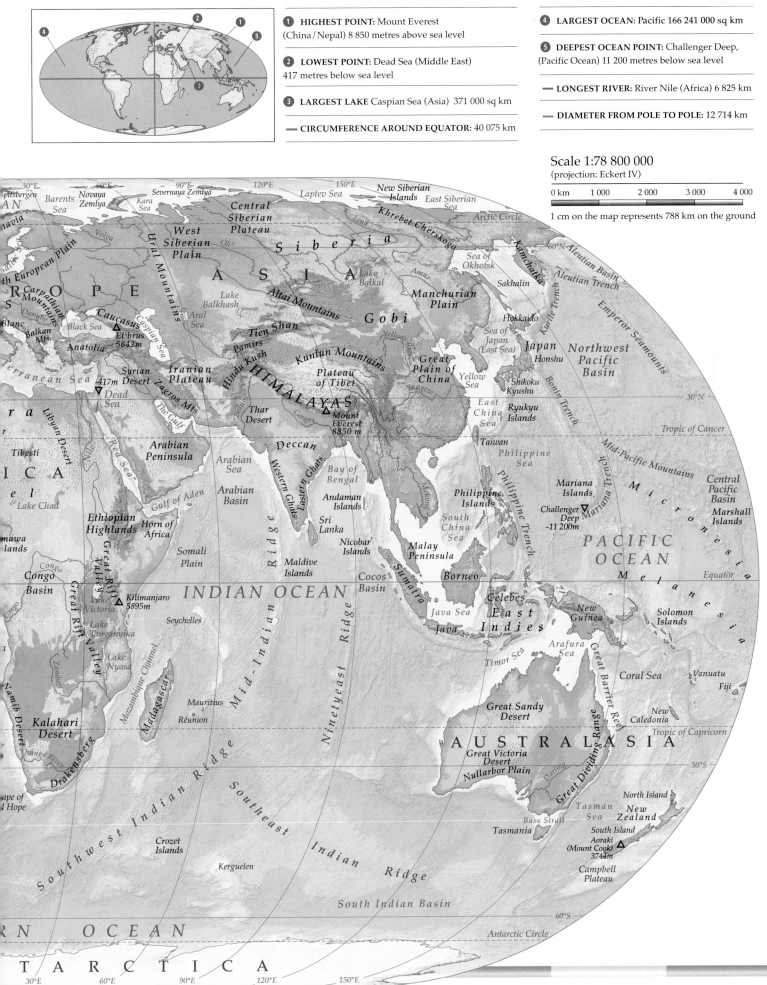

1 HIGHEST POINT: Mount Everest (China / Nepal) 8 850 metres above sea level

2 LOWEST POINT: Dead Sea (Middle East) 417 metres below sea level

3 LARGEST LAKE Caspian Sea (Asia) 371 000 sq km

— **CIRCUMFERENCE AROUND EQUATOR:** 40 075 km

4 LARGEST OCEAN: Pacific 166 241 000 sq km

5 DEEPEST OCEAN POINT: Challenger Deep, (Pacific Ocean) 11 200 metres below sea level

— **LONGEST RIVER:** River Nile (Africa) 6 825 km

— **DIAMETER FROM POLE TO POLE:** 12 714 km

Scale 1:78 800 000
(projection: Eckert IV)

0 km   1 000   2 000   3 000   4 000

1 cm on the map represents 788 km on the ground

TECTONIC PLATES

The Earth's crust is not a continuous unbroken shell. It is divided into several major (and a number of smaller) slabs of rock called tectonic plates. These move in different ways on the liquid rock of the mantle below the Earth's surface. The majority of the world's volcanoes and fault lines are found at or near the plate boundaries.

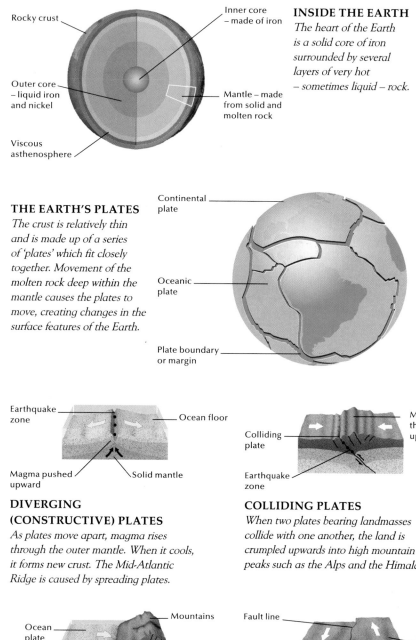

Rocky crust

Inner core – made of iron

Outer core – liquid iron and nickel

Mantle – made from solid and molten rock

Viscous asthenosphere

INSIDE THE EARTH
The heart of the Earth is a solid core of iron surrounded by several layers of very hot – sometimes liquid – rock.

THE EARTH'S PLATES
The crust is relatively thin and is made up of a series of 'plates' which fit closely together. Movement of the molten rock deep within the mantle causes the plates to move, creating changes in the surface features of the Earth.

Continental plate

Oceanic plate

Plate boundary or margin

Earthquake zone

Ocean floor

Magma pushed upward

Solid mantle

DIVERGING (CONSTRUCTIVE) PLATES
As plates move apart, magma rises through the outer mantle. When it cools, it forms new crust. The Mid-Atlantic Ridge is caused by spreading plates.

Colliding plate

Mountains thrust upward

Earthquake zone

COLLIDING PLATES
When two plates bearing landmasses collide with one another, the land is crumpled upwards into high mountain peaks such as the Alps and the Himalayas.

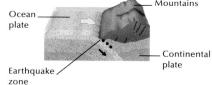

Ocean plate

Mountains

Continental plate

Earthquake zone

SUBDUCTING (DESTRUCTIVE) PLATES
When an ocean-bearing plate collides with a continental plate it is forced downwards under the other plate and into the mantle. Volcanoes occur along these boundaries.

Fault line

Plate

Earthquake zone

SLIDING PLATES
As two plates slide past each other, great friction occurs along the fault line that lies between them. This can lead to powerful earthquakes.

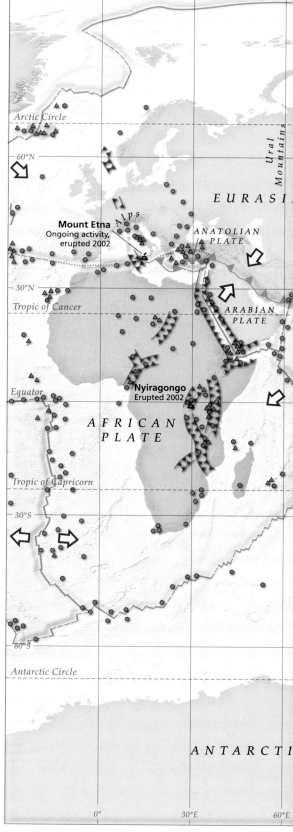

Mount Etna
Ongoing activity, erupted 2002

EURASI

ANATOLIAN PLATE

ARABIAN PLATE

Nyiragongo
Erupted 2002

AFRICAN PLATE

ANTARCTI

Scale 1:137 000 000
(projection: Gall Stereographic)

0 km   2 000   4 000   6 000   8 000

1 cm on the map represents 1 370 km on the ground

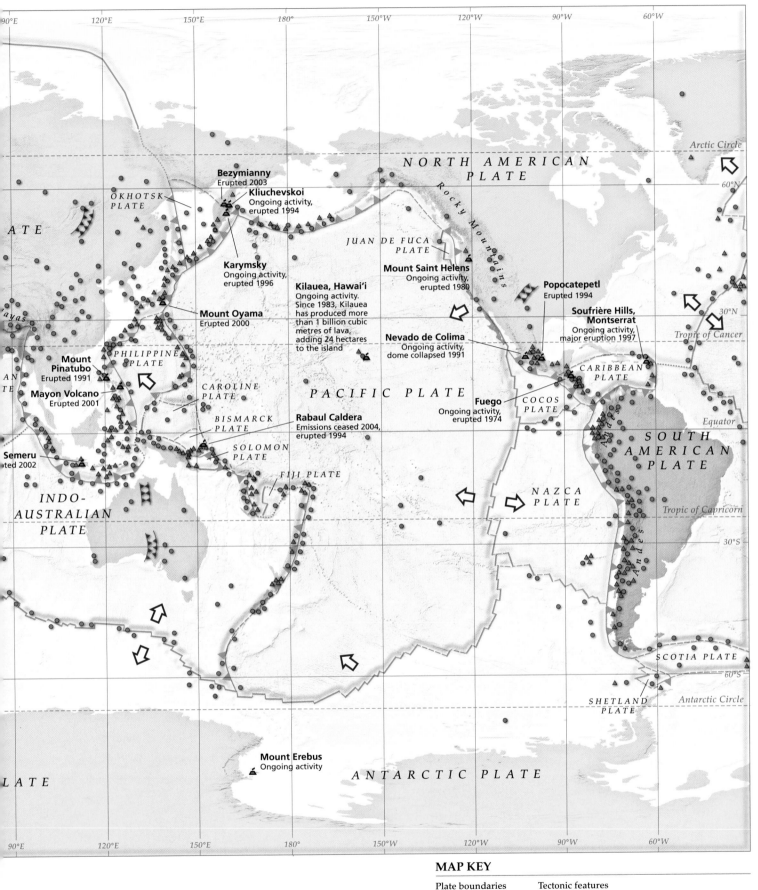

Bezymianny
Erupted 2003

Kliuchevskoi
Ongoing activity,
erupted 1994

OKHOTSK PLATE

Karymsky
Ongoing activity,
erupted 1996

JUAN DE FUCA PLATE

Mount Saint Helens
Ongoing activity,
erupted 1980

NORTH AMERICAN PLATE

Kilauea, Hawai'i
Ongoing activity.
Since 1983, Kilauea
has produced more
than 1 billion cubic
metres of lava,
adding 24 hectares
to the island

Popocatepetl
Erupted 1994

Mount Oyama
Erupted 2000

**Soufrière Hills,
Montserrat**
Ongoing activity,
major eruption 1997

Nevado de Colima
Ongoing activity,
dome collapsed 1991

PHILIPPINE PLATE

**Mount
Pinatubo**
Erupted 1991

CARIBBEAN PLATE

CAROLINE PLATE

PACIFIC PLATE

Fuego
Ongoing activity,
erupted 1974

COCOS PLATE

Mayon Volcano
Erupted 2001

BISMARCK PLATE

Rabaul Caldera
Emissions ceased 2004,
erupted 1994

SOLOMON PLATE

SOUTH AMERICAN PLATE

Semeru
ted 2002

FIJI PLATE

*INDO-
AUSTRALIAN
PLATE*

NAZCA PLATE

SCOTIA PLATE

Mount Erebus
Ongoing activity

SHETLAND PLATE

ANTARCTIC PLATE

Arctic Circle
60°N
30°N
Tropic of Cancer
Equator
Tropic of Capricorn
30°S
60°S
Antarctic Circle

90°E   120°E   150°E   180°   150°W   120°W   90°W   60°W

MAP KEY

Plate boundaries
— constructive
▲▲ destructive
----- conservative
.... uncertain

Tectonic features
⛰ major volcanic events since 1980
▲ volcanic zone
● hot spot
● major earthquake

⇨ direction of plate movement
〰 rift valley

OCEANS

Over two thirds of the Earth's surface is covered by seas and oceans. These contain over 97 per cent of the world's water. The depth of water varies considerably, with many land areas having fairly shallow water close to them where continental shelves extend out from the coast. The oceans are not still – ocean currents have a major effect on world climate patterns, carrying warm or cold water around the globe.

SEA LEVEL

If the influence of tides, winds, currents and variations in gravity were ignored, the surface of the Earth's oceans would closely follow the topography of the ocean floor.

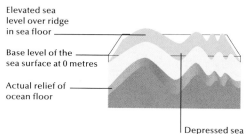

Elevated sea level over ridge in sea floor

Base level of the sea surface at 0 metres

Actual relief of ocean floor

Depressed sea level over trough in ocean floor

SEA FLOOR FEATURES

The continental shelf is a shallow, flat sea bed surrounding the Earth's continents. It extends to the continental slope, which falls to the ocean floor. Here, the flat abyssal plains are interrupted by vast, underwater mountain ranges, mid-ocean ridges and ocean trenches, which plunge to depths of up to 11 200 metres.

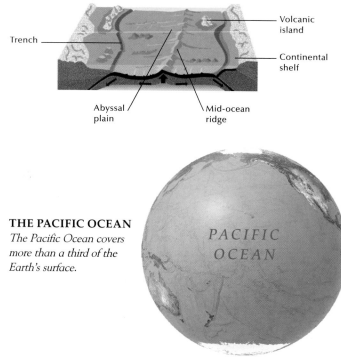

Trench

Volcanic island

Continental shelf

Abyssal plain

Mid-ocean ridge

THE PACIFIC OCEAN

The Pacific Ocean covers more than a third of the Earth's surface.

PACIFIC OCEAN

AGES OF THE OCEAN FLOOR

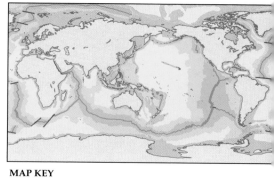

MAP KEY

Ages of the ocean floor (million years before present [Ma])

Quaternary 1.6 Ma to present	Mesozoic 180 to 61 Ma
Neogene 23 to 1.6 Ma	
Paleogene 60 to 24 Ma	continental shelf
	uncertain age

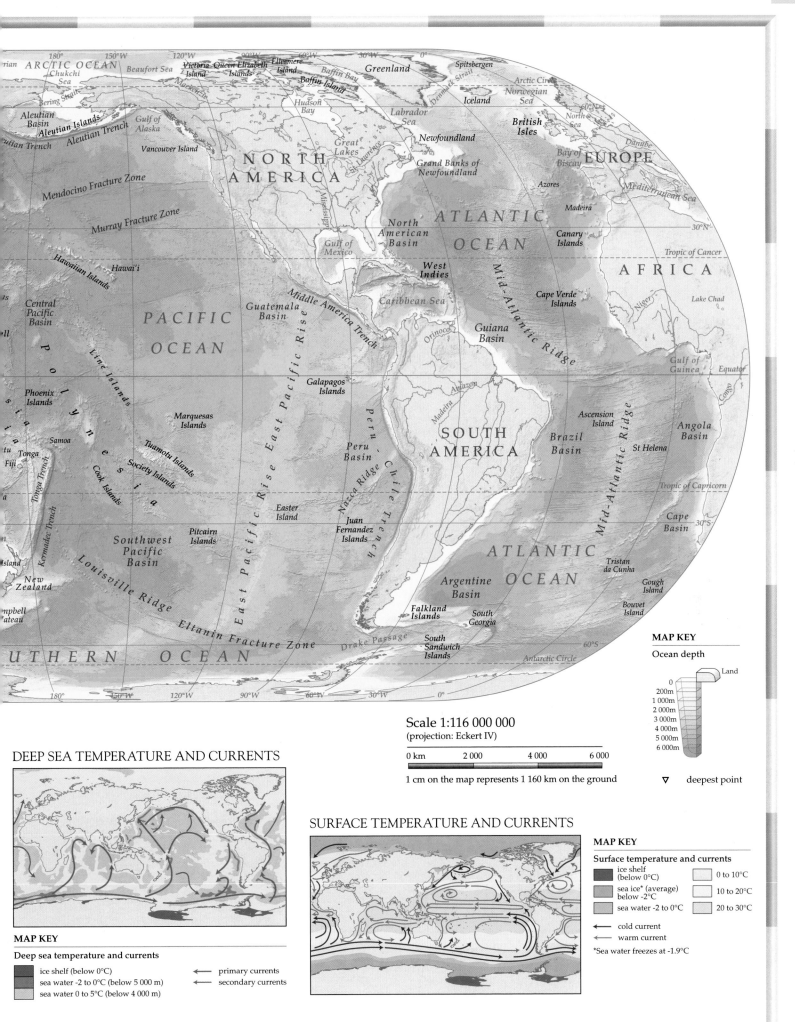

Scale 1:116 000 000
(projection: Eckert IV)

0 km	2 000	4 000	6 000

1 cm on the map represents 1 160 km on the ground

MAP KEY

Ocean depth

- 0 — Land
- 200m
- 1 000m
- 2 000m
- 3 000m
- 4 000m
- 5 000m
- 6 000m

▽ deepest point

DEEP SEA TEMPERATURE AND CURRENTS

MAP KEY

Deep sea temperature and currents

- ice shelf (below 0°C)
- sea water -2 to 0°C (below 5 000 m)
- sea water 0 to 5°C (below 4 000 m)
- ← primary currents
- ← secondary currents

SURFACE TEMPERATURE AND CURRENTS

MAP KEY

Surface temperature and currents

- ice shelf (below 0°C)
- sea ice* (average) below -2°C
- sea water -2 to 0°C
- 0 to 10°C
- 10 to 20°C
- 20 to 30°C
- ← cold current
- ← warm current

*Sea water freezes at -1.9°C

CLIMATE

The world's atmospheric systems are driven by the energy of the Sun. The distribution of this energy and therefore variations in climate across the world depend upon: distance from the Equator (latitude); height above sea level (altitude); winds; ocean currents and distance from the sea. Tropical climates along the Equator are separated from the two polar regions by a large temperate zone.

MAP KEY

Climate regions

- polar
- tundra
- sub-arctic
- cool continental
- temperate
- warm temperate
- mediterranean
- semi-arid
- arid
- tropical
- humid equatorial
- mountain

Scale 1:113 000 000
(projection: Eckert IV)

0 km   2 000   4 000   6 000

1 cm on the map represents 1 130 km on the ground

PRECIPITATION

MAP KEY

Average annual precipitation (mm)

- above 3 500 mm
- 2 500 to 3 500 mm
- 2 000 to 2 500 mm
- 1 500 to 2 000 mm
- 1 000 to 1 500 mm
- 500 to 1 000 mm
- 200 to 500 mm
- 0 to 200 mm

AVERAGE JANUARY TEMPERATURE

MAP KEY

Average January temperature

- above 30 °C
- 20 to 30 °C
- 10 to 20 °C
- 0 to 10 °C
- -10 to 0 °C
- -20 to -10 °C
- -30 to -20 °C
- below -30 °C

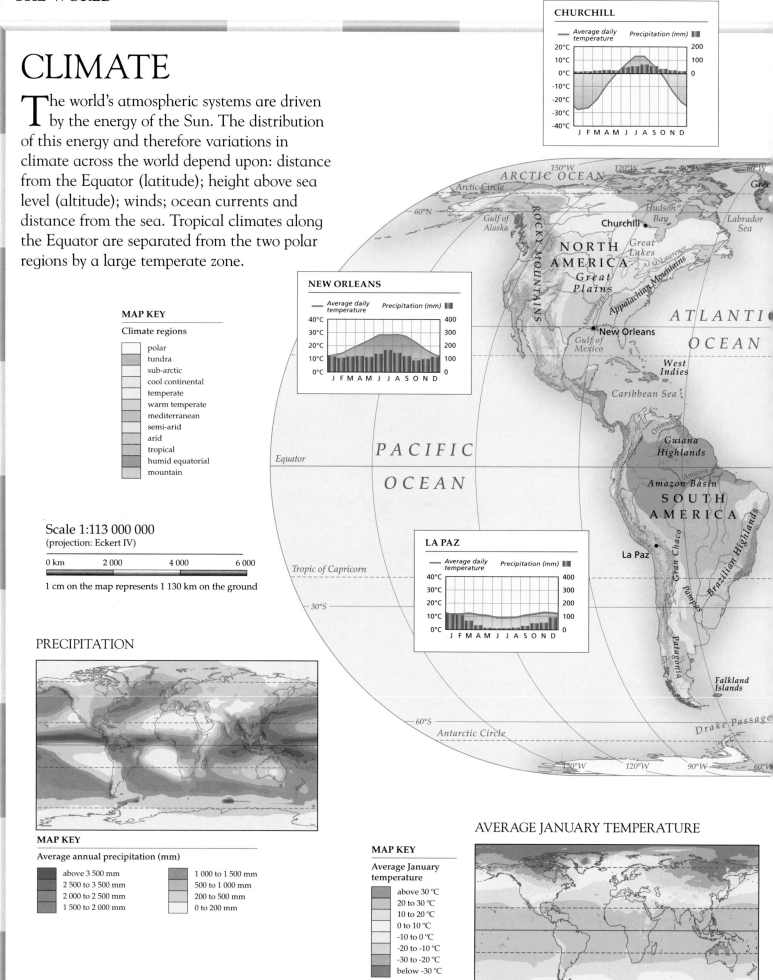

CHURCHILL

Average daily temperature   Precipitation (mm)

NEW ORLEANS

Average daily temperature   Precipitation (mm)

LA PAZ

Average daily temperature   Precipitation (mm)

EDINBURGH

Average daily temperature — Precipitation (mm) ▮

OLENËK

Average daily temperature — Precipitation (mm) ▮

BEIJING

Average daily temperature — Precipitation (mm) ▮

BANJARMASIN

Average daily temperature — Precipitation (mm) ▮

CAPE TOWN

Average daily temperature — Precipitation (mm) ▮

ONSLOW

Average daily temperature — Precipitation (mm) ▮

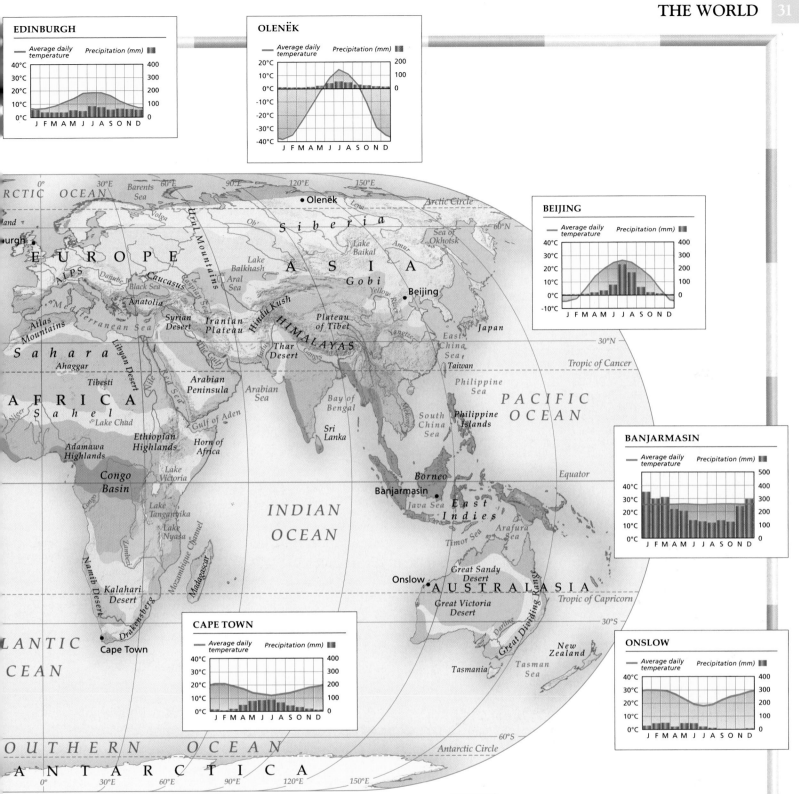

AVERAGE JULY TEMPERATURE

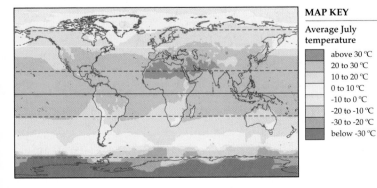

MAP KEY

Average July temperature

- above 30 °C
- 20 to 30 °C
- 10 to 20 °C
- 0 to 10 °C
- -10 to 0 °C
- -20 to -10 °C
- -30 to -20 °C
- below -30 °C

WINDS

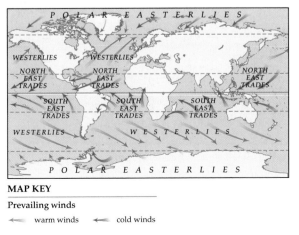

MAP KEY

Prevailing winds

← warm winds   ← cold winds

CLIMATE CHANGE

The Earth's climate is a dynamic, constantly changing system. It is the result of complicated interactions between the atmosphere, biosphere, hydrosphere and lithosphere, which are known as the geosphere. Throughout the Earth's history there have been several periods when it has been much warmer or colder than today. Some of the variations and changes appear in fairly regular cycles, for example Ice Ages have occurred roughly every 100 000 years. Other events that affect the climate on a short timescale, like El Niño, sunspots and major volcanic eruptions, occur more frequently.

THE GEOSPHERE

The physical systems on or near the Earth's surface can be divided into four 'spheres'. They interact with one another to determine climate.

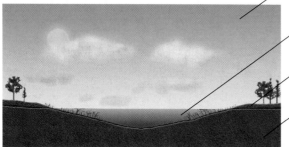

The atmosphere, which contains all of the Earth's air. The atmosphere is made up of different layers.

The hydrosphere, which contains all of the Earth's solid, liquid and gaseous water.

The biosphere, which contains all of the Earth's living organisms.

The lithosphere, which contains the solid rock of the Earth's crust and the uppermost layer of the mantle.

EVIDENCE OF CLIMATE CHANGE

It is only in more recent times that accurate measurements of weather and climate have been made. This has allowed scientists to identify changes and trends over the past 100–150 years and make predictions about future changes. On average the world is 0.6 degrees Celsius warmer than it was 100 years ago. In order 1998, 2002, 1997 and 2001 were the warmest four years since records began 150 years ago. Other evidence of climate change includes:

• sea level rises;

• temperature rises and the melting of ice sheets;

• the thinning of the Arctic sea ice;

• extended periods of drought;

• more severe storms and flooding.

Higher temperatures have already led to the shrinking of the world's major glaciers. In Greenland ice sheets are melting at an increasing rate and the extent of Arctic pack ice is shrinking. In Antarctica, especially around the peninsula, sections of the ice sheet are breaking off as temperatures rise.

TEMPERATURE CHANGE RELATIVE TO THE 1961–1990 AVERAGE

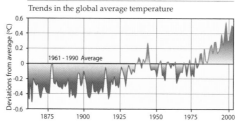

Trends in the global average temperature

WHY ARE SCIENTISTS CONCERNED?

Whilst the Earth's climate has experienced many changes over time, it is the speed and causes of the recent changes that concern scientists. There has been debate amongst scientists about why temperatures have risen, but many now believe that the main cause is an increase of certain gases in the Earth's atmosphere, commonly known as the 'greenhouse gases'.

THE MAIN GREENHOUSE GASES AND THEIR CAUSES	
Gas	Human causes
Carbon dioxide CO_2	Burning of fossil fuels, solid waste and wood; deforestation resulting in less carbon dioxide being removed from the atmosphere
Methane CH_4	Decay of organic matter e.g. waste in landfill sites; raising of livestock; extraction of fossil fuels and rice cultivation
Nitrous Oxide N_2O	Use of nitrogen fertilisers; burning of fossil fuels and wood
Ozone O_3	Air pollution
Halocarbons HFCs, CFCs, HCFCs	Use in solvents, cleaners and coolants, e.g. in spray cans and fridges

WHAT IS THE GREENHOUSE EFFECT?

The Earth's atmosphere is made up of several naturally occurring gases – including carbon dioxide, water vapour, methane and nitrous oxide, which together are called the greenhouse gases. They are essential in controlling and maintaining the Earth's temperature. This process is known as the 'greenhouse effect'.

THE INCREASING GREENHOUSE EFFECT

Measurements show a dramatic increase in the amount of greenhouse gases – carbon dioxide levels alone have increased by 50 per cent since 1800. As a result, the layer of greenhouse gases in the atmosphere is trapping more solar radiation, so more solar heat is reaching the Earth than is being radiated back out. This increases the greenhouse effect, leading to the temperature changes known as global warming.

THE GREENHOUSE EFFECT

Without the greenhouse effect, heat would radiate straight back into space and the Earth would be 20–30 degrees Celsius colder.

Radiation is re-emitted from the atmosphere back to Earth.

Some radiation is reflected back into space.

Greenhouse gases absorb outgoing radiation, trapping heat in the atmosphere.

Greenhouse gases allow sufficient solar radiation through to warm the Earth's surface.

PREDICTED CHANGES IN SURFACE AIR TEMPERATURES BY 2070–2100

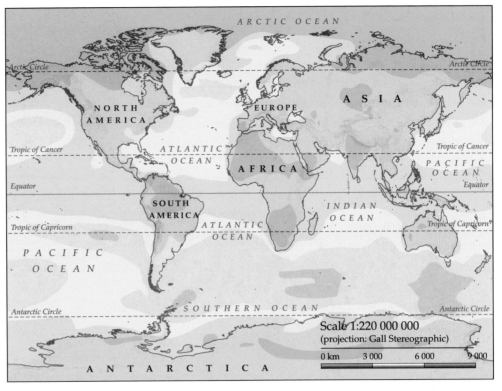

INCREASE IN CARBON EMISSIONS 1900–2000

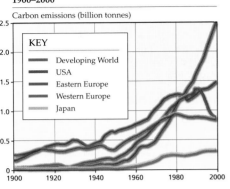

Carbon emissions (billion tonnes)

KEY
- Developing World
- USA
- Eastern Europe
- Western Europe
- Japan

HUMAN IMPACT ON GLOBAL WARMING

Most scientists now agree that human activity has significantly contributed to global warming. Greenhouse gases are produced and released by farming and industry. Carbon dioxide is the main cause of concern as it makes up over two thirds of the current levels of greenhouse gases. Factory emissions, burning fossil fuels such as oil, coal and gas in power stations, and exhaust emissions from motor vehicles are the major sources of 'extra' emissions. The main producers of greenhouse gases are MEDCs, with the USA alone responsible for 36 per cent of all greenhouse gas emissions.

POSSIBLE EFFECTS OF GLOBAL WARMING

With emissions of greenhouse gases continuing to rise, a number of leading organisations suggest that by 2100, global temperatures could be between 1.4 and 5.8 degrees Celsius higher than they are today. Some of the possible effects of this temperature rise could include:

- melting of pack ice and ice sheets, causing sea levels to rise, widespread flooding and the displacement of millions of people;

- less solar radiation being reflected back into space from ice and snow. More radiation will be absorbed by the Earth's surface, increasing warming;

- rising ocean temperatures, potentially changing patterns of ocean currents and altering global climatic patterns;

MAP KEY

Change in average surface air temperature between 1960–1990 and 2070–2100 in degrees Celsius

- 4 to 5
- 3 to 4
- 2 to 3
- 1 to 2
- 0 to 1

- hot regions becoming hotter with less rainfall, making human settlement virtually impossible. Deserts will spread;

- increasing occurrence of floods, drought and other extreme weather conditions;

- changing distribution of natural vegetation zones and ecosystems;

- habitat loss, resulting in the extinction of thousands of land plants and animals.

EFFORTS TO TACKLE GLOBAL WARMING

At the Kyoto summit, held in Japan in 1997, a new treaty was set out to try and put into practice recommendations made by the United Nations Framework for Climate Change (UNFCC). It requires countries to cut their emissions of greenhouse gases by an average of 5 per cent by 2012 (based on 1990 emissions levels). The Kyoto Protocol was seen as essential to reducing greenhouse gases and slowing down global warming.

However, the success of Kyoto has been limited. Countries unlikely to exceed their quota of emissions can trade their 'spare' quota with countries that will exceed their targets. Countries can also offset their emissions totals against carbon 'sinks' – forested areas. This means that countries like Russia, which is very dependent on fossil fuels, but which also has large areas of forest can continue to produce high levels of carbon dioxide emissions.

The Kyoto Protocol was finally ratified in February 2005 but emissions in many countries continue to rise. The refusal of the USA (the world's largest producer of carbon dioxide emissions) to sign the treaty means that it may only have a small impact on future climate change. The problems surrounding the treaty have also highlighted the difficulties of trying to take worldwide action on environmental issues.

THE BIG ISSUES

1 Are current agreements like the Kyoto Protocol on greenhouse gas emissions doing enough to reduce global warming sufficiently to halt climate change?

2 What are the possible consequences of failing to reduce greenhouse gas emissions?

3 Should we just accept the fact that the world's climate is always changing and concentrate on preparing for and adapting to it?

LIFE ON EARTH

The world can be divided into a number of major biomes. These are regions with a specific combination of natural vegetation, animals, climates, soils and landscapes, which combine to give each its unique character. Some biomes have a far greater plant and animal biodiversity than others: many are under threat from human activity.

Tundra on Clavering Island, North East Greenland National Park, Greenland.

WORLD BIOMES

MAP KEY

World biomes

	polar
	tundra
	coniferous forest
	deciduous forest
	temperate grassland
	mediterranean
	savanna
	tropical forest
	hot desert
	cold desert
	mountain

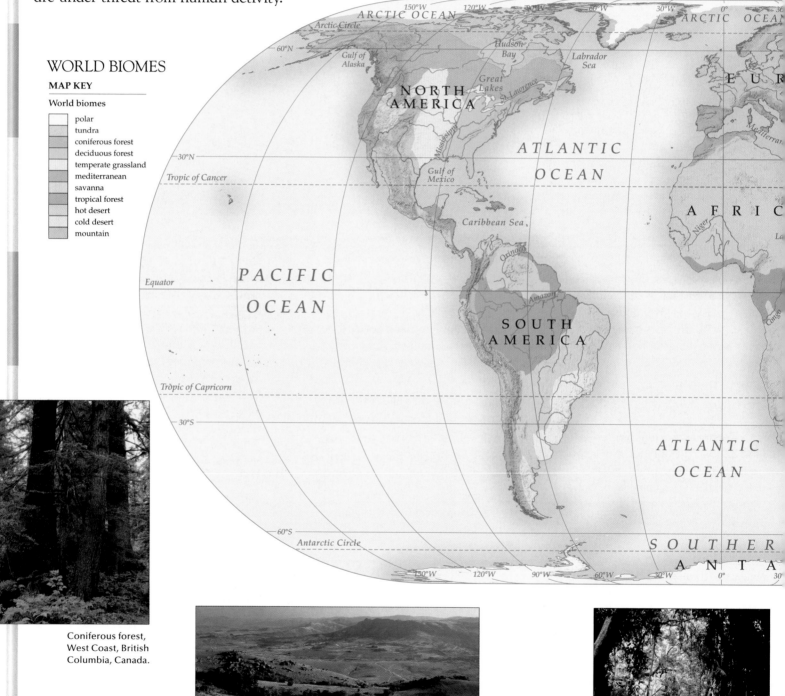

Coniferous forest, West Coast, British Columbia, Canada.

Savanna in Swaziland, South Africa.

Tropical rainforest in the Gambia, Africa.

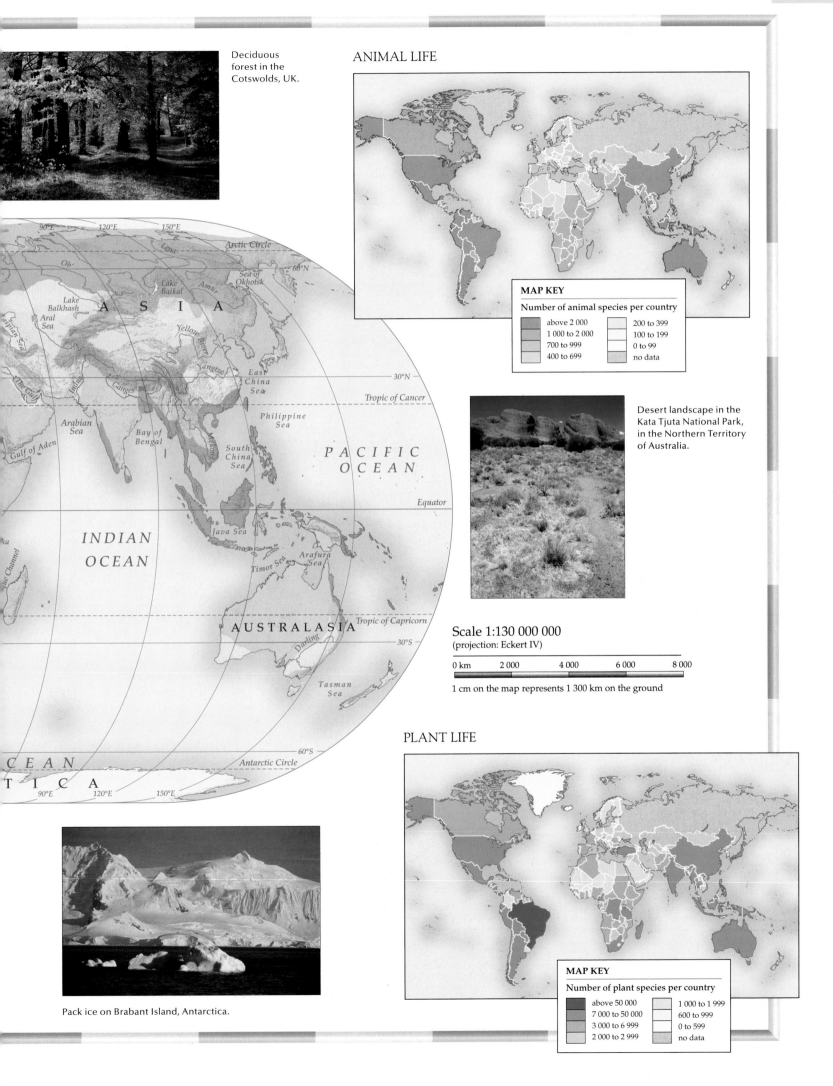

Deciduous forest in the Cotswolds, UK.

ANIMAL LIFE

MAP KEY

Number of animal species per country

above 2 000	200 to 399
1 000 to 2 000	100 to 199
700 to 999	0 to 99
400 to 699	no data

Desert landscape in the Kata Tjuta National Park, in the Northern Territory of Australia.

Scale 1:130 000 000

(projection: Eckert IV)

| 0 km | 2 000 | 4 000 | 6 000 | 8 000 |

1 cm on the map represents 1 300 km on the ground

PLANT LIFE

Pack ice on Brabant Island, Antarctica.

MAP KEY

Number of plant species per country

above 50 000	1 000 to 1 999
7 000 to 50 000	600 to 999
3 000 to 6 999	0 to 599
2 000 to 2 999	no data

Map labels

Arctic Circle
Lena
Ob·
66°N
Sea of Okhotsk
Lake Baikal
Amur
A S I A
Lake Balkhash
Aral Sea
Yellow River
Yangtze
East China Sea
30°N
Tropic of Cancer
The Gulf
Indus
Ganges
Arabian Sea
Bay of Bengal
Mekong
Philippine Sea
South China Sea
PACIFIC OCEAN
Gulf of Aden
Java Sea
Equator
INDIAN OCEAN
Timor Sea
Arafura Sea
...que Channel
AUSTRALASIA
Tropic of Capricorn
Darling
30°S
Tasman Sea
OCEAN
...TICA
60°S
Antarctic Circle
90°E 120°E 150°E

BRITISH ISLES POLITICAL

The United Kingdom comprises England, Wales, Scotland and Northern Ireland. Together with Ireland, which gained independence in 1921, it makes up the British Isles. The political map of the UK has changed considerably since 1997. There is now a mixture of unitary authorities and counties responsible for local government. Both Scotland and Wales have their own elected Parliament and Assembly.

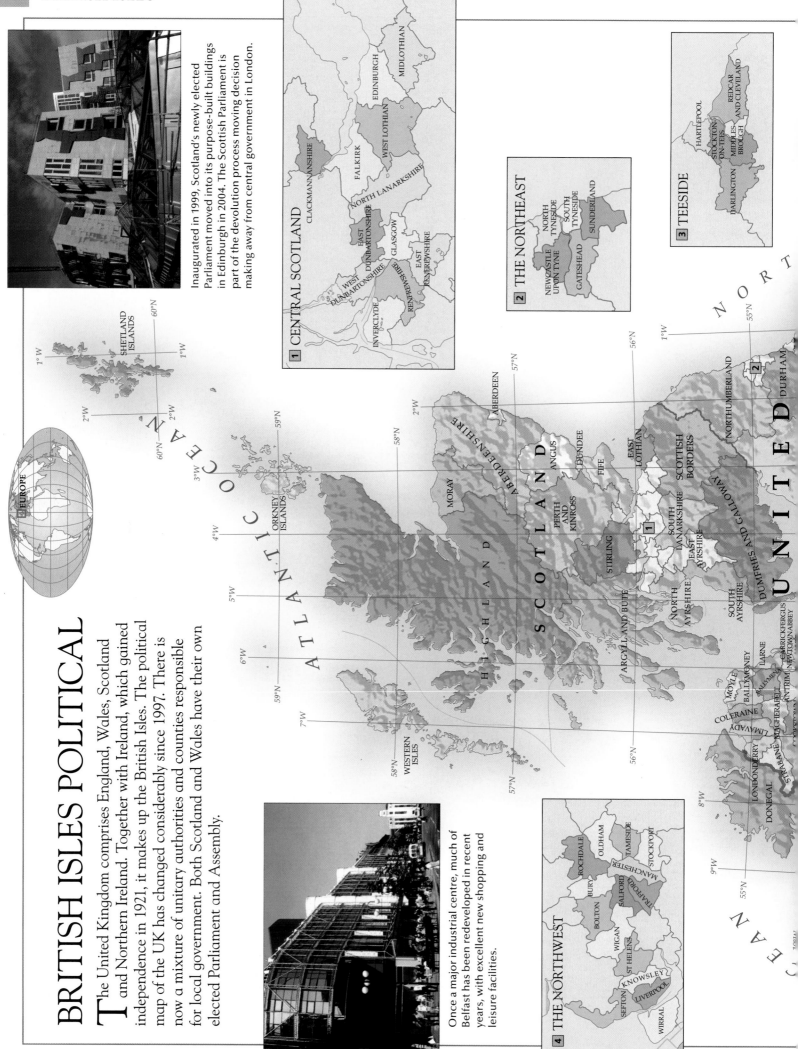

Inaugurated in 1999, Scotland's newly elected Parliament moved into its purpose-built buildings in Edinburgh in 2004. The Scottish Parliament is part of the devolution process moving decision making away from central government in London.

Once a major industrial centre, much of Belfast has been redeveloped in recent years, with excellent new shopping and leisure facilities.

1 CENTRAL SCOTLAND

CLACKMANNANSHIRE
FALKIRK
WEST LOTHIAN
EDINBURGH
MIDLOTHIAN
NORTH LANARKSHIRE
WEST DUNBARTONSHIRE
EAST DUNBARTONSHIRE
GLASGOW
EAST RENFREWSHIRE
RENFREWSHIRE
INVERCLYDE

2 THE NORTHEAST

NEWCASTLE UPON TYNE
NORTH TYNESIDE
SOUTH TYNESIDE
GATESHEAD
SUNDERLAND

3 TEESIDE

HARTLEPOOL
STOCKTON-ON-TEES
MIDDLESBROUGH
REDCAR AND CLEVELAND
DARLINGTON

4 THE NORTHWEST

ROCHDALE
OLDHAM
BURY
TAMESIDE
STOCKPORT
BOLTON
SALFORD
MANCHESTER
TRAFFORD
WIGAN
ST HELENS
KNOWSLEY
SEFTON
LIVERPOOL
WIRRAL

EUROPE

ATLANTIC OCEAN

SHETLAND ISLANDS
ORKNEY ISLANDS
WESTERN ISLES

HIGHLAND
MORAY
ABERDEENSHIRE
ABERDEEN
ANGUS
DUNDEE
PERTH AND KINROSS
FIFE
STIRLING
EAST LOTHIAN
SCOTTISH BORDERS
SOUTH LANARKSHIRE
EAST AYRSHIRE
NORTH AYRSHIRE
SOUTH AYRSHIRE
ARGYLL AND BUTE
DUMFRIES AND GALLOWAY
NORTHUMBERLAND
DURHAM

SCOTLAND
UNITED

NORTH

MOYLE
COLERAINE
LIMAVADY
BALLYMONEY
BALLYMENA
LARNE
MAGHERAFELT
ANTRIM
NEWTOWNABBEY
CARRICKFERGUS
STRABANE
LONDONDERRY
DONEGAL

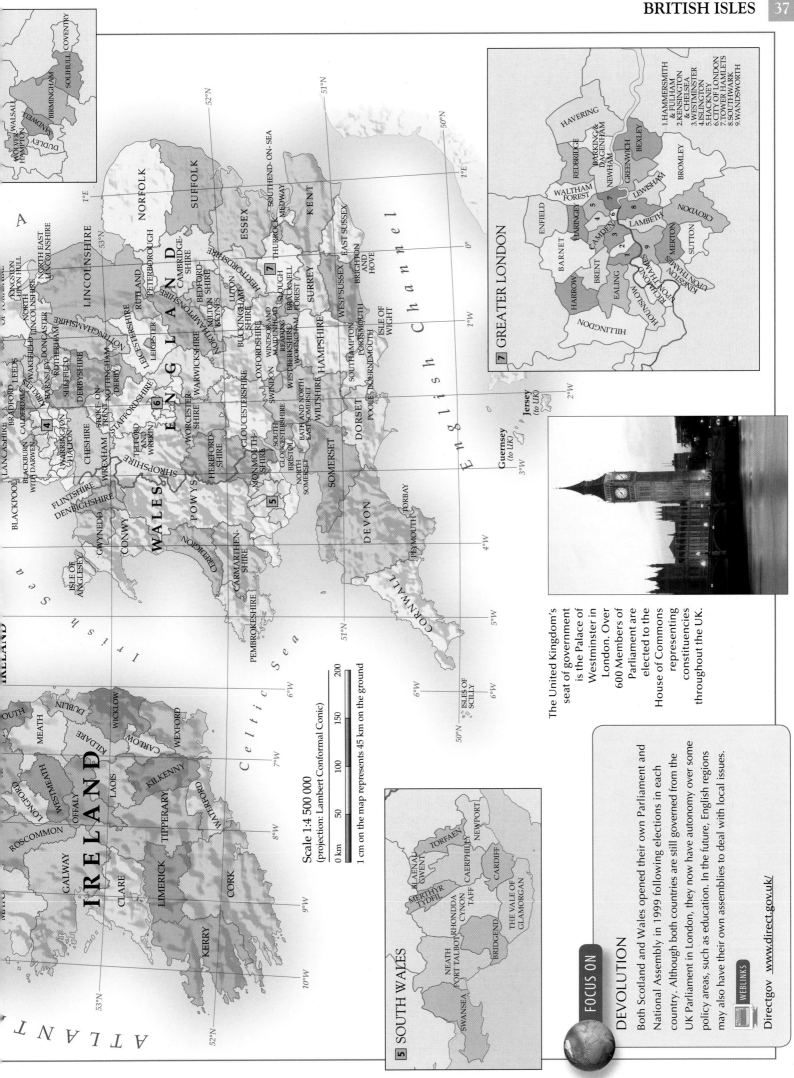

Scale 1:4 500 000
(projection: Lambert Conformal Conic)

0 km   50   100   150   200

1 cm on the map represents 45 km on the ground

7 GREATER LONDON

1. HAMMERSMITH & FULHAM
2. KENSINGTON & CHELSEA
3. WESTMINSTER
4. ISLINGTON
5. HACKNEY
6. CITY OF LONDON
7. TOWER HAMLETS
8. SOUTHWARK
9. WANDSWORTH

The United Kingdom's seat of government is the Palace of Westminster in London. Over 600 Members of Parliament are elected to the House of Commons representing constituencies throughout the UK.

FOCUS ON

DEVOLUTION

Both Scotland and Wales opened their own Parliament and National Assembly in 1999 following elections in each country. Although both countries are still governed from the UK Parliament in London, they now have autonomy over some policy areas, such as education. In the future, English regions may also have their own assemblies to deal with local issues.

WEBLINKS

Directgov www.direct.gov.uk/

5 SOUTH WALES

BRITISH ISLES PHYSICAL

Once connected to mainland Europe, the British Isles are now separated from the rest of the continent by the English Channel. To the north and west the land is mainly mountainous. In the south and east the land is much lower and flatter.

GLACIATION IN THE BRITISH ISLES

Much of the British Isles' present day physical landscape was shaped by the last Ice Age, which ended 10 000 years ago.

Southern limit of glaciation 10 000–70 000 years ago

PHYSICAL FACTFILE

1 HIGHEST POINT: Ben Nevis, 1 343 metres above sea level

2 LOWEST POINT: The Fenlands, 4 metres below sea level

3 LARGEST LAKE: Lough Neagh, 396 km²

— LONGEST RIVER: River Shannon, 370 km

— LENGTH OF COASTLINE: 13 880 km (19 716 km including all islands)

MAP KEY

Elevation

4 000m
2 000m
1 000m
500m
250m
100m
0
250m
2 000m
4 000m

Below sea level

△ mountain

▽ depression

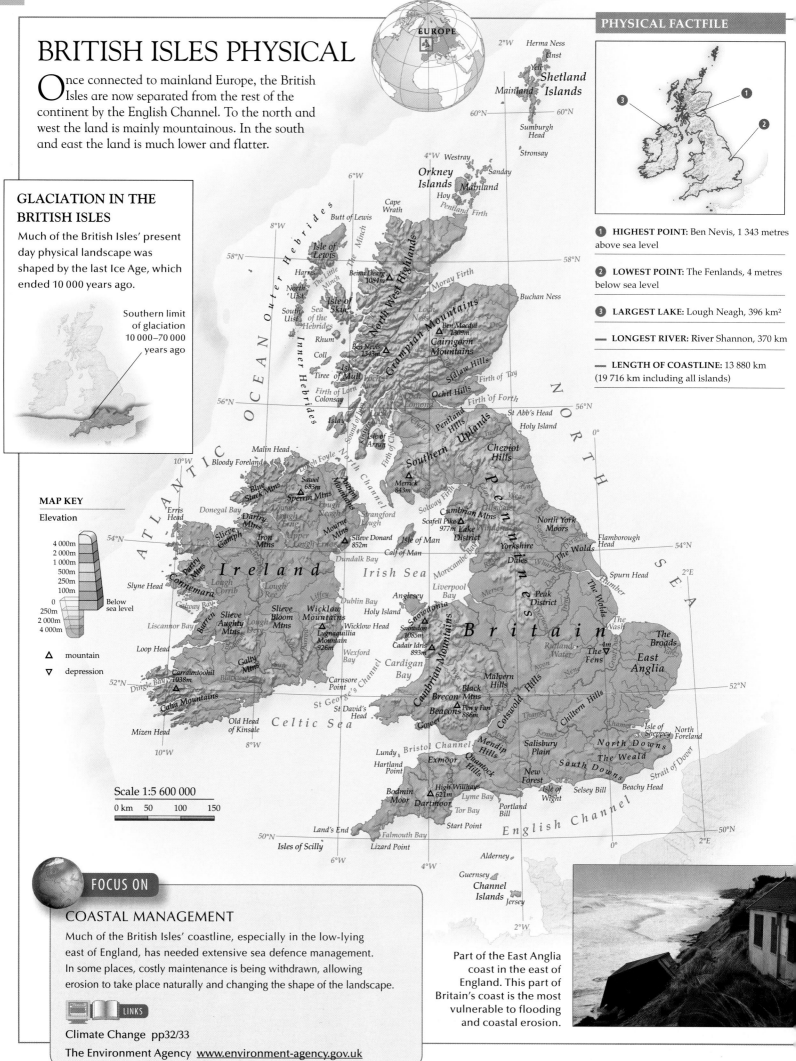

Scale 1:5 600 000

0 km   50   100   150

FOCUS ON

COASTAL MANAGEMENT

Much of the British Isles' coastline, especially in the low-lying east of England, has needed extensive sea defence management. In some places, costly maintenance is being withdrawn, allowing erosion to take place naturally and changing the shape of the landscape.

LINKS

Climate Change pp32/33

The Environment Agency www.environment-agency.gov.uk

Part of the East Anglia coast in the east of England. This part of Britain's coast is the most vulnerable to flooding and coastal erosion.

BRITISH ISLES GEOLOGY

The oldest – and hardest – rocks are found in the north and west of the British Isles. Metamorphic and igneous rocks make up much of the Scottish Highlands, north Wales and Northern Ireland. To the south and east, the rocks become progressively younger with softer clays and sands separated by harder limestone ridges.

MAP KEY

Sedimentary rocks

- unconsolidated sand and shell banks
- clay
- chalk
- oolitic limestone
- massive limestone
- friable sandstone
- hard sandstone
- greywacke and slate
- mixed hard sediments
- coal measures

Igneous rocks

- extrusive (volcanic), lava, basalt etc.
- intrusive, granite etc.

Metamorphic rocks

- gneiss, schist, quartzite etc.

Scale 1:5 000 000

0 km   50   100   150

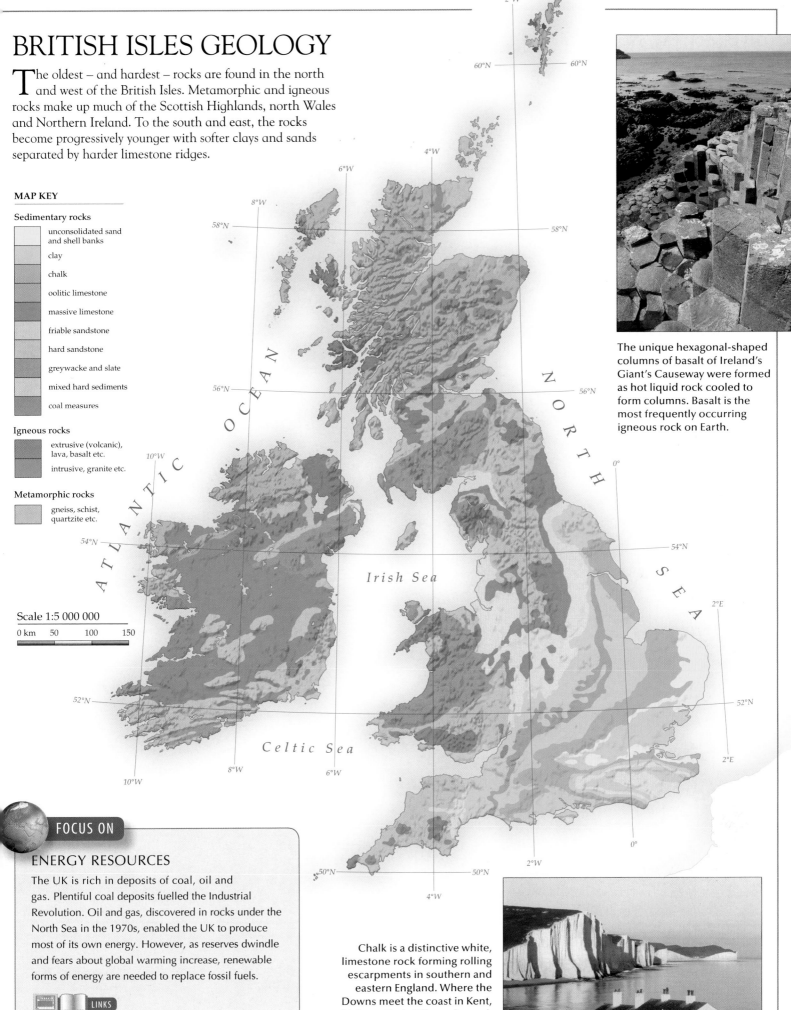

The unique hexagonal-shaped columns of basalt of Ireland's Giant's Causeway were formed as hot liquid rock cooled to form columns. Basalt is the most frequently occurring igneous rock on Earth.

ATLANTIC OCEAN

NORTH SEA

Irish Sea

Celtic Sea

FOCUS ON

ENERGY RESOURCES

The UK is rich in deposits of coal, oil and gas. Plentiful coal deposits fuelled the Industrial Revolution. Oil and gas, discovered in rocks under the North Sea in the 1970s, enabled the UK to produce most of its own energy. However, as reserves dwindle and fears about global warming increase, renewable forms of energy are needed to replace fossil fuels.

LINKS

Climate Change pp32/33

British Geological Survey www.bgs.ac.uk

Chalk is a distinctive white, limestone rock forming rolling escarpments in southern and eastern England. Where the Downs meet the coast in Kent, high, vertical cliffs are formed.

UK CLIMATE

The UK has a temperate maritime climate. Temperatures are rarely extreme, partly because the warm water from the North Atlantic Drift raises winter temperatures. The mountainous north and west are wetter than the south and east.

EUROPE

The River Ouse flooded the city of York in 2000 after prolonged rainfall. River levels rose by over five metres, causing extensive damage.

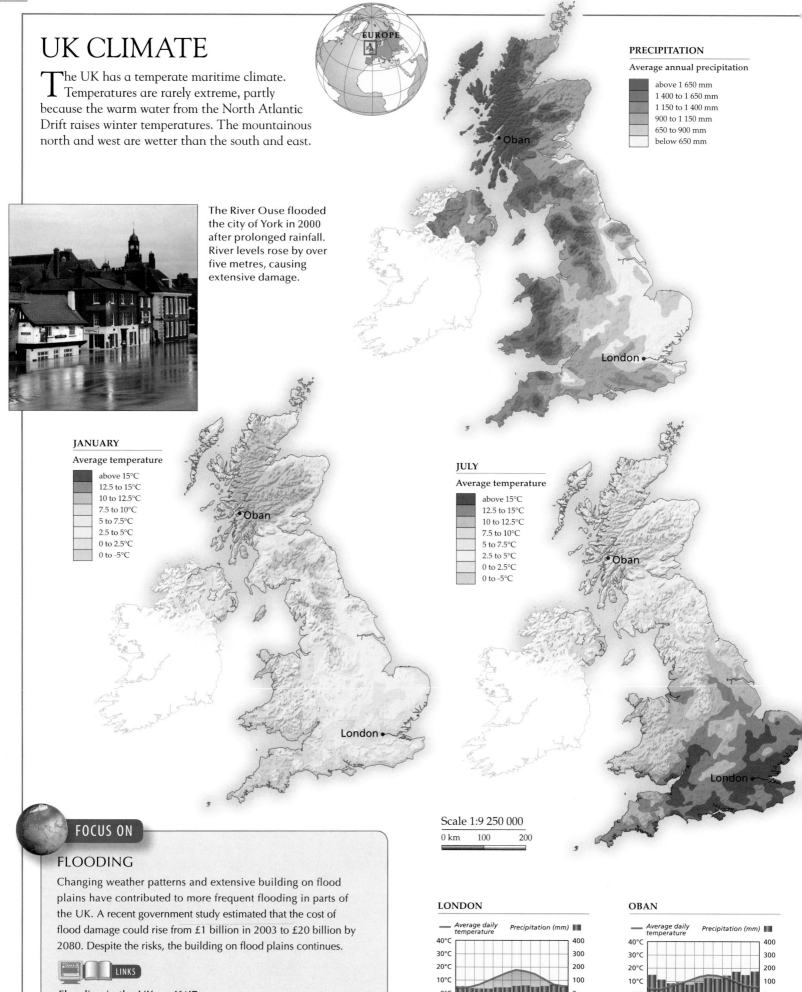

PRECIPITATION

Average annual precipitation

- above 1 650 mm
- 1 400 to 1 650 mm
- 1 150 to 1 400 mm
- 900 to 1 150 mm
- 650 to 900 mm
- below 650 mm

• Oban

London •

JANUARY

Average temperature

- above 15°C
- 12.5 to 15°C
- 10 to 12.5°C
- 7.5 to 10°C
- 5 to 7.5°C
- 2.5 to 5°C
- 0 to 2.5°C
- 0 to -5°C

• Oban

London •

JULY

Average temperature

- above 15°C
- 12.5 to 15°C
- 10 to 12.5°C
- 7.5 to 10°C
- 5 to 7.5°C
- 2.5 to 5°C
- 0 to 2.5°C
- 0 to -5°C

• Oban

London •

Scale 1:9 250 000

0 km   100   200

FOCUS ON

FLOODING

Changing weather patterns and extensive building on flood plains have contributed to more frequent flooding in parts of the UK. A recent government study estimated that the cost of flood damage could rise from £1 billion in 2003 to £20 billion by 2080. Despite the risks, the building on flood plains continues.

LINKS

Flooding in the UK pp46/47

United Nations Framework Convention on Climate Change http://unfccc.int/

The Environment Agency www.environment-agency.gov.uk

LONDON

— Average daily temperature   Precipitation (mm) ■■

40°C — 400
30°C — 300
20°C — 200
10°C — 100
0°C — 0
J F M A M J J A S O N D

☼ 1 daily hours of sunshine, January   ☼ 6 daily hours of sunshine, July

OBAN

— Average daily temperature   Precipitation (mm) ■■

40°C — 400
30°C — 300
20°C — 200
10°C — 100
0°C — 0
J F M A M J J A S O N D

☼ 1 daily hours of sunshine, January   ☼ 4 daily hours of sunshine, July

UK POPULATION

The UK's 60 million population is unevenly distributed. The majority of people live in the large urban areas, with one in four in London and the Southeast. In contrast, much of the highland regions of Wales and Scotland are very sparsely populated.

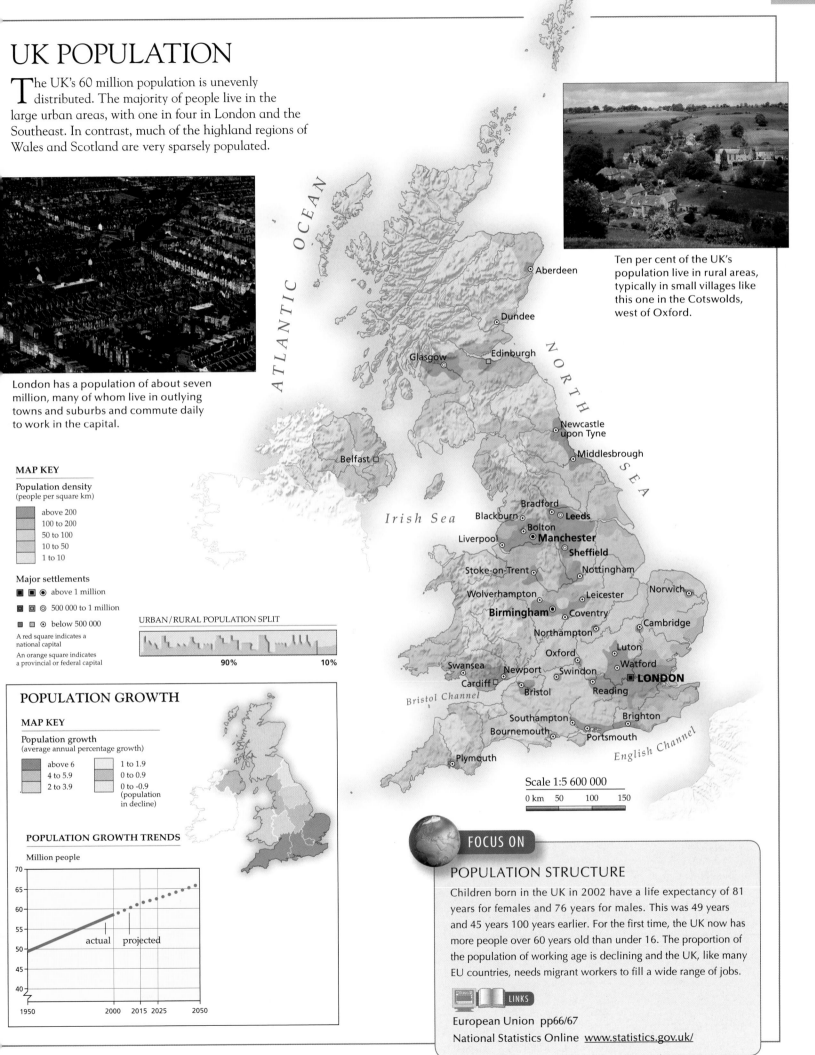

Ten per cent of the UK's population live in rural areas, typically in small villages like this one in the Cotswolds, west of Oxford.

London has a population of about seven million, many of whom live in outlying towns and suburbs and commute daily to work in the capital.

MAP KEY

Population density
(people per square km)

- above 200
- 100 to 200
- 50 to 100
- 10 to 50
- 1 to 10

Major settlements

- ■ ■ ⊙ above 1 million
- ■ □ ◎ 500 000 to 1 million
- ■ □ ⊙ below 500 000

A red square indicates a national capital

An orange square indicates a provincial or federal capital

URBAN / RURAL POPULATION SPLIT

90%   10%

POPULATION GROWTH

MAP KEY

Population growth
(average annual percentage growth)

- above 6
- 4 to 5.9
- 2 to 3.9
- 1 to 1.9
- 0 to 0.9
- 0 to -0.9 (population in decline)

POPULATION GROWTH TRENDS

Million people

actual | projected

1950 ... 2000 2015 2025 ... 2050

(graph axis values: 70, 65, 60, 55, 50, 45, 40)

Map labels

Aberdeen
Dundee
Glasgow   Edinburgh
Belfast
Newcastle upon Tyne
Middlesbrough
Bradford
Blackburn   Leeds
Bolton
Liverpool   Manchester
Sheffield
Stoke-on-Trent   Nottingham
Wolverhampton   Leicester   Norwich
Birmingham   Coventry
Northampton   Cambridge
Oxford   Luton
Swansea   Newport   Swindon   Watford
Cardiff   LONDON
Bristol   Reading
Southampton   Brighton
Bournemouth   Portsmouth
Plymouth

ATLANTIC OCEAN
NORTH SEA
Irish Sea
Bristol Channel
English Channel

Scale 1:5 600 000

0 km   50   100   150

FOCUS ON

POPULATION STRUCTURE

Children born in the UK in 2002 have a life expectancy of 81 years for females and 76 years for males. This was 49 years and 45 years 100 years earlier. For the first time, the UK now has more people over 60 years old than under 16. The proportion of the population of working age is declining and the UK, like many EU countries, needs migrant workers to fill a wide range of jobs.

LINKS

European Union pp66/67

National Statistics Online www.statistics.gov.uk/

UK LAND USE

The UK is highly urban and industrialised. The location of different types of farming reflects different physical features and climate. Most arable farming is found near the warmer, drier and flatter east, whilst livestock, pasture and hill farming is found in the wetter, higher north and west. Many major industrial areas originally developed close to fossil fuel resources, but concentrate today on light or service industries.

MAP KEY

Land use type

- forest
- pasture
- cropland
- livestock rearing
- hill farming
- market gardening, pigs and poultry
- urban area

Industry

- industrial area
- major conurbation

Arable farming – barley and wheat – on the Lincolnshire Wolds. Warm, dry summers and flat, fertile soils make eastern England the UK's main cereal growing region.

MINERAL RESOURCES

There are numerous small deposits of other minerals such as tin, copper, iron ore, gold and silver, which are worked depending on their commerical viability.

MAP KEY

- oil field
- gas field
- coal field

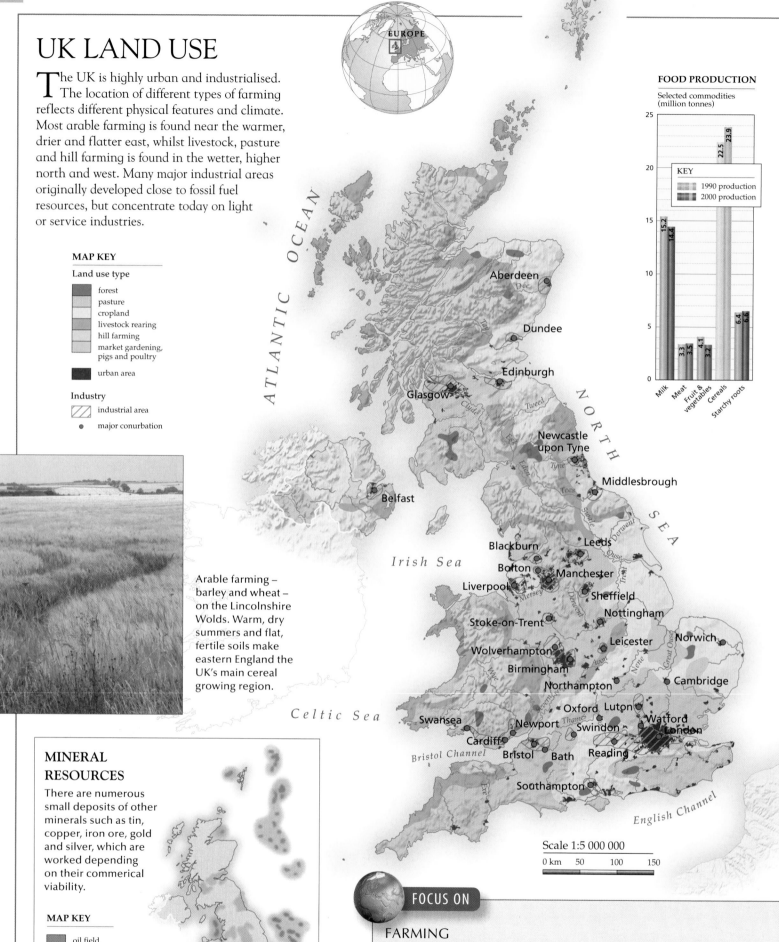

FOOD PRODUCTION

Selected commodities
(million tonnes)

KEY
- 1990 production
- 2000 production

Commodity	1990	2000
Milk	15.2	14.4
Meat	3.3	3.5
Fruit & vegetables	4.1	3.2
Cereals	22.5	23.9
Starchy roots	6.4	6.6

 FOCUS ON

FARMING

UK farming has undergone major changes since the middle of the twentieth century. Farms are now typically highly mechanised, capital intensive businesses, employing few people. Many farmers have gone out of business since the mid 1990s.

LINKS

Genetically Modified Crops pp148/149
Department for Environment Food and Rural Affairs www.defra.gov.uk

Scale 1:5 000 000

0 km　50　100　150

UK ENVIRONMENT

The UK is a densely populated country. It suffers from a range of environmental problems, many associated with pollution from the production of waste from industry and homes. Emissions from vehicles, spillages from industry and the transport of goods, such as oil, also cause damage to the environment.

One of the main causes of atmospheric pollution – and acid rain – are emissions of SO_2 and NO_2 from thermal power stations. This is a coal-fired station at Radcliffe on Soar, Nottinghamshire.

MAP KEY

2001 CO² Emissions
(tonnes per sq km)

- high (above 100)
- medium (33 to 100)
- low (0 to 32)

Marine pollution

- heavy marine pollution
- light marine pollution
- major oil spill (over 500 tonnes)

Environment

- nuclear power station
- nuclear accident
- polluted river

MAP KEY

- Blue Flag beaches, 2004

UK BLUE FLAG BEACHES

The Blue Flag Award is a measure of cleanliness and quality for beaches in Europe. To gain Blue Flag status, a beach has to meet strict criteria for both the beach area and water quality.

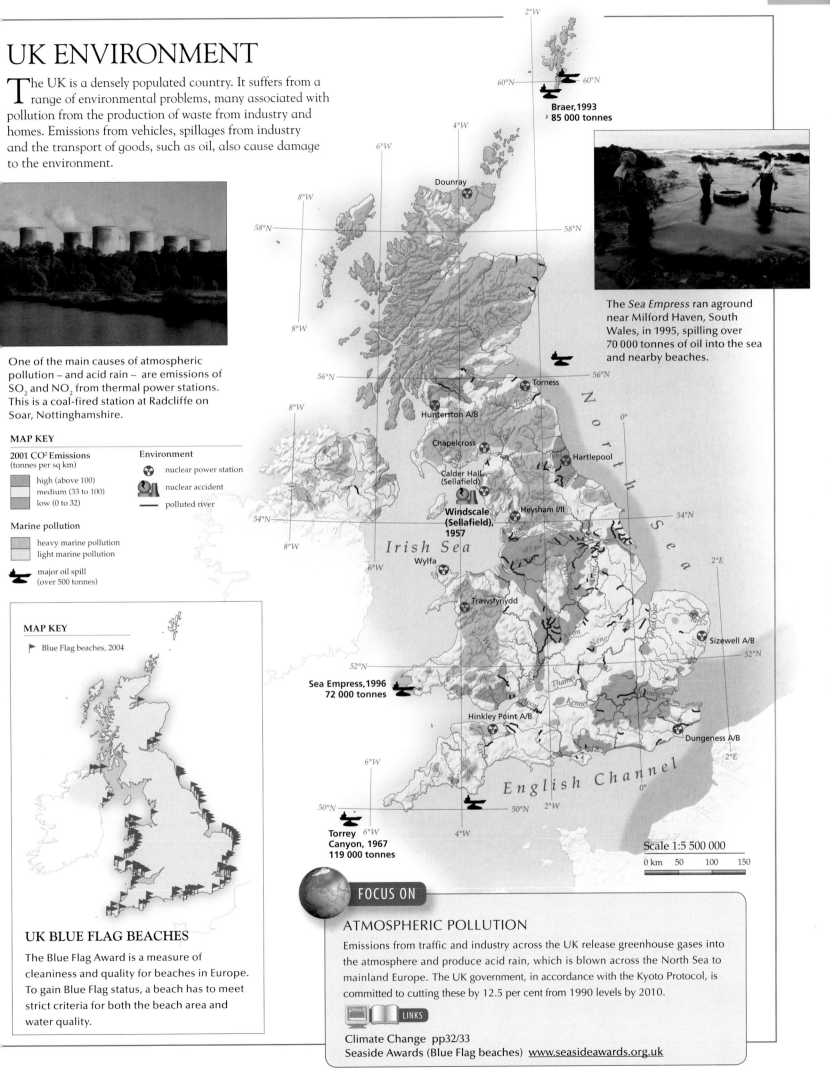

The *Sea Empress* ran aground near Milford Haven, South Wales, in 1995, spilling over 70 000 tonnes of oil into the sea and nearby beaches.

Braer, 1993
85 000 tonnes

Dounray

Torness

Hunterston A/B

Chapelcross

Calder Hall (Sellafield)

Windscale (Sellafield), 1957

Heysham I/II

Hartlepool

Wylfa

Trawsfynydd

Sizewell A/B

Sea Empress, 1996
72 000 tonnes

Hinkley Point A/B

Dungeness A/B

Torrey Canyon, 1967
119 000 tonnes

Irish Sea

North Sea

English Channel

Scale 1:5 500 000

0 km   50   100   150

FOCUS ON

ATMOSPHERIC POLLUTION

Emissions from traffic and industry across the UK release greenhouse gases into the atmosphere and produce acid rain, which is blown across the North Sea to mainland Europe. The UK government, in accordance with the Kyoto Protocol, is committed to cutting these by 12.5 per cent from 1990 levels by 2010.

LINKS

Climate Change pp32/33
Seaside Awards (Blue Flag beaches) www.seasideawards.org.uk

UK TRANSPORT

In the UK the majority of people travel by road, creating pressure on the existing road and motorway network, especially around major cities. As an island nation, traffic via sea and air is significant and set to increase.

EUROPE

Average traffic flows in London are twice that for the UK as a whole, especially on the M25 orbital motorway.

Construction of the Channel Tunnel Rail Link from St Pancras, London to Paris. Trains will be able to make the journey in 2 hours, 20 minutes.

TRAFFIC GROWTH

Road traffic by type of vehicle
(billion vehicle kilometres)

560	
480	
400	
320	
340	
160	
80	

1950 1960 1970 1980 1990 2000

Source: DfT

KEY
— all motor vehicles
— cars and taxis
— other vehicles

MAP KEY

- **M6** motorway
- **A1** main road
- — railway
- --- ferry route
- ● major port
- ● other port
- ✈ airport

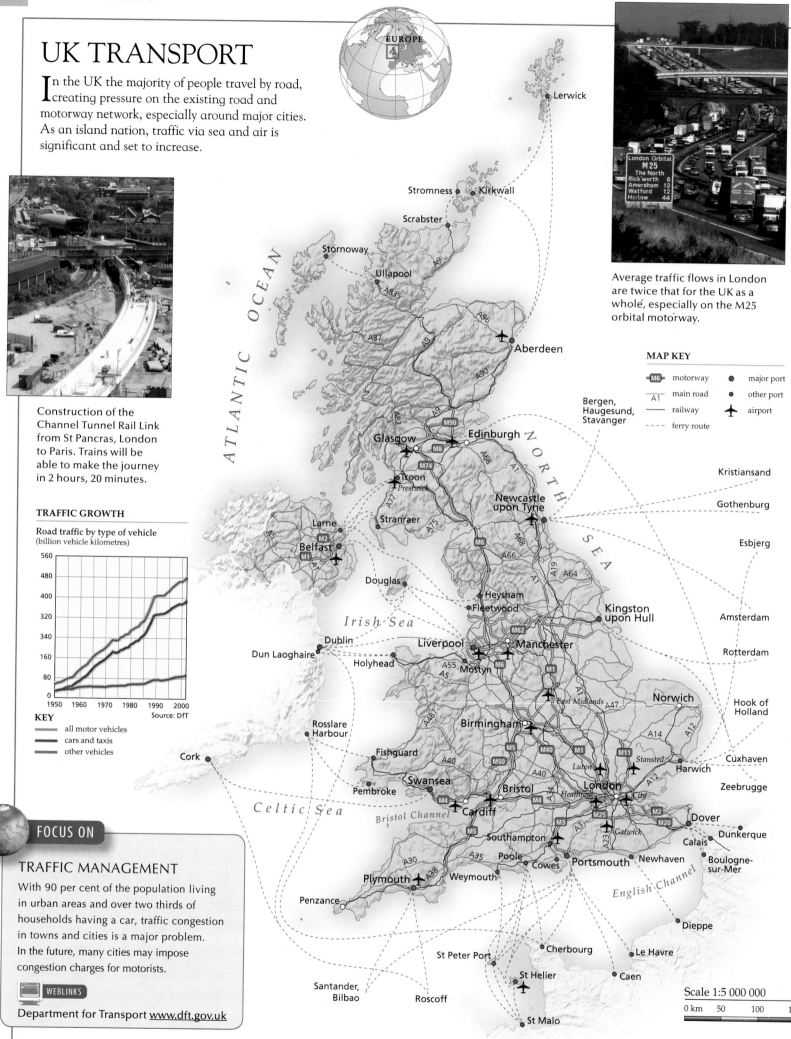

FOCUS ON

TRAFFIC MANAGEMENT

With 90 per cent of the population living in urban areas and over two thirds of households having a car, traffic congestion in towns and cities is a major problem. In the future, many cities may impose congestion charges for motorists.

WEBLINKS

Department for Transport www.dft.gov.uk

Scale 1:5 000 000

0 km   50   100

UK TOURISM

The UK remains in the top ten most popular tourist destinations worldwide, with over 25 million overseas visitors each year. Despite its relatively small size, the UK has a wide range of tourist attractions including historic buildings, National Parks with a wide variety of physical landscapes and world-famous art galleries, museums and theatres.

The pleasure beach at Blackpool on England's northwest coast, with the famous Blackpool Tower in the background. Over six million people visit here every year, making it the most visited free visitor attraction in the UK.

The Royal Botanic Gardens in Kew, west London were awarded World Heritage Site status in 2003. Visitors are attracted to its plant and tree collections, galleries and glasshouses. The oldest glasshouse is the Palm House (above), which is over 150 years old.

MAP KEY

Protected areas

- National Park
- Forest Park
- Areas of Outstanding Natural Beauty
- ○ World Heritage Site
- heritage coastline
- .... long-distance footpath
- —— canal

UK'S TOP TEN TOURIST SITES

(Number of visitors for 2004 shown in brackets)

1. Blackpool Pleasure Beach (6 200 000)
2. Strathclyde Country Park (5 131 000)
3. Tate Modern (4 618 632)
4. British Museum (4 607 311)
5. National Gallery (4 130 973)
6. British Airways London Eye (4 090 000)
7. Natural History Museum (2 957 501)
8. Victoria and Albert Museum (2 661 331)
9. Science Museum (2 628 374)
10. Pleasureland Theme Park (2 000 000)

LONDON

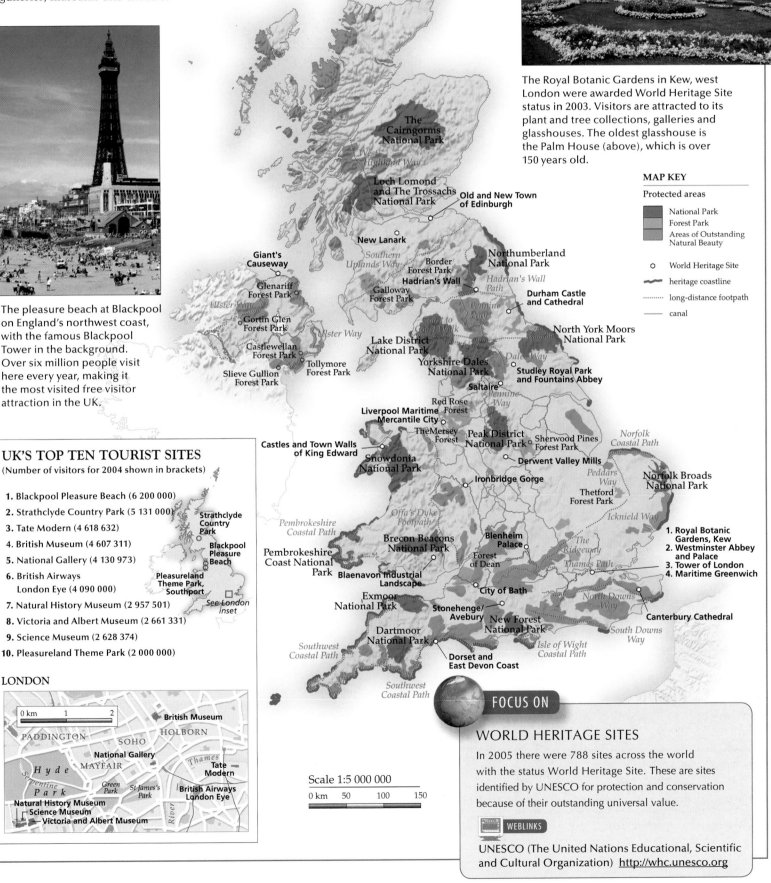

Map labels:
Heart of Neolithic Orkney
The Cairngorms National Park
West Highland Way
Loch Lomond and The Trossachs National Park
Old and New Town of Edinburgh
New Lanark
Southern Uplands Way
Giant's Causeway
Border Forest Park
Northumberland National Park
Hadrian's Wall
Hadrian's Wall Path
Glenariff Forest Park
Galloway Forest Park
Durham Castle and Cathedral
Ulster Way
Gortin Glen Forest Park
Pennine Way
Coast to Coast Walk
North York Moors National Park
Ulster Way
Lake District National Park
Castlewellan Forest Park
Tollymore Forest Park
Yorkshire Dales National Park
Dales Way
Studley Royal Park and Fountains Abbey
Slieve Gullion Forest Park
Saltaire
Pennine Way
Red Rose Forest
Liverpool Maritime Mercantile City
The Mersey Forest
Peak District National Park
Sherwood Pines Forest Park
Norfolk Coastal Path
Castles and Town Walls of King Edward
Snowdonia National Park
Derwent Valley Mills
Peddars Way
Norfolk Broads National Park
Ironbridge Gorge
Thetford Forest Park
Icknield Way
Offa's Dyke Footpath
Pembrokeshire Coastal Path
Brecon Beacons National Park
Blenheim Palace
The Ridgeway
Royal Botanic Gardens, Kew
Pembrokeshire Coast National Park
Forest of Dean
Thames Path
1. Royal Botanic Gardens, Kew
2. Westminster Abbey and Palace
3. Tower of London
4. Maritime Greenwich
Blaenavon Industrial Landscape
City of Bath
North Downs Way
Exmoor National Park
Stonehenge/Avebury
New Forest National Park
Canterbury Cathedral
Dartmoor National Park
Isle of Wight Coastal Path
South Downs Way
Southwest Coastal Path
Dorset and East Devon Coast
Southwest Coastal Path

London inset labels:
Strathclyde Country Park
Blackpool Pleasure Beach
Pleasureland Theme Park, Southport
See London inset

London inset map:
0 km 1 2
PADDINGTON
SOHO
HOLBORN
British Museum
National Gallery
MAYFAIR
Thames
Tate Modern
Hyde Park
Green Park
St James's Park
British Airways London Eye
Serpentine
Natural History Museum
Science Museum
Victoria and Albert Museum
River

Scale 1:5 000 000

0 km 50 100 150

FOCUS ON

WORLD HERITAGE SITES

In 2005 there were 788 sites across the world with the status World Heritage Site. These are sites identified by UNESCO for protection and conservation because of their outstanding universal value.

WEBLINKS

UNESCO (The United Nations Educational, Scientific and Cultural Organization) http://whc.unesco.org

FLOODING IN THE UK

Flooding is one of the world's most common natural hazards. In some countries vast areas of land are flooded every year, affecting millions of people. Over 4.5 million people in China were killed by floods in the twentieth century alone. Although flooding in the UK is rarely fatal, about five million people in two million properties are at risk.

TYPES AND CAUSES OF FLOODING

Rivers: The main physical cause of river flooding in the UK is prolonged heavy rainfall. This leads to ground saturation, increased surface runoff and river channels overflowing. Sometimes this is made worse by melting snow, especially in upland areas, and by human action. Channelling rivers in urban areas and building on river flood plains has increased the risk of flooding.

The River Ouse floods Lewes, October 2000

Flash floods: Sudden incidences of flooding occur when water cannot drain away or be absorbed. This can happen in small, steeply sloping river basins e.g. Lynmouth (1952) and Boscastle (2004). They are almost impossible to predict and can cause severe, localised damage.

Boscastle, August 2004

Intra-urban (drains and sewers): The drainage and sewage systems in most of the UK's major urban areas are old. Many are not large enough to cope with the volume of waste water produced or the amount of surface runoff after sudden downpours or periods of heavy rain. The resulting flooding is a major health risk as floods bring large amounts of raw sewage to the surface.

Coastal/tidal: As an island nation, coastal flooding is a major risk, especially along the mainly low-lying east coast of England. Both coastal areas and tidal estuaries are at risk from flooding. The southeast of the British Isles is also sinking very slowly at the same time that sea levels are rising. This could result in high tides along the Thames in central London being up to 2.5 metres higher in 100 years time. Along the North Sea coast, a combination of high tides, low pressure and high winds from storms can create storm surges that bring widespread flooding e.g. in 1953 when 300 people were killed.

Whitstable during the Great Flood, 1953

MANAGING FLOODING

It is impossible to stop flooding, as it is a natural process. Many of the UK's flood defences, especially coastal ones, were constructed after the 1953 Great Flood. To continue to be effective they need to be maintained and, with likely climate changes, strengthened – at considerable cost.

THE 1953 GREAT FLOOD

The worst floods to hit the UK in recent times took place in January 1953 along the east coast and Thames estuary. Over 300 people died, 25 000 homes were damaged and 40 000 people had to be rescued or evacuated from their homes. The combination of a low pressure system in the North Sea and a high spring tide created a surge of water off the east coast that overwhelmed coastal defences when it reached land. It devastated parts of Lincolnshire, East Anglia, Essex and Kent. The floods prompted coastal defence building on a large scale. It also led to the construction of the Thames Flood Barrier to the east of London.

AREAS AFFECTED BY THE 1953 GREAT FLOOD

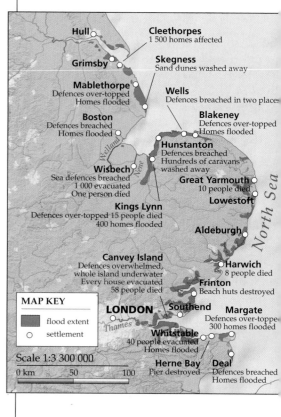

Hull

Cleethorpes
1 500 homes affected

Grimsby

Skegness
Sand dunes washed away

Mablethorpe
Defences over-topped
Homes flooded

Wells
Defences breached in two places

Boston
Defences breached
Homes flooded

Blakeney
Defences over-topped
Homes flooded

Hunstanton
Defences breached
Hundreds of caravans washed away

Wisbech
Sea defences breached
1 000 evacuated
One person died

Great Yarmouth
10 people died

Lowestoft

Kings Lynn
Defences over-topped 15 people died
400 homes flooded

Aldeburgh

Canvey Island
Defences overwhelmed,
whole island underwater
Every house evacuated
58 people died

Harwich
8 people died

Frinton
Beach huts destroyed

MAP KEY

☐ flood extent
○ settlement

LONDON

Southend

Margate
Defences over-topped
300 homes flooded

Whitstable
40 people evacuated
Homes flooded

Scale 1:3 300 000
0 km   50   100

Herne Bay
Pier destroyed

Deal
Defences breached
Homes flooded

The Thames Flood Barrier in London

THAMES FLOOD BARRIER

The Thames Barrier (above) was opened in 1983, construction having begun in 1974. Designed to stop tidal surges from flooding London, it spans 520 metres of the River Thames at Woolwich. There are 10 massive gates separated by concrete piers. These sit on the river bed until they need to be raised in response to a flood warning. Warnings are issued by the Storm Tide Forecasting Service (STFS), which closely monitors east coast tides and weather. The barrier was designed to withstand flood levels predicted until 2030. The Environment Agency is already studying what may need to be done to enable the barrier to cope with potential flooding after that date.

MANAGING THE FLOOD RISK

In England and Wales, the Environment Agency is responsible for managing the risk of flooding, maintaining flood defences and providing a flood warning system. It is now concentrating on the management of flood risk, rather than defending against it — reducing the likelihood and impact of flooding and the risk to people, property and the environment. This means working with local authorities, for example, to prevent new homes being built on flood plains. It may also mean allowing coastal erosion to take place in some areas, rather than maintaining costly sea defences.

LONDON FLOOD DEFENCES

Thames Barrier: number of closures per year (1983–2003)

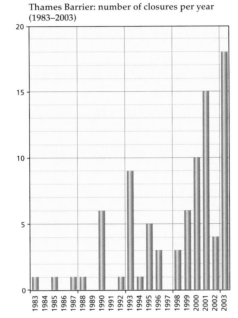

THE FUTURE

One of the greatest challenges facing the Environment Agency is the likely increase in flood risk. The maps below were produced by the Foresight Flood and Coastal Defence Project in 2004, and estimate the annual cost of flood damage in 2080. The different predictions are based on variations in the amount of development in flood-prone areas, the strength of the economy and climate change.

COST OF DAMAGE IF CO_2 EMISSIONS ARE LOW

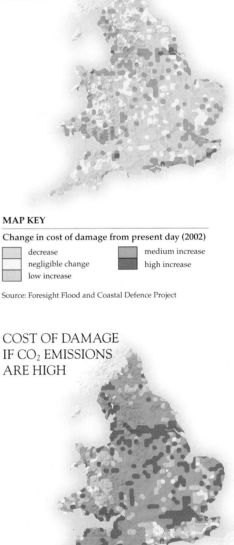

MAP KEY

Change in cost of damage from present day (2002)

decrease	medium increase
negligible change	high increase
low increase	

Source: Foresight Flood and Coastal Defence Project

COST OF DAMAGE IF CO_2 EMISSIONS ARE HIGH

FLOOD RISKS AND MANAGEMENT COSTS 2004			
	Properties at risk	Average annual damage per year (£ millions)	Flood management costs 2003–2004 (£ millions)
River and coastal flooding			
England and Wales	1 740 000	1 040	439
Scotland	180 000	32	14
Northern Ireland	45 000	16	11
Intra-urban flooding			
All UK	80 000	270	320
Total	**2 045 000**	**1 358**	**884**

THE BIG ISSUES

1 What combination of factors caused the flooding of 1953?

2 What are the main effects of, and dangers resulting from, urban flooding?

3 Why is it better to 'manage' flood risk, rather than just try to 'defend' against it?

4 Flood risk in the UK is increasing. What can be done to minimise this risk?

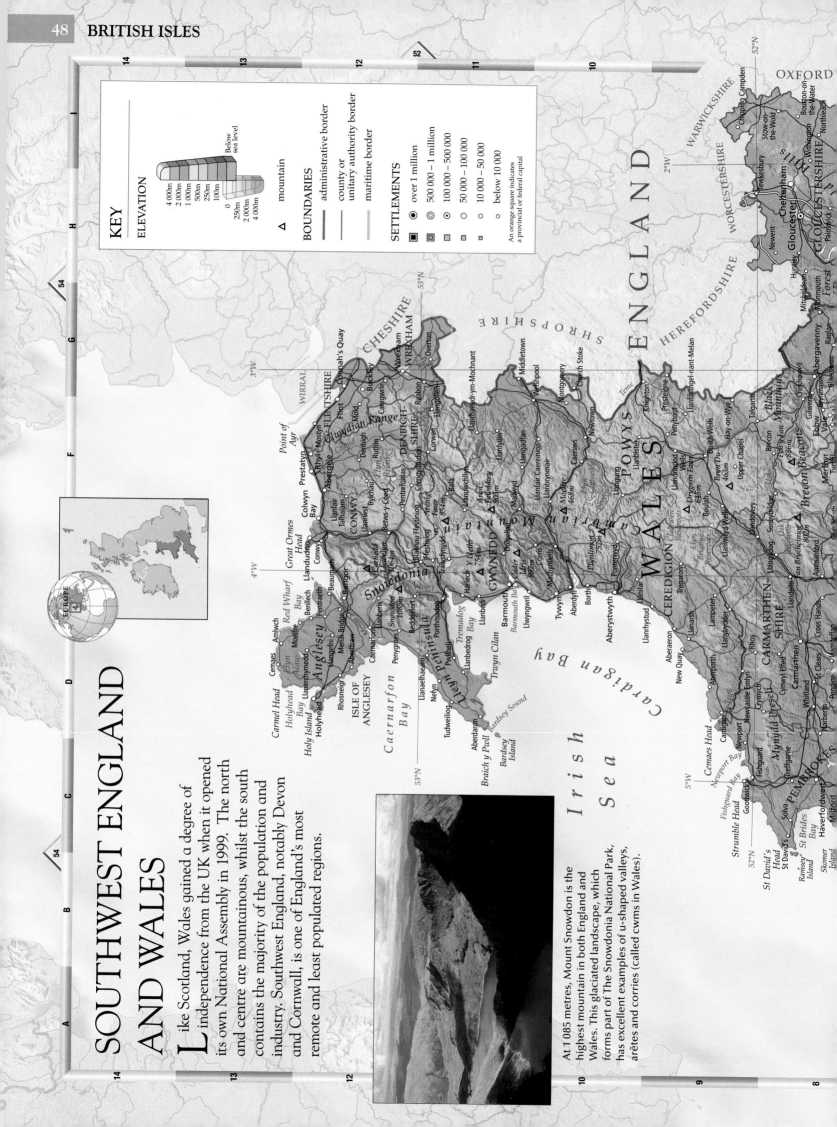

SOUTHWEST ENGLAND AND WALES

Like Scotland, Wales gained a degree of independence from the UK when it opened its own National Assembly in 1999. The north and centre are mountainous, whilst the south contains the majority of the population and industry. Southwest England, notably Devon and Cornwall, is one of England's most remote and least populated regions.

At 1 085 metres, Mount Snowdon is the highest mountain in both England and Wales. This glaciated landscape, which forms part of The Snowdonia National Park, has excellent examples of u-shaped valleys, arêtes and corries (called cwms in Wales).

KEY

ELEVATION

4 000m
2 000m
1 000m
500m
250m
100m
0
250m
2 000m
4 000m
Below sea level

△ mountain

BOUNDARIES

—— administrative border

—— county or unitary authority border

—— maritime border

SETTLEMENTS

◉ over 1 million

◎ 500 000 – 1 million

⊙ 100 000 – 500 000

○ 50 000 – 100 000

○ 10 000 – 50 000

∘ below 10 000

An orange square indicates a provincial or federal capital

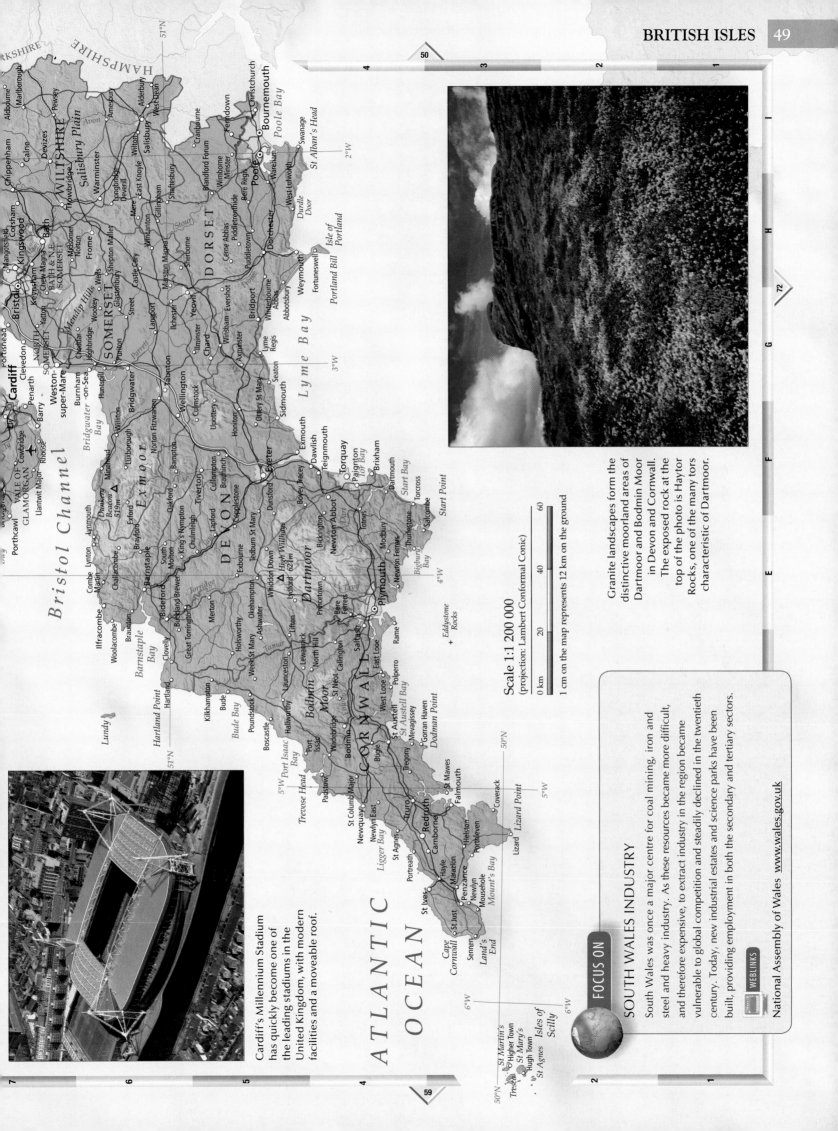

Cardiff's Millennium Stadium has quickly become one of the leading stadiums in the United Kingdom, with modern facilities and a moveable roof.

Granite landscapes form the distinctive moorland areas of Dartmoor and Bodmin Moor in Devon and Cornwall. The exposed rock at the top of the photo is Haytor Rocks, one of the many tors characteristic of Dartmoor.

Scale 1:1 200 000
(projection: Lambert Conformal Conic)

0 km 20 40 60

1 cm on the map represents 12 km on the ground

+ Eddystone
  Rocks

FOCUS ON

SOUTH WALES INDUSTRY

South Wales was once a major centre for coal mining, iron and steel and heavy industry. As these resources became more difficult, and therefore expensive, to extract industry in the region became vulnerable to global competition and steadily declined in the twentieth century. Today, new industrial estates and science parks have been built, providing employment in both the secondary and tertiary sectors.

WEBLINKS

National Assembly of Wales www.wales.gov.uk

SOUTHEAST ENGLAND

The southeast of England is the most densely populated region in the UK, dominated by the capital city, London. London is one of the world's leading cities, especially for finance and associated service industries. Close to mainland Europe, it is also an important tourist centre with a wide variety of attractions, including world-renowned museums, galleries and historic sites.

The tertiary sector is the fastest growing sector of the economy in the Southeast. Many of the 'new' high-tech industries have located outside London, along the M4's 'Silicon Corridor', between Reading and Bristol.

KEY

ELEVATION

4 000m
2 000m
1 000m
500m
250m
100m
0
250m   Below
2 000m   sea level
4 000m

△   mountain

BOUNDARIES

──── national border

──── administrative border

SETTLEMENTS

■ ⊙   over 1 million

▣ ◎   500 000 – 1 million

▪ ⊙   100 000 – 500 000

▪ ○   50 000 – 100 000

▪ ○   below 50 000

A red square indicates a
national capital

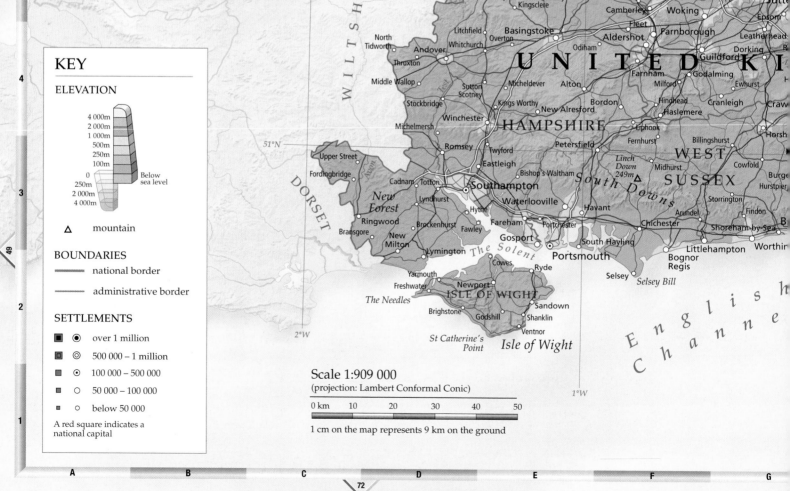

Scale 1:909 000
(projection: Lambert Conformal Conic)

0 km   10   20   30   40   50

1 cm on the map represents 9 km on the ground

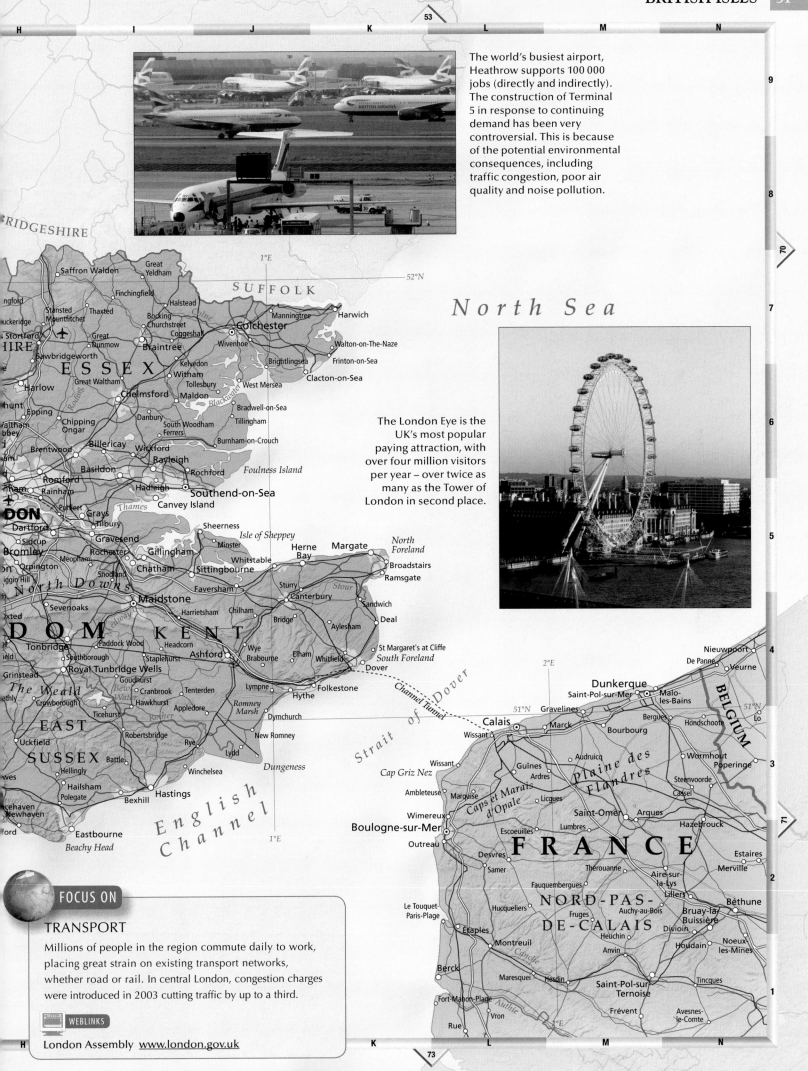

The world's busiest airport, Heathrow supports 100 000 jobs (directly and indirectly). The construction of Terminal 5 in response to continuing demand has been very controversial. This is because of the potential environmental consequences, including traffic congestion, poor air quality and noise pollution.

The London Eye is the UK's most popular paying attraction, with over four million visitors per year – over twice as many as the Tower of London in second place.

FOCUS ON

TRANSPORT

Millions of people in the region commute daily to work, placing great strain on existing transport networks, whether road or rail. In central London, congestion charges were introduced in 2003 cutting traffic by up to a third.

WEBLINKS

London Assembly www.london.gov.uk

CENTRAL ENGLAND

One of the UK's most diverse regions, Central England stretches from the flat, predominantly farming areas of East Anglia and Lincolnshire in the east to the densely populated industrial urban centres of Birmingham, Nottingham and Leicester. To the north lies Derbyshire's Peak District National Park at the southern end of the Pennines.

The most visited of all the National Parks, with over 22 million visitors per year, the Peak District has some of England's most attractive scenery, predominantly limestone and millstone grit, like the outcrops at Kinder Scout (above).

Scale 1:1 055 000
(projection: Lambert Conformal Conic)

0 km   20   40   60

1 cm on the map represents 10.5 km on the ground

KEY

ELEVATION

4 000m
2 000m
1 000m
500m
250m
100m
0
250m
2 000m   Below
4 000m   sea level

△ mountain
▽ depression

BOUNDARIES

——— administrative border

——— county or unitary authority border

········· maritime border

SETTLEMENTS

◉ over 1 million
◎ 500 000 – 1 million
☉ 100 000 – 500 000
○ 50 000 – 100 000
○ 10 000 – 50 000
∘ below 10 000

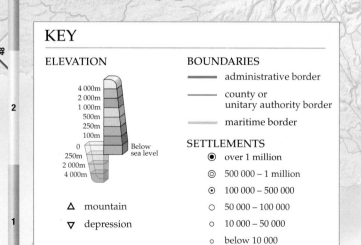

The multi-million pound regeneration scheme in the heart of Birmingham is one of the largest such schemes in Europe. The old Bullring shopping centre has been transformed by the construction of modern buildings like the new Selfridges store (right).

WALES

EUROPE

OLDHAM

CHESHIRE

DERBYS

STAFFORDSHIRE

POWYS

SHROPSHIRE

WORCESTERSHIRE

HEREFORDSHIRE

WARWICKS

GLOUCESTERSHIRE

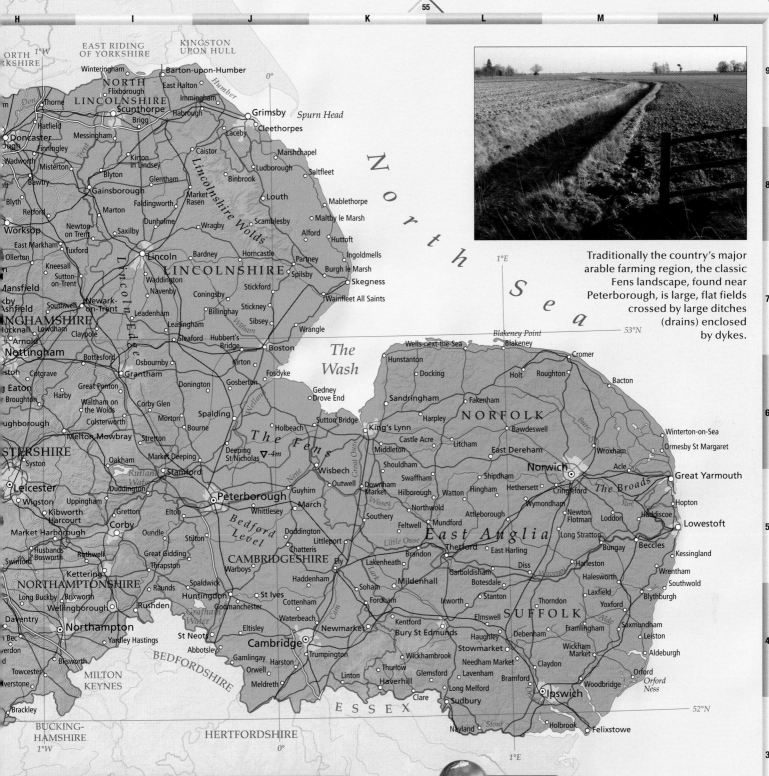

Traditionally the country's major arable farming region, the classic Fens landscape, found near Peterborough, is large, flat fields crossed by large ditches (drains) enclosed by dykes.

FOCUS ON

NATIONAL PARKS

The National Parks Act of 1949 paved the way for the establishment of what are now 12 such areas in England and Wales. Although often made up of private land, they are subject to strict planning regulations. In 2004 the New Forest became the twelfth National Park. The South Downs were also under consideration by the Countryside Agency in 2004.

WEBLINKS

Association of National Park Authorities
www.anpa.gov.uk/

Nottingham's new tramway system was opened in 2004 and has contributed to the city's increased attraction and property boom for both housing and service industries.

NORTHERN ENGLAND

Northern England was once one of the UK's major industrial regions, but the development and growth of newer high-tech and service industries have replaced the heavy industry of the past. Regeneration schemes have radically changed the urban landscape of major cities such as Manchester, Leeds and Newcastle.

The unique landscape of the largest of the UK's National Parks, the Lake District – a mixture of peaks, ridges, passes and lakes – attracts millions of visitors every year.

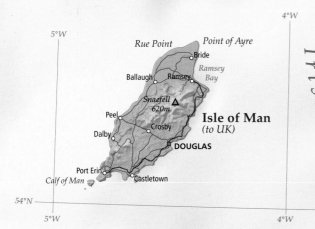

Manchester is the second most populous metropolitan region in the UK. As derelict mills and warehouses have been redeveloped for housing, the population of the city centre itself has started to rise.

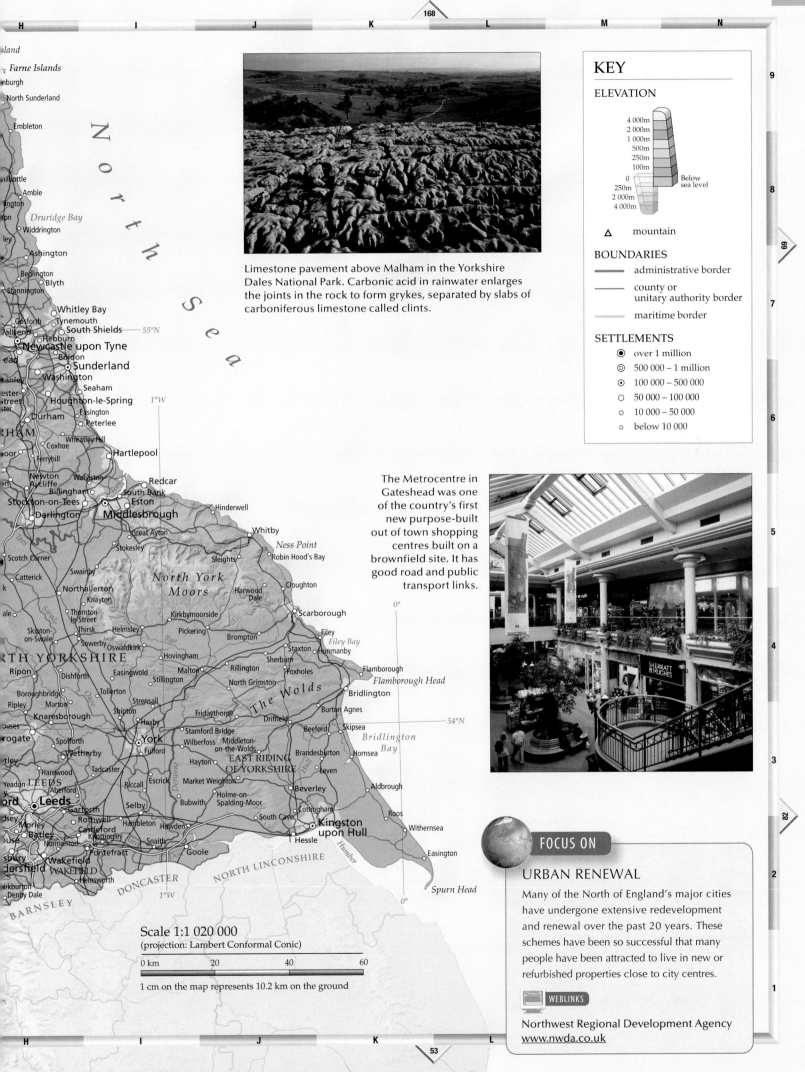

Limestone pavement above Malham in the Yorkshire Dales National Park. Carbonic acid in rainwater enlarges the joints in the rock to form grykes, separated by slabs of carboniferous limestone called clints.

KEY

ELEVATION

4 000m
2 000m
1 000m
500m
250m
100m
0
250m
2 000m
4 000m
Below sea level

△　mountain

BOUNDARIES

—— administrative border

—— county or unitary authority border

—— maritime border

SETTLEMENTS

◉ over 1 million

◎ 500 000 – 1 million

⊙ 100 000 – 500 000

○ 50 000 – 100 000

○ 10 000 – 50 000

○ below 10 000

The Metrocentre in Gateshead was one of the country's first new purpose-built out of town shopping centres built on a brownfield site. It has good road and public transport links.

Scale 1:1 020 000
(projection: Lambert Conformal Conic)

0 km   20   40   60

1 cm on the map represents 10.2 km on the ground

FOCUS ON

URBAN RENEWAL

Many of the North of England's major cities have undergone extensive redevelopment and renewal over the past 20 years. These schemes have been so successful that many people have been attracted to live in new or refurbished properties close to city centres.

WEBLINKS

Northwest Regional Development Agency
www.nwda.co.uk

SCOTLAND

Scotland is one of Europe's most sparsely populated countries. Over 75 per cent of the land is mountainous, with the Highlands and Islands in the north and the Southern Uplands to the south. These are separated by the Central Lowlands, where the majority of the population live and work.

SHETLAND ISLANDS

Scale 1:2 350 000

0 km   20   40

1 cm on the map represents 23.5 km on the ground

Herma Ness
Unst
Baltasound
Yell
Fetlar
Out Skerries
Whalsay
Bressay
Lerwick
Isbister
Yell Sound
Esha Ness
Brae
St Magnus Bay
Muckle Roe
Mainland
Papa Stour
Scousburgh
Foula
West Burra
Fitful Head
Sumburgh
Sumburgh Head
ATLANTIC OCEAN
North Sea
Fair Isle

60°N

2°W   1°W   2°W

EUROPE

Fair Isle

North Ronaldsay
Mull Head
Papa Westray
Sanday
Rackwick
Westray
Stronsay
Braeswick
Rousay Firth
Shapinsay
Stronsay
Firth
Westray Firth
Eday
The North Sound
Brough Head
Mainland
Kirkwall
Rousay
Stromness
St Mary's
Scapa Flow
St Margaret's Hope
Rora Head
Hoy
Lyness
South Ronaldsay

Orkney Islands

Sule Skerry
Stack Skerry

ATLANTIC OCEAN

ATLANTIC OCEAN

Duncansby Head
John o'Groats
Ness Head
Wick
Pentland Firth
Dunnet Head
Thurso
Halkirk
Latheron
Helmsdale
Dounreay
Halladale
Strathy Point
Portskerra
Kinbrace
Brora
Golspie
Tarbat Ness
Tongue
Ben Klibreck 721m
Helmsdale
Dornoch
Balintore
Cromarty
Ben Hope 927m
Altnaharra
Loch Shin
Bonar Bridge
Clashmore
Tain
Durness
Loch Eriboll
Laird
Invergordon
Nairn
Archiemore
Ben More Assynt 998m
Ledmore
Oykel
Beauly
Dingwall
Fore
Inverness
Kinlochbervie
Scourie
Lochinver
Beinn Dearg 1084m
Garve
Eddrachillis Bay
Ullapool
Achnasheen
Fort Augustus
Enard Bay
Dundonnell
Taagan
Carn Eige 1182m
Sgurr Na Lapaich 1150m
Reiff
Summer Isles
Loch Maree
Torridon
Kyle of Lochalsh
Invergarry
Gairloch
Rubha Reidh
Loch Torridon
Shiel Bridge
Maillaig
Inner Sound
Broadford
Ardvasar
Raasay
Kyle of Lochalsh

North West Highlands

HIGHLAND

SCOTLAND

Fraserburgh
Rattray Head
Buchan Ness
Cruden Bay
Mintlaw
Peterhead
New Pitsligo
Turriff
Ellon
Inverurie
Aberdeen
Cullen
Banff
Macduff
Buckie
Keith
Huntly
Pitcaple
Inverurie
Stonehaven
Fochabers
Rothes
Colpy
Banchory
Lossiemouth
Elgin
Tomintoul
Crathie
Ballater
Aboyne
Burghead
Forres
Cairngorm Mountains
Ben Macdui 1309m
Braemar
Lochnagar 1154m
Charlestown of Aberlour
Grantown-on-Spey
Lettoch
Aviemore
Carrbridge
Moy
Kingussie
Dalwhinnie
Laggan
Drumnadrochit
Loch Ness
Invermoriston
Loch Lochy
Cairn Gorm
Mullardoch
Monadhliath Mountains
Grampian Mountains

MORAY
ABERDEENSHIRE

Moray Firth
Ythan
Ugie
Don
Dee
Deveron
Spey

North Sea

Port of Ness
Butt of Lewis
Eye Peninsula
Broad Bay
Stornoway
Carloway
Galson
Loch Roag
Timsgarry
Isle of Lewis
Loch Seaforth
Tarbet
Clisham 799m

EILEAN SIAR

Husinish
Scarp
Tarransay
Harris
Rodel
Sound of Harris
Pabbay
Berneray
Grimnish Point
Monach Islands
North Uist
Lochmaddy
Balivanich
Benbecula
South Uist
Lochboisdale
Eriskay
Barra
Castlebay

Shiant Islands
Rubha Hunish
The Little Minch
Uig
Loch Snizort
The Storr 719m
Portree
Isle of Skye
Soay
Rhum
Canna
Harris
Eigg

Sea of the Hebrides

The Minch

Outer Hebrides

58°N
57°N

6°W   7°W

58°N
57°N

FOCUS ON

TOURISM

The Highlands and Islands region of northwest Scotland is a popular tourist destination, containing spectacular mountain scenery and unspoilt beaches and coastline. The main island groups of the Hebrides, Orkneys and Shetlands attract a wide range of visitors, despite their remote location.

WEBLINKS

Scottish Executive www.scotland.gov.uk

Scale 1:1 400 000
(projection: Lambert Conformal Conic)

1 cm on the map represents 14.0 km on the ground

Scotland has numerous islands, large and small, like Raasay (shown above), which is part of the Inner Hebrides Islands. Faced with the challenge of sustaining remote communities, many islands have successfully developed local craft industries and encouraged tourism.

KEY

ELEVATION

4 000m
2 000m
1 000m
500m
250m
100m
0
Below sea level
250m
2 000m
4 000m

△ mountain

BOUNDARIES

administrative border
county or unitary authority border
maritime border

SETTLEMENTS

■ over 1 million
◉ 500 000 – 1 million
◉ 100 000 – 500 000
○ 50 000 – 100 000
○ 10 000 – 50 000
○ below 10 000

An orange square indicates a provincial or federal capital

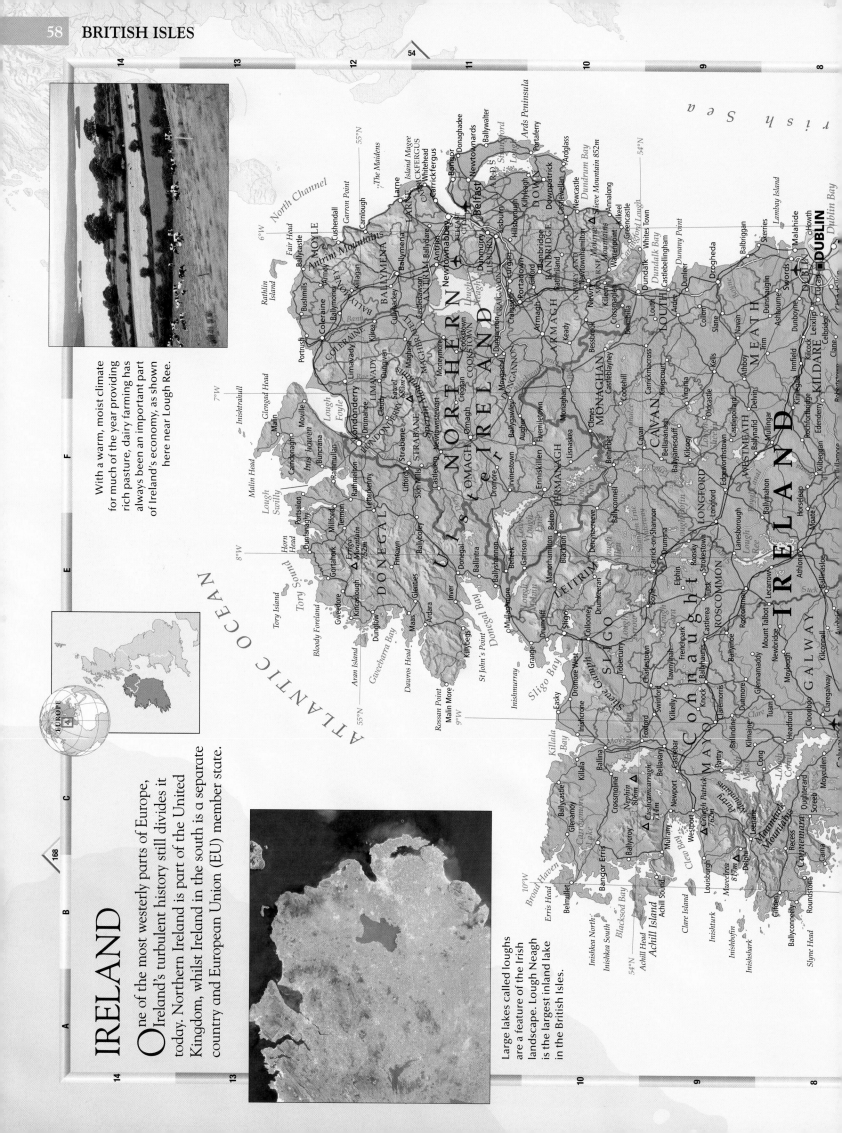

IRELAND

One of the most westerly parts of Europe, Ireland's turbulent history still divides it today. Northern Ireland is part of the United Kingdom, whilst Ireland in the south is a separate country and European Union (EU) member state.

With a warm, moist climate for much of the year providing rich pasture, dairy farming has always been an important part of Ireland's economy, as shown here near Lough Ree.

Large lakes called loughs are a feature of the Irish landscape. Lough Neagh is the largest inland lake in the British Isles.

ATLANTIC OCEAN

Irish Sea

EUROPE

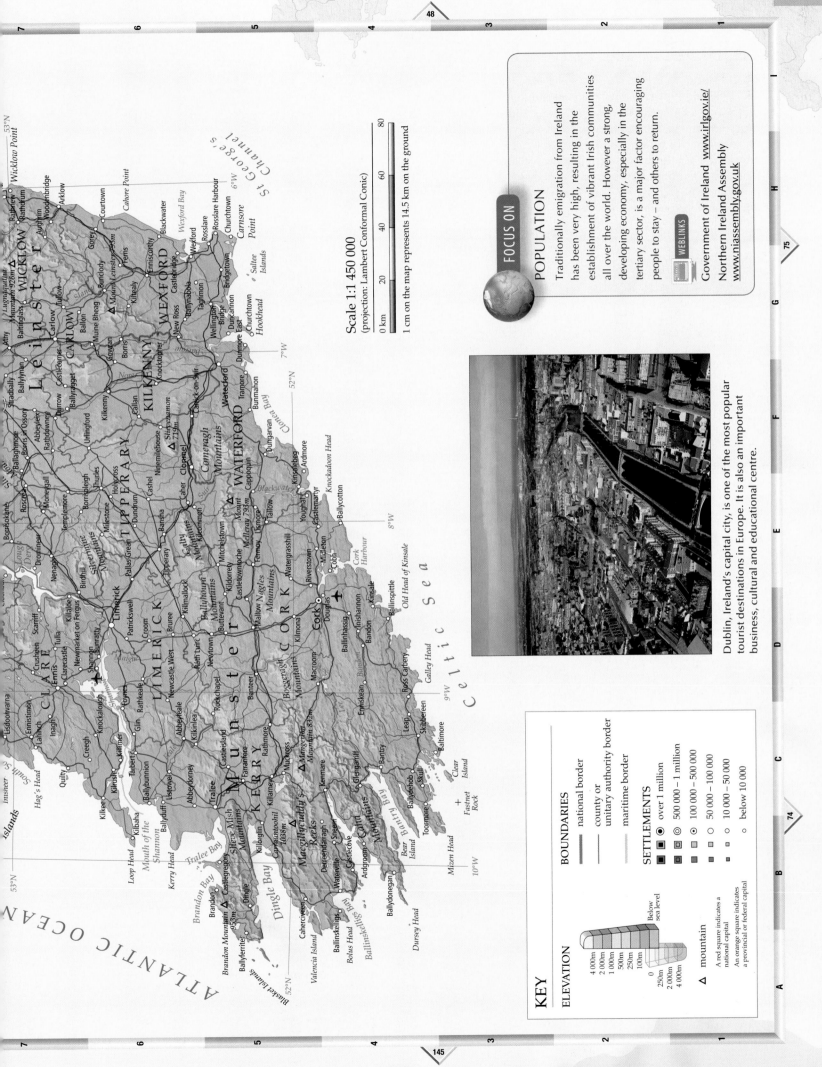

Scale 1:1 450 000
(projection: Lambert Conformal Conic)

0 km   20   40   60   80

1 cm on the map represents 14.5 km on the ground

FOCUS ON

POPULATION

Traditionally emigration from Ireland has been very high, resulting in the establishment of vibrant Irish communities all over the world. However a strong, developing economy, especially in the tertiary sector, is a major factor encouraging people to stay – and others to return.

WEBLINKS

Government of Ireland www.irlgov.ie/
Northern Ireland Assembly
www.niassembly.gov.uk

Dublin, Ireland's capital city, is one of the most popular tourist destinations in Europe. It is also an important business, cultural and educational centre.

KEY

ELEVATION

4 000m
2 000m
1 000m
500m
250m
100m
0
Below sea level

250m
2 000m
4 000m

△ mountain

A red square indicates a national capital

An orange square indicates a provincial or federal capital

BOUNDARIES

—— national border

—— county or unitary authority border

········ maritime border

SETTLEMENTS

■⊙ over 1 million
◎ 500 000 – 1 million
⊙ 100 000 – 500 000
○ 50 000 – 100 000
○ 10 000 – 50 000
○ below 10 000

EUROPE POLITICAL

The break up of the Soviet Union between 1989 and 1991 ended the political division of Eastern and Western Europe. This greatly changed the map of Europe creating a number of newly independent countries and democracies. Shifting and changing borders are not uncommon in European history. European countries have a history of forming alliances amongst themselves, for example NATO, the Warsaw Pact and the European Union.

By 2004, the majority of European countries were members of the European Union (EU), with several others waiting to join.

MAP KEY

Settlements

■ over 1 million
▪ 500 000 to 1 million
▪ 100 000 to 500 000
▫ 50 000 to 100 000
▫ below 50 000

A red square indicates a national capital

Boundaries

—— international border
✱✱✱ ceasefire line

MAP KEY

UN Human Development Index (HDI)

high
medium
low
no data

Source: UN, 2004

QUALITY OF LIFE

EUROPE circa 1985

North Atlantic Treaty Organization (NATO)
established 1949, allied with Canada and the USA

1. Iceland	8. France
2. Norway	9. West Germany
3. Denmark	10. Portugal
4. United Kingdom	11. Spain
5. Belgium	12. Italy
6. Netherlands	13. Greece
7. Luxembourg	14. Turkey

Warsaw Pact established 1955

15. Soviet Union (USSR)
16. East Germany
17. Poland
18. Czechoslovakia
19. Hungary
20. Romania
21. Bulgaria
22. Albania
    (left in 1968)

—— Iron Curtain

Scale 1:25 700 000

0 km 250 500 750 1 000

FOCUS ON

THE EUROPEAN UNION

The European Union is an important economic, political and legislative body. In 2005 it numbered 25 member countries. For further information and a map of EU countries see pp 66/67.

LINKS

European Union pp66/67

EUROPE PHYSICAL

Europe is classed as a continent, although it is part of the Asia land mass. It is the smallest continent in terms of land mass after Australasia and Oceania, yet it has a wide range of landscape and scenery. The North European Plain is an area of unbroken lowland stretching for 4 000 km across central and eastern Europe, bordered to the south by the Alps and Pyrenees and eroded plateaux or massifs. To the north are the older mountains of Scandinavia and northern Britain.

PHYSICAL FACTFILE

1 HIGHEST POINT: Mount El'brus, 5 642 metres above sea level

2 LOWEST POINT: Caspian Sea, 28 metres below sea level

3 LARGEST LAKE: Lake Ladoga, 18 400 km²

— **LONGEST RIVER:** River Volga, 3 531 km

— **LENGTH OF COASTLINE:** 224 393 km

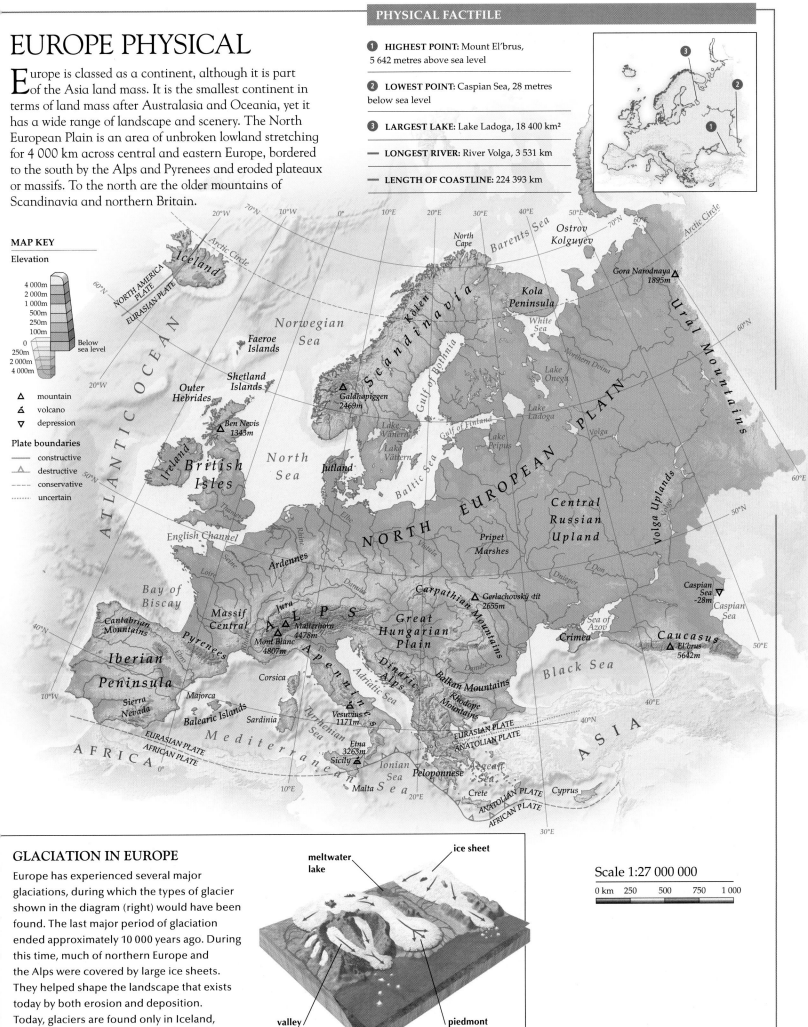

MAP KEY

Elevation

4 000m
2 000m
1 000m
500m
250m
100m
0
Below sea level
250m
2 000m
4 000m

△ mountain
▵ volcano
▽ depression

Plate boundaries

constructive
destructive
conservative
uncertain

GLACIATION IN EUROPE

Europe has experienced several major glaciations, during which the types of glacier shown in the diagram (right) would have been found. The last major period of glaciation ended approximately 10 000 years ago. During this time, much of northern Europe and the Alps were covered by large ice sheets. They helped shape the landscape that exists today by both erosion and deposition. Today, glaciers are found only in Iceland, Scandinavia, the Alps and parts of Spain.

meltwater lake
ice sheet
valley glacier
piedmont glacier

Scale 1:27 000 000

0 km   250   500   750   1 000

EUROPE CLIMATE

Most of western Europe has a temperate climate, changing to a drier, more extreme continental climate in the east and inland. The north is colder, with a mixture of tundra and sub-arctic conditions. The south has a mediterranean climate, which has warm, wet winters and hot, dry summers.

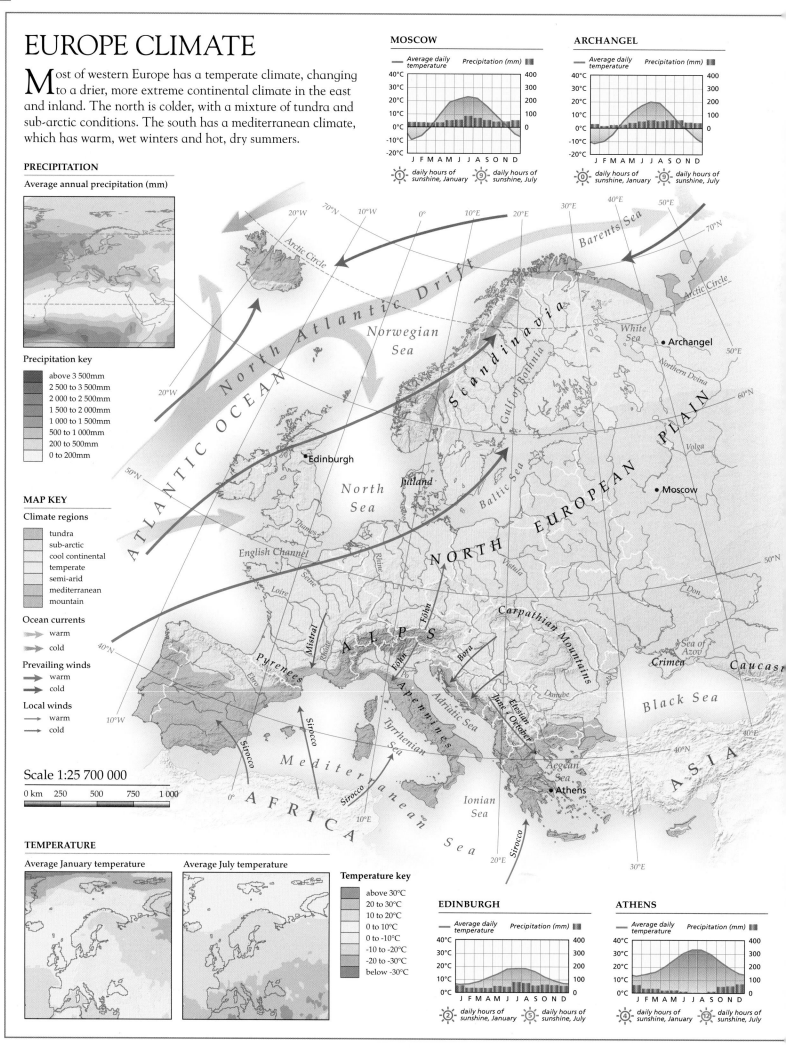

PRECIPITATION

Average annual precipitation (mm)

Precipitation key

	above 3 500mm
	2 500 to 3 500mm
	2 000 to 2 500mm
	1 500 to 2 000mm
	1 000 to 1 500mm
	500 to 1 000mm
	200 to 500mm
	0 to 200mm

MAP KEY

Climate regions

	tundra
	sub-arctic
	cool continental
	temperate
	semi-arid
	mediterranean
	mountain

Ocean currents

→ warm
→ cold

Prevailing winds

→ warm
→ cold

Local winds

→ warm
→ cold

Scale 1:25 700 000

0 km   250   500   750   1 000

TEMPERATURE

Average January temperature

Average July temperature

Temperature key

	above 30°C
	20 to 30°C
	10 to 20°C
	0 to 10°C
	0 to -10°C
	-10 to -20°C
	-20 to -30°C
	below -30°C

MOSCOW

Average daily temperature — Precipitation (mm)

daily hours of sunshine, January ①
daily hours of sunshine, July ⑨

ARCHANGEL

Average daily temperature — Precipitation (mm)

daily hours of sunshine, January ⓪
daily hours of sunshine, July ⑨

EDINBURGH

Average daily temperature — Precipitation (mm)

daily hours of sunshine, January ②
daily hours of sunshine, July ⑤

ATHENS

Average daily temperature — Precipitation (mm)

daily hours of sunshine, January ④
daily hours of sunshine, July ⑫

EUROPE POPULATION

Of Europe's 700 million plus population, 73 per cent live in urban areas – some of the most densely populated regions in the world. In contrast, there are also many rural settlements in the more isolated fringes and mountainous regions of the continent.

Urban areas account for more than 27 per cent of the total land use in Europe. Many of these are rapidly spreading outwards as a continuous urban sprawl between one town or city and the next.

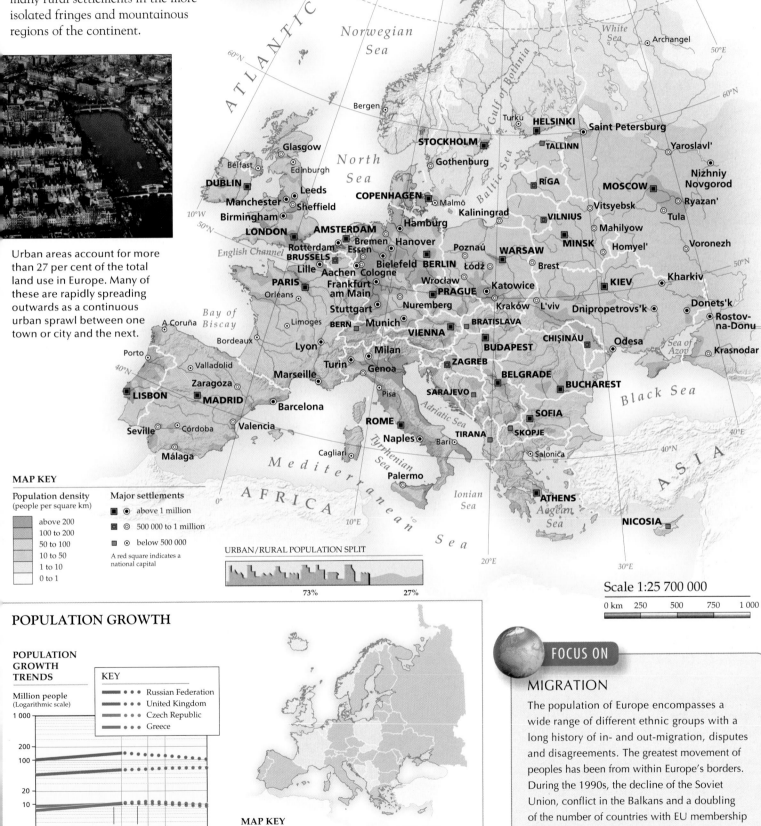

MAP KEY

Population density
(people per square km)

- above 200
- 100 to 200
- 50 to 100
- 10 to 50
- 1 to 10
- 0 to 1

Major settlements

- ■ ◉ above 1 million
- ■ ◉ 500 000 to 1 million
- ■ ◉ below 500 000

A red square indicates a national capital

URBAN/RURAL POPULATION SPLIT

73%   27%

Scale 1:25 700 000

0 km   250   500   750   1 000

POPULATION GROWTH

POPULATION GROWTH TRENDS

Million people
(Logarithmic scale)

KEY
- ••• Russian Federation
- ••• United Kingdom
- ••• Czech Republic
- ••• Greece

1 000
200
100
20
10
2
1

1950   2000   2015 2025   2050

actual   projected

MAP KEY

Population growth (average annual percentage growth)

- above 2.5
- 2 to 2.4
- 1.5 to 1.9
- 1 to 1.4
- 0 to 0.9
- 0 to -0.9 (population in decline)

FOCUS ON

MIGRATION

The population of Europe encompasses a wide range of different ethnic groups with a long history of in- and out-migration, disputes and disagreements. The greatest movement of peoples has been from within Europe's borders. During the 1990s, the decline of the Soviet Union, conflict in the Balkans and a doubling of the number of countries with EU membership increased awareness of the issue of migration.

LINKS

European Union pp66/67

EUROPE LAND USE

Land use across Europe varies greatly. Lowland regions tend to be densely populated, with highly industrialised areas and intensive arable and livestock farming. Coniferous forests are found in mountainous regions, especially across Scandinavia in the north and in the Alps and Pyrenees where the climate is colder and wetter.

FOOD PRODUCTION

Selected commodities (million tonnes)

	1990 production	2000 production
Milk	174	165
Meat	44	45
Fruit & vegetables	138	148
Cereals	284	290
Starchy roots	97	87

KEY
1990 production
2000 production

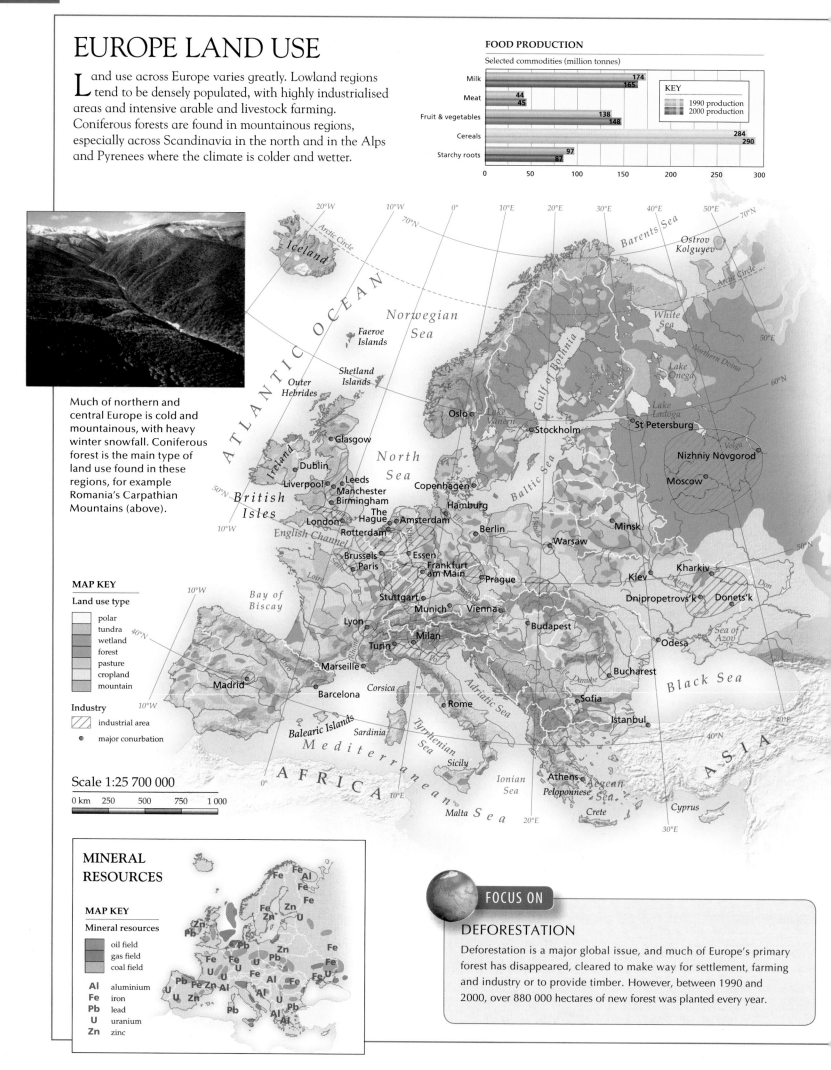

Much of northern and central Europe is cold and mountainous, with heavy winter snowfall. Coniferous forest is the main type of land use found in these regions, for example Romania's Carpathian Mountains (above).

MAP KEY

Land use type

- polar
- tundra
- wetland
- forest
- pasture
- cropland
- mountain

Industry

- industrial area
- major conurbation

Scale 1:25 700 000

0 km   250   500   750   1 000

MINERAL RESOURCES

MAP KEY

Mineral resources

- oil field
- gas field
- coal field

Al	aluminium
Fe	iron
Pb	lead
U	uranium
Zn	zinc

FOCUS ON

DEFORESTATION

Deforestation is a major global issue, and much of Europe's primary forest has disappeared, cleared to make way for settlement, farming and industry or to provide timber. However, between 1990 and 2000, over 880 000 hectares of new forest was planted every year.

EUROPE ENVIRONMENT

Europe is a highly industrialised and densely populated continent. Emissions and discharges from power stations, factories, vehicles and homes have created widespread pollution of air and water. Major spills from oil tankers and the release of radioactivity from nuclear power stations have had a lasting impact, not just on the locality where they occurred, but across Europe.

Oil tanker spills in the seas and oceans around Europe have caused widespread pollution of both marine and coastal ecosystems, damaging local fishing and tourist industries. The *Prestige*, which broke up in December 2002, affected a large section of Spain's North Atlantic coast.

Braer, 1993
85 000 tonnes

Glasgow
Dublin
Windscale (Sellafield), 1957
Sea Empress, 1996
72 000 tonnes
Birmingham
Torrey Canyon, 1967
119 000 tonnes
London
Brussels
Essen
Berlin
Leipzig
Greifswald, 1976
Bydgoszcz
Warsaw
Chernobyl, 1986
Saint Petersburg
Moscow
Volgograd
Donets'k
Paris
Frankfurt am Main
Prague
Kraków
Kiev
Dnipropetrovs'k
Amoco Cadiz, 1978
223 000 tonnes
Jakob Maersk, 1975
88 000 tonnes
Budapest
Miskolc
Milan
Zagreb
Bucharest
Ruse
Lisbon
Madrid
Haven, 1991
144 000 tonnes
Independenta, 1979
95 000 tonnes
Athens
Irenes Serenade, 1980
100 000 tonnes

1. Prestige, 2002, 77 000 tonnes
2. Aegean Sea, 1992, 74 000 tonnes
3. Urquiola, 1976, 100 000 tonnes

Scale 1:30 250 000

0 km   500   1 000

MAP KEY

Environmental issues

- marine pollution
- heavy marine pollution
- acid deposition
- polluted river
- poor urban air quality
- major oil spill
- nuclear accident

CHERNOBYL DISASTER

The world's worst nuclear accident occurred at Chernobyl in the Ukraine in 1986. The toxic radioactive material released was carried by the wind, spreading across Europe as far as northwest England.

A concrete shield or Sarcophagus was built to contain contamination. Officials are concerned that it is crumbling and may collapse.

Chernobyl

MAP KEY

Levels of caesium 137 deposition
(Ci per square km)

- above 5
- 1.08 to 5
- 0.27 to 1.07
- 0.054 to 0.26
- below 0.054

FOCUS ON

MARINE POLLUTION

The coastline of western Europe is one of the most polluted in the world. Industrial discharge and shipping are the main causes of pollution along the Noth Sea, Baltic and Atlantic coasts. A narrow entrance and minimal tides in the Mediterranean Sea mean that pollution can build up quickly – oil, chemicals, garbage and sewage being the main components.

EUROPEAN UNION

The European Union is a unique organisation of democratic countries, established to enable economic and political cooperation between member states. Based on a series of treaties, the EU is unlike other trade blocs because it has developed common institutions, to which member states delegate some of their decision-making powers.

The European flag was introduced in 1955. The twelve gold stars, arranged in a circle, symbolise solidarity, perfection and unity. There has – and always will be – twelve stars, irrespective of the number of members.

MAP KEY

EU member countries

- **1957** Belgium, France, Germany, Italy, Luxembourg, Netherlands
- **1973** Denmark, Ireland, United Kingdom
- **1981** Greece
- **1986** Portugal, Spain
- **1995** Austria, Finland, Sweden
- **2004** Czech Republic, Cyprus, Estonia, Hungary, Latvia, Lithuania, Malta, Poland, Slovakia, Slovenia
- Likely future new members: Bulgaria, Romania, Turkey, Croatia, Macedonia
- non-members

Scale 1:38 500 000
(projection: Lambert Azimuthal Equal Area)

0 km   500   1 000   1 500

THE ORIGINS OF THE EU

The EU has its roots in the aftermath of the Second World War. In an attempt to secure a lasting peace after centuries of conflict, in 1951 six countries agreed to pool control of their coal and steel production. This was so successful that in 1957 the six countries signed the Treaty of Rome, establishing a common market (EEC) and removing trade barriers. Since then there have been several waves of expansion, so that by 2004 there were 25 member states.

In 1992 a single market was established, enabling the free movement of goods, services and people between member states. Economic integration culminated in the establishment of a common currency, the Euro, in 12 countries in January 2002.

THE CHANGING ROLE OF THE EU

Over time the scope of the EU's role has expanded. Political cooperation between states has increased, and the development of common institutions has enabled joint decision making in some policy areas.

The basis of today's European Union was established in the Maastricht Treaty, signed in 1992. The treaty outlines the policy areas that countries cooperate on, commonly known as the 'three pillars' of the EU:

- **The European Community:** European institutions are responsible for managing the single market, freedom of movement across borders, economic and monetary union and cooperation on agricultural and environmental policy. Member states have given up some of their sovereignty over these areas and EU institutions can act independently of national governments on them.

- **Common Foreign and Security Policy:** Member states try to develop common policies and take joint action on foreign and security issues.

- **Justice and Home Affairs:** Member states try to integrate their policies on crime, customs and asylum.

THE ROLE OF EU INSTITUTIONS		
Institution	**Role**	**Accountability**
European Commission	Manages the operation of the EU and proposes new legislation. It is also responsible for implementing policy. There are 25 Commissioners, each overseeing an area of policy.	Politically independent. Answerable only to the European Parliament. Commissioners are appointed by national governments.
European Parliament	Shares responsibility with the European Council for approving legislation and the EU budget. It has the power to sack the Commission.	Directly elected by EU citizens. Elections are held every five years.
Council of Ministers	Shares responsibility with the European Parliament for approving legislation and the EU budget.	Made up of ministers from member states.

MIGRATION AND THE EU

Europe has a long history of migration. Millions of Europeans have emigrated to other continents or moved within Europe and the EU. At the same time, others have migrated into the continent, including many from former colonies.

The growth of Transnational companies with offices in several countries has encouraged increased migration by professional workers.

MIGRATION WITHIN THE EU

EU citizens have the right to travel, work and study in any member country. Migration has also been made easier by the ending of border controls between member states and better transport and communications links.

Between 1992 and 1996 Germany admitted nearly 350 000 Bosnian refugees, who were fleeing conflict in the former Yugoslavia.

However, potential migrants, especially from post-communist new member states, are subject to restrictions from existing members. This is because some western EU countries are concerned that there will be mass migration from the newer members. Others argue that enlargement will improve the economies of new members, eventually leading to a reduction in those wanting to move.

MIGRATION FROM THE EU

Europe was the source of most of the world's international migrants in the nineteenth and early twentieth centuries, with 35 to 40 million people migrating to the USA alone between 1820 and 1924. Europeans continue to migrate to countries outside the EU, with most moving to developed countries, particularly the USA. In the UK, commonwealth countries such as Australia and New Zealand receive a large proportion of UK migrants. This type of migration is voluntary and motivated by economic and social incentives, such as better employment and education opportunities.

MIGRATION INTO THE EU

The EU is attractive to migrants because of its economic prosperity and political stability. There are two main groups of migrants into the EU from non-EU countries:

- Economic migrants, who migrate to seek work or a better quality of life.

- Forced migrants, who are forced to leave their homes because of war, persecution or natural disaster. They often seek asylum in other countries as refugees.

There has been an increase in both types of migrants over the last 50 years. Civil war and the break up of Yugoslavia (1990s), and conflict in Chechnya (1999–), Afghanistan (2001) and Iraq (2003–4) have forced thousands to flee to the EU for safety.

Fruit and vegetable farms in Andalucia, Spain, depend on the labour of seasonal agriculture workers from Morocco.

Many businesses in the EU depend on – and actively recruit – migrant workers, in both skilled and unskilled work. Governments have sought to manage migration by allowing companies to recruit unskilled migrants, who are needed to fill temporary or seasonal vacancies (often in sectors that are unattractive to national workers), whilst denying them the right to permanently settle. Border controls have also been tightened to try and prevent people entering the EU illegally.

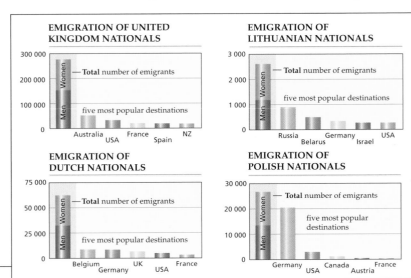

EMIGRATION OF UNITED KINGDOM NATIONALS

— Total number of emigrants

five most popular destinations

Australia USA France Spain NZ

EMIGRATION OF DUTCH NATIONALS

— Total number of emigrants

five most popular destinations

Belgium Germany UK USA France

EMIGRATION OF LITHUANIAN NATIONALS

— Total number of emigrants

five most popular destinations

Russia Belarus Germany Israel USA

EMIGRATION OF POLISH NATIONALS

— Total number of emigrants

five most popular destinations

Germany USA Canada Austria France

THE BIG ISSUES

1 What have been the main achievements of the EU since its beginnings in 1951?

2 What are the arguments for and against further enlargement of the EU?

3 How have Europeans benefited from migration?

4 How do you think the EU might evolve in the future?

SCANDINAVIA AND THE BALTIC STATES

Norway, Sweden, Finland, Denmark and Iceland are Europe's Nordic states. Norway, Sweden and Denmark are also known collectively as Scandinavia. They are amongst the most northerly, coldest and most sparsely populated countries in the continent. To the southeast of Scandinavia, separated by the Baltic Sea, are the Baltic states of Estonia, Latvia and Lithuania, all of whom joined the European Union (EU) in 2004.

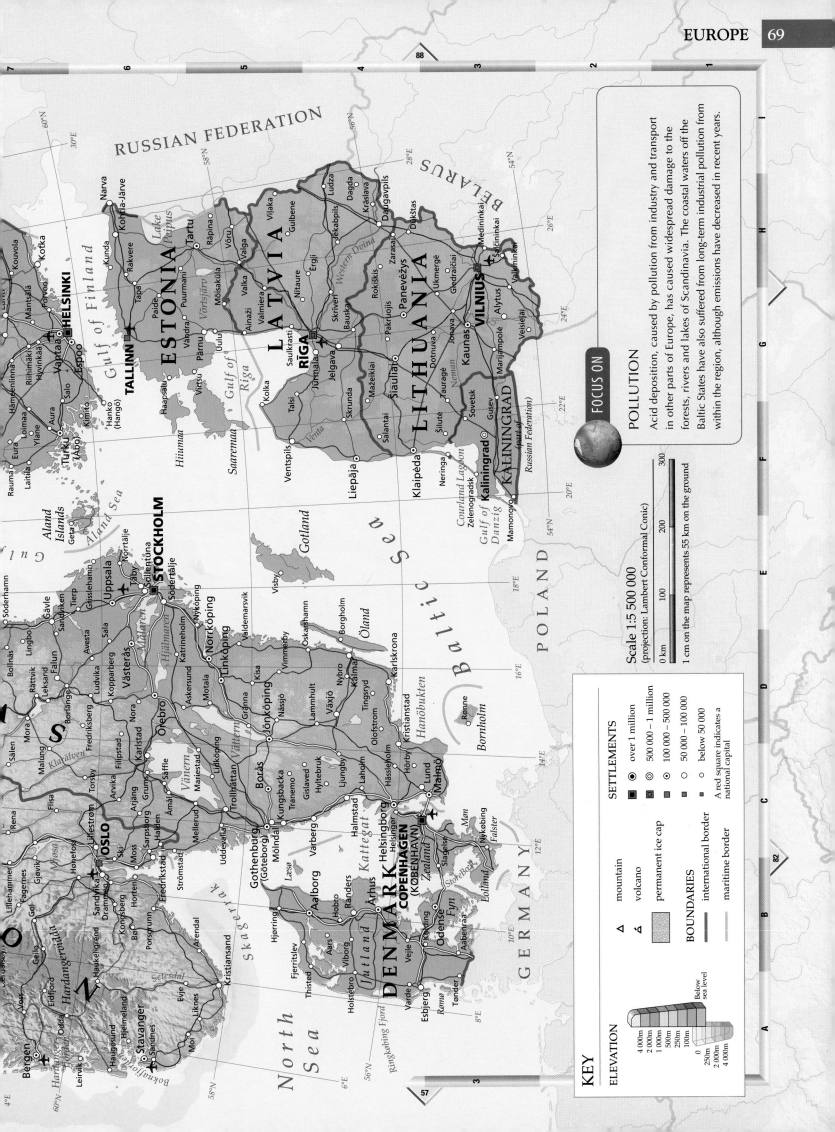

NETHERLANDS, BELGIUM AND LUXEMBOURG

The Netherlands, Belgium and Luxembourg are known collectively as the Low Countries because much of the region is very flat and just above or even below sea level. Also called Benelux, the three countries were founder members of the EEC, later to become the European Union (EU).

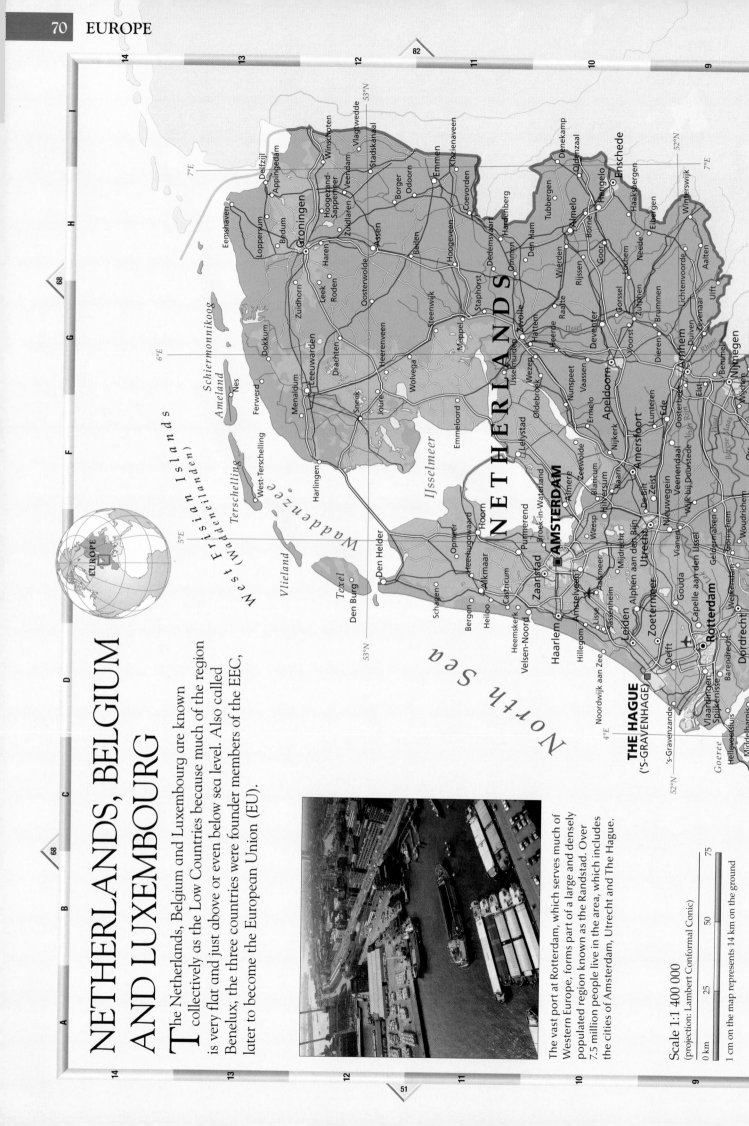

The vast port at Rotterdam, which serves much of Western Europe, forms part of a large and densely populated region known as the Randstad. Over 7.5 million people live in the area, which includes the cities of Amsterdam, Utrecht and The Hague.

Scale 1:1 400 000
(projection: Lambert Conformal Conic)

0 km   25   50   75

1 cm on the map represents 14 km on the ground

EUROPE

NETHERLANDS

North Sea

IJsselmeer

Waddenzee

West (Waddeneilanden) Frisian Islands

Schiermonnikoog
Ameland
Terschelling
West-Terschelling
Vlieland
Texel
Den Burg

Eemshaven
Delfzijl
Appingedam
Loppersum
Bedum
Groningen
Haren
Hoogezand-Sappemeer
Zuidlaren
Assen
Winschoten
Vlagtwedde
Stadskanaal
Veendam
Borger
Odoorn
Emmen
Klazienaveen
Coevorden
Denekamp
Oldenzaal
Enschede
Haaksbergen
Hengelo
Almelo
Borne
Tubbergen
Den Ham
Hardenberg
Dedemsvaart
Ommen
Wierden
Rijssen
Raalte
Goor
Lochem
Neede
Eibergen
Winterswijk
Aalten
Ulft

Delfzijl
Zuidhorn
Leek
Roden
Oosterwolde
Dokkum
Ferwerd
Nes
Menaldum
Leeuwarden
Drachten
Harlingen
Sneek
Joure
Wolvega
Heerenveen
Meppel
Staphorst
Steenwijk
Hoogeveen
Beilen
Zwolle
Hattem
Heerde
Deventer
Zutphen
Gorssel
Brummen
Dieren
Doesburg
Lichtenvoorde
Zevenaar

Den Helder
Schagen
Bergen
Heerhugowaard
Opmeer
Hoorn
Heiloo
Alkmaar
Heemskerk
Castricum
Velsen-Noord
Beverwijk
Haarlem
Zaanstad
Purmerend
Broek-in-Waterland
AMSTERDAM
Amstelveen
Hillegom
Lisse
Sassenheim
Leiden
Noordwijk aan Zee
Zoetermeer
THE HAGUE ('S-GRAVENHAGE)
's-Gravenzande
Delft
Vlaardingen
Spijkenisse
Rotterdam
Barendrecht
Dordrecht

Lelystad
Emmeloord
Almere
Zeewolde
Blaricum
Hilversum
Bussum
Weesp
Naarden
Baarn
Amersfoort
Soest
Zeist
De Bilt
UTRECHT
Nieuwegein
Veenendaal
Wijk bij Duurstede
Ede
Lunteren
Apeldoorn
Nijkerk
Harderwijk
Ermelo
Nunspeet
Vaassen
Wezep
IJsselmuiden

Arnhem
Duiven
Nijmegen
Beuningen
Groesbeek
Gennep
Nieuw-Bergen
Cuijck
Boxmeer
Grave
Oss
's-Hertogenbosch
Rosmalen
Sint-Michielsgestel
Schijndel
Oirschot
Tilburg
Breda
Oosterhout
Made
Raamsdonksveer
Waalwijk
Vijmen
Woudrichem
Gorinchem
Alphen aan den Rijn
Gouda
Capelle aan den IJssel
Vianen
Mijdrecht
Werkendam

Middelharnis
Helleveotsluis
Goeree
Overflakkee
Zierikzee
Schouwen
Zevenbergen
Roosendaal
Zevenbergschen
Tholen
Noord-Beveland
Eastern Scheldt
Goes
Middelburg

Rhine
Waal
Lek
Ussel
Neder Rijn
Benedenmaas
Ussel

G

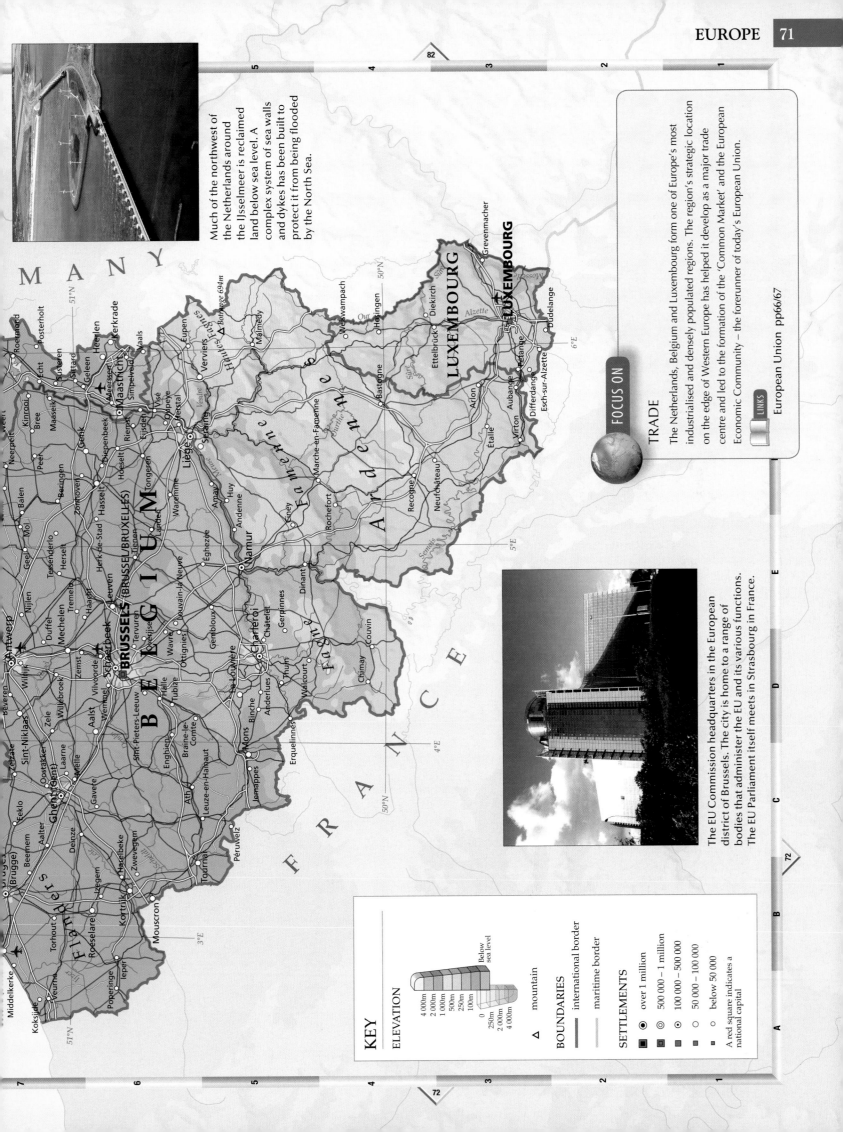

Much of the northwest of the Netherlands around the IJsselmeer is reclaimed land below sea level. A complex system of sea walls and dykes has been built to protect it from being flooded by the North Sea.

FOCUS ON

TRADE

The Netherlands, Belgium and Luxembourg form one of Europe's most industrialised and densely populated regions. The region's strategic location on the edge of Western Europe has helped it develop as a major trade centre and led to the formation of the 'Common Market' and the European Economic Community – the forerunner of today's European Union.

LINKS
European Union pp66/67

The EU Commission headquarters in the European district of Brussels. The city is home to a range of bodies that administer the EU and its various functions. The EU Parliament itself meets in Strasbourg in France.

KEY

ELEVATION

4 000m
2 000m
1 000m
500m
250m
100m
0
250m
2 000m
4 000m
Below sea level

△ mountain

BOUNDARIES

international border
maritime border

SETTLEMENTS

over 1 million
500 000 – 1 million
100 000 – 500 000
50 000 – 100 000
below 50 000

A red square indicates a national capital

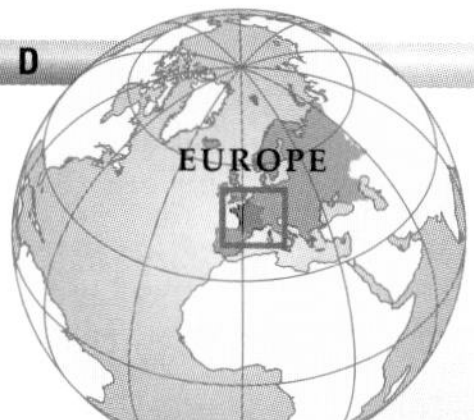

FRANCE

France is the largest country in western Europe. Flat lowland river basins surround the plateau of the Massif Central, whilst the mountains of the Pyrenees and Alps form the borders with Spain and Italy. A founder member of the European Union (EU), France is a leading industrial and farming country.

EUROPE

REGIONAL FRANCE

There are 22 regions in France, including the island of Corsica. These are further divided into smaller areas called departements. The capital city, Paris, is located in the Île-de-France, part of the Paris Basin.

Regional map labels:
NORD-PAS-DE-CALAIS · Lille · HAUTE-NORMANDIE · Amiens · PICARDIE · Caen · Rouen · CHAMPAGNE-ARDENNE · BASSE-NORMANDIE · PARIS · ÎLE-DE-FRANCE · LORRAINE · Châlons-en-Champagne · Nancy · Strasbourg · BRETAGNE · Rennes · ALSACE · PAYS DE LA LOIRE · Orléans · BOURGOGNE · FRANCHE-COMTÉ · Nantes · CENTRE · Dijon · Besançon · Poitiers · POITOU-CHARENTES · LIMOUSIN · Clermont-Ferrand · Limoges · Lyon · RHÔNE-ALPES · Bordeaux · AUVERGNE · AQUITANE · MIDI-PYRÉNÉES · Toulouse · Montpellier · PROVENCE-ALPES-CÔTE D'AZURE · LANGUEDOC-ROUSILLION · Marseille · CORSE · Ajaccio

PARIS

Paris and its suburbs, part of the Île-de-France region, are shown in white and blue on this false colour satellite image. The River Seine can clearly be seen running across the centre of the built up area. Small patches of farmland are visible around the edges, shown in red.

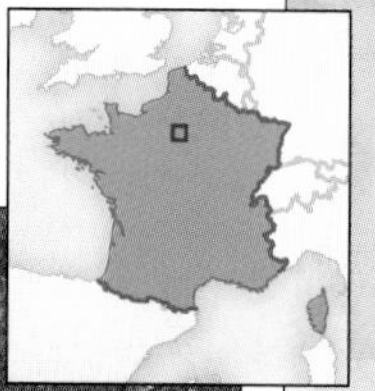

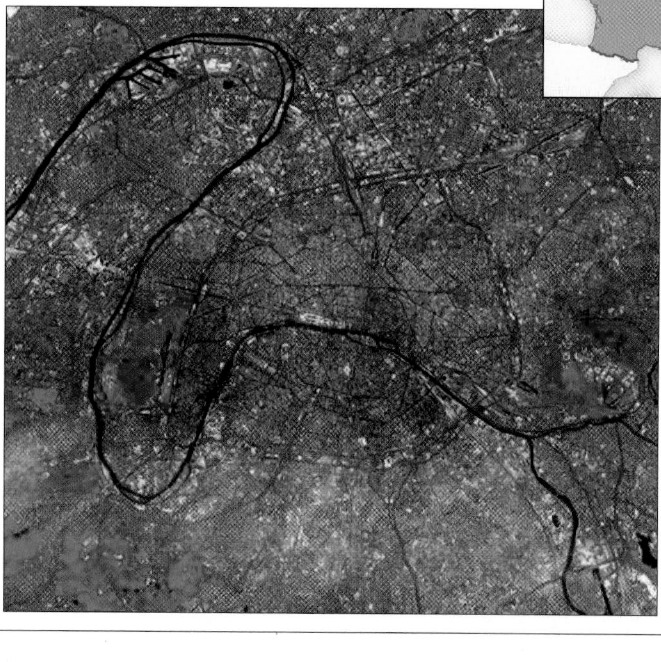

Main map labels:
UNITED KINGDOM · Channel Tunnel · Strait of Dover · Calais · Boulogne-sur-Mer · le Portel · Berck-Plage · English Channel · Abbeville · Dieppe · Amiens · Alderney · Cap de la Hague · Cherbourg · Fécamp · Picardy (Picardie) · Beauvais · Guernsey (to UK) · Baie de la Seine · le Havre · Barentin · Rouen · Channel Islands · Jersey (to UK) · Bayeux · Caen · Louviers · Golfe de St-Malo · St-Lô · Coutances · Lisieux · Évreux · Argenteuil · PARIS · Île d'Ouessant · Granville · Avranches · Normandy (Normandie) · Argentan · Dreux · Versailles · Brest · Morlaix · St-Malo · Domfront · Chartres · Landerneau · Plérin · St-Brieuc · Dinan · Fougères · Alençon · Châteaudun · Île-de-France · Iroise · Brittany (Bretagne) · Loudéac · Vitré · Laval · Maine · Orléans · Pointe du Raz · Quimper · Quimperlé · Pontivy · Rennes · le Mans · Vendôme · Olivet · Concarneau · Hennebont · Auray · Vannes · Redon · Châteaubriant · Sarthe · la Flèche · Touraine · Blois · Orléans · Lorient · Belle Île · la Baule-Escoublac · St-Nazaire · Angers · Anjou · Saumur · Tours · Vierzon · Belle Île · Rezé · Nantes · Cholet · Thouars · Berry · Île d'Yeu · Challans · les Herbiers · Châtellerault · Châteauroux · St-Am... · la Roche-sur-Yon · Poitiers · FRANCE · les Sables-d'Olonne · Fontenay-le-Comte · Poitou · Bourbonna... · Île de Ré · Niort · Vienne · Mon... · la Rochelle · Bellac · Guéret · Rochefort · Civray · Île d' Oléron · Saintes · Cognac · Limoges · Aubuss... · Royan · Charente · Angoulême · Limousi... · Bay of Biscay · Angoumois · Charente · Thiviers · Médoc · Périgueux · Tulle · Isle · Brive-la-Gaillarde · Cenon · Libourne · Dordogne · Auri... · Mérignac · Bordeaux · Bergerac · Dordogne · Arcachon · Pessac · Cancon · Lot · la Teste · Marmande · Houilles · Cahors · Landes · Garonne · Lot · Agen · Moissac · Aquitaine · Castelsarrasin · Aveyron · Gaillac · Gulf of Gascony · Mont-de-Marsan · Eauze · Montauban · Adour · Armagnac · Auch · Toulouse · Anglet · Dax · Orthez · Gascony (Gascogne) · Lombez · Biarritz · Bayonne · Pau · Tarbes · St-Gaudens · Castelnauda... · Lourdes · Pamiers · Carcas... · Balaïtous 3144m · Foix · Pyrenees · SPAIN · Rob... · ANDORRA

POPULATION DENSITY

The regions forming the Paris Basin and coastal areas are the most densely populated in France, in marked contrast to the more sparsely populated mountain regions of Limousin, Auvergne and the Rhone-Alpes.

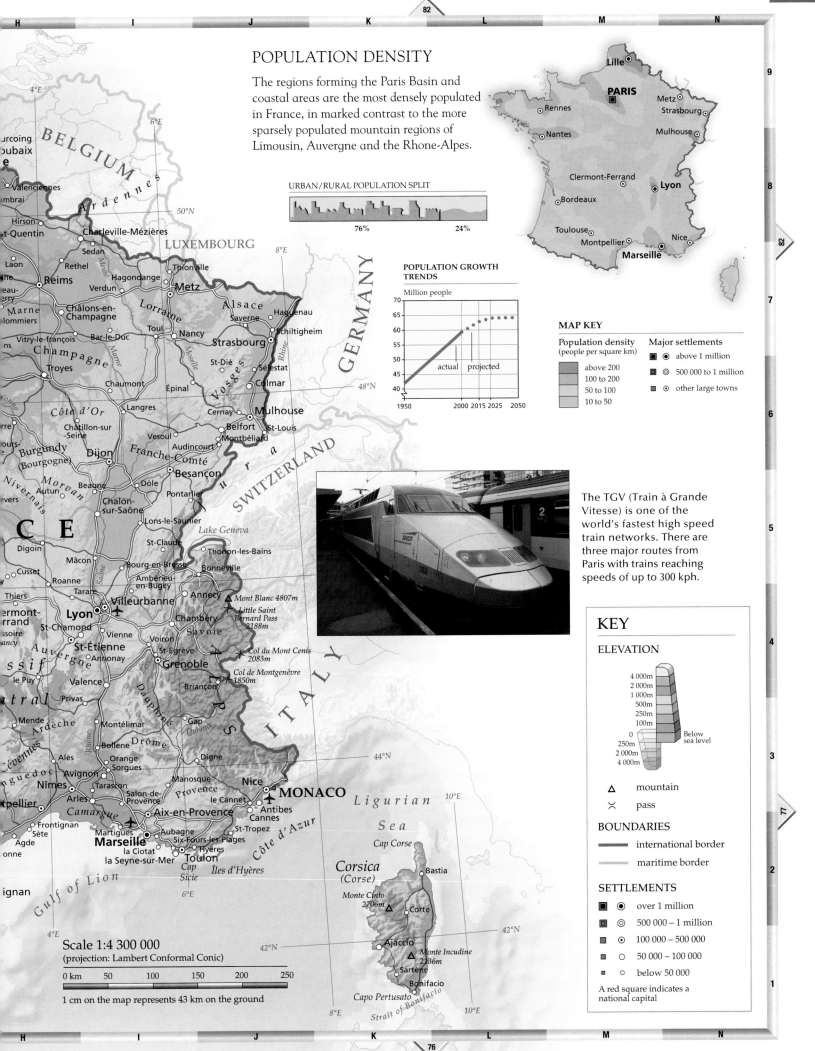

URBAN/RURAL POPULATION SPLIT

76%   24%

POPULATION GROWTH TRENDS

Million people

actual   projected

1950   2000 2015 2025   2050

MAP KEY

Population density (people per square km)
- above 200
- 100 to 200
- 50 to 100
- 10 to 50

Major settlements
- ■ ◉ above 1 million
- ▣ ◎ 500 000 to 1 million
- ▪ ⊙ other large towns

The TGV (Train à Grande Vitesse) is one of the world's fastest high speed train networks. There are three major routes from Paris with trains reaching speeds of up to 300 kph.

KEY

ELEVATION

4 000m
2 000m
1 000m
500m
250m
100m
0
250m
2 000m
4 000m

Below sea level

△ mountain
⋈ pass

BOUNDARIES

─── international border
─── maritime border

SETTLEMENTS

- ■ ◉ over 1 million
- ▣ ◎ 500 000 – 1 million
- ▪ ⊙ 100 000 – 500 000
- ▪ ○ 50 000 – 100 000
- ▪ ○ below 50 000

A red square indicates a national capital

Scale 1:4 300 000
(projection: Lambert Conformal Conic)

0 km   50   100   150   200   250

1 cm on the map represents 43 km on the ground

SPAIN AND PORTUGAL

Spain and Portugal together make up the Iberian Peninsula and are both members of the European Union (EU). The mountains of the Pyrenees form Spain's northern border with France. The central area of Spain is a large, arid plateau called the Meseta. From here a few rivers drain towards the coastal areas, providing some flat land. The Balearic and Canary Islands are also part of Spain.

REGIONAL AREAS

Many Spanish regions have strong identities and allegiances, notably the Basques (País Vasco) and Catalans (Cataluña), which has been the cause of conflict. Portuguese administrative names are derived from the appropriate settlement name, so for example, Faro is the administrative capital of the FARO administrative region.

Barcelona is one of Spain's major cities. Home to the 1992 Olympic Games, it also attracts visitors to Las Ramblas, a thriving thoroughfare linking the port to the old Gothic quarter.

POPULATION DENSITY

Most of Spain's 40 million people live along the Mediterranean coast or around the capital city, Madrid. Its overall population density is one of the lowest in the EU.

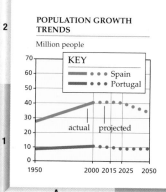

POPULATION GROWTH TRENDS

Million people

KEY
• • • Spain
• • • Portugal

actual | projected

1950 2000 2015 2025 2050

MAP KEY

Population density
(people per square km)

- above 200
- 100 to 200
- 50 to 100
- 10 to 50

Major settlements
- ■ ● above 1 million
- ▣ ◎ 500 000 to 1 million
- ▪ ⊙ below 500 000

A red square indicates a national capital

URBAN/RURAL POPULATION SPLIT

78%   22%

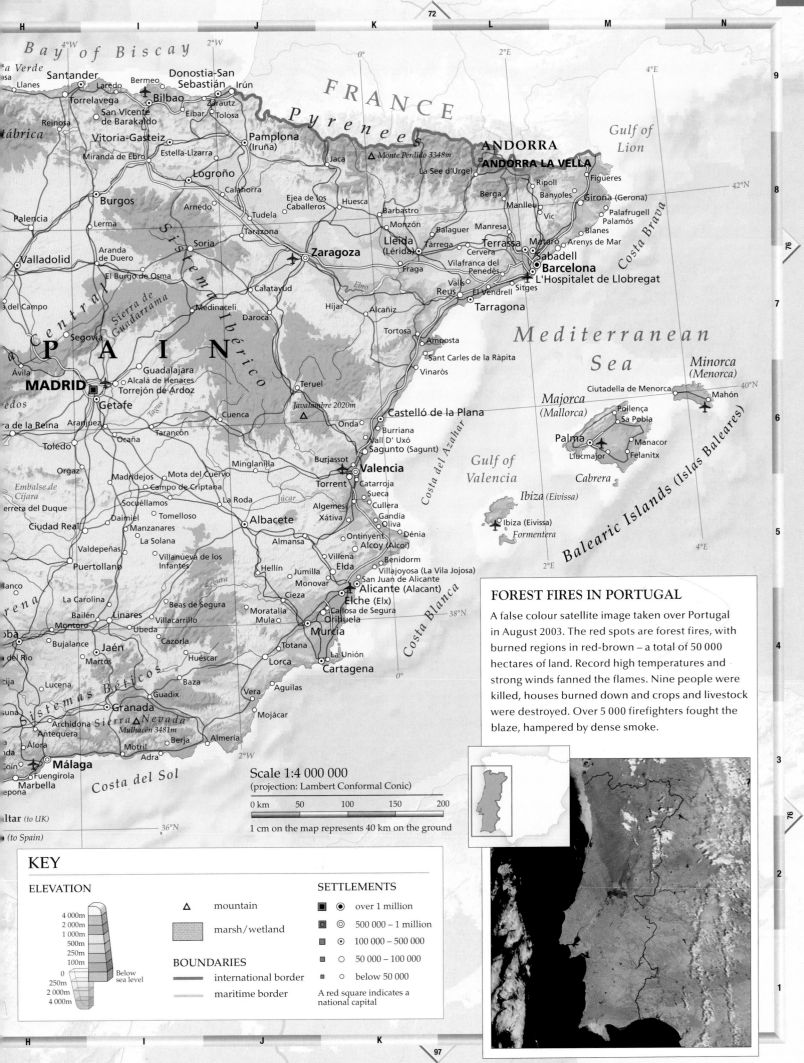

ITALY

Italy's famous boot-shaped peninsula, part of mainland Europe, juts out into the Mediterranean Sea from the Alps, which form its northern border. The Apennine Mountains run down the spine of the country, separated from the Alps by the fertile lowlands of the Po Valley.

REGIONAL MAP

Italy is divided into 20 regions, including the islands of Sicily and Sardinia. There is a very marked north/south divide in Italy, the urban north being more industrialised compared to the less wealthy, rural south.

Fiat's Lingotto building in Turin, built in 1923. It operated for 60 years before being converted into a modern arts, leisure and shopping complex. Turin remains one of Italy's major industrial cities.

MOUNT ETNA

A true colour satellite image of Sicily's Mount Etna. An active volcano, this shows the fourth successive day of eruptions in October 2002. The plume of ash, clearly visible, extended over 400 km southwards towards North Africa.

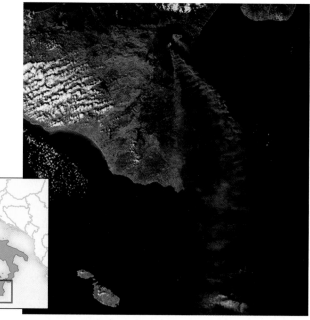

Scale 1:4 250 000
(projection: Lambert Conformal Conic)

| 0 km | 50 | 100 | 150 | 200 | 250 |

1 cm on the map represents 42.5 km on the ground

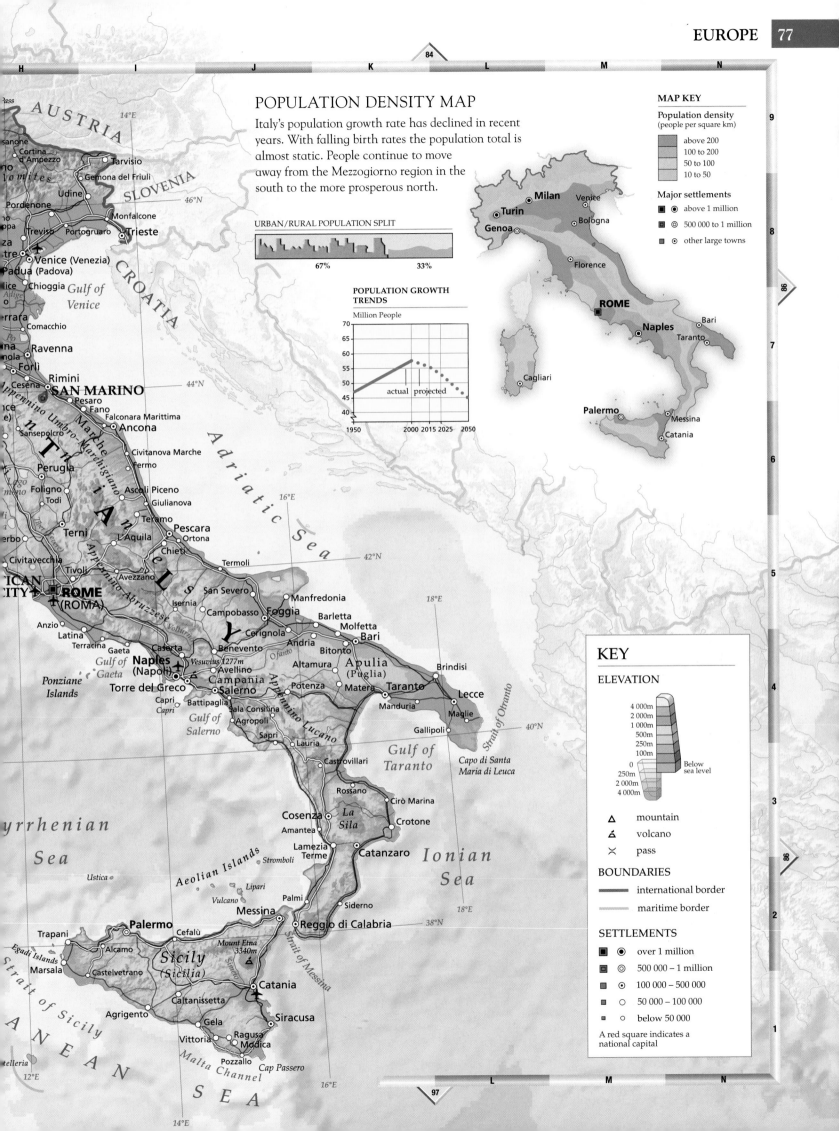

POPULATION DENSITY MAP

Italy's population growth rate has declined in recent years. With falling birth rates the population total is almost static. People continue to move away from the Mezzogiorno region in the south to the more prosperous north.

URBAN/RURAL POPULATION SPLIT

67%   33%

POPULATION GROWTH TRENDS

Million People

actual   projected

1950   2000 2015 2025 2050

MAP KEY

Population density (people per square km)
- above 200
- 100 to 200
- 50 to 100
- 10 to 50

Major settlements
- ■ ⊙ above 1 million
- ▣ ⊚ 500 000 to 1 million
- ▪ ⊙ other large towns

KEY

ELEVATION

4 000m
2 000m
1 000m
500m
250m
100m
0
250m
2 000m
4 000m

Below sea level

- △ mountain
- ⧊ volcano
- ⋈ pass

BOUNDARIES
- —— international border
- —— maritime border

SETTLEMENTS
- ■ ⊙ over 1 million
- ▣ ⊚ 500 000 – 1 million
- ▪ ⊙ 100 000 – 500 000
- ▪ ○ 50 000 – 100 000
- ▪ ○ below 50 000

A red square indicates a national capital

THE MEDITERRANEAN

Stretching 4 000 km from east to west, the Mediterranean Sea was once a much larger sea, squeezed out by the collision of two major tectonic plates. Almost 30 countries share its coastline or form island nations within it, creating an historically important cultural mix. The Mediterranean also gives its name to the very distinctive type of climate found here and in other parts of the world.

The western entrance to the Mediterranean is the very narrow Strait of Gibraltar, just 13 km wide, separating Spain and Morocco. As a result, the sea has a very small tidal range and is very salty.

EUROPE

Scale 1:9 200 000
(projection: Gall)

0 km   100   200   300   400   500

1 cm on the map represents 92 km on the ground

KEY

ELEVATION

4 000m
2 000m
1 000m
500m
250m
100m
0
250m   Below
2 000m   sea level
4 000m

△ mountain   ⏚ volcano

sandy desert

seasonal lake

BOUNDARIES

international border
disputed border
×—×—× ceasefire line
maritime border

SETTLEMENTS

■ ⦿ over 1 million
▣ ◎ 500 000 – 1 million
▦ ⊙ 100 000 – 500 000
▪ ○ 50 000 – 100 000
▫ ○ below 50 000

A red square indicates a national capital

FOCUS ON

TOURISM

The warm sunny weather and scenery of the Mediterranean attracts millions of tourists every year – more tourists visit here than any other destination in the world. This has created conflict between the economic benefits of tourism and the effect on the natural environment and resources of the Mediterranean.

📖 LINKS

Tourism pp80/81

Both the EU and the UN are involved in trying to resolve the conflict in Cyprus. The island has been divided since 1974 when tension between the Greek and Turkish communities led to armed conflict. UN peacekeeping forces have been on the island for more than 40 years after tensions boiled over in the early 1960s.

CYPRUS

TURKISH REPUBLIC OF NORTHERN CYPRUS
(recognised only by Turkey)

Agialousa (Yenierenköy)
Lápithos (Lapta)
Kerýneia (Girne)
Mórfou (Güzelyurt)
Kythréa (Değirmenlik)
NICOSIA
Famagusta Bay
Famagusta (Ammóchostos) (Gazimağusa)
Pólis
CYPRUS
Dhekelia Sovereign Base Area *(to UK)*
Troodos
Lárnaca (Lárnaka)
Páfos
Limassol (Lemesós)
Akrotiri Sovereign Base Area *(to UK)*
Mediterranean Sea

Scale 1:3 300 000
0 km 25 50 75

HUNGARY
SLOVENIA
LJUBLJANA
ZAGREB
CROATIA
Sava
BOSNIA & HERZEGOVINA
SARAJEVO
Split
Adriatic Sea
Dinaric Alps
SERBIA & MONTENEGRO (YUGOSLAVIA)
Niš
Priština
SOFIA (SOFIYA)
BULGARIA
Burgas
Danube
Balkan Mountains
SKOPJE
MACEDONIA
Plovdiv
Rhodope Mountains
Erdine
Black Sea
Bosporus
Zonguldak
Bari
TIRANA (TIRANË)
ALBANIA
İstanbul
Sea of Marmara
Bursa
Kızıl Irmak
Taranto
1277m
Gulf of Taranto
Strait of Otranto
Pindus Mountains
Salonica (Thessaloniki)
Limnos
Balikesir
Eskişehir
ANKARA
Cosenza
Catanzaro
Corfu
Lárisa
GREECE
Aegean Sea
Lesbos
T U R K E Y
A n a t o l i a
Kayseri
Reggio di Calabria
Lefkada
Kefaloniá
Euboea
Chios
İzmir
ATHENS (ATHINA)
Samos
Büyükmenderes Nehri
Konya
Taurus Mountains
Gaziantep
Mount Etna 3340m
Catania
Siracusa
Zakynthos
Pátra
Peloponnese
Andros
Mirtoan Sea
Cyclades
Dodecanese
Antalya
Gulf of Antalya
Mersin
Adana
Ionian Sea
Kythira
Rhodes
Aleppo (Halab)
Sea of Crete
Kárpathos
Irakleio
TURKISH REPUBLIC OF NORTHERN CYPRUS
(recognised only by Turkey)
NICOSIA
SYRIA
Crete
CYPRUS
Lárnaca
Limassol
LEBANON
BEIRUT (BEYROUTH)
DAMASCUS (DIMASHQ)
Hefa
Darnah
Mişrātah
Benghazi (Banghāzī)
Al Jabal al Akhdar
Tobruk
ISRAEL
Tel Aviv-Yafo
West Bank
'AMMAN
Gulf of Sirte
Surt
Sidi Barrani
Nile Delta
JERUSALEM
Gaza Strip
Gaza
Dead Sea
Alexandria
Port Said
JORDAN
Ajdabiyā
LIBYA
E G Y P T
Suez Canal
CAIRO
Suez
El Giza
Sinai
Qattara Depression
-133m
Nile
Gulf of Suez

The 160 km-long Suez Canal, opened in 1869, links Port Said in Egypt to Suez and the Red Sea. It provides a route from Europe to Asia without having to sail around Africa.

TOURISM

Tourism is one of the fastest growing industries in the world. In 2002, it employed nearly 200 million people worldwide – just under 8 per cent of the world's total workforce. Although the growth of tourism has brought many economic and cultural benefits to tourist destinations, these have to be balanced against the environmental and social costs.

GROWTH OF INTERNATIONAL TOURISM

The rapid rise of international tourism, especially to long-haul destinations, has been made possible by cheaper, readily available air travel. In addition, many tourists from MEDCs now have more leisure time and disposable income, and often take several holidays or short breaks each year.

The number of international tourists and the income they have generated has grown steadily since 1950. However, economic factors can affect growth. For example, tourism and airlines were badly affected by the terrorist attacks on New York and Washington on 11 September 2001 – an event now universally referred to as 9/11. Tourist numbers fell by 3 per cent and over 3 million jobs were lost, although visitor numbers and income were increasing again by 2004.

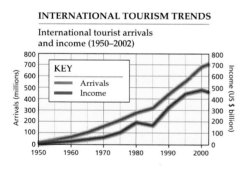

INTERNATIONAL TOURISM TRENDS
International tourist arrivals and income (1950–2002)

INTERNATIONAL TOURISM RECEIPTS IN 2002

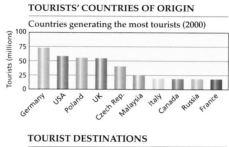

TOURISTS' COUNTRIES OF ORIGIN
Countries generating the most tourists (2000)

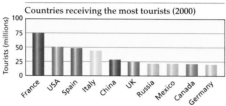

TOURIST DESTINATIONS
Countries receiving the most tourists (2000)

SUSTAINABLE TOURISM

Most of the world's tourists live in MEDCs and the majority travel to holiday destinations in other MEDCs, especially Europe and the USA. However, this is beginning to change as significant numbers now visit locations in LEDCs, such as China.

Particularly in LEDCs, the growth of the tourism industry can threaten the natural environment and traditional way of life, often the very things that attract visitors to a region. However, the importance of tourism to many countries' economies means that they cannot afford to discourage it. Instead, some destinations are increasingly promoting sustainable tourism or eco-tourism. These types of holidays ensure that money spent is of direct benefit to the local community and that the often fragile environments that tourists come to see are properly protected.

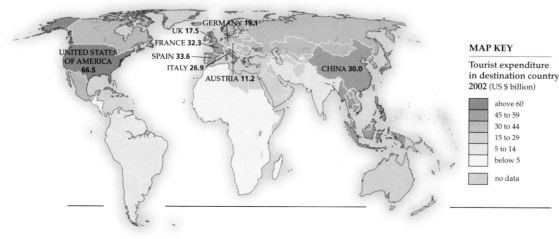

MAP KEY

Tourist expenditure in destination country 2002 (US $ billion)

- above 60
- 45 to 59
- 30 to 44
- 15 to 29
- 5 to 14
- below 5
- no data

MEDITERRANEAN TOURISM

Europe is still the world's most popular tourist destination, claiming roughly 60 per cent of the world market. The majority of tourists who visit choose either mountain or coastal locations. By far the most visited coastal regions are those of the Mediterranean countries and islands, especially France, Italy, Spain and Greece.

TOURISM IN THE MEDITERRANEAN
The Mediterranean region has high levels of plant diversity, with 25 000 different species, 13 000 of which are endemic, i.e. unique to the region. Many of these biodiversity 'hotspots' experience high levels of tourist activity, threatening biodiversity in the region.

PRESSURES ON THE REGION

The high number of visitors to the region, often concentrated into just part of the year, has created a range of problems, placing increasing pressure on what are often quite limited resources. Some of the major impacts of tourism are:

- High demand for water in areas where it is often a scarce resource. Tourists typically use almost twice as much water per day as local residents.

- The production (and disposal) of over 40 million tonnes of waste each year.

VISITOR NUMBERS

Over five million people have jobs related to tourism in the Mediterranean, with the industry providing 7 per cent of the GDP of the region. 135 million international visitors came in 1990, rising to 220 million in 2002. This is expected to increase to 350 million by 2020.

Resorts on the southeast coast of Spain, like Benidorm (above), continue to attract large numbers of tourists, despite heavy development.

PROTECTING THE ENVIRONMENT

For many years there was no central planning or strategy for the development of tourism in the region. In 1975 the Mediterranean Action Plan (MAP) was set up, part of the United Nations Environment Programme (UNEP). Its first aim was to protect the marine environment but, since 1995, it has widened its brief to include sustainable development, biodiversity and management of coastal regions.

Some areas, such as the Balearic Islands, are considering implementing a visitor eco-tax to fund environment-friendly developments. This is an initiative that could help many tourist areas in the Mediterranean, especially if the money raised is reinvested in protecting and managing the environment that attracts visitors.

MAP KEY

Tourism activity in the Mediterranean 2005
- very high
- high
- medium

Plant biodiversity (endemic rate)
- above 20%
- 10% to 20%

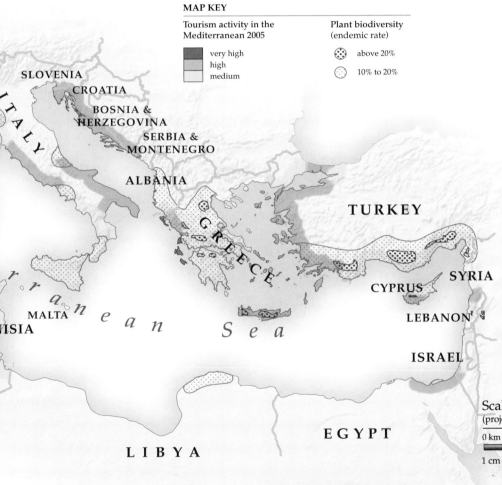

Scale 1:16 000 000
(projection: Lambert Azimuthal Equal Area)

0 km   200   400   600   800

1 cm on the map represents 160 km on the ground

- Increased urbanisation of coastal regions as more hotels and tourist facilities are built, damaging local ecosystems.

- An increase in the number of second or holiday homes, which take up much more land than hotels but are usually only occupied for short periods of each year.

- High levels of pollution, particularly from cars, aircraft and boats.

Waste washed up onto a beach in the Maddalena National Park, Sardinia, Italy.

THE BIG ISSUES

1 Why do so many tourists visit Europe – and the Mediterranean – in particular?

2 Why did the events of 9/11 affect the tourist industry?

3 What are the main benefits and costs, and to whom, of a rapidly expanding tourist industry?

4 How can fragile sites be protected from too many visitors, whilst raising much needed money for local communities in LEDCs?

GERMANY AND THE ALPINE STATES

Germany is the most populous country in Europe, and one of the founder members of the European Union (EU). In 1990 East and West Germany were reunited as a single country. Lowland in the north gives way to the central plateaux, including the Harz Mountains. On the southern border lie the Alps, which run through the other Alpine states of Switzerland, Austria and Slovenia.

POPULATION DENSITY

With the exception of the Berlin area, all the former East German states have seen a decrease in population as people have migrated to the west in search of work and a perceived better quality of life.

MAP KEY

Population density
(people per square km)

- above 200
- 100 to 200
- 50 to 100
- 10 to 50

Major settlements
- above 1 million
- 500 000 to 1 million
- other large towns

POPULATION GROWTH TRENDS

Million people

95
90
85
80
75
70
65

1950 2000 2015 2025 2050

actual projected

URBAN/RURAL POPULATION SPLIT

12%

88%

12%

REGIONAL MAP

Germany is divided into 16 separate states, 6 of which made up the former East Germany, including the capital Berlin.

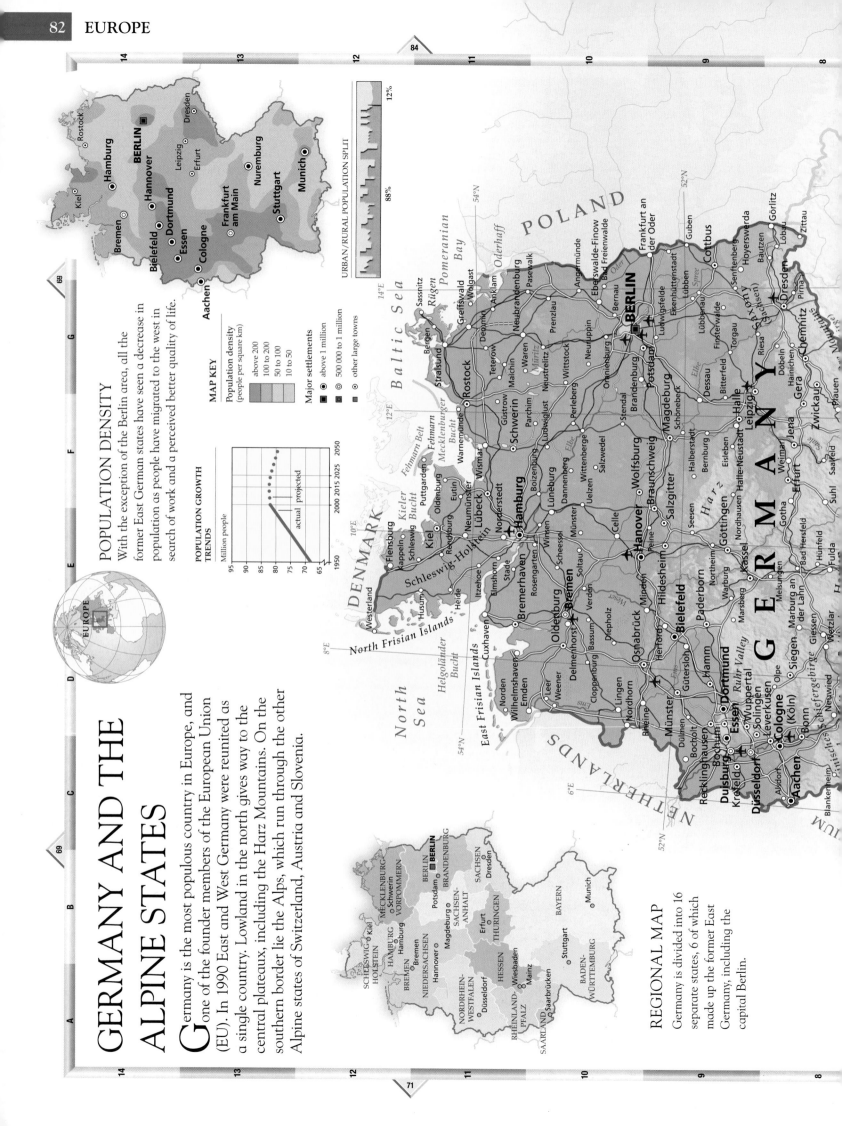

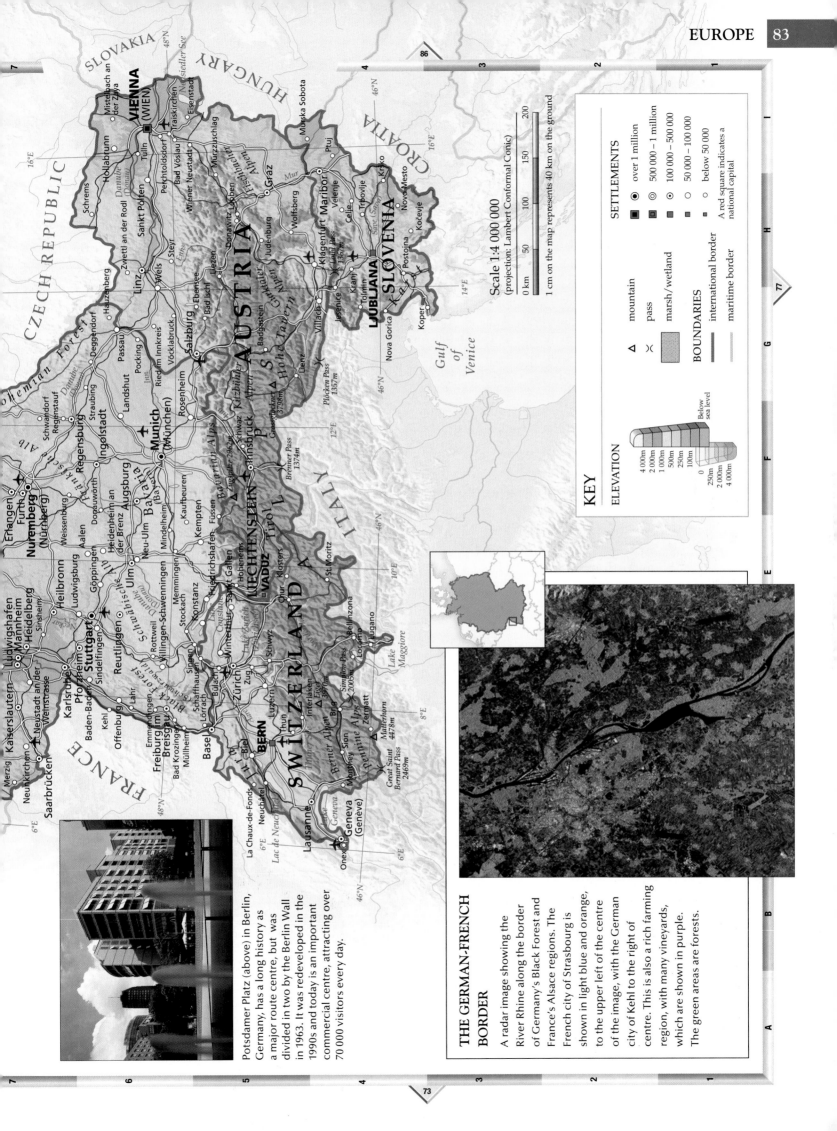

Potsdamer Platz (above) in Berlin, Germany, has a long history as a major route centre, but was divided in two by the Berlin Wall in 1963. It was redeveloped in the 1990s and today is an important commercial centre, attracting over 70 000 visitors every day.

THE GERMAN-FRENCH BORDER

A radar image showing the River Rhine along the border of Germany's Black Forest and France's Alsace regions. The French city of Strasbourg is shown in light blue and orange, to the upper left of the centre of the image, with the German city of Kehl to the right of centre. This is also a rich farming region, with many vineyards, which are shown in purple. The green areas are forests.

Scale 1:4 000 000
(projection: Lambert Conformal Conic)

1 cm on the map represents 40 km on the ground

KEY

ELEVATION

4 000m
2 000m
1 000m
500m
250m
100m
0
Below sea level

250m
2 000m
4 000m

SETTLEMENTS

- ◉ over 1 million
- ◎ 500 000 – 1 million
- ◉ 100 000 – 500 000
- ○ 50 000 – 100 000
- ∘ below 50 000

A red square indicates a national capital

△ mountain
✕ pass
marsh/wetland

BOUNDARIES

international border
maritime border

CENTRAL EUROPE

During the twentieth century, Central Europe suffered enormous conflict. Following the end of Communist rule in the 1980s and early 1990s, all four countries in the region established democratic governments and sought closer links with Western Europe. They finally joined the European Union in 2004. Today, the region is an important one both for farming and industry.

The capital city of the Czech Republic, Prague is an historic city that attracts large numbers of visitors. It has so many churches it is called 'the city of a hundred spires'.

Poland's heavy industries have played an important part in its economic development. However, its coal industry – the second largest in Europe – is heavily in debt. Many mines are closing, leading to job losses.

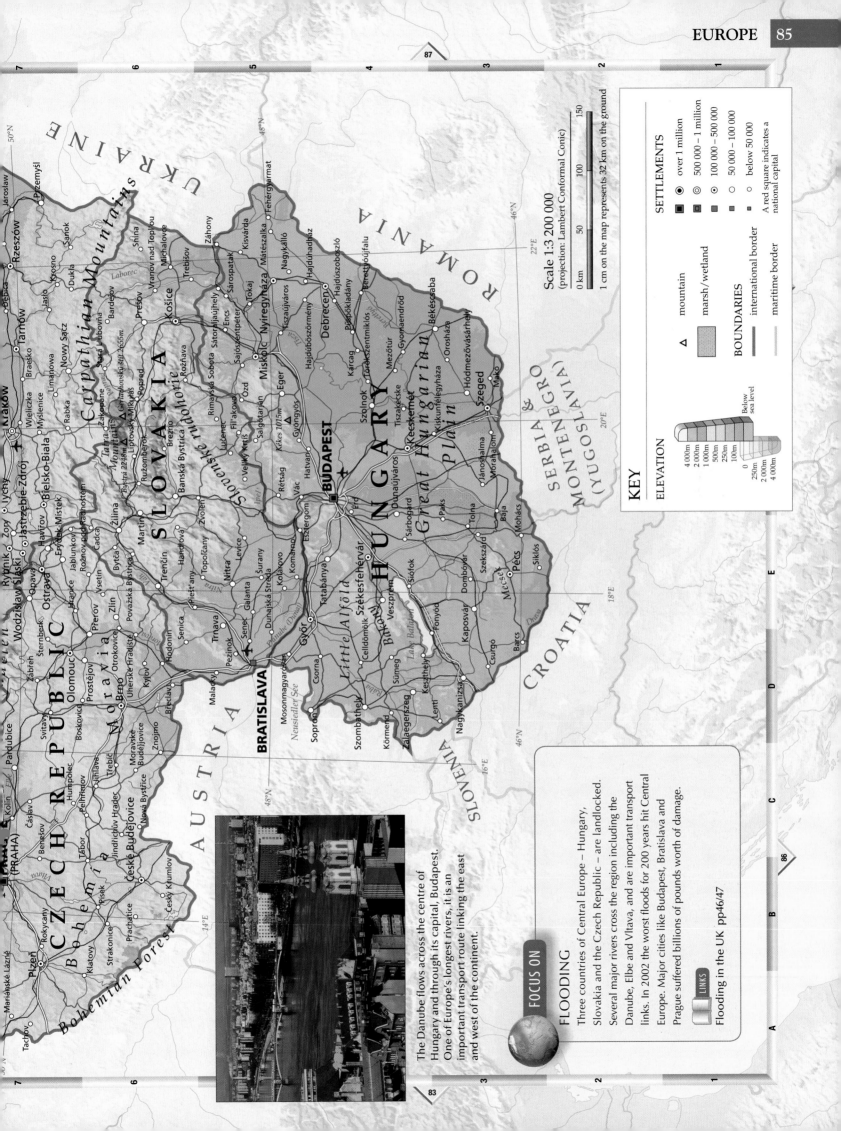

FOCUS ON

FLOODING

The Danube flows across the centre of Hungary and through its capital, Budapest. One of Europe's longest rivers, it is an important transport route linking the east and west of the continent.

Three countries of Central Europe – Hungary, Slovakia and the Czech Republic – are landlocked. Several major rivers cross the region including the Danube, Elbe and Vltava, and are important transport links. In 2002 the worst floods for 200 years hit Central Europe. Major cities like Budapest, Bratislava and Prague suffered billions of pounds worth of damage.

LINKS
Flooding in the UK pp46/47

SOUTHEAST EUROPE

Greece, once the centre of western civilisation, has enjoyed relatively peaceful conditions during modern times, although it is still involved in a dispute with Turkey over the control of Cyprus. In the north of the region, civil war during the 1990s led to the break-up of former Yugoslavia into five new independent countries and the displacement of many people.

EUROPE

The old walled city of Dubrovnik was badly damaged during fighting with Serbia in the 1990s. Always a popular tourist resort, visitors are returning to the city, on the Adriatic coast of what is now Croatia.

The civil war in what was once Yugoslavia lasted throughout the 1990s. Thousands were killed in the fighting or murdered. Thousands more fled – like these refugees from Kosovo.

KEY

ELEVATION

4 000m
2 000m
1 000m
500m
250m
100m
0
250m   Below
2 000m   sea level
4 000m

△ mountain

marsh/wetland

BOUNDARIES

—— international border

—— maritime border

—— administrative border

SETTLEMENTS

■ ■ ◉ over 1 million

▣ ▣ ◎ 500 000 – 1 million

▨ ▨ ◉ 100 000 – 500 000

▪ ▪ ○ 50 000 – 100 000

▫ ▫ ○ below 50 000

A red square indicates a national capital

An orange square indicates a provincial or federal capital

Map labels:

HUNGARY
SLOVENIA
Varazdin
ZAGREB
Virovitica
Karlovac
Osijek
VOJVODINA
Subotica
Kikinda
Arad
Timişoara
Vrbas
Zrenjanin
CROATIA
Papuk
Great Hungarian Plain
Maros
Rijeka
Kvarner
Krk
Cres
Pag
Bosanski Novi
Slavonski Brod
Vukovar
Novi Sad
Reşi
Pula
Kozara
Vršac
Lošinj
Bihać
Banja Luka
REPUBLIKA SRPSKA
Gradačac
Zemun
Pančevo
Smederevo
Zadar
Tuzla
Šabac
BELGRADE (BEOGRAD)
Dugi Otok
Zenica
BOSNIA AND
Valjevo
Smederevska
Troglav 1913m
HERZEGOVINA
SARAJEVO
Kragujevac
Ralanka
SER
Adriatic Sea
Split
FEDERACIJA BOSNA HERCEGOVINA
Foča
SERBIA &
Brač
Mostar
MONTENEGRO
Vis
Hvar
Bijelo Polje
Niš
Korčula
MONTENEGRO
(YUGOSLAV
Leskovac
Mljet
Dubrovnik
Nikšić
Peć
Kosovska M
Priština
Palagruža
Podgorica
Đeravica 2656m
KOSOVO
Bajram Curri
Lake Scutari
Prizren
Shkodër
SKOPJE
Kur
ALBANIA
MACEDO
Durrës
Pri
TIRANA
Lake Ohri
Fier
Berat
Bito
Vlorë
Korçë
Strait of Otranto
Gjirokastër
Neapoli
Konitsa
Sarandë
Corfu (Kerkyra)
Metsovo
Corfu (Kerkyra)
Ioannina
Igoumenitsa
Pindus Mountains
Arta
Ionian Sea
Paxoi
Preveza
GR
Ionian Islands (Ionioi Nisoi)
Lefkada
Vasiliki
Kefallinia
Poros
Lechaina
Zakynthos
Keri
Pyrgo
Medit
Kalam

Gulf of Venice

48°N
46°N
44°N
42°N
40°N
38°N
36°N
14°E
16°E
18°E
20°E

Europe's largest Roma population live in Romania, often in poverty. Many have attempted to migrate to other parts of Europe and face hostility and prejudice there.

When Athens hosted the 2004 Olympic Games, many new facilities were constructed, like the main stadium here in the Marousi suburbs. Infrastructure in the city, including transport, was also redeveloped to cope with the influx of athletes and spectators.

Scale 1:5 300 000
(projection: Lambert Conformal Conic)

| 0 km | 100 | 200 | 300 |

1 cm on the map represents 53 km on the ground

FOCUS ON

CONFLICT

The civil war which spread throughout the former Yugoslavia in the 1990s not only caused many deaths through 'ethnic cleansing', it also led to widespread migration across Europe as people fled for their lives.

📖 LINKS

European Union pp66/67

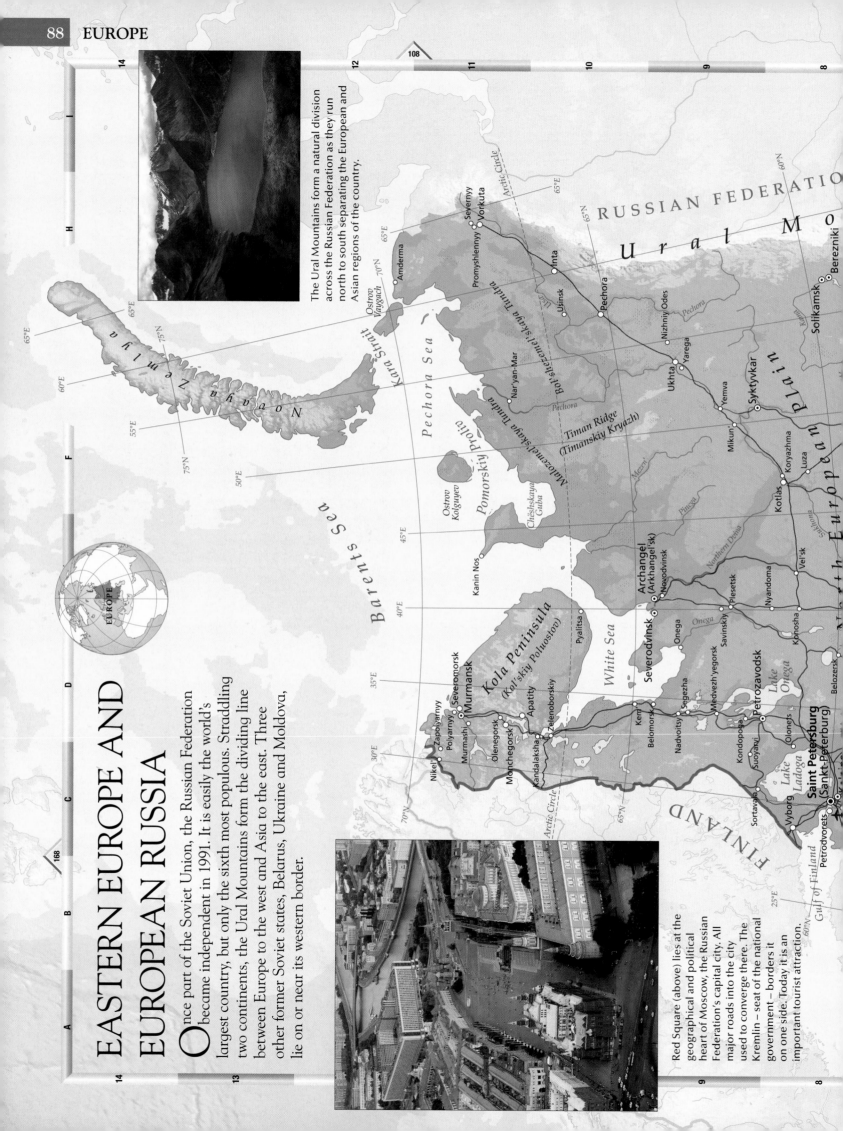

EASTERN EUROPE AND EUROPEAN RUSSIA

Once part of the Soviet Union, the Russian Federation became independent in 1991. It is easily the world's largest country, but only the sixth most populous. Straddling two continents, the Ural Mountains form the dividing line between Europe to the west and Asia to the east. Three other former Soviet states, Belarus, Ukraine and Moldova, lie on or near its western border.

EUROPE

The Ural Mountains form a natural division across the Russian Federation as they run north to south separating the European and Asian regions of the country.

Red Square (above) lies at the geographical and political heart of Moscow, the Russian Federation's capital city. All major roads into the city used to converge there. The Kremlin – seat of the national government – borders it on one side. Today it is an important tourist attraction.

RUSSIAN FEDERATION

Ural Mo

North European Plain

Barents Sea

Pechora Sea

Kara Strait

Novaya Zemlya

Ostrov Vaygach

Amderma

Severnyy
Vorkuta
Promyshlennyy
Inta

Usinsk
Pechora

Nar'yan-Mar
Nizhniy Odes
Pechora

Bol'shezemel'skaya Tundra

Yarega
Ukhta

Pechora

Malozemel'skaya Tundra

Timan Ridge
(Timanskiy Kryazh)

Yemva
Syktyvkar

Mikun'

Koryazhma
Kotlas
Luza

Ostrov Kolguyev

Pomorskiy Proliv

Chëshskaya Guba

Kanin Nos

Mezen'

Pinega

Northern Dvina

Archangel
(Arkhangel'sk)
Novodvinsk

Vel'sk

Onega

Plesetsk
Nyandoma

Konosha

Kola Peninsula
(Kol'skiy Poluostov)

Pyalitsa

White Sea

Severodvinsk

Onega

Medvezh'yegorsk
Savinskiy

Lake Onega

Petrozavodsk

Nikel'
Zapolyarnyy
Polyarnyy
Murmashi
Murmansk
Severomorsk

Olenegorsk
Monchegorsk
Apatity
Zelenoborskiy
Kandalaksha

Kem'
Belomorsk
Nadvoitsy
Segezha

Kondopoga

Suoyarvi

Lake Ladoga

Sortavala
Olonets

Vyborg

Saint Petersburg
(Sankt-Peterburg)

Petrodvorets

Gulf of Finland

FINLAND

Berezniki
Solikamsk

Arctic Circle

108

168

14 13 12 11 10 9 8

70°N 65°N 60°N

30°E 35°E 40°E 45°E 50°E 55°E 60°E 65°E

25°E

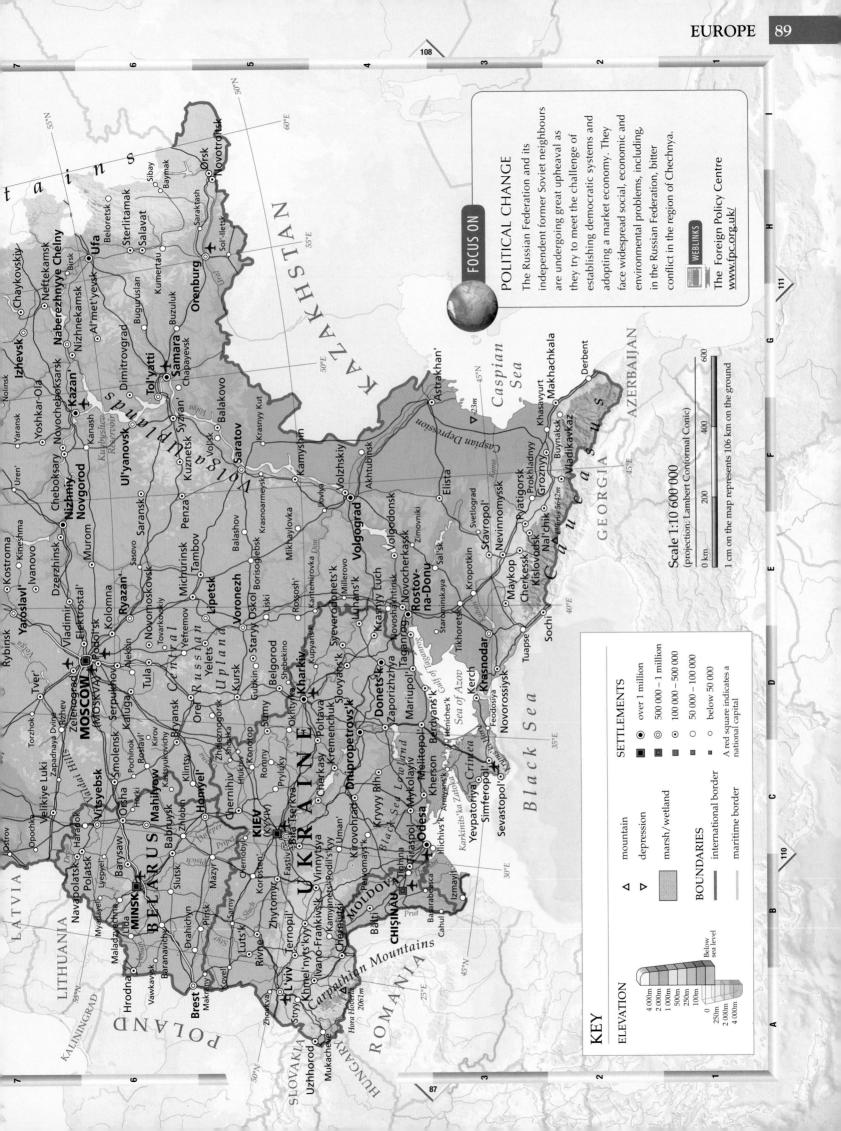

FOCUS ON

POLITICAL CHANGE

The Russian Federation and its independent former Soviet neighbours are undergoing great upheaval as they try to meet the challenge of establishing democratic systems and adopting a market economy. They face widespread social, economic and environmental problems, including, in the Russian Federation, bitter conflict in the region of Chechnya.

WEBLINKS

The Foreign Policy Centre
www.fpc.org.uk/

Scale 1:10 600 000
(projection: Lambert Conformal Conic)

0 km   200   400   600

1 cm on the map represents 106 km on the ground

KEY

ELEVATION

4 000m
2 000m
1 000m
500m
250m
100m
0
Below sea level
250m
2 000m
4 000m

△ mountain
▽ depression
marsh/wetland

BOUNDARIES
—— international border
—— maritime border

SETTLEMENTS

⬤ over 1 million
◉ 500 000 – 1 million
⊙ 100 000 – 500 000
○ 50 000 – 100 000
○ below 50 000

A red square indicates a national capital

AFRICA POLITICAL

There are 54 countries in Africa, 32 of which are amongst the poorest nations in the world. With development a key priority in the region, the UN and other agencies are working with African governments and local communities in an attempt to eradicate the causes of poverty.

QUALITY OF LIFE

MAP KEY

UN Human Development Index (HDI)

- high
- medium
- low
- no data

Source: UN, 2004

Scale 1:46 000 000

0 km   500   1 000   1 500

MAP KEY

Settlements

- over 1 000 000
- 500 000 to 1 000 000
- 100 000 to 500 000
- 50 000 to 100 000
- under 50 000

A red square indicates a national capital

Boundaries

- international border
- disputed border

COLONIAL AFRICA

Today's political map of Africa is very different to the one of 70 years ago. Gradually colonial rule has been replaced, but many new democracies are still seeking political stability. A large number of African countries continue to use a European language, often French or English, as their official language.

MAP KEY

Territory controlled by European nations in 1914

- Belgium
- United Kingdom
- France
- Germany
- Italy
- Portugal
- Spain
- Ottoman, under UK control
- Independent

Many of the people of northern Africa are of Arabic origin, with Islam the main religion. Mosques like this one in Casablanca, Morocco are a common sight. Southern Africa is mainly Christian, predominantly Roman Catholic.

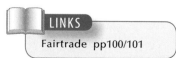

LINKS

Fairtrade pp100/101

AFRICA PHYSICAL

Africa is the second largest of the world's continents, separated from mainland Europe by the Mediterranean Sea to the north, and from Asia by the Red Sea to the east. The Sahara Desert covers the majority of the north of the continent whilst the Great Rift Valley and mountain plateaux dominate the south.

PHYSICAL FACTFILE

1 HIGHEST POINT : Mount Kilimanjaro, 5 895 metres above sea level

2 LOWEST POINT : Lake Assal, 156 metres below sea level

3 LARGEST LAKE : Lake Victoria 69 500 km²

— LONGEST RIVER : River Nile, 6 825 km

— LENGTH OF COASTLINE : 77 667 km

MAP KEY

Elevation

4 000m
2 000m
1 000m
500m
250m
100m
0
250m — Below sea level
2 000m
4 000m

△ mountain
⬟ volcano
▽ depression

Plate boundaries
— constructive
△ destructive
- - - conservative
······ uncertain

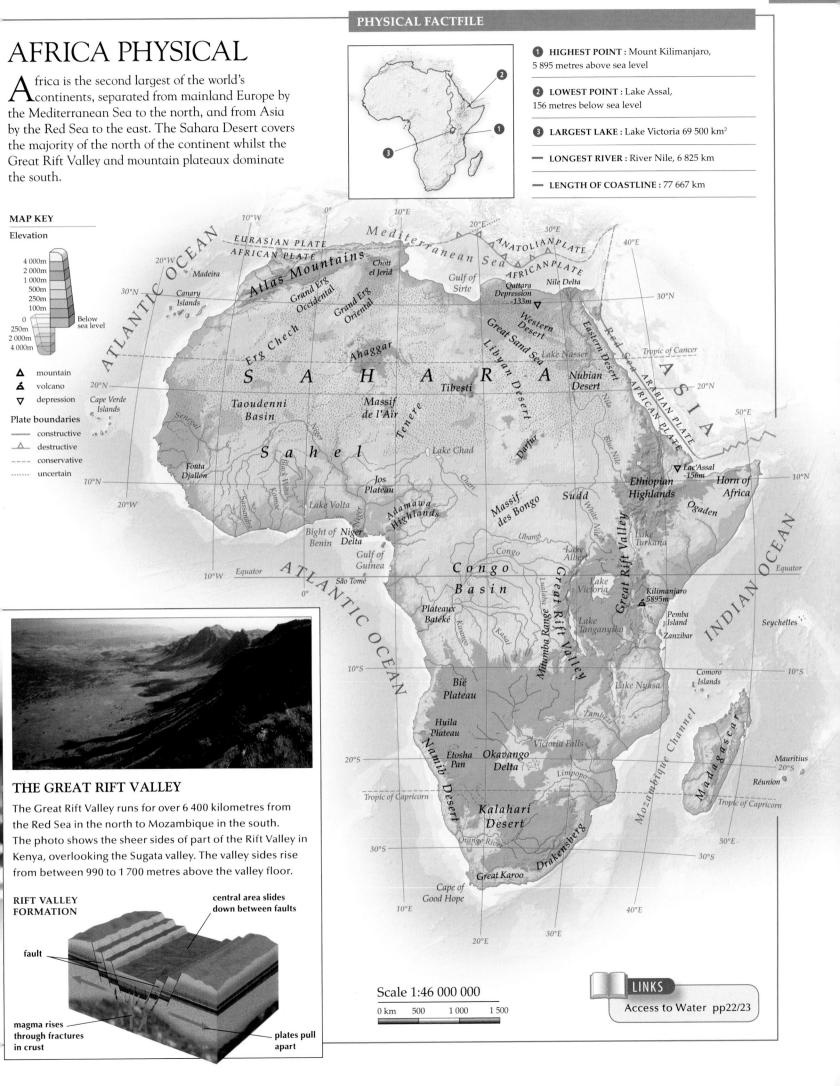

THE GREAT RIFT VALLEY

The Great Rift Valley runs for over 6 400 kilometres from the Red Sea in the north to Mozambique in the south. The photo shows the sheer sides of part of the Rift Valley in Kenya, overlooking the Sugata valley. The valley sides rise from between 990 to 1 700 metres above the valley floor.

RIFT VALLEY FORMATION

central area slides down between faults

fault

magma rises through fractures in crust

plates pull apart

Scale 1:46 000 000

0 km   500   1 000   1 500

LINKS

Access to Water pp22/23

AFRICA CLIMATE

With much of the continent lying within the Tropics, most climate types found in Africa experience high temperatures for all or part of the year. There is a much greater variety in annual precipitation totals, the tropical climates of central Africa contrasting with hot, arid deserts covering large areas around the Tropics of Cancer and Capricorn.

MAP KEY

Climate regions

- warm temperate
- mediterranean
- semi-arid
- arid
- tropical
- humid equatorial
- mountain

Local winds

- → cold wind
- → hot wind

CAIRO

Average daily temperature
Precipitation (mm)

40°C / 400
30°C / 300
20°C / 200
10°C / 100
0°C / 0

J F M A M J J A S O N D

☀7 daily hours of sunshine, January
☀12 daily hours of sunshine, July

PRECIPITATION

Average annual precipitation (mm)

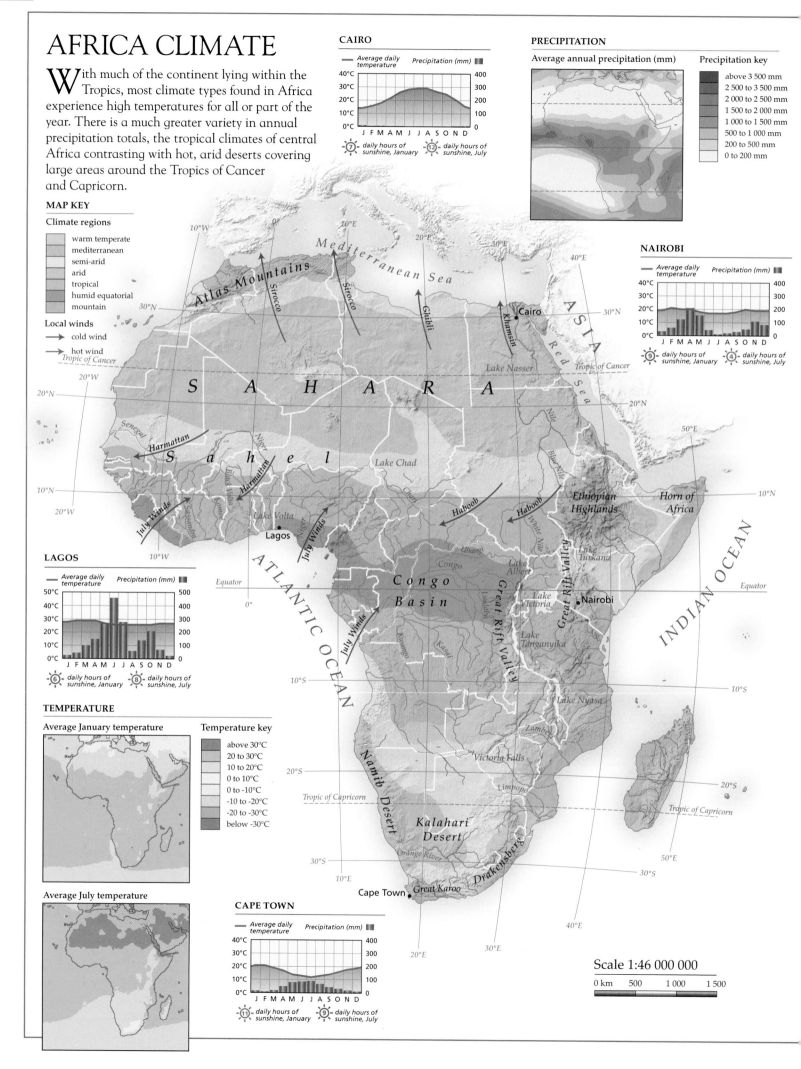

Precipitation key

- above 3 500 mm
- 2 500 to 3 500 mm
- 2 000 to 2 500 mm
- 1 500 to 2 000 mm
- 1 000 to 1 500 mm
- 500 to 1 000 mm
- 200 to 500 mm
- 0 to 200 mm

NAIROBI

Average daily temperature
Precipitation (mm)

40°C / 400
30°C / 300
20°C / 200
10°C / 100
0°C / 0

J F M A M J J A S O N D

☀9 daily hours of sunshine, January
☀4 daily hours of sunshine, July

LAGOS

Average daily temperature
Precipitation (mm)

50°C / 500
40°C / 400
30°C / 300
20°C / 200
10°C / 100
0°C / 0

J F M A M J J A S O N D

☀6 daily hours of sunshine, January
☀8 daily hours of sunshine, July

TEMPERATURE

Average January temperature

Temperature key

- above 30°C
- 20 to 30°C
- 10 to 20°C
- 0 to 10°C
- 0 to -10°C
- -10 to -20°C
- -20 to -30°C
- below -30°C

Average July temperature

CAPE TOWN

Average daily temperature
Precipitation (mm)

40°C / 400
30°C / 300
20°C / 200
10°C / 100
0°C / 0

J F M A M J J A S O N D

☀11 daily hours of sunshine, January
☀9 daily hours of sunshine, July

Scale 1:46 000 000

0 km 500 1 000 1 500

AFRICA POPULATION

Population density in most of Africa is low, as few people live in the extreme heat and aridity of desert areas. The most densely populated regions are close to reliable water supplies, for example in Cairo on Egypt's River Nile or in wetter tropical countries like Nigeria.

URBAN/RURAL POPULATION SPLIT
37%   63%

MAP KEY

Population density
(people per square km)

- above 200
- 100 to 200
- 50 to 100
- 10 to 50
- 1 to 10
- 0 to 1

Major settlements

- ■ ● above 1 million
- ▨ ◎ 500 000 to 1 million
- ▪ ⊙ 100 000 to 500 000

A red square indicates a national capital

The majority of people still live in rural areas, maintaining aspects of their cultures. For many of Kenya's Masai people, nomadic herding of cattle is still the traditional way of life.

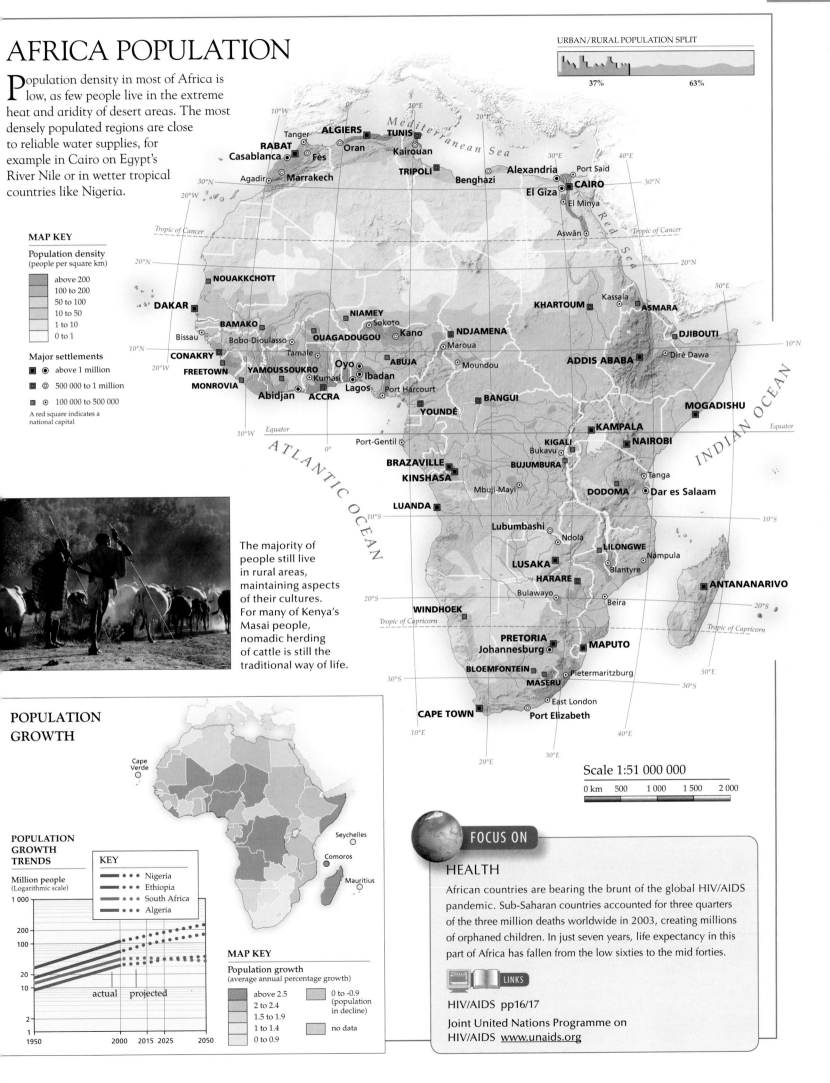

POPULATION GROWTH

POPULATION GROWTH TRENDS

KEY
- Nigeria
- Ethiopia
- South Africa
- Algeria

Million people (Logarithmic scale)

actual | projected

1950 2000 2015 2025 2050

MAP KEY

Population growth
(average annual percentage growth)

- above 2.5
- 2 to 2.4
- 1.5 to 1.9
- 1 to 1.4
- 0 to 0.9
- 0 to -0.9 (population in decline)
- no data

Scale 1:51 000 000

0 km 500 1 000 1 500 2 000

FOCUS ON

HEALTH

African countries are bearing the brunt of the global HIV/AIDS pandemic. Sub-Saharan countries accounted for three quarters of the three million deaths worldwide in 2003, creating millions of orphaned children. In just seven years, life expectancy in this part of Africa has fallen from the low sixties to the mid forties.

LINKS

HIV/AIDS pp16/17

Joint United Nations Programme on HIV/AIDS www.unaids.org

AFRICA LAND USE

With large areas of unproductive, sparsely populated, arid land, industry and commercial farming are mainly found in tropical areas or near major rivers. Many West African countries near the Equator rely on income from exporting plantation crops like cacao and coffee. Extracting and processing a range of mineral resources is an important contributor to a number of countries' economies.

Most of Egypt relies on water from the River Nile for industrial and domestic use. The flat, fertile flood plains next to the river are used intensively for farming. The annual floods are now controlled upstream by the Aswan High Dam.

MAP KEY

Land use type
- forest
- pasture
- cropland
- wetland
- hot desert

Industry
- industrial area
- major conurbation

FOOD PRODUCTION

Selected commodities (million tonnes)

KEY
- 1990 production
- 2000 production

Commodity	1990	2000
Milk	21	27
Meat	9	11
Fruit & vegetables	81	107
Cereals	89	106
Starchy roots	110	168

Scale 1:48 500 000

0 km   500   1 000   1 500

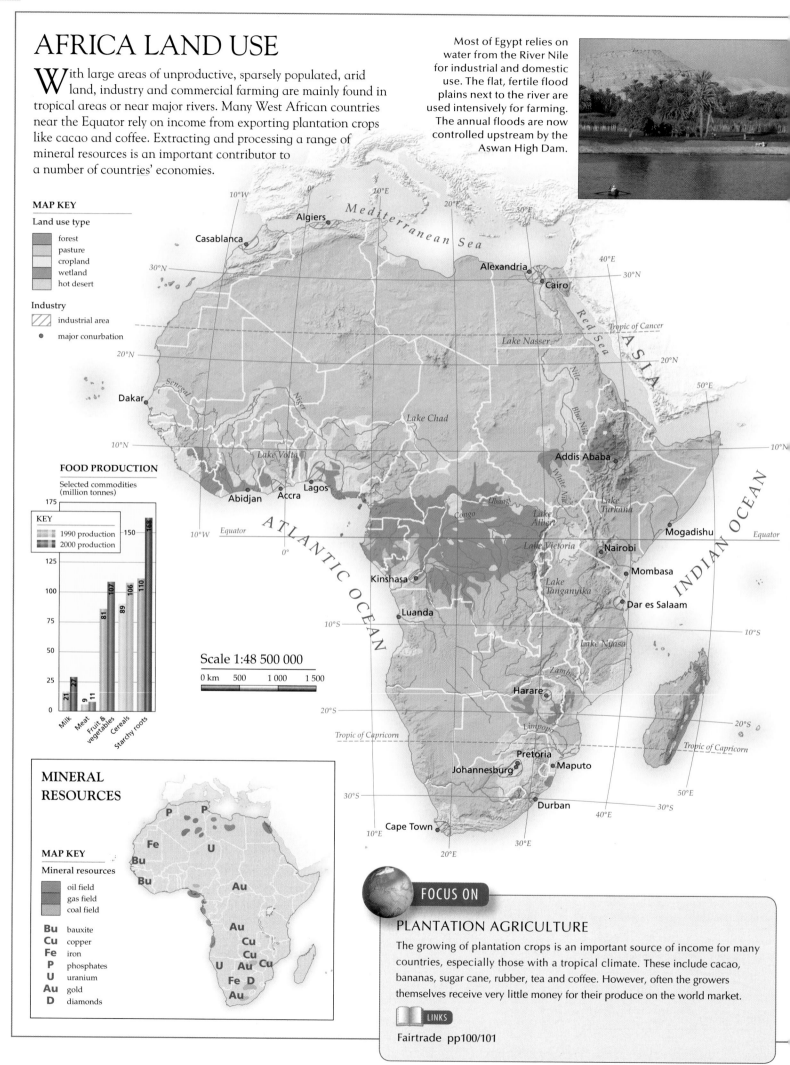

MINERAL RESOURCES

MAP KEY

Mineral resources
- oil field
- gas field
- coal field

- **Bu** bauxite
- **Cu** copper
- **Fe** iron
- **P** phosphates
- **U** uranium
- **Au** gold
- **D** diamonds

FOCUS ON

PLANTATION AGRICULTURE

The growing of plantation crops is an important source of income for many countries, especially those with a tropical climate. These include cacao, bananas, sugar cane, rubber, tea and coffee. However, often the growers themselves receive very little money for their produce on the world market.

LINKS

Fairtrade pp100/101

AFRICA ENVIRONMENT

Many environmental issues in Africa are connected with high temperatures and arid conditions. Marginal areas on the edges of Africa's deserts are becoming degraded as wood is removed for fuel, exposing the dry soil to erosion. Along the coast of West Africa, oil and chemical industries are causing widespread pollution on land and at sea.

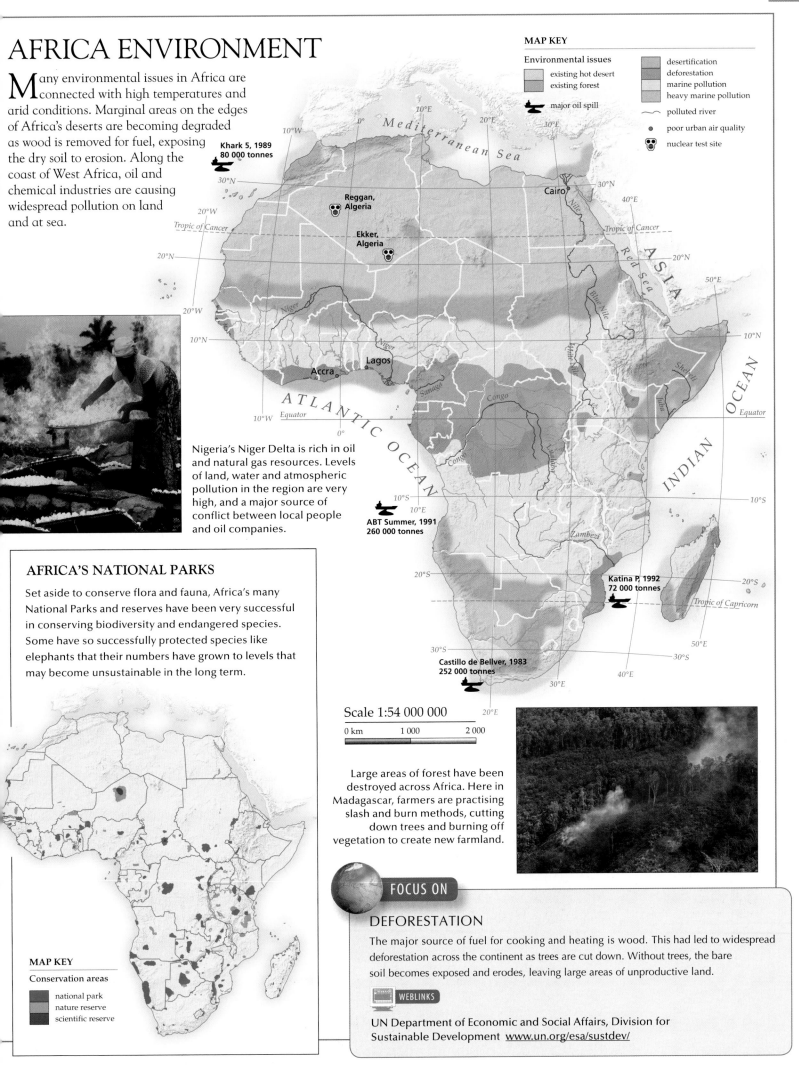

MAP KEY

Environmental issues

- existing hot desert
- existing forest
- major oil spill
- desertification
- deforestation
- marine pollution
- heavy marine pollution
- polluted river
- poor urban air quality
- nuclear test site

Khark 5, 1989
80 000 tonnes

Reggan, Algeria

Ekker, Algeria

Cairo

Accra Lagos

ABT Summer, 1991
260 000 tonnes

Katina P, 1992
72 000 tonnes

Castillo de Bellver, 1983
252 000 tonnes

Scale 1:54 000 000

0 km   1 000   2 000

Nigeria's Niger Delta is rich in oil and natural gas resources. Levels of land, water and atmospheric pollution in the region are very high, and a major source of conflict between local people and oil companies.

AFRICA'S NATIONAL PARKS

Set aside to conserve flora and fauna, Africa's many National Parks and reserves have been very successful in conserving biodiversity and endangered species. Some have so successfully protected species like elephants that their numbers have grown to levels that may become unsustainable in the long term.

MAP KEY

Conservation areas

- national park
- nature reserve
- scientific reserve

Large areas of forest have been destroyed across Africa. Here in Madagascar, farmers are practising slash and burn methods, cutting down trees and burning off vegetation to create new farmland.

FOCUS ON

DEFORESTATION

The major source of fuel for cooking and heating is wood. This had led to widespread deforestation across the continent as trees are cut down. Without trees, the bare soil becomes exposed and erodes, leaving large areas of unproductive land.

WEBLINKS

UN Department of Economic and Social Affairs, Division for Sustainable Development www.un.org/esa/sustdev/

NORTH AFRICA

The geography of North Africa is one of extremes of climate and landscape. From west to east across the middle of the region is the Sahara – the world's largest desert and one of the hottest and most arid parts of the world. In contrast, several countries along the west coast experience a hot and humid tropical climate and rich rainforests are found there.

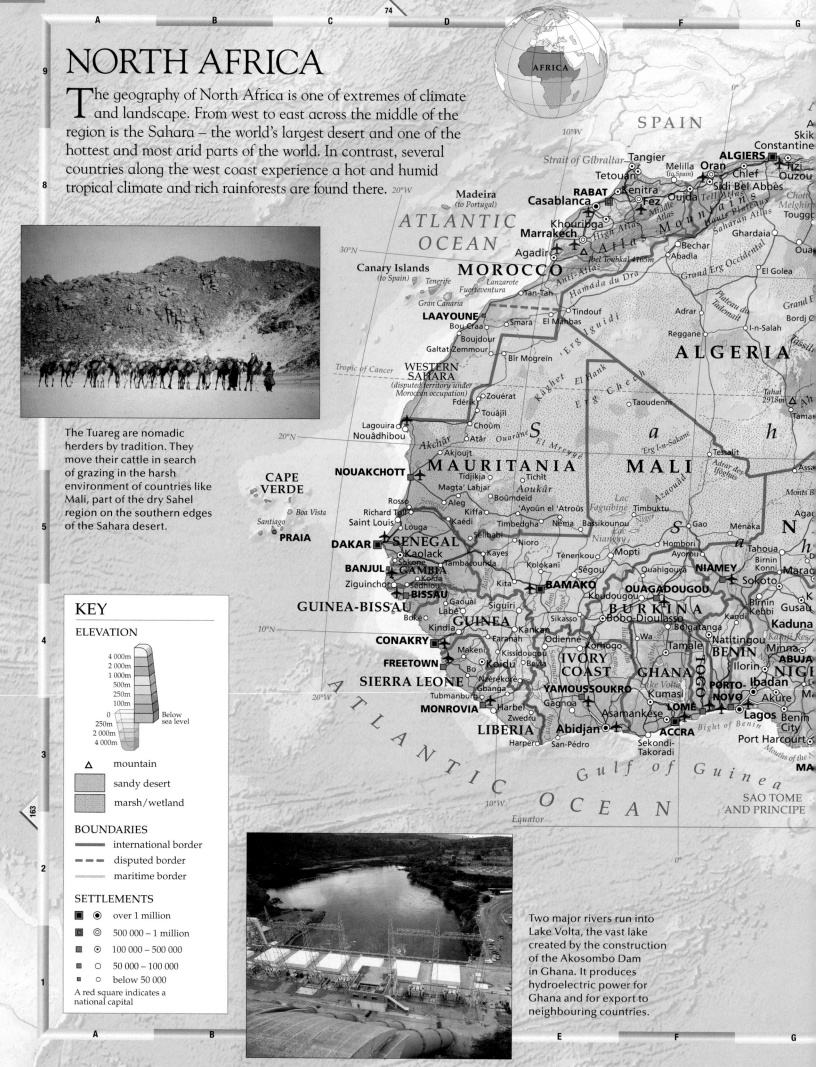

The Tuareg are nomadic herders by tradition. They move their cattle in search of grazing in the harsh environment of countries like Mali, part of the dry Sahel region on the southern edges of the Sahara desert.

KEY

ELEVATION

4 000m	
2 000m	
1 000m	
500m	
250m	
100m	
0	Below sea level
250m	
2 000m	
4 000m	

△ mountain

sandy desert

marsh/wetland

BOUNDARIES

——— international border

– – – disputed border

——— maritime border

SETTLEMENTS

◙ ⊙ over 1 million

◙ ◎ 500 000 – 1 million

▪ ⊙ 100 000 – 500 000

▪ ○ 50 000 – 100 000

▪ ○ below 50 000

A red square indicates a national capital

Two major rivers run into Lake Volta, the vast lake created by the construction of the Akosombo Dam in Ghana. It produces hydroelectric power for Ghana and for export to neighbouring countries.

SPAIN

ATLANTIC OCEAN

Strait of Gibraltar · Tangier
Tetouan · Melilla (to Spain) · Oran · ALGIERS · Constantine · Skik · Tizi Ouzou
RABAT · Kenitra · Oujda
Casablanca · Fez · Sidi Bel Abbès · Chlef
Khouribga
Marrakech · MOROCCO
Agadir · Jbel Toubkal 4165m · Béchar · Abadla
Madeira (to Portugal)
Canary Islands (to Spain)
Tenerife · Lanzarote
Gran Canaria · Fuerteventura
Tan-Tan · Hamada du Dra · El Golea
LAAYOUNE · Tindouf · Adrar
Bou Craa · Smara · El Mahbas · Reggane · I-n-Salah
Boujdour
Galtat Zemmour · Bîr Mogreïn
WESTERN SAHARA (disputed territory under Moroccan occupation)
Zouérat · Taoudenni
Fdérik
Touâjîl
Lagouira · Choûm
Nouâdhibou · Atâr · Ouarâne · El Mreyyé · Tessalit
Akjoujt
MAURITANIA · MALI · Adrar des Ifoghas
Tidjikja · Tichît
CAPE VERDE
Boa Vista
Santiago
PRAIA
NOUAKCHOTT · Magta' Lahjar · Aoukâr · Timbuktu · Gao
Rosso · Aleg · Kiffa · Boûmdeid · 'Ayoûn el 'Atroûs · Ménaka
Richard Toll · Kaédi · Nioro · Néma · Bassikounou
Saint Louis · Louga · Sélibabi · Timbedgha · Hombori · Tahoua
DAKAR · SENEGAL · Kayes · Nioro · Ténenkou · Ayorou · Birnin Konni
Kaolack · Tambacounda · Kolokani · Mopti · Ouahigouya · NIAMEY
BANJUL · GAMBIA · Kolda · Kita · SÉGOU · Sokoto · Marad
Ziguinchor · Sédhiou · BAMAKO · OUAGADOUGOU · Birnin Kebbi · Gusa
BISSAU · Gaoual · Koudougou · BURKINA · Kaduna
GUINEA-BISSAU · Labé · Siguiri · Bobo-Dioulasso · Bolgatanga · Kandi · ABUJA · NIG
Boké · Kindia · GUINEA · Sikasso · Wa · Natitingou · Minna
CONAKRY · Faranah · Kankan · Odienné · Korhogo · Tamale · BENIN · Ilorin · Ibadan
Makeni · Kissidougou · IVORY COAST · GHANA · PORTO-NOVO · Lagos
FREETOWN · Koidu · Beyla · Kumasi · TOGO · Akure · Benin City
SIERRA LEONE · Bo · Nzérékoré · YAMOUSSOUKRO · LOMÉ · Port Harcourt
Tubmanburg · Gbanga · Gagnoa · Asamankese · ACCRA · Bight of Benin
MONROVIA · Harbel · Abidjan · Sekondi-Takoradi
LIBERIA · Zwedru · San-Pédro · Mouths of the N
Harper

ALGERIA · Sahara

Tropic of Cancer
30°N
20°N
10°N
20°W
10°W
0°
Equator

ATLANTIC OCEAN

Gulf of Guinea

SAO TOME AND PRINCIPE

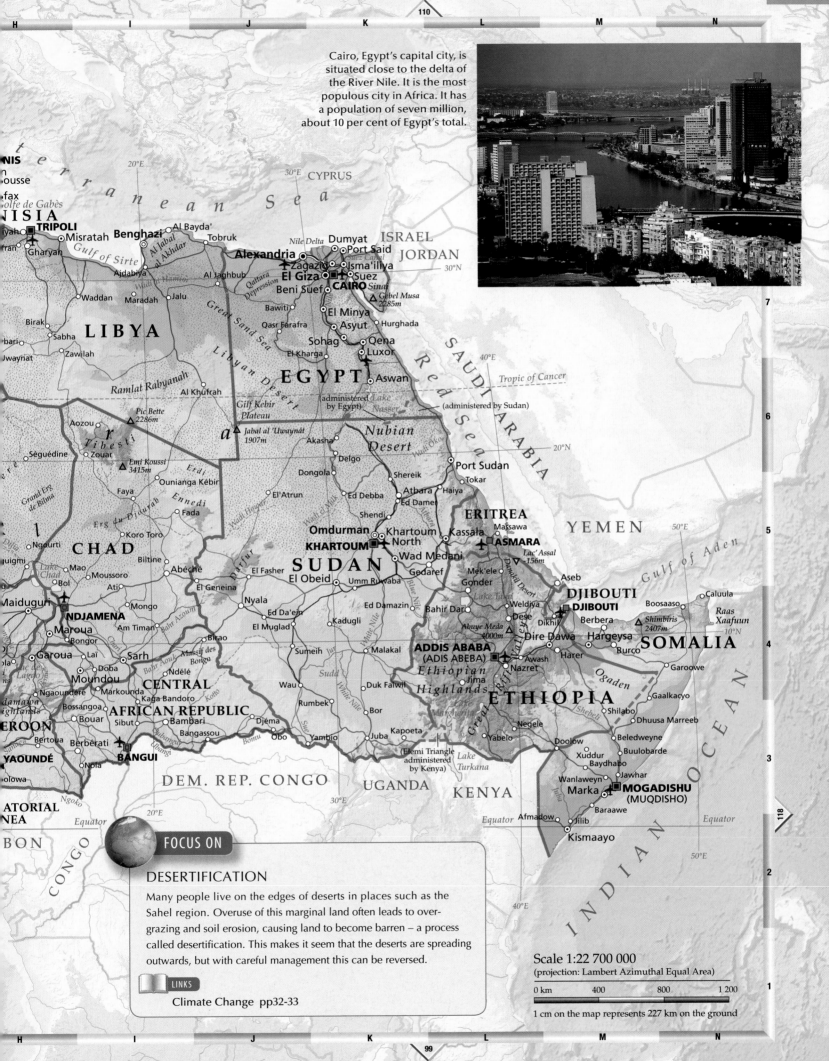

Cairo, Egypt's capital city, is situated close to the delta of the River Nile. It is the most populous city in Africa. It has a population of seven million, about 10 per cent of Egypt's total.

FOCUS ON

DESERTIFICATION

Many people live on the edges of deserts in places such as the Sahel region. Overuse of this marginal land often leads to over-grazing and soil erosion, causing land to become barren – a process called desertification. This makes it seem that the deserts are spreading outwards, but with careful management this can be reversed.

LINKS

Climate Change pp32-33

Scale 1:22 700 000
(projection: Lambert Azimuthal Equal Area)

| 0 km | 400 | 800 | 1 200 |

1 cm on the map represents 227 km on the ground

SOUTHERN AFRICA

Apart from the Congo Basin in the north of the region and areas of lowland along the coast, much of Southern Africa is covered by upland plateaux. Economically, South Africa is the wealthiest and most industrialised country in the continent.

Both Namibia and South Africa have internationally renowned diamond industries. The photo above shows part of the Oranjemund Diamond Mine in Namibia.

KEY

ELEVATION

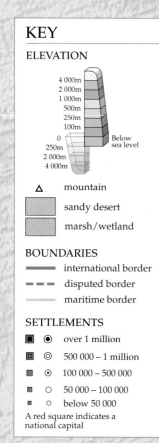

4 000m
2 000m
1 000m
500m
250m
100m
0
250m
2 000m
4 000m
Below sea level

△ mountain

sandy desert

marsh/wetland

BOUNDARIES

—— international border

- - - disputed border

—— maritime border

SETTLEMENTS

■⊙ over 1 million
▣◎ 500 000 – 1 million
▪⊙ 100 000 – 500 000
▪○ 50 000 – 100 000
▪○ below 50 000

A red square indicates a national capital

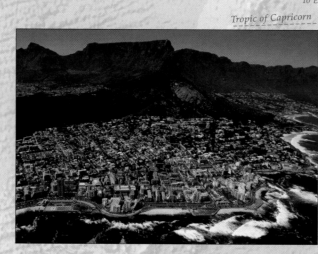

Cape Town, the legislative capital city of South Africa, is overlooked by the distinctively shaped Table Mountain. The city occupies the coastal lowlands between the Atlantic Ocean and the mountains inland.

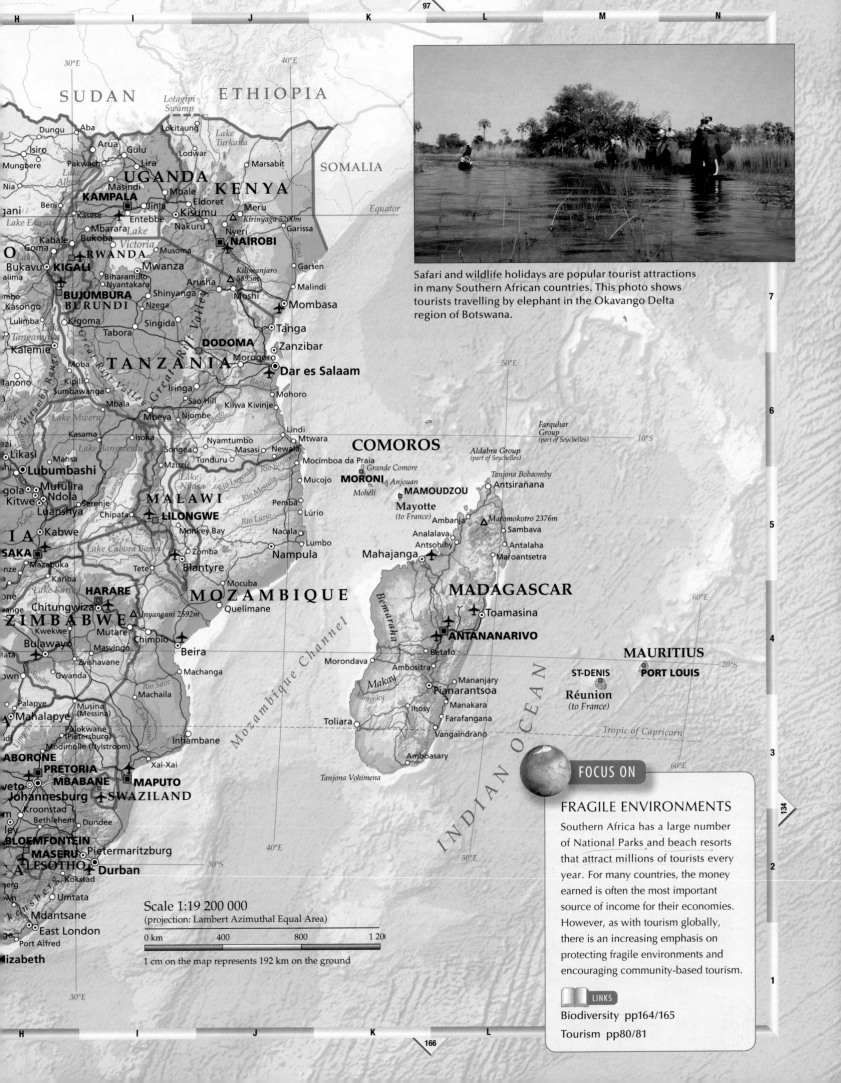

Safari and wildlife holidays are popular tourist attractions in many Southern African countries. This photo shows tourists travelling by elephant in the Okavango Delta region of Botswana.

SUDAN

ETHIOPIA

Lotagipi Swamp

Lake Turkana

SOMALIA

Dungu
Aba
Isiro
Arua
Gulu
Lokitaung
Lodwar
Marsabit
Mungbere
Pakwach
Lira
Nia
Beni
Masindi
Mbale
Eldoret
Meru
Kasese
KAMPALA
Jinja
Equator
UGANDA
KENYA
Lake Albert
Kabale
Entebbe
Nakuru
Kirinyaga 5200m
Garissa
Goma
Bukoba
KIGALI
Musoma
NAIROBI
RWANDA
Lake Victoria
Mwanza
Garsen
Bukavu
Biharamulo
Nyantakara
Arusha
Kilimanjaro
5895m
Malindi
BUJUMBURA
Shinyanga
Moshi
BURUNDI
Nzega
Mombasa
Kigoma
Singida
Tabora
Tanga
Kalemie
Moba
DODOMA
Zanzibar
Kipili
Morogoro
Sumbawanga
TANZANIA
Iringa
Dar es Salaam
Mbala
Sao Hill
Kilwa Kivinje
Mbeya
Njombe
Mohoro
Kasama
Isoka
Lindi
Nyamtumbo
Mtwara
COMOROS
Lake Bangweulu
Songea
Masasi
Newala
Farquhar Group (part of Seychelles)
Mansa
Mzuzu
Tunduru
Mocímboa da Praia
Grande Comore
Aldabra Group (part of Seychelles)
Lubumbashi
Mucojo
MORONI
Anjouan
MALAWI
Lake Nyasa
Pemba
Mohéli
MAMOUDZOU
Tanjona Bobaomby
Mufulira
LILONGWE
Lúrio
Mayotte (to France)
Antsirañana
Ndola
Rio Messalo
Nacala
Ambanja
Kitwe
Serenje
Monkey Bay
Lumbo
Analalava
Sambava
Luanshya
Chipata
Antsohihy
Antalaha
Kabwe
Nampula
Maromokotro 2376m
Maroantsetra
Lake Cabora Bassa
Zomba
Mahajanga
Mazabuka
Tete
Blantyre
MADAGASCAR
Kariba
Mocuba
HARARE
MOZAMBIQUE
Quelimane
ANTANANARIVO
Toamasina
Chitungwiza
Inyangani 2592m
Betafo
ZIMBABWE
Mutare
MAURITIUS
Kwekwe
Chimoio
Beira
Morondava
Ambositra
ST-DENIS
PORT LOUIS
Bulawayo
Masvingo
Ambatofinandrahana
Zvishavane
Machanga
Makay
Mananjary
Réunion (to France)
Gwanda
Machaila
Fianarantsoa
Palapye
Musina (Messina)
Machaila
Ihosy
Manakara
Mahalapye
Palokwane (Pietersburg)
Xai-Xai
Toliara
Farafangana
Modimolle (Nylstroom)
Inhambane
Vangaindrano
GABORONE
Amboasary
PRETORIA
MBABANE
MAPUTO
Johannesburg
SWAZILAND
Tanjona Vohimena
Kroonstad
Dundee
BLOEMFONTEIN
MASERU
Pietermaritzburg
LESOTHO
Durban
Kokstad
Mdantsane
East London
Port Alfred
Elizabeth

Great Rift Valley
Mirumba Range
Lake Tanganyika
Lake Mweru
Lake Malawi
Mozambique Channel
Bemaraha
Mangoky
INDIAN OCEAN

30°E   40°E   50°E   60°E
Equator
10°S
20°S
Tropic of Capricorn
30°S

Scale 1:19 200 000
(projection: Lambert Azimuthal Equal Area)

0 km   400   800   1 200

1 cm on the map represents 192 km on the ground

FOCUS ON

FRAGILE ENVIRONMENTS

Southern Africa has a large number of National Parks and beach resorts that attract millions of tourists every year. For many countries, the money earned is often the most important source of income for their economies. However, as with tourism globally, there is an increasing emphasis on protecting fragile environments and encouraging community-based tourism.

LINKS

Biodiversity pp164/165
Tourism pp80/81

FAIRTRADE

Many of the world's most popular foodstuffs are grown in tropical regions in LEDCs. Crops such as tea, coffee, cocoa, bananas and sugar cane are grown on large plantations or small farms and exported worldwide. Since the 1980s there have been increasing efforts to give farmers a fairer share of the wealth generated by these cash crops.

WHY FAIRTRADE?

Cash crops are usually exported as unprocessed primary products. Most of the processing, packaging, marketing and sales are undertaken by large Transnational companies (TNCs) in their home countries. TNCs are usually based in MEDCs, meaning that it is richer countries that benefit most in terms of jobs and profits. Because a small number of large companies dominate the commodity markets (where prices for primary products are set), farmers themselves typically receive little money for what they produce. They have no control over prices, which often fluctuate considerably from year to year and, until recently, no alternative but to sell on the world market.

For many years, development agencies such as Oxfam, CAFOD, Christian Aid and Traidcraft campaigned against the low prices paid to farmers and workers in LEDCs. They believed that consumers in some MEDCs would be prepared to pay more if this extra money would directly benefit the poorest producers. This way of trading became known as 'Fairtrade'.

The FAIRTRADE Mark can only be carried by products following strict guidelines set down and monitored by the Fairtrade Labelling Organizations International (FLO).

FAIRTRADE PRODUCTS

Today, 19 organisations are involved in the Fairtrade Labelling Organizations International (FLO). Farmers and producers register with the FLO to receive the FAIRTRADE Mark. The Mark is a guarantee to consumers that farmers receive a fair price for their produce, plus an additional premium used to the benefit of the local community.

The sale of Fairtrade products in the UK has increased rapidly since they were first introduced in 1994. In 2004, over 250 Fairtrade products including tea, coffee, chocolate, fruit, wine, roses and footballs were sold in the UK at a value of £92 million.

DEFINITION OF FAIRTRADE

In 1999, the International Federation of Fair Trade (IFAT), an affiliation of over 150 Fairtrade organisations worldwide, agreed the following definition of Fairtrade:

• *Fairtrade is an alternative approach to conventional international trade. It is a trading partnership which aims at sustainable development for excluded and disadvantaged producers. It seeks to do this by providing better trading conditions, by awareness raising and by campaigning.*

The FAIRTRADE Mark can only be carried by products following strict guidelines set down and monitored by the Fairtrade Labelling Organizations International (FLO).

COCOA FARMING IN GHANA

Ghana's cocoa farmers produce some of the world's best quality beans – of little direct use to the people of Ghana themselves, who don't eat chocolate, but a major source of income for the country when exported to produce chocolate in richer MEDCs.

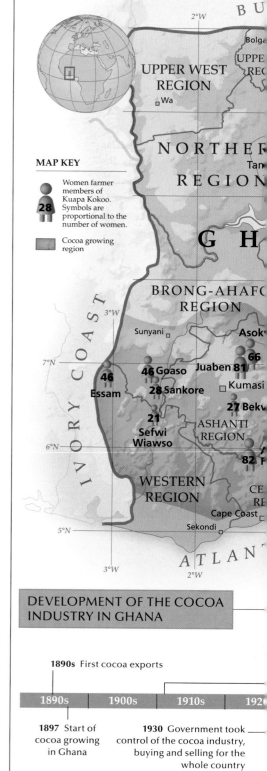

MAP KEY

Women farmer members of Kuapa Kokoo. **28** Symbols are proportional to the number of women.

Cocoa growing region

DEVELOPMENT OF THE COCOA INDUSTRY IN GHANA

1890s First cocoa exports

| 1890s | 1900s | 1910s | 192• |

1897 Start of cocoa growing in Ghana

1930 Government took control of the cocoa industry, buying and selling for the whole country

AFRICA'S CLIMATE

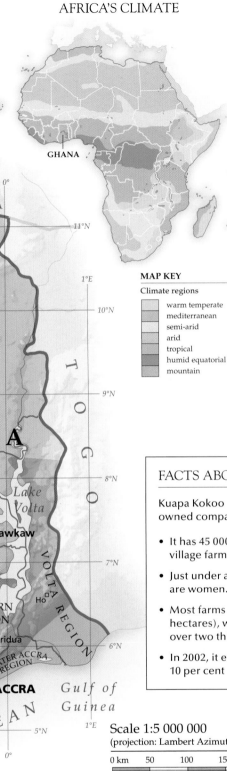

GHANA

MAP KEY

Climate regions

- warm temperate
- mediterranean
- semi-arid
- arid
- tropical
- humid equatorial
- mountain

Scale 1:5 000 000

(projection: Lambert Azimuthal Equal Area)

| 0 km | 50 | 100 | 150 | 200 | 250 |

1 cm on the map represents 50 km on the ground

KUAPA KOKOO

The Kuapa Kokoo cocoa farmers' co-operative in Ghana's Ashanti region was formed in 1993 in partnership with the Twin Trading Company in the UK. In 1995 it became a registered Fairtrade producer organisation.

Kuapa Kokoo buys the cocoa produced by its farmers to sell to the government Cocoa Buying Board. It receives a minimum price of US $1600 per tonne for Fairtrade cocoa, plus a premium of US $150 per tonne. If world prices rise above this, then the higher price is paid plus the premium.

FAIRTRADE VERSUS CONVENTIONAL COCOA PRICES

Fairtrade price versus New York 2nd Position price
(US $ per tonne)

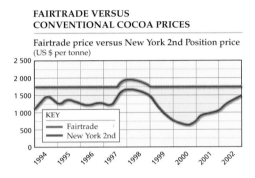

KEY
— Fairtrade
— New York 2nd

FACTS ABOUT KUAPA KOKOO

Kuapa Kokoo is the only farmer-owned company in Ghana:

- It has 45 000 members from 950 village farmer societies.

- Just under a third of the members are women.

- Most farms are small, (about 1.6 hectares), with cocoa providing over two thirds of the farmer's income.

- In 2002, it exported over 37 000 tonnes of cocoa beans, 10 per cent of Ghana's total production.

The motto 'Pa Pa Paa' means 'the best of the best'.

A farmer spreading out cocoa beans to dry in the Ashanti region, Ghana.

DEVELOPMENT BENEFITS

In addition to the main company, Kuapa Kokoo Limited, the cooperative runs a Farmer's Union, Farmer's Trust and Credit Union. The Kuapa Kokoo Farmer's Trust has used the premiums to provide a range of benefits. These include end of year bonuses to farmers and the provision of community amenities such as classrooms and mobile cinemas for its farmer education programme. It has funded over 150 water projects, soap-making businesses and corn mills.

In the UK, cocoa from Kuapa Kokoo is used by the Day Chocolate Company, (part owned by Kuapa Kokoo) for their Divine chocolate brand and Dubble bars. It is also used by the Co-op and Starbucks' own brand chocolate.

Products produced by the Day Chocolate Company, using Kuapa Kokoo cocoa, are now sold in more than 4 000 shops since it was launched in 1998.

1911–76 World's leading cocoa producer

1970s World cocoa prices dropped by almost 70%. Many Ghanaians stopped growing cocoa

1980s Drought and fires added to the problem of low prices. Ghana's share of the world market dropped to 12%

1990s World Bank and IMF brought in a rescue package for the Ghanaian economy. The cocoa industry was liberalised, enabling private companies to trade in cocoa

2004 3.2 million people were employed in the cocoa industry. Ghana was the world's second largest producer and third largest exporter of cocoa

2001 219 000 tonnes of cocoa was produced. Worth US $222 million, it accounted for 30% of export income

| 1940s | 1950s | 1960s | 1970s | 1980s | 1990s | 2000s |

THE BIG ISSUES

1 The purchase of Fairtrade products is increasing rapidly, especially in the UK, but they will probably only ever have a small share of the world market. Why?

2 How do farmers like those who belong to Kuapa Kokoo benefit from Fairtrade?

3 Is Fairtrade a long-term solution to the poverty of cash crop farmers in LEDCs?

POLITICAL ASIA

Asia is made up of 49 countries, many emerging from the break up of the USSR in 1991. In the west, the continent is separated from Europe by the Ural Mountains and Turkey. On the eastern edge are the island nations of Japan, Indonesia and the Philippines. The northern regions of the Russian Federation reach beyond the Arctic Circle, whilst Indonesia in the south lies across the Equator.

MAP KEY

Settlements

- ■ over 1 million
- ◉ 500 000 to 1 million
- ■ 100 000 to 500 000
- ▪ 50 000 to 100 000
- ▫ under 50 000

A red square indicates a national capital

Boundaries

- —— international border
- --- disputed border
- ××× ceasefire line
- ···· territorial claim
- —— maritime border

GROSS DOMESTIC PRODUC

Billion US dollars (Logarithmic scale)

KEY
- 1975
- 2003

Japan   China   India   Banglade

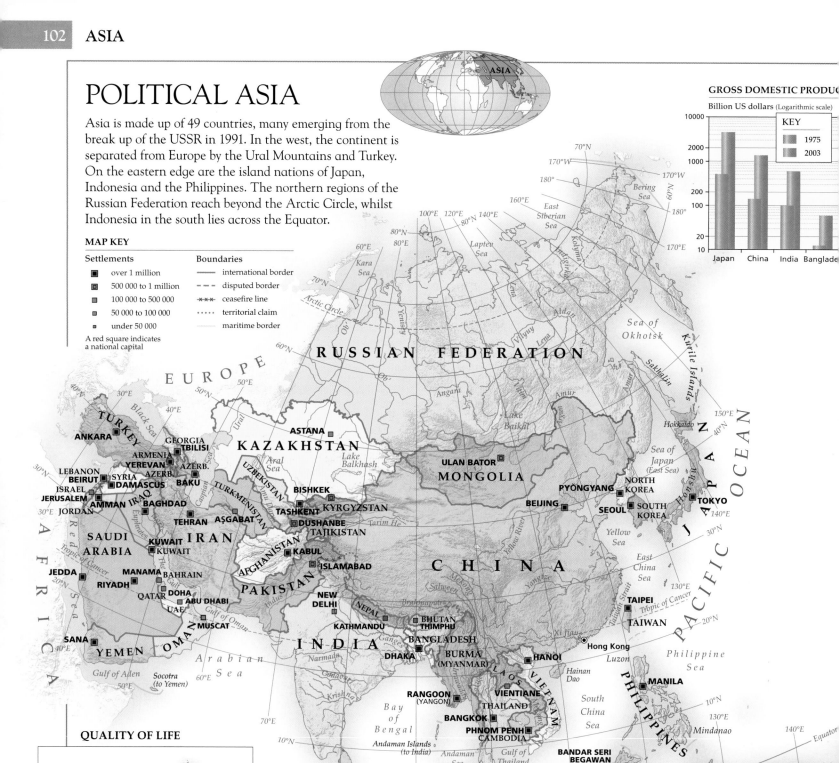

QUALITY OF LIFE

Maldives

MAP KEY

UN Human Development Index (HDI)

- high
- medium
- low
- no data

Source: UN, 2004

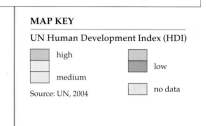

Scale 1:56 000 000

0 km   500   1 000   1 500

In 1997, Hong Kong, once a colony of the UK, returned to Chinese rule as a Special Administrative Area. Although just over 1 000 km² in size, it is home to nearly seven million people and is a densely populated city of skyscrapers. It is also a major world commercial centre.

PHYSICAL ASIA

Asia is the world's largest continent. Geologically, the mountains and plateaux of the north are much older than the landscapes in the south. The south has the world's highest and youngest fold mountain range, the Himalayas. These are still rising as the Indo-Australian tectonic plate pushes against the Eurasian plate.

PHYSICAL FACTFILE

1 HIGHEST POINT: Mount Everest, Himalayas 8 850 metres above sea level

2 LOWEST POINT: Dead Sea shore, 417 metres below sea level

3 LARGEST LAKE: Caspian Sea, 371 000 km²

— **LONGEST RIVER:** Yangtze, 6 300 km

— **LENGTH OF COASTLINE:** 422 698 km

Much of Bangladesh is located on the delta of the Ganges and Brahmaputra rivers. A low-lying area it is prone to flooding from the two rivers overflowing and also from coastal flooding from cyclones.

MAP KEY

Elevation

4 000m
2 000m
1 000m
500m
250m
100m
0
250m — Below sea level
2 000m
4 000m

△ mountain
⊿ volcano
▽ depression

Plate boundaries
— constructive
—△— destructive
— — — conservative
.... uncertain

THE HIMALAYAS

The Himalayas are located where the Indo-Australian and Eurasian plates converge. Both are continental plates with the same density, meaning that neither can be forced beneath the other. Instead of subduction occurring, the plates have collided and crumpled upwards, forming the Himalayas.

Himalayas
Present day
20 million years ago
60 million years ago
80 million years ago

crust buckled upwards to form mountain range

high plateau

ancient oceanic crust

Scale 1:56 000 000

0 km   500   1 000   1 500

ASIA CLIMATE

Asia covers a wide range of latitudes and therefore experiences many different types of climate. Sub-arctic and tundra cover the north of the continent. Moving south, temperatures gradually increase but annual precipitation totals vary greatly. Inland the climate is mainly continental, but there are also extensive hot desert regions. Tropical or monsoon climates dominate the coastal regions and islands in the south.

MAP KEY

Climate regions
- tundra
- sub-arctic
- cool continental
- warm temperate
- mediterranean
- semi-arid
- arid
- tropical
- humid equatorial
- mountain

Local winds
- → cold
- ⋯▶ warm/wet monsoon
- ⋯▶ cold/dry monsoon
- ➔ direction of tropical storms

TEHRAN
— Average daily temperature   Precipitation (mm) ▩
daily hours of sunshine, January: 6
daily hours of sunshine, July: 11

PRECIPITATION
Average annual precipitation (mm)

Precipitation key
- above 3 500 mm
- 2 500 to 3 500 mm
- 2 000 to 2 500 mm
- 1 500 to 2 000 mm
- 1 000 to 1 500 mm
- 500 to 1 000 mm
- 200 to 500 mm
- 0 to 200 mm

VLADIVOSTOCK
— Average daily temperature   Precipitation (mm) ▩
daily hours of sunshine, January: 6
daily hours of sunshine, July: 4

SHANGHAI
— Average daily temperature   Precipitation (mm) ▩
daily hours of sunshine, January: 4
daily hours of sunshine, July: 7

NEW DELHI
— Average daily temperature   Precipitation (mm) ▩
daily hours of sunshine, January: 7
daily hours of sunshine, July: 6

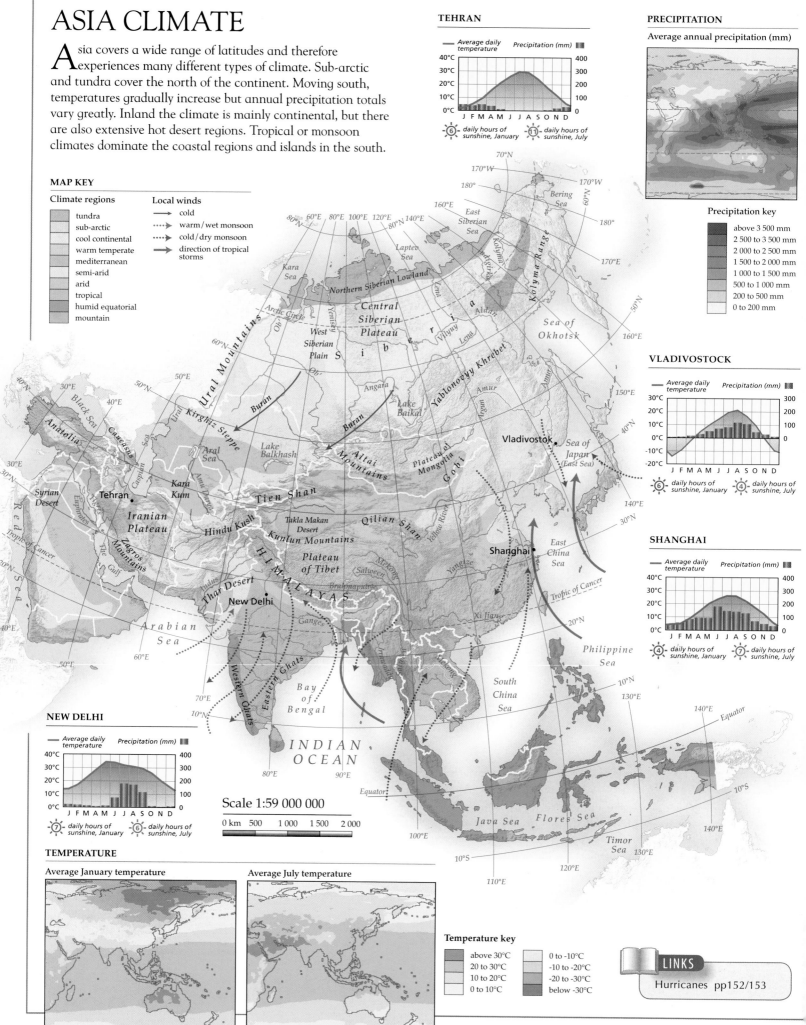

Scale 1:59 000 000

0 km   500   1 000   1 500   2 000

TEMPERATURE

Average January temperature

Average July temperature

Temperature key
- above 30°C
- 20 to 30°C
- 10 to 20°C
- 0 to 10°C
- 0 to -10°C
- -10 to -20°C
- -20 to -30°C
- below -30°C

LINKS

Hurricanes pp152/153

ASIA POPULATION

China and India account for just under 40 per cent of the total world population, with over a billion people in each country. Many parts of Asia, like Japan, have very high population densities, whilst the sub-arctic north and desert and mountain interiors of the continent have very few people.

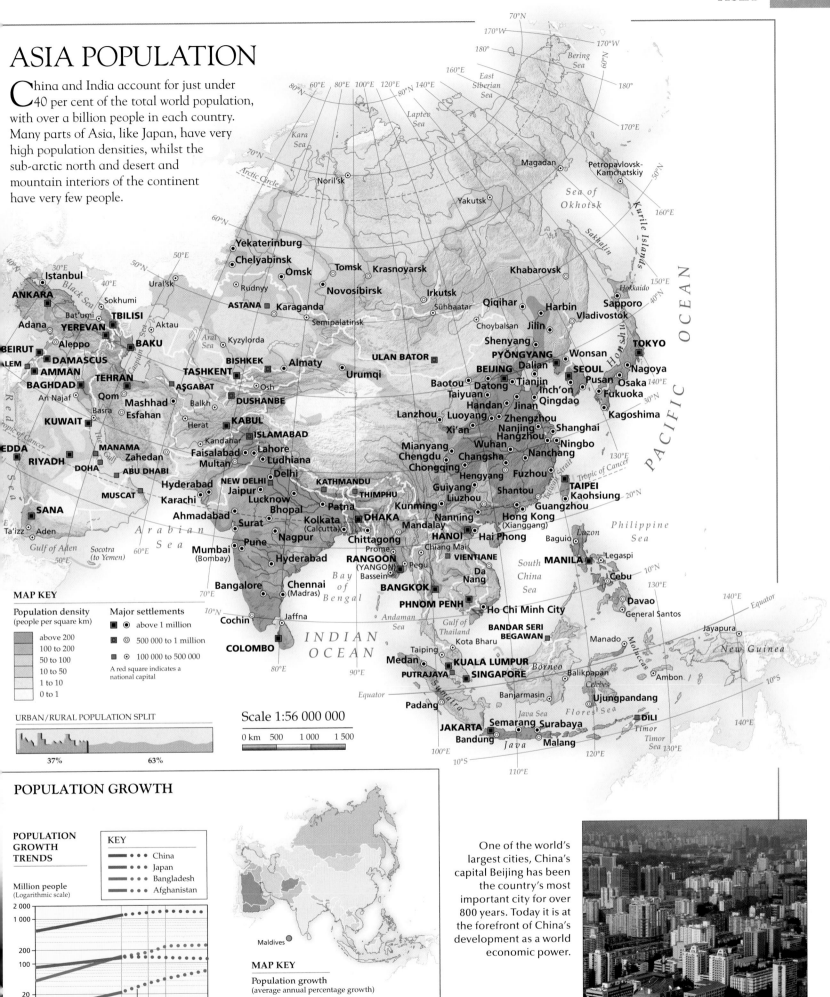

MAP KEY

Population density
(people per square km)

- above 200
- 100 to 200
- 50 to 100
- 10 to 50
- 1 to 10
- 0 to 1

Major settlements

- ■ ● above 1 million
- ■ ◎ 500 000 to 1 million
- ■ ● 100 000 to 500 000

A red square indicates a national capital

URBAN/RURAL POPULATION SPLIT

37%   63%

Scale 1:56 000 000

0 km   500   1 000   1 500

POPULATION GROWTH

POPULATION GROWTH TRENDS

KEY
- ● ● ● China
- ● ● ● Japan
- ● ● ● Bangladesh
- ● ● ● Afghanistan

Million people
(Logarithmic scale)

2 000
1 000
200
100
20
10
2

actual   projected

1950   2000   2015   2025   2050

Maldives

MAP KEY

Population growth
(average annual percentage growth)

- above 2.5
- 2 to 2.4
- 1.5 to 1.9
- 1 to 1.4
- 0 to 0.9
- 0 to -0.9 (population in decline)

One of the world's largest cities, China's capital Beijing has been the country's most important city for over 800 years. Today it is at the forefront of China's development as a world economic power.

ASIA LAND USE

Extensive areas of desert, mountains and frozen land across Asia are of limited use for farming. Some of the most fertile land is found in eastern China and India, particularly along river valleys. However, Arctic Russia and the deserts of the Arabian Peninsula contain major deposits of fossil fuels and are important sources of income for their respective countries.

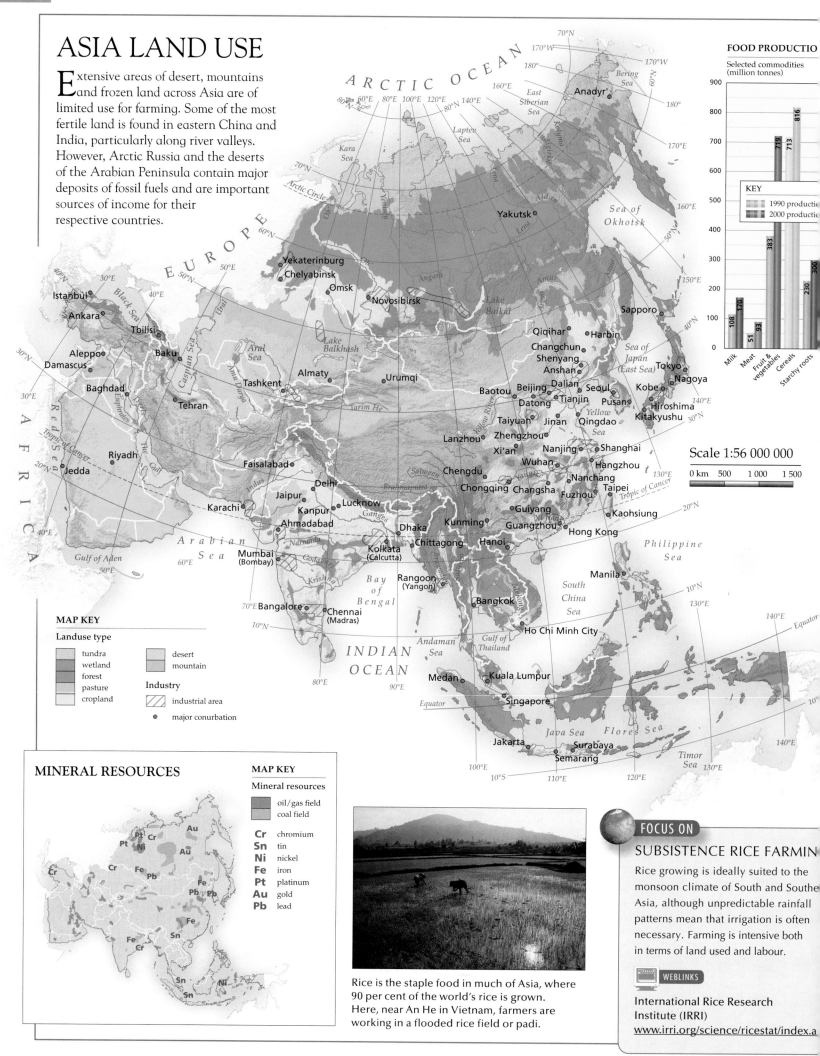

FOOD PRODUCTIO

Selected commodities
(million tonnes)

KEY
1990 productio
2000 productio

	Milk	Meat	Fruit & vegetables	Cereals	Starchy roots
1990	108	51	383	719	230
2000	170	93		713 / 816	300

Scale 1:56 000 000

0 km 500 1 000 1 500

MAP KEY

Landuse type

- tundra
- wetland
- forest
- pasture
- cropland
- desert
- mountain

Industry

- industrial area
- major conurbation

MINERAL RESOURCES

MAP KEY

Mineral resources

- oil/gas field
- coal field

Cr	chromium
Sn	tin
Ni	nickel
Fe	iron
Pt	platinum
Au	gold
Pb	lead

Rice is the staple food in much of Asia, where 90 per cent of the world's rice is grown. Here, near An He in Vietnam, farmers are working in a flooded rice field or padi.

FOCUS ON

SUBSISTENCE RICE FARMIN

Rice growing is ideally suited to the monsoon climate of South and Southe Asia, although unpredictable rainfall patterns mean that irrigation is often necessary. Farming is intensive both in terms of land used and labour.

WEBLINKS

International Rice Research Institute (IRRI)
www.irri.org/science/ricestat/index.a

ENVIRONMENT OF ASIA

Deforestation and atmospheric pollution are major issues for the island nations of Southeast Asia. Over-extraction of water to feed the cotton industry has resulted in the Aral Sea shrinking by 40 per cent. Elsewhere, rapid industrialisation in recent years has polluted rivers and coastal regions.

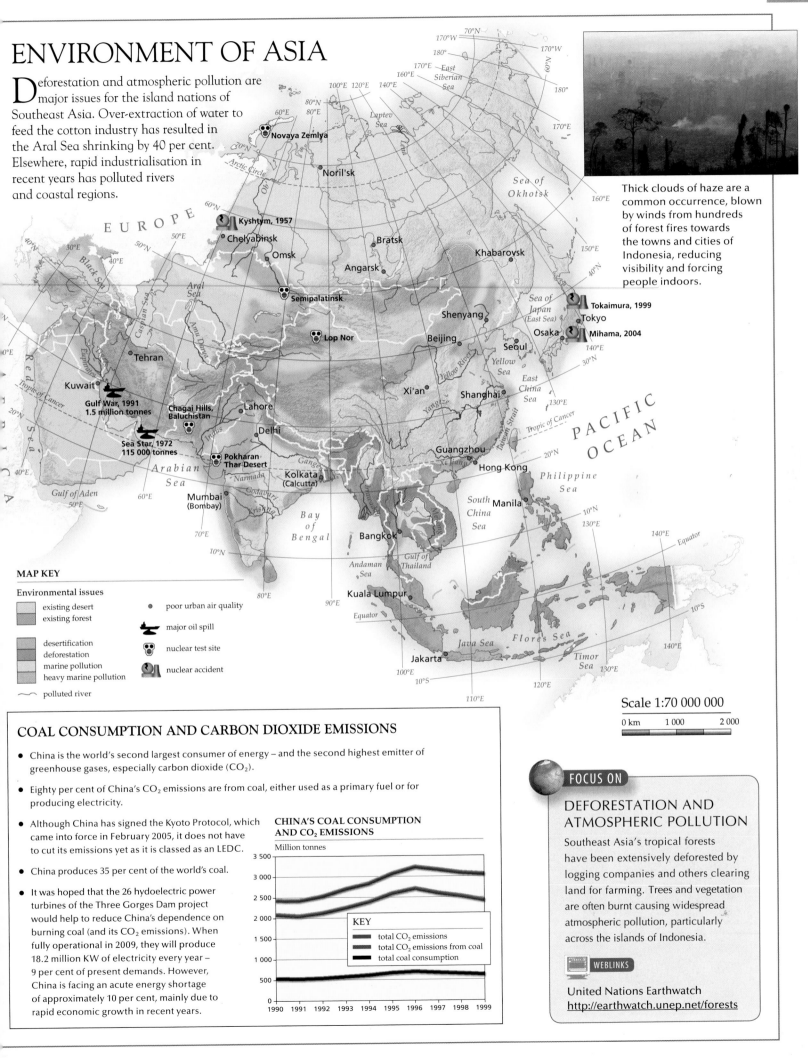

Thick clouds of haze are a common occurrence, blown by winds from hundreds of forest fires towards the towns and cities of Indonesia, reducing visibility and forcing people indoors.

MAP KEY

Environmental issues

- existing desert
- existing forest
- desertification
- deforestation
- marine pollution
- heavy marine pollution
- ～ polluted river
- poor urban air quality
- major oil spill
- nuclear test site
- nuclear accident

Scale 1:70 000 000

0 km   1 000   2 000

COAL CONSUMPTION AND CARBON DIOXIDE EMISSIONS

- China is the world's second largest consumer of energy – and the second highest emitter of greenhouse gases, especially carbon dioxide (CO_2).

- Eighty per cent of China's CO_2 emissions are from coal, either used as a primary fuel or for producing electricity.

- Although China has signed the Kyoto Protocol, which came into force in February 2005, it does not have to cut its emissions yet as it is classed as an LEDC.

- China produces 35 per cent of the world's coal.

- It was hoped that the 26 hydoelectric power turbines of the Three Gorges Dam project would help to reduce China's dependence on burning coal (and its CO_2 emissions). When fully operational in 2009, they will produce 18.2 million KW of electricity every year – 9 per cent of present demands. However, China is facing an acute energy shortage of approximately 10 per cent, mainly due to rapid economic growth in recent years.

CHINA'S COAL CONSUMPTION AND CO_2 EMISSIONS

Million tonnes

KEY
- total CO_2 emissions
- total CO_2 emissions from coal
- total coal consumption

1990 1991 1992 1993 1994 1995 1996 1997 1998 1999

FOCUS ON

DEFORESTATION AND ATMOSPHERIC POLLUTION

Southeast Asia's tropical forests have been extensively deforested by logging companies and others clearing land for farming. Trees and vegetation are often burnt causing widespread atmospheric pollution, particularly across the islands of Indonesia.

WEBLINKS

United Nations Earthwatch
http://earthwatch.unep.net/forests

Map labels: Novaya Zemlya, Noril'sk, Kyshtym, 1957, Chelyabinsk, Omsk, Bratsk, Khabarovsk, Angarsk, Semipalatinsk, Lop Nor, Shenyang, Tokaimura, 1999, Tokyo, Osaka, Mihama, 2004, Beijing, Seoul, Tehran, Kuwait, Gulf War, 1991 1.5 million tonnes, Chagai Hills, Baluchistan, Lahore, Xi'an, Shanghai, Sea Star, 1972 115 000 tonnes, Delhi, Pokharan Thar Desert, Guangzhou, Kolkata (Calcutta), Hong Kong, Mumbai (Bombay), Manila, Bangkok, Kuala Lumpur, Jakarta, EUROPE, PACIFIC OCEAN, Black Sea, Caspian Sea, Aral Sea, Arabian Sea, Gulf of Aden, Bay of Bengal, Andaman Sea, Gulf of Thailand, South China Sea, Philippine Sea, Java Sea, Flores Sea, Timor Sea, East China Sea, Yellow Sea, Sea of Japan (East Sea), Sea of Okhotsk, Laptev Sea, East Siberian Sea, Red Sea, Arctic Circle, Tropic of Cancer, Equator

RUSSIAN FEDERATION AND KAZAKHSTAN

The Russian Federation is the largest country in the world, spanning 12 time zones. The vast size of the country, its harsh climate – and the resulting problems of developing infrastructure – have limited settlement and economic development east of the Ural Mountains. Kazakhstan to the south is the second largest of the former Soviet states.

Russia has one of the world's largest fishing fleets, with the majority of its marine catch in the Pacific Ocean and Bering Sea. Although output has declined, it is still one of the world's top five fish producers.

In 2003, the Aral Sea on the border of Kazakhstan and Uzbekistan was only half the size it was in 1989 and badly polluted.

1989

2003

Scale 1:25 000 000
(projection: Lambert Conformal Conic)

| 0 km | 250 | 500 | 750 | 1 000 | 1 250 |

1 cm on the map represents 250 km on the ground

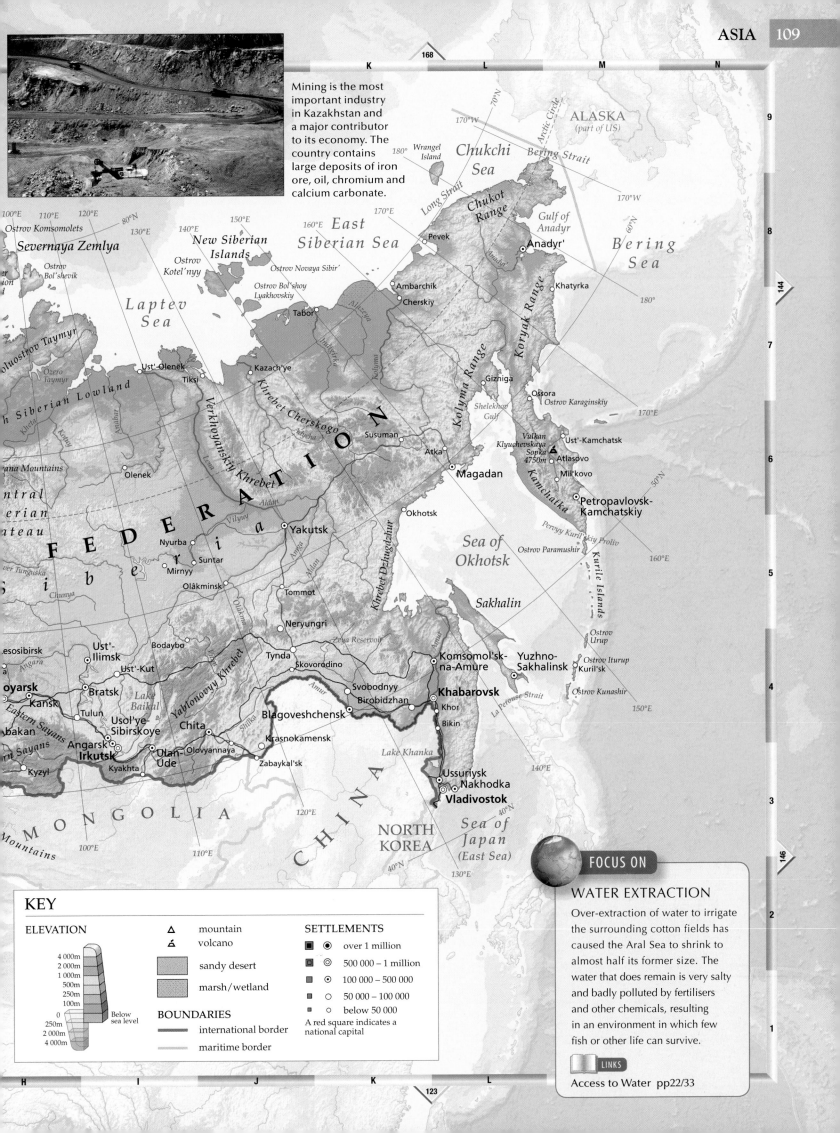

Mining is the most important industry in Kazakhstan and a major contributor to its economy. The country contains large deposits of iron ore, oil, chromium and calcium carbonate.

ALASKA
(part of US)

Chukchi Sea

East Siberian Sea

Bering Sea

Laptev Sea

New Siberian Islands

Severnaya Zemlya

Ostrov Komsomolets

Ostrov Bol'shevik

Ostrov Kotel'nyy

Ostrov Novaya Sibir'

Ostrov Bol'shoy Lyakhovskiy

Poluostrov Taymyr

Ozero Taymyr

h Siberian Lowland

Khrebet Cherskogo

Verkhoyanskiy Khrebet

Kolyma Range

Koryak Range

Chukot Range

Gulf of Anadyr

Bering Strait

Wrangel Island

Long Strait

Pevek

Anadyr'

Khatyrka

Ambarchik

Cherskiy

Tabor

Tiksi

Ust'-Olenëk

Kazach'ye

Ust'-Kamchatsk

Gizhiga

Ossora

Ostrov Karaginskiy

Shelekhov Gulf

Vulkan Klyuchevskaya Sopka 4750m

Atlasovo

Mil'kovo

Susuman

Atka

Magadan

Okhotsk

Petropavlovsk-Kamchatskiy

Kamchatka

Sea of Okhotsk

Sakhalin

Kurile Islands

Ostrov Paramushir

Pervyy Kuril'skiy Proliv

Ostrov Urup

Ostrov Iturup

Ostrov Kunashir

Ostrov Urup

Kuril'sk

Yuzhno-Sakhalinsk

FEDERATION

Siberia

Yakutsk

Nyurba

Suntar

Mirnyy

Olëkminsk

Tommot

Neryungri

Olenek

Aldan

Vilyuy

Amga

Zeya Reservoir

Ust'-Ilimsk

Bodaybo

Tynda

Skovorodino

Svobodnyy

Birobidzhan

Komsomol'sk-na-Amure

Khabarovsk

Khor

Bikin

Lake Khanka

Ussuriysk

Nakhodka

Vladivostok

La Pérouse Strait

Amur

esosibirsk

oyarsk

Kansk

Bratst

Tulun

Usol'ye-Sibirskoye

Angarsk

Irkutsk

Ust'-Kut

Lake Baikal

Chita

Ulan-Ude

Kyakhta

Kyzyl

Olovyannaya

Krasnokamensk

Zabaykal'sk

Blagoveshchensk

Yablonovyy Khrebet

Khrebet Dzhugdzhur

MONGOLIA

CHINA

NORTH KOREA

Sea of Japan (East Sea)

Eastern Sayans

Sayans

abakan

Kyzyl

KEY

ELEVATION

4 000m
2 000m
1 000m
500m
250m
100m
0
Below sea level
250m
2 000m
4 000m

△ mountain
⚐ volcano

sandy desert

marsh/wetland

BOUNDARIES

international border
maritime border

SETTLEMENTS

■ ◉ over 1 million
▣ ◎ 500 000 – 1 million
▪ ⊙ 100 000 – 500 000
▪ ○ 50 000 – 100 000
▪ ○ below 50 000

A red square indicates a national capital

FOCUS ON

WATER EXTRACTION

Over-extraction of water to irrigate the surrounding cotton fields has caused the Aral Sea to shrink to almost half its former size. The water that does remain is very salty and badly polluted by fertilisers and other chemicals, resulting in an environment in which few fish or other life can survive.

LINKS

Access to Water pp22/33

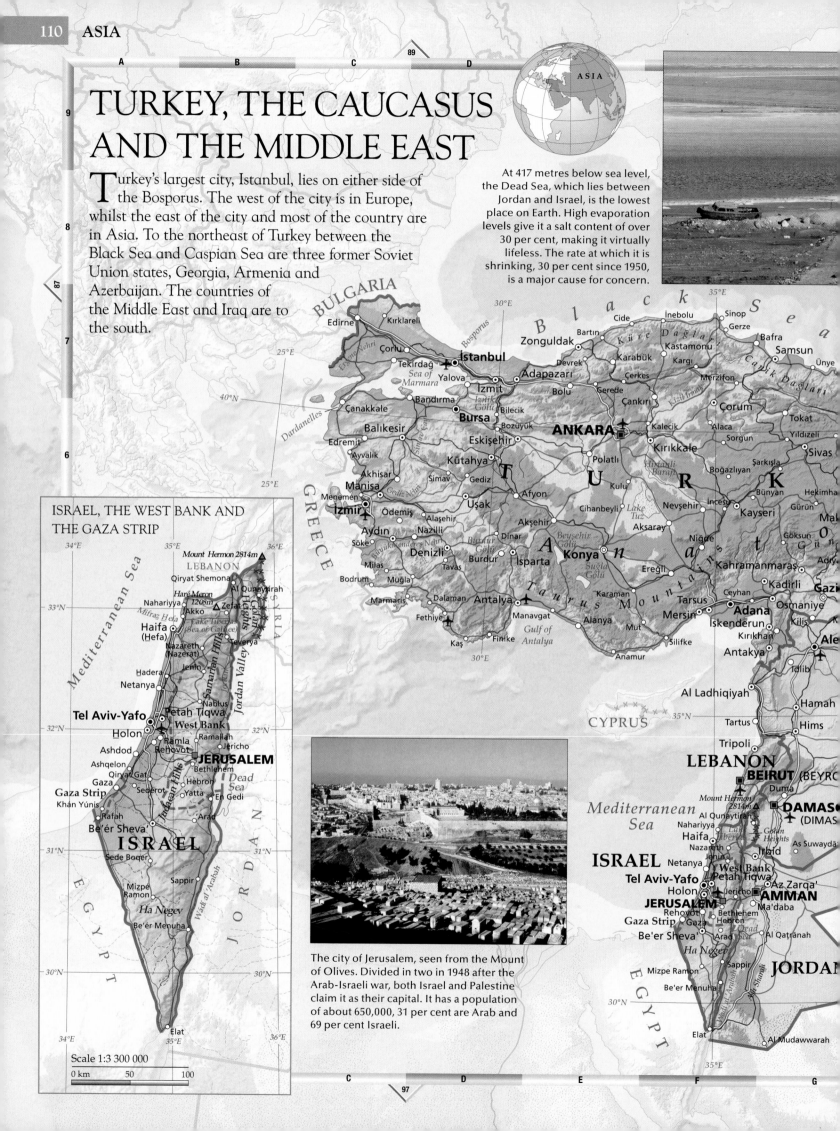

TURKEY, THE CAUCASUS AND THE MIDDLE EAST

Turkey's largest city, Istanbul, lies on either side of the Bosporus. The west of the city is in Europe, whilst the east of the city and most of the country are in Asia. To the northeast of Turkey between the Black Sea and Caspian Sea are three former Soviet Union states, Georgia, Armenia and Azerbaijan. The countries of the Middle East and Iraq are to the south.

At 417 metres below sea level, the Dead Sea, which lies between Jordan and Israel, is the lowest place on Earth. High evaporation levels give it a salt content of over 30 per cent, making it virtually lifeless. The rate at which it is shrinking, 30 per cent since 1950, is a major cause for concern.

ISRAEL, THE WEST BANK AND THE GAZA STRIP

Mount Hermon 2814m
LEBANON
Qiryat Shemona
Haré Meron 1208m
Nahariyya   Al Qunaytirah
Akko   Golan Heights
Haifa (Hefa)   Zefat
Lake Tiberias (Sea of Galilee)
Mifraz Hefa
Nazareth (Nazerat)   Teverya
Hadera   Jenin
Netanya   SYRIA
Nablus
Tel Aviv-Yafo   Petah Tiqwa
Holon   West Bank
Ramla   Ramallah
Rehovot   Jericho
Ashdod
Ashqelon   JERUSALEM
Qiryat Gat   Bethlehem
Gaza   Hebron
Gaza Strip   Sederot   Yatta
Khán Yúnis   En Gedi
Rafah   Arad
Be'ér Sheva'   Dead Sea
ISRAEL
Sede Boqer
Mizpe Ramon   Sappir
Ha Negev
Be'ér Menuha   Elat

Mediterranean Sea
Samarian Hills
Jordan Valley
Judean Hills
Wádi al 'Arabah
EGYPT
JORDAN

34°E · 35°E · 36°E
33°N · 32°N · 31°N · 30°N

Scale 1:3 300 000
0 km   50   100

The city of Jerusalem, seen from the Mount of Olives. Divided in two in 1948 after the Arab-Israeli war, both Israel and Palestine claim it as their capital. It has a population of about 650,000, 31 per cent are Arab and 69 per cent are Israeli.

BULGARIA
Edirne   Kirklareli
Çorlu
Tekirdağ   İSTANBUL
Yalova   İzmit
Sea of Marmara   Adapazari
Bandirma   Bolu
Çanakkale   Bilecik
Balikesir   BURSA   Bozüyük
Edremit   Eskişehir   ANKARA
Ayvalik
Akhisar   Kütahya   Polatlı
Manisa   Simav   Gediz
Menemen   Uşak   Afyon
İzmir   Ödemiş   Akşehir
Aydın   Alaşehir   Cihanbeyli
Nazilli   Dinar   Konya
Söke   Denizli   Isparta   Ereğli
Milas   Burdur
Bodrum   Muğla   Tavas
Marmaris   Dalaman   Antalya   Manavgat
Fethiye   Alanya   Mut
Kaş   Finike   Silifke
Anamur
Gulf of Antalya

Black Sea
Zonguldak   Cide   İnebolu   Sinop
Bartin   Gerze
Devrek   Karabük   Kastamonu   Bafra   Samsun
Gerede   Kargı   Ünye
Çankırı   Merzifon   Çanlik Dağları
Kalecik   Çorum   Tokat
Kırıkkale   Alaca   Sorgun   Yıldızeli
Kulu   Boğazlıyan   Şarkışla   Sivas
Nevşehir   İncesu   Bünyan   Hekimhan
Aksaray   Kayseri   Gürün   Ma...
Niğde   Göksun   O...
Kahramanmaraş
Karaman   Tarsus   Ceyhan   Kadirli
Mersin   Adana   Osmaniye   Gazi...
İskenderun   Kilis
Kırıkhan   Ale...
Antakya
İdlib
TURK... Mountains
Küre Dağları
Kızıl Irmak
Hirfanli Baraji
Lake Tuz
Beyşehir Gölü
Suğla Gölü
Taurus Mountains
30°E · 35°E
40°N · 35°N

GREECE
CYPRUS

Al Ladhiqiyah
Hamah
Hims
Tartus
Tripoli
LEBANON
BEIRUT (BEYR...
Duma
Mount Hermon 2814m
DAMAS... (DIMAS...)
Al Qunaytirah
Nahariyya   Golan Heights
Haifa   As Suwaydá
Nazareth   Irbid
ISRAEL   Jenin
Netanya   West Bank
Tel Aviv-Yafo   Petah Tiqwa
Holon   Jericho   Az Zarqa'
JERUSALEM   AMMAN
Rehovot   Ma'daba
Gaza Strip   Bethlehem
Be'er Sheva'   Hebron   Al Qatranah
Arad   Dead Sea
Mizpe Ramon   Sappir   JORDAN
Ha Negev
Be'ér Menuha
Elat   Al Mudawwarah

Mediterranean Sea
EGYPT
Wádi al 'Arabah
33°N · 32°N · 31°N · 30°N
35°E

H   I   J   K   L   M   N

KEY

ELEVATION

4 000m
2 000m
1 000m
500m
250m
100m
0
250m
2 000m
4 000m

Below sea level

△ mountain

sandy desert

marsh/wetland

BOUNDARIES

——— international border
– – – disputed border
· · · · territorial claim
×××× ceasefire line
——— maritime border

SETTLEMENTS

■ ⊙ over 1 million
▣ ◎ 500 000 – 1 million
▪ ⊙ 100 000 – 500 000
▪ ○ 50 000 – 100 000
▫ ○ below 50 000

A red square indicates a national capital

RUSSIAN FEDERATION

Caucasus

Caucasus

Kazbek 5047m △

45°E

daut'a

Sokhumi   Mestia

Och'amch'ire

GEORGIA   K'ut'aisi   Gori

P'ot'i   Samtredia   ●TBILISI
                              Rust'avi

K'obulet'i   Akhalts'ikhe

Bat'umi   Lesser Caucasus

Hopa   AZERBAIJAN

Rize   Pazar   Artvin   Gyumri   Vanadzor   Sevan

Of   Kars   Artik   Ganca

Ardenic Daglari   Sarıkamış   ARMENIA   YEREVAN ■
                                        Artashat

ne   İspir   Pasinler   Horasan   Mount Ararat 5137m △

Aşkale   Erzurum   Ağrı   Doğubayazit   Naxçivan   AZERBAIJAN

rzincan   Tercan   Patnos   Muradiye

Bingöl   Muş   Ercis

azığ   Toros   Tatvan   Van

Silvan   Bitlis   Gevaş

barkır   Batman   Siirt

Mardin   Şırnak   Kurdistan

şehir   Nusaybin   Zākhō   Al Amādīyah

Cizre   Rawāndiz

rfa   Al Qāmishli   Tall Zāhir

npinar   Al Hasakah   Sinjār   Dokan

Raqqah   Tall Afar   Arbil

Al Jazirah   Al Bādī   ●Mosul   Chamchamāl

Al Ḩaḑr   Kirkuk   Tāza Khurmātū

A   Ash Sharqāţ   Tūz Khurmātū

Bayjī   Khānaqīn

Tikrīt   Sārihah

Al 'Ubaydī   Sāmarrā'   Al Muqdādīyah

Alūs   Al Khāliş   Mandalī

Al Fuḩaymī   Bāzīyah   Ba'qūbah   Tursāq

Muḩaywīr   Hīt   Shaykh Ḩātim

Ar Ramādī   ■BAGHDAD   Badrah

Al Fallūjah

Buḩayrat ar Razāzah   Aş Şuwayrah

Ar Ruţbah   Al Musayyib   An Numānīyah   Alī al Gharbī

Karbalā'   Al Kut

Ukhayḑir   Al Hillah   Al Ḩayy   Al 'Amārah

IRAQ   Al Kūfah   Ar Rifā'ī

An Nukhayb   An Najaf   Abū Şukhayr   Qalat Şālih

Ash Shanāfiyah   Ash Shaţrah

As Samāwah   Al Qurnah

Al Barīt   An Nasiriyah   Basra ●

As Salmān   Jalīb Shahāb

Al Ma'āniyah   Al 'Athāmīn   Safwān   Ar Ruḑaymah

AUDI ARABIA   Zahrat al Baṭn

KUWAIT

sert

40°E

30°N

45°E

TURKMENISTAN

50°E

Xaçmaz

Zaqatala   Quba

Saki   Siyazan

AZERBAIJAN   Sumqayit

Mingaçevir   Maraza   BAKU (BAKI) ■

Yevlax   Qazimammad

Ganca   40°N

Nagorno-   Xankandi   Ali-Bayramli

Karabakh   İmisli

Goris   Bilasuvar

Lankaran   50°E

Lake Van (Van Gölü)

Caspian Sea

IRAN

35°N

Hawr as Sa'dīyah

Hawr al Hammar

Scale 1:7 000 000
(Projection: Lambert Conformal Conic)

0   100   200   300   400

1 cm on the map represents 70 km on the ground

Earthquakes are common in Turkey, an active tectonic region. In 1999, a quake measuring 7.4 on the Richter scale occurred along the North Anatolian fault. Centred near Izmit, in the northwest of Turkey, 17 000 people were killed.

FOCUS ON

WATER WARS

Conflict between Israel and its Palestinian neighbours over territorial rights and borders has continued since the State of Israel was formed in 1948. This conflict extends to rights to water from the aquifers beneath the West Bank, which are monopolised by Israel whilst a quarter of the Palestinian households in the West Bank have no connection to piped water.

📖 LINKS

Conflict in the Middle East pp112/113

CONFLICT IN THE MIDDLE EAST

The roots of the Israeli-Palestinian conflict date back many years. However, it was the failed attempt to establish two separate states in 1948 that began the current dispute over land rights in the region. Today there is still no Palestinian state, and conflict centres around Israeli attempts to control much of the disputed territories that would form a new Palestine – the West Bank and Gaza strip.

1920–30

Following World War I, the former Ottoman Empire was split up and Palestine was put under a British mandate. Increasing anti-Semitism in Europe led to mass Jewish migration. Over 75 000 Jews moved to Palestine, forcing many Arabs to leave.

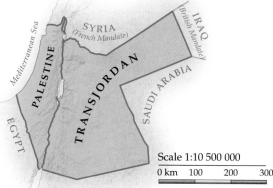

Scale 1:10 500 000
0 km   100   200   300

1947

Britain gave up its mandate over Palestine, passing responsibility to the United Nations (UN). It produced a new plan to divide up the area into separate Jewish and Arab states. The Arabs rejected the plan.

MAP KEY

1947 UN Partition Plan

- Arab State
- Jewish State
- Jerusalem: International City

Scale 1:7 000 000
0 km   100   200

1948–1949

The new State of Israel was formed. Surrounding Arab countries invaded but were driven back. Many Palestinian Arabs fled to nearby countries as Israel claimed more territory. A new armistice line was agreed and the UN negotiated a ceasefire, but no peace agreement.

MAP KEY

1948–1949 Armistice Line

- Jewish State
- Jordanian controlled
- Egyptian controlled
- Jerusalem: International City
- - - Armistice line

Scale 1:7 000 000
0 km   100   200

1967

The Six Day War. Israel attacked Arab troops on its borders and seized control of more land – the Golan Heights from Syria, Sinai and Gaza from Egypt and the West Bank and the Old City of Jerusalem from Jordan. Peace talks have since centred on a return to the pre-1967 borders. There is still no lasting peace in the region.

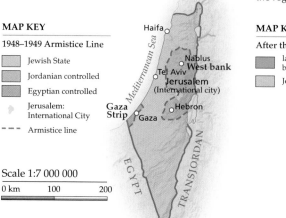

MAP KEY

After the 1967 war

- land occupied by Israel
- Jewish State

Scale 1:10 500 000
0 km   100   200   300

PEACE EFFORTS

Despite the Oslo Accords (and a follow up, Oslo II in 1995) violence has continued, with suicide bombings and attacks by militant Palestinian groups, and assassinations and blockades by the Israeli army. In 2001 Ariel Sharon became Israel's new Prime Minister, elected on a promise to be much tougher in dealings with the Palestinians. Violence escalated along traditional lines. By mid 2002, Israel

had re-occupied most of the West Bank. The peace process again stalled until the UN, USA, EU and Russia introduced the 'road map' for the Middle East in 2003.

Whether this latest peace effort will succeed will depend on the desire of both sides for a lasting settlement, and an agreement on the main obstacles, which will not be addressed until stage three of the road map.

The Jewish West Bank settlement of Homesh, next to the Palestinian village of Burqua. The settlement is one of the four in the West Bank that may be removed as part of Israel's plan to pull out from Gaza and areas of the West Bank.

KEY DATES SINCE 1967	
1979	Israel and Egypt signed a peace deal returning Sinai to Egypt.
1980s	Israel continued to build Jewish settlements in the West Bank and Gaza. In 1987 Palestinians there launched the Intifada (popular uprising) against Israel.
1988	The PLO formally recognises Israel's right to exist, but Israel continued to view the PLO as a terrorist organisation.
1993	The Oslo Accords provided limited self-rule for Palestinians in the disputed territories of Gaza and the West Bank.
1998/99	In the Wye River Accords Israel promised further withdrawals from the West Bank.
2000	Israel withdrew from Lebanon after 22 years.

THE ROAD MAP TO PEACE 2003

Aim	To set up an independent Palestinian state in the Occupied Territories of the West Bank and Gaza, side by side with Israel in three stages by 2005
Stage 1	• Immediate halt to Palestinian violence • Reform of Palestinian political institutions • Dismantling of Israeli settlements built since March 2001 • Gradual withdrawal of Israelis from the Occupied Territories
Stage 2	• Creation of an independent Palestine • International conference about the plan/road map
Stage 3	• Permanent end to conflict • Agreement on final borders • Status of Jerusalem • Decision about four million Palestinian refugees and Israeli settlements • Other Arab states agree peace deal with Israel

THE REGION IN 2005

Scale 1:2 600 000

0 km   25   50   75   100

AP KEY

oundaries

— international border

-- disputed border

x—x ceasefire line

Settlements

■ ⊙ over 1 million
▣ ◎ 500 000 – 1 million
▪ ⊙ 100 000 – 500 000
▪ ○ 50 000 – 100 000
▪ ○ below 50 000

A red square indicates a national capital

WATER WARS

Much of the Middle East is arid and suffers from extended periods of drought. Many commentators have voiced the opinion that if a major war were to start in the Middle East, the most probable cause would be access to water.

THE JORDAN BASIN

MAP KEY

••• watershed

← direction of water flow

Scale 1:2 300 000

0 km   25   50

CONTROLLING THE WATER SUPPLY

Both Israel and Palestine are heavily dependent on water from the major aquifers that hold water beneath the West Bank. Since the 1967 war Israel has controlled this area.

At the World Water Conference in Kyoto in 2003, former Soviet President Mikhail Gorbachev stated that in recent years there had been 21 armed conflicts over water and 18 of these involved Israel:

• water has always been a major problem in Israeli-Palestinian peace talks;

• water has been the main stumbling block in Israeli peace talks with Syria;

• water tensions are cited as the background reason to the Six Day War;

• the peace agreement between Israel and Jordan included provision of water supplies.

Israeli military operations in Palestinian controlled areas, in response to terrorist attacks, have damaged the infrastructure, including water supplies.

Although Israel is legally bound to supply Palestinians with water, they receive only a third of that supplied to Israelis. Whilst Israelis enjoy mains supplies and irrigation for farming, Palestinians often have to rely on water tankers for basic water needs. These are frequently stopped and turned back at the many Israeli-controlled checkpoints. As more and more pressure is placed on limited and diminishing water resources, 'water wars' may become a major source of Israeli-Palestinian conflict.

RAINFALL IN THE REGION

• Annual rainfall in Israel ranges between 1 000 mm at the northernmost point and 31 mm at the southern tip – nearly all of it coming between November and February.

• As much as 60 per cent of Israel's total rainfall evaporates, 5 per cent runs into the sea, and the remaining 35 per cent seeps into the ground, where it gathers in natural aquifers.

Farming in the Negev Desert (above) is only possible with irrigation.

THE BIG ISSUES

1 What are the main issues preventing a lasting peace settlement in the region?

2 Why is water an increasing source of tension between Israelis and Palestinians?

3 What measures must be taken to ensure equal access to water supplies?

THE ARABIAN PENINSULA

The majority of the Arabian Peninsula is desert, located inland in Saudi Arabia and Yemen. Most of the population lives along the cooler, wetter highlands of the coastal areas. The largest reserves of oil and gas in the world are found in this region, bringing immense wealth to a small minority.

Desert covers much of the Arabian Peninsula. In the west it is mainly a high, rocky plateau. To the centre and east this gives way to large, shifting sand dunes.

KEY

ELEVATION

4 000m
2 000m
1 000m
500m
250m
100m
0
250m   Below
2 000m   sea level
4 000m

△   mountain

▨   sandy desert

BOUNDARIES

——   international border

——   maritime border

SETTLEMENTS

■ ⊙   over 1 million

▣ ◎   500 000 – 1 million

▦ ⊙   100 000 – 500 000

▪ ○   50 000 – 100 000

▫ ○   below 50 000

A red square indicates a
national capital

The holy city of Mecca is located near the Red Sea coast of Saudi Arabia. Over two million Muslims make the pilgrimage or *haj* here every year.

ASIA

110

Turayf
Al Qurayyāt
'Ar'ar
Al Harrah
IRAQ
Sakākah
Al Labbah
Rafhah
Nis
Haql
JORDAN
Al Jawf
Jabal al Lawz △ 2580m
Tabūk
Al Qalibah
An Nafād
Ash Sharmah
Jabal ash Shifā
Taymā'
Al Mayyāh
Ḍubā
Ad Dār al Ḥamrā'
Ha'il
EGYPT
Al 'Ulā
Najd
Buraydah
Al Wajh
Khaybar
'Uqlat aş Şuqūr
'Unayzah
Al
Wādī al Hamd
Hadīyah
Wādī ar Rimā
Umm Lajj
Al Ḥanākīyah
S   A
Al Hijāz
Medina
Ad Daw
Yanbu 'al Bahr
Al Q
Badr Ḥunayn
Mahd adh Dhahab
'Afīf
Ḥalabān
Rābigh
A   R   A
Zalim
Al Khurmah
JEDDA (JIDDAH)
Mecca
At Ta'if
Ar Rawdah
'Asīr
Al Lith
Al Bahah
Qal 'at Bīshah
Tathlith
Al Qunfudhah
Al Birk
Abha
Zahrān
Ad Darb
Na
Jīzān
Sa'dah
Jaza'ir Farasan
Hūth
Khamir
Al Luhayyah
'Amrān
Az Zaydīyah
Hodeida
Bājil
Dhamār
ERITREA
Zabid
Ta'izz
Al Mukhā
Al Turbah
Bab el Mandeb
DJIBOUTI

40°E
30°N
35°E
25°N
35°E
Tropic of Cancer
20°N
40°E
15°N

Gulf of Suez
Gulf of Aqaba
Red   Sea

Scale 1:8 700 000
(projection: Lambert Conformal Conic)

0 km   100   200   300   400

1 cm on the map represents 87 km on the ground

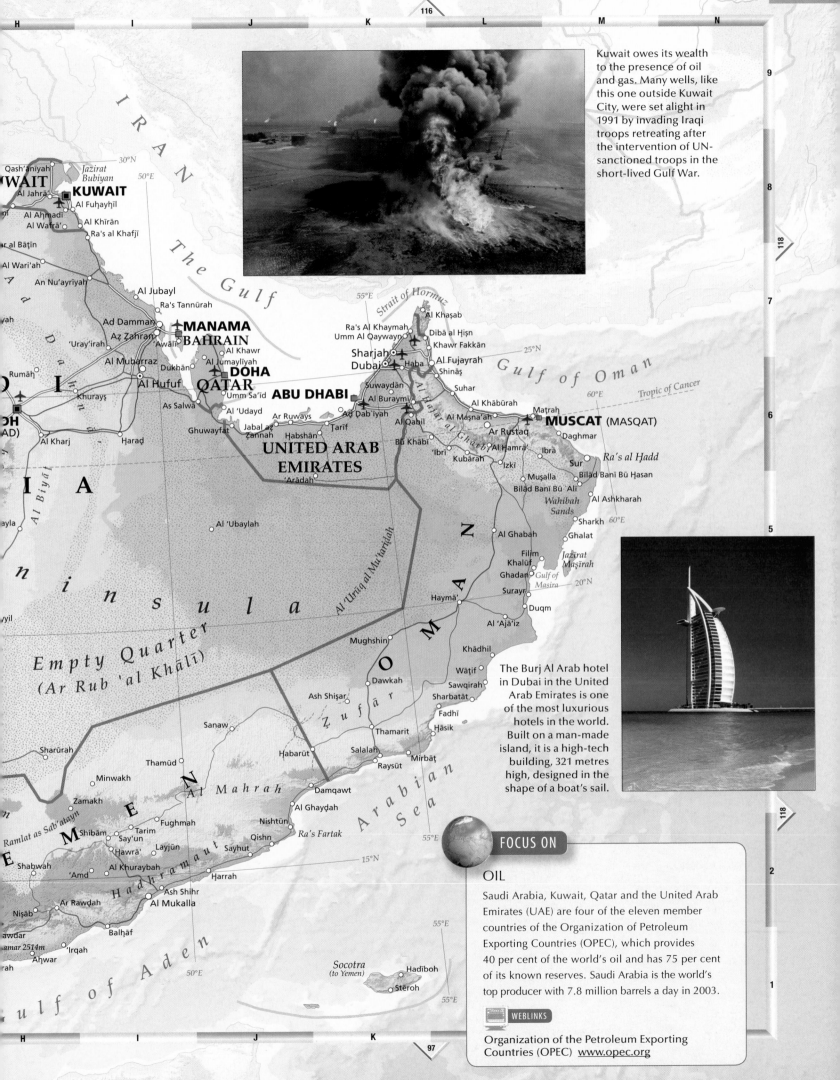

Kuwait owes its wealth to the presence of oil and gas. Many wells, like this one outside Kuwait City, were set alight in 1991 by invading Iraqi troops retreating after the intervention of UN-sanctioned troops in the short-lived Gulf War.

The Burj Al Arab hotel in Dubai in the United Arab Emirates is one of the most luxurious hotels in the world. Built on a man-made island, it is a high-tech building, 321 metres high, designed in the shape of a boat's sail.

FOCUS ON

OIL

Saudi Arabia, Kuwait, Qatar and the United Arab Emirates (UAE) are four of the eleven member countries of the Organization of Petroleum Exporting Countries (OPEC), which provides 40 per cent of the world's oil and has 75 per cent of its known reserves. Saudi Arabia is the world's top producer with 7.8 million barrels a day in 2003.

WEBLINKS

Organization of the Petroleum Exporting Countries (OPEC) www.opec.org

CENTRAL ASIA

Kyrgyzstan and Tajikistan are predominantly mountainous, whilst Uzbekistan and Turkmenistan are a mixture of desert and steppe. All four countries were formed following the 1991 break up of the Soviet Union. Iran is a major world oil producer and the world's largest Islamic republic. Afghanistan has suffered continual conflict since the 1970s, and is rebuilding after the Taliban were ousted in 2001.

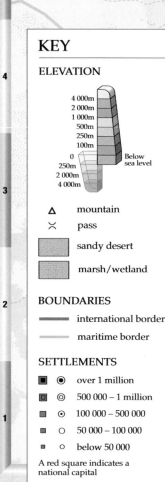

The world's largest inland sea or lake, the Caspian Sea is 371 000 km². It has a wide variety of fish species, including sturgeon, the eggs of which provide caviar.

KEY

ELEVATION

4 000m
2 000m
1 000m
500m
250m
100m
0
250m
2 000m
4 000m
Below sea level

△ mountain
✕ pass
sandy desert
marsh/wetland

BOUNDARIES

international border
maritime border

SETTLEMENTS

■ ⊙ over 1 million
▣ ◎ 500 000 – 1 million
▪ ⊙ 100 000 – 500 000
▪ ○ 50 000 – 100 000
▪ ○ below 50 000

A red square indicates a national capital

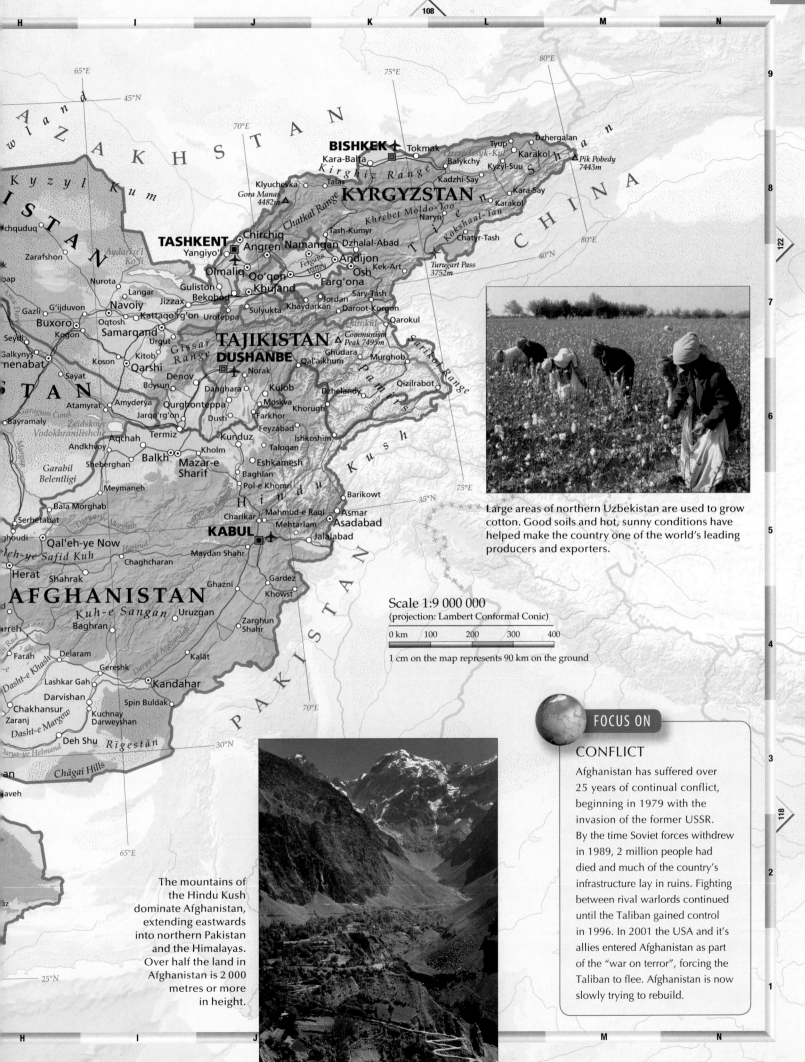

Large areas of northern Uzbekistan are used to grow cotton. Good soils and hot, sunny conditions have helped make the country one of the world's leading producers and exporters.

Scale 1:9 000 000
(projection: Lambert Conformal Conic)

| 0 km | 100 | 200 | 300 | 400 |

1 cm on the map represents 90 km on the ground

The mountains of the Hindu Kush dominate Afghanistan, extending eastwards into northern Pakistan and the Himalayas. Over half the land in Afghanistan is 2 000 metres or more in height.

FOCUS ON

CONFLICT

Afghanistan has suffered over 25 years of continual conflict, beginning in 1979 with the invasion of the former USSR. By the time Soviet forces withdrew in 1989, 2 million people had died and much of the country's infrastructure lay in ruins. Fighting between rival warlords continued until the Taliban gained control in 1996. In 2001 the USA and it's allies entered Afghanistan as part of the "war on terror", forcing the Taliban to flee. Afghanistan is now slowly trying to rebuild.

SOUTH ASIA

India is the dominant country of South Asia, home to one billion of the world's six billion people and a fast-growing economy. In the north of the region are the Himalayas, the world's highest and youngest mountains, which contrast with the low-lying delta of the Ganges and Brahmaputra rivers in Bangladesh.

The historic town of Leh is in the disputed territory of Kashmir on the Pakistan-Indian border. The region has been a regular source of conflict and sporadic fighting between the two countries since independence in 1947, when Kashmir's ruler could not decide which country to join. This eventually resulted in both India and Pakistan claiming the territory.

Typical of many Indian cities, Mumbai (Bombay) is a mixture of modern tower blocks and shanty settlements, which house many of the city's 18 million inhabitants.

FOCUS ON

GLOBALISATION

The worldwide distribution of jobs and manufacturing processes is one of the most recognisable signs of globalisation. Advances in communication technologies in particular have led to a new range of jobs being 'outsourced'. A good example of this is the growth of call centres in India servicing the customers of companies in the UK.

📖 LINKS

Globalisation pp120/121

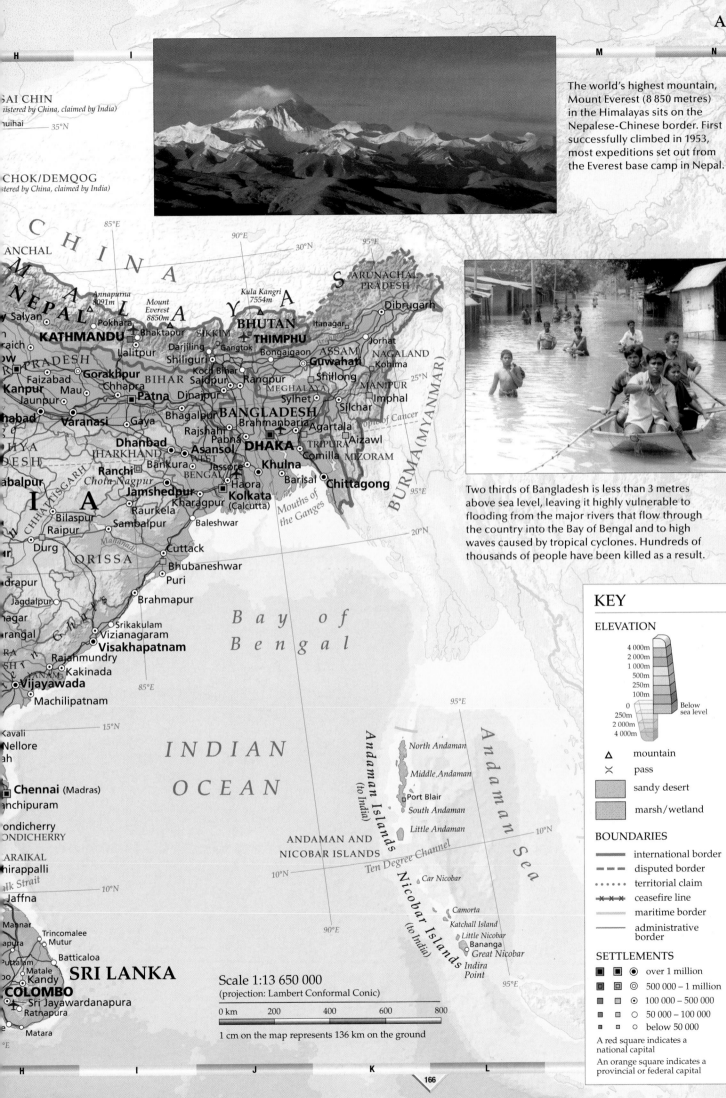

The world's highest mountain, Mount Everest (8 850 metres) in the Himalayas sits on the Nepalese-Chinese border. First successfully climbed in 1953, most expeditions set out from the Everest base camp in Nepal.

Two thirds of Bangladesh is less than 3 metres above sea level, leaving it highly vulnerable to flooding from the major rivers that flow through the country into the Bay of Bengal and to high waves caused by tropical cyclones. Hundreds of thousands of people have been killed as a result.

KEY

ELEVATION

4 000m
2 000m
1 000m
500m
250m
100m
0
250m
2 000m
4 000m
Below sea level

△ mountain
✕ pass
sandy desert
marsh/wetland

BOUNDARIES

international border
disputed border
territorial claim
ceasefire line
maritime border
administrative border

SETTLEMENTS

over 1 million
500 000 – 1 million
100 000 – 500 000
50 000 – 100 000
below 50 000

A red square indicates a national capital

An orange square indicates a provincial or federal capital

Scale 1:13 650 000
(projection: Lambert Conformal Conic)

0 km   200   400   600   800

1 cm on the map represents 136 km on the ground

AKSAI CHIN
(administered by China, claimed by India)
Banghzhuihai   35°N

HUTIAN/DEMQOG
(administered by China, claimed by India)

CHINA

HIMALAYAS

NEPAL
Salyan
Annapurna 8091m
Mount Everest 8850m
Pokhara
KATHMANDU
Bhaktapur
Lalitpur
Darjiling
Shiliguri
SIKKIM
Gangtok
Kula Kangri 7554m
BHUTAN
THIMPHU
Itanagar
ARUNACHAL PRADESH
Dibrugarh
Jorhat
NAGALAND
Kohima
ASSAM
Guwahati
Shillong
MEGHALAYA
MANIPUR
Imphal
25°N
Silchar
NAGALAND

ANCHAL
30°N
85°E
90°E
95°E

PRADESH
Gorakhpur
Faizabad
Mau
Kanpur
Jaunpur
Chhapra
Patna
BIHAR
Saidpur
Rangpur
Dinajpur
Koch Bihar
Bongaigaon
Kohima

habad
Varanasi
Gaya
Bhagalpur
Brahmanbaria
Agartala
Tropic of Cancer
Aizawl
MIZORAM
Comilla

MADHYA PRADESH
Dhanbad
Asansol
Rajshahi
Pabna
DHAKA
TRIPURA
BANGLADESH

jabalpur
JHARKHAND
Bankura
Jassore
Khulna
Haora
Barisal
Chittagong
BURMA (MYANMAR)
95°E

Ranchi
Chota Nagpur
Jamshedpur
WEST BENGAL
Kolkata (Calcutta)
Kharagpur
Mouths of the Ganges

Bilaspur
Raipur
Raurkela
Sambalpur
Baleshwar
20°N

Durg
ORISSA
Cuttack
Bhubaneshwar
Puri
Brahmapur
Mahanadi

drapur
Jagdalpur

nagar
Srikakulam
Vizianagaram
Visakhapatnam

Bay of Bengal

rangal
Rajahmundry
Kakinada
YANAM
Vijayawada
Machilipatnam
85°E

Kavali
Nellore
ah
15°N

INDIAN OCEAN

Andaman Islands (to India)
North Andaman
Middle Andaman
Port Blair
South Andaman
Little Andaman
Andaman Sea
95°E
10°N

Chennai (Madras)
anchipuram
ondicherry
PONDICHERRY
ARAIKAL
hirappalli
alk Strait
Jaffna
10°N

ANDAMAN AND NICOBAR ISLANDS
Ten Degree Channel
10°N
90°E

Nicobar Islands (to India)
Car Nicobar
Camorta
Katchall Island
Little Nicobar
Bananga
Great Nicobar
Indira Point
95°E

Mannar
Trincomalee
apura
Mutur
Batticaloa
Puttalam
Matale
Kandy
SRI LANKA
COLOMBO
Sri Jayawardanapura
Ratnapura
Matara

GLOBALISATION

There is no generally accepted definition of globalisation, although it is usually used to describe the way in which world trade and culture are becoming more closely integrated. There is also debate as to whether it is a beneficial process, or one that increases the gap between richer and poorer countries.

Mass global communication, the rapid spreading of ideas and greater interaction between cultures are some of the ways in which the internet has encouraged globalisation. In countries like Vietnam (left) it has also enabled economic development in industries like tourism.

WHAT IS GLOBALISATION?

Although the term globalisation has only been used since the 1960s, some people argue that the process itself has been taking place for many centuries – since people started travelling and trading between countries. A useful definition comes from the geographer Peter Haggett who defines globalisation as, '*the process by which events, activities and decisions in one part of the world can have significant consequences for communities in distant parts of the globe.*'

Globalisation has been made possible by new communication and transport technologies, which have helped remove the major obstacles to globalisation – geographical distance and cultural differences. The establishment of international institutions such as the World Trade Organization and the removal of trade barriers has also enabled globalisation to spread.

There are many different aspects to globalisation. The growth of international trade, the electronic transfer of money around the world, the growth of transnational companies and increased foreign investment by businesses are major features of globalisation. Other aspects include the spread of global brands, greater cultural exchange between countries and the sharing of knowledge.

THE GLOBALISATION DEBATE

Most of the debate about globalisation has focused on international trade and the activities of transnational companies. Supporters of globalisation point out that

some LEDCs have benefited from opening up to world trade, by enjoying cheaper imports. Since China opened up to the world market income per capita rose from US $1460 in 1980 to US $4129 by 1999. They also argue that because LEDCs have lower labour costs than in MEDCs, they are able to attract investment from foreign companies, creating millions of jobs across the world.

Opponents of free trade argue that whilst it is potentially a powerful force for improving development levels, there are too many inequalities in the current trading systems. Far from being 'free', many countries still operate trade policies supported by duties, tariffs and subsidies to protect their own industries. MEDCs that subsidise farmers

Today the free movement of money is perhaps the key to globalisation – £670 billion moves through global currency markets like this one in Brazil, every day.

GLOBAL TRADE: TRADE FLOWS TO AND FROM CHINA

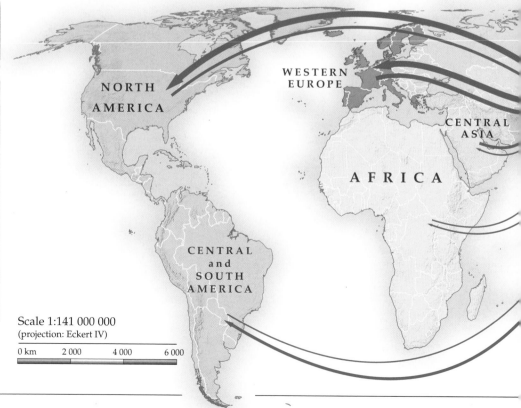

NORTH AMERICA

WESTERN EUROPE

CENTRAL ASIA

AFRICA

CENTRAL and SOUTH AMERICA

Scale 1:141 000 000
(projection: Eckert IV)

0 km   2 000   4 000   6 000

include the USA, which subsidises cotton farmers and the EU countries, which subsidise the production of milk and sugar. As a result, farmers can sell their produce more cheaply than farmers in LEDCs who have no subsidies. This makes it almost impossible for poorer LEDCs to compete. Since the late 1980s LEDCs have lobbied to get rid of subsidies and tariffs so their industries could compete fairly.

Regular world trade talks by the World Trade Organization (WTO) have become a focus for anti-globalisation protesters. They argue that it is dominated by a small group of rich MEDCs who act to support their own interests.

MAP KEY

Trade flow to and from China
(US $ billion)

Exports from China   Imports into China

0.25 to 10
10 to 50
50 to 100
100 to 275

ASTERN EUROPE and
USSIAN FEDERATION

JAPAN

IINA

SOUTHEAST
ASIA

AUSTRALIA
and
OCEANIA

GLOBALISATION IN INDIA

One group benefiting from globalisation are the educated middle classes in the cities of the 'new' India. Over 300 million of India's one billion population are in the middle classes, many of whom are highly educated and able to speak good English. Technology and communications industries have expanded rapidly, exploiting the availability of this highly skilled labour force.

Call centres are one of the most rapidly growing areas for Indian BPO (Business Process Outsourcing) companies. The first overseas call centre was set up in 1998 near New Delhi dealing with work outsourced by General Electric.

GROWTH OF OUTSOURCING

Growth in these industries in India has been driven mainly by demand from businesses based in MEDCs. For many years companies in MEDCs have 'outsourced' areas of their business to other countries, mainly in order to benefit from lower labour costs. However, most of the work was unskilled.

Recent improvements in communications technologies (such as the Internet) have enabled companies to outsource service sector jobs. The driving force to outsource is the lower wages in India, which mean that labour costs can be reduced by up to 40 per cent. Although salaries are low compared to those in MEDCs, these jobs are still well paid relative to other sectors in India, and can therefore attract the best graduates. Seventy per cent or more of major companies in the USA and Europe have outsourced either manufacturing or service jobs overseas, with many going to India.

A large number of these jobs are in the computer software industry (Microsoft's Bill Gates believes that India is the next 'software superpower'). Others are in another growth area – call centres. By 2008 it is predicted that jobs in IT and call centre outsourcing in India will increase by 500 per cent, employing four million people. Many of these will be in Cyberabad, a suburb in the city of Hyderabad where companies like Microsoft, Dell, GE, HSBC and IBM are based.

The offices of a software company based in Electronics City in Bangalore.

Economic growth rates of 7 per cent a year and the availability of well paid jobs mean people have more disposable income in cities like Hyderabad. Modern shopping malls have been built and shops now stock a wide range of global consumer goods. However, this prosperity is not shared by the majority of India's poor.

GROWTH OF THE INDIAN SOFTWARE INDUSTRY 1995–2000

Value of sales (US $ million)

KEY
— total software sales
— software export sales
— domestic software sales

10 000
9 000
8 000
7 000
6 000
5 000
4 000
3 000
2 000
1 000
0

1995-96 1996-97 1997-98 1998-99 1999-00 2000-2001

THE BIG ISSUES

1 What are the benefits of globalisation?

2 Is globalisation a mainly beneficial process? Why?

3 How can the benefits of globalisation be more equally shared?

CHINA AND MONGOLIA

With 1.3 billion people, China is the world's most populous and third largest country. Since it opened up to foreign investment in 1978 the country has rapidly industrialised and started to develop a market economy. Today, the eastern coastal regions are the most economically developed, whilst the rural interior remains poor. Mongolia, to the north of China, is a sparsely populated, mainly arid country.

The Gobi Desert forms the southern half of Mongolia. Extremely hot in summer, winter temperatures are frequently below freezing, creating a harsh physical environment.

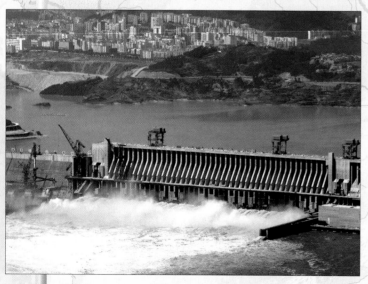

The first sections of the world's largest hydroelectric power scheme, the Three Gorges Dam project opened in 2003. A controversial scheme, over a million people had to be moved to make way for various dams and reservoirs on the river Yangtze, like this one at Yichang, Hubei Province.

FOCUS ON

MULTI-PURPOSE RIVER MANAGEMENT

Hydroelectric power from China's Three Gorges Dam scheme will replace some of the country's coal-fired power stations, but the project will also help control the river Yangtze. The river regularly floods large areas of China, causing widespread damage to settlements and farmland and putting millions of people at risk. The environmental impacts of the dam are yet to be seen.

WEBLINKS

International Rivers Network
www.irn.org/programs/threeg

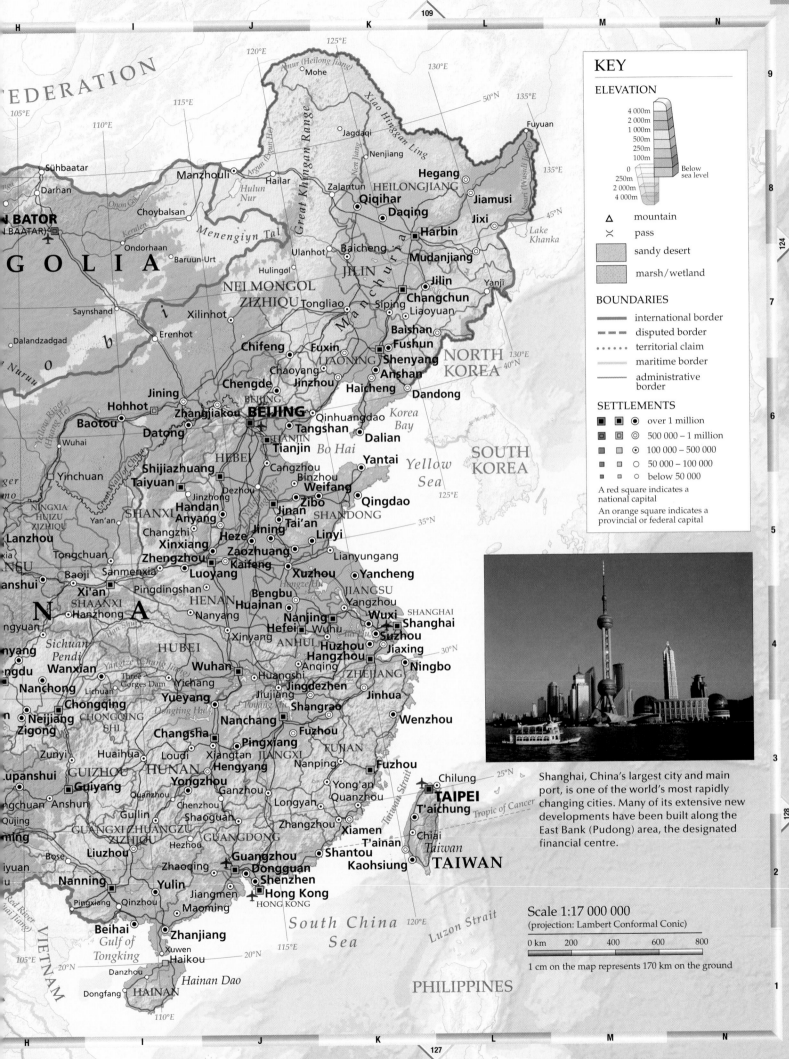

KEY

ELEVATION

4 000m
2 000m
1 000m
500m
250m
100m
0
Below sea level
250m
2 000m
4 000m

△ mountain
⋈ pass
sandy desert
marsh/wetland

BOUNDARIES

international border
disputed border
territorial claim
maritime border
administrative border

SETTLEMENTS

- ■ ■ ◉ over 1 million
- ■ ◉ 500 000 – 1 million
- ◉ 100 000 – 500 000
- ○ 50 000 – 100 000
- ○ below 50 000

A red square indicates a national capital

An orange square indicates a provincial or federal capital

Shanghai, China's largest city and main port, is one of the world's most rapidly changing cities. Many of its extensive new developments have been built along the East Bank (Pudong) area, the designated financial centre.

Scale 1:17 000 000
(projection: Lambert Conformal Conic)

0 km   200   400   600   800

1 cm on the map represents 170 km on the ground

KOREA AND JAPAN

Japan is a country made up of over 3 000 islands. Most of its people live on the coastal lowlands on the four largest islands of Honshu, Kyushu, Hokkaido and Shikoku. Tectonically active, almost three quarters of Japan is mountainous, formed from volcanoes rising from the sea bed. South Korea's manufacturing and high–tech industries grew rapidly during the late 1990s, whilst the communist North Korea remains underdeveloped and isolated.

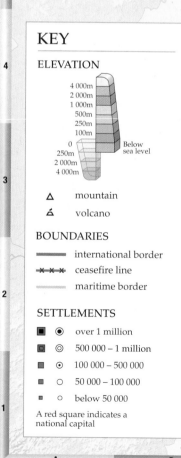

Although the border with the South remains closely guarded, many North Koreans have fled to South Korea to try to escape poverty and food shortages.

KEY

ELEVATION

4 000m
2 000m
1 000m
500m
250m
100m
0
250m   Below
2 000m   sea level
4 000m

△   mountain

⌂   volcano

BOUNDARIES

——————   international border

×××   ceasefire line

——————   maritime border

SETTLEMENTS

■ ⊙   over 1 million

▣ ◎   500 000 – 1 million

▪ ⊙   100 000 – 500 000

▪ ○   50 000 – 100 000

▫ ○   below 50 000

A red square indicates a national capital

Strong government support has led to the rapid growth of industries such as electronics in South Korea. Modern factories produce a range of goods like TVs, selling at competitive prices on the world market.

N

Over 5 000 people died when an earthquake struck Kobe and the surrounding area in Japan in January 1995. Buildings and roads collapsed and fire destroyed many homes.

Kurile Islands
(administered by Russian Federation, claimed by Japan)

Sea of Okhotsk

Wakkanai
Rebun-to
Esashi
Rishiri-to
Nayoro   Monbetsu
Shibetsu   Abashiri
Asahikawa   Kitami
Takikawa   △ *Asahi-dake 2290m*   Nemuro
Otaru   Akkeshi
Sapporo Ebetsu Obihiro   Kushiro
Suttsu   Chitose   △ *Horoshiri-dake 2052m*
Okushiri-to   Mori   Noboribetsu
Tomakomai
Uchiura-wan   **Muroran**

Hokkaido

Tsugaru-kaikyo
Hakodate
Mutsu

Aomori
Goshogawara   Hachinohe
Hirosaki
Odate   Kuji
Noshiro
Gojome   Iwate
Akita   Miyako
Honjo   Morioka
Yokote
Sakata Shinjo   Kesennuma
Tsuruoka   Shizugawa
Furukawa   Ishinomaki
Yamagata   **Sendai**
Niigata   *Sendai-wan*
Sado   Fukushima   Soma
Nagaoka   Haramachi
Suzu   *Inawashiro-ko* Koriyama
Togi   Joetsu   Sukagawa
Itoigawa   Iwaki
Takaoka Nagano   Hitachi
Kanazawa
Komatsu Toyama   Utsunomiya
Matsumoto Maebashi Mito
Fukui   *Hida-*   Oyama *Kasumiga-ura*
sanmyaku   **TOKYO**
Tsuruga Kofu   Choshi
Tottori   Nakatsugawa   Chiba
Ogaki Gifu Mount Fuji **Yokohama**
Kyoto Otsu **Nagoya** (*Fuji-san*) Hiratsuka
Himeji Okazaki Toyota 3776m Fuji
Osaka Tsu Shizuoka *Izu-hanto*
urashiki **Kobe** Ise **Hamamatsu** *Sagami-nada*
Wakayama *Ise-wan* *O-shima*
Gobo *Nii-jima*
Tanabe Owase *Kozu-shima*
Shingu *Mikura-jima*

Shikoku

Izu-shoto

Hachijo-jima

Sea of Japan (East Sea)

JAPAN

JAPANESE ALPS

Ou-sanmyaku

Biwa-ko
Kii-suido
Awaji-shima
Naikai

PACIFIC OCEAN

Tokyo is one of the world's leading financial centres, located at the northeastern end of a continuous built-up area known as the Tokaido megalopolis. It was home to more than 33.7 million people in 2000.

Scale 1:6 500 000
(projection: Lambert Conformal Conic)

0 km   100   200   300   400

1 cm on the map represents 65 km on the ground

FOCUS ON

NUCLEAR POWER

With few of its own energy resources, Japan is the world's third biggest nuclear power producer, with 54 operational reactors and 2 more planned. However, a series of minor accidents has re-opened the debate about the safety of nuclear power.

LINKS

Geothermal power pp137

Federation of Electric Power Companies of Japan www.japannuclear.com

H   I   J   K   L   M   N

SOUTHEAST ASIA

Southeast Asia is made up of five mainland countries, plus the peninsula and islands of Malaysia, Indonesia and the Philippines. A tropical region, rainforests once covered much of the southern areas, giving way to mountain ranges in the north. One of the world's newest nations, East Timor, gained its independence from Indonesia in 2002.

Malaysia's capital city, Kuala Lumpur with its well-known Petronas Towers, sits at the northern end of a fast-developing high-tech corridor called Cyberjaya.

KEY

ELEVATION

4 000m
2 000m
1 000m
500m
250m
100m
0
250m — Below sea level
2 000m
4 000m

△ mountain
⌃ volcano
marsh/wetland

BOUNDARIES

international border
maritime border

SETTLEMENTS

■ ⊙ over 1 million
▣ ◎ 500 000 – 1 million
▢ ⊙ 100 000 – 500 000
▪ ○ 50 000 – 100 000
▪ ○ below 50 000

A red square indicates a national capital

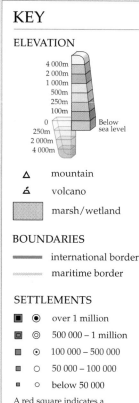

Phuket in Thailand was one of the many resorts damaged by the Asian Tsunami in December 2004. This photograph was taken before the disaster, showing some of the attractions Thailand offers to over 11 million tourists who visit annually.

K   L   M   N

124

One hundred kilometres northwest of the Philippines' capital Manila, Mount Pinatubo had been inactive for 600 years until June 1991. Despite advance warnings and the evacuation of the area, 350 people were killed when it finally erupted.

FOCUS ON

NEWLY INDUSTRIALISED COUNTRIES (NICs)

In the last quarter of the twentieth century, a number of countries in Southeast Asia experienced rapid industrialisation, moving their economies from ones dependent on primary industries like farming and forestry to secondary (manufacturing) and tertiary industries. The best example of these new 'Tiger economies' is Malaysia, although progress has slowed since 2000.

Terraces, like these growing rice in Bali, Indonesia, are usually constructed so that as much land as possible can be cultivated. This allows even quite steep-sloping land to be used for agriculture.

Scale 1:18 750 000
(projection: Mercator)

0 km   250   500   750   1000

1 cm on the map represents 187 km on the ground

PACIFIC OCEAN

Luzon Strait
20°N   20°N
Babuyan Channel   Babuyan Island
125°E
Luzon   Cordillera Central   Tuguegarao
Baguio   Ilagan
Dagupan   Cabanatuan
Mount Pinatubo 1485m   Angeles
MANILA   Lucena
Batangas
Calapan   Naga   Legaspi
Mindoro   *Sibuyan*
Mindoro Strait   *Sea*   Masbate   Calbayog
Roxas City   *Samar*   Tacloban
PHILIPPINES   Iloilo   Cadiz   *Leyte*
Panay Island   **Cebu**
Negros   *Bohol Sea*
Puerto Princesa   Butuan
Palawan   Iligan   Cagayan de Oro
Bislig
Zamboanga   *Moro Gulf*   **Davao**   *Mindanao*
Basilan   Lebak   *Davao Gulf*
General Santos

Philippine Sea

15°N   15°N

10°N   10°N

Babeldaob

130°E

PALAU

5°N

el Islands
ted by China,
n & Vietnam)

South China Sea

y Islands
ted by China,
, Philippines,
& Vietnam)
115°E

Palawan Passage

Balabac Strait

Gunung Kinabalu 4101m
Kota Kinabalu   Sandakan
BANDAR SERI BEGAWAN
BRUNEI   Sabah
Miri   Tawau

Sulu Archipelago

Sulu Sea

Celebes Sea

135°E

Pulau Morotai

140°E

ntulu   *Banjaran Tamabu*
ak   *Borneo*
Batang Rajang
Aman   *Pegunungan Muller*
nantan   Samarinda
Balikpapan
Amuntai   Kandangan
Pulau Laut
anjarmasin   Parepare

Manado

Gorontalo   *Molucca Sea*
Mafa
Halmahera Sea
Waigeo
Sorong   Selat Dampier
Misool   *Doberai Peninsula*
Fakfak   *Teluk Berau*

Pulau Halmahera

Waflia   Wahai   *Ceram Sea*
Palu   Ambon   *Pulau Seram*
Celebes (Sulawesi)   *Kepulauan Banggai*
Kepulauan Sula

Equator

Pulau Biak
Pulau Yapen
Sarmi
Pegunungan Maoke
Jayapura

Teluk Cenderawasih

D   *O*   *N*   *E*   *S*   *I*   *A*
Danau Towuti   Kendari
Teluk Bone   *Pulau Buru*
Moluccas (Maluku)
Puncak Jaya 5040m
Tembagapura
Amamapare   *Pegunungan Maoke*

Ujungpandang   *Pulau Buton*   *Banda Sea*
Bulukumba   *Kepulauan Kai*   *New Guinea*
Papua (Irian Jaya)   **PAPUA NEW GUINEA**
a Sea
arang   *Pulau Madura*   *Kepulauan Aru*
Surabaya   *Flores Sea*   *Pulau Wetar*
Probolinggo   *Pulau Lombok*   *Lesser Sunda Islands*   *Kepulauan Alor*   *Pulau Yamdena*   *Kepulauan Leti*
Malang   Jember   *Bali*   *Flores*   *Kepulauan Tanimbar*
Kediri   Mataram   *Sumbawa*   **DILI**
Madiun   Denpasar   *Selat Sumba*   Endeh   **EAST TIMOR**
akarta   *Sumba*   Waikabubak   *Savu Sea*   *Timor*
Pulau Sumba   Kupang   Nikiniki

Arafura Sea

5°S

10°S   10°S   10°S

Torres Strait

115°E   120°E   125°E   130°E   135°E   140°E

H   I   J   K   L   M   N

9

8

128

7

4

3

128

2

1

AUSTRALASIA AND OCEANIA POLITICAL

Australia, New Zealand, Papua New Guinea and thousands of smaller islands make up the continent of Australasia and Oceania, spread over the southern Pacific. Many were settled by colonial powers such as the UK and France, but have since become independent.

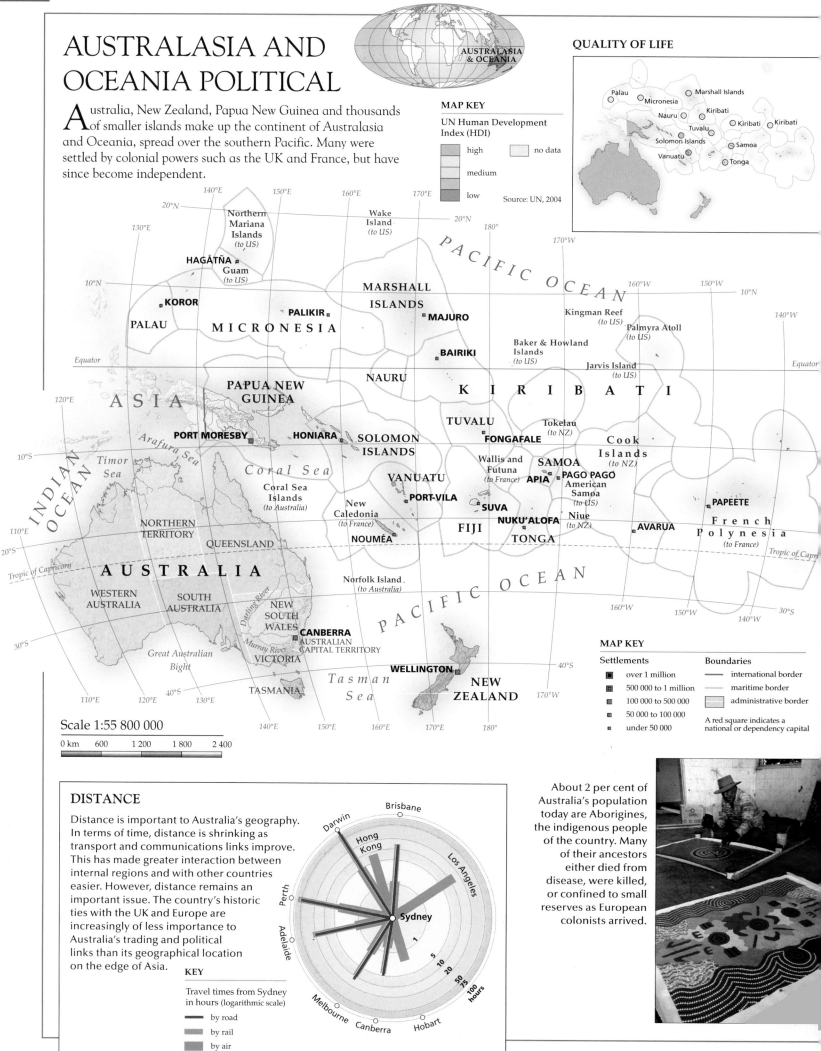

AUSTRALASIA & OCEANIA

MAP KEY

UN Human Development Index (HDI)

- high
- medium
- low
- no data

Source: UN, 2004

QUALITY OF LIFE

Palau · Micronesia · Marshall Islands · Nauru · Kiribati · Tuvalu · Kiribati · Kiribati · Solomon Islands · Samoa · Vanuatu · Tonga

MAP KEY

Settlements		Boundaries	
■	over 1 million	——	international border
▣	500 000 to 1 million	——	maritime border
▪	100 000 to 500 000	▨	administrative border
▪	50 000 to 100 000		A red square indicates a
▪	under 50 000		national or dependency capital

Scale 1:55 800 000

0 km   600   1 200   1 800   2 400

DISTANCE

Distance is important to Australia's geography. In terms of time, distance is shrinking as transport and communications links improve. This has made greater interaction between internal regions and with other countries easier. However, distance remains an important issue. The country's historic ties with the UK and Europe are increasingly of less importance to Australia's trading and political links than its geographical location on the edge of Asia.

KEY

Travel times from Sydney in hours (logarithmic scale)

- by road
- by rail
- by air

About 2 per cent of Australia's population today are Aborigines, the indigenous people of the country. Many of their ancestors either died from disease, were killed, or confined to small reserves as European colonists arrived.

AUSTRALASIA AND OCEANIA PHYSICAL

Whilst Australia is tectonically stable, New Zealand and many of the islands of Oceania lie on or close to plate boundaries and are volcanic in origin. A large number of the Pacific islands of Polynesia, Micronesia and Melanesia are coral atolls.

PHYSICAL FACTFILE

1 HIGHEST POINT: Mount Wilhelm, 4 509 metres above sea level

2 LOWEST POINT: Lake Eyre, 16 metres below sea level

3 LARGEST LAKE: Lake Eyre, 9 690 km²

— **LONGEST RIVER:** River Murray, 2 520 km

— **LENGTH OF COASTLINE:** 137 773 km

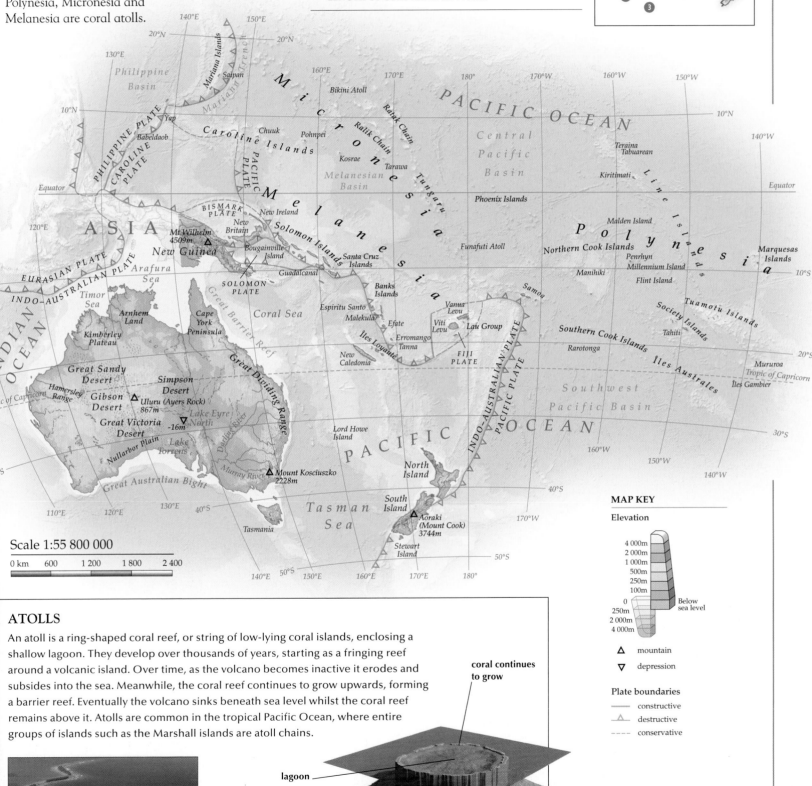

Scale 1:55 800 000

0 km   600   1 200   1 800   2 400

MAP KEY

Elevation

4 000m
2 000m
1 000m
500m
250m
100m
0
250m
2 000m
4 000m
Below sea level

△ mountain

▽ depression

Plate boundaries

— constructive

△ destructive

---- conservative

ATOLLS

An atoll is a ring-shaped coral reef, or string of low-lying coral islands, enclosing a shallow lagoon. They develop over thousands of years, starting as a fringing reef around a volcanic island. Over time, as the volcano becomes inactive it erodes and subsides into the sea. Meanwhile, the coral reef continues to grow upwards, forming a barrier reef. Eventually the volcano sinks beneath sea level whilst the coral reef remains above it. Atolls are common in the tropical Pacific Ocean, where entire groups of islands such as the Marshall islands are atoll chains.

coral continues to grow

lagoon

submerged volcanic island

The Funafuti atoll, Tuvalu

LINKS

Geothermal Energy p137

AUSTRALASIA CLIMATE

Not surprisingly for a continent that covers most of the South Pacific, Australasia has a wide variety of climatic types. The centre of Australia is hot desert, whilst Papua New Guinea and many smaller Pacific islands experience a tropical climate. New Zealand's climate is mainly temperate.

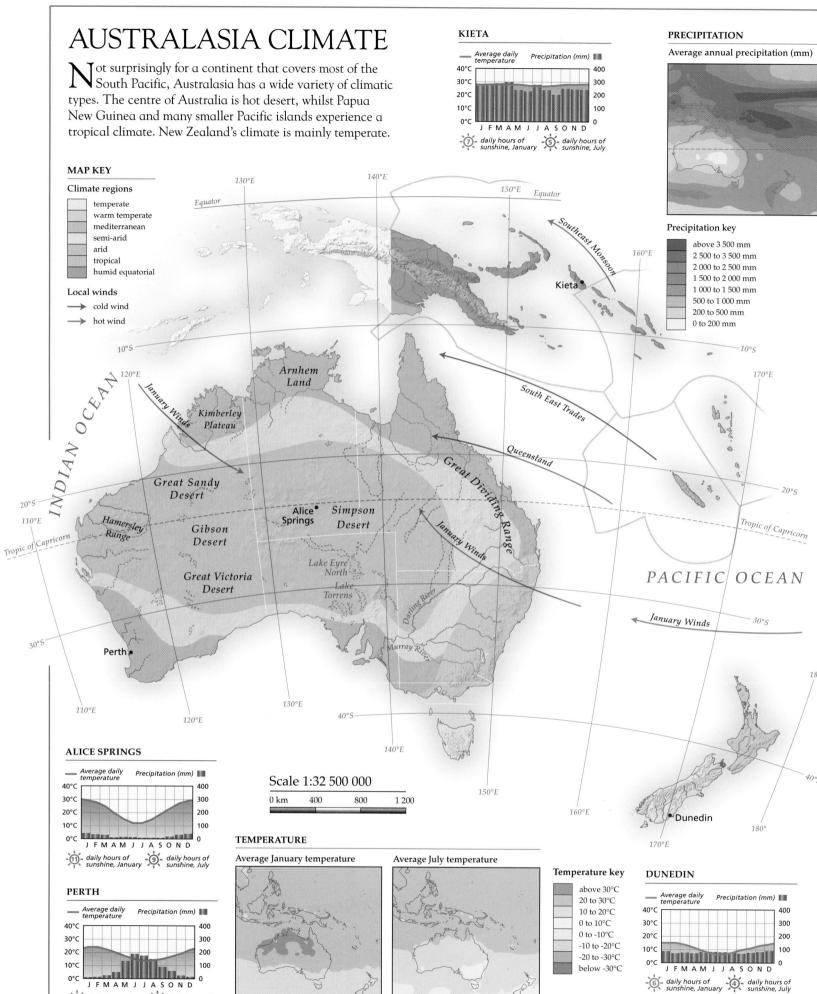

KIETA

Average daily temperature — Precipitation (mm)

daily hours of sunshine, January — 7
daily hours of sunshine, July — 5

PRECIPITATION

Average annual precipitation (mm)

Precipitation key
- above 3 500 mm
- 2 500 to 3 500 mm
- 2 000 to 2 500 mm
- 1 500 to 2 000 mm
- 1 000 to 1 500 mm
- 500 to 1 000 mm
- 200 to 500 mm
- 0 to 200 mm

MAP KEY

Climate regions
- temperate
- warm temperate
- mediterranean
- semi-arid
- arid
- tropical
- humid equatorial

Local winds
- → cold wind
- → hot wind

ALICE SPRINGS

Average daily temperature — Precipitation (mm)

daily hours of sunshine, January — 11
daily hours of sunshine, July — 9

PERTH

Average daily temperature — Precipitation (mm)

daily hours of sunshine, January — 11
daily hours of sunshine, July — 5

Scale 1:32 500 000

0 km   400   800   1 200

TEMPERATURE

Average January temperature

Average July temperature

Temperature key
- above 30°C
- 20 to 30°C
- 10 to 20°C
- 0 to 10°C
- 0 to -10°C
- -10 to -20°C
- -20 to -30°C
- below -30°C

DUNEDIN

Average daily temperature — Precipitation (mm)

daily hours of sunshine, January — 6
daily hours of sunshine, July — 4

AUSTRALASIA POPULATION

Population density is low throughout the region. Most of the population is concentrated in the cities of Australia and New Zealand. In Papua New Guinea over 80 per cent of the population live in rural areas. The smaller islands of the region range from sparsely populated or uninhabited to the occasional quite densely populated main islands within the major island groups.

Sydney is Australia's largest city and first main settlement. Like the majority of Australian cities it is located on the coast and is famous for landmarks such as the Harbour Bridge and Sydney Opera House.

MAP KEY

Population density
(people per square km)

- 50 to 100
- 10 to 50
- 1 to 10
- 0 to 1

Major settlements

- ■ ■ ◉ above 1 million
- ▣ ▢ ◎ 500 000 to 1 million
- ▩ ▢ ◉ 100 000 to 500 000

A red square indicates a national capital

An orange square indicates a provincial or federal capital

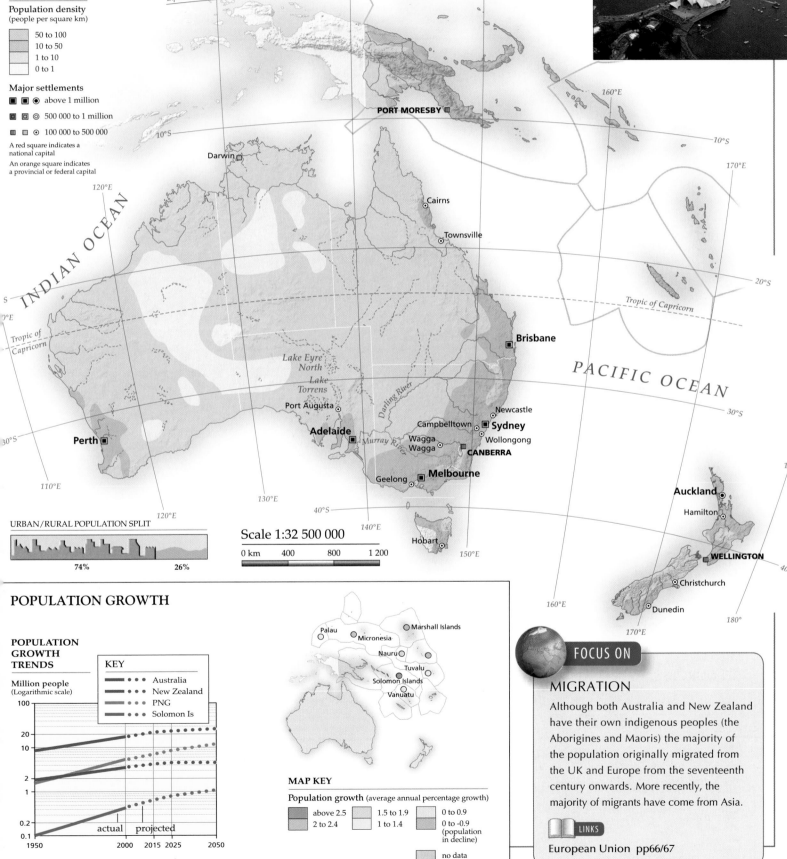

Scale 1:32 500 000

0 km 400 800 1 200

URBAN/RURAL POPULATION SPLIT

74%   26%

POPULATION GROWTH

POPULATION GROWTH TRENDS

Million people
(Logarithmic scale)

KEY
- ● ● ● Australia
- ● ● ● New Zealand
- ● ● ● PNG
- ● ● ● Solomon Is

100
20
10
2
1
0.2
0.1

1950   2000 2015 2025   2050

actual   projected

MAP KEY

Population growth (average annual percentage growth)

- above 2.5
- 2 to 2.4
- 1.5 to 1.9
- 1 to 1.4
- 0 to 0.9
- 0 to -0.9 (population in decline)
- no data

FOCUS ON

MIGRATION

Although both Australia and New Zealand have their own indigenous peoples (the Aborigines and Maoris) the majority of the population originally migrated from the UK and Europe from the seventeenth century onwards. More recently, the majority of migrants have come from Asia.

📖📖 LINKS

European Union pp66/67

AUSTRALASIA LAND USE

Many of the inhabitants of the islands of Australasia rely on fishing for a living, whilst Australia and New Zealand are the world's largest sheep farmers, producing both meat and wool. Plantation crops such as coffee and coconuts are grown in Papua New Guinea's tropical climate.

Located in one of the wetter and more humid parts of Australasia, three quarters of Papua New Guinea is covered by tropical rainforest. Like many such forests, its future is threatened by logging, deforestation and soil erosion.

MAP KEY

Land use type

- forest
- pasture
- cropland
- barren land
- desert
- mountain region

Industry

- industrial area
- major conurbation

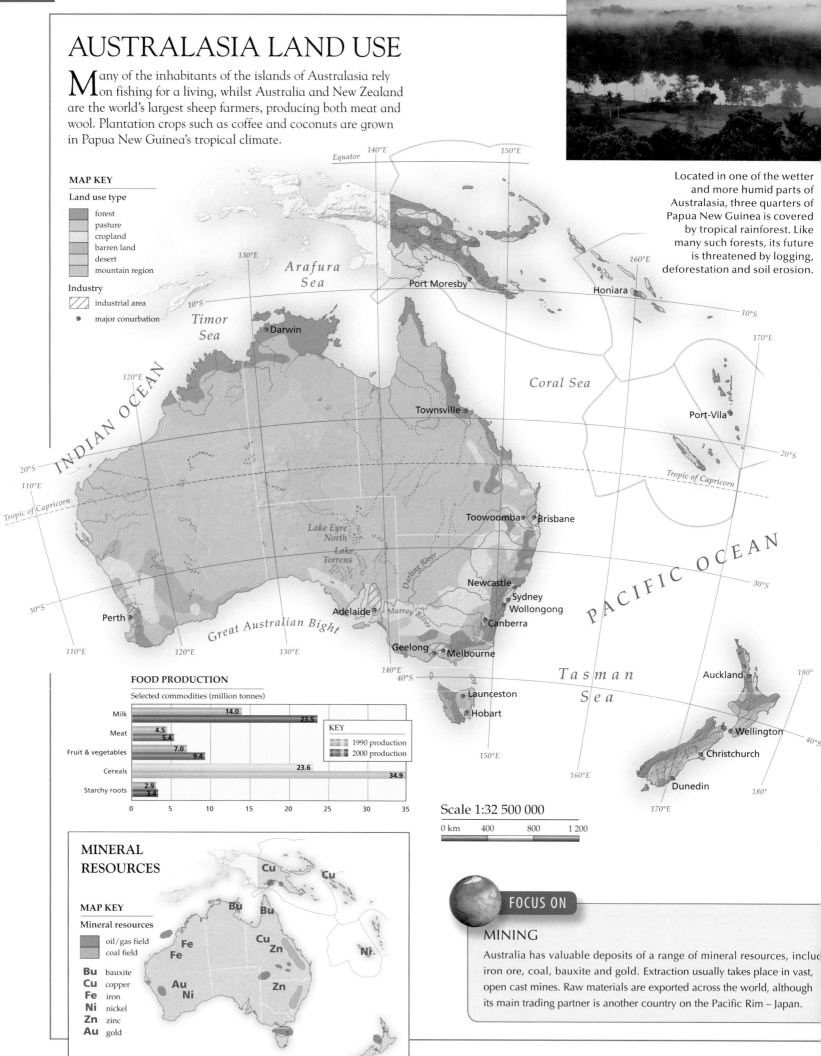

FOOD PRODUCTION

Selected commodities (million tonnes)

Milk	14.0	23.5
Meat	4.5	5.4
Fruit & vegetables	7.0	9.4
Cereals	23.6	34.9
Starchy roots	2.9	3.4

KEY
- 1990 production
- 2000 production

0 5 10 15 20 25 30 35

Scale 1:32 500 000

0 km   400   800   1 200

MINERAL RESOURCES

MAP KEY

Mineral resources

- oil/gas field
- coal field

Bu bauxite
Cu copper
Fe iron
Ni nickel
Zn zinc
Au gold

FOCUS ON

MINING

Australia has valuable deposits of a range of mineral resources, includ iron ore, coal, bauxite and gold. Extraction usually takes place in vast, open cast mines. Raw materials are exported across the world, although its main trading partner is another country on the Pacific Rim – Japan.

AUSTRALASIA ENVIRONMENT

Many of the environmental issues faced by countries within Australasia are climate related. Arid conditions are found in over two thirds of Australia, and dry conditions and high temperatures regularly produce bush or forest fires. Increasing sea temperatures threaten coral reefs, whilst global warming may see island life threatened by rising sea levels.

Australia's Great Barrier Reef is the most extensive coral reef system on Earth, stretching more than 2 300 km off the northeast coast of Australia. It is the largest of all the World Heritage Sites.

MAP KEY

Environmental issues

existing hot desert
existing forest

desertification
deforestation
marine pollution
heavy marine pollution

~ polluted river

• poor urban air quality

☢ nuclear test site

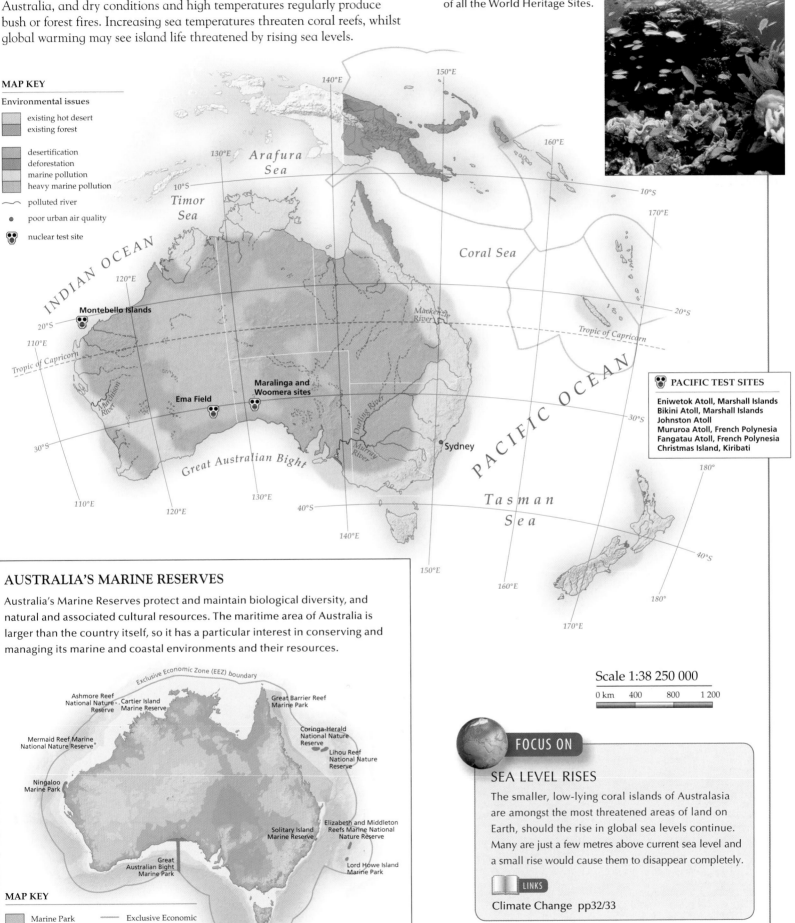

INDIAN OCEAN

Arafura Sea

Timor Sea

Montebello Islands ☢

Ema Field ☢

Maralinga and Woomera sites ☢

Coral Sea

Mackenzie River

Tropic of Capricorn

PACIFIC OCEAN

Darling River

Murray River

Sydney

Great Australian Bight

Tasman Sea

☢ **PACIFIC TEST SITES**

**Eniwetok Atoll, Marshall Islands
Bikini Atoll, Marshall Islands
Johnston Atoll
Mururoa Atoll, French Polynesia
Fangatau Atoll, French Polynesia
Christmas Island, Kiribati**

AUSTRALIA'S MARINE RESERVES

Australia's Marine Reserves protect and maintain biological diversity, and natural and associated cultural resources. The maritime area of Australia is larger than the country itself, so it has a particular interest in conserving and managing its marine and coastal environments and their resources.

Exclusive Economic Zone (EEZ) boundary

Ashmore Reef National Nature Reserve — Cartier Island Marine Reserve

Mermaid Reef Marine National Nature Reserve

Ningaloo Marine Park

Great Barrier Reef Marine Park

Coringa-Herald National Nature Reserve

Lihou Reef National Nature Reserve

Solitary Island Marine Reserve

Elizabeth and Middleton Reefs Marine National Nature Reserve

Great Australian Bight Marine Park

Lord Howe Island Marine Park

Tasmanian Seamounts Marine Reserve

MAP KEY

Marine Park — Exclusive Economic Zone boundary

Marine Reserve

Scale 1:38 250 000

0 km   400   800   1 200

FOCUS ON

SEA LEVEL RISES

The smaller, low-lying coral islands of Australasia are amongst the most threatened areas of land on Earth, should the rise in global sea levels continue. Many are just a few metres above current sea level and a small rise would cause them to disappear completely.

LINKS

Climate Change pp32/33

AUSTRALIA

Australia is the world's sixth largest country, a very flat, stable land mass. It is one of the most sparsely populated countries in the world. With over two thirds of the centre, or outback, classed as arid, most of the population live in cities around the coast.

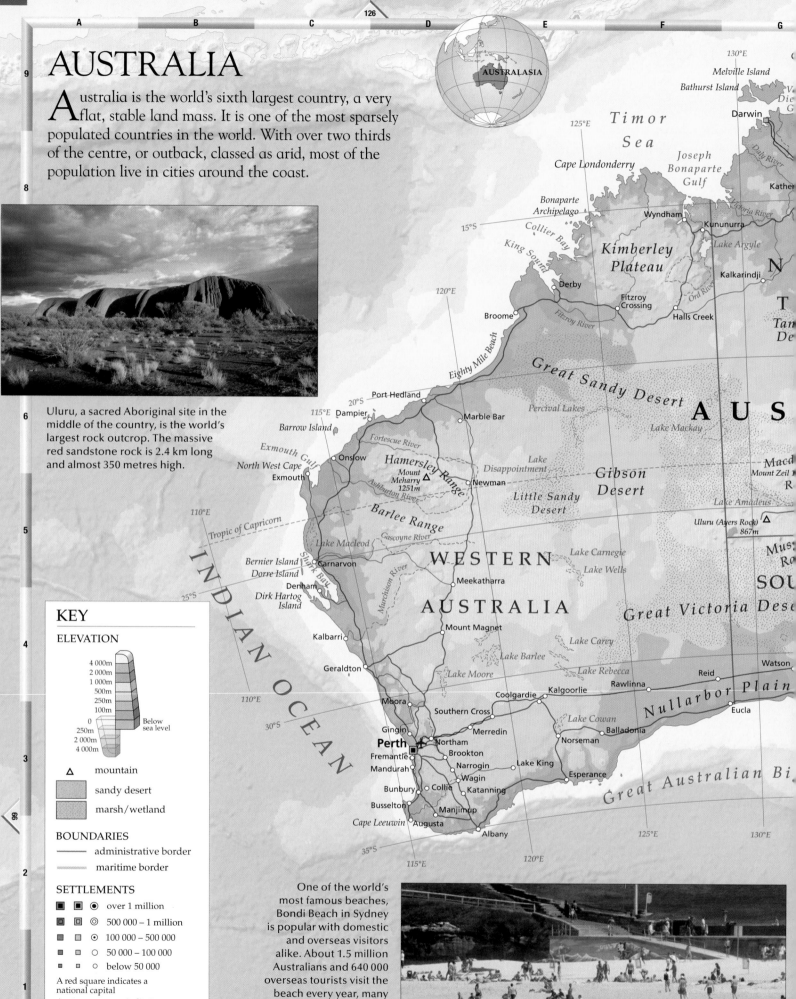

Uluru, a sacred Aboriginal site in the middle of the country, is the world's largest rock outcrop. The massive red sandstone rock is 2.4 km long and almost 350 metres high.

KEY

ELEVATION

4 000m
2 000m
1 000m
500m
250m
100m
0
250m
2 000m
4 000m

Below sea level

△ mountain

sandy desert

marsh/wetland

BOUNDARIES

administrative border

maritime border

SETTLEMENTS

■ ■ ⊙ over 1 million
▣ ▣ ◎ 500 000 – 1 million
▪ ▫ ⊙ 100 000 – 500 000
▪ ▫ ○ 50 000 – 100 000
▪ ▫ ○ below 50 000

A red square indicates a national capital

An orange square indicates a provincial or federal capital

One of the world's most famous beaches, Bondi Beach in Sydney is popular with domestic and overseas visitors alike. About 1.5 million Australians and 640 000 overseas tourists visit the beach every year, many of whom come to surf.

AUSTRALASIA

Timor Sea

Melville Island
Bathurst Island
Darwin

Cape Londonderry

Joseph Bonaparte Gulf

Daly River

Kather

Bonaparte Archipelago
Wyndham
Kununurra
Victoria River

Collier Bay
King Sound
Kimberley Plateau
Lake Argyle
Kalkarindji

Derby
Fitzroy Crossing
Halls Creek
Ord River

Broome
Fitzroy River

Tan De

Eighty Mile Beach
Great Sandy Desert
A U S

Port Hedland
Marble Bar
Percival Lakes
Lake Mackay

Dampier
Barrow Island

Lake Disappointment
Macd
Mount Zeil
R

Onslow
Fortescue River
Hamersley Range
Mount Meharry 1251m
Newman
Gibson Desert

Exmouth Gulf
North West Cape
Exmouth
Ashburton River

Little Sandy Desert
Lake Amadeus

Barlee Range
Uluru (Ayers Rock) 867m

Tropic of Capricorn
Lake Macleod
Gascoyne River

Lake Carnegie
Mus
Ro

Bernier Island
Dorre Island
Carnarvon
Shark Bay
Murchison River

WESTERN
Lake Wells
SOU

Denham
Dirk Hartog Island

Meekatharra
AUSTRALIA
Great Victoria Dese

Kalbarri
Mount Magnet
Lake Carey

Lake Barlee
Watson

Geraldton
Lake Moore
Lake Rebecca
Reid

Moora
Coolgardie
Kalgoorlie
Rawlinna
Nullarbor Plain

Southern Cross
Eucla

Gingin
Merredin
Lake Cowan
Balladonia

Perth
Northam
Norseman

Fremantle
Brookton
Lake King

Mandurah
Narrogin
Esperance
Great Australian Bi

Bunbury
Wagin

Collie
Katanning

Busselton
Manjimup

Cape Leeuwin
Augusta

Albany

INDIAN OCEAN

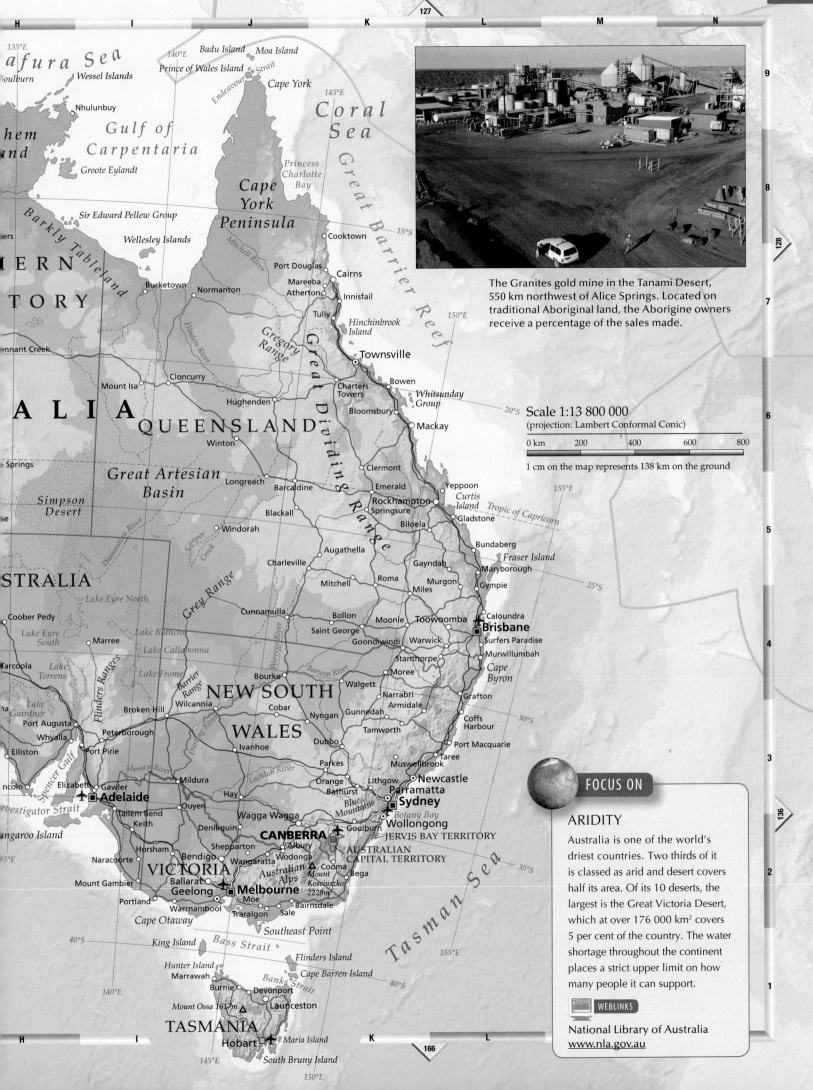

H   I   J   K   L   M   N

Arafura Sea

135°E
140°E
Wessel Islands
Nhulunbuy
Badu Island
Moa Island
Prince of Wales Island
Endeavour Strait
Cape York

Gulf of
Carpentaria

Groote Eylandt

Coral
Sea

Cape
York
Peninsula

*Princess
Charlotte
Bay*

Sir Edward Pellew Group
Wellesley Islands

Burketown
Normanton

Cooktown
Port Douglas
Mareeba
Atherton
Cairns
Innisfail
Tully

*Hinchinbrook
Island*

145°E

15°S

150°E

Barkly Tableland

Great Barrier Reef

The Granites gold mine in the Tanami Desert,
550 km northwest of Alice Springs. Located on
traditional Aboriginal land, the Aborigine owners
receive a percentage of the sales made.

NORTHERN
TERRITORY

nnant Creek

Mount Isa
Cloncurry
Hughenden

Mitchell River
Flinders River

*Gregory
Range*

Townsville

Charters
Towers
Bowen

Great Dividing Range

*Whitsunday
Group*

20°S

QUEENSLAND

AUSTRALIA

Winton

Bloomsbury
Mackay

Scale 1:13 800 000
(projection: Lambert Conformal Conic)

0 km   200   400   600   800

1 cm on the map represents 138 km on the ground

Springs

*Great Artesian
Basin*

Longreach
Barcaldine
Blackall

Clermont
Emerald
Rockhampton
Springsure

Yeppoon
*Curtis
Island*
Gladstone

155°E

Tropic of Capricorn

*Simpson
Desert*

Windorah

Charleville

Biloela

Bundaberg

Fraser Island

Cooper Creek
Diamantina River

Augathella

Gayndah
Maryborough

SOUTH
AUSTRALIA

Lake Eyre North

Mitchell
Roma
Miles
Murgon
Gympie

25°S

Coober Pedy

Grey Range

Cunnamulla

Bollon
Moonie
Toowoomba
Caloundra
Brisbane

*Lake Eyre
South*

Marree

Saint George
Warwick
Goondiwindi

Surfers Paradise
Murwillumbah

Lake Blanche

Stanthorpe

*Cape
Byron*

arcoola
*Lake
Torrens*

Lake Callabonna

Bourke

Moree

Grafton

Flinders Ranges
Lake Frome

*Barrier
Range*

Wilcannia

Walgett
Narrabri
Armidale

NEW SOUTH

Barwon River

Broken Hill

Cobar

Gunnedah
Coffs
Harbour

*Lake
Gairdner*

Peterborough

WALES

Nyngan
Tamworth

30°S

Port Augusta
Whyalla
Lincoln
Elliston

Port Pirie

Ivanhoe

Warrego River

Dubbo

Port Macquarie

Murray River

Gawler
Elizabeth
Adelaide

Mildura

Hay

Darling River

Lachlan River

Parkes
Orange
Bathurst
Lithgow
*Blue
Mountains*

Taree
Muswellbrook

Newcastle
Parramatta
Sydney

Spencer Gulf
Investigator Strait
angaroo Island

Tallem Bend
Keith

Ouyen
Deniliquin

Wagga Wagga

Goulburn

Wollongong
Botany Bay

JERVIS BAY TERRITORY

Naracoorte

Horsham
Bendigo

Shepparton
Wangaratta

CANBERRA
Albury
Wodonga
*AUSTRALIAN
CAPITAL TERRITORY*

35°S

VICTORIA

Ballarat
Geelong

Melbourne
Moe

*Australian
Alps*
Cooma
*Mount
Kosciuszko
2228m*

Bega

Mount Gambier
Portland

Warrnambool
Traralgon
Sale
Bairnsdale

Cape Otaway

Southeast Point

155°E

King Island

Bass Strait

Flinders Island

40°S

40°S

Tasman Sea

Hunter Island
Marrawah
Burnie
Devonport
Launceston

Banks Strait
Cape Barren Island

Mount Ossa 1617m

TASMANIA

Hobart
Maria Island

South Bruny Island

145°E
150°E

H   I   J   K   L   M

9
128
8
7
6
5
136
4
3
2
1

FOCUS ON

ARIDITY

Australia is one of the world's
driest countries. Two thirds of it
is classed as arid and desert covers
half its area. Of its 10 deserts, the
largest is the Great Victoria Desert,
which at over 176 000 km^2 covers
5 per cent of the country. The water
shortage throughout the continent
places a strict upper limit on how
many people it can support.

WEBLINKS

National Library of Australia
www.nla.gov.au

NEW ZEALAND

New Zealand is made up of two main islands. Most people live on the smaller North Island. A major plate boundary runs through South Island, so the country experiences a wide range of tectonic activity. Although the population of just under four million is predominantly urban, farming is an important part of the economy.

AUSTRALASIA AND OCEANIA

There are over 50 million sheep and 6 million dairy cattle in New Zealand, its temperate climate providing good pasture for both. Sheep and dairy farming generates almost a third of the country's export income.

Champagne Pool, Waiotapu, Rotorua, North Island. The pool has arsenic-rich green water bubbling with carbon dioxide. Minerals are deposited as hot water flows out of the pool.

Map labels

Cape Reinga, North Cape, Te Kao, Great Exhibition Bay, Kaitaia, Kerikeri, Paihia, Okaihau, Kaikohe, Hikurangi, Hokianga Harbour, Whangarei, Dargaville, Little Barrier Island, Ruawai, Great Barrier Island, Wellsford, Kaipara Harbour, Warkworth, Colville Channel, Helensville, Hauraki Gulf, Coromandel, Whitianga, Takapuna, Auckland, Manurewa, Papakura, Waiuku, Pukekohe, Thames, Paeroa, Mayor Island, Huntly, Katikati, Bay of Plenty, Morrinville, Tauranga, East Cape, Hamilton, Matamata, Whakatane, Cambridge, Kawerau, Opotiki, Ruatoria, Otorohanga, Lake Rotorua, Rotorua, Raukumara Range, Te Kuiti, Tokoroa, Murupara

North Island, North Taranaki Bight, Ohura, Taumarunui, Taupo, Gisborne, New Plymouth, Waitara, Lake Taupo, Lake Waikaremoana, Poverty Bay, Cape Egmont, Mount Taranaki (Mount Egmont) 2518m, Stratford, Turangi, Mount Ruapehu 2797m, Wairoa, Mahia Peninsula, Raetihi, Waiouru, Hawke Bay, Hawera, Tajhape, Hastings, Napier, Patea, Havelock North, South Taranaki Bight, Wanganui, Waipawa, Marton, Feilding, Waipukurau, Dannevirke, Palmerston North, Woodville, Levin, Pahiatua, Cape Farewell, D'Urville Island, Otaki, Masterton, Golden Bay, Paraparaumu, Porirua, Lower Hutt, WELLINGTON, Cape Palliser

Motueka, Tasman Bay, Nelson, Picton, Cook Strait, Karamea Bight, Mount Owen 1875m, Richmond, Seddonville, Blenheim, Westport, Richmond Range, Seddon, Reefton, Clarence, Springs Junction, Kaikoura, Runanga, Greymouth, Hanmer Springs, Hokitika, Lake Brunner, Otira, Arthur's Pass 920m, Waipara, Pegasus Bay, Ross, Rangiora, Kaiapoi, Whataroa, Oxford, Christchurch, Fox Glacier, Darfield, Lyttelton, Aoraki (Mount Cook) 3744m, Banks Peninsula, Southern Alps, Mayfield, Canterbury Plains, Haast, Mount Cook, Hinds, Lake Ellesmere, Geraldine, Ashburton, Fairlie, Canterbury Bight, Temuka, Timaru, Milford Sound, Mount Aspiring 3027m, Wanaka, Waimate, Studholme, Livingstone Mts, Lake Wanaka, Lake Hawea, Queenstown, Oamaru, Eyre Mts, Cromwell, Fiordland, Lake Te Anau, Lake Wakatipu, Alexandra, Hampden, Te Anau, Lumsden, Mosgiel, Dunedin, Lake Manapouri, West Cape, Gore, Milton, Winton, Mataura, Balclutha, Te Waewae Bay, Riverton, Invercargill, Tokanui, Foveaux Strait, Ruapuke Island, Codfish Island, Halfmoon Bay, Stewart Island, South West Cape

North Island, NEW ZEALAND, South Island

Tasman Sea, PACIFIC OCEAN

Scale

Scale 1:5 700 000
(projection: Lambert Conformal Conic)

0 km 50 100 150 200 250

1 cm on the map represents 57 km on the ground

KEY

ELEVATION

4 000m
2 000m
1 000m
500m
250m
100m
0
250m
2 000m
4 000m
Below sea level

SETTLEMENTS

- over 1 million
- 500 000 – 1 million
- 100 000 – 500 000
- 50 000 – 100 000
- below 50 000

A red square indicates a national capital

△ mountain   ⌓ volcano   ⋈ pass

GEOTHERMAL ENERGY

New Zealand is rich in energy resources. It has deposits of coal, oil and gas, but almost one third of its electricity production is via renewable resources. Of the total energy supply, 11 per cent comes from hydroelectric power, with 7 per cent from geothermal sources.

TOTAL PRIMARY ENERGY SUPPLY IN NEW ZEALAND (2004)

30%
11%
33%
11% 7% 8%

gas	hydro
oil	geothermal
coal	other

HOW GEOTHERMAL POWER WORKS

The availability of geothermal power is a direct result of New Zealand's physical geography. It lies on the boundary of the Pacific and Indo-Australian tectonic plates, which runs through the centre of the country from the southwest to the northeast. New Zealand itself was formed by the collision of these two plates, which are still moving towards each other today. There is a high level of tectonic activity, with many active volcanoes, especially in an arc in the middle of North Island.

It is this tectonic activity that generates heat underground, which is then used to produce geothermal energy. To do this on a commercial scale, engineers need to be able to access this heat. Suitable areas, where the heat is close to the surface, can be identified by the presence of geysers and sulphur springs.

A GEOTHERMAL POWER STATION
Geothermal systems extend under large areas of land making it very expensive to find, develop and extract geothermal energy.

6. Turbine produces power

5. Hot water goes through production well

2. Groundwater percolates downwards

3. Water temperature is raised by contact with hot rocks

4. Hot water is taken from underground well

PACIFIC OCEAN

WAIKATO
Hamilton
Cambridge
Te Awamutu
Tokoroa
Ohaaki
Mokai
Taupo
Rotokawa
Wairakei and
Mclahlan-Wairakei
Lake Taupo
Ngawha
Kakaramea 1301m
Tongariro 1968m
Mount Ruapehu 2797m
Kawerau

WAIKATO
Mount Taranaki (Mount Egmont) 2518m
Mount Ruapehu 2797m
INDO-AUSTRALIAN PLATE
ALPINE FAULT
PACIFIC PLATE

MAP KEY
— plate boundary
⌂ volcano
◆ geothermal power station

GEOTHERMAL POWER PRODUCTION

New Zealand has seven geothermal power stations. In 2000 they generated 437 MW of electricity. This is 5.5 per cent of the world total for geothermal energy, placing it ninth in the list of producers from 22 countries. Ninety per cent of this is produced in the Waikato region. Unfortunately only about ten per cent of the geothermal energy extracted is in useable form. Some of the 'waste' heat is used to heat local homes or tourist accommodation, but the rest is either re-injected underground or lost to the atmosphere.

1. Rainfall adds to groundwater

7. Excess steam is released

Geyser

Super-heated water rising to the surface

8. Excess water is put back into the ground through injection well

Heat from the Earth's interior

GEOTHERMAL POWER PRODUCTION		
Location of power station	Production in 2000 (MW)	Year built
Wairakei	162.2	1950s
Ohaaki	114.4	1988
Mclahlan-Wairakei	55	1996
Mokai	55	2000
Rotokawa	25.5	1998
Kawerau	15.9	1966
Ngawha	9.0	1997
Total	437	

Power from the Kawerau station is used directly in the local paper and pulp mill as well as for national use. In addition to generating electricity, the heat from geothermal activity is used for domestic heating in the area around Rotorua. It can also be used to dry crops. Hot springs are often used for bathing and swimming.

These pipelines in the Wairakei Valley, near Rotorua, carry super-heated steam to the Wairakei geothermal station.

EFFECTS

Although the production of geothermal power produces only very small amounts of greenhouse gases, it can have a considerable effect on the local environment. Geysers and springs associated with geothermal activity may disappear because both the water and heat they need are being used up. Land subsidence can also occur, for example an area near the Ohaaki station is sinking and may well be drowned by the nearby Waikato river. There can also be problems from associated toxic elements such as arsenic, boron and mercury.

THE BIG ISSUES

1 How does New Zealand's physical geography help provide the necessary conditions for the production of geothermal energy?

2 What efforts have been made to make geothermal power as efficient as possible?

3 Why is geothermal power not a truly 'clean' renewable energy source?

NORTH AMERICA POLITICAL

North America stretches almost the entire length of the Northern Hemisphere from the Arctic Circle in northern Canada to the border with South America near the Equator. Canada and the USA are the second and third largest countries in the world respectively, but the continent also includes Greenland and the countries of Central America and the Caribbean.

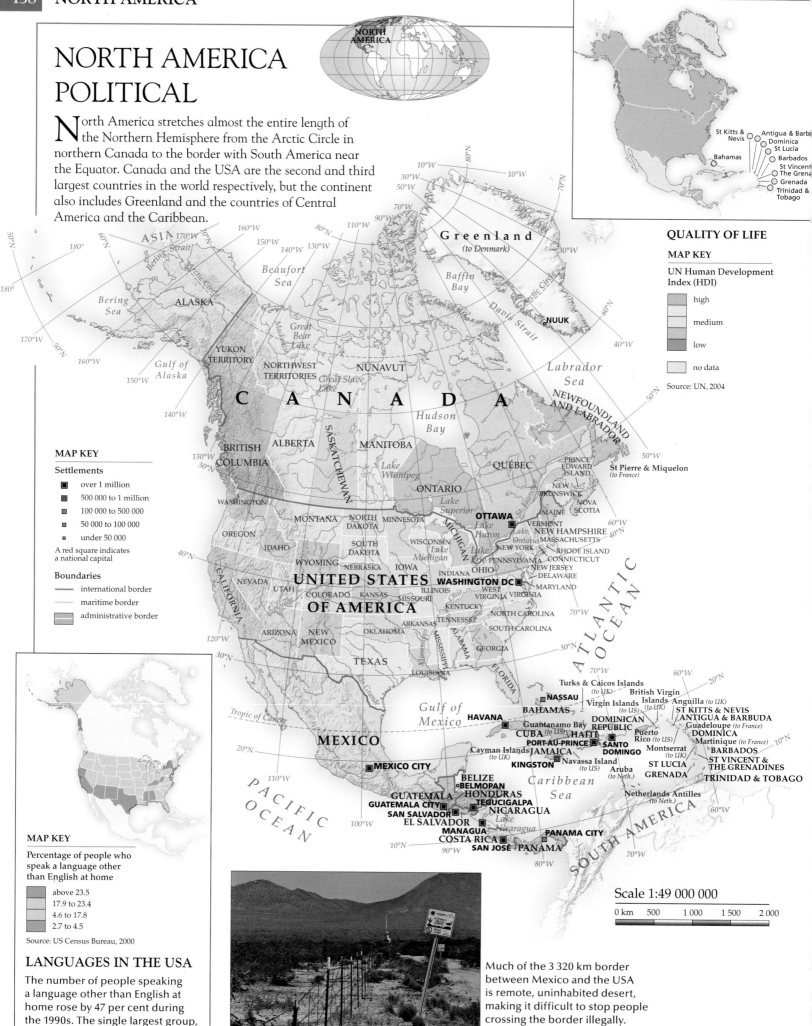

St Kitts & Nevis
Antigua & Barbuda
Dominica
St Lucia
Barbados
St Vincent & The Grenadines
Grenada
Trinidad & Tobago
Bahamas

QUALITY OF LIFE

MAP KEY

UN Human Development Index (HDI)

- high
- medium
- low
- no data

Source: UN, 2004

MAP KEY

Settlements

- over 1 million
- 500 000 to 1 million
- 100 000 to 500 000
- 50 000 to 100 000
- under 50 000

A red square indicates a national capital

Boundaries

- international border
- maritime border
- administrative border

Scale 1:49 000 000

0 km   500   1 000   1 500   2 000

MAP KEY

Percentage of people who speak a language other than English at home

- above 23.5
- 17.9 to 23.4
- 4.6 to 17.8
- 2.7 to 4.5

Source: US Census Bureau, 2000

LANGUAGES IN THE USA

The number of people speaking a language other than English at home rose by 47 per cent during the 1990s. The single largest group, accounting for 12.5 per cent of the population, is Spanish.

Much of the 3 320 km border between Mexico and the USA is remote, uninhabited desert, making it difficult to stop people crossing the border illegally.

NORTH AMERICA PHYSICAL

The world's third largest continent, North America can be divided into a number of distinctive physical regions. The major mountains of the Western Cordillera in the west give way to the Great Plains in central Canada and the USA, drained by the Mississippi River into the Gulf of Mexico.

PHYSICAL FACTFILE

① HIGHEST POINT: Mount McKinley, 6 194 metres above sea level

② LOWEST POINT: Death Valley, 86 metres below sea level

③ LARGEST LAKE: Lake Superior, 82 100 km²

— **LONGEST RIVER:** Mississippi River/Missouri River, 5 971 km

— **LENGTH OF COASTLINE:** 473 538 km

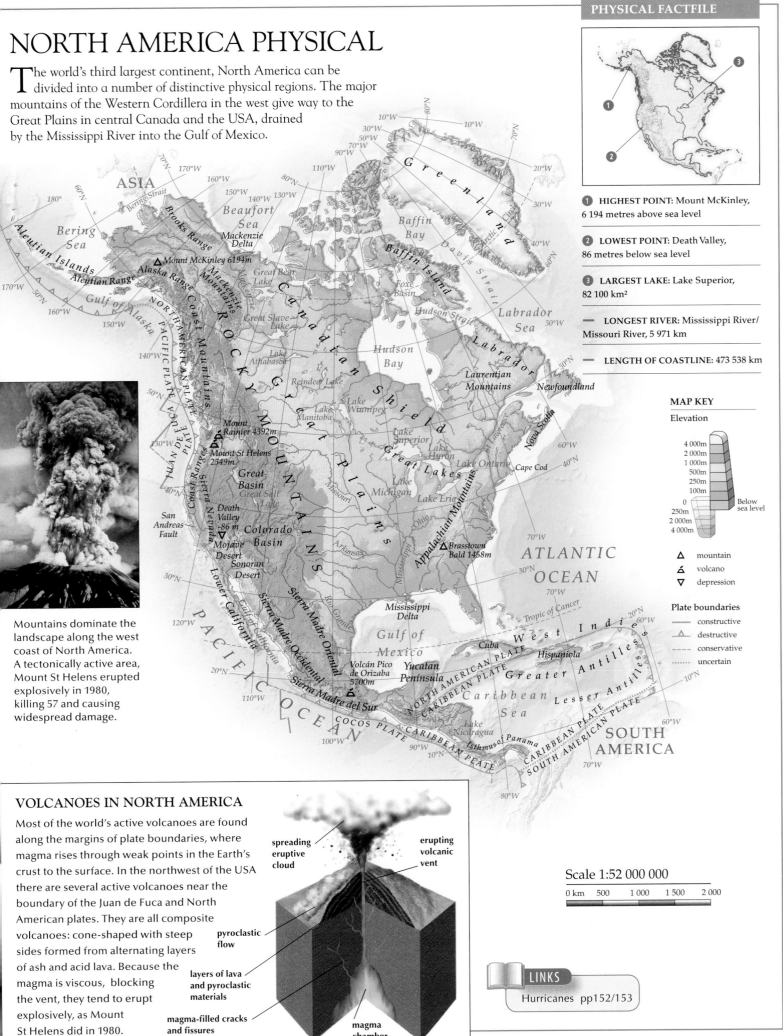

Mountains dominate the landscape along the west coast of North America. A tectonically active area, Mount St Helens erupted explosively in 1980, killing 57 and causing widespread damage.

MAP KEY

Elevation

4 000m
2 000m
1 000m
500m
250m
100m
0
250m
2 000m
4 000m
Below sea level

△ mountain
⌂ volcano
▽ depression

Plate boundaries

— constructive
△ destructive
--- conservative
···· uncertain

VOLCANOES IN NORTH AMERICA

Most of the world's active volcanoes are found along the margins of plate boundaries, where magma rises through weak points in the Earth's crust to the surface. In the northwest of the USA there are several active volcanoes near the boundary of the Juan de Fuca and North American plates. They are all composite volcanoes: cone-shaped with steep sides formed from alternating layers of ash and acid lava. Because the magma is viscous, blocking the vent, they tend to erupt explosively, as Mount St Helens did in 1980.

spreading eruptive cloud

erupting volcanic vent

pyroclastic flow

layers of lava and pyroclastic materials

magma-filled cracks and fissures

magma chamber

Scale 1:52 000 000

0 km   500   1 000   1 500   2 000

LINKS

Hurricanes pp152/153

NORTH AMERICA CLIMATE

North America experiences a wide range of climate types. In the north, Canada's (predominately) polar and sub-arctic climates contrast with the tropical and hot, humid conditions found in Central America and the Caribbean. Warm temperate conditions dominate on the USA's eastern coast, changing to cool continental inland.

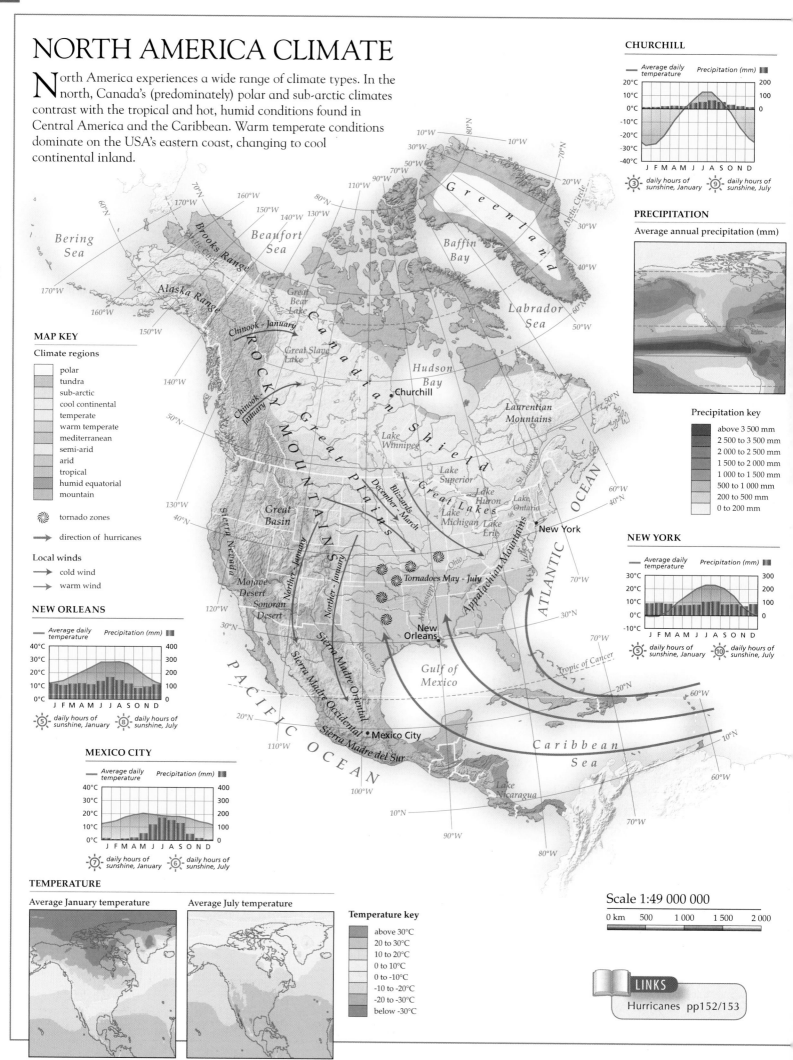

CHURCHILL

— Average daily temperature   Precipitation (mm) ▮▮

daily hours of sunshine, January ☀ 3
daily hours of sunshine, July ☀ 9

PRECIPITATION

Average annual precipitation (mm)

Precipitation key

above 3 500 mm
2 500 to 3 500 mm
2 000 to 2 500 mm
1 500 to 2 000 mm
1 000 to 1 500 mm
500 to 1 000 mm
200 to 500 mm
0 to 200 mm

NEW YORK

— Average daily temperature   Precipitation (mm) ▮▮

daily hours of sunshine, January ☀ 5
daily hours of sunshine, July ☀ 10

MAP KEY

Climate regions

polar
tundra
sub-arctic
cool continental
temperate
warm temperate
mediterranean
semi-arid
arid
tropical
humid equatorial
mountain

🌀 tornado zones

→ direction of hurricanes

Local winds

→ cold wind
→ warm wind

NEW ORLEANS

— Average daily temperature   Precipitation (mm) ▮▮

daily hours of sunshine, January ☀ 5
daily hours of sunshine, July ☀ 8

MEXICO CITY

— Average daily temperature   Precipitation (mm) ▮▮

daily hours of sunshine, January ☀ 7
daily hours of sunshine, July ☀ 6

TEMPERATURE

Average January temperature

Average July temperature

Temperature key

above 30°C
20 to 30°C
10 to 20°C
0 to 10°C
0 to -10°C
-10 to -20°C
-20 to -30°C
below -30°C

Scale 1:49 000 000

0 km   500   1 000   1 500   2 000

LINKS

Hurricanes pp152/153

NORTH AMERICA POPULATION

In terms of population distribution and density, North America is a continent of extremes. Many regions are sparsely populated or even empty, especially the far north and high mountains. However, the conurbations along the east and west coasts of the USA are amongst the most densely populated anywhere.

MAP KEY

Population density
(people per square km)

- above 200
- 100 to 200
- 50 to 100
- 10 to 50
- 1 to 10
- 0 to 1

Major settlements

- ■ ⊙ above 1 million
- ▣ ◎ 500 000 to 1 million
- ▪ ⊙ 100 000 to 500 000

A red square indicates a national capital

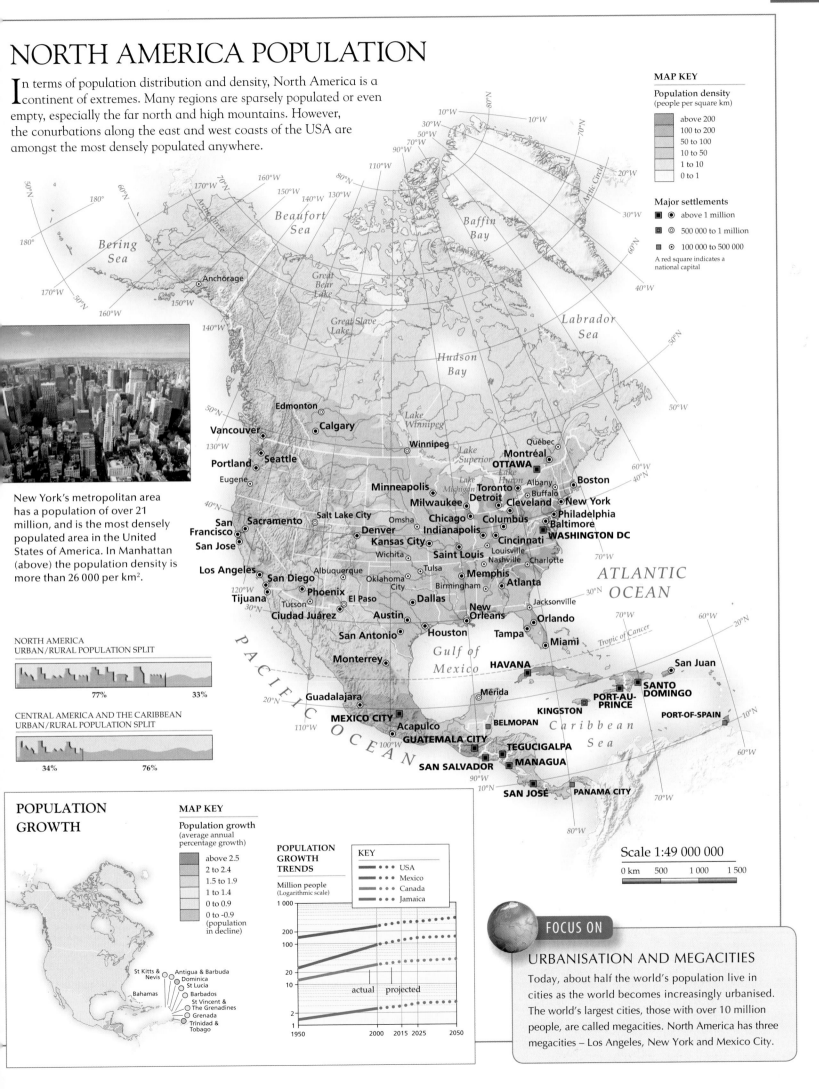

New York's metropolitan area has a population of over 21 million, and is the most densely populated area in the United States of America. In Manhattan (above) the population density is more than 26 000 per km².

NORTH AMERICA URBAN/RURAL POPULATION SPLIT

77%   33%

CENTRAL AMERICA AND THE CARIBBEAN URBAN/RURAL POPULATION SPLIT

34%   76%

Scale 1:49 000 000

0 km   500   1 000   1 500

POPULATION GROWTH

MAP KEY

Population growth
(average annual percentage growth)

- above 2.5
- 2 to 2.4
- 1.5 to 1.9
- 1 to 1.4
- 0 to 0.9
- 0 to -0.9 (population in decline)

St Kitts & Nevis
Antigua & Barbuda
Dominica
St Lucia
Barbados
St Vincent & The Grenadines
Grenada
Trinidad & Tobago
Bahamas

POPULATION GROWTH TRENDS

Million people (Logarithmic scale)

KEY
- USA
- Mexico
- Canada
- Jamaica

1 000
200
100
20
10
2
1

actual   projected

1950   2000   2015   2025   2050

FOCUS ON

URBANISATION AND MEGACITIES

Today, about half the world's population live in cities as the world becomes increasingly urbanised. The world's largest cities, those with over 10 million people, are called megacities. North America has three megacities – Los Angeles, New York and Mexico City.

NORTH AMERICA LAND USE

Much of Canada, the USA and the Caribbean is rich farmland producing a range of crops and livestock. There are, however, large parts of the continent that are desert, mountain and ice, which are largely unproductive. Both Canada and the USA have a great variety of natural resources, providing a base for industrial activity and economic development.

A tractor spraying GM cotton with herbicide on a farm in Arkansas, USA. This type of GM cotton is resistant to herbicides, so weeds can be killed without damaging the crop. The USA grows 70 per cent of the world's GM crops.

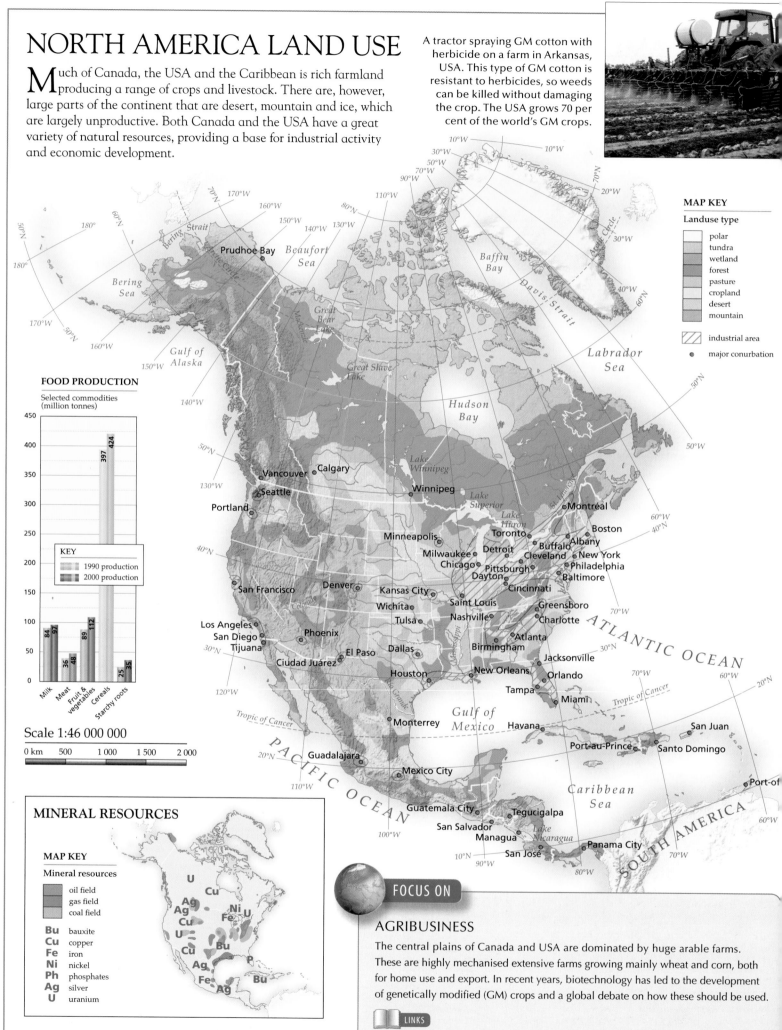

FOOD PRODUCTION

Selected commodities (million tonnes)

KEY
- 1990 production
- 2000 production

Commodity	1990	2000
Milk	84	97
Meat	36	48
Fruit & vegetables	89	112
Cereals	397	424
Starchy roots	25	35

Scale 1:46 000 000

0 km 500 1 000 1 500 2 000

MAP KEY

Landuse type
- polar
- tundra
- wetland
- forest
- pasture
- cropland
- desert
- mountain

industrial area

major conurbation

MINERAL RESOURCES

MAP KEY

Mineral resources
- oil field
- gas field
- coal field

Bu	bauxite
Cu	copper
Fe	iron
Ni	nickel
Ph	phosphates
Ag	silver
U	uranium

FOCUS ON

AGRIBUSINESS

The central plains of Canada and USA are dominated by huge arable farms. These are highly mechanised extensive farms growing mainly wheat and corn, both for home use and export. In recent years, biotechnology has led to the development of genetically modified (GM) crops and a global debate on how these should be used.

LINKS

Genetically Modified Crops pp148/149

NORTH AMERICA ENVIRONMENT

North America has a number of fragile, endangered ecosystems – notably the Arctic wilderness and dwindling rainforests of Central America. It suffers from a wide variety of environmental problems, with industry and transport the major contributors to atmospheric pollution. Oil spills have also caused damage both on land and sea.

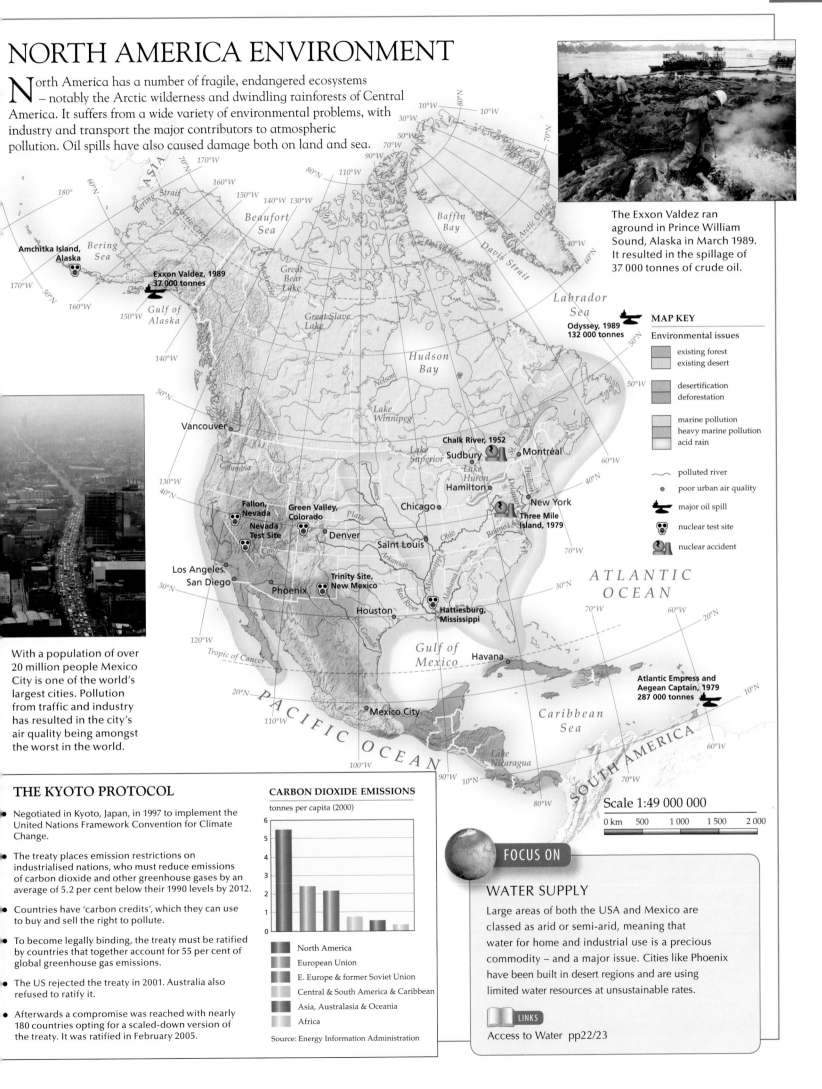

The Exxon Valdez ran aground in Prince William Sound, Alaska in March 1989. It resulted in the spillage of 37 000 tonnes of crude oil.

With a population of over 20 million people Mexico City is one of the world's largest cities. Pollution from traffic and industry has resulted in the city's air quality being amongst the worst in the world.

MAP KEY

Environmental issues
- existing forest
- existing desert
- desertification
- deforestation
- marine pollution
- heavy marine pollution
- acid rain
- ~~~ polluted river
- • poor urban air quality
- ⚓ major oil spill
- ☠ nuclear test site
- ☢ nuclear accident

Scale 1:49 000 000

0 km   500   1 000   1 500   2 000

THE KYOTO PROTOCOL

- Negotiated in Kyoto, Japan, in 1997 to implement the United Nations Framework Convention for Climate Change.

- The treaty places emission restrictions on industrialised nations, who must reduce emissions of carbon dioxide and other greenhouse gases by an average of 5.2 per cent below their 1990 levels by 2012.

- Countries have 'carbon credits', which they can use to buy and sell the right to pollute.

- To become legally binding, the treaty must be ratified by countries that together account for 55 per cent of global greenhouse gas emissions.

- The US rejected the treaty in 2001. Australia also refused to ratify it.

- Afterwards a compromise was reached with nearly 180 countries opting for a scaled-down version of the treaty. It was ratified in February 2005.

CARBON DIOXIDE EMISSIONS

tonnes per capita (2000)

- North America
- European Union
- E. Europe & former Soviet Union
- Central & South America & Caribbean
- Asia, Australasia & Oceania
- Africa

Source: Energy Information Administration

FOCUS ON

WATER SUPPLY

Large areas of both the USA and Mexico are classed as arid or semi-arid, meaning that water for home and industrial use is a precious commodity – and a major issue. Cities like Phoenix have been built in desert regions and are using limited water resources at unsustainable rates.

LINKS

Access to Water pp22/23

CANADA

The second largest country in the world, much of Canada's Arctic north is uninhabited, with most of the population concentrated along the southern border with the USA, especially around the Great Lakes.

NORTH AMERICA

One of the world's most famous – and visited – tourist sites, Niagara Falls straddles the border between Canada and the USA. Horseshoe Falls, Ontario, is over 750 metres wide and drops down vertically 56 metres.

KEY

ELEVATION

4 000m
2 000m
1 000m
500m
250m
100m
0
250m
2 000m
4 000m

Below sea level

△ mountain

marsh/wetland

BOUNDARIES

——— international border

——— maritime border

——— administrative border

SETTLEMENTS

■ ■ ⊙ over 1 million

▣ ▣ ◎ 500 000 – 1 million

▪ ▪ ⊙ 100 000 – 500 000

▪ ▫ ○ 50 000 – 100 000

▪ ▫ ○ below 50 000

A red square indicates a national capital

An orange square indicates a provincial or federal capital

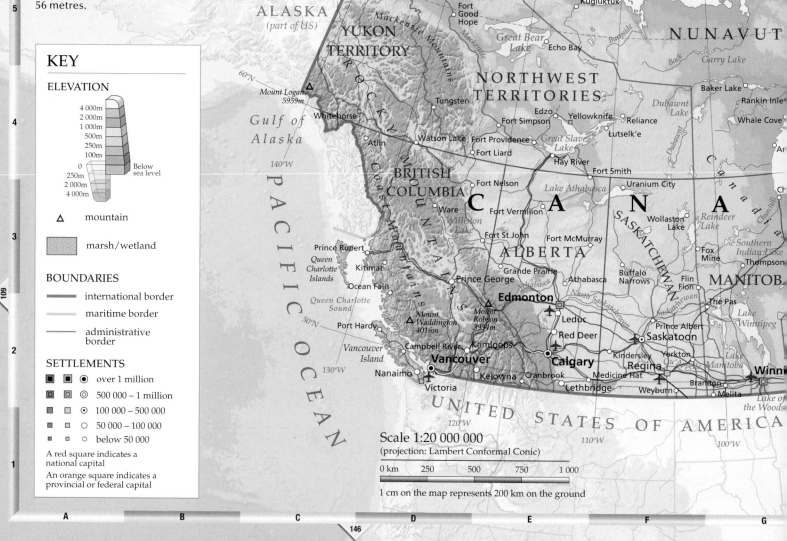

ARCTIC OCEAN

Beaufort Sea

Queen Elizabeth Island

Axel Heiberg Island

Ellef Ringnes Island

Amund Ringnes Island

Isachsen

Prince Patrick Island

Mould Bay

Bathurst Island

Cornwallis Island

Devon

Melville Island

Viscount Melville Sound

Resolute

Banks Island

Prince of Wales Island

Somerset Island

Boothia Peninsula

Sachs Harbour

McClintock Channel

Gulf of

Amundsen Gulf

Holman

Victoria Island

King William Island

Pelly Ba

Tuktoyaktuk

Cambridge Bay

Gjoa Haven

Aklavik

Inuvik

Paulatuk

Kugluktuk

Fort McPherson

ALASKA (part of US)

Fort Good Hope

NUNAVUT

YUKON TERRITORY

Mackenzie Mountains

Great Bear Lake

Echo Bay

Back

Garry Lake

Mount Logan 5959m

NORTHWEST TERRITORIES

Baker Lake

Rankin Inle

Tungsten

Edzo

Yellowknife

Reliance

Dubawnt Lake

Whale Cove

Whitehorse

Fort Simpson

Lutselk'e

Gulf of Alaska

Atlin

Watson Lake

Fort Providence

Great Slave Lake

Ar

Fort Liard

Dubawnt

Hay River

Fort Smith

BRITISH COLUMBIA

Fort Nelson

Uranium City

Canada

PACIFIC OCEAN

Ware

C A N A D A

Lake Athabasca

Fort Vermilion

Wollaston Lake

Reindeer Lake

SASKATCHEWAN

Williston Lake

Fort St. John

Fort McMurray

Fox Mine

Southern Indian Lake

Prince Rupert

Queen Charlotte Islands

Kitimat

ALBERTA

Grande Prairie

Athabasca

Buffalo Narrows

Thompson

Prince George

Flin Flon

MANITOBA

Ocean Falls

Athabasca

The Pas

Queen Charlotte Sound

Edmonton

North Saskatchewan

Port Hardy

Mount Waddington 4016m

Mount Robson 3954m

Leduc

Red Deer

Prince Albert

Saskatoon

Lake Winnipeg

Campbell River

Kamloops

Kindersley

Yorkton

Lake Manitob

Vancouver Island

Vancouver

Calgary

Regina

Winni

Nanaimo

Kelowna

Cranbrook

Medicine Hat

Brandon

Victoria

Lethbridge

Weyburn

Melita

Lake of the Woods

UNITED STATES OF AMERICA

Scale 1:20 000 000
(projection: Lambert Conformal Conic)

0 km   250   500   750   1 000

1 cm on the map represents 200 km on the ground

Greenland
(to Denmark)

Gunnbjørn
Fjeld
3700m △

Ammassalik

*Baffin
Bay*

Davis Strait

ffin Island

Kong Christian IX Land

Kong Frederik VIII Land

Knud Rasmussen Land

NUUK

Qaqortoq

olik

*Prince
Charles
Island*

*Nettilling
Lake*

Cumberland Sound

*Hall
Peninsula*

*Foxe
Basin*

*Amadjuak
Lake*

Iqaluit

*Meta Incognita
Peninsula*

*Resolution
Island*

Coral Harbour

*Charles
Island*

Hudson Strait

Ivujivik

*Akpatok
Island*

Button Islands

Labrador Sea

Kuujjuaq

Nain

Hopedale

Makkovik

Cape Harrison

Cartwright

Labrador

NEWFOUNDLAND & LABRADOR

St.Anthony

Gander

Grand
Falls

St. Johns

Corner Brook

Newfoundland

Cape Race

Channel-Port
aux Basques

St Pierre and
Miquelon
(to France)

QUÉBEC

*James
Bay*

Laurentian Mountains

Schefferville

*Smallwood
Reservoir*

Labrador
City

*Réservoir de
Caniapiscau*

Havre-St-Pierre

Île d'Anticosti

*Gulf of
St. Lawrence*

Sept-Îles

Gaspé

Sydney

Glace Bay

Cape Breton Island

Cabot Strait

Baie-Comeau

Rimouski

Bathurst

PRINCE
EDWARD
ISLAND

Charlottetown

Sable Island

Moncton

Amherst

Dartmouth

ONTARIO

Fort Albany

Moosonee

Chibougamau

Jonquière

Chicoutimi

Rivière-du-Loup

Fredericton

NOVA SCOTIA

Halifax

Hearst

Cochrane

Amos

Charlesbourg

Québec

St-Georges

St.John

Liverpool

Yarmouth

Bay of Fundy

NEW
BRUNSWICK

Kapuskasing

Val-d'Or

La Tuque

Trois-Rivières

Sherbrooke

Kirkland Lake

Timmins

Laval

Montréal

OTTAWA

Gatineau

Nepéan

Sudbury

North Bay

Peterborough

Oshawa

Lake Ontario

Toronto

St. Catharines

Niagara Falls

Hamilton

London

Windsor

Lake Erie

ATLANTIC OCEAN

In 1995 the Canadian government agreed to negotiate with native peoples over issues of self-governance. The Nunavut region, covering a fifth of Canada's total land area, became the first self-governing native region, holding its first election in 1999.

Toronto, Ontario, is Canada's largest city and economic capital. It is also one of the most ethnically diverse cities in the world with more than 55 languages recorded as being spoken in the 2001 census.

FOCUS ON

ENERGY

Canada has rich reserves of oil, gas and coal and is a major exporter of fossil fuels. However, with regular rainfall and a choice of suitable sites, it produces 60 per cent of its own electricity via cleaner, renewable, hydroelectric power.

LINKS

Geothermal Energy pp136/137

THE UNITED STATES OF AMERICA

Of the USA's 50 states, 2 are separated from the mainland area – Alaska, northwest of Canada and the islands of Hawai'i in the Pacific Ocean. Today the USA is the world's only real superpower, with a strong industrial economy and its people generally enjoying a high quality of life.

ALASKA

Scale 1:38 000 000

0 km   500   1 000

Maroon Lake in the Rocky Mountains National Park. The Rockies run north to south in the west of the USA. They are relatively young fold mountains formed by the movement of tectonic plates along the Pacific coast.

KEY

ELEVATION

4 000m
2 000m
1 000m
500m
250m
100m
0
250m
2 000m
4 000m
Below sea level

△ mountain
⩟ volcano
marsh/wetland

BOUNDARIES

—— international border
—— maritime border
—— administrative border

SETTLEMENTS

■ ■ ⊙ over 1 million
▣ ▢ ◎ 500 000 – 1 million
▪ ⊡ 100 000 – 500 000
▪ ▫ 50 000 – 100 000
▪ ▫ below 50 000

A red square indicates a national capital

An orange square indicates a provincial or federal capital

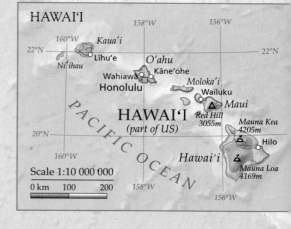

HAWAI'I

HAWAI'I (part of US)

Scale 1:10 000 000

0 km   100   200

Oil is a crucial commodity for the USA's economy. Alaska has large reserves of oil, which are transported 1 285 km from Northern Alaska to the port of Valdez via the Trans-Alaskan pipeline.

FOCUS ON

RESOURCE CONSUMPTION

The USA has about five per cent of the population – but uses over a quarter of the world's energy. In doing so it produces almost a quarter of the world's total emissions of carbon dioxide. The average water consumption of an American is 600 litres per day, compared to 30 litres for someone living in Africa.

LINKS

Climate Change pp32/33
UN Framework Convention on Climate Change
www.unfccc.int

Scale 1:13 000 000
(projection: Lambert Conformal Conic)

0 km   200   400   600   800

1 cm on the map represents 130 km on the ground

GENETICALLY MODIFIED CROPS

The first genetically modified (GM) crops were grown and sold in the early 1990s. However, growing 'improved' varieties of plants (and animals) has been happening since farming began. Farmers, then scientists and researchers, have tried to produce 'better' plants to improve flavour, size and, very importantly, yield. Traditionally this has been by cross-pollinating different species of the same plant. However, such work has been very 'hit and miss' in terms of producing a successful new plant.

USEFUL DEFINITIONS	
Genetic Modification (GM)	Altering the genetic composition of cells or organisms by introducing 'foreign' genes. (Genetically modified or GM crops are also known as transgenic crops.)
Genetically modified food	Food product which has some genetically modified organism(s) as an ingredient
DNA	Deoxyribonucleic acid – the genetic base of cells and organisms
Gene	A specific sequence of DNA code carrying inherited characteristics
Biotechnology	The application of technology to modify the products or processes of living systems

THE SCIENCE OF GM CROPS

In the 1950s scientists discovered that DNA carried the genetic detail of all living things. By the 1980s, individual genes with specific characteristics could be identified, located and transferred. From this, biotechnology companies began to research and develop GM crops.

GM crops are designed to be resistant to competition or destruction by animals, insects and other plants. Genes controlling resistance are bred into the new GM crop, but these genes can come from a wide range of different sources – not all from other plants. A frost-resistant GM tomato has been produced by taking the 'anti-freeze' gene from a cold-water fish.

Some GM crops are designed to be resistant to herbicides, so weeds can be killed with general spray that won't kill or damage the growing crop. 'BT corn' and 'BT cotton' are examples of GM crops which produce toxins in their pollen that kill pests trying to feed off it, reducing the need for pesticides.

COUNTRIES GROWING GM CROPS

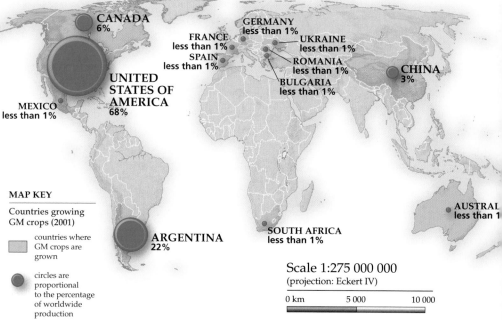

CANADA 6%

GERMANY less than 1%

FRANCE less than 1%

SPAIN less than 1%

UKRAINE less than 1%

ROMANIA less than 1%

BULGARIA less than 1%

CHINA 3%

UNITED STATES OF AMERICA 68%

MEXICO less than 1%

AUSTRAL less than 1

ARGENTINA 22%

SOUTH AFRICA less than 1%

MAP KEY

Countries growing GM crops (2001)

▢ countries where GM crops are grown

⬤ circles are proportional to the percentage of worldwide production

Scale 1:275 000 000
(projection: Eckert IV)

0 km   5 000   10 000

This maize crop has been genetically modified to resist herbicides. Herbicide has been used to kill pigweed, leaving the maize unaffected.

WHERE GM CROPS ARE GROWN

By 2004, 40 countries were growing GM crops (including non-food crops like cotton) commercially or under trial conditions. The majority of crops grown are soybeans, oilseed rape and maize (corn), to be used for human consumption and animal fodder. There has been a twenty-fold increase in the amount of land used to grow GM crops since they were first grown in 1994.

WORLD LAND USE – GM CROPS

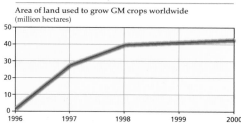

Area of land used to grow GM crops worldwide (million hectares)

THE GM DEBATE

The growth and use of GM crops has provoked widespread debate. Some of the benefits and disadvantages claimed by those on either side of the debate include:

For: GM crops will:
- give higher crop yields;
- provide cheaper food;
- be of a better quality than non-GM crops;
- need fewer herbicides and pesticides;
- could be a major factor in feeding the world's hungry.

Against: GM crops will:
- be too expensive for poorer LEDCs;
- contaminate ordinary crops;
- create 'superweeds' resistant to pesticides;
- affect human health e.g. allergic reactions to imported genes;
- adversely affect biodiversity.

GM CROPS IN THE USA

Unlike the fierce debate underway in the European Union and other countries there has been little real opposition to GM crops in the USA. This may be partly due to the fact that GM foods have been on sale for over ten years and there has been no measured effect on human health.

This farm in Arkansas grows 'Roundup Ready' soya, which is resistant to the 'Roundup' herbicide being sprayed on it.

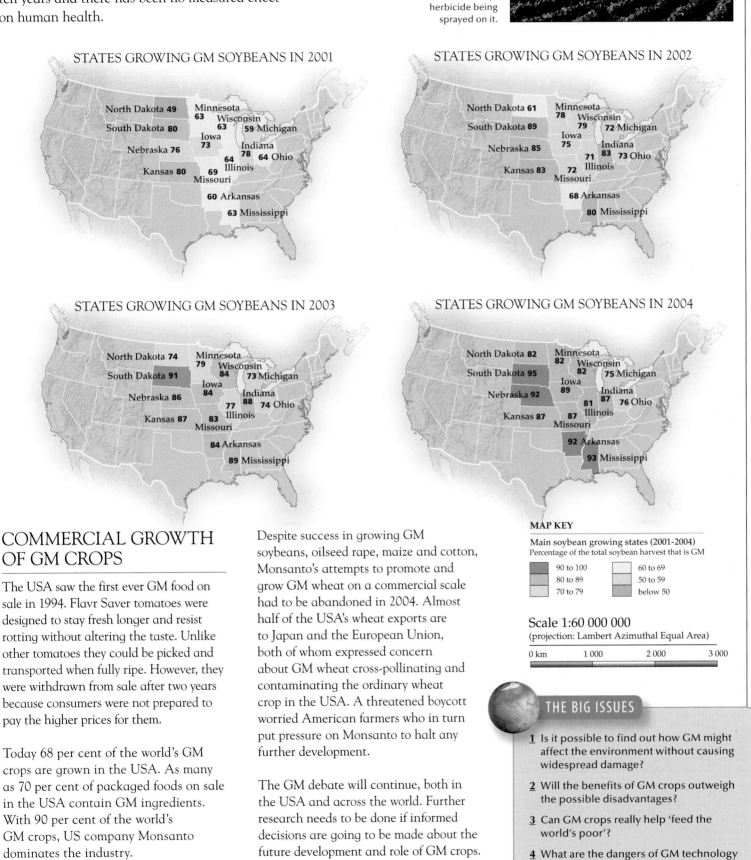

STATES GROWING GM SOYBEANS IN 2001

North Dakota **49**
South Dakota **80**
Nebraska **76**
Kansas **80**
Minnesota **63**
Wisconsin **63**
59 Michigan
Iowa **73**
Indiana **78**
64 Ohio
64 Illinois
Missouri **69**
60 Arkansas
63 Mississippi

STATES GROWING GM SOYBEANS IN 2002

North Dakota **61**
South Dakota **89**
Nebraska **85**
Kansas **83**
Minnesota **78**
Wisconsin **79**
72 Michigan
Iowa **75**
Indiana **83**
71 **73** Ohio
Illinois **72**
Missouri
68 Arkansas
80 Mississippi

STATES GROWING GM SOYBEANS IN 2003

North Dakota **74**
South Dakota **91**
Nebraska **86**
Kansas **87**
Minnesota **79**
Wisconsin **84**
73 Michigan
Iowa **84**
Indiana **88**
77 **74** Ohio
83 Illinois
Missouri
84 Arkansas
89 Mississippi

STATES GROWING GM SOYBEANS IN 2004

North Dakota **82**
South Dakota **95**
Nebraska **92**
Kansas **87**
Minnesota **82**
Wisconsin **82**
75 Michigan
Iowa **89**
Indiana **87**
81 **76** Ohio
Illinois **87**
Missouri
92 Arkansas
93 Mississippi

COMMERCIAL GROWTH OF GM CROPS

The USA saw the first ever GM food on sale in 1994. Flavr Saver tomatoes were designed to stay fresh longer and resist rotting without altering the taste. Unlike other tomatoes they could be picked and transported when fully ripe. However, they were withdrawn from sale after two years because consumers were not prepared to pay the higher prices for them.

Today 68 per cent of the world's GM crops are grown in the USA. As many as 70 per cent of packaged foods on sale in the USA contain GM ingredients. With 90 per cent of the world's GM crops, US company Monsanto dominates the industry.

Despite success in growing GM soybeans, oilseed rape, maize and cotton, Monsanto's attempts to promote and grow GM wheat on a commercial scale had to be abandoned in 2004. Almost half of the USA's wheat exports are to Japan and the European Union, both of whom expressed concern about GM wheat cross-pollinating and contaminating the ordinary wheat crop in the USA. A threatened boycott worried American farmers who in turn put pressure on Monsanto to halt any further development.

The GM debate will continue, both in the USA and across the world. Further research needs to be done if informed decisions are going to be made about the future development and role of GM crops.

MAP KEY

Main soybean growing states (2001-2004)
Percentage of the total soybean harvest that is GM

90 to 100	60 to 69
80 to 89	50 to 59
70 to 79	below 50

Scale 1:60 000 000
(projection: Lambert Azimuthal Equal Area)

0 km   1 000   2 000   3 000

THE BIG ISSUES

1 Is it possible to find out how GM might affect the environment without causing widespread damage?

2 Will the benefits of GM crops outweigh the possible disadvantages?

3 Can GM crops really help 'feed the world's poor'?

4 What are the dangers of GM technology being controlled by a few powerful Transnational companies?

CENTRAL AMERICA AND THE CARIBBEAN

The predominantly mountainous countries of Central America link North and South America via a relatively long, narrow strip of land within the Tropics. To the east lie the islands of the Caribbean. The region is tectonically very active, with a constant threat of earthquakes or volcanic eruptions.

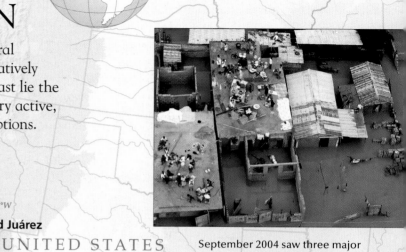

September 2004 saw three major hurricanes and Tropical Storm Jeanne ravage the Caribbean. Floods following Jeanne killed more than 1 500 people in Haiti and left at least 200 000 homeless. The effects of the torrential rain were considered to have been made far worse because of extensive deforestation in Haiti.

Scale 1:15 000 000
(projection: Lambert Conformal Conic)

0 km	200	400	600	800

1 cm on the map represents 150 km on the ground

KEY

ELEVATION

4 000m
2 000m
1 000m
500m
250m
100m
0
250m — Below sea level
2 000m
4 000m

△ mountain
▲ volcano
▨ marsh/wetland

BOUNDARIES
━━━ international border
━━━ maritime border

SETTLEMENTS
■ ⊙ over 1 million
▣ ◎ 500 000 – 1 million
▣ ⊙ 100 000 – 500 000
▪ ○ 50 000 – 100 000
▫ ○ below 50 000

A red square indicates a national capital

Volcanic activity began in the Soufrière Hills in 1995, resulting in ash falling on Montserrat's capital Plymouth. Two years later on 25 June 1997, a pyroclastic surge swept through the area. About 12 000 people left the island and although some are returning much of the area is still uninhabitable.

The islands of the Caribbean are popular tourist destinations, offering hot, sunny weather, sandy beaches and clear seas. St Lucia, although a relatively small island, is a common stopping place for cruise liners.

FOCUS ON

NATURAL HAZARDS – HURRICANES

Up to a dozen hurricanes form each year in the western Atlantic, many finding landfall in the Caribbean or Central America. Even if casualties are low, it often takes many years to recover from the damage done to buildings, industry and farmland in what are generally quite poor countries.

LINKS

Hurricanes pp152/153

HURRICANES

Tropical storms or cyclones are large areas of low air pressure that bring torrential rain and very strong winds to tropical regions. In the North Atlantic they are called hurricanes once wind speeds exceed 120 kph. Up to 20 tropical storms may reach hurricane strength during the hurricane season, which runs from June to October.

THE SAFFIR-SIMPSON CLASSIFICATION				
Category	Wind speed (kph)	Pressure (mb)	Storm surge (m)	Damage
1	120–153	> 980	1.0–1.7	Minor: trees; mobile homes
2	154–177	979–965	1.8–2.6	Moderate: roof; windows; small boats ripped from moorings; flooding
3	178–209	964–945	2.7–3.8	Extensive: structural damage to buildings; flooding on land less than 1.7 metres above sea level to 10 km inland
4	210–249	944–920	3.9–5.6	Extreme: destroys buildings; beaches; flooding on land less than 3.3 metres above sea level to 5 km inland
5	> 250	< 920	over 5.7	Catastrophic: destruction on land less than 5 metres above sea level; mass evacuation needed

STORM SURGE (IN METRES)

Typical storm surge height (m) / Wind speed in kph

IMPACT OF HURRICANES

Tropical storms or hurricanes last an average of ten days, but the biggest can last for up to four weeks. They cause damage in three main ways: winds, storm surges (in coastal areas) and floods. Winds can destroy crops, buildings, power and communications infrastructure. Storm surges along coastal areas can be devastating. Torrential rainfall can last for several hours or days, causing widespread flooding inland. This can trigger landslides and mudslides.

Although hurricanes will inevitably cause damage, how well an area or a country recovers is usually dependent on how wealthy it is. The USA uses satellites to track hurricanes and issue warnings. Properties are boarded up and areas evacuated in advance of approaching storms. Government aid is usually made available to help clear up the damage, rebuild homes and restore business and economic activity after the event. Countries in the Caribbean and Central America (predominately LEDCs) can be devastated by the effects of a hurricane. With buildings, infrastructure and farmland ruined and little money available for rebuilding, it can take years for the people and economy to recover. Even then, an LEDC may often be dependent on international aid both for short- and mid-term help and long-term rebuilding.

HOW HURRICANES DEVELOP
North Atlantic hurricanes begin as tropical depressions and storms in warm waters (over 27 degrees Celsius) off the West African coast.

As the water heats the air above it, warm, moist air starts to spiral rapidly upwards, turning and spinning inwards

This creates an area of very low pressure in the centre, called the 'eye'

Wind speeds can reach over 250 kph around the edges of the central eye

The eye itself is calm

The rising air quickly cools down, forming thick, dense, vertical cumulo-nimbus clouds that bring heavy rainfall

Tropical storms need warm water for energy. Once they reach land they quickly lose power

These masses of rotating low pressure can be over 100 km wide and travel at up to 50 kph

KEEPING TRACK

To help identify and track hurricanes, especially as there may be more than one happening at a time, meteorologists use alternate male and female names from agreed alphabetical lists, rotated over a six year cycle. If a hurricane has been particularly destructive its name is retired and replaced.

TRACKING HURRICANE MITCH

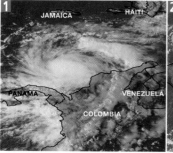

21.10.1998 Mitch began as a tropical depression south of the Caribbean. The next day it was upgraded to a tropical storm, then a hurricane as wind speeds increased.

26.10.1998 Mitch was now a category 5 hurricane with speeds of over 250 kph, moving west across the Caribbean.

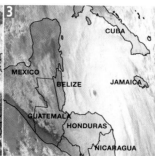

27.10.1998 Meteorologists tracked Mitch via satellite, but could not predict which direction it would take or where it would make landfall.

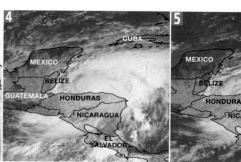

28.10.1998 Wind speeds, although still high, had started to fall as it headed towards Honduras. Unfortunately, the entire system was moving very slowly.

29.10.1998 As a resu[lt] 1 800 cm of rain fell [in] just three days over Honduras, Nicaragu[a] and El Salvador.

HURRICANE MITCH

Central America was hit by its most destructive hurricane for 200 years in October 1998. Over three million people were directly affected by Hurricane Mitch across Central America. Mudslides triggered by torrential rain destroyed villages, schools, health facilities, power supplies, roads, bridges and farmland. The final death toll was estimated at 20 000, but many bodies were never recovered.

Hurricane Mitch was the...
second longest-lasting category 5 hurricane (33 hours)
third longest continuous period of high winds (15 hours)
fourth strongest hurricane (winds of 249 kph)
fourth lowest air pressure ever measured (905 mb)

Onlookers stand by the Choluteca river in Honduras as it is turned into a raging torrent after days of heavy rain brought by Hurricane Mitch.

The aftermath of Hurricane Mitch in Tegucigalpa, the capital of Honduras. Mudslides triggered by torrential rain killed thousands of people and destroyed homes and possessions.

MEXICO
0 dead/missing
thousands evacuated

BELIZE
0 dead/missing
10 000 evacuated

HONDURAS
14 000 dead/missing
2 million homeless

GUATEMALA
200 dead/missing
80 000 evacuated

EL SALVADOR
400 dead/missing
50 000 homeless

NICARAGUA
3 000 dead/missing
750 000 homeless

COSTA RICA
7 dead/missing
3 000 homeless

PANAMA

MAP KEY

Storm strength
(Saffir-Simpson classification)

- category five
- category four
- category three
- category two
- category one
- tropical storm
- tropical depression

— international border

1 numbers correspond to satellite images below

Scale 1:18 750 000
(projection: Lambert Conformal Conic)

0 km   200   400   600   800

EFFECTS

After Mitch hit Central America, short-term emergency aid – medicines, food, water and shelter – came from governments and non-government organisations (NGOs) across the world. However, its effects are still being felt over five years later.

The overall cost of the destruction caused by Mitch has been estimated at £7 billion. Most of the countries in Central America are LEDCs, with economies based primarily on farming. The money needed to repair the damage is simply not available from within the region.

Funding needed to rebuild homes and infrastructure has come mainly from international aid agencies or organisations like the World Bank. Much of this has been organised via the Central America Emergency Trust Fund. Honduras is likely to take at least 20 years to repair the damage, which made 20 per cent of its five million population homeless.

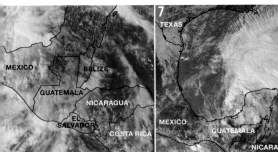

02.11.1998 Mitch turned northeast across the Gulf of Mexico, regaining strength.

03.11.1998 Mitch reaches the coast of Florida in the USA before dying out.

All satellite images supplied by the National Oceanic and Atmospheric Association (NOAA)

THE BIG ISSUES

1 Hurricanes can not be stopped – but what can be done to lessen damage and reduce the number of deaths?

2 How can the long-term impact of hurricanes on LEDCs be reduced?

3 Research suggests that the number and intensity of hurricanes could increase as ocean temperatures rise. How might this affect the Caribbean?

4 Why do people live in areas at high risk of hurricane damage? Should they be discouraged from doing so?

SOUTH AMERICA POLITICAL

South America is made up of 12 countries and is the fourth largest continent. It stretches from 12 degrees north of the Equator to the island of Cape Horn 56 degrees south. Over half the total land area is found in Brazil.

There is a large gap between the wealthiest and poorest people in many countries in South America, with large variations in living standards in cities such as Buenos Aires (above).

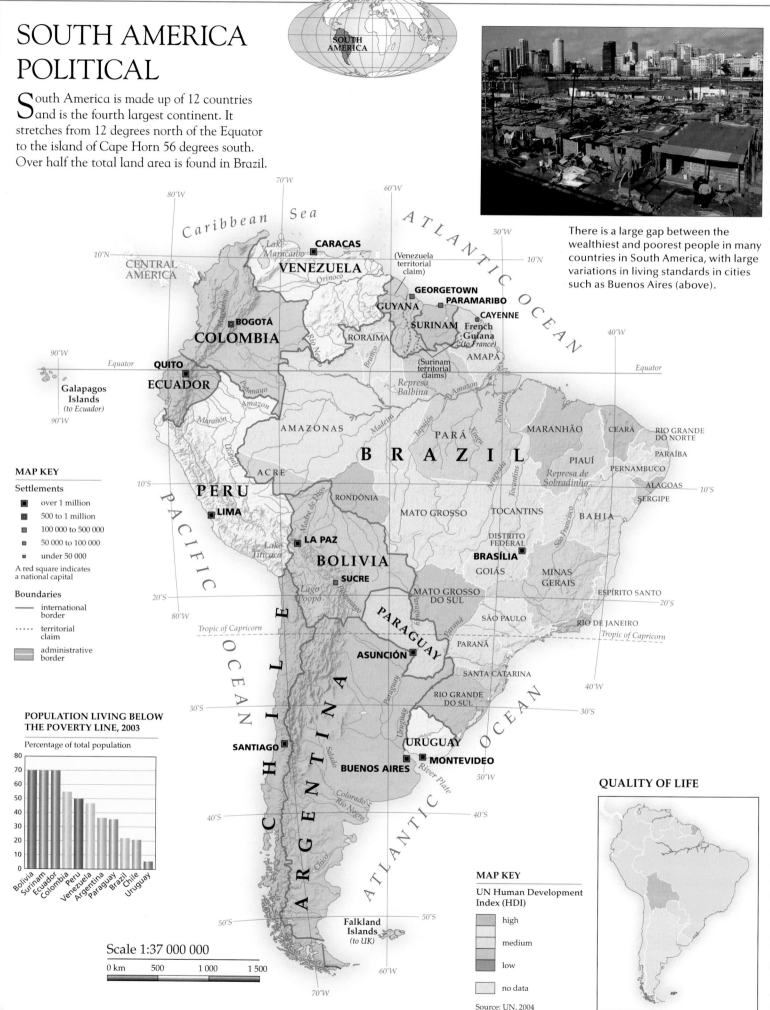

MAP KEY

Settlements

■ over 1 million
▣ 500 to 1 million
▪ 100 000 to 500 000
▪ 50 000 to 100 000
▫ under 50 000

A red square indicates a national capital

Boundaries

—— international border

····· territorial claim

▭ administrative border

POPULATION LIVING BELOW THE POVERTY LINE, 2003

Percentage of total population

Bolivia, Surinam, Ecuador, Colombia, Peru, Venezuela, Argentina, Paraguay, Brazil, Chile, Uruguay

Scale 1:37 000 000

0 km　500　1 000　1 500

QUALITY OF LIFE

MAP KEY

UN Human Development Index (HDI)

▨ high
▨ medium
▨ low
▢ no data

Source: UN, 2004

SOUTH AMERICA PHYSICAL

The Amazon Basin and the Andes mountain range dominate the physical landscape of the continent. Regions of highland plateaux, such as the Mato Grosso, have been formed from older, eroded shield mountains.

PHYSICAL FACTFILE

1 **HIGHEST POINT:** Cerro Aconcagua, 6 959 metres above sea level

2 **LOWEST POINT:** Peninsula Valdés, 40 metres below sea level

3 **LARGEST LAKE:** Lake Titicaca, 8 340 km²

— **LONGEST RIVER:** Amazon, 6 430 km

— **LENGTH OF COASTLINE:** 144 567 km

MAP KEY

Elevation

4 000m
2 000m
1 000m
500m
250m
100m
0
250m   Below
2 000m   sea level
4 000m

△ mountain
◬ volcano
▽ depression

Plate boundaries

——   constructive
—△— destructive
- - - conservative
······ uncertain

Scale 1:41 000 000

0 km   500   1 000   1 500

PLATE BOUNDARIES

The Andes are located at a destructive plate margin along the Pacific coast of South America. The oceanic Nazca plate is sinking beneath the continental South American plate, which has been forced upwards to form the young fold mountains of the Andes. Many of these are active volcanoes, and plate collisions also result in frequent earthquakes.

ocean trench

continent's edge thickens and buckles upwards

subducting oceanic plate

continental plate

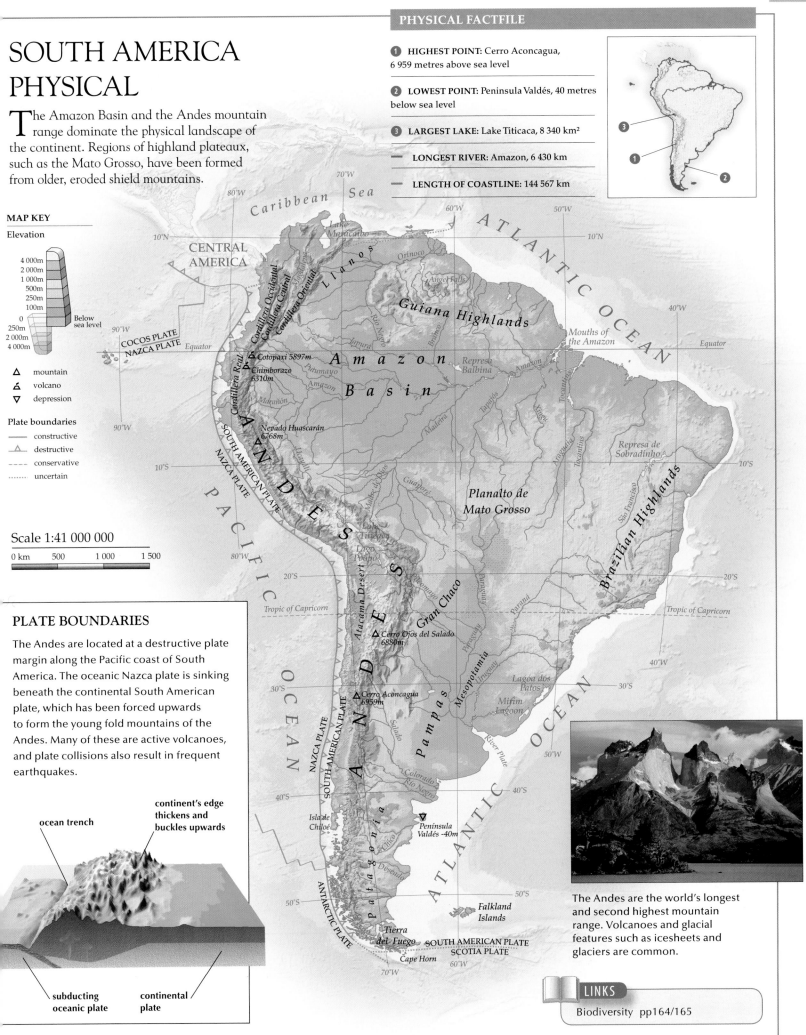

The Andes are the world's longest and second highest mountain range. Volcanoes and glacial features such as icesheets and glaciers are common.

LINKS

Biodiversity pp164/165

SOUTH AMERICA CLIMATE

Much of the north of the continent experiences a hot, wet tropical climate. Conditions along the west coast are much drier, with semi-arid and hot desert in places. Tundra is found in the extreme south, where the Patagonia ice sheet and several glaciers are found.

MAP KEY

Climate regions

- temperate
- warm temperate
- mediterranean
- semi-arid
- arid
- tropical
- humid equatorial
- mountain/tundra

Local winds

→ cold

MANAUS

Average daily temperature — Precipitation (mm)

40°C 30°C 20°C 10°C 0°C | 400 300 200 100 0

J F M A M J J A S O N D

☀4 daily hours of sunshine, January   ☀8 daily hours of sunshine, July

PRECIPITATION

Average annual precipitation (mm)

Precipitation key

- above 3 500 mm
- 2 500 to 3 500 mm
- 2 000 to 2 500 mm
- 1 500 to 2 000 mm
- 1 000 to 1 500 mm
- 500 to 1 000 mm
- 200 to 500 mm
- 0 to 200 mm

LIMA

Average daily temperature — Precipitation (mm)

40°C 30°C 20°C 10°C 0°C | 400 300 200 100 0

J F M A M J J A S O N D

☀6 daily hours of sunshine, January   ☀1 daily hours of sunshine, July

LA PAZ

Average daily temperature — Precipitation (mm)

40°C 30°C 20°C 10°C 0°C | 400 300 200 100 0

J F M A M J J A S O N D

☀6 daily hours of sunshine, January   ☀9 daily hours of sunshine, July

TEMPERATURE

Average January temperature

Temperature key

- above 30°C
- 20 to 30°C
- 10 to 20°C
- 0 to 10°C
- 0 to -10°C
- -10 to -20°C
- -20 to -30°C
- below -30°C

Average July temperature

BUENOS AIRES

Average daily temperature — Precipitation (mm)

40°C 30°C 20°C 10°C 0°C | 400 300 200 100 0

J F M A M J J A S O N D

☀9 daily hours of sunshine, January   ☀5 daily hours of sunshine, July

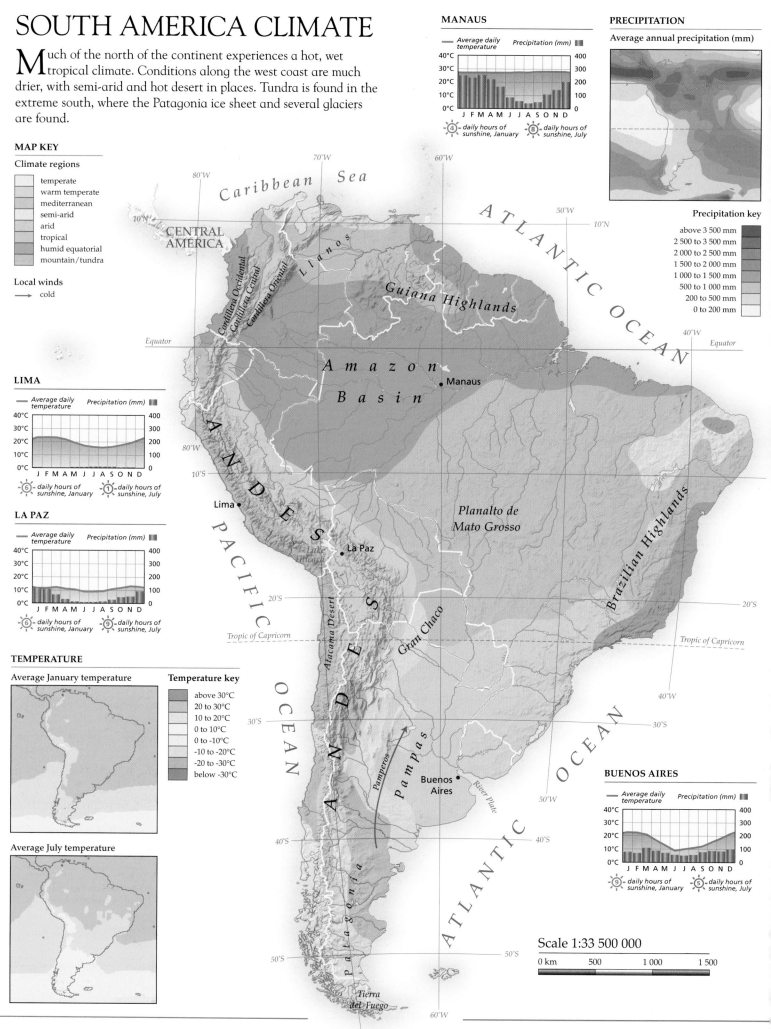

Caribbean Sea

CENTRAL AMERICA

ATLANTIC OCEAN

Cordillera Occidental
Cordillera Central
Cordillera Oriental

Llanos

Guiana Highlands

Amazon Basin

Manaus

Equator

A N D E S

PACIFIC OCEAN

Lima

La Paz

Lake Titicaca

Planalto de Mato Grosso

Brazilian Highlands

Atacama Desert

Gran Chaco

Tropic of Capricorn

Pamperos

Pampas

Buenos Aires

River Plate

ATLANTIC OCEAN

Patagonia

Tierra del Fuego

Scale 1:33 500 000

0 km   500   1 000   1 500

SOUTH AMERICA POPULATION

The population of South America is very unevenly distributed; there are high population densities along the coasts and in the North, whilst much of the interior is empty or sparsely populated. After 50 years of rapid growth, many countries' population growth rates have now significantly slowed.

The majority of South America's people are now city dwellers. Chile's capital Santiago is home to a third of the country's 15 million people.

MAP KEY

Population density
(people per square km)

- above 200
- 100 to 200
- 50 to 100
- 10 to 50
- 1 to 10

Major settlements

- ▣ ⊙ above 1 million
- ▣ ◎ 500 000 to 1 million
- ▪ ⊙ 100 000 to 500 000

A red square indicates a national capital

URBAN/RURAL POPULATION SPLIT

80%   20%

POPULATION GROWTH

MAP KEY

Population growth
(average annual percentage growth)

- above 2.5
- 2 to 2.4
- 1.5 to 1.9
- 1 to 1.4
- 0 to 0.9
- 0 to -0.9 (population in decline)

POPULATION GROWTH TRENDS

Million people
(Logarithmic scale)

KEY
- • • • Argentina
- • • • Paraguay
- • • • Colombia
- • • • Uruguay

1 000
200
100
20
10
2
1

actual   projected

1950   2000 2015 2025   2050

Scale 1:33 500 000

0 km   500   1 000   1 500

FOCUS ON

URBANISATION

Rapid, large-scale urbanisation has meant that cities have been unable to provide sufficient employment or services to migrants. As a result, shanty towns have developed on the edge of major cities, housing the poorest people in the city.

Map labels:

Caribbean Sea

Barranquilla, Cartagena, Maracaibo, CARACAS, Valencia, Maracay, Cumaná, San Cristóbal, Bucaramanga, Medellín, GEORGETOWN, PARAMARIBO, CAYENNE, BOGOTÁ, Boa Vista, Cali, Pasto, Esmeraldas, QUITO, Guayaquil, Iquitos, Belém, São Luís, Manaus, Santarém, Piura, Fortaleza, Natal, Trujillo, Porto Velho, Palmas, Recife, Maceió, Aracaju, Callao, LIMA, Cusco, Salvador, Cuiabá, BRASÍLIA, La Paz, Arequipa, Oruro, Santa Cruz, Goiânia, Arica, SUCRE, Campo Grande, Belo Horizonte, Vitória, Campinas, Rio de Janeiro, Antofagasta, Salta, ASUNCIÓN, São Paulo, Curitiba, Córdoba, Corrientes, Florianópolis, Coquimbo, Porto Alegre, Mendoza, Paraná, Rosario, SANTIAGO, BUENOS AIRES, MONTEVIDEO, La Plata, Concepción, Mar del Plata, Bahía Blanca, River Plate, Punta Arenas

PACIFIC OCEAN, ATLANTIC OCEAN, Equator, Tropic of Capricorn

SOUTH AMERICA LAND USE

South America is rich in mineral resources and a wide range of tropical foodstuffs. Although many countries rely heavily on these primary industries, others like Brazil, Argentina and Venezuela have also developed a wide range of manufacturing and high-tech industries.

The Pampas of eastern Argentina is a large area of flat grassland. Cattle are reared for beef, much of it exported to the USA.

MAP KEY

Land use type

- forest
- pasture
- cropland
- desert
- barren land
- mountain

- industrial area
- major conurbation

FOOD PRODUCTION

Selected commodities (million tonnes)

- 1990 production
- 2000 production

Commodity	1990	2000
Milk	32	45
Meat	16	26
Fruit & vegetables	68	88
Cereals	64	97
Starchy roots	42	46

MINERAL RESOURCES

MAP KEY

Mineral resources

- oil field
- gas field
- coal field

Bu bauxite
Cu copper
Fe iron
Pb lead
Ag silver
Sn tin

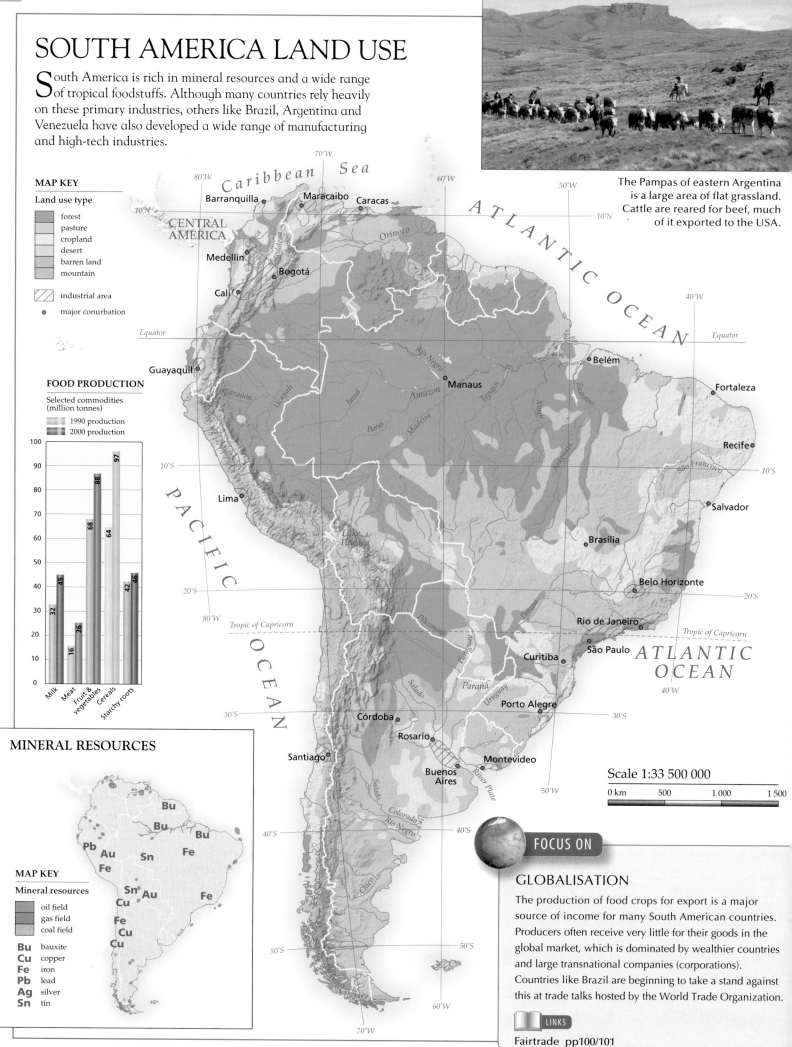

Scale 1:33 500 000

0 km   500   1 000   1 500

FOCUS ON

GLOBALISATION

The production of food crops for export is a major source of income for many South American countries. Producers often receive very little for their goods in the global market, which is dominated by wealthier countries and large transnational companies (corporations). Countries like Brazil are beginning to take a stand against this at trade talks hosted by the World Trade Organization.

LINKS

Fairtrade pp100/101

SOUTH AMERICA ENVIRONMENT

South America has a wide range of ecosystems. Many have been protected because of their remoteness, but are now becoming accessible. Vast tracts of rainforest have been destroyed for farming and industry, whilst ancient heritage sites are threatened by rising tourist numbers. The rapid growth of urban areas and industry has significantly increased atmospheric pollution.

The famous Inca remains in Machu Picchu, Peru, high in the Andes are an increasingly popular tourist destination. Whilst the local economy benefits from extra visitors, the environment is becoming damaged.

MAP KEY

Environmental issues

- existing forest
- existing desert
- desertification
- deforestation
- marine pollution
- heavy marine pollution
- ~~~ polluted river
- ● poor urban air quality

Scale 1:37 000 000

0 km   500   1 000   1 500

DEFORESTATION

The images here show how an area in Rôndonia in Brazil's Amazon rainforest has changed since the building of the Cuiabá-Porta Velho highway. From 1975 to 1986 settlements were established in Ariquemas, close to the road. The pattern seen is the result of logging activity. This, and large areas of land cleared for farming can be seen clearly in the 1999 image.

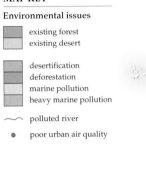

BRAZIL

Rôndônia region

1975

1986

1999

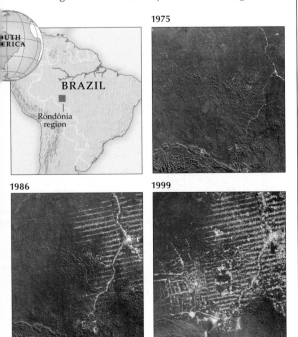

FOCUS ON

DEFORESTATION

Amazonia is the world's largest rainforest. A unique ecosystem containing the world's greatest biodiversity, between 1970 and 2002 up to 20 per cent of the forest was lost. Farming, logging and mining have all contributed to deforestation. It is estimated that less than 30 per cent of the original forest will remain unaffected by 2020.

📖 LINKS

Biodiversity pp164/165

SOUTH AMERICA

South America contains the world's largest rainforest through which the world's second longest river flows – the Amazon. The west coast is dominated by the Andes Mountains. Despite its fairly harsh physical geography, the continent has a long history of settlement. Today it contains some of the largest and most densely populated urban areas in the world.

KEY

ELEVATION

4 000m
2 000m
1 000m
500m
250m
100m
0
250m
2 000m
4 000m

Below sea level

△ mountain
⋏ volcano

sandy desert

marsh/wetland

BOUNDARIES

—— international border
⋯⋯ territorial claim
······ administrative border
—— maritime border

SETTLEMENTS

■ over 1 million
◉ 500 000 – 1 million
⊙ 100 000 – 500 000
○ 50 000 – 100 000
○ below 50 000

A red square indicates a national capital

An orange square indicates a provincial or federal capital

An offshore rig near Maracaibo, 500 km from Venezuela's capital city, Caracas. The country has the world's sixth largest proven oil resources, much of it located under the Caribbean Sea.

SOUTH AMERICA

ATLANTIC OCEAN

PACIFIC OCEAN

Caribbean Sea

PANAMA

COLOMBIA

VENEZUELA

GUYANA

SURINAM

French Guiana (to France)

ECUADOR

PERU

BRAZIL

ANDES

Guiana Highlands

Amazon

Mouths of the Amazon

CARACAS
BOGOTÁ
QUITO
LIMA
GEORGETOWN
PARAMARIBO
CAYENNE

Recife
Maceió
Fortaleza
Natal
João Pessoa
Campina Grande
Teresina
São Luís
Belém
Macapá
Manaus

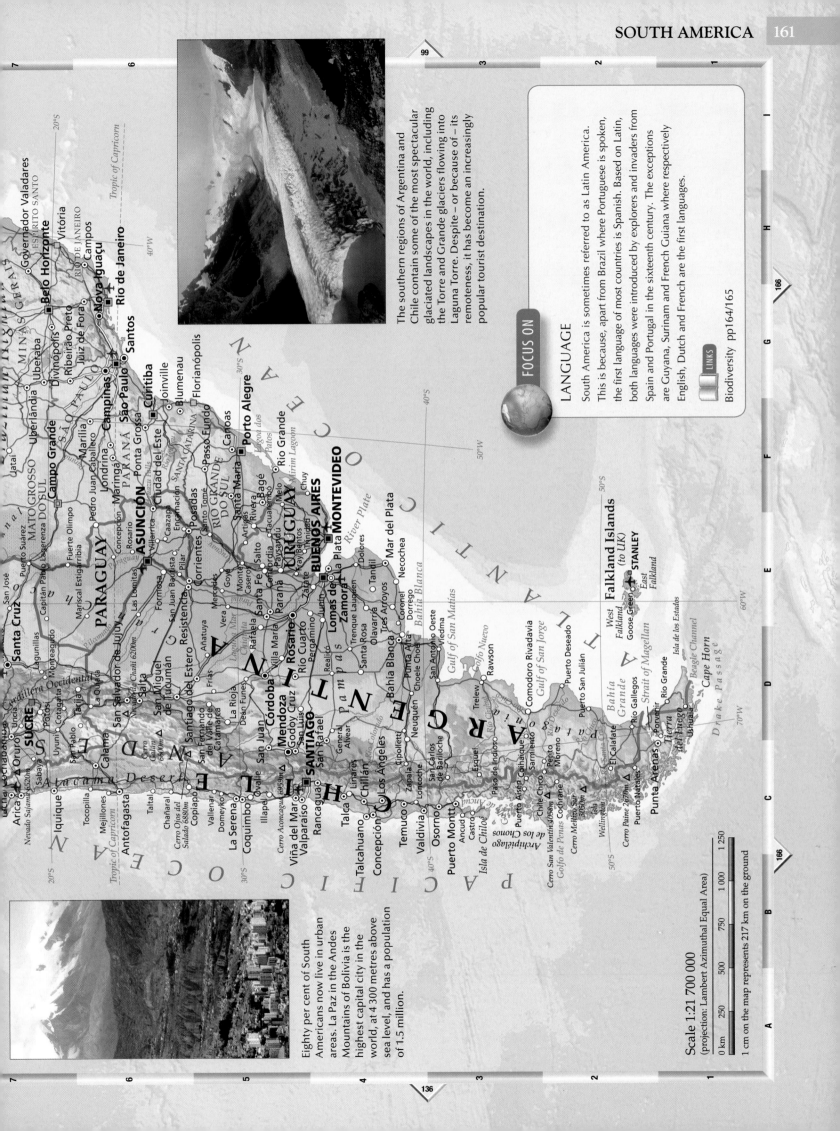

The southern regions of Argentina and Chile contain some of the most spectacular glaciated landscapes in the world, including the Torre and Grande glaciers flowing into Laguna Torre. Despite – or because of – its remoteness, it has become an increasingly popular tourist destination.

FOCUS ON

LANGUAGE

South America is sometimes referred to as Latin America. This is because, apart from Brazil where Portuguese is spoken, the first language of most countries is Spanish. Based on Latin, both languages were introduced by explorers and invaders from Spain and Portugal in the sixteenth century. The exceptions are Guyana, Surinam and French Guiana where respectively English, Dutch and French are the first languages.

LINKS
Biodiversity pp164/165

Eighty per cent of South Americans now live in urban areas. La Paz in the Andes Mountains of Bolivia is the highest capital city in the world, at 4 300 metres above sea level, and has a population of 1.5 million.

Scale 1:21 700 000
(projection: Lambert Azimuthal Equal Area)

0 km   250   500   750   1 000   1 250

1 cm on the map represents 217 km on the ground

BRAZIL

Brazil is the sixth most populous country in the world and home to over half of South America's population, over 80 per cent of whom live in urban areas. With a third of the land tropical rainforest, Brazil is rich in mineral deposits and natural resources, which have provided a base for economic development.

SOUTH AMERICA

The River Amazon flows east from the Andes to the Atlantic Ocean. The world's second longest river, much of it surrounded by tropical rainforest, it contains 20 per cent of the world's fresh water.

KEY

ELEVATION

4 000m
2 000m
1 000m
500m
250m
100m
0
250m
2 000m
4 000m

Below sea level

△ mountain

marsh/wetland

BOUNDARIES

━━━ international border

─── administrative border

SETTLEMENTS

▪ ▪ ⊙ over 1 million

▣ ▣ ◎ 500 000 – 1 million

▪ ▪ ⊙ 100 000 – 500 000

▫ ▫ ○ 50 000 – 100 000

▪ ▫ ○ below 50 000

A red square indicates a national capital

An orange square indicates a provincial or federal capital

Rapid and large-scale urban development has resulted in the growth of makeshift shanty towns, known in Brazil as favelas. In Rio de Janeiro favelas like Rocinha (pictured above), are home to about 20 per cent of the city's 12 million population.

Mount Roraima 2810m
Boa Vista
Conceição do Maú
RORAIMA
GUYANA
Missão Catrimani
Caracaraí
Vista Alegre
VENEZUELA
Pico da Neblina 3014m
Boiaçu
COLOMBIA
Santa Isabel do Rio Negro
Barcelos
Represa Balbina
Rio Negro
Rio Branco
Serra do Jatapu
Vila Bittencourt
Japurá
Novo Airão
Manaus
Urucará
Itacoatiara
Foz do Mamoriá
Rio Japurá
Santo Antônio do Içá
Tefé
Rio Solimões
Careiro
Benjamin Constant
Jutaí
Rio Juruá
Rio Teié
Coari
Rio Purus
Rio Madeira
Jacaré-a-Canga
Itamarati
Rio Coari
Tapauá
Manicoré
Barra do São Manuel
Elvira
Eirunepé
AMAZONAS
Rio Purus
Lábrea
Humaitá
Serra
Envira
Cruzeiro do Sul
Feijó
Boca do Acre
Porto Velho
B R
Japiim
Rio Iraí
Jaciparaná
Peixoto de
Foz do Breu
ACRE
Rio Acre
Rio Abunã
Ariquemes
Juruena
Rio Branco
Guajará-Mirim
RONDÔNIA
PERU
Rio Mamoré
Pimenta Bueno
Vilhena
Rio Guaporé
Chapada dos Pareçis
M
Mato Grosso
Nobre
Cáceres
PARAGUA
Phi
Coru
Porto Murtinho
D
PARAGUAY
Foz d
ARGENTINA
Uruguaiana
URU
Santa Livrar

Equator
5°N
60°W
65°W
70°W
5°S
10°S
70°W
15°S
65°W
20°S
Tropic of Capricorn
25°S
30°S
60°W

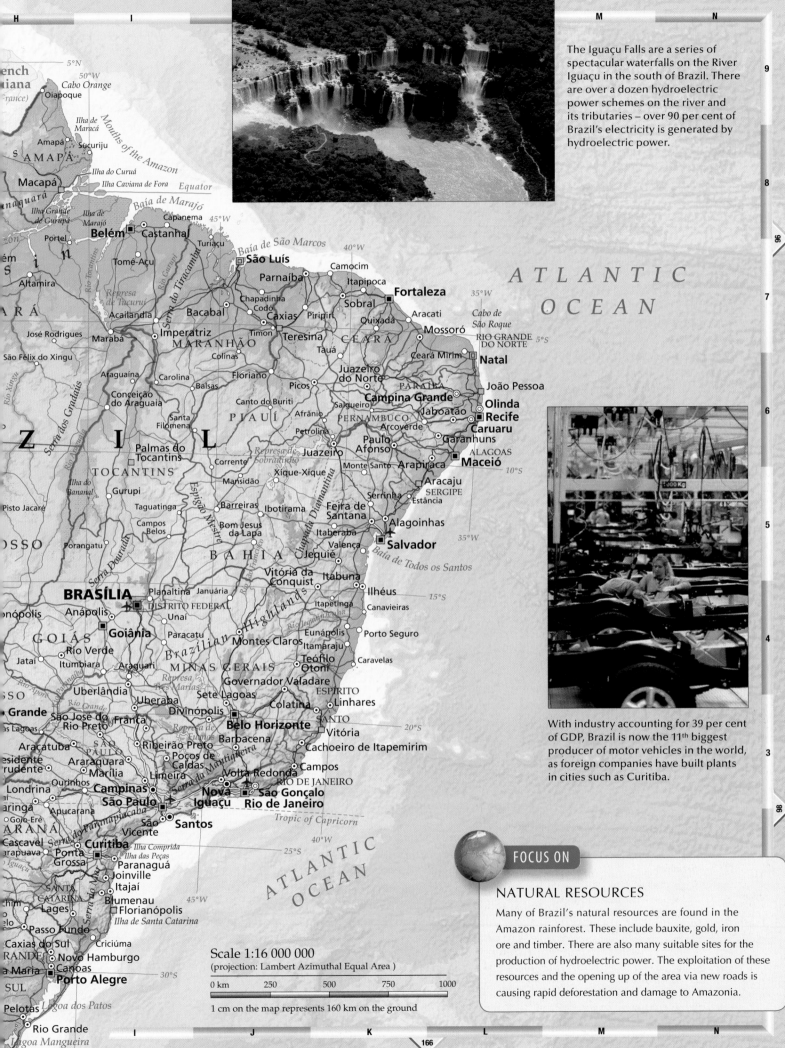

The Iguaçu Falls are a series of spectacular waterfalls on the River Iguaçu in the south of Brazil. There are over a dozen hydroelectric power schemes on the river and its tributaries – over 90 per cent of Brazil's electricity is generated by hydroelectric power.

With industry accounting for 39 per cent of GDP, Brazil is now the 11th biggest producer of motor vehicles in the world, as foreign companies have built plants in cities such as Curitiba.

FOCUS ON

NATURAL RESOURCES

Many of Brazil's natural resources are found in the Amazon rainforest. These include bauxite, gold, iron ore and timber. There are also many suitable sites for the production of hydroelectric power. The exploitation of these resources and the opening up of the area via new roads is causing rapid deforestation and damage to Amazonia.

Scale 1:16 000 000
(projection: Lambert Azimuthal Equal Area)

0 km 250 500 750 1000

1 cm on the map represents 160 km on the ground

(Map labels)

ATLANTIC OCEAN

French Guiana (France)

5°N
50°W
45°W
40°W
35°W
Equator
5°S
10°S
15°S
20°S
Tropic of Capricorn
25°S
30°S
50°W

Cabo Orange
Oiapoque
Amapá
Sucuriju
AMAPÁ
Macapá
Macquará
Ilha de Maracá
Ilha do Curuá
Ilha Caviana de Fora
Ilha Grande de Gurupá
Portel
Ilha de Marajó
Baía de Marajó
Mouths of the Amazon
Belém
Castanhal
Capanema
Turiaçu
Baía de São Marcos
São Luís
Baía de São Marcos
Camocim
Itapipoca
Fortaleza
Parnaíba
Tomé-Açu
Altamira
CARÁ
José Rodrigues
Acailândia
Chapadinha
Codó
Caxias
Piripiri
Sobral
Quixadá
Aracati
Mossoró
Cabo de São Roque
São Félix do Xingu
Marabá
Imperatriz
Bacabal
Timon
Teresina
Tauá
CEARÁ
Ceará Mirim
RIO GRANDE DO NORTE
Natal
MARANHÃO
Colinas
Picos
Juazeiro do Norte
Araguaína
Carolina
Floriano
Balsas
Canto do Buriti
Salgueiro
PARAIBA
Campina Grande
João Pessoa
BRAZIL
Conceição do Araguaia
Santa Filomena
PIAUÍ
Afrânio
PERNAMBUCO
Arcoverde
Olinda
Recife
Jaboatão
Caruaru
Garanhuns
Palmas do Tocantins
Petrolina
Juazeiro
Paulo Afonso
ALAGOAS
Maceió
Pisto Jacaré
TOCANTINS
Correnté
Represa de Sobradinho
Monte Santo
Arapiraca
Ilha do Bananal
Gurupi
Mansidão
Xique-Xique
Serrinha
Aracaju
SERGIPE
Estância
Taguatinga
Barreiras
Ibotirama
Feira de Santana
Alagoinhas
OSSO
Porangatu
Campos Belos
Bom Jesus da Lapa
Itaberaba
Valença
Salvador
BAHIA
Jequié
Baía de Todos os Santos
BRASÍLIA
Planaltina
Januária
Vitória da Conquist
Itabuna
Ilhéus
ónópolis
DISTRITO FEDERAL
Unaí
Itapetinga
Canavieiras
Anápolis
Brazilian Highlands
Porto Seguro
GOIÁS
Goiânia
Paracatu
Montes Claros
Eunápolis
Itamaraju
Rio Verde
Itumbiara
MINAS GERAIS
Teófilo Otoni
Caravelas
Jataí
Araguari
Represa Três Marias
Governador Valadare
ESPIRITO SANTO
SSO
Uberlândia
Sete Lagoas
Linhares
Grande
Uberaba
Divinópolis
Colatina
Vitória
São José do Rio Preto
França
Belo Horizonte
Araçatuba
Ribeirão Preto
Barbacena
Cachoeiro de Itapemirim
esidente Prudente
Araraquara
Poços de Caldas
RIO DE JANEIRO
Campos
Marília
Limeira
Volta Redonda
Ourinhos
Campinas
Nova Iguaçu
São Gonçalo
Londrina
São Paulo
Rio de Janeiro
aringá
SÃO PAULO
Apucarana
Santos
São Vicente
Gojo-Erê
PARANÁ
Curitiba
Ilha Comprida
Cascavel
Ponta Grossa
Ilha das Peças
arapuava
Paranaguá
Joinville
Itajaí
Blumenau
SANTA CATARINA
Lages
Florianópolis
Ilha de Santa Catarina
Passo Fundo
Caxias do Sul
Criciúma
RANDE
Novo Hamburgo
Maria
Canoas
SUL
Porto Alegre
Pelotas
Lagoa dos Patos
Rio Grande
Lagoa Mangueira

Serra do Tiracambu
Rio Tocantins
Rio Curupi
Rio Gurupi
Represa de Tucuruí
Serra dos Gradaús
Rio Xingu
Rio Araguaia
Espigão Mestre
Serra Dourada
Chapada Diamantina
Rio Jequitinhonha
Rio Pardo
Rio Paranaíba
Rio Grande
Rio São Francisco
Serra da Mantiqueira
Serra do Paranapiacaba
Serra do Mar

H I J K L M N
9 8 7 6 5 4 3
96 98

BIODIVERSITY

Biodiversity is generally defined as the number and variety of plant and animal species that make up the Earth's ecosystems. By counting the number of different species in a region, the level of biodiversity can be measured. If this is repeated over time any changes that are taking place can be assessed. Of particular importance are the number of endemic species found in a given location. A major cause of loss of biodiversity is when endemic species begin to disappear. This may be the result of human activity or competition from introduced species.

BIODIVERSITY IN SOUTH AMERICA

The Amazon rainforest in South America is said to have the greatest biodiversity of anywhere in the world, although some scientists dispute this. There are thought to be several million different species in this region, the majority of which – especially insects – have yet to be discovered and classified. This makes it very difficult to monitor and study accurately.

The volcanic island of San Bartolme lies off the coast of Santiago, one of the larger islands. The beach at Shark Cove is a popular destination for visitors.

USEFUL DEFINITIONS

Endemic	Found in one place – unique to that location
Native/resident	Found in several locations, but arrived there by natural means, especially plants and invertebrates
Introduced	Brought to a place by people, either deliberately or accidentally
Migrant	Regular visitor e.g. birds in winter
Flora	The plants of a region
Fauna	The animals of a region

DARWIN'S FINCHES

The Galapagos Islands were made famous by Charles Darwin, who visited them in 1831 as part of an expedition. The observations he made on the islands' endemic species, particularly finches, led him to study how species evolve. This culminated in his ground-breaking theory of evolution by natural selection.

THE GALAPAGOS ISLANDS

The Galapagos Islands cover a small area. Their very remoteness in the Pacific Ocean, over 1 000 km away from the nearest land, meant that they lay undiscovered until just under 500 years ago. By the time the first settlers arrived in 1832 when they were claimed by Ecuador, the islands had over 7 100 species of plants and animals, 30 per cent of which are endemic to the Galapagos.

The 13 main islands and hundreds of smaller ones form an archipelago covering just over 7 400 km². They sit on the northern edge of the Nazca Plate and were formed as volcanoes rose from the ocean floor where two submarine ridges meet to form a 'hot spot'. Only five of the islands are inhabited, with a total population estimated at 20 000, half of whom live in Puerto Ayora on Santa Cruz.

BIODIVERSITY IN THE GALAPAGOS

The unique range of plants and animals on the islands developed partly because of their isolation from the rest of the world and lack of competition. Because of this the Galapagos Islands are of particular interest to scientists studying evolution and so efforts have been made to protect the islands' biodiversity.

Pinta

PACIFI

Santiag

Fernandina

Rab

Isabela

Galapagos Islands

Scale 1:2 600 000
(projection: Lambert Azimuthal Equal Area)

0 km	25	50	75	100

1 cm on the map represents 26 km on the ground

THE NATIONAL PARK AND MARINE RESERVE

The Galapagos National Park (GNP) was set up with the main aim of protecting the islands' biodiversity. The GNP covers 97 per cent of the land, with the other 3 per cent reserved for human use. The GNP has produced a number of 'Master Plans' for the protection and use of the islands. Part of this includes land use zoning within the National Park.

TIMELINE OF THE GALAPAGOS ISLANDS' PROTECTION

1959 Ecuador declared the Galapagos Islands a National Park

1968 The Galapag National Park (GN was set

1950s	1960s

ENDEMIC PLANTS AND ANIMALS

Flightless Cormorant – evolved in an environment free from predators, where it had no need to fly.

Lava Cactus – endemic to the islands. Cacti thrive in the dry, hostile environment of the island's inland areas.

Marine Iguana – the only species of marine lizard in the world.

Sally Lightfoot Crab – a climbing crab that is found in large numbers on the islands.

MAP KEY

Introduced species

cattle	
cat	
dog	
donkey	
goat	
horse	
pig	
black rat	
✕	eradicated species
- - -	Marine Reserve boundary

GNP AND MARINE RESERVE OBJECTIVES

- To maintain the biodiversity and unique natural resources of the islands via an agreed management plan
- Protect and conserve the land and marine coastal ecosystems
- Manage the sustainability of commercial fishing resources whilst protecting biodiversity
- Manage and control tourist activity to prevent it impacting on the environment
- Involve residents and visitors in the conservation process
- Promote sustainability and provide scientific programmes
- Repopulate the islands with captive-bred endemic species

INTRODUCED SPECIES

Introduced species of animals and plants are a serious threat to biodiversity. Grazing cattle, donkeys and goats have stripped bare the vegetation on many islands, leaving little for the giant tortoises and land iguanas to feed on. Tens of thousands of these introduced species are still found on the islands, especially Isabela, despite a

largescale eradication programme. Equally destructive have been pigs, dogs, cats and rats, which attack and kill iguanas, lizards, turtles and birds, and take eggs and fledglings from nests.

Newly introduced plant species have quickly colonised some areas, altering the natural ecosystems. Elephant grass on Santa Cruz has wiped out several endemic plant species in just 30 years.

The GNP has tackled these problems by undertaking eradication programmes, using targeted poison and herbicides and by physically digging up introduced plants. It has also set up captive breeding programmes for giant tortoises and land iguanas at the Charles Darwin Research Foundation on Santa Cruz to re-introduce these animals onto islands where they have been wiped out.

FISHING AND TOURISM

The other main threats to the islands' biodiversity come from two major economic activities – fishing and tourism. The number of legal fishing boats has trebled in eight years. The harvesting of sea cucumbers has caused most concern. They help purify seawater and are an important food source for plankton, which itself serves the main food chain. Despite the imposition of quotas, patrol boats and a legal fishing season of two months, stocks are thought to have decreased by 80 per cent since over four million were taken in 1999.

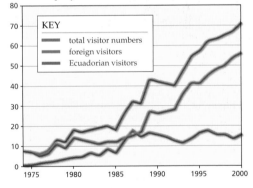

GROWTH IN VISITOR NUMBERS 1974–2000

Visitors per year since 1974 (thousands)

KEY
— total visitor numbers
— foreign visitors
— Ecuadorian visitors

THE BIG ISSUES

1 How has the GNP sought to protect the islands' biodiversity?

2 How can the GNP reduce illegal fishing?

3 Are biodiversity and the protection of endemic species more important than economic development?

4 Should the islanders receive more funding so they can improve their lives whilst being encouraged to protect the endemic plants and animals fully?

1978 UNESCO declared the Galapagos a World Heritage Site	**1985** UNESCO awarded the islands 'Biosphere Reserve' status	**1998** The Galapagos Marine Reserve (the world's second largest) was set up, extending 60 km around the islands	**2001** The Marine Reserve became a UNESCO World Heritage Site in 2001
1970s	1980s	1990s	2000s

ANTARCTICA

Antarctica's size, remoteness, lack of indigenous people and severe physical geography combine to make it a unique continent – and a fragile one. At 14 million km², it is 58 times the size of the UK, with over 99 per cent covered by permanent ice. In winter, pack ice forms around the coast, doubling the size of the continent.

ANTARCTICA

There are between 40 and 50 Scientific Research Stations in Antarctica. Some are permanently staffed – like the British base of Rothera on the Antarctic Peninsula – whilst others are only used during the summer months.

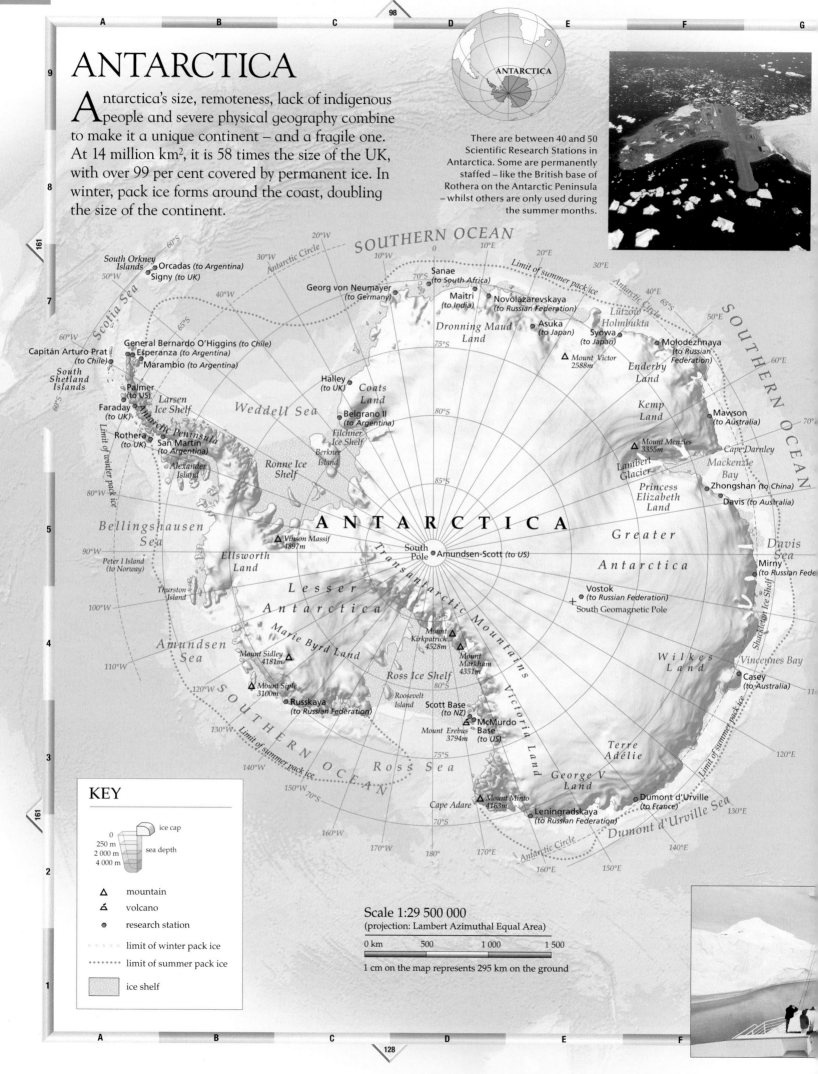

KEY

- ice cap
  - 0
  - 250 m
  - 2 000 m — sea depth
  - 4 000 m
- △ mountain
- ⌂ volcano
- ● research station
- ⋯⋯ limit of winter pack ice
- ⋯⋯ limit of summer pack ice
- ▨ ice shelf

Scale 1:29 500 000
(projection: Lambert Azimuthal Equal Area)

| 0 km | 500 | 1 000 | 1 500 |

1 cm on the map represents 295 km on the ground

A FRAGILE ENVIRONMENT

Antarctica is one of the most pristine places on Earth, but despite its extreme physical conditions and remoteness it still faces a range of environmental problems. Although efforts have been made to limit human activity on the continent, tourism, over-fishing and the possible future mining of minerals are amongst the main threats to Antartica's fragile environment.

The Southern Ocean surrounding Antarctica is rich in krill, small shrimp-like plankton. The possibility of commercial fishing for krill in the future could have a major impact on the Antarctic food chain, which relies almost exclusively on them.

ANTARCTIC TREATY

Over 40 research stations are based on Antarctica and are home to up to 10 000 scientists and support staff in summer, falling to just a few thousand in winter. Their work, and the use of the continent, is strictly controlled by the Antarctic Treaty System, first introduced in 1961.

The Treaty's objectives are broadly:

- to demilitarise Antarctica, to establish it as a zone free of nuclear tests and the disposal of radioactive waste, and to ensure that it is used for peaceful purposes only;

- to promote international scientific cooperation in Antarctica;

- to set aside disputes over territorial sovereignty.

The Treaty has been signed by 44 countries, 27 of whom have 'Consultative Status' and meet annually. Under the terms of the Treaty, all countries have set aside territorial claims and agreed that Antarctica is a *'natural reserve devoted to peace and science'*.

TOURIST TRENDS 1992–2005

Number of tourists landed (thousands)

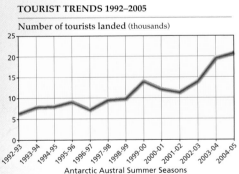

Antarctic Austral Summer Seasons
Source: IAATO (International Association of Antarctic Tour Operators)

Currently tourism in the Antarctic (mostly in the form of cruises) has only a limited impact on the environment – visitor numbers are small, there are only 200 landing sites and tour operators are well-regulated. However, tourist numbers are increasing, and with them, damage to the environment.

CLIMATE CHANGE

The greatest threats come from human activity, not on Antarctica itself but in other continents. In 1981 British scientists discovered a hole in the ozone layer over Antarctica. Ozone in the stratosphere protects the Earth from harmful ultraviolet radiation, but the release of gases like chlorofluorocarbons (CFCs) into the atmosphere has damaged the ozone layer. The hole appears over Antarctica every spring when ice crystals in the air react with the returning sun. The Montreal Protocol of 1987 has led to a reduction in the use of CFCs, but it could take 30 years before the ozone hole closes.

THE HOLE IN THE OZONE LAYER

The ozone hole at its maximum extent in 2004.

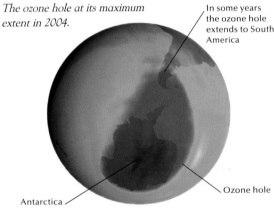

In some years the ozone hole extends to South America

Antarctica

Ozone hole

Climate change, whether caused by atmospheric pollution leading to global warming or natural fluctuations, could have a devastating impact on Antarctica. Although the vast interior of Antarctica still remains well below freezing all year, temperatures on the Antarctic Peninsula have risen by 2.5 degrees Celsius in just 60 years, causing the break up of a number of ice shelves. If temperatures continue to rise, melting sea ice, glaciers and ice sheets could not only impact on Antarctica, but disrupt world climatic patterns and lead to global rises in sea level.

BREAK-UP OF THE LARSEN-B ICE SHELF

In 2002 a 3 250 km² section of the Larsen-B ice shelf disintegrated in just over a month. Scientists had predicted its eventual collapse, due to rising temperatures in the region, but not the speed with which it occured.

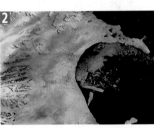

31.01.2002

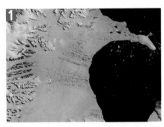

17.02.2002

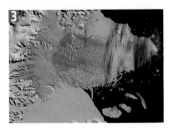

05.03.2002

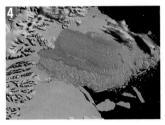

07.03.2002

THE BIG ISSUES

1 Can the Antarctic Treaty fully safeguard the future of the continent?

2 Why can properly regulated tourism be considered good for Antarctica?

3 Why are the major threats to Antarctica from activity on the world's other continents?

4 What would be your 10 point plan to protect Antarctica?

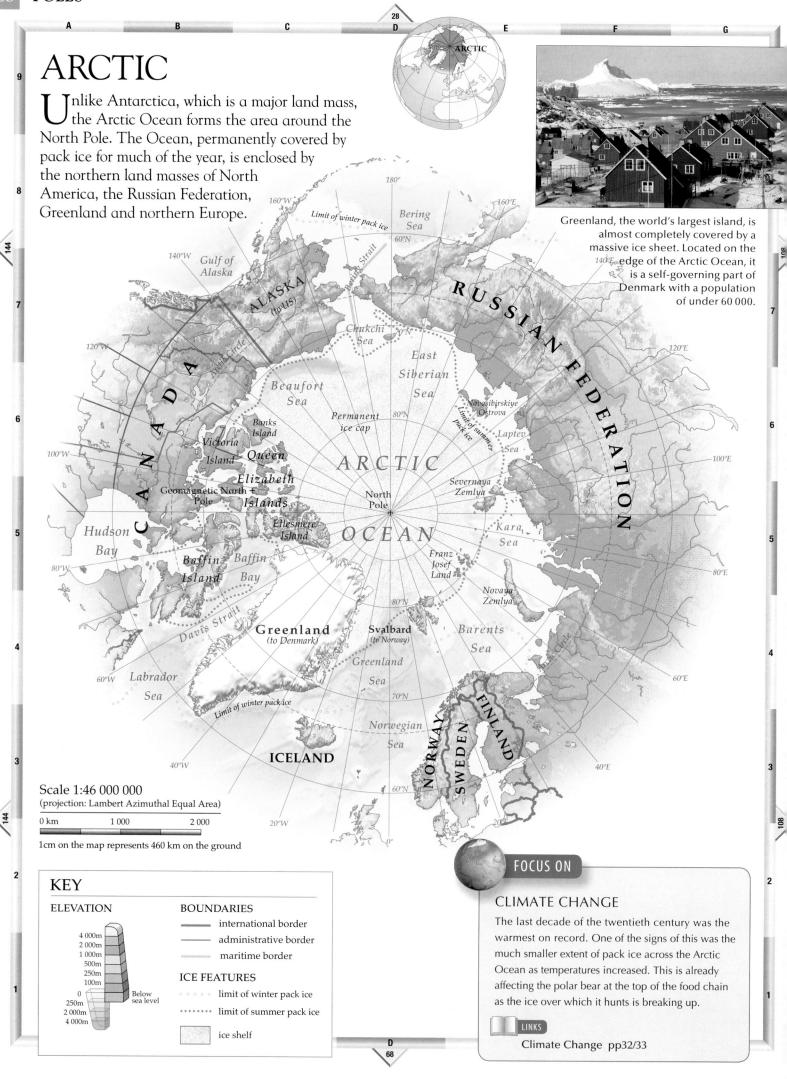

ARCTIC

Unlike Antarctica, which is a major land mass, the Arctic Ocean forms the area around the North Pole. The Ocean, permanently covered by pack ice for much of the year, is enclosed by the northern land masses of North America, the Russian Federation, Greenland and northern Europe.

ARCTIC

Greenland, the world's largest island, is almost completely covered by a massive ice sheet. Located on the edge of the Arctic Ocean, it is a self-governing part of Denmark with a population of under 60 000.

180°
160°W
160°E
140°W
140°E
120°W
120°E
100°W
100°E
80°W
80°E
60°W
60°E
40°W
40°E
20°W
20°E
0°
60°N
70°N
80°N
Limit of winter pack ice
Bering Sea
Bering Strait
Gulf of Alaska
ALASKA (to US)
RUSSIAN FEDERATION
Chukchi Sea
East Siberian Sea
Arctic Circle
CANADA
Beaufort Sea
Permanent ice cap
Novosibirskiye Ostrova
Limit of summer pack ice
Banks Island
Victoria Island
Queen Elizabeth Islands
Laptev Sea
ARCTIC OCEAN
Severnaya Zemlya
Geomagnetic North Pole
North Pole
Hudson Bay
Ellesmere Island
Kara Sea
Franz Josef Land
Baffin Island
Baffin Bay
Novaya Zemlya
Davis Strait
Greenland (to Denmark)
Svalbard (to Norway)
Barents Sea
Labrador Sea
Greenland Sea
FINLAND
Norwegian Sea
NORWAY
SWEDEN
ICELAND

Scale 1:46 000 000
(projection: Lambert Azimuthal Equal Area)

0 km 1 000 2 000

1cm on the map represents 460 km on the ground

KEY

ELEVATION

4 000m
2 000m
1 000m
500m
250m
100m
0
Below sea level
250m
2 000m
4 000m

BOUNDARIES

- international border
- administrative border
- maritime border

ICE FEATURES

- limit of winter pack ice
- limit of summer pack ice
- ice shelf

FOCUS ON

CLIMATE CHANGE

The last decade of the twentieth century was the warmest on record. One of the signs of this was the much smaller extent of pack ice across the Arctic Ocean as temperatures increased. This is already affecting the polar bear at the top of the food chain as the ice over which it hunts is breaking up.

LINKS

Climate Change pp32/33

28 144 108 68

NDEX

rid Systems and Location' on page 10
guide to using this index.

A

raa 69 B3 Denmark 55°3'N 9°26'E
n 82 C8 Germany 50°47'N 6°6'E
rg 69 B4 Denmark 57°3'N 9°56'E
83 E6 Germany 48°50'N 10°6'E
eer 70 E10 Netherlands 52°17'N 4°43'E
71 D6 Belgium 50°57'N 4°3'E
n 70 H9 Netherlands 51°56'N 6°35'E
71 C7 Belgium 51°5'N 3°28'E
koski 68 G8 Finland 62°34'N 25°45'E
83 D5 ≈ W Switzerland
69 B4 Denmark 56°49'N 9°32'E
99 I9 Dem. Rep. Congo 3°52'N 30°14'E
an 116 C3 Iran 30°24'N 48°18'E
a 96 F7 Algeria 31°4'N 2°39'W
an 109 H4 Russian Fed. 53°43'N 91°25'E
ū 116 E4 Iran 31°7'N 53°17'E
iri 125 L9 Japan 44°N 144°15'E
ville 72 G8 France 50°6'N 1°50'E
dorney 59 C6 Ireland 52°21'N 9°40'W
feale 59 C6 Ireland 52°24'N 9°21'W
leix 59 F7 Ireland 52°55'N 7°20'W
tsbury 49 H5 England, UK 50°39'N 2°40'W
tsley 53 J4 England, UK 52°12'N 0°19'W
né 97 I5 Chad 13°49'N 20°49'E
aeron 48 E9 Wales, UK 52°15'N 4°15'W
dare 48 F8 Wales, UK 51°42'N 3°32'W
daron 48 D11 Wales, UK 52°49'N 4°47'W
deen 56 I8 Scotland, UK 57°10'N 2°4'W
deen, City of 36 ◈ Unitary authority
tland, UK
deenshire 56 H8 ◈ Unitary authority
tland, UK
dyfi 48 E10 Wales, UK 52°33'N 4°7'W
feldy 57 F7 Scotland, UK 56°38'N 3°49'W
fraw 48 D12 Wales, UK 53°12'N 4°33'W
ford 55 H3 England, UK 53°50'N 1°28'W
gavenny 48 G8 Wales, UK 51°50'N 3°W
gele 48 F12 Wales, UK 53°16'N 3°33'W
kenfig 49 F7 Wales, UK 51°33'N 3°41'W
porth 48 D9 Wales, UK 52°8'N 4°37'W
tillery 48 G8 Wales, UK 51°43'N 3°9'W
ystwyth 48 E10 Wales, UK 52°25'N 4°5'W
114 F3 Saudi Arabia 18°16'N 42°32'E
87 I4 Turkey 40°4'N 26°13'E
an 96 E3 Ivory Coast 5°19'N 4°1'W
ne 147 I4 Texas, USA 32°27'N 99°44'W
gdon 50 E6 England, UK 51°41'N 1°17'W
gton 57 F4 Scotland, UK 55°30'N 3°42'W
ko 68 E12 Sweden 68°21'N 18°50'E
ne 56 H8 Scotland, UK 57°4'N 2°46'W
ntes 74 F5 Portugal 39°28'N 8°12'W
zzese, Appennino 77 I5 ▲ C Italy
hirīn 116 E5 Iran 34°17'N 51°17'E
Dhabi 115 K6 ● United Arab Emirates
°30'N 54°20'E
a 96 G4 ● Nigeria 9°4'N 7°28'E
nã, Rio 160 D8 ≈ Bolivia/Brazil
Şukhayr 111 J2 Iraq 31°54'N 44°27'E
ye Meda 97 L4 ▲ C Ethiopia
andia 163 I7 Brazil 4°51'S 47°26'W
oneta 150 C5 Mexico 22°30'N 105°21'W
ulco 150 D3 Mexico 16°51'N 99°53'W
a 96 F3 ● Ghana 5°33'N 0°15'W
ington 54 F2 England, UK 53°46'N 2°21'W
hoish 57 D5 Scotland, UK 55°57'N 5°30'W
l Head 58 B9 Headland W Ireland
l Island 58 B9 Island W Ireland
l Sound 58 B9 Ireland 53°55'N 9°56'W
asheen 56 E9 Scotland, UK 57°34'N 5°W
ns Island 151 J5 Island SE Bahamas
53 M5 England, UK 52°38'N 1°29'E
ncagua, Cerro 161 C5 ▲ W Argentina
ruña 74 F9 Spain 43°22'N 8°24'W
162 D6 ◈ State Brazil
, Rio 162 E6 ≈ W Brazil
n see Aden
na 110 F5 Turkey 37°N 35°19'E
pazarī 110 D7 Turkey 40°49'N 30°24'E
re, Cape 166 D3 Headland Antarctica
ab'īyah 115 K6 United Arab Emirates
°17'N 54°8'E
Dahna 115 H7 Desert E Saudi Arabia
Dammam 115 I7 Saudi Arabia
°23'N 50°5'E
Dār al Ḥamrā' 114 E7 Saudi Arabia
°22'N 37°46'E
Darb 114 F3 Saudi Arabia 17°45'N 42°15'E
Dawādimī 114 G6 Saudi Arabia
°32'N 44°21'E
is Ababa 97 L4 ● Ethiopia 9°N 38°43'E
laide 135 I3 South Australia
°56'S 138°36'E
n 114 G1 Yemen 12°51'N 45°5'E
n, Gulf of 115 I1 Gulf SW Arabian Sea
ge 77 H8 ≈ N Italy
rondack Mountains 147 M7 ▲▲ New York,
E USA
aman 110 G5 Turkey 37°46'N 38°15'E
a 75 I3 Spain 36°45'N 3°1'W
ar 96 F7 Algeria 27°56'N 0°12'W
atic Sea 79 H7 Sea N Mediterranean Sea
cha 109 J6 ≈ NE Russian Fed.
hanistan 117 I4 ◆ Islamic state C Asia
114 G6 Saudi Arabia 23°57'N 42°57'E
adow 97 M2 Somalia 0°24'N 42°4'E
nio 163 K6 Brazil 8°32'S 40°54'W
ca 91 Continent
ca, Horn of 91 Physical region Ethiopia/
omalia
on 110 D6 Turkey 38°46'N 30°32'E
dez 96 G5 Niger 16°57'N 7°56'E
dir 96 E7 Morocco 30°30'N 9°37'W

Agartala 119 J6 India 23°49'N 91°15'E
Agathónisi 87 J2 *Island* Dodecanese, Greece, Aegean Sea
Agde 73 H2 France 43°19'N 3°29'E
Agen 72 F3 France 44°12'N 0°37'E
Agialousa 79 N9 Cyprus 35°33'N 34°13'E
Ágios Efstrátios 87 I3 *Island* E Greece
Agios Nikolaos 87 I1 Greece 35°12'N 25°43'E
Agra 118 G7 India 27°9'N 78°E
Ağrī 111 I6 Turkey 39°44'N 43°4'E
Agrigento 77 I1 Italy 37°19'N 13°33'E
Agropoli 77 J4 Italy 40°22'N 14°59'E
Agua Prieta 150 B7 Mexico 31°16'N 109°33'W
Aguascalientes 150 D4 Mexico 21°54'N 102°17'W
Aguilas 75 J4 Spain 37°24'N 1°36'W
Ahaggar 96 G6 ▲▲ SE Algeria
Ahmadabad 118 F6 India 23°3'N 72°40'E
Ahmadnagar 118 F5 India 19°8'N 74°48'E
Ahvaz 116 D4 Iran 31°20'N 48°38'E
Aḥwar 115 H1 Yemen 13°34'N 46°41'E
Ailsa Craig 57 D4 *Island* SW Scotland, UK
Ainaži 69 G5 Latvia 57°51'N 24°24'E
Ainsdale 54 E2 England, UK 53°37'N 3°8'W
Airdrie 57 F5 Scotland, UK 55°52'N 3°59'W
Aire 55 I2 ≈ N England, UK
Aïr, Massif de l' 97 H5 ▲▲ NC Niger
Aix-en-Provence 73 I3 France 43°31'N 5°27'E
Āīzawl 119 K6 India 23°41'N 92°45'E
Ajaccio 73 K1 France 41°54'N 8°43'E
Ajaureforsen 69 D10 Sweden 65°31'N 15°44'E
Aj Bogd Uul 122 F7 ▲ SW Mongolia
Ajdabiya 97 I7 Libya 30°46'N 20°14'E
Ajmer 118 G7 India 26°29'N 74°40'E
Akasha 97 K6 Sudan 21°3'N 30°46'E
Akchâr 96 D6 *Desert* W Mauritania
Akhalts'ikhe 111 I7 Georgia 41°39'N 43°4'E
Akhisar 110 C6 Turkey 38°54'N 27°50'E
Akhtubinsk 89 F4 Russian Fed. 48°17'N 46°14'E
Akimiski Island 145 I3 *Island* Northwest Territories, C Canada
Akita 125 J6 Japan 39°44'N 140°6'E
Akjoujt 96 D6 Mauritania 19°42'N 14°28'W
Akkeshi 125 L8 Japan 43°3'N 144°49'E
Aklavik 144 D5 Northwest Territories, Canada 68°15'N 135°2'W
Akpatok Island 145 I4 *Island* Northwest Territories, E Canada
Akron 147 L6 Ohio, USA 41°5'N 81°31'W
Akrotiri Sovereign Base Area 79 M8 *Air base* S Cyprus
Aksai Chin 119 H9 *Disputed region* China/India
Aksaray 110 F5 Turkey 38°23'N 33°50'E
Akşehir 110 E5 Turkey 38°22'N 31°24'E
Aksu 122 D7 China 41°17'N 80°15'E
Aksu He 122 D7 ≈ China/Kyrgyzstan
Aktau 108 D3 Kazakhstan 43°37'N 51°14'E
Aktobe 108 E4 Kazakhstan 50°18'N 57°10'E
Akure 96 G4 Nigeria 7°18'N 5°13'E
Akureyri 68 B11 Iceland 65°40'N 18°7'W
Alabama 147 K4 ◈ State USA
Alabama River 147 K4 ≈ Alabama, S USA
Alaca 110 F6 Turkey 40°10'N 34°52'E
Alacant see Alicante
Alagoas 163 L6 ◈ State Brazil
Alagoinhas 163 K5 Brazil 12°9'S 38°21'W
Al Aḥmadī 115 H8 Kuwait 29°2'N 48°1'E
Al 'Ajā'iz 115 L4 Oman 19°33'N 57°12'E
Al 'Amādīyah 111 I5 Iraq 37°6'N 43°29'E
Al 'Amarah 111 K3 Iraq 31°51'N 47°10'E
Alamo 146 E5 Nevada, USA 37°21'N 115°8'W
Aland Islands 69 F6 *Island group* SW Finland
Aland Sea 69 E6 *Strait* Baltic Sea/Gulf of Bothnia
Alanya 110 E5 Turkey 36°32'N 32°2'E
Al Arṭāwīyah 115 H7 Saudi Arabia 26°34'N 45°20'E
Alaşehir 110 D5 Turkey 38°19'N 28°30'E
Al Ashkharah 115 M5 Oman 21°47'N 59°30'E
Alaska 146 B7 ◈ State USA
Alaska, Gulf of 146 C6 *Gulf* Canada/USA
Alaska Peninsula 146 B6 *Coastal feature* Alaska, USA
Alaska Range 146 B7 ▲▲ Alaska, USA
Al 'Athāmīn 111 J2 Iraq 30°27'N 43°41'E
Alavus 68 F8 Finland 62°33'N 23°38'E
Alaw, Llyn 48 D12 ◎ NW Wales, UK
Alazeya 109 K7 ≈ NE Russian Fed.
Albacete 75 J5 Spain 39°N 1°52'W
Al Bādī 111 I4 Iraq 35°57'N 41°37'E
Al Bāḥah 114 F4 Saudi Arabia 20°1'N 41°29'E
Alba Iulia 87 H8 Romania 46°6'N 23°33'E
Albania 86 F5 ◆ *Republic* SE Europe
Albany 147 L4 Georgia, USA 31°35'N 84°9'W
Albany 146 D8 Oregon, USA 44°38'N 123°6'W
Albany 134 D2 Western Australia 35°3'S 117°54'E
Albany 147 N7 New York, USA 42°39'N 73°45'W
Albany 145 H2 ≈ Ontario, S Canada
Al Barīt 111 I2 Iraq 31°16'N 42°28'E
Al Bayḍa' 97 I8 Libya 32°46'N 21°43'E
Al Bayḍa' 115 H1 Yemen 13°58'N 45°38'E
Albergaria-a-Velha 74 E7 Portugal 40°42'N 8°28'W
Albert 72 G8 France 50°N 2°38'E
Alberta 144 E3 ◈ *Province* Canada
Albert, Lake 99 I8 ◎ Uganda/Dem. Rep. Congo
Albi 72 G3 France 43°55'N 2°9'E
Al Birk 114 F3 Saudi Arabia 18°13'N 41°36'E
Alborz, Reshteh-ye Kūhhā-ye 116 E5 ▲▲ N Iran
Albuquerque 146 G5 New Mexico, USA 35°5'N 106°38'W
Al Buraymī 115 K6 Oman 24°16'N 55°48'E
Albury 135 J2 New South Wales, Australia 36°3'S 146°53'E
Alcácer do Sal 74 E4 Portugal 38°22'N 8°29'W
Alcalá de Henares 75 I6 Spain 40°28'N 3°22'W
Alcamo 77 I2 Italy 37°58'N 12°58'E
Alcañiz 75 K7 Spain 41°3'N 0°9'W
Alcántara, Embalse de 74 G6 ⊠ W Spain
Alcester 52 F4 England, UK 52°12'N 1°55'W
Alcoi see Alcoy
Alcoy 75 K5 Spain 38°42'N 0°29'W
Aldabra Group 99 L6 *Island group* SW Seychelles
Aldan 109 J6 ≈ NE Russian Fed.
Aldbourne 49 I7 England, UK 51°29'N 1°45'W
Aldbrough 55 K3 England, UK 53°50'N 0°8'W

Alde 53 M4 ≈ E England, UK
Aldeburgh 53 M4 England, UK 52°12'N 1°36'E
Alderbury 49 I6 England, UK 51°2'N 1°50'W
Aldermaston 50 E5 England, UK 51°23'N 1°10'W
Alderney 72 E8 *Island* Channel Islands
Aldershot 50 F4 England, UK 51°15'N 0°47'W
Aldford 52 E7 England, UK 53°8'N 2°53'W
Aleg 96 D5 Mauritania 17°3'N 13°53'W
Aleksin 89 D6 Russian Fed. 54°30'N 37°8'E
Alençon 72 F7 France 48°26'N 0°4'E
Aleppo 110 G4 Syria 36°14'N 37°10'E
Alert 145 H9 Northwest Territories, Canada 82°28'N 62°13'W
Alès 73 H3 France 44°8'N 4°5'E
Alessandria 76 F8 Italy 44°54'N 8°37'E
Ålesund 68 A8 Norway 62°28'N 6°11'E
Aleutian Basin 25 *Undersea feature* Bering Sea
Aleutian Islands 146 A5 *Island group* Alaska, USA
Aleutian Trench 25 *Undersea feature* S Bering Sea
Alexander Archipelago 146 C6 *Island group* Alaska, USA
Alexander Island 166 B6 *Island* Antarctica
Alexandra 136 B2 New Zealand 45°15'S 169°25'E
Alexandria 57 E5 Scotland, UK 56°0'N 4°33'W
Alexandria 147 J4 Louisiana, USA 31°19'N 92°27'W
Alexandria 97 J7 Egypt 31°7'N 29°51'E
Alexandroupoli 87 I4 Greece 40°52'N 25°53'E
Al Fallūjah 111 J3 Iraq 33°21'N 43°46'E
Alfeios 86 G2 ≈ S Greece
Alford 53 J8 England, UK 53°15'N 0°9'E
Alfreton 52 G7 England, UK 53°5'N 1°30'W
Al Fuḥayḥīl 115 H8 Kuwait 29°1'N 48°5'E
Al Fuḥaymī 111 I4 Iraq 34°18'N 42°9'E
Al Fujayrah 115 L6 United Arab Emirates 25°9'N 56°18'E
Alga 108 E4 Kazakhstan 49°56'N 57°19'E
Algeciras 74 G3 Spain 36°8'N 5°27'W
Algemesí 75 K5 Spain 39°11'N 0°27'W
Algeria 96 F7 ◆ *Republic* N Africa
Al Ghabah 115 L5 Oman 21°22'N 57°14'E
Al Ghayḍah 115 J3 Yemen 16°15'N 52°13'E
Alghero 76 F4 Italy 40°34'N 8°19'E
Algiers 96 G8 ● Algeria 36°47'N 2°58'E
Al Hadr 111 I4 Iraq 35°34'N 42°44'E
Al Hajār al Gharbī 115 L6 ▲▲ N Oman
Al Ḥamrā' 115 L6 Oman 23°7'N 57°23'E
Al Ḥanākīyah 114 F6 Saudi Arabia 24°55'N 40°31'E
Al Ḥarrah 114 E9 *Desert* NW Saudi Arabia
Al Hasakah 111 H5 Syria 36°22'N 40°44'E
Al Ḥayy 111 K3 Iraq 32°11'N 46°3'E
Al Hijāz 114 E6 *Physical region* NW Saudi Arabia
Al Hillah 111 J3 Iraq 32°28'N 44°29'E
Al Hufuf 115 I6 Saudi Arabia 25°21'N 49°34'E
'Alī al Gharbī 111 K3 Iraq 32°28'N 46°42'E
Aliartos 87 H3 Greece 38°23'N 23°6'E
Ali-Bayramli 111 K7 Azerbaijan 39°57'N 48°54'E
Alicante 75 K4 Spain 38°21'N 0°29'W
Alice Springs 135 H6 Northern Territory, Australia 23°42'S 133°52'E
Al Jaghbub 97 J7 Libya 29°45'N 24°31'E
Al Jahrā' 115 H8 Kuwait 29°18'N 47°36'E
Al Jawf 114 F8 Saudi Arabia 29°51'N 39°49'E
Al Jubayl 115 I7 Saudi Arabia 27°N 49°36'E
Al Jumaylīyah 115 J7 Qatar 25°37'N 51°5'E
Al Khābūrah 115 L6 Oman 23°57'N 57°6'E
Al Khāliş 111 J3 Iraq 33°51'N 44°33'E
Al Kharj 115 H6 Saudi Arabia 24°12'N 47°12'E
Al Khaşab 115 K7 Oman 26°11'N 56°18'E
Al Khawr 115 J7 Qatar 25°40'N 51°33'E
Al Khīrān 115 I8 Kuwait 28°34'N 48°21'E
Al Khufrah 97 J6 Libya 24°11'N 23°19'E
Al Khuraybah 115 I2 Yemen 15°5'N 48°17'E
Al Khurmah 114 F5 Saudi Arabia 21°59'N 42°0'E
Alkmaar 70 E11 Netherlands 52°37'N 4°45'E
Al Kūfah 111 J3 Iraq 32°2'N 44°25'E
Al Kut 111 K3 Iraq 32°30'N 45°51'E
Al Labbah 114 F8 *Physical region* N Saudi Arabia
Al Lādhiqīyah 110 F4 Syria 35°31'N 35°47'E
Allahabad 119 H6 India 25°27'N 81°50'E
Allegheny Plateau 147 M7 ▲▲ New York/Pennsylvania, NE USA
Allendale Town 54 G6 England, UK 54°55'N 2°16'W
Allenheads 54 G6 England, UK 54°48'N 2°11'W
Allen, Lough 58 E10 ◎ NW Ireland
Allentown 147 M7 Pennsylvania, USA 40°37'N 75°30'W
Alleppey 118 G2 India 9°30'N 76°22'E
Al Lith 114 F4 Saudi Arabia 21°N 41°E
Alloa 57 F6 Scotland, UK 56°7'N 3°49'W
Allonby 54 D6 England, UK 54°46'N 3°31'W
Al Luḥayyah 114 F2 Yemen 15°44'N 42°45'E
Al Ma'ānīyah 111 J2 Iraq 30°45'N 42°58'E
Almada 74 E5 Portugal 38°40'N 9°9'W
Al Mahrah 115 J3 ▲▲ E Yemen
Al Majma'ah 114 G7 Saudi Arabia 25°55'N 45°19'E
Almansa 75 J5 Spain 38°52'N 1°6'W
Al Maṣna'ah 115 L6 Oman 23°45'N 57°38'E
Almaty 108 F2 Kazakhstan 43°19'N 76°55'E
Al Mayyāh 114 G7 Saudi Arabia 27°57'N 42°53'E
Almelo 70 H10 Netherlands 52°22'N 6°42'E
Almendra, Embalse de 74 G7 ⊠ Castilla-León, NW Spain
Almendralejo 74 G5 Spain 38°41'N 6°25'W
Almere 70 F10 Netherlands 52°22'N 5°12'E
Almería 75 J3 Spain 36°50'N 2°26'W
Al'met'yevsk 89 G6 Russian Fed. 54°53'N 52°20'E
Almondsbury 49 H7 England, UK 51°33'N 2°41'W
Al Mubarraz 115 I6 Saudi Arabia 25°28'N 49°34'E
Al Mudawwarah 110 G1 Jordan 29°20'N 36°E
Al Mukalla 115 I2 Yemen 14°36'N 49°7'E
Al Mukhā 114 G1 Yemen 13°18'N 43°17'E
Al Muqdādīyah 111 J3 Iraq 33°58'N 44°58'E
Al Musayyib 111 J3 Iraq 32°47'N 44°20'E
Aln 54 G8 ≈ N England, UK
Alness 56 F10 Scotland, UK 57°42'N 4°18'W

Alnwick 55 H8 England, UK 55°27'N 1°44'W
Alonnisos 87 H3 *Island* Northern Sporades, Greece, Aegean Sea
Álora 75 H3 Spain 36°50'N 4°43'W
Alor, Kepulauan 127 J1 *Island group* E Indonesia
Alphen aan den Rijn 70 E10 Netherlands 52°8'N 4°40'E
Alps 83 F5 ▲▲ C Europe
Al Qābil 115 K6 Oman 23°55'N 55°50'E
Al Qalībah 114 E8 Saudi Arabia 28°29'N 37°40'E
Al Qamishli 111 I5 Syria 37°N 41°E
Al Qash'ānīyah 115 H8 Kuwait 29°59'N 47°42'E
Al Qaṭrānah 110 G2 Jordan 31°14'N 36°3'E
Al Qunaytirah 110 B5 Syria 33°8'N 35°49'E
Al Qunfudhah 114 F4 Saudi Arabia 19°19'N 41°3'E
Al Qurayyāt 114 E9 Saudi Arabia 31°25'N 37°26'E
Al Qurnah 111 K2 Iraq 31°1'N 47°27'E
Al Quwayīyah 114 G6 Saudi Arabia 24°6'N 45°18'E
Alsager 52 F7 England, UK 53°6'N 2°17'W
Alsdorf 82 C8 Germany 50°52'N 6°9'E
Alston 54 F6 England, UK 54°49'N 2°25'W
Alta 68 F13 Norway 69°58'N 23°17'E
Altai Mountains 103 ▲▲ Asia/Europe
Altamaha River 147 L4 ≈ Georgia, SE USA
Altamira 163 H7 Brazil 3°13'S 52°15'W
Altamura 77 K4 Italy 40°50'N 16°33'E
Altar, Desierto de 150 B7 *Desert* Mexico/USA see also Sonoran Desert
Altay 122 G7 Mongolia 46°23'N 96°17'E
Altnaharra 56 E11 Scotland, UK 58°17'N 4°31'W
Alton 50 E4 England, UK 51°9'N 1°4'W
Altoona 147 M6 Pennsylvania, USA 40°32'N 78°23'W
Altun Shan 122 E6 ▲▲ NW China
Al 'Ubaydī 111 I4 Iraq 34°22'N 41°15'E
Al 'Ubaylah 115 J5 Saudi Arabia 22°2'N 50°57'E
Al 'Udayd 115 J6 United Arab Emirates 24°34'N 51°27'E
Al 'Ulā 114 E7 Saudi Arabia 26°39'N 37°55'E
Al 'Urūq al Mu'tariḍah 115 K5 *Salt lake* SE Saudi Arabia
Ālūs 111 I3 Iraq 34°5'N 42°27'E
Al 'Uwaynat 97 H7 Libya 25°47'N 10°34'E
Al Wafrā' 115 H8 Kuwait 28°38'N 47°57'E
Al Wajh 114 D7 Saudi Arabia 26°16'N 36°30'E
Alwar 118 G7 India 27°32'N 76°35'E
Al Wari'ah 115 H7 Saudi Arabia 27°54'N 47°23'E
Alytus 69 G3 Lithuania 54°24'N 24°2'E
Alzette 71 G3 ≈ S Luxembourg
Amadeus, Lake 134 G5 ◎ Northern Territory, C Australia
Amadjuak Lake 145 I5 ◎ Baffin Island, Northwest Territories, N Canada
Amakusa-nada 124 F2 *Gulf* Kyūshū, SW Japan
Åmål 69 C6 Sweden 59°4'N 12°41'E
Amamapare 127 M2 Indonesia 4°51'S 136°44'E
Amantea 77 K3 Italy 39°6'N 16°5'E
Amapá 163 H8 ◈ *State* Brazil
Amarapura 126 E7 Burma 21°54'N 96°1'E
Amarillo 147 H4 Texas, USA 35°13'N 101°50'W
Amay 71 F5 Belgium 50°33'N 5°19'E
Amazon 163 H8 ≈ Brazil/Peru
Amazonas 162 F7 ◈ *State* Brazil
Amazon Basin 162 G7 *Basin* N South America
Ambanja 99 L5 Madagascar 13°40'S 48°27'E
Ambarchik 109 K8 Russian Fed. 69°33'N 162°8'E
Ambérieu-en-Bugey 73 I5 France 45°57'N 5°21'E
Amble 55 H8 England, UK 55°20'N 1°33'W
Ambleside 54 E5 England, UK 54°26'N 2°58'W
Amboasary 99 K3 Madagascar 25°1'S 46°23'E
Ambon 127 K2 Indonesia 3°41'S 128°10'E
Ambositra 99 L4 Madagascar 20°31'S 47°15'E
Ambriz 98 E6 Angola 7°55'S 13°11'E
'Amd 115 I2 Yemen 15°10'N 47°58'E
Amderma 88 H12 Russian Fed. 69°45'N 61°36'E
Amdo 122 E4 China 32°15'N 91°43'E
Ameland 70 F13 *Island* Waddeneilanden, N Netherlands
American Samoa 128 US ◇ Polynesia
Amersfoort 70 F10 Netherlands 52°9'N 5°23'E
Amersham 50 F6 England, UK 51°40'N 0°37'W
Amesbury 49 I6 England, UK 51°9'N 1°54'W
Amga 109 J5 ≈ NE Russian Fed.
Amherst 145 K2 Nova Scotia, Canada 45°50'N 64°14'W
Amiens 72 G8 France 49°54'N 2°18'E
Amindivi Islands 118 F3 *Island group* Lakshadweep, India, N Indian Ocean
Amlwch 48 D13 Wales, UK 53°25'N 4°23'W
Amman 110 F2 ● Jordan 31°57'N 35°56'E
Ammanford 48 E8 Wales, UK 51°48'N 4°3'W
Ämmänsaari 68 H10 Finland 64°51'N 28°58'E
Ammassalik 145 K7 Greenland 65°51'N 37°30'W
Ammochostos see Famagusta
Āmol 116 E6 Iran 36°31'N 52°24'E
Amorgos 87 I2 *Island* Cyclades, Greece, Aegean Sea
Amos 145 I2 Québec, Canada 48°34'N 78°8'W
Ampato, Nevado 161 C7 ▲ S Peru
Amposta 75 K7 Spain 40°43'N 0°34'E
'Amrān 114 G2 Yemen 15°39'N 43°59'E
Amravati 118 G5 India 20°56'N 77°45'E
Amritsar 118 G8 India 31°38'N 74°55'E
Amstelveen 70 E10 Netherlands 52°18'N 4°50'E
Amsterdam 70 E10 ● Netherlands 52°22'N 4°54'E
Am Timan 97 I4 Chad 11°2'N 20°17'E
Amu Darya 117 H7 ≈ C Asia
Amund Ringnes Island 144 G7 *Island* Northwest Territories, Sverdrup Islands, N Canada
Amundsen Gulf 144 E6 *Gulf* Northwest Territories, N Canada
Amundsen Sea 166 B4 *Sea* S Pacific Ocean
Amuntai 127 H2 Indonesia 2°24'S 115°14'E
Amur 109 K4 ≈ China/Russian Fed.
Amyderya 117 I6 Turkmenistan 37°58'N 65°14'E
Anabar 109 I6 ≈ NE Russian Fed.
Anadyr' 109 L8 Russian Fed. 64°41'N 177°22'E

Anafi 87 I1 *Island* Cyclades, Greece, Aegean Sea
Analalava 99 L5 Madagascar 14°38'S 47°46'E
Anamur 110 E4 Turkey 36°6'N 32°49'E
Anantapur 118 G3 India 14°41'N 77°36'E
Anápolis 163 I4 Brazil 16°19'S 48°58'W
Anar 116 F3 Iran 30°49'N 55°18'E
Anārak 116 E4 Iran 33°21'N 53°43'E
Anar Darreh 117 H4 Afghanistan 32°45'N 61°38'E
Añatuya 161 D5 Argentina 28°28'S 62°52'W
Anchorage 146 B6 Alaska, USA 61°13'N 149°52'W
Ancona 77 I6 Italy 43°38'N 13°30'E
Ancud 161 C3 Chile 41°53'S 73°50'W
Åndalsnes 68 B8 Norway 62°33'N 7°42'E
Andaman and Nicobar Islands 119 K3 ◈ *Union territory* India
Andaman Islands 119 K3 *Island group* India, NE Indian Ocean
Andaman Sea 126 E5 *Sea* NE Indian Ocean
Andenne 71 E5 Belgium 50°29'N 5°6'E
Anderlues 71 D5 Belgium 50°24'N 4°16'E
Andes 161 C6 ▲▲ W South America
Andhra Pradesh 119 H4 ◈ *State* India
Andijon 117 K7 Uzbekistan 40°46'N 72°19'E
Andkhvoy 117 I6 Afghanistan 36°56'N 65°8'E
Andong 124 F4 South Korea 36°34'N 128°44'E
Andorra 75 L8 ◆ *Monarchy* SW Europe
Andorra la Vella 75 L8 ● Andorra 42°30'N 1°30'E
Andover 50 D4 England, UK 51°13'N 1°28'W
Andøya 68 D12 *Island* C Norway
Andreanof Islands 146 A6 *Island group* Aleutian Islands, Alaska, USA
Andria 77 K5 Italy 41°13'N 16°17'E
Andros 87 I2 *Island* Cyclades, Greece, Aegean Sea
Andros Island 151 I5 *Island* NW Bahamas
Andros Town 151 I5 Bahamas 24°40'N 77°47'W
Angara 109 H4 ≈ C Russian Fed.
Angarsk 109 I3 Russian Fed. 52°31'N 103°55'E
Ånge 68 D8 Sweden 62°31'N 15°40'E
Ángel de la Guarda, Isla 150 B7 *Island* NW Mexico
Angeles 127 I6 Philippines 15°16'N 120°37'E
Ångermanälven 68 E9 ≈ N Sweden
Angermünde 82 H10 Germany 53°2'N 13°59'E
Angers 72 F6 France 47°30'N 0°33'W
Angle 48 C8 Wales, UK 51°41'N 5°9'W
Anglesey 48 D12 *Island* NW Wales, UK
Anglet 72 E3 France 43°29'N 1°30'W
Ang Nam Ngum 126 F4 ◎ C Laos
Angola 98 F6 ◆ *Republic* SW Africa
Angola Basin 25 *Undersea feature* E Atlantic Ocean
Angostura, Presa 150 F3 ⊠ Sonora, NW Mexico Central America
Angostura, Presa de la 150 F3 ⊠ SE Mexico
Angoulême 72 F4 France 45°39'N 0°10'E
Angoumois 72 F4 *Cultural region* France
Angren 117 J7 Uzbekistan 41°5'N 70°18'E
Anguilla 151 M4 *UK* ◇ West Indies
Angus 57 G7 ◈ *Unitary authority* Scotland, UK
Anhui 123 J4 ◈ *Province* China
Anjou 72 F6 *Cultural region* France
Anjouan 99 K5 *Island* SE Comoros
Ankara 110 E6 ● Turkey 39°55'N 32°50'E
Anklam 82 G11 Germany 53°51'N 13°42'E
Annaba 96 G8 Algeria 36°55'N 7°47'E
An Nafud 114 F8 *Desert* NW Saudi Arabia
An Najaf 111 J2 Iraq 31°59'N 44°19'E
Annalee 58 F10 ≈ N Ireland
Annalong 58 H10 Northern Ireland, UK 54°6'N 5°53'W
Annan 57 G3 Scotland, UK 55°N 3°20'W
Annapolis 147 M6 Maryland, USA 38°59'N 76°30'W
Annapurna 119 I7 ▲ C Nepal
Ann Arbor 147 L7 Michigan, USA 42°17'N 83°45'W
An Nasiriyah 111 K2 Iraq 31°4'N 46°17'E
Annecy 73 I5 France 45°53'N 6°9'E
An Nu'ayrīyah 115 I7 Saudi Arabia 27°30'N 48°30'E
An Nukhayb 111 I2 Iraq 32°2'N 42°15'E
An Nu'mānīyah 111 J3 Iraq 32°34'N 45°23'E
Anqing 123 J4 China 30°32'N 116°59'E
Anshan 123 K6 China 41°6'N 122°55'E
Anshun 123 H3 China 26°15'N 105°58'E
Anston 53 H8 England, UK 53°21'N 1°15'W
Antakya 110 G4 Turkey 36°12'N 36°10'E
Antalaha 99 L5 Madagascar 14°53'S 50°16'E
Antalya 110 D5 Turkey 36°53'N 30°42'E
Antananarivo 99 L4 ● Madagascar 18°52'S 47°30'E
Antarctica 166 *Continent*
Antarctic Peninsula 166 B6 *Coastal feature* Antarctica
Antequera 75 H3 Spain 37°1'N 4°34'W
Antibes 73 J3 France 43°35'N 7°7'E
Anticosti, Île d' 145 K3 *Island* Québec, E Canada
Antigua 151 M4 *Island* S Antigua and Barbuda, Leeward Islands
Antigua and Barbuda 151 M4 ◆ *Commonwealth republic* E West Indies
Antikythira 87 H1 *Island* S Greece
Antofagasta 161 C6 Chile 23°40'S 70°23'W
Antony 72 G7 France 48°45'N 2°17'E
Antrim 58 H11 Northern Ireland, UK 54°43'N 6°13'W
Antrim 58 H11 ◈ *District* Northern Ireland, UK
Antrim Mountains 58 H12 ▲▲ NE Northern Ireland, UK
Antsirañana 99 L5 Madagascar 12°19'S 49°17'E
Antsohihy 99 L5 Madagascar 14°50'S 47°58'E
Antwerp 71 D7 Belgium 51°13'N 4°25'E
Anuradhapura 119 H2 Sri Lanka 8°20'N 80°25'E
Anyang 123 J5 China 36°11'N 114°18'E
A'nyêmaqên Shan 122 G5 ▲▲ C China
Anzio 77 H5 Italy 41°28'N 12°38'E
Aomori 125 K7 Japan 40°50'N 140°43'E
Aoraki 136 C3 ▲ South Island, New Zealand 43°38'S 170°5'E
Aosta 76 E8 Italy 45°43'N 7°20'E
Aoukâr 96 E5 *Plateau* C Mauritania
Aouk, Bahr 97 I4 ≈ Central African Republic/Chad
Aozou 97 I6 Chad 22°1'N 17°11'E

◆ Country ● Country capital ◇ Dependent territory ○ Dependent territory capital ◈ Administrative region ▲ Mountain ▲▲ Mountain range ⚲ Volcano ≈ River ◎ Lake ⊠ Reservoir

170 Apalachee Bay - Bargoed

Apalachee Bay 147 L3 Bay Florida, SE USA
Apaporis, Río 160 C10 ≈ Brazil/Colombia
Apatity 88 D11 Russian Fed. 67°34'N 33°26'E
Apeldoorn 70 G10 Netherlands 52°13'N 5°57'E
Apia 128 ● Samoa 13°50'S 171°47'W
Aporé, Rio 163 H4 ≈ SW Brazil
Apostle Islands 147 J8 Island group Wisconsin, N USA
Appalachian Mountains 147 L5 ⛰ E USA
Appingedam 70 H13 Netherlands 53°18'N 6°52'E
Appleby-in-Westmorland 54 F5 England, UK 54°35'N 2°26'W
Appledore 51 J3 England, UK 51°1'N 0°46'E
Apucarana 163 H3 Brazil 23°34'S 51°28'W
Apuseni, Munţii 87 H8 ⛰ W Romania
Aqaba, Gulf of 114 D8 Gulf NE Red Sea
Aqchah 117 I6 Afghanistan 37°N 66°7'E
Aquitaine 72 F3 Cultural region France
'Arabah, Wadi al 110 B2 Dry watercourse Israel/Jordan
Arabian Basin 25 Undersea feature N Arabian Sea
Arabian Peninsula 114 G5 Coastal feature SW Asia
Arabian Sea 115 K2 Sea NW Indian Ocean
Aracaju 163 K5 Brazil 10°45'S 37°7'W
Aracati 163 K7 Brazil 4°32'S 37°45'W
Araçatuba 163 H3 Brazil 21°12'S 50°24'W
Arad 86 G8 Romania 46°12'N 21°20'E
'Arad 110 B3 Israel 31°16'N 35°9'E
'Arādah 115 K5 United Arab Emirates 22°57'N 53°24'E
Araguaia, Rio 163 I6 ≈ C Brazil
Araguaína 163 I6 Brazil 7°16'S 48°18'W
Araguari 163 I4 Brazil 18°38'S 48°13'W
Arak 116 D5 Iran 34°7'N 49°39'E
Arakan Yoma 126 D7 ⛰ W Burma
Aral Sea 116 G9 Inland sea Kazakhstan/Uzbekistan
Aral'sk 108 E3 Kazakhstan 46°48'N 61°40'E
Ārān 116 E5 Iran 34°3'N 51°30'E
Aranda de Duero 75 I7 Spain 41°40'N 3°41'W
Aran Fawddwy 48 F11 ▲ NW Wales, UK
Aran Island 58 D12 Island NW Ireland
Aran Islands 59 C7 Island group W Ireland
Aranjuez 75 I6 Spain 40°2'N 3°37'W
Arapiraca 163 L6 Brazil 9°45'S 36°40'W
'Ar'ar 114 F9 Saudi Arabia 31°N 41°E
Araraquara 163 I3 Brazil 21°46'S 48°8'W
Araras 162 H7 Brazil 6°4'S 54°34'W
Arbil 111 J5 Iraq 36°12'N 44°1'E
Arbroath 57 H7 Scotland, UK 56°34'N 2°35'W
Arcachon 72 E3 France 44°40'N 1°11'W
Archangel 88 E9 Russian Fed. 64°32'N 40°40'E
Archidona 75 H3 Spain 37°6'N 4°23'W
Arco 76 G8 Italy 45°53'N 10°52'E
Arcoverde 163 K6 Brazil 8°23'S 37°W
Arda 87 I5 ≈ Bulgaria/Greece see also Ardas
Ardabil 116 D6 Iran 38°15'N 48°18'E
Ardara 58 E11 Ireland 54°46'N 8°25'W
Ardas 87 I5 ≈ Bulgaria/Greece see also Arda
Ardèche 73 H3 Cultural region France
Ardee 58 G9 Ireland 53°52'N 6°33'W
Ardestān 116 E4 Iran 33°29'N 52°17'E
Ardglass 58 I10 Northern Ireland, UK 54°16'N 5°33'W
Ardgroom 59 B4 Ireland 51°43'N 9°52'W
Ardlussa 57 C6 Scotland, UK 56°2'N 5°50'W
Ardmolich 57 D7 Scotland, UK 56°48'N 5°41'W
Ardmore 59 F5 Ireland 51°56'N 7°42'W
Ardnamurchan, Point of 57 C7 Headland N Scotland, UK
Ardrahan 59 D7 Ireland 53°9'N 8°48'W
Ards 58 I11 ◐ District Northern Ireland, UK
Ards Peninsula 58 I11 Coastal feature E Northern Ireland, UK
Arduaine 57 D6 Scotland, UK 56°14'N 5°29'W
Ardvasar 56 C8 Scotland, UK 57°4'N 5°58'W
Arendal 69 B5 Norway 58°27'N 8°45'E
Arenig Fawr 48 E11 ▲ NW Wales, UK
Arenys de Mar 75 M8 Spain 41°35'N 2°33'E
Areopoli 86 G1 Greece 36°40'N 22°24'E
Arequipa 161 C7 Peru 16°24'S 71°33'W
Arezzo 77 H6 Italy 43°28'N 11°50'E
Argenteuil 72 G7 France 48°57'N 2°13'E
Argentina 161 D4 ◆ Republic S South America
Argentine Basin 24 Undersea feature SW Atlantic Ocean
Arghandab, Darya-ye 117 I4 ≈ SE Afghanistan
Argun 123 J8 ≈ China/Russian Fed.
Argyle, Lake 134 F8 Salt lake Western Australia
Argyll and Bute 57 D6 ◐ Unitary authority Scotland, UK
Århus 69 B4 Denmark 56°9'N 10°11'E
Arica 161 C7 Chile 18°31'S 70°18'W
Arinagour 57 B7 Scotland, UK 56°38'N 6°28'W
Ariquemes 162 F6 Brazil 9°55'S 63°6'W
Arisaig 56 C8 Scotland, UK 56°55'N 5°48'W
Arizona 146 F4 ◐ State USA
Årjäng 68 C6 Sweden 59°24'N 12°9'E
Arjeplog 68 E10 Sweden 66°4'N 18°E
Arkansas 147 J5 ◐ State USA
Arkansas River 147 J4 ≈ C USA
Arkhangel'sk see Archangel
Arklow 59 H7 Ireland 52°48'N 6°9'W
Arles 73 I3 France 43°41'N 4°38'E
Arlington 147 I4 Texas, USA 32°44'N 97°5'W
Arlington 147 M6 Virginia, USA 38°54'N 77°9'W
Arlon 71 G3 Belgium 49°41'N 5°49'E
Armagh 58 G10 Northern Ireland, UK 54°15'N 6°33'W
Armagh 58 G10 ◐ District Northern Ireland, UK
Armagnac 72 F3 Cultural region France
Armando Laydner, Represa 163 I3 ⊠ S Brazil
Armenia 160 B11 Colombia 4°32'N 75°40'W
Armenia 111 J7 ◆ Republic SW Asia
Armidale 135 L3 New South Wales, Australia 30°32'S 151°40'E
Armoy 58 H12 Northern Ireland, UK 55°8'N 6°19'W
Armstrong 145 H2 Ontario, Canada 50°20'N 89°2'W
Armyans'k 89 C3 Ukraine 46°5'N 33°43'E
Arnedo 75 J8 Spain 42°14'N 2°5'W
Arnhem 70 G9 Netherlands 51°59'N 5°54'E
Arnhem Land 135 H8 Physical region Northern Territory, N Australia
Arno 76 G7 ≈ C Italy
Arnold 53 H7 England, UK 53°N 1°10'W
Ar Ramādī 111 J3 Iraq 33°27'N 43°19'E
Arran, Isle of 57 D5 Island SW Scotland, UK
Ar Raqqah 111 H4 Syria 35°57'N 39°3'E
Arras 72 G8 France 50°17'N 2°46'E
Ar Rawḍah 114 G5 Saudi Arabia 21°19'N 42°48'E
Ar Rawḍah 115 H2 Yemen 14°26'N 47°14'E
Arriaga 150 E3 Mexico 16°14'N 93°54'W
Ar Rifā'ī 111 K2 Iraq 31°47'N 46°7'E
Ar Riyad see Riyadh
Arrochar 57 E6 Scotland, UK 56°12'N 4°41'W
Arrow, Lough 58 E10 ◎ N Ireland
Ar Rub 'al Khālī 115 I4 Desert SW Asia
Ar Ruḍaymah 111 K2 Iraq 30°20'N 45°26'E
Ar Rustaq 115 L6 Oman 23°34'N 57°25'E
Ar Ruṭbah 111 H3 Iraq 33°3'N 40°16'E
Ar Ruways 115 J6 United Arab Emirates 24°9'N 52°57'E
Árta 86 G3 Greece 39°8'N 20°59'E
Artashat 111 J6 Armenia 39°57'N 44°34'E
Artemisa 151 H4 Cuba 22°49'N 82°47'W
Artigas 161 E5 Uruguay 30°25'S 56°28'W
Art'ik 111 I7 Armenia 40°38'N 43°58'E
Artois 72 G8 Cultural region France
Artvin 111 I7 Turkey 41°12'N 41°48'E
Arua 99 I8 Uganda 3°2'N 30°56'E
Aruba 151 K3 Dutch ◇ West Indies
Aru, Kepulauan 127 L2 Island group E Indonesia
Arunachal Pradesh 119 K7 ◐ State India
Arundel 50 F3 England, UK 50°51'N 0°34'W
Arusha 99 J7 Tanzania 3°23'S 36°40'E
Arviat 144 G4 Northwest Territories, Canada 61°10'N 94°15'W
Arvidsjaur 68 E10 Sweden 65°34'N 19°12'E
Arvika 68 C6 Sweden 59°41'N 12°38'E
Arys' 108 F2 Kazakhstan 42°26'N 68°49'E
Asadabad 117 K5 Afghanistan 34°52'N 71°9'E
Asahi-dake 125 K8 ▲ Hokkaidō, N Japan
Asahikawa 125 K8 Japan 43°46'N 142°23'E
Asamankese 96 F3 Ghana 5°47'N 0°41'W
Asansol 119 I6 India 23°40'N 86°59'E
Ascension Island 13 St. Helena ◇ Atlantic Ocean
Ascoli Piceno 77 I6 Italy 42°51'N 13°34'E
Aseb 97 M5 Eritrea 13°4'N 42°36'E
Aşgabat 116 G6 ● Turkmenistan 37°58'N 58°22'E
Ashbourne 58 H8 Ireland 53°29'N 6°35'W
Ashbourne 52 G7 England, UK 53°1'N 1°45'W
Ashburton 136 C3 New Zealand 43°55'S 171°47'E
Ashburton River 134 D5 ≈ Western Australia
Ashby de la Zouch 52 G6 England, UK 52°43'N 1°30'W
Ashdod 110 A3 Israel 31°48'N 34°38'E
Asheville 147 L5 North Carolina, USA 35°36'N 82°33'W
Ashford 51 J4 England, UK 51°9'N 0°52'E
Ashington 55 H7 England, UK 55°10'N 1°31'W
Ashmore and Cartier Islands 13 Australian ◇ Indian Ocean
Ash Shanāfīyah 111 J2 Iraq 31°35'N 44°38'E
Ash Sharmah 114 D8 Saudi Arabia 28°2'N 35°16'E
Ash Sharqāṭ 111 I4 Iraq 35°31'N 43°15'E
Ash Shaṭrah 111 K2 Iraq 31°26'N 46°10'E
Ash Shiḥr 115 I2 Yemen 14°45'N 49°24'E
Ash Shişar 115 K3 Oman 18°13'N 53°35'E
Ashton-under-Lyne 54 G2 England, UK 53°29'N 2°6'W
Ashwater 49 D5 England, UK 50°45'N 4°14'W
Asia 103 Continent
'Asīr 114 F4 ⛰ SW Saudi Arabia
Aşkale 111 H6 Turkey 39°56'N 40°39'E
Askern 53 H9 England, UK 53°37'N 1°15'W
Askersund 69 D6 Sweden 58°55'N 14°55'E
Askrigg 54 G4 England, UK 54°19'N 2°7'W
Asmar 117 K5 Afghanistan 34°59'N 71°29'E
Asmara 97 L5 ● Eritrea 15°15'N 38°58'E
Aspatria 54 E6 England, UK 54°45'N 3°21'W
As Salimi 115 H8 Kuwait 29°7'N 46°41'E
As Salmān 111 J2 Iraq 30°29'N 44°34'E
As Salwā 115 J6 Qatar 24°44'N 50°52'E
Assam 119 K7 ◐ State India
Assamakka 96 G6 Niger 19°24'N 5°53'E
As Samāwah 111 J2 Iraq 31°17'N 45°6'E
Assen 70 H12 Netherlands 53°N 6°34'E
Assenede 71 C7 Belgium 51°15'N 3°43'E
As Sulaymaniyah 111 J4 Iraq 35°32'N 45°27'E
As Sulayyil 115 H4 Saudi Arabia 20°29'N 45°33'E
As Suwaydā' 110 G3 Syria 32°43'N 36°33'E
Aş Şuwayrah 111 J3 Iraq 32°57'N 44°47'E
Astana 108 F3 ● Kazakhstan 51°13'N 71°25'E
Asti 76 F8 Italy 44°54'N 8°11'E
Astorga 74 G8 Spain 42°27'N 6°4'W
Astoria 146 D8 Oregon, USA 46°12'N 123°50'W
Astrakhan' 89 F3 Russian Fed. 46°20'N 48°1'E
Astwood Bank 52 F4 England, UK 52°16'N 2°1'W
Astypalaia 87 I2 Island Cyclades, Greece, Aegean Sea
Asunción 161 E6 ● Paraguay 25°17'S 57°36'W
Aswān 97 K6 Egypt 24°3'N 32°59'E
Asyut 97 K7 Egypt 27°6'N 31°11'E
Atacama Desert 161 C6 Desert N Chile
Atamyrat 117 I6 Turkmenistan 37°52'N 65°6'E
Aţâr 96 D6 Mauritania 20°30'N 13°3'W
Atas Bogd 122 G7 ▲ SW Mongolia
Atbara 97 K5 Sudan 17°42'N 34°E
Atbara 97 L5 ≈ Eritrea/Sudan
Atbasar 108 F4 Kazakhstan 51°49'N 68°18'E
Ath 71 C6 Belgium 50°38'N 3°47'E
Athabasca 144 E3 Alberta, Canada 54°44'N 113°15'W
Athabasca 144 E3 ≈ Alberta, SW Canada
Athabasca, Lake 144 F3 ◎ Alberta/Saskatchewan, SW Canada
Athboy 58 G9 Ireland 53°38'N 6°55'W
Athens 87 H2 ● Greece 37°59'N 23°44'E
Atherstone 52 G5 England, UK 52°34'N 1°36'W
Atherton 135 K7 Queensland, Australia 17°18'S 145°29'E
Atherton 54 F2 England, UK 53°32'N 2°28'W
Athína see Athens
Athlone 58 E8 Ireland 53°25'N 7°56'W
Athy 59 G7 Ireland 52°59'N 6°59'W
Ati 97 I5 Chad 13°11'N 18°20'E
Atikokan 145 H2 Ontario, Canada 48°45'N 91°38'W
Atka 146 A6 Alaska, USA 52°12'N 174°14'W
Atka 109 L6 Russian Fed. 60°45'N 151°35'E
Atlanta 147 L4 Georgia, USA 33°45'N 84°23'W
Atlantic Ocean 24 Ocean
Atlas Mountains 96 F8 ⛰ NW Africa
Atlasovo 109 M6 Russian Fed. 55°42'N 159°35'E
Atlin 144 D4 British Columbia, Canada 59°31'N 133°41'W
Aṭ Ṭā'if 114 F5 Saudi Arabia 21°50'N 40°50'E
Attawapiskat 145 H3 Ontario, Canada 52°55'N 82°26'W
Attawapiskat 145 H2 ≈ Ontario, S Canada
Attleborough 53 L5 England, UK 52°30'N 1°1'E
At Turbah 114 G1 Yemen 12°42'N 43°31'E
Atyrau 108 D3 Kazakhstan 47°7'N 51°56'E
Aubagne 73 I2 France 43°17'N 5°35'E
Aubange 71 G3 Belgium 49°35'N 5°49'E
Auch 72 F3 France 43°40'N 0°37'E
Auckland 136 E7 New Zealand 36°53'S 174°46'E
Audincourt 73 J6 France 47°29'N 6°50'E
Audley 52 F7 England, UK 53°4'N 2°16'W
Augathella 135 K5 Queensland, Australia 25°54'S 146°38'E
Augher 58 F11 Northern Ireland, UK 54°26'N 7°9'W
Aughrim 58 E8 Ireland 53°19'N 8°27'W
Aughrim 59 H7 Ireland 52°52'N 6°28'W
Augsburg 83 F6 Germany 48°22'N 10°54'E
Augusta 147 N8 Maine, USA 44°20'N 69°44'W
Augusta 134 D2 Western Australia 34°18'S 115°10'E
Augustów 84 H11 Poland 53°52'N 22°58'E
Auob 98 F3 ≈ Namibia/South Africa
Aura 69 F7 Finland 60°37'N 22°35'E
Auray 72 D6 France 47°40'N 2°59'W
Aurillac 72 G4 France 44°56'N 2°26'E
Aurora 147 H6 Colorado, USA 39°42'N 104°51'W
Aurora 147 K6 Illinois, USA 41°46'N 88°19'W
Aus 98 F3 Namibia 26°38'S 16°19'E
Austin 147 I3 Texas, USA 30°16'N 97°45'W
Australia 135 H6 ◆ Commonwealth republic
Australia 129 Continent
Australian Alps 135 J2 ⛰ SE Australia
Australian Capital Territory 135 K2 ◐ Territory Australia
Austria 83 H5 ◆ Republic C Europe
Auvergne 73 H4 Cultural region France
Auxerre 73 H6 France 47°48'N 3°35'E
Aveiro 74 E7 Portugal 40°38'N 8°40'W
Avellino 77 J4 Italy 40°54'N 14°46'E
Avesta 69 D6 Sweden 60°9'N 16°10'E
Aveyron 72 G3 ≈ S France
Avezzano 77 I5 Italy 42°2'N 13°26'E
Aviemore 56 F8 Scotland, UK 57°6'N 4°1'W
Avignon 73 I3 France 43°57'N 4°49'E
Ávila 75 H6 Spain 40°39'N 4°42'W
Avilés 74 G9 Spain 43°33'N 5°55'W
Avonmouth 49 G7 England, UK 51°29'N 2°43'W
Avranches 72 E7 France 48°42'N 1°21'W
Awaji-shima 125 H3 Island SW Japan
'Awālī 115 I7 Bahrain 26°7'N 50°33'E
Awash 97 L4 Ethiopia 8°59'N 40°16'E
Awbārī 97 H7 Libya 26°35'N 12°46'E
Awe, Loch 57 D6 ◎ W Scotland, UK
Axe 49 G5 ≈ SW England, UK
Axel 71 C7 Netherlands 51°16'N 3°55'E
Axel Heiberg Island 144 F8 Island Northwest Territories, N Canada
Axminster 49 G5 England, UK 50°47'N 3°0'W
Ayacucho 160 B8 Peru 13°10'S 74°15'W
Ayagoz 108 G3 Kazakhstan 47°54'N 80°25'E
Ayamonte 74 F3 Spain 37°13'N 7°24'W
Aydarko'l Ko'li 117 I7 ◎ C Uzbekistan
Aydın 110 C5 Turkey 37°51'N 27°51'E
Ayers Rock see Uluru
Aylesbury 50 F7 England, UK 51°50'N 0°50'W
Aylesham 51 K4 England, UK 51°13'N 1°11'E
Ayorou 96 F5 Niger 14°45'N 0°54'E
'Ayoûn el 'Atroûs 96 E5 Mauritania 16°38'N 9°36'W
Ayr 57 E4 Scotland, UK 55°28'N 4°38'W
Ayr 57 F4 ≈ W Scotland, UK
Ayre, Point of 54 B5 Headland N Isle of Man
Ayr, Point of 48 F13 Headland N Wales, UK
Aytos 87 J6 Bulgaria 42°43'N 27°14'E
Ayvalık 110 C6 Turkey 39°18'N 26°42'E
Azahar, Costa del 75 L6 Physical region E Spain
Azaouâd 96 F5 Desert C Mali
Azerbaijan 111 K7 ◆ Republic SE Asia
Azoum, Bahr 97 I4 ≈ SE Chad
Azov 108 C4 Russian Fed. 47°7'N 39°26'E
Azov, Sea of 89 D3 Sea NE Black Sea
Azuaga 74 G4 Spain 38°16'N 5°40'W
Azuero, Península de 151 I1 Coastal feature S Panama
Az Zahrān 115 I7 Saudi Arabia 26°18'N 50°2'E
Az Zarqā' 110 G2 Jordan 32°4'N 36°6'E
Az Zāwiyah 97 H8 Libya 32°45'N 12°44'E
Az Zaydīyah 114 G2 Yemen 15°20'N 43°3'E
Az Zilfī 114 G7 Saudi Arabia 26°17'N 44°48'E

B

Baarle-Hertog 70 E8 Belgium 51°26'N 4°56'E
Baarn 70 F10 Netherlands 52°13'N 5°16'E
Babayevo 88 D8 Russian Fed. 59°23'N 35°52'E
Babeldaob 127 L4 Island N Palau
Bab el Mandeb 114 G1 Strait Gulf of Aden/Red Sea
Bābol 116 E6 Iran 36°34'N 52°39'E
Babruysk 89 C6 Belarus 53°7'N 29°13'E
Babuyan Channel 127 J7 Channel N Philippines
Babuyan Island 127 J7 Island N Philippines
Bacabal 163 J7 Brazil 4°15'S 44°45'W
Bacău 87 I8 Romania 46°36'N 26°56'E
Back 144 F5 ≈ Northwest Territories, N Canada
Bacton 53 M6 England, UK 52°52'N 1°28'E
Badajoz 74 F5 Spain 38°53'N 6°58'W
Baden-Baden 83 D6 Germany 48°46'N 8°14'E
Bad Freienwalde 82 H10 Germany 52°47'N 14°4'E
Badgastein 83 G5 Austria 47°7'N 13°9'E
Bad Hersfeld 82 E8 Germany 50°52'N 9°42'E
Bad Homburg vor der Höhe 82 D8 Germany 50°14'N 8°37'E
Bad Ischl 83 G5 Austria 47°43'N 13°36'E
Bad Krozingen 83 D6 Germany 47°55'N 7°43'E
Badlands 147 H8 Physical region North Dakota, N USA
Badrah 111 K3 Iraq 33°6'N 45°58'E
Badr Ḥunayn 114 E6 Saudi Arabia 23°46'N 38°45'E
Badu Island 135 J9 Island Queensland, NE Australia
Bad Vöslau 83 I6 Austria 47°58'N 16°13'E
Baffin Bay 145 H7 Bay Canada/Greenland
Baffin Island 145 H6 Island Northwest Territories, NE Canada
Bafing 96 D4 ≈ W Africa
Bafra 110 F7 Turkey 41°34'N 35°56'E
Bagé 163 H1 Brazil 31°22'S 54°6'W
Baghdād 111 J3 ● Iraq 33°20'N 44°26'E
Baghlan 117 J6 Afghanistan 36°11'N 68°44'E
Baghran 117 I4 Afghanistan 32°55'N 64°57'E
Bagoé 96 E4 ≈ Ivory Coast/Mali
Baguio 127 I6 Philippines 16°25'N 120°36'E
Bagzane, Monts 96 G5 ▲ N Niger
Bahamas 151 I6 ◆ Commonwealth republic N West Indies
Bahamas 151 I6 Island group N West Indies
Bäharly 116 F6 Turkmenistan 38°30'N 57°18'E
Bahawalpur 118 F7 Pakistan 29°25'N 71°40'E
Bahia 163 J5 ◐ State Brazil
Bahía Blanca 161 D4 Argentina 38°43'S 62°19'W
Bahir Dar 97 L4 Ethiopia 11°34'N 37°23'E
Bahraich 119 H7 India 27°35'N 81°36'E
Bahrain 115 I7 ◆ Monarchy SW Asia
Baia Mare 87 H9 Romania 47°40'N 23°35'E
Baicheng 123 K7 China 45°32'N 122°51'E
Baie-Comeau 145 J2 Québec, Canada 49°12'N 68°10'W
Bailén 75 I4 Spain 38°6'N 3°46'W
Bairiki 128 ● Kiribati 1°20'N 173°1'E
Bairnsdale 135 J2 Victoria, Australia 37°51'S 147°38'E
Baishan 123 L7 China 41°57'N 126°31'E
Baja 85 F3 Hungary 46°13'N 18°56'E
Bājil 114 G2 Yemen 15°5'N 43°16'E
Bajram Curri 86 F5 Albania 42°23'N 20°6'E
Baker and Howland Islands 128 US ◇ Polynesia
Baker Lake 144 G4 Northwest Territories, Canada 64°20'N 96°10'W
Bakersfield 146 E5 California, USA 35°22'N 119°1'W
Bakewell 52 G7 England, UK 53°12'N 1°42'W
Baki see Baku
Bakkaflói 68 B12 Sea area W Norwegian Sea
Bakony 85 E4 ⛰ W Hungary
Baku 111 L7 ● Azerbaijan 40°24'N 49°51'E
Bala 48 F11 Wales, UK 52°54'N 3°31'W
Balabac Strait 127 I4 Strait Malaysia/Philippines
Balaguer 75 L8 Spain 41°48'N 0°48'E
Balaïtous 72 F2 ▲ France/Spain
Balakovo 89 F5 Russian Fed. 52°3'N 47°47'E
Bala Morghab 117 H5 Afghanistan 35°38'N 63°21'E
Balashov 89 E5 Russian Fed. 51°32'N 43°14'E
Balaton, Lake 85 E4 ◎ W Hungary
Balbina, Represa 162 F8 ⊠ NW Brazil
Balbriggan 58 H9 Ireland 53°37'N 6°11'W
Balclutha 136 C1 New Zealand 46°15'S 169°45'E
Baldock 50 G7 England, UK 51°59'N 0°12'W
Balearic Islands 75 M5 Island group Spain, W Mediterranean Sea
Baleine, Rivière à la 145 J4 ≈ Québec, E Canada
Balen 71 F7 Belgium 51°12'N 5°12'E
Baleshwar 119 I5 India 21°31'N 86°59'E
Balḥāf 115 I2 Yemen 14°2'N 48°16'E
Bali 127 H1 Island C Indonesia
Balıkesir 110 C6 Turkey 39°38'N 27°52'E
Balikpapan 127 I3 Indonesia 1°15'S 116°50'E
Balintore 56 F10 Scotland, UK 57°46'N 3°56'W
Balivanich 56 A9 Scotland, UK 57°28'N 7°26'W
Balkanabat 116 F7 Turkmenistan 39°33'N 54°19'E
Balkan Mountains 87 H6 ⛰ Bulgaria/Serbia and Montenegro
Balkh 117 I6 Afghanistan 36°46'N 66°54'E
Balkhash 108 F3 Kazakhstan 46°52'N 74°55'E
Balladonia 134 E3 Western Australia 32°21'S 123°32'E
Ballaghmore 59 F7 Ireland 52°58'N 7°41'W
Ballantrae 57 E3 Scotland, UK 55°5'N 5°W
Ballarat 135 J2 Victoria, Australia 37°36'S 143°51'E
Ballater 56 G8 Scotland, UK 57°2'N 3°1'W
Ballaugh 54 B4 Isle of Man 54°19'N 4°40'W
Ballina 58 D10 Ireland 54°7'N 9°9'W
Ballinasloe 58 E8 Ireland 53°20'N 8°13'W
Ballindine 58 D9 Ireland 53°40'N 8°57'W
Ballinhassig 59 D4 Ireland 51°48'N 8°43'W
Ballinskelligs 59 B4 Ireland 51°49'N 10°28'W
Ballinskelligs Bay 59 B4 Inlet SW Ireland
Ballinspittle 59 D4 Ireland 51°39'N 8°34'W
Ballintra 58 E11 Ireland 54°35'N 8°7'W
Ballon 59 G7 Ireland 52°43'N 6°52'W
Ballybofey 58 F11 Ireland 54°49'N 7°47'W
Ballybunnion 59 C6 Ireland 52°31'N 9°51'W
Ballycastle 58 H12 Northern Ireland, UK 55°12'N 6°14'W
Ballycastle 58 C10 Ireland 54°18'N 9°23'W
Ballyclare 58 H11 Northern Ireland, UK 54°45'N 6°W
Ballyconneely 58 B8 Ireland 53°27'N 10°18'W
Ballyconnell 58 F10 Ireland 54°7'N 7°35'W
Ballycotton 59 E4 Ireland 51°48'N 8°0'W
Ballycroy 58 C10 Ireland 54°1'N 9°49'W
Ballydehob 59 C4 Ireland 51°33'N 9°35'W
Ballydonegan 59 B4 Ireland 51°37'N 10°15'W
Ballyduff 59 C6 Ireland 52°27'N 9°48'W
Ballyferriter 59 B5 Ireland 52°10'N 10°35'W
Ballygawley 58 G11 Northern Ireland, UK 54°28'N 7°2'W
Ballyhaunis 58 D9 Ireland 53°45'N 8°45'W
Ballyhoura Mountains 59 D5 ⛰ S Ireland
Ballyjamesduff 58 F9 Ireland 53°52'N 7°2
Ballylynan 59 G7 Ireland 52°57'N 7°2'W
Ballymahon 58 F8 Ireland 53°33'N 7°45'W
Ballymena 58 H12 Northern Ireland, UK 54°52'N 6°17'W
Ballymena 58 H12 ◐ District Northern Ireland, UK
Ballymoe 58 E9 Ireland 53°42'N 8°38'W
Ballymoney 58 G12 Northern Ireland, UK 55°10'N 6°30'W
Ballymoney 58 G12 ◐ District Northern Ireland, UK
Ballynabola 59 G6 Ireland 52°57'N 6°50'W
Ballynafid 58 F9 Ireland 53°36'N 7°25'W
Ballyragget 59 F7 Ireland 52°47'N 7°31'W
Ballyshannon 58 E11 Ireland 54°30'N 8°1
Ballyvaghan 59 C7 Ireland 53°6'N 9°15'W
Ballywalter 58 I11 Northern Ireland, UK 54°33'N 5°26'W
Balsas 163 I6 Brazil 7°30'S 46°W
Balsas, Río 150 D3 ≈ S Mexico
Baltasound 56 I12 Scotland, UK 60°46'N 0°58'W
Bălţi 89 B4 Moldova 47°45'N 27°57'E
Baltic Sea 69 E3 Sea N Europe
Baltimore 59 C4 Ireland 51°28'N 9°19'W
Baltimore 147 M6 Maryland, USA 39°17'N 76°37'W
Baltinglass 59 G7 Ireland 52°55'N 6°43'W
Balykchy 117 L8 Kyrgyzstan 42°29'N 76°8
Bam 116 G3 Iran 29°8'N 58°27'E
Bamako 96 E4 ● Mali 12°39'N 8°2'W
Bambari 97 I3 Central African Republic 5°45'N 20°37'E
Bamberg 83 F7 Germany 49°54'N 10°53'E
Bamburgh 55 H9 England, UK 55°37'N 1°4
Bampton 49 F6 England, UK 50°59'N 3°29
Bampton 50 D6 England, UK 51°43'N 1°32
Bananal, Ilha do 163 I5 Island C Brazil
Bananga 119 L2 India 6°57'N 93°54'E
Banbridge 58 H10 Northern Ireland, UK 54°21'N 6°16'W
Banbridge 58 H10 ◐ District Northern Ireland, UK
Banbury 50 E7 England, UK 52°4'N 1°20'W
Banchory 56 H8 Scotland, UK 58°5'N 0°35
Bandaaceh 126 E4 Indonesia 5°30'N 95°2
Bandar-e 'Abbas 116 F2 Iran 27°11'N 56°
Bandar-e Langeh 116 E2 Iran 26°34'N 54°
Bandarlampung 126 G2 Indonesia 5°28'S 105°16'E
Bandar Seri Begawan 127 H4 ● Brunei 4°56'N 114°58'E
Banda Sea 127 K2 Sea E Indonesia
Bandırma 110 D7 Turkey 40°21'N 27°58'E
Bandon 59 D4 Ireland 51°44'N 8°44'W
Bandon 59 D4 ≈ S Ireland
Bandundu 98 F7 Dem. Rep. Congo 3°19'S 17°24'E
Bandung 126 G1 Indonesia 6°47'S 107°28'
Banff 56 H10 Scotland, UK 57°39'N 2°33'W
Bangalore 118 G3 India 12°58'N 77°35'E
Bangassou 97 J3 Central African Republic 4°51'N 22°55'E
Banggai, Kepulauan 127 J3 Island group C Indonesia
Banghāzī 97 I8 Libya 32°7'N 20°4'E
Bangka, Pulau 126 G2 Island W Indonesia
Bangkok 126 E6 ● Thailand 13°44'N 100°3
Bangladesh 119 J6 ◆ Republic S Asia
Bangor 58 H11 Northern Ireland, UK 54°40'N 5°40'W
Bangor 48 E12 Wales, UK 53°13'N 4°8'W
Bangor 147 N8 Maine, USA 44°48'N 68°47'
Bangor Erris 58 C10 Ireland 54°10'N 9°45'
Bangui 97 I3 ● Central African Republic 4°21'N 18°35'E
Bangweulu, Lake 99 I6 ◎ N Zambia
Bani 96 E4 ≈ S Mali
Banja Luka 86 E7 Bosnia and Herzegovina 44°47'N 17°10'E
Banjarmasin 127 H2 Indonesia 3°22'S 114°
Banjul 96 D5 ● Gambia 13°26'N 16°43'W
Banks Island 144 E6 Island Banks Island, Northwest Territories, NW Canada
Banks Peninsula 136 D3 Coastal feature So Island, New Zealand
Banks Strait 135 J1 Strait SW Tasman Sea
Bankura 119 I6 India 23°14'N 87°5'E
Banmauk 126 E8 Burma 24°26'N 95°54'E
Bann 58 G12 ≈ N Northern Ireland, UK
Ban Nadou 126 G6 Laos 15°51'N 105°38'E
Bansha 59 E6 Ireland 52°26'N 8°2'W
Banská Bystrica 85 F6 Slovakia 48°46'N 19°
Banteer 59 D5 Ireland 52°7'N 8°54'W
Bantry 59 C4 Ireland 51°41'N 9°27'W
Bantry Bay 59 C4 Bay SW Ireland
Banyak, Kepulauan 126 E3 Island group NW Indonesia
Banyoles 75 M8 Spain 42°7'N 2°46'E
Baoji 123 H5 China 34°23'N 107°16'E
Baoshan 122 G2 China 25°5'N 99°7'E
Baotou 123 I6 China 40°38'N 109°59'E
Ba'qūbah 111 J3 Iraq 33°45'N 44°40'E
Baraawe 97 M3 Somalia 1°10'N 43°59'E
Baranavichy 89 B6 Belarus 53°8'N 26°2'E
Barbacena 163 J3 Brazil 21°13'S 43°47'W
Barbados 151 N3 ◆ Commonwealth republi SE West Indies
Barbastro 75 K8 Spain 42°2'N 0°7'E
Barbate de Franco 74 G3 Spain 36°11'N 5°55'W
Barbuda 151 M4 Island N Antigua and Barbu
Barcaldine 135 J5 Queensland, Australia 23°33'S 145°21'E
Barcelona 75 L7 Spain 41°25'N 2°10'E
Barcelona 160 D12 Venezuela 10°8'N 64°43
Barcelos 162 F8 Brazil 0°59'S 62°58'W
Barcs 85 D3 Hungary 45°58'N 17°26'E
Bardejov 85 G6 Slovakia 49°17'N 21°18'E
Bardney 53 I7 England, UK 53°13'N 0°25'W
Bardsey Island 48 D11 Island NW Wales, UK
Bardsey Sound 48 D11 Sound NW Wales, U
Bareilly 119 H7 India 28°20'N 79°24'E
Barendrecht 70 D9 Netherlands 51°52'N 4°3
Barentin 72 F8 France 49°33'N 0°57'E
Barents Sea 168 E4 Sea Arctic Ocean
Bargoed 48 F8 Wales, UK 51°42'N 3°13'W

◆ Country ● Country capital ◇ Dependent territory ○ Dependent territory capital ◐ Administrative region ▲ Mountain ⛰ Mountain range ♨ Volcano ≈ River ◎ Lake ⊠ Reservoir

Bari - Bose 171

77 K5 Italy 41°6'N 16°52'E
owt 117 K5 Afghanistan 35°18'N 71°36'E
as 160 C12 Venezuela 8°36'N 70°15'W
al 119 J6 Bangladesh 22°41'N 90°20'E
an, Pegunungan 126 F2 ▲▲ Sumatra,
ndonesia
, Sungai 127 H2 ≈ Borneo, C Indonesia
ng and Dagenham 37 ◈ London Borough
land, UK
Tableland 135 H8 Plateau Northern
itory/Queensland, N Australia
d 87 J8 Romania 46°12'N 27°39'E
-Duc 73 I7 France 48°46'N 5°10'E
e, Lake 134 E4 ◎ Western Australia
e Range 134 D5 ▲▲ Western Australia
tta 77 K5 Italy 41°20'N 16°17'E
ek 84 C10 Poland 53°N 15°11'E
outh 48 E11 Wales, UK 52°44'N 4°4'W
outh Bay 48 E11 Bay NW Wales, UK
rd Castle 54 G5 England, UK
35'N 1°55'W
aul 108 G4 Russian Fed. 53°21'N 83°45'E
et 50 G6 England, UK 51°38'N 0°12'W
et 37 ◈ London Borough England, UK
oldswick 54 G3 England, UK
55'N 2°13'W
sley 52 G8 England, UK 53°33'N 1°25'W
sley 37 ◈ Unitary authority England, UK
staple 49 E6 England, UK 51°5'N 4°4'W
staple Bay 49 D6 Bay SW England, UK
uisimeto 160 C12 Venezuela
3'N 69°18'W
56 A8 Island NW Scotland, UK
de Rio Grande 151 H2 Nicaragua
56'N 83°30'W
do São Manuel 162 G6 Brazil
2'S 58°3'W
anca 160 B8 Peru 10°46'S 77°46'W
ancabermeja 160 B11 Colombia
'N 73°51'W
anquilla 160 B12 Colombia
59'N 74°48'W
eiras 163 J5 Brazil 12°9'S 44°58'W
eiro 74 E5 Portugal 38°40'N 9°5'W
grennan 57 E3 Scotland, UK 55°3'N 4°42'W
er Range 135 J4 Hill range New South
les, SE Australia
er Reef 150 G4 Reef E Belize
ow 146 B7 Alaska, USA 71°17'N 156°47'W
ow 59 G6 ≈ SE Ireland
ow-in-Furness 54 E4 England, UK
7'N 3°14'W
ow Island 134 C6 Island Western Australia
y 49 F7 Wales, UK 51°24'N 3°18'W
ang 117 K6 ≈ SE Tajikistan
in 110 E7 Turkey 41°37'N 32°20'E
on-upon-Humber 53 I9 England, UK
40'N 0°21'W
oszyce 84 G12 Poland 54°16'N 20°49'E
un-Urt 123 I7 Mongolia 46°40'N 113°17'E
, Volcán 151 H1 ⛰ W Panama
a, Volcán 151 H1 ⛰ NW Costa Rica
von River 135 K4 ≈ New South Wales,
Australia
saw 89 B6 Belarus 54°14'N 28°30'E
rabeasca 89 B4 Moldova 46°22'N 28°56'E
hurch 52 D6 England, UK 52°48'N 2°55'W
l 83 D5 Switzerland 47°33'N 7°36'E
an 127 J4 Island SW Philippines
ldon 51 I6 England, UK 51°34'N 0°25'E
ngstoke 50 E4 England, UK 51°16'N 1°8'W
a 111 L2 Iraq 30°30'N 47°50'E
sano del Grappa 77 H8 Italy
5°45'N 11°45'E
sein 126 D6 Burma 16°46'N 94°45'E
senthwaite Lake 54 E6 ◎ NW England, UK
se-Terre 151 M4 ○ Guadeloupe
5°8'N 61°40'W
seterre 151 M4 ● Saint Kitts and Nevis
7°16'N 62°45'W
se Terre 151 M4 Island W Guadeloupe
sikounou 96 E5 Mauritania 15°55'N 5°59'W
s Strait 135 J1 Strait SE Australia
sum 82 E10 Germany 52°52'N 8°44'E
ia 73 K2 France 42°42'N 9°27'E
ogne 71 F4 Belgium 50°N 5°43'E
utäsk 68 E9 Sweden 64°47'N 20°5'E
a 97 H3 Equatorial Guinea 1°51'N 9°48'E
angas 127 J6 Philippines 13°47'N 121°3'E
dambang 126 F5 Cambodia 13°6'N 103°13'E
éké, Plateaux 98 F7 Plateau S Congo
h 49 H7 England, UK 51°23'N 2°22'W
Bathinda 118 G8 India 30°14'N
4°54'E
hurst 135 K3 New South Wales, Australia
3°32'S 149°35'E
hurst 145 J2 New Brunswick, Canada
7°37'N 65°40'W
hurst Island 134 G9 Island Northern Territory,
Australia
hurst Island 144 F7 Island Parry Islands,
orthwest Territories, N Canada
n, Wādī al 114 G7 Dry watercourse SW Asia
ey 55 H2 England, UK 53°43'N 1°38'W
man 111 H5 Turkey 37°52'N 41°6'E
on Rouge 147 K3 Louisiana, USA
0°28'N 91°9'W
sfjord 68 G13 Norway 70°37'N 29°42'E
ticaloa 119 H2 Sri Lanka 7°44'N 81°43'E
tipaglia 77 J4 Italy 40°36'N 14°59'E
tle 51 I3 England, UK 50°55'N 0°28'E
umi 111 I7 Georgia 41°39'N 41°38'E
u Pahat 126 F3 Malaysia 1°51'N 102°56'E
uchi 97 H4 Nigeria 10°18'N 9°46'E
ska 69 G4 Latvia 56°25'N 24°11'E
tzen 82 H8 Germany 51°11'N 14°29'E
aria 83 F6 Cultural region Germany
arian Alps 83 F5 ▲▲ Austria/Germany
ispe, Río 150 B7 ≈ NW Mexico
wdeswell 53 L6 England, UK 52°44'N 1°0'E
witi 97 J7 Egypt 28°19'N 28°53'E
wtry 53 H8 England, UK 53°26'N 1°3'W
Islands 150 G3 Island group N Honduras
amo 151 I4 Cuba 20°21'N 76°38'W
an Har Shan 122 F5 ▲▲ C China
yanhongor 122 G7 Mongolia
6°8'N 100°42'E
dhabo 97 M3 Somalia 3°8'N 43°39'E

Bayeux 72 F7 France 49°16'N 0°42'W
Bayjī 111 J4 Iraq 34°56'N 43°29'E
Baymak 89 H6 Russian Fed. 52°34'N 58°20'E
Bayonne 72 E3 France 43°30'N 1°28'W
Bayramaly 117 H6 Turkmenistan 37°33'N 62°8'E
Bayreuth 83 F7 Germany 49°57'N 11°34'E
Baza 75 I4 Spain 37°30'N 2°45'W
Bāzīyah 111 I3 Iraq 33°50'N 42°41'E
Beachy Head 51 H2 Headland SE England, UK
Beaconsfield 50 F6 England, UK
51°36'N 0°49'W
Beagle Channel 161 D1 Channel Argentina/Chile
Beal 54 G9 England, UK 55°41'N 1°54'W
Bear Lake 146 G6 ◎ Idaho/Utah, NW USA
Beas de Segura 75 I4 Spain 38°16'N 2°54'W
Beattock 57 G4 Scotland, UK 55°18'N 3°35'W
Beaufort Sea 146 C7 Sea Arctic Ocean
Beaufort West 98 G2 South Africa
32°21'S 22°35'E
Beauly 56 E9 Scotland, UK 57°29'N 4°29'W
Beaumaris 48 E12 Wales, UK 53°16'N 4°12'W
Beaumont 147 J3 Texas, USA 30°5'N 94°6'W
Beaune 73 I5 France 47°2'N 4°50'E
Beauvais 72 G7 France 49°27'N 2°4'E
Beaver River 147 I5 ≈ Oklahoma, C USA
Beawar 118 F7 India 26°8'N 74°22'E
Bebington 52 D8 England, UK 53°22'N 3°1'W
Beccles 53 M5 England, UK 52°27'N 1°32'E
Béchar 96 F8 Algeria 31°38'N 2°11'W
Beckfoot 54 D6 England, UK 54°50'N 3°31'W
Bedale 55 H4 England, UK 54°17'N 1°43'W
Beddgelert 48 E11 Wales, UK 53°1'N 4°12'W
Bedford 50 G8 England, UK 52°8'N 0°29'W
Bedford Level 53 J5 Physical region
E England, UK
Bedfordshire 50 G7 ◈ County England, UK
Bedlington 55 H7 England, UK 55°8'N 1°36'W
Bedum 70 H13 Netherlands 53°18'N 6°36'E
Bedworth 52 G5 England, UK 52°28'N 1°26'W
Beeford 55 K3 England, UK 53°59'N 0°23'W
Be'er Menuha 110 B2 Israel 30°22'N 35°9'E
Beernem 71 B7 Belgium 51°9'N 3°18'E
Be'er Sheva' 110 A3 Israel 31°15'N 34°47'E
Beesel 71 G7 Netherlands 51°16'N 6°2'E
Beeston 53 H6 England, UK 52°55'N 1°10'W
Bega 135 K2 New South Wales, Australia
36°43'S 149°50'E
Behābād 116 F4 Iran 32°23'N 59°50'E
Behbahān 116 D3 Iran 30°38'N 50°7'E
Beihai 123 I2 China 21°29'N 109°10'E
Beijing 123 J6 ● China 39°58'N 116°23'E
Beilen 70 H12 Netherlands 52°52'N 6°27'E
Beinn Dearg 56 E10 ▲ N Scotland, UK
Beira 99 I4 Mozambique 19°45'S 34°56'E
Beirut 110 F3 ● Lebanon 33°55'N 35°31'E
Beja 74 F4 Portugal 38°1'N 7°52'W
Béjar 74 G6 Spain 40°24'N 5°45'W
Békéscsaba 85 G3 Hungary 46°40'N 21°5'E
Bekobod 117 J7 Uzbekistan 40°17'N 69°11'E
Belarus 89 B6 ◆ Republic E Europe
Bełchatów 84 F8 Poland 51°23'N 19°20'E
Belcher Islands 145 I3 Island group Northwest
Territories, SE Canada
Belcoo 58 E10 Northern Ireland, UK
54°17'N 7°53'W
Beledweyne 97 M3 Somalia 4°39'N 45°12'E
Belém 163 I8 Brazil 1°27'S 48°29'W
Belfast 58 H11 Northern Ireland, UK
54°35'N 5°55'W
Belfast City 58 H11 ◈ District
Northern Ireland, UK
Belford 54 G9 England, UK 55°36'N 1°53'W
Belfort 73 J6 France 47°38'N 6°52'E
Belgaum 118 F4 India 15°52'N 74°30'E
Belgium 71 E6 ◆ Monarchy NW Europe
Belgorod 89 D5 Russian Fed. 50°38'N 36°37'E
Belgrade 86 G7 ● Serbia and Montenegro
44°48'N 20°27'E
Belitung, Pulau 126 G2 Island W Indonesia
Belize 150 G3 ◆ Commonwealth republic
Central America
Belize City 150 G3 Belize 17°29'N 88°10'W
Belkofski 146 B6 Alaska, USA 55°7'N 162°4'W
Bellananagh 58 F9 Ireland 53°55'N 7°24'W
Bellavary 58 D9 Ireland 53°55'N 9°19'W
Belleek 58 E11 Northern Ireland, UK
54°28'N 8°6'W
Belle Île 72 D6 Island NW France
Belle Isle, Strait of 145 K3 Strait Newfoundland
and Labrador, E Canada
Bellingham 54 G7 England, UK 55°9'N 2°16'W
Bellingham 146 E9 Washington, USA
48°46'N 122°29'W
Bellingshausen Sea 166 A5 Sea Antarctica
Bellinzona 83 E4 Switzerland 46°12'N 9°2'E
Bello 160 B11 Colombia 6°19'N 75°34'W
Bellshill 55 H9 England, UK 55°34'N 1°47'W
Bellville 98 G1 South Africa 33°50'S 18°43'E
Belmopan 150 G3 ● Belize 17°13'N 88°48'W
Belmullet 58 B10 Ireland 54°14'N 9°59'W
Belo Horizonte 161 G7 Brazil 19°54'S 43°54'W
Belomorsk 88 D9 Russian Fed. 64°30'N 34°43'E
Beloretsk 89 H6 Russian Fed. 53°56'N 58°26'E
Belozersk 88 D8 Russian Fed. 59°59'N 37°49'E
Belper 52 G7 England, UK 53°1'N 1°34'W
Belsay 54 G7 England, UK 55°6'N 1°51'W
Belturbet 58 F10 Ireland 54°6'N 7°26'W
Belukha, Gora 108 G3 ▲ Kazakhstan/
Russian Fed.
Belyy, Ostrov 108 G7 Island N Russian Fed.
Bemaraha 99 K4 ▲▲ W Madagascar
Bemmel 70 G9 Netherlands 51°53'N 5°54'E
Benavente 74 G8 Spain 42°N 5°40'W
Benbecula 56 A9 Island NW Scotland, UK
Bend 146 E7 Oregon, USA 44°4'N 121°19'W
Bendigo 135 J2 Victoria, Australia
36°46'S 144°19'E
Benešov 85 C7 Czech Republic 49°48'N 14°41'E
Benevento 77 J4 Italy 41°7'N 14°45'E
Bengbu 123 J4 China 32°57'N 117°17'E
Bengkulu 126 F2 Indonesia 3°46'S 102°16'E
Benguela 98 E5 Angola 12°35'S 13°30'E
Ben Hope 56 E12 ▲ N Scotland, UK
Beni 99 H8 Dem. Rep. Congo 0°31'N 29°30'E
Benidorm 75 K5 Spain 38°33'N 0°9'W
Benin 96 F4 ◆ Republic W Africa
Benin, Bight of 96 F3 Gulf W Africa
Benin City 96 G3 Nigeria 6°23'N 5°40'E

Beni Suef 97 K7 Egypt 29°9'N 31°4'E
Benjamin Constant 162 D7 Brazil
4°22'S 70°2'W
Ben Klibreck 56 F11 ▲ N Scotland, UK
Ben Lawers 57 F7 ▲ C Scotland, UK
Benllech 48 E12 Wales, UK 53°20'N 4°12'W
Ben Lui 57 E6 ▲ C Scotland, UK
Ben Macdui 56 G8 ▲ C Scotland, UK
Ben More Assynt 56 E11 ▲ N Scotland, UK
Ben Nevis 57 E7 ▲ N Scotland, UK
Bentley 53 H9 England, UK 53°32'N 1°12'W
Benue 97 H4 ≈ Cameroon/Nigeria
Beograd see Belgrade
Berat 86 F4 Albania 40°43'N 19°58'E
Berau, Teluk 127 L2 Bay Irian Jaya, E Indonesia
Berbera 97 M4 Somalia 10°24'N 45°2'E
Berbérati 97 I3 Central African Republic
4°14'N 15°50'E
Berck-Plage 72 G8 France 50°24'N 1°35'E
Berdyans'k 89 D4 Ukraine 46°46'N 36°49'E
Bere Ferrers 49 E4 England, UK 50°28'N 4°6'W
Bereket 116 F7 Turkmenistan 39°17'N 55°27'E
Bere Regis 49 H5 England, UK 50°44'N 2°15'W
Berettyó 85 G4 ≈ Hungary/Romania
Berettyóújfalu 85 H4 Hungary 47°15'N 21°33'E
Berezniki 88 H8 Russian Fed. 59°26'N 56°49'E
Berga 75 L8 Spain 42°6'N 1°41'E
Bergamo 76 G8 Italy 45°42'N 9°40'E
Bergen 82 G11 Germany 54°25'N 13°25'E
Bergen 70 E11 Netherlands 52°40'N 4°42'E
Bergen 69 A7 Norway 60°24'N 5°19'E
Bergerac 72 F4 France 44°51'N 0°30'E
Bergeyk 71 F7 Netherlands 51°19'N 5°21'E
Bergse Maas 70 F9 ≈ S Netherlands
Beringen 71 F7 Belgium 51°4'N 5°14'E
Bering Sea 109 M8 Sea N Pacific Ocean
Bering Strait 146 A7 Strait Bering Sea/
Chukchi Sea
Berja 75 I3 Spain 36°51'N 2°56'W
Berkeley 146 D6 California, USA
37°52'N 122°16'W
Berkhamsted 50 F6 England, UK
51°44'N 0°45'W
Berkner Island 166 C6 Island Antarctica
Berlin 82 G10 ● Germany 52°31'N 13°26'E
Bermeo 75 I9 Spain 43°25'N 2°44'W
Bermuda 12 UK ◇ Atlantic Ocean
Bern 83 D5 ● Switzerland 46°57'N 7°26'E
Bernau 82 G10 Germany 52°41'N 13°36'E
Bernburg 82 G9 Germany 51°47'N 11°45'E
Berner Alpen 83 D4 ▲▲ SW Switzerland
Berneray 56 A8 Island NW Scotland, UK
Bernier Island 134 C5 Island Western Australia
Berry 72 G6 Cultural region France
Bertoua 97 H3 Cameroon 4°34'N 13°42'E
Berwick-upon-Tweed 54 G10 England, UK
55°46'N 2°W
Besançon 73 I6 France 47°14'N 6°1'E
Bessbrook 58 G10 Northern Ireland, UK
54°13'N 6°28'W
Betafo 99 L4 Madagascar 19°50'S 46°50'E
Betanzos 74 F9 Spain 43°17'N 8°17'W
Bethlehem 99 H2 South Africa 28°12'S 28°16'E
Bethlehem 110 B3 West Bank 31°43'N 35°12'E
Béticos, Sistemas 75 H3 ▲▲ S Spain
Bétou 98 F8 Congo 3°8'N 18°31'E
Bette, Pic 97 I6 ▲ S Libya
Betws-y-Coed 48 E12 Wales, UK 53°5'N 3°45'W
Beulah 48 F9 Wales, UK 52°9'N 3°38'W
Beveren 71 D7 Belgium 51°13'N 4°15'E
Beverley 55 J3 England, UK 53°51'N 0°26'W
Bexhill 51 I3 England, UK 50°50'N 0°28'E
Bexley 37 ◈ London Borough England, UK
Beyla 96 E4 Guinea 8°43'N 8°41'W
Beyneu 108 D3 Kazakhstan 45°20'N 55°11'E
Beyrouth see Beirut
Béziers 73 H2 France 43°21'N 3°13'E
Bhadravati 118 G3 India 13°52'N 75°43'E
Bhagalpur 119 I6 India 25°14'N 86°59'E
Bhaktapur 119 I7 Nepal 27°47'N 85°21'E
Bharuch 118 F5 India 21°48'N 72°55'E
Bhavnagar 118 F5 India 21°46'N 72°14'E
Bhopal 118 G6 India 23°17'N 77°25'E
Bhubaneshwar 119 I5 India 20°16'N 85°51'E
Bhusawal 118 G5 India 21°1'N 75°50'E
Bhutan 119 J7 ◆ Monarchy S Asia
Biak, Pulau 127 L3 Island E Indonesia
Biała Podlaska 84 H9 Poland 52°3'N 23°8'E
Białogard 84 D11 Poland 54°1'N 15°59'E
Białystok 84 H10 Poland 53°8'N 23°9'E
Biarritz 72 E2 France 43°25'N 1°40'W
Bicester 50 E7 England, UK 51°53'N 1°17'W
Bickington 49 F4 England, UK 50°33'N 3°49'W
Biddulph 52 F7 England, UK 53°7'N 2°10'W
Bideford 49 E6 England, UK 51°1'N 4°12'W
Bidford-on-Avon 52 F4 England, UK
52°9'N 1°49'W
Biel 83 C5 Switzerland 47°9'N 7°16'E
Bielefeld 82 E9 Germany 52°1'N 8°32'E
Bielsko-Biała 85 F7 Poland 49°49'N 19°1'E
Bielsk Podlaski 84 H10 Poland 52°45'N 23°11'E
Bien Hoa 126 G5 Vietnam 10°58'N 106°50'E
Bienville, Lac 145 I3 ◎ Québec, C Canada
Bigbury Bay 49 E4 Bay SW England, UK
Big Cypress Swamp 147 M3 Wetland Florida,
SE USA
Biggin Hill 51 H5 England, UK 51°20'N 0°1'E
Biggleswade 50 G8 England, UK 52°5'N 0°16'W
Bighorn Mountains 146 G7 ▲▲ Wyoming,
C USA
Bihać 86 D7 Bosnia and Herzegovina
44°49'N 15°53'E
Bihār 119 I7 ◈ State India
Biharamulo 99 I7 Tanzania 2°37'S 31°20'E
Bijelo Polje 86 F6 Serbia and Montenegro
43°3'N 19°44'E
Bikaner 118 F7 India 28°1'N 73°22'E
Bikin 109 L4 Russian Fed. 46°45'N 134°6'E
Bilād Banī Bū 'Alī 115 M5 Oman
22°2'N 59°18'E
Bilād Banī Bū Ḥasan 115 M5 Oman
22°9'N 59°14'E
Bilaspur 119 H5 India 22°6'N 82°8'E
Biläsuvar 111 K6 Azerbaijan 39°26'N 48°34'E
Bila Tserkva 89 C5 Ukraine 49°49'N 30°8'E
Bilauktaung Range 126 E6 ▲▲ Burma/Thailand
Bilbao 75 I9 Spain 43°15'N 2°56'W
Bilecik 110 D6 Turkey 39°59'N 29°54'E

Billericay 51 I6 England, UK 51°37'N 0°19'E
Billingham 55 I5 England, UK 54°36'N 1°17'W
Billinghay 53 J7 England, UK 53°5'N 0°20'W
Billings 146 G7 Montana, USA
45°47'N 108°32'W
Billingshurst 50 G3 England, UK 51°N 0°27'W
Billingsley 52 E5 England, UK 52°28'N 2°30'W
Bilma, Grand Erg de 97 H5 Desert NE Niger
Biloela 135 L5 Queensland, Australia
24°27'S 150°31'E
Biltine 97 I5 Chad 14°30'N 20°53'E
Binbrook 53 J8 England, UK 53°25'N 0°12'W
Binche 71 D5 Belgium 50°25'N 4°10'E
Binghamton 147 M7 New York, USA
42°6'N 75°55'W
Bingley 55 H3 England, UK 53°51'N 1°47'W
Bingöl 111 H6 Turkey 38°54'N 40°29'E
Bintulu 127 H4 Malaysia 3°12'N 113°1'E
Binzhou 123 J5 China 37°23'N 118°3'E
Bioco, Isla de 96 G3 Island
NW Equatorial Guinea
Birāk 97 H7 Libya 27°32'N 14°17'E
Birao 97 J4 Central African Republic
10°14'N 22°49'E
Birdhill 59 E7 Ireland 52°45'N 8°25'W
Birjand 116 G4 Iran 32°54'N 59°14'E
Birkenfeld 83 D7 Germany 49°39'N 7°10'E
Birkenhead 52 D8 England, UK 53°24'N 3°2'W
Birmingham 52 F5 England, UK 52°30'N 1°50'W
Birmingham 147 K4 Alabama, USA
33°30'N 86°47'W
Birmingham 37 ◈ Unitary authority
England, UK
Bîr Mogreïn 96 E7 Mauritania 25°10'N 11°35'W
Birnin Kebbi 96 G4 Nigeria 12°28'N 4°8'E
Birnin Konni 96 G5 Niger 13°51'N 5°15'E
Birobidzhan 109 K4 Russian Fed.
48°42'N 132°55'E
Birr 59 E7 Ireland 53°6'N 7°55'W
Birsk 89 H7 Russian Fed. 55°24'N 55°33'E
Biscay, Bay of 72 D5 Bay France/Spain
Bishkek 117 K8 ● Kyrgyzstan 42°54'N 74°27'E
Bishop Auckland 55 H6 England, UK
54°41'N 1°41'W
Bishop's Castle 52 D5 England, UK
52°29'N 3°4'W
Bishop's Stortford 51 H7 England, UK
51°45'N 0°11'E
Bishop's Waltham 50 E3 England, UK
50°56'N 1°16'W
Biskupiec 84 G11 Poland 53°52'N 20°57'E
Bislig 127 K5 Philippines 8°10'N 126°19'E
Bismarck 147 H8 North Dakota, USA
46°49'N 100°47'W
Bissau 96 D4 ● Guinea-Bissau 11°52'N 15°39'W
Bistriţa 87 H8 Romania 47°10'N 24°31'E
Bitam 98 E8 Gabon 2°5'N 11°30'E
Bitburg 83 C7 Germany 49°58'N 6°31'E
Bitlis 111 I6 Turkey 38°23'N 42°4'E
Bitola 86 G4 Macedonia 41°1'N 21°22'E
Bitonto 77 K5 Italy 41°7'N 16°41'E
Bitterfeld 82 G9 Germany 51°37'N 12°18'E
Bitterley 52 E5 England, UK 52°24'N 2°36'W
Bitterroot Range 146 F8 ▲▲ Idaho/Montana,
NW USA
Biwa-ko 125 I4 ◎ Honshū, SW Japan
Blackall 135 J5 Queensland, Australia
24°26'S 145°32'E
Blackburn 54 F2 England, UK 53°45'N 2°29'W
Blackburn and Darwen 37 ◈ Unitary authority
England, UK
Black Drin 86 G5 ≈ Albania/Macedonia
Blackford 57 F6 Scotland, UK 56°15'N 3°44'W
Blacklion 58 E10 Ireland 54°17'N 7°53'W
Black Mountains 48 G8 ▲▲ SE Wales, UK
Blackpool 54 E3 England, UK 53°50'N 3°3'W
Blackpool 37 ◈ Unitary authority England, UK
Black Sea 61 Sea Asia/Europe
Black Sea Lowland 89 C4 Depression SE Europe
Blacksod Bay 58 B10 Inlet W Ireland
Black Volta 96 E4 ≈ W Africa
Blackwater 59 H6 Ireland 52°26'N 6°20'W
Blaenau Ffestiniog 48 E11 Wales, UK
53°0'N 3°56'W
Blaenau Gwent 37 ◈ Unitary authority
Wales, UK
Blaenavon 48 G8 Wales, UK 51°45'N 3°6'W
Blagoevgrad 87 H5 Bulgaria 42°1'N 23°5'E
Blagoveshchensk 109 K4 Russian Fed.
50°19'N 127°30'E
Blair Atholl 57 F7 Scotland, UK 56°46'N 3°49'W
Blairgowrie 57 G7 Scotland, UK
56°19'N 3°25'W
Blakeney 53 L7 England, UK 52°57'N 0°53'E
Blakeney Point 53 L7 Headland E England, UK
Blanca, Bahía 161 E4 Bay E Argentina
Blanca, Costa 75 K4 Physical region SE Spain
Blanche, Lake 135 I4 ◎ South Australia
Blanco, Cape 146 D7 Headland Oregon,
NW USA
Blandford Forum 49 H5 England, UK
50°51'N 2°11'W
Blanes 75 M8 Spain 41°41'N 2°48'E
Blankenberge 71 B7 Belgium 51°19'N 3°8'E
Blankenheim 82 C8 Germany 50°26'N 6°41'E
Blantyre 99 I5 Malawi 15°45'S 35°4'E
Blaricum 70 F10 Netherlands 52°16'N 5°15'E
Blasket Islands 59 A5 Island group W Ireland
Blaydon 55 H7 England, UK 54°57'N 1°48'W
Blenheim 136 D4 New Zealand 41°32'S 174°E
Blessington 58 G8 Ireland 53°9'N 6°32'W
Bletchley 50 F7 England, UK 52°N 0°46'W
Blisworth 53 H4 England, UK 52°10'N 0°57'W
Bloemfontein 99 H2 ● South Africa
29°7'S 26°14'E
Blois 72 G6 France 47°36'N 1°20'E
Błonie 84 G9 Poland 52°13'N 20°36'E
Bloody Foreland 58 E12 Headland NW Ireland
Bloomsbury 135 K6 Queensland, Australia
20°47'S 148°35'E
Bloxham 50 E7 England, UK 52°0'N 1°24'W
Blubberhouses 55 H3 England, UK
54°0'N 1°52'W
Bluefields 151 H2 Nicaragua 12°1'N 83°47'W
Blue Mountains 135 K3 ▲▲ New South Wales,
SE Australia
Blue Nile 97 K4 ≈ Ethiopia/Sudan
Blumenau 163 I2 Brazil 26°55'S 49°7'W

Blyth 53 H8 England, UK 53°23'N 1°9'W
Blyth 55 H7 England, UK 55°7'N 1°30'W
Blythburgh 53 M4 England, UK 52°19'N 1°28'E
Blyton 53 I8 England, UK 53°27'N 0°42'W
Bø 69 B6 Norway 59°24'N 9°4'E
Bo 96 D4 Sierra Leone 7°58'N 11°45'W
Boaco 151 G2 Nicaragua 12°28'N 85°45'W
Boa Vista 162 F9 Brazil 2°51'N 60°43'W
Bobaomby, Tanjona 99 L5 Headland
N Madagascar
Bobo-Dioulasso 96 E4 Burkina 11°12'N 4°21'W
Bobolice 84 D11 Poland 53°56'N 16°37'E
Boca do Acre 162 E6 Brazil 8°45'S 67°23'W
Bocay 151 G2 Nicaragua 14°19'N 85°8'W
Bocholt 82 C9 Germany 51°50'N 6°37'E
Bochum 82 D9 Germany 51°29'N 7°13'E
Bocking Churchstreet 51 I7 England, UK
51°55'N 0°28'E
Bodaybo 109 I4 Russian Fed. 57°52'N 114°5'E
Boden 68 F10 Sweden 65°50'N 21°44'E
Bodmin 49 D4 England, UK 50°29'N 4°43'W
Bodmin Moor 49 D4 Heathland SW England, UK
Bodø 68 D11 Norway 67°17'N 14°22'E
Bodrum 110 C5 Turkey 37°1'N 27°28'E
Boende 98 G8 Dem. Rep. Congo 0°12'S 20°54'E
Bofin, Lough 58 E9 ◎ N Ireland
Bogatynia 84 C8 Poland 50°53'N 14°55'E
Boğazlıyan 110 F6 Turkey 39°13'N 35°17'E
Boggeragh Mountains 59 D5 ▲▲ S Ireland
Bognor Regis 50 F3 England, UK
50°47'N 0°41'W
Bogor 126 G2 Indonesia 6°34'S 106°45'E
Bogotá 160 B11 ● Colombia 4°38'N 74°5'W
Bo Hai 123 K6 Gulf NE China
Bohemia 85 B7 Cultural region Czech Republic
Bohemian Forest 85 A6 ▲▲ C Europe
Bohol Sea 127 J5 Sea S Philippines
Bohoro Shan 122 D7 ▲▲ NW China
Boiaçu 162 F8 Brazil 0°27'S 61°46'W
Boise 146 F7 Idaho, USA 43°39'N 116°14'W
Boizenburg 82 F10 Germany 53°23'N 10°43'E
Bojnūrd 116 F6 Iran 37°31'N 57°24'E
Boké 96 D4 Guinea 10°56'N 14°18'W
Boknafjorden 69 A6 Fjord S Norway
Bol 97 H5 Chad 13°27'N 14°40'E
Boldon 55 H7 England, UK 54°56'N 1°32'W
Bolesławiec 84 C8 Poland 51°16'N 15°34'E
Bolgatanga 96 F4 Ghana 10°45'N 0°52'W
Bolivia 161 D7 ◆ Republic W South America
Bollene 73 I3 France 44°16'N 4°45'E
Bollnäs 69 D7 Sweden 61°18'N 16°27'E
Bollon 135 K4 Queensland, Australia
28°7'S 147°28'E
Bologna 77 H7 Italy 44°30'N 11°20'E
Bol'shevik, Ostrov 109 H8 Island Severnaya
Zemlya, N Russian Fed.
Bol'shezemel'skaya Tundra 88 G10
Physical region NW Russian Fed.
Bol'shoy Lyakhovskiy, Ostrov 109 J7 Island
NE Russian Fed.
Bolton 54 F2 England, UK 53°35'N 2°26'W
Bolton 36 ◈ Unitary authority England, UK
Bolu 110 E7 Turkey 40°45'N 31°38'E
Bolungarvík 68 A12 Iceland 66°9'N 23°17'W
Bolus Head 59 B4 Headland SW Ireland
Bolzano 77 H9 Italy 46°30'N 11°22'E
Boma 98 E7 Dem. Rep. Congo 5°42'S 13°5'E
Bombay see Mumbai
Bom Jesus da Lapa 163 J5 Brazil
13°16'S 43°23'W
Bomu 98 G9 ≈ Central African Republic/
Dem. Rep. Congo
Bonaire 151 L2 Island E Netherlands Antilles
Bonaparte Archipelago 134 E8 Island group
Western Australia
Bonar Bridge 56 F10 Scotland, UK
57°54'N 4°22'W
Bondo 98 G9 Dem. Rep. Congo 3°52'N 23°41'E
Bone, Teluk 127 I2 Bay Celebes, C Indonesia
Bongaigaon 119 J7 India 26°30'N 90°31'E
Bongo, Massif des 97 J4 ▲▲
NE Central African Republic
Bongor 97 H4 Chad 10°18'N 15°20'E
Bonifacio 73 K1 France 41°24'N 9°9'E
Bonifacio, Strait of 76 F5 Strait
C Mediterranean Sea
Bonin Trench 25 Undersea feature
NW Pacific Ocean
Bonn 82 D8 Germany 50°44'N 7°6'E
Boosaaso 97 N4 Somalia 11°26'N 49°37'E
Boothia, Gulf of 144 G6 Gulf Northwest
Territories, NE Canada
Boothia Peninsula 144 G6 Coastal feature
Northwest Territories, NE Canada
Bootle 54 E1 England, UK 53°27'N 2°57'W
Boppard 82 D8 Germany 50°13'N 7°36'E
Boquillas 150 D6 Mexico 29°10'N 102°55'W
Bor 86 G6 Serbia and Montenegro 44°5'N 22°7'E
Bor 97 K3 Sudan 6°12'N 31°33'E
Borah Peak 146 F7 ▲ Idaho, NW USA
Borås 69 C5 Sweden 57°44'N 12°55'E
Borāzjān 116 D3 Iran 29°19'N 51°12'E
Bordeaux 72 F4 France 44°49'N 0°33'W
Bordj Omar Driss 96 G7 Algeria 28°9'N 6°52'E
Bordon 50 F4 England, UK 51°5'N 0°56'W
Borgarnes 68 A11 Iceland 64°33'N 21°55'W
Børgefjelt 68 D10 ▲▲ C Norway
Borger 70 H12 Netherlands 52°54'N 6°48'E
Borgholm 69 D4 Sweden 56°50'N 16°41'E
Borisoglebsk 89 E5 Russian Fed. 51°23'N 42°0'E
Borlänge 69 D7 Sweden 60°29'N 15°25'E
Borne 70 H10 Netherlands 52°18'N 6°45'E
Borneo 127 H3 Island SE Asia
Bornholm 69 D3 Island E Denmark
Boroughbridge 55 H4 England, UK
54°6'N 1°25'W
Borovichi 89 D7 Russian Fed. 58°24'N 33°56'E
Borris 59 G6 Ireland 52°35'N 6°53'W
Borris in Ossory 59 F7 Ireland 52°56'N 7°37'W
Borrisokane 59 E7 Ireland 52°59'N 8°7'W
Borrisoleigh 59 E7 Ireland 52°44'N 8°8'W
Borth 48 E10 Wales, UK 52°30'N 4°6'W
Borūjen 116 D4 Iran 32°N 51°9'E
Borūjerd 116 D5 Iran 33°55'N 48°46'E
Bosanski Novi 86 E7 Bosnia and Herzegovina
45°3'N 16°23'E
Boscastle 49 D5 England, UK 50°42'N 4°44'W
Bose 123 H2 China 23°55'N 106°32'E

◆ Country ● Country capital ◇ Dependent territory ○ Dependent territory capital ◈ Administrative region ▲ Mountain ▲▲ Mountain range ⛰ Volcano ≈ River ◎ Lake ▣ Reservoir

174 Connaught - Drumsna

Connaught **58 D9** *Cultural region* Ireland
Connecticut **147 N7** ◈ *State* USA
Connel **57 D7** Scotland, UK *56°26'N 5°23'W*
Connemara **58 C8** *Physical region* W Ireland
Conn, Lough **58 C10** ◎ W Ireland
Consett **54 G6** England, UK *54°50'N 1°53'W*
Constance, Lake **83 E5** ◎ C Europe
Constanţa **87 J7** Romania *44°9'N 28°37'E*
Constantine **96 G8** Algeria *36°23'N 6°44'E*
Conwy **48 E12** Wales, UK *53°17'N 3°51'W*
Conwy **48 F12** ◈ *Unitary authority* Wales, UK
Conwy **48 E12** ≈ N Wales, UK
Coober Pedy **135 H4** South Australia *29°1'S 134°47'E*
Cook Islands **128** *NZ* ◇ Pacific Ocean
Cook Islands **24** *Island group* Cook Islands, Cook Islands C Pacific Ocean
Cookstown **58 G11** Northern Ireland, UK *54°39'N 6°45'W*
Cookstown **58 G11** ◈ *District* Northern Ireland, UK
Cook Strait **136 D4** *Strait* New Zealand
Cooktown **135 K8** Queensland, Australia *15°28'S 145°15'E*
Coolgardie **134 E3** Western Australia *31°1'S 121°12'E*
Cooma **135 K2** New South Wales, Australia *36°16'S 149°9'E*
Coon Rapids **147 J7** Minnesota, USA *45°12'N 93°18'W*
Cooper Creek **135 J5** ≈ Queensland/ South Australia
Cootehill **58 G10** Ireland *54°4'N 7°5'W*
Copacabana **161 C7** Bolivia *16°11'S 69°2'W*
Copenhagen **69 C4** ● Denmark *55°43'N 12°34'E*
Copiapó **161 C5** Chile *23°40'S 70°23'W*
Copplestone **49 E5** England, UK *50°49'N 3°45'W*
Coquimbo **161 C5** Chile *30°S 71°18'W*
Coral Harbour **145 H5** Northwest Territories, Canada *64°10'N 83°15'W*
Coral Sea **135 K9** *Sea* SW Pacific Ocean
Coral Sea Islands **128** *Australian* ◇ Pacific Ocean
Corbridge **54 G7** England, UK *54°58'N 2°1'W*
Corby **53 I5** England, UK *52°30'N 0°41'W*
Corby Glen **53 I6** England, UK *52°25'N 0°32'W*
Córdoba **161 D5** Argentina *31°25'S 64°11'W*
Córdoba **75 H4** Spain *37°53'N 4°46'W*
Corfu **86 F3** Greece *39°37'N 19°56'E*
Coria **74 G6** Spain *39°59'N 6°32'W*
Corinth **87 H2** Greece *37°56'N 22°55'E*
Cork **59 D5** Ireland *51°54'N 7°6'W*
Çorlu **110 C7** Turkey *41°11'N 27°48'E*
Corner Brook **145 K3** Newfoundland and Labrador, Canada *48°58'N 57°58'W*
Cornwall **37** ◈ *County* England, UK
Cornwall, Cape **49 B3** *Headland* SW England, UK
Cornwallis Island **144 G7** *Island* Northwest Territories, Parry Islands, N Canada
Coro **160 C12** Venezuela *11°27'N 69°41'W*
Corocoro **161 C7** Bolivia *17°10'S 68°28'W*
Coromandel **136 E7** New Zealand *36°47'S 175°30'E*
Coronel Dorrego **161 E4** Argentina *38°38'S 61°15'W*
Corozal **150 G3** Belize *18°23'N 88°23'W*
Corpus Christi **147 I2** Texas, USA *27°48'N 97°24'W*
Corrente **163 J6** Brazil *10°29'S 45°11'W*
Corrib, Lough **58 C8** ◎ W Ireland
Corrientes **161 E5** Argentina *27°29'S 58°42'W*
Corris **48 E10** Wales, UK *52°39'N 3°54'W*
Corsham **49 H7** England, UK *51°25'N 2°12'W*
Corsica **73 K2** *Island* France, C Mediterranean Sea
Corsock **57 F3** Scotland, UK *55°4'N 3°57'W*
Cortegana **74 F4** Spain *37°55'N 6°49'W*
Cortina d'Ampezzo **77 H9** Italy *46°33'N 12°9'E*
Coruche **74 E5** Portugal *38°58'N 8°31'W*
Çorum **110 F7** Turkey *40°31'N 34°57'E*
Corumbá **162 G4** Brazil *19°S 57°35'W*
Corwen **48 F11** Wales, UK *52°59'N 3°21'W*
Cosenza **77 K3** Italy *39°17'N 16°15'E*
Cosne-Cours-sur-Loire **73 H6** France *47°25'N 2°57'E*
Costa Rica **151 H1** ◆ *Republic* Central America
Cotagaita **161 D7** Bolivia *20°47'S 65°40'W*
Côte d'Ivoire *see* Ivory Coast
Cotgrave **53 H6** England, UK *52°55'N 1°3'W*
Cotswold Hills **48 H8** *Hill range* S England, UK
Cottbus **82 H9** Germany *51°42'N 14°22'E*
Cottenham **53 J4** England, UK *52°16'N 0°0'E*
Cottingham **55 J3** England, UK *53°46'N 0°26'W*
Council Bluffs **147 I6** Iowa, USA *41°16'N 95°52'W*
Courland Lagoon **69 F3** *Lagoon* Lithuania/ Russian Fed.
Courtown **59 H6** Ireland *52°38'N 6°13'W*
Coutances **72 E7** France *49°4'N 1°27'W*
Couvin **71 D4** Belgium *50°3'N 4°30'E*
Coventry **52 G5** England, UK *52°25'N 1°30'W*
Coventry **37** ◈ *Unitary authority* England, UK
Coverack **49 C3** England, UK *50°2'N 5°2'W*
Covilhã **74 F6** Portugal *40°17'N 7°30'W*
Cowan, Lake **134 E3** ◎ Western Australia
Cowbridge **49 F7** Wales, UK *51°27'N 3°26'W*
Cowes **50 E2** England, UK *50°45'N 1°19'W*
Cowfold **50 G3** England, UK *50°59'N 0°22'W*
Cowley **50 E6** England, UK *51°43'N 1°12'W*
Cowshill **54 G6** England, UK *54°46'N 2°13'W*
Coxhoe **55 H6** England, UK *54°43'N 1°30'W*
Coxim **163 H4** Brazil *18°28'S 54°45'W*
Cozumel, Isla **150 G4** *Island* SE Mexico
Cradock **99 H2** South Africa *32°7'S 25°38'E*
Craigavon **58 H11** Northern Ireland, UK *54°28'N 6°25'W*
Craigavon **58 G11** ◈ *District* Northern Ireland, UK
Crail **57 H6** Scotland, UK *56°15'N 2°36'W*
Craiova **87 H7** Romania *44°19'N 23°49'E*
Cranbourne **49 I5** England, UK *50°54'N 2°3'W*
Cranbrook **144 E2** British Columbia, Canada *49°29'N 115°48'W*
Cranbrook **51 I4** England, UK *51°5'N 0°31'E*
Cranleigh **50 G4** England, UK *51°7'N 0°30'W*
Crathie **56 G8** Scotland, UK *57°2'N 3°11'W*
Craughwell **58 D8** Ireland *53°14'N 8°43'W*
Craven Arms **52 E5** England, UK *52°26'N 2°51'W*
Crawley **50 G4** England, UK *51°7'N 0°12'W*
Creegh **59 C6** Ireland *52°44'N 9°25'W*
Creggan **58 G11** Northern Ireland, UK *53°42'N 9°51'W*
Cremona **76 G8** Italy *45°8'N 10°2'E*
Cres **86 D7** *Island* W Croatia
Crescent City **146 D7** California, USA *41°45'N 124°14'W*
Cressage **52 E5** England, UK *52°38'N 2°40'W*
Créteil **72 G7** France *48°47'N 2°28'E*
Crete, Sea of **87 I1** *Sea* Greece, Aegean Sea
Creuse **72 F5** ≈ C France
Crewe **52 E7** England, UK *53°5'N 2°27'W*
Crianlarich **57 E6** Scotland, UK *56°23'N 4°40'W*
Criciúma **163 I1** Brazil *28°39'S 49°23'W*
Crickhowell **48 G8** Wales, UK *51°52'N 3°8'W*
Crieff **57 F6** Scotland, UK *56°22'N 3°49'W*
Cringleford **53 M5** England, UK *52°36'N 1°15'E*
Croagh Patrick **58 C9** ▲ W Ireland
Croatia **86 E7** ◆ *Republic* SE Europe
Croker Island **134 G9** *Island* Northern Territory, N Australia
Cromarty **56 F10** Scotland, UK *57°40'N 4°2'W*
Cromer **53 M6** England, UK *52°56'N 1°6'E*
Cromwell **136 B2** New Zealand *45°3'S 169°14'E*
Crookham **54 G9** England, UK *55°37'N 2°13'W*
Crookston **147 I8** Minnesota, USA *47°47'N 96°36'W*
Croom **59 D6** Ireland *52°31'N 8°42'W*
Crosby **54 B4** Isle of Man *54°10'N 4°35'W*
Crosby **54 E2** England, UK *53°30'N 3°2'W*
Crosby Ravensworth **54 F5** England, UK *54°31'N 2°36'W*
Cross Fell **54 F6** ▲ N England, UK
Cross Hands **48 E8** Wales, UK *51°48'N 4°13'W*
Crossmaglen **58 G10** Northern Ireland, UK *54°6'N 6°31'W*
Crossmolina **58 C10** Ireland *54°5'N 9°32'W*
Crotone **77 K3** Italy *39°5'N 17°7'E*
Crowborough **51 H4** England, UK *51°3'N 0°0'E*
Crowle **52 F4** England, UK *52°11'N 2°8'W*
Croydon **51 H5** England, UK *51°21'N 0°6'W*
Croydon **37** ◈ *London Borough* England, UK
Crozet Islands **25** *Island group* French Southern and Antarctic Territories
Cruden Bay **56 I9** Scotland, UK *57°25'N 1°46'W*
Crudgington **52 E6** England, UK *52°46'N 2°36'W*
Crusheen **59 D7** Ireland *52°55'N 8°52'W*
Cruz Alta **163 H1** Brazil *28°38'S 53°38'W*
Cruzeiro do Sul **162 D6** Brazil *7°40'S 72°39'W*
Crymych **48 D8** Wales, UK *51°59'N 4°37'W*
Csorna **85 D4** Hungary *47°37'N 17°14'E*
Csurgó **85 D3** Hungary *46°16'N 17°9'E*
Cuando **98 G4** ≈ S Africa
Cuango **98 F6** ≈ Angola/Dem. Rep. Congo *see also* Kwango
Cuanza **98 F6** ≈ C Angola
Cuauhtémoc **150 C6** Mexico *28°22'N 106°52'W*
Cuautla **150 D4** Mexico *18°48'N 98°56'W*
Cuba **151 H4** ◆ *Republic* W West Indies
Cubal **98 E5** Angola *12°58'S 14°16'E*
Cubango **98 F5** Angola *14°27'S 16°18'E*
Cubango **98 F5** ≈ S Africa *see also* Okavango
Cúcuta **160 C11** Colombia *7°55'N 72°31'W*
Cuddapah **119 H3** India *14°30'N 78°50'E*
Cudworth **52 G9** England, UK *53°34'N 1°26'W*
Cuenca **160 B10** Ecuador *2°54'S 79°W*
Cuenca **75 J6** Spain *40°4'N 2°7'W*
Cuernavaca **150 D4** Mexico *18°57'N 99°15'W*
Cuiabá **162 G4** Brazil *15°32'S 56°5'W*
Cuijck **70 G8** Netherlands *51°41'N 5°56'E*
Cuito **98 G4** ≈ SE Angola
Culiacán **150 C5** Mexico *24°48'N 107°25'W*
Cullen **56 H10** Scotland, UK *57°42'N 2°47'W*
Cullera **75 K5** Spain *39°10'N 0°15'W*
Cullompton **49 F5** England, UK *50°51'N 3°31'W*
Cullybackey **58 H12** Northern Ireland, UK *54°54'N 6°28'W*
Culmstock **49 F5** England, UK *50°55'N 3°17'W*
Cumberland, Lake **147 L5** ▣ Kentucky, S USA
Cumberland Sound **145 I5** *Inlet* Baffin Island, Northwest Territories, NE Canada
Cumbernauld **57 F5** Scotland, UK *55°57'N 4°W*
Cumbria **54 E6** ◈ *County* England, UK
Cumbrian Mountains **54 E5** ▲▲ NW England, UK
Cumnock **57 F4** Scotland, UK *55°32'N 4°28'W*
Cumpas **150 B7** Mexico *30°N 109°48'W*
Cumrew **54 F6** England, UK *54°50'N 2°40'W*
Cunene **98 E4** ≈ Angola/Namibia *see also* Kunene
Cuneo **76 E7** Italy *44°23'N 7°32'E*
Cunnamulla **135 J4** Queensland, Australia *28°9'S 145°44'E*
Cupar **57 G6** Scotland, UK *56°19'N 3°1'W*
Curaçao **151 K2** *Island* Netherlands Antilles
Curitiba **163 I2** Brazil *25°25'S 49°25'W*
Curtis Island **135 L5** *Island* Queensland, SE Australia
Curuá, Ilha do **163 I8** *Island* NE Brazil
Cusco **160 C8** Peru *13°35'S 72°2'W*
Cushcamcarragh **58 C9** ▲ NW Ireland
Cushendall **58 H12** Northern Ireland, UK *55°5'N 6°1'W*
Cusset **73 H5** France *46°8'N 3°27'E*
Cuttack **119 I5** India *20°28'N 85°53'E*
Cuxhaven **82 E11** Germany *53°51'N 8°43'E*
Cwmbran **48 G8** Wales, UK *51°39'N 3°W*
Cyclades **87 I2** *Island group* SE Greece
Cynwyl Elfed **48 D8** Wales, UK *51°55'N 4°25'W*
Cyprus **79 M8** ◆ *Republic* E Mediterranean Sea
Czech Republic **85 C7** ◆ *Republic* C Europe
Czersk **84 E11** Poland *53°48'N 17°58'E*
Częstochowa **84 F8** Poland *50°49'N 19°07'E*
Człopa **84 D10** Poland *53°5'N 16°5'E*
Człuchów **84 D11** Poland *53°41'N 17°20'E*

D

Dąbrowa Tarnowska **85 G7** Poland *50°10'N 21°E*
Dādra and Nagar Haveli **118 F5** ◈ *Union territory* India
Dagda **69 H4** Latvia *56°6'N 27°36'E*
Dagenham **51 H5** England, UK *51°31'N 0°9'E*
Daghmar **115 M6** Oman *23°9'N 59°1'E*
Dagupan **127 I6** Philippines *16°5'N 120°21'E*
Dahm, Ramlat **114 G3** *Desert* NW Yemen
Daimiel **75 I5** Spain *39°4'N 3°37'W*
Dakar **96 C5** ● Senegal *14°44'N 17°27'W*
Dakoro **96 G5** Niger *14°29'N 6°45'E*
Dalaman **110 D5** Turkey *36°47'N 28°47'E*
Dalandzadgad **123 H7** Mongolia *43°35'N 104°23'E*
Da Lat **126 G5** Vietnam *11°56'N 108°25'E*
Dalby **54 B4** Isle of Man *54°9'N 4°49'W*
Dale **48 C8** Wales, UK *51°42'N 5°13'W*
Dali **122 G2** China *25°34'N 100°11'E*
Dalian **123 K6** China *38°53'N 121°37'E*
Dalkeith **57 G5** Scotland, UK *55°53'N 3°1'W*
Dallas **147 I4** Texas, USA *32°47'N 96°48'W*
Dalmally **57 E7** Scotland, UK *56°24'N 4°56'W*
Dalmellington **57 E4** Scotland, UK *55°20'N 4°21'W*
Dalwhinnie **56 F8** Scotland, UK *56°56'N 4°23'W*
Daly River **134 G8** ≈ Northern Territory, N Australia
Daly Waters **135 H8** Northern Territory, Australia *16°21'S 133°22'E*
Daman **118 F5** India *20°25'N 72°58'E*
Damān and Diu **118 F5** ◈ *Union territory* India
Damascus **110 G3** ● Syria *33°30'N 36°19'E*
Damavand, Qolleh-ye **116 E5** ▲ N Iran
Dāmghān **116 F5** Iran *36°13'N 54°22'E*
Dampier **134 C6** Western Australia *20°40'S 116°40'E*
Dampier, Selat **127 L3** *Strait* Irian Jaya, E Indonesia
Damqawt **115 J3** Yemen *16°35'N 52°39'E*
Damxung **122 E4** China *30°29'N 91°2'E*
Danakil Desert **97 L5** *Desert* E Africa
Da Nang **126 G6** Vietnam *16°4'N 108°14'E*
Danbury **51 I6** England, UK *51°43'N 0°34'E*
Dandong **123 K6** China *40°10'N 124°23'E*
Danghara **117 J6** Tajikistan *38°5'N 69°14'E*
Dângrêk, Chuŏr Phnum **126 F6** ▲▲ Cambodia/ Thailand
Dangriga **150 G3** Belize *16°59'N 88°13'W*
Danlí **150 G2** Honduras *14°2'N 86°34'W*
Dannenberg **82 F10** Germany *53°5'N 11°6'E*
Dannevirke **136 E5** New Zealand *40°14'S 176°5'E*
Danube **61** ≈ C Europe
Danxian **123 I1** China *19°31'N 109°31'E*
Danzig, Gulf of **69 E3** *Gulf* N Poland
Da Qaidam **122 F5** China *37°50'N 95°18'E*
Daqing **123 K8** China *46°29'N 125°7'E*
Dar es Salaam **99 J6** Tanzania *6°51'S 39°18'E*
Darfield **136 D3** New Zealand *43°29'S 172°7'E*
Darfur **97 J5** *Cultural region* Sudan
Dargaville **136 D7** New Zealand *35°19'S 173°53'E*
Darhan **123 H8** Mongolia *49°24'N 105°57'E*
Darien, Gulf of **151 J1** *Gulf* S Caribbean Sea
Darjiling **119 J7** India *27°0'N 88°13'E*
Darling River **135 J3** ≈ New South Wales, SE Australia
Darlington **55 H5** England, UK *54°31'N 1°34'W*
Darlington **36** ◈ *Unitary authority* England, UK
Darmstadt **83 D7** Germany *49°52'N 8°39'E*
Darnley, Cape **166 F6** *Headland* Antarctica
Daroca **75 J7** Spain *41°7'N 1°25'W*
Daroot-Korgon **117 K7** Kyrgyzstan *39°35'N 72°13'E*
Dart **49 F4** ≈ SW England, UK
Dartford **51 H5** England, UK *51°27'N 0°13'E*
Dartmoor **49 E5** *Heathland* SW England, UK
Dartmouth **145 K2** Nova Scotia, Canada *44°40'N 63°35'W*
Dartmouth **49 F4** England, UK *50°21'N 3°34'W*
Darvishan **117 I3** Afghanistan *31°2'N 64°12'E*
Darwaza **116 G7** Turkmenistan *40°10'N 58°27'E*
Darwen **54 F2** England, UK *53°42'N 2°25'W*
Darwin **134 G9** Northern Territory, Australia *12°28'S 130°52'E*
Daşoguz **116 G8** Turkmenistan *41°51'N 59°53'E*
Datong **123 I6** China *40°9'N 113°17'E*
Daugavpils **69 H4** Latvia *55°53'N 26°34'E*
Dauphiné **73 I3** *Cultural region* France
Davangere **118 G3** India *14°30'N 75°52'E*
Davao **127 J4** Philippines *7°6'N 125°36'E*
Davao Gulf **127 J4** *Gulf* Mindanao, S Philippines
Davenport **147 J6** Iowa, USA *41°31'N 90°35'W*
Daventry **53 H4** England, UK *52°15'N 1°16'W*
David **151 H1** Panama *8°26'N 82°26'W*
Davis Sea **166 G5** *Sea* Antarctica
Davis Strait **145 I6** *Strait* Baffin Bay/Labrador Sea
Dawkah **115 K4** Oman *18°32'N 54°3'E*
Dawlish **49 F4** England, UK *50°35'N 3°28'W*
Dawros Head **58 D11** *Headland* N Ireland
Dax **72 E3** France *43°43'N 1°3'W*
Dayton **147 L6** Ohio, USA *39°46'N 84°12'W*
Daytona Beach **147 M3** Florida, USA *29°12'N 81°3'W*
De Aar **98 G2** South Africa *30°40'S 24°1'E*
Dead Sea **110 B3** *Salt lake* Israel/Jordan
Deal **51 K4** England, UK *51°14'N 1°23'E*
Dean, Forest of **48 H8** *Forest* C England, UK
Deán Funes **161 D5** Argentina *30°25'S 64°22'W*
Death Valley **146 E5** *Valley* California, W USA
Debenham **53 M4** England, UK *52°14'N 1°4'E*
Dębica **85 G7** Poland *50°4'N 21°24'E*
De Bilt **70 F9** Netherlands *52°6'N 5°11'E*
Dęblin **84 H9** Poland *51°34'N 21°50'E*
Debrecen **85 H4** Hungary *47°32'N 21°38'E*
Deccan **118 G4** *Plateau* C India
Děčín **84 B8** Czech Republic *50°48'N 14°15'E*
Deddington **50 E7** England, UK *51°59'N 1°27'W*
Dedemsvaart **70 H11** Netherlands *52°36'N 6°28'E*
Deeping St Nicholas **53 J6** England, UK *52°44'N 0°17'W*
Deggendorf **83 G6** Germany *48°50'N 12°58'E*
Değirmenlik *see* Kythrea
Dehra Dun **118 G8** India *30°19'N 78°4'E*
Deh Shu **117 H3** Afghanistan *30°28'N 63°21'E*
Deinze **71 C7** Belgium *50°59'N 3°32'E*
Delaram **117 H4** Afghanistan *32°11'N 63°27'E*
Delaware **147 N6** ◈ *State* USA
Delft **70 D9** Netherlands *52°1'N 4°22'E*
Delfzijl **70 H13** Netherlands *53°20'N 6°55'E*
Delgo **97 K6** Sudan *20°8'N 30°35'E*
Delhi **118 G7** India *28°40'N 77°11'E*
Delicias **150 C6** Mexico *28°9'N 105°22'W*
Delmenhorst **82 E10** Germany *53°3'N 8°38'E*
Delphi **58 C9** Ireland *53°37'N 9°52'W*
Delvin **58 G9** Ireland *53°35'N 7°7'W*
Demba **98 G7** Dem. Rep. Congo *5°24'S 22°16'E*
Demmin **82 G11** Germany *53°53'N 13°3'E*
Demqog **119 H9** *Disputed* China/India
Denbigh **48 F12** Wales, UK *53°11'N 3°25'W*
Denbighshire **48 F12** ◈ *Unitary authority* Wales, UK
Den Burg **70 E12** Netherlands *53°3'N 4°47'E*
Denby Dale **55 H2** England, UK *53°36'N 1°41'W*
Dender **71 D6** ≈ W Belgium
Denekamp **70 I10** Netherlands *52°23'N 7°E*
Denham **134 C4** Western Australia *25°56'S 113°35'E*
Den Ham **70 H11** Netherlands *52°30'N 6°31'E*
Den Helder **70 E12** Netherlands *52°54'N 4°45'E*
Dénia **75 K5** Spain *38°51'N 0°7'E*
Deniliquin **135 J2** New South Wales, Australia *35°33'S 144°58'E*
Denizli **110 D5** Turkey *37°46'N 29°5'E*
Denmark **69 B4** ◆ *Monarchy* N Europe
Denny **57 F6** Scotland, UK *56°2'N 3°58'W*
Denov **117 J6** Uzbekistan *38°20'N 67°48'E*
Denpasar **127 H1** Indonesia *8°40'S 115°14'E*
Denton **147 I4** Texas, USA *33°11'N 97°8'W*
Denver **147 H6** Colorado, USA *39°45'N 105°W*
Dera Ghazi Khan **118 F8** Pakistan *30°1'N 70°37'E*
Đeravica **86 F5** ▲ S Serbia and Montenegro
Derbent **89 G2** Russian Fed. *42°1'N 48°16'E*
Derby **134 E7** Western Australia *17°18'S 123°37'E*
Derby **52 G6** England, UK *52°55'N 1°30'W*
Derby, City of **37** ◈ *Unitary authority* England, UK
Derbyshire **52 G7** ◈ *County* England, UK
Derg **58 F11** ≈ Ireland/Northern Ireland, UK
Derg, Lough **59 E7** ◎ W Ireland
Ḑerkeş **110 E7** Turkey *40°52'N 32°52'E*
Derreendarragh **59 C4** Ireland *51°53'N 9°54'W*
Derrynacreeve **58 F10** Ireland *54°9'N 7°43'W*
Derwent **54 E6** ≈ N England, UK
Dese **97 L4** Ethiopia *11°2'N 39°39'E*
Deseado, Río **161 D2** ≈ S Argentina
Des Moines **147 J6** Iowa, USA *41°36'N 93°37'W*
Desna **89 C5** ≈ Russian Fed./Ukraine
Dessau **82 G9** Germany *51°51'N 12°15'E*
Detroit **147 L7** Michigan, USA *42°20'N 83°3'W*
Deurne **70 G8** Netherlands *51°28'N 5°47'E*
Deva **87 H8** Romania *45°55'N 22°55'E*
Deventer **70 G10** Netherlands *52°15'N 6°10'E*
Deveron **56 H10** ≈ NE Scotland, UK
Devizes **49 I7** England, UK *51°21'N 2°0'W*
Devon **49 E5** ◈ *County* England, UK
Devon Island **144 G7** *Island* Parry Islands, Northwest Territories, NE Canada
Devonport **135 J1** Tasmania, Australia *41°14'S 146°21'E*
Devrek **110 E7** Turkey *41°14'N 31°57'E*
Dewsbury **55 H2** England, UK *53°42'N 1°37'W*
Dezful **116 D4** Iran *32°23'N 48°28'E*
Dezhou **123 J5** China *37°28'N 116°18'E*
Dhaka **119 J6** ● Bangladesh *23°42'N 90°22'E*
Dhamār **114 G2** Yemen *14°31'N 44°25'E*
Dhanbad **119 I6** India *23°48'N 86°27'E*
Dhekelia Sovereign Air Base **79 M8** *Air base* SE Cyprus
Dhuusa Marreeb **97 M3** Somalia *5°33'N 46°24'E*
Diamantina, Chapada **163 K5** ▲▲ E Brazil
Diamantina River **135 I5** ≈ Queensland/ South Australia
Dibā al Ḩişn **115 K7** United Arab Emirates *25°35'N 56°16'E*
Dibrugarh **119 K7** India *27°29'N 94°49'E*
Dickinson **147 H8** North Dakota, USA *46°54'N 102°48'W*
Didcot **50 E6** England, UK *51°35'N 1°15'W*
Didymoteicho **87 I5** Greece *41°22'N 26°29'E*
Diekirch **71 G4** Luxembourg *49°52'N 6°10'E*
Diepenbeek **71 F6** Belgium *50°54'N 5°25'E*
Diepholz **82 D10** Germany *52°36'N 8°23'E*
Dieppe **72 G8** France *49°55'N 1°5'E*
Dieren **70 G9** Netherlands *52°3'N 6°6'E*
Differdange **71 G3** Luxembourg *49°32'N 5°53'E*
Digne **73 J3** France *44°5'N 6°14'E*
Digoin **73 H5** France *46°30'N 4°E*
Digul, Sungai **127 M2** ≈ Irian Jaya, E Indonesia
Dijon **73 I6** France *47°21'N 5°4'E*
Dikhil **97 M4** Djibouti *11°8'N 42°19'E*
Dikson **108 G7** Russian Fed. *73°30'N 80°35'E*
Dikti **87 I1** ▲▲ Kriti, Greece, E Mediterranean Sea
Dili **127 J1** ● East Timor *8°33'S 125°34'E*
Dilia **97 H5** ≈ SE Niger
Dilolo **98 G6** Dem. Rep. Congo *10°42'S 22°21'E*
Dimashq *see* Damascus
Dimitrovgrad **87 I5** Bulgaria *42°3'N 25°36'E*
Dimitrovgrad **89 G6** Russian Fed. *54°14'N 49°37'E*
Dimovo **87 H6** Bulgaria *43°46'N 22°47'E*
Dinajpur **119 J7** Bangladesh *25°38'N 88°40'E*
Dinan **72 E7** France *48°27'N 2°2'W*
Dinant **71 E5** Belgium *50°16'N 4°55'E*
Dinar **110 D5** Turkey *38°5'N 30°9'E*
Dinaric Alps **86 E6** ▲▲ Bosnia and Herzegovina/ Croatia
Dindigul **118 G2** India *10°23'N 78°E*
Dingle **59 B5** Ireland *52°9'N 10°16'W*
Dingle Bay **59 B5** *Bay* SW Ireland
Dingwall **56 E9** Scotland, UK *57°36'N 4°26'W*
Dippen **57 D4** Scotland, UK *55°35'N 5°35'W*
Dire Dawa **97 M4** Ethiopia *9°35'N 41°53'E*
Dirk Hartog Island **134 C4** *Island* Western Australia
Disappointment, Lake **134 E6** *Salt lake* Western Australia
Dishforth **55 H4** England, UK *54°9'N 1°31'W*
Diss **53 L5** England, UK *52°23'N 1°6'E*
Distrito Federal **163 I4** ◈ *Federal district* Brazil
Ditchling **50 G3** England, UK *50°54'N 0°8'W*
Divinópolis **163 J3** Brazil *20°8'S 44°55'W*
Diyarbakır **111 H5** Turkey *37°55'N 40°14'E*
Djambala **98 F7** Congo *2°32'S 14°43'E*
Djanet **97 H6** Algeria *24°34'N 9°33'E*
Djéma **97 J3** Central African Republic *6°4'N 25°20'E*
Djerba **78 G4** *Island* E Tunisia
Djibouti **97 M4** ● Djibouti *11°33'N 42°55'E*
Djibouti **97 M4** ◆ *Republic* E Africa
Djourab, Erg du **97 I5** *Desert* N Chad
Djúpivogur **68 C11** Iceland *64°40'N 14°18'*
Dnieper **89 C5** ≈ E Europe
Dniester **89 B4** ≈ Moldova/Ukraine
Dnipropetrovs'k **89 D4** Ukraine *48°28'N 3*
Doba **97 I4** Chad *8°40'N 16°50'E*
Döbeln **82 G8** Germany *51°7'N 13°7'E*
Dobre Miasto **84 G11** Poland *53°59'N 20°2*
Dobrich **87 J6** Bulgaria *43°35'N 27°49'E*
Docking **53 K6** England, UK *52°54'N 0°39'*
Doddington **53 J5** England, UK *52°28'N 0°*
Dodecanese **87 J2** *Island group* SE Greece
Dodge City **147 I5** Kansas, USA *37°45'N 100°1'W*
Dodman Point **49 D3** *Headland* SW England, UK
Dodoma **99 J7** ● Tanzania *6°11'S 35°45'E*
Dogai Coring **122 E5** ◎ W China
Dogo **125 H4** *Island* Oki-shotō, SW Japan
Doğubayazit **111 J6** Turkey *39°33'N 44°7'E*
Doha **115 J6** ● Qatar *25°15'N 51°36'E*
Dokan **111 J4** Iraq *35°55'N 44°58'E*
Dokkum **70 G13** Netherlands *53°20'N 6°E*
Dôle **73 I6** France *47°5'N 5°30'E*
Dolgellau **48 E11** Wales, UK *52°45'N 3°54'*
Dolisie **98 E7** Congo *4°12'S 12°41'E*
Dolores **161 E4** Argentina *36°21'S 57°39'W*
Dombås **68 B8** Norway *62°4'N 9°7'E*
Dombóvár **85 E3** Hungary *46°24'N 18°9'E*
Domeyko **161 C5** Chile *28°58'S 70°54'W*
Dominica **151 M4** ◆ *Republic* E West Indies
Dominican Republic **151 K4** ◆ *Republic* C West Indies
Don **89 E4** ≈ SW Russian Fed.
Don **53 H9** ≈ N England, UK
Donaghadee **58 I11** Northern Ireland, UK *54°39'N 5°31'W*
Donauwörth **83 F6** Germany *48°43'N 10°4*
Donawitz **83 H5** Austria *47°23'N 15°0'E*
Don Benito **74 G5** Spain *38°57'N 5°52'W*
Doncaster **53 H8** England, UK *53°32'N 1°7'*
Doncaster **37** ◈ *Unitary authority* England, U
Donegal **58 E11** Ireland *54°39'N 8°6'W*
Donegal **58 E12** ◈ *County* Ireland
Donegal Bay **58 E11** *Bay* NW Ireland
Donets'k **89 D4** Ukraine *47°58'N 37°50'E*
Dongchuan **123 H3** China *26°9'N 103°10'E*
Dongfang **123 I1** China *19°5'N 108°40'E*
Dongguan **123 J2** China *23°3'N 113°43'E*
Dongola **97 K6** Sudan *19°10'N 30°27'E*
Dongou **98 F8** Congo *2°5'N 18°E*
Dongting Hu **123 I3** ◎ S China
Donington **53 J6** England, UK *52°55'N 0°1*
Donostia-San Sebastián **75 J9** Spain *43°19'N 1°59'W*
Doolow **97 M3** Ethiopia *4°10'N 42°5'E*
Dorchester **49 H5** England, UK *50°43'N 2°2*
Dordogne **72 F4** *Cultural region* France
Dordogne **72 F4** ≈ W France
Dordrecht **70 E9** Netherlands *51°48'N 4°40'*
Dorking **50 G4** England, UK *51°13'N 0°27'*
Dornoch **56 F10** Scotland, UK *57°52'N 4°1'*
Dorotea **68 D9** Sweden *64°17'N 16°30'E*
Dorre Island **134 C5** *Island* Western Australi
Dorset **49 H5** ◈ *County* England, UK
Dortmund **82 D9** Germany *51°31'N 7°28'E*
Dos Hermanas **74 G3** Spain *37°16'N 5°55'*
Dotnuva **69 G3** Lithuania *55°23'N 23°53'E*
Douai **73 H8** France *50°22'N 3°4'E*
Douala **97 H3** Cameroon *4°4'N 9°43'E*
Douglas **59 D4** Ireland *51°52'N 8°25'W*
Douglas **54 B4** ○ Isle of Man *54°9'N 4°28'W*
Dounreay **56 F12** Scotland, UK *58°35'N 3°4*
Dourada, Serra **163 I5** ▲▲ S Brazil
Dourados **162 G3** Brazil *22°9'S 54°52'W*
Douro **74 G7** ≈ Portugal/Spain
Dover **51 K4** England, UK *51°8'N 3°E*
Dover **147 M6** Delaware, USA *39°9'N 75°31*
Dover, Strait of **51 K3** *Strait* England, UK/Fra
Dovrefjell **68 B8** ▲▲ S Norway
Down **58 H10** ◈ *District* Northern Ireland, UK
Downham Market **53 K5** England, UK *52°35'N 0°23'E*
Downpatrick **58 I10** Northern Ireland, UK *54°20'N 5°43'W*
Dozen **124 G4** *Island* Oki-shotō, SW Japan
Drachten **70 G12** Netherlands *53°7'N 6°6'E*
Drag **68 D11** Norway *68°2'N 16°E*
Dra, Hamada du **96 E7** *Plateau* W Algeria
Drahichyn **89 B6** Belarus *52°11'N 25°10'E*
Drakensberg **99 I2** ▲▲ Lesotho/South Africa
Drake Passage **161 D1** *Passage* Atlantic Ocea Pacific Ocean
Drama **87 H5** Greece *41°9'N 24°10'E*
Drammen **69 B6** Norway *59°44'N 10°12'E*
Drava **85 E3** ≈ SE Europe
Drawsko Pomorskie **84 C11** Poland *53°32'N 15°48'E*
Dresden **82 G8** Germany *51°3'N 13°43'E*
Drezdenko **84 C10** Poland *52°51'N 15°50'E*
Driffield **55 J3** England, UK *54°0'N 0°28'W*
Drinit, Lumi i **86 F5** ≈ NW Albania
Drobeta-Turnu Severin **87 H7** Romania *44°39'N 22°40'E*
Drogheda **58 H9** Ireland *53°43'N 6°21'W*
Droitwich **52 F4** England, UK *52°15'N 2°5'W*
Drôme **73 I3** *Cultural region* France
Dromineer **59 E7** Ireland *52°54'N 8°16'W*
Dromore **58 F11** Northern Ireland, UK *54°25'N 6°9'W*
Dromore West **58 D10** Ireland *54°14'N 8°55*
Dronfield **52 G8** England, UK *53°17'N 1°27'*
Dronning Maud Land **166 D7** *Physical regior* Antarctica
Drumahoe **58 F12** Northern Ireland, UK *54°58'N 7°16'W*
Drumbilla **58 G10** Ireland *54°1'N 6°34'W*
Drumcliff **58 D10** Ireland *54°19'N 8°30'W*
Drumkeeran **58 E10** Ireland *54°9'N 8°21'W*
Drummore **57 E3** Scotland, UK *54°42'N 4°52*
Drumnadrochit **56 E9** Scotland, UK *57°20'N 4°33'W*
Drumsna **58 E9** Ireland *53°56'N 8°0'W*

◆ Country ● Country capital ◇ Dependent territory ○ Dependent territory capital ◈ Administrative region ▲ Mountain ▲▲ Mountain range Volcano ≈ River ◎ Lake ▣ Reservoir

Druridge Bay - Flamborough 175

ge Bay 55 H8 Bay N England, UK
144 G2 Ontario, Canada
'8'N 92°48'W
n Fawr 48 F9 ▲ E Wales, UK
89 C7 ⟿ N Belarus
, Pico 151 K4 ▲ C Dominican Republic
114 D7 Saudi Arabia 27°26'N 35°42'E
115 K6 United Arab Emirates
1'N 55°18'E
nt 144 F4 ⟿ Northwest Territories,
Canada
135 K3 New South Wales, Australia
6'S 148°41'E
58 H8 ● Ireland 53°20'N 6°15'W
58 H8 ◈ County Ireland
Bay 58 H8 Bay E Ireland
vnik 86 E6 Croatia 42°40'N 18°6'E
ue 147 J6 Iowa, USA 42°30'N 90°40'W
ngton 53 I5 England, UK 52°36'N 0°32'W
ange 71 G3 Luxembourg 49°28'N 6°5'E
52 F5 England, UK 52°30'N 2°5'W
37 ◈ Unitary authority England, UK
71 D7 Belgium 51°6'N 4°30'E
tok 86 D6 Island W Croatia
rg 82 C9 Germany 51°25'N 6°47'E
70 G9 Netherlands 51°57'N 6°2'E
iwil 97 K4 Sudan 7°30'N 31°27'E
n 115 I6 Qatar 25°29'N 50°48'E
85 H7 Poland 49°33'N 21°40'E
s 69 H4 Lithuania 55°32'N 26°21'E
122 G5 China 36°11'N 97°51'E
n 82 D9 Germany 51°51'N 7°17'E
87 J6 Bulgaria 43°51'N 27°10'E
147 J8 Minnesota, USA 46°47'N 92°6'W
110 G3 Syria 33°33'N 36°24'E
arton 57 E5 Scotland, UK
7'N 4°31'W
ies 57 G3 Scotland, UK 55°4'N 3°37'W
ies and Galloway 57 F3 ◈
ary authority Scotland, UK
nt d'Urville Sea 166 F3 Sea
cific Ocean
at 97 K7 Egypt 31°26'N 31°48'E
ská Streda 85 D5 Slovakia 48°N 17°28'E
ay Point 58 H9 Headland NE Ireland
ajváros 85 F4 Hungary 47°N 18°55'E
ane 57 F6 Scotland, UK 56°12'N 3°56'W
oyne 58 G8 Ireland 53°24'N 6°28'W
nnon 59 G5 Ireland 52°13'N 6°54'W
nsby Head 56 G12 Headland
otland, UK
urch 53 H4 England, UK 52°20'N 1°21'W
alk 58 H10 Ireland 54°1'N 6°25'W
ee 99 I2 South Africa 28°9'S 30°12'E
ee 57 G7 Scotland, UK 56°28'N 3°W
ee, City of 36 ◈ Unitary authority
land, UK
onnell 56 D10 Scotland, UK
47'N 5°13'W
um 59 E6 Ireland 52°33'N 8°1'W
din 136 C2 New Zealand 45°52'S 170°31'E
naghy 58 E12 Ireland 55°11'N 7°59'W
rmline 57 G6 Scotland, UK 56°4'N 3°29'W
annon 58 G11 Northern Ireland, UK
31'N 6°46'W
annon 58 G11 ◈ District
thern Ireland, UK
arvan 59 F5 Ireland 52°5'N 7°37'W
eness 51 J3 Headland SE England, UK
ven 58 G12 Northern Ireland, UK
56'N 6°54'W
ow 58 E12 Ireland 54°57'N 8°22'W
u 99 H8 Dem. Rep. Congo 3°40'N 28°32'E
olme 53 I8 England, UK 53°17'N 0°32'W
erque 72 G9 France 51°6'N 2°34'E
ery Beacon 49 F6 ▲ SW England, UK
aoghaire 58 H8 Ireland 53°17'N 6°8'W
avin 59 G7 Ireland 53°4'N 6°45'W
er 58 H9 Ireland 53°50'N 6°25'W
ore 58 D9 Ireland 53°37'N 8°44'W
ore East 59 G5 Ireland 52°9'N 7°4'W
urry 58 H11 Northern Ireland, UK
35'N 6°2'W
et Head 56 G12 Headland N Scotland, UK
57 H5 Scotland, UK 55°46'N 2°13'W
ford 49 F5 England, UK 50°42'N 3°48'W
haughlin 58 G8 Ireland 53°31'N 6°41'W
able 50 G7 England, UK 51°53'N 0°32'W
115 L4 Oman 19°42'N 57°40'E
nce 73 J3 ⟿ SE France
ngo 150 C5 Mexico 24°3'N 104°38'W
an 99 I2 South Africa 29°51'S 31°E
e Door 49 H5 Natural arch S England, UK
119 H5 India 21°12'N 81°20'E
am 55 H6 England, UK 54°47'N 1°34'W
am 147 M5 North Carolina, USA
'N 78°54'W
am 55 H6 ◈ County England, UK
ess 56 E12 Scotland, UK 58°34'N 4°46'W
s 86 F5 Albania 41°20'N 19°26'E
ow 59 F7 Ireland 52°50'N 7°23'W
ey Head 59 B4 Headland S Ireland
ey 48 H8 England, UK 51°41'N 2°25'W
ville Island 136 D5 Island C New Zealand
anbe 117 J6 ● Tajikistan 38°35'N 68°44'E
eldorf 82 C9 Germany 51°14'N 6°49'E
117 J6 Tajikistan 37°22'N 68°41'E
Harbor 146 A6 Alaska, USA
51'N 166°33'W
48 E10 ⟿ W Wales, UK
church 51 J3 England, UK 51°0'N 0°58'E
zhinsk 89 E7 Russian Fed. 56°20'N 43°22'E
al-Abad 117 K7 Kyrgyzstan
56'N 73°0'E
landy 117 K6 Tajikistan 37°34'N 72°35'E
rgalan 117 L8 Kyrgyzstan 42°37'N 78°56'E
gdzhur, Khrebet 109 K5 ▲▲ E Russian Fed.
saly 108 E3 Kazakhstan 45°29'N 64°4'E
dowo 84 F11 Poland 53°13'N 20°12'E
122 G8 Mongolia 49°37'N 95°46'E

E

g 37 ◈ London Borough England, UK
ton 57 H5 Scotland, UK 55°38'N 2°45'W
57 F6 ⟿ N Scotland, UK
Easington 55 K2 England, UK 53°40'N 0°5'E
Easington 55 H6 England, UK 54°47'N 1°21'W
Easingwold 55 I4 England, UK 54°8'N 1°9'W
Easky 58 D10 Ireland 54°18'N 8°58'W
East Anglia 53 L5 Physical region E England, UK
East Ayrshire 57 F4 ◈ Unitary authority Scotland, UK
Eastbourne 51 H2 England, UK 50°46'N 0°16'E
East Cape 136 F6 Headland North Island, New Zealand
East China Sea 124 E1 Sea W Pacific Ocean
East Dereham 53 L6 England, UK 52°41'N 0°55'E
East Dunbartonshire 36 ◈ Unitary authority Scotland, UK
Easter Island 24 Island E Pacific Ocean
Eastern Desert 91 Desert E Egypt
Eastern Ghats 119 H4 ▲▲ SE India
Eastern Sayans 109 H4 ▲▲ Mongolia/Russian Fed.
East Falkland 161 E2 Island E Falkland Islands
East Grinstead 51 H4 England, UK 51°8'N 0°0'W
East Halton 53 J9 England, UK 53°40'N 0°18'W
East Harling 53 L5 England, UK 52°25'N 0°52'E
East Ilsley 50 E5 England, UK 51°31'N 1°18'W
East Kilbride 57 F5 Scotland, UK 55°46'N 4°10'W
East Knoyle 49 H6 England, UK 51°3'N 2°11'W
East Korea Bay 124 F6 Bay E North Korea
Eastleigh 50 E3 England, UK 50°58'N 1°22'W
East Linton 57 H5 Scotland, UK 56°N 2°41'W
East London 99 H1 South Africa 33°S 27°54'E
East Looe 49 D4 England, UK 50°22'N 4°26'W
East Lothian 36 ◈ Unitary authority Scotland, UK
Eastmain 145 I3 ⟿ Québec, C Canada
East Markham 53 H8 England, UK 53°15'N 0°58'W
East Pacific Rise 24 Undersea feature E Pacific Ocean
East Renfrewshire 36 ◈ Unitary authority Scotland, UK
East Riding of Yorkshire 55 J3 ◈ Unitary authority England, UK
East Saint Louis 147 K5 Illinois, USA 38°35'N 90°7'W
East Sea 125 H6 Sea NW Pacific Ocean see also Japan, Sea of
East Siberian Sea 25 Sea Arctic Ocean
East Sussex 51 H3 ◈ County England, UK
East Timor 127 K1 ◆ Republic SE Asia
Eau Claire 147 J7 Wisconsin, USA 44°50'N 91°30'W
Ebbw Vale 48 F8 Wales, UK 51°48'N 3°13'W
Ebensee 83 H5 Austria 47°48'N 13°46'E
Eberswalde-Finow 82 H10 Germany 52°50'N 13°48'E
Ebetsu 125 K8 Japan 43°8'N 141°37'E
Ebolowa 97 H3 Cameroon 2°56'N 11°11'E
Ebro 75 K7 ⟿ NE Spain
Ecclefechan 57 G3 Scotland, UK 55°4'N 3°17'W
Eccleshall 52 F6 England, UK 52°52'N 2°19'W
Echo Bay 144 E5 Northwest Territories, Canada 66°4'N 118°W
Echt 71 G7 Netherlands 51°7'N 5°52'E
Ecija 75 H4 Spain 37°33'N 5°4'W
Ecuador 160 B10 ◆ Republic NW South America
Eday 56 H14 Island NE Scotland, UK
Ed Da'ein 97 J4 Sudan 11°25'N 26°8'E
Ed Damazin 97 K4 Sudan 11°45'N 34°20'E
Ed Damer 97 K5 Sudan 17°37'N 33°59'E
Ed Debba 97 K5 Sudan 18°2'N 30°56'E
Eddleston 57 G5 Scotland, UK 55°42'N 3°10'W
Eddrachillis Bay 56 D11 Bay NW Scotland, UK
Eddystone Rocks 49 D3 Island group SW England, UK
Ede 70 F9 Netherlands 52°3'N 5°40'E
Eden 54 E6 ⟿ NW England, UK
Edenbridge 51 H4 England, UK 51°11'N 0°3'E
Edenderry 58 G8 Ireland 53°21'N 7°3'W
Edgeworthstown 58 F9 Ireland 53°41'N 7°53'W
Edinburgh 57 G5 Scotland, UK 55°57'N 3°13'W
Edinburgh, City of 36 ◈ Unitary authority Scotland, UK
Edirne 110 C7 Turkey 41°40'N 26°34'E
Edmonton 144 E2 Alberta, Canada 53°34'N 113°25'W
Edolo 76 G9 Italy 46°13'N 10°20'E
Edremit 110 C6 Turkey 39°34'N 27°1'E
Edward, Lake 99 H8 ◎ Uganda/Dem. Rep. Congo
Edwards Plateau 147 I3 Plain Texas, SW USA
Edzo 144 E4 Northwest Territories, Canada 62°44'N 115°55'W
Eeklo 71 C7 Belgium 51°11'N 3°34'E
Eemshaven 70 H13 Netherlands 53°28'N 6°50'E
Eersel 70 F8 Netherlands 51°22'N 5°19'E
Egadi Is. 77 H2 Island group S Italy
Eger 85 G5 Hungary 47°54'N 20°22'E
Éghezée 71 E5 Belgium 50°36'N 4°55'E
Egilsstadhir 68 C11 Iceland 65°14'N 14°21'W
Egmont, Cape 136 D5 Headland North Island, New Zealand
Egypt 97 K6 ◆ Republic NE Africa
Eibar 75 I9 Spain 43°11'N 2°28'W
Eibergen 70 H9 Netherlands 52°6'N 6°39'E
Eidfjord 69 A7 Norway 60°26'N 7°5'E
Eifel 82 C8 Plateau W Germany
Eiger 83 D4 ▲ C Switzerland
Eigg 56 C8 Island W Scotland, UK
Eight Degree Channel 118 F1 Channel India/Maldives
Eighty Mile Beach 134 D7 Coastal feature Western Australia
Eijsden 71 F6 Netherlands 50°47'N 5°41'E
Eindhoven 70 F8 Netherlands 51°26'N 5°30'E
Eirunepé 162 D6 Brazil 6°38'S 69°53'W
Eisenhüttenstadt 82 H9 Germany 52°9'N 14°36'E
Eisenstadt 83 I5 Austria 47°50'N 16°32'E
Eisleben 82 F9 Germany 51°32'N 11°33'E
Ejea de los Caballeros 75 J8 Spain 42°7'N 1°9'W
Ejin Qi 122 G6 China 41°59'N 101°4'E
El Golea 96 G7 Algeria 30°35'N 2°59'E
Elat 110 A1 Israel 29°33'N 34°57'E
El'Atrun 97 J5 Sudan 18°11'N 26°40'E
Elâzığ 111 H6 Turkey 38°41'N 39°14'E
Elba 76 G6 Island Archipelago Toscano, C Italy
Elbe 61 ⟿ Czech Republic/Germany
Elbert, Mount 146 G6 ▲ Colorado, C USA
Elbląg 84 F12 Poland 54°10'N 19°25'E
El'brus 89 E2 ▲ SW Russian Fed.
El Burgo de Osma 75 I7 Spain 41°36'N 3°4'W
El Calafate 161 C2 Argentina 50°20'S 72°13'W
Elche 75 K4 Spain 38°16'N 0°41'W
El Chichónal, Volcán 150 F3 ✱ SE Mexico
Elda 75 K5 Spain 38°29'N 0°47'W
El Dorado 150 C5 Mexico 24°19'N 107°23'W
Eldoret 99 J8 Kenya 0°31'N 35°17'E
Elektrostal' 89 D6 Russian Fed. 55°47'N 38°24'E
Eleuthera Island 151 I5 Island N Bahamas
El Fasher 97 J5 Sudan 13°37'N 25°22'E
El Geneina 97 J5 Sudan 13°27'N 22°30'E
Elgin 56 G10 Scotland, UK 57°39'N 3°20'W
El Giza 97 K7 Egypt 30°1'N 31°13'E
Elham 51 J4 England, UK 51°8'N 1°5'E
El Hank 96 E6 Cliff N Mauritania
Elista 89 F3 Russian Fed. 46°18'N 44°9'E
Elizabeth 135 I3 South Australia 34°44'S 138°39'E
Ełk 84 H11 Poland 53°51'N 22°20'E
El Kharga 97 K7 Egypt 25°31'N 30°36'E
Elland 54 G2 England, UK 53°41'N 1°54'W
Ellef Ringnes Island 144 F8 Island Northwest Territories, N Canada
Ellen, Mount 146 F5 ▲ Utah, W USA
Ellesmere Island 144 G8 Island Queen Elizabeth Islands, Northwest Territories, N Canada
Ellesmere, Lake 136 D3 ◎ South Island, New Zealand
Ellesmere Port 52 D8 England, UK 53°17'N 2°54'W
Elliston 135 H3 South Australia 33°40'S 134°56'E
Ellon 56 I9 Scotland, UK 57°22'N 2°6'W
Ellsworth Land 166 B5 Physical region Antarctica
El Mahbas 96 E7 Western Sahara 27°26'N 9°9'W
El Minya 97 K7 Egypt 28°6'N 30°40'E
El Mreyyé 96 E6 Desert E Mauritania
Elmshorn 82 E11 Germany 53°45'N 9°39'E
Elmswell 53 L4 England, UK 52°14'N 0°53'E
El Muglad 97 J4 Sudan 11°2'N 27°44'E
El Obeid 97 K5 Sudan 13°11'N 30°10'E
El Paso 146 G4 Texas, USA 31°45'N 106°30'W
Elphin 58 E9 Ireland 53°51'N 8°55'W
El Porvenir 151 I1 Panama 9°33'N 78°56'W
El Progreso 150 G3 Honduras 15°25'N 87°49'W
El Puerto de Santa María 74 G3 Spain 36°36'N 6°13'W
El Salvador 150 F2 ◆ Republic Central America
El Sáuz 150 C6 Mexico 29°3'N 106°15'W
Elst 70 G9 Netherlands 51°55'N 5°51'E
Elstree 50 G6 England, UK 51°38'N 0°15'W
El Sueco 150 C6 Mexico 29°53'N 106°24'W
Eltanin Fracture Zone 24 Undersea feature SE Pacific Ocean
Eltisley 53 J4 England, UK 52°12'N 0°14'W
Elton 53 I5 England, UK 52°32'N 0°23'W
Elvas 74 F5 Portugal 38°53'N 7°10'W
El Vendrell 75 L7 Spain 41°13'N 1°32'E
Elvira 162 C6 Brazil 7°12'S 69°56'W
Elx see Elche
Ely 53 K5 England, UK 52°24'N 0°15'E
Ely 49 F7 Wales, UK 51°29'N 3°15'W
Ely 49 F7 ⟿ SE Wales, UK
Emba 108 E3 Kazakhstan 48°50'N 58°10'E
Embleton 55 H9 England, UK 55°30'N 1°36'W
Emden 82 D11 Germany 53°22'N 7°12'E
Emerald 135 K5 Queensland, Australia 23°33'S 148°11'E
Emi Koussi 97 I5 ▲ N Chad
Emmeloord 70 F11 Netherlands 52°43'N 5°46'E
Emmen 70 H11 Netherlands 52°48'N 6°57'E
Emmendingen 83 D6 Germany 48°7'N 7°51'E
Emory Peak 147 H3 ▲ Texas, SW USA
Empalme 150 B6 Mexico 27°57'N 110°49'W
Emperor Seamounts 25 Undersea feature NW Pacific Ocean
Ems 82 D10 ⟿ NW Germany
Enafors 68 C8 Sweden 63°17'N 12°24'E
Enard Bay 56 D11 Bay NW Scotland, UK
Encarnación 161 E6 Paraguay 27°20'S 55°50'W
Encs 85 G5 Hungary 48°21'N 21°9'E
Endeavour Strait 135 J9 Strait Queensland, NE Australia
Endeh 127 J1 Indonesia 8°48'S 121°37'E
Enderby Land 166 F7 Physical region Antarctica
Enfield 51 H6 England, UK 51°39'N 0°1'W
Enfield 37 ◈ London Borough England, UK
Enghien 71 D6 Belgium 50°42'N 4°3'E
England 37 ◈ National region, UK
English Channel 51 J3 Channel NW Europe
Enid 147 I5 Oklahoma, USA 36°25'N 97°53'W
Ennedi 97 J5 Plateau E Chad
Ennis 59 D7 Ireland 52°50'N 8°59'W
Enniscorthy 59 G6 Ireland 52°30'N 6°34'W
Enniskean 59 D4 Ireland 51°44'N 8°56'W
Enniskillen 58 F10 Northern Ireland, UK 54°21'N 7°38'W
Ennistimon 59 C7 Ireland 52°57'N 9°17'W
Enns 83 H5 ⟿ C Austria
Enschede 70 H10 Netherlands 52°13'N 6°55'E
Ensenada 150 A7 Mexico 31°52'N 116°32'W
Entebbe 99 I8 Uganda 0°7'N 32°30'E
Enterkinfoot 57 F4 Scotland, UK 55°19'N 3°57'W
Entroncamento 74 E5 Portugal 39°28'N 8°28'W
Enugu 96 G3 Nigeria 6°24'N 7°24'E
Envira 162 D6 Brazil 7°12'S 69°59'W
Epéna 98 F8 Congo 1°28'N 17°29'E
Épinal 73 J6 France 48°10'N 6°28'E
Epping 51 H6 England, UK 51°41'N 0°6'E
Epsom 50 G5 England, UK 51°19'N 0°23'W
Equatorial Guinea 97 H3 ◆ Republic C Africa
Erciş 111 I6 Turkey 39°2'N 43°21'E
Érd 85 F4 Hungary 47°22'N 18°56'E
Erdenet 123 H8 Mongolia 49°1'N 104°7'E
Erdi 97 J5 Plateau NE Chad
Erebus, Mount 166 D3 ✱ Ross Island, Antarctica
Erechim 163 H2 Brazil 27°35'S 52°15'W
Ereğli 110 F5 Turkey 37°30'N 34°2'E
Erenhot 123 I7 China 43°35'N 112°E
Erfurt 82 F8 Germany 50°59'N 11°2'E
Ergene Irmaği 87 J5 ⟿ NW Turkey
Ērgli 69 H4 Latvia 56°55'N 25°38'E
Eriboll, Loch 56 E12 Inlet NW Scotland, UK
Ericht, Loch 56 F8 ◎ C Scotland, UK
Erie 147 L7 Pennsylvania, USA 42°7'N 80°4'W
Erie, Lake 147 L7 ◎ Canada/USA
Eriskay 56 A8 Island NW Scotland, UK
Eritrea 97 L5 ◆ Transitional government E Africa
Erlangen 83 F7 Germany 49°36'N 11°E
Erldunda Roadhouse 135 H5 Northern Territory, Australia 25°13'S 133°13'E
Ermelo 70 F10 Netherlands 52°18'N 5°38'E
Ermioni 87 H2 Greece 37°24'N 23°15'E
Ernakulam 118 G2 India 10°4'N 76°18'E
Erne 58 E10 ⟿ Ireland/Northern Ireland, UK
Erquelinnes 71 D5 Belgium 50°18'N 4°8'E
Errigal Mountain 58 E12 ▲ N Ireland
Erris Head 58 B10 Headland W Ireland
Errol 57 G6 Scotland, UK 56°24'N 3°12'W
Erzincan 111 H6 Turkey 39°44'N 39°30'E
Erzurum 111 H6 Turkey 39°57'N 41°17'E
Esashi 125 K9 Japan 44°57'N 142°32'E
Esbjerg 69 A4 Denmark 55°28'N 8°28'E
Esch-sur-Alzette 71 G3 Luxembourg 49°30'N 5°59'E
Escrick 55 I3 England, UK 53°53'N 1°10'W
Escuinapa 150 C5 Mexico 22°50'N 105°46'W
Escuintla 150 F2 Guatemala 14°17'N 90°46'W
Esenguly 116 E6 Turkmenistan 37°29'N 53°57'E
Esha Ness 56 I12 Headland NE Scotland, UK
Eshkamesh 117 J6 Afghanistan 36°25'N 69°11'E
Eskişehir 110 D6 Turkey 39°46'N 30°30'E
Esmeraldas 160 A10 Ecuador 0°55'N 79°40'W
Esperance 134 E3 Western Australia 33°49'S 121°52'E
Espírito Santo 163 K4 ◈ State Brazil
Espoo 69 G6 Finland 60°10'N 24°42'E
Esquel 161 C3 Argentina 42°55'S 71°20'W
Essen 70 D8 Belgium 51°28'N 4°28'E
Essen 82 D9 Germany 51°28'N 7°1'E
Essex 51 I7 ◈ County England, UK
Estacado, Llano 147 H4 Plain New Mexico/Texas, SW USA
Estados, Isla de los 161 D1 Island S Argentina
Estância 163 K5 Brazil 11°15'S 37°28'W
Estelí 150 G2 Nicaragua 13°5'N 86°21'W
Estella-Lizarra 75 J8 Spain 42°41'N 2°2'W
Estepona 75 H3 Spain 36°26'N 5°9'W
Eston 55 I5 England, UK 54°34'N 1°7'W
Estonia 69 G6 ◆ Republic NE Europe
Estrela, Serra da 74 F6 ▲▲ C Portugal
Estremoz 74 F5 Portugal 38°50'N 7°35'W
Esztergom 85 E5 Hungary 47°47'N 18°44'E
Étalle 71 F3 Belgium 49°41'N 5°36'E
Ethiopia 97 M3 ◆ Republic E Africa
Ethiopian Highlands 97 L4 Plateau N Ethiopia
Etosha Pan 98 F4 Salt lake N Namibia
Etrek 116 F6 ⟿ Iran/Turkmenistan
Ettelbrück 71 G3 Luxembourg 49°51'N 6°6'E
Eucla 134 G3 Western Australia 31°41'S 128°51'E
Eugene 146 D7 Oregon, USA 44°3'N 123°5'W
Eunápolis 163 K4 Brazil 16°20'S 39°36'W
Eupen 71 G6 Belgium 50°38'N 6°2'E
Eura 69 F7 Finland 61°7'N 22°12'E
Europe 61 Continent
Eutin 82 F11 Germany 54°8'N 10°38'E
Evansville 147 K5 Indiana, USA 37°58'N 87°33'W
Evaz 116 E2 Iran 27°48'N 53°58'E
Everard, Lake 135 H4 Salt lake South Australia
Everdon 53 H4 England, UK 52°12'N 1°11'W
Everest, Mount 122 D3 ▲ China/Nepal
Everett 146 E8 Washington, USA 47°59'N 122°12'W
Everglades, The 147 M2 Wetland Florida, SE USA
Evershot 49 H5 England, UK 50°50'N 2°43'W
Evesham 52 F4 England, UK 52°6'N 1°57'W
Evje 69 A5 Norway 58°35'N 7°49'E
Évora 74 F5 Portugal 38°34'N 7°54'W
Évreux 72 G7 France 49°2'N 1°10'E
Ewhurst 50 G4 England, UK 51°9'N 0°27'W
Exbourne 49 E5 England, UK 50°48'N 4°2'W
Exe 49 F6 ⟿ SW England, UK
Exeter 49 F5 England, UK 50°43'N 3°31'W
Exford 49 F6 England, UK 51°7'N 3°43'W
Exmoor 49 F6 Heathland SW England, UK
Exmouth 134 C6 Western Australia 22°1'S 114°6'E
Exmouth 49 F5 England, UK 50°36'N 3°25'W
Exmouth Gulf 134 C6 Gulf Western Australia
Exuma Sound 151 I5 Sound C Bahamas
Eyemouth 57 I5 Scotland, UK 55°52'N 2°7'W
Eye Peninsula 56 C11 Coastal feature NW Scotland, UK
Eynsham 50 E6 England, UK 51°47'N 1°25'W
Eyre Mountains 136 B2 ▲▲ South Island, New Zealand
Eyre North, Lake 135 I4 Salt lake South Australia
Eyre South, Lake 135 H4 Salt lake South Australia

F

Fada 97 I5 Chad 17°14'N 21°32'E
Fadhī 115 L3 Oman 17°54'N 55°30'E
Faenza 77 H7 Italy 44°17'N 11°53'E
Faeroe Islands 13 Danish ◇ Atlantic Ocean
Fagernes 69 B7 Norway 60°59'N 9°14'E
Fagne 71 D4 Hill range S Belgium
Faguibine, Lac 96 E5 ◎ NW Mali
Fairbanks 146 B7 Alaska, USA 64°48'N 147°47'W
Fairford 48 I8 England, UK 51°41'N 1°48'W
Fair Head 58 H13 Headland N Northern Ireland, UK
Fair Isle 56 I14 Island NE Scotland, UK
Fairlie 136 C3 New Zealand 44°6'S 170°50'E
Faisalabad 118 F8 Pakistan 31°26'N 73°6'E
Faizabad 119 H7 India 26°46'N 82°8'E
Fakenham 53 L6 England, UK 52°50'N 0°51'E
Fakfak 127 L2 Indonesia 2°55'S 132°17'E
Falam 126 D7 Burma 22°58'N 93°45'E
Falconara Marittima 77 I6 Italy 43°37'N 13°23'E
Faldingworth 53 I8 England, UK 53°20'N 0°25'W
Falkirk 57 F5 Scotland, UK 56°N 3°48'W
Falkirk 36 ◈ Unitary authority Scotland, UK
Falkland Islands 161 E2 UK ◇ Atlantic Ocean
Falmouth 49 C3 England, UK 50°8'N 5°4'W
Falster 69 C3 Island SE Denmark
Falun 69 D7 Sweden 60°36'N 15°36'E
Famagusta 79 M9 Cyprus 35°7'N 33°57'E
Famagusta Bay 79 N9 Bay E Cyprus
Famenne 71 F5 Physical region SE Belgium
Fan Brycheiniog 48 F8 ▲ E Wales, UK
Fannich, Loch 56 E10 ◎ NW Scotland, UK
Fano 77 I7 Italy 43°50'N 13°E
Farafangana 99 L3 Madagascar 22°50'S 47°50'E
Farah 117 H4 Afghanistan 32°22'N 62°7'E
Farah Rud 117 H4 ⟿ W Afghanistan
Faranah 96 D4 Guinea 10°2'N 10°44'W
Farasan, Jaza'ir 114 F3 Island group SW Saudi Arabia
Fareham 50 E3 England, UK 50°51'N 1°10'W
Farewell, Cape 136 D5 Headland South Island, New Zealand
Fargo 147 I8 North Dakota, USA 46°53'N 96°47'W
Farg'ona 117 K7 Uzbekistan 40°28'N 71°44'E
Faringdon 50 D6 England, UK 51°39'N 1°41'W
Farkhor 117 J6 Tajikistan 37°32'N 69°22'E
Farmington 146 G5 New Mexico, USA 36°44'N 108°13'W
Farnborough 50 F4 England, UK 51°17'N 0°46'W
Farne Islands 55 H9 Island group N England, UK
Farnham 50 F4 England, UK 51°13'N 0°49'W
Farnworth 54 F2 England, UK 53°33'N 2°20'W
Faro 74 F3 Portugal 37°1'N 7°56'W
Farquhar Group 99 M6 Island group S Seychelles
Farranfore 59 C5 Ireland 52°10'N 9°31'W
Fastiv 89 C5 Ukraine 50°8'N 29°59'E
Fastnet Rock 59 C3 Island SW Ireland
Fauske 68 D11 Norway 67°15'N 15°27'E
Faversham 51 J5 England, UK 51°18'N 0°44'E
Fawley 50 E3 England, UK 50°50'N 1°27'W
Faxaflói 68 A11 Bay W Iceland
Faya 97 I5 Chad 17°58'N 19°6'E
Fayetteville 147 M5 North Carolina, USA 35°3'N 78°53'W
Fdérik 96 D6 Mauritania 22°40'N 12°41'W
Feale 59 C6 ⟿ SW Ireland
Fear, Cape 147 M5 Headland Bald Head Island, North Carolina, SE USA
Fécamp 72 F8 France 49°45'N 0°22'E
Fehérgyarmat 85 H5 Hungary 47°59'N 22°29'E
Fehmarn Bælt 82 F12 Strait Denmark/Germany
Feijó 162 D6 Brazil 8°7'S 70°27'W
Feilding 136 E5 New Zealand 40°15'S 175°34'E
Feira de Santana 163 K5 Brazil 12°17'S 38°53'W
Felanitx 75 M6 Spain 39°28'N 3°8'E
Felipe Carrillo Puerto 150 G4 Mexico 19°34'N 88°2'W
Felixstowe 53 M3 England, UK 51°58'N 1°20'E
Felton 55 H8 England, UK 55°17'N 1°40'W
Feltwell 53 K5 England, UK 52°29'N 0°31'E
Femunden 68 C8 ◎ S Norway
Fens, The 53 J6 Wetland E England, UK
Feodosiya 89 D3 Ukraine 45°3'N 35°24'E
Feolin Ferry 57 C5 Scotland, UK 55°52'N 6°0'W
Fergana Valley 117 K7 Basin Tajikistan/Uzbekistan
Fermanagh 58 F10 ◈ District Northern Ireland, UK
Fermo 77 I6 Italy 43°9'N 13°44'E
Fermoy 59 E5 Ireland 52°8'N 8°16'W
Ferndown 49 I5 England, UK 50°48'N 1°55'W
Fernhurst 50 F4 England, UK 51°2'N 0°44'W
Ferns 59 G6 Ireland 52°36'N 6°33'W
Ferrara 77 H7 Italy 44°50'N 11°36'E
Ferrol 74 F9 Spain 43°29'N 8°14'W
Ferryhill 55 H6 England, UK 54°40'N 1°37'W
Ferwerd 70 G13 Netherlands 53°21'N 5°47'E
Fethiye 110 D5 Turkey 36°37'N 29°8'E
Fetlar 56 I12 Island NE Scotland, UK
Feyzabad 117 J6 Afghanistan 37°6'N 70°34'E
Fez 96 F8 Morocco 34°6'N 4°57'W
Ffestiniog 48 E11 Wales, UK 52°55'N 3°54'W
Fianarantsoa 99 L4 Madagascar 21°27'S 47°5'E
Fier 86 F4 Albania 40°44'N 19°34'E
Fife 57 G6 ◈ Unitary authority Scotland, UK
Fife Ness 57 H6 Headland E Scotland, UK
Figeac 72 G3 France 44°37'N 2°1'E
Figueira da Foz 74 E6 Portugal 40°9'N 8°51'W
Figueres 75 M8 Spain 42°16'N 2°57'E
Fiji 128 ◆ Republic SW Pacific Ocean
Fil'akovo 85 F5 Slovakia 48°15'N 19°53'E
Filchner Ice Shelf 166 C6 Ice feature Antarctica
Filey 55 K4 England, UK 54°12'N 0°19'W
Filey Bay 55 K4 Bay N England, UK
Filim 115 L5 Oman 20°37'N 58°11'E
Filipstad 69 D6 Sweden 59°44'N 14°10'E
Finale Ligure 76 F7 Italy 44°11'N 8°22'E
Finchingfield 51 I7 England, UK 51°58'N 0°18'E
Findhorn 56 F9 ⟿ N Scotland, UK
Findon 50 G3 England, UK 50°51'N 0°25'W
Finike 110 D4 Turkey 36°18'N 30°8'E
Finland 68 G10 ◆ Republic N Europe
Finland, Gulf of 69 G6 Gulf E Baltic Sea
Finningley 53 H8 England, UK 53°29'N 1°2'W
Finnmarksvidda 68 F12 Physical region N Norway
Finsterwalde 82 G9 Germany 51°38'N 13°43'E
Fintown 58 E12 Ireland 54°54'N 8°9'W
Fionnphort 57 C6 Scotland, UK 56°20'N 6°17'W
Firenze see Florence
Fischbacher Alpen 83 I5 ▲▲ E Austria
Fish 98 F3 ⟿ S Namibia
Fishguard 48 C9 Wales, UK 51°59'N 4°49'W
Fishguard Bay 48 C9 Bay SW Wales, UK
Fisterra, Cabo 74 E9 Headland NW Spain
Fitful Head 56 I11 Headland NE Scotland, UK
Fitzroy Crossing 134 F7 Western Australia 18°10'S 125°40'E
Fitzroy River 134 E7 ⟿ Western Australia
Fivemiletown 58 F10 Northern Ireland, UK 54°23'N 7°18'W
Fjällåsen 68 E11 Sweden 67°31'N 20°8'E
Fjerritslev 69 B4 Denmark 57°6'N 9°17'E
Flamborough 55 K4 England, UK 54°7'N 0°9'W

◆ Country ● Country capital ◇ Dependent territory ○ Dependent territory capital ◈ Administrative region ▲ Mountain ▲▲ Mountain range ✱ Volcano ⟿ River ◎ Lake ⊞ Reservoir

Great Gidding - Hope 177

idding 53 I5 England, UK
5'N 0°22'W
larwood 54 F3 England, UK
7'N 2°29'W
lungarian Plain 85 F3 *Plain* SE Europe
nagua 151 J4 *Island* S Bahamas
Caroo 98 G1 *Physical region*
th Africa
akes 139 *Lakes* Ontario, Canada/USA
Malvern 52 F4 England, UK
N 2°19'W
Nicobar 119 L2 *Island* Nicobar Islands,
, NE Indian Ocean
Offley 50 G7 England, UK
5'N 0°20'W
Ormes Head 48 E12 *Headland*
ales, UK
Ouse 53 K6 ≈ E England, UK
lains 147 H6 *Physical region*
da/USA
Ponton 53 I6 England, UK
1'N 0°42'W
Rift Valley 99 I6 *Depression* Africa/Asia
Saint Bernard Pass 76 E8 *Pass* Italy/
erland
Salt Lake 146 F6 *Salt lake* Utah, W USA
Salt Lake Desert 146 F6 *Plain* Utah,
SA
Sand Sea 97 J7 *Desert* Egypt/Libya
Sandy Desert 134 E6 *Desert*
ern Australia
Slave Lake 144 F4 ◎ Northwest
ories, NW Canada
Torrington 49 E6 England, UK
8'N 4°9'W
Victoria Desert 134 F4 *Desert*
Australia/Western Australia
Wall of China 123 I5 *Ancient monument*
ina
Waltham 51 I6 England, UK
6'N 0°23'E
Yarmouth 53 N5 England, UK
7'N 1°44'E
Yeldham 51 I7 England, UK 52°1'N 0°33'E
, Sierra de 75 H6 ▲▲ W Spain
87 H3 ◆ *Republic* SE Europe
Bay 147 K7 Wisconsin, USA
2'N 88°W
Bay 147 K7 *Lake bay* Michigan/Wisconsin,
A
castle 58 H10 Northern Ireland, UK
'N 6°5'W
head 54 F7 England, UK 54°59'N 2°32'W
and 145 I8 *Danish* ◇ North America
and Sea 68 B12 *Sea* Arctic Ocean
aw 57 H5 Scotland, UK 55°43'N 2°32'W
Mountains 147 N8 ▲▲ Vermont, NE USA
ock 57 E5 Scotland, UK 55°57'N 4°45'W
River 146 G6 Wyoming, USA
3'N 109°27'W
sboro 147 M5 North Carolina, USA
'N 79°48'W
ville 147 L5 South Carolina, USA
1'N 82°24'W
wich 37 ⬖ *London Borough* England, UK
ry Range 135 J7 ▲▲ Queensland,
stralia
wald 82 G11 Germany 54°4'N 13°24'E
da 151 M3 ◆ *Commonwealth republic*
dines, The 151 M3 *Island group* Grenada/
Vest Indies
incent and the Grenadines
ble 73 I4 France 45°11'N 5°42'E
Bridge 54 G5 England, UK
0'N 1°56'W
a 57 G3 Scotland, UK 54°59'N 3°4'W
n 53 I5 England, UK 52°32'N 0°38'W
nmacher 71 H3 Luxembourg
1'N 6°27'E
mouth 136 C4 New Zealand
29'S 171°14'E
Range 135 J4 ▲▲ New South Wales/
ensland, E Australia
tones 58 H7 Ireland 53°8'N 6°5'W
by 53 J9 England, UK 53°35'N 0°5'W
ey 68 B12 *Island* N Iceland
ehamn 68 E6 Sweden 60°4'N 18°50'E
beek 70 G9 Netherlands 51°47'N 5°56'E
: 84 G9 Poland 51°11'N 20°52'E
68 C9 Norway 64°29'N 12°19'E
ngen 70 H12 Netherlands 53°13'N 6°35'E
e Eylandt 135 I8 *Island* Northern Territory,
ustralia
fontein 98 F4 Namibia 19°32'S 18°5'E
Karasberge 98 F2 ▲▲ S Namibia
eto 76 G6 Italy 42°45'N 11°7'E
glockner 83 G5 ▲ W Austria
yy 89 F2 Russian Fed. 43°20'N 45°43'E
iądz 84 E11 Poland 53°29'N 18°45'E
s 69 C6 Sweden 59°22'N 13°11'E
e 84 C11 Poland 53°55'N 15°11'E
to 151 H1 Panama 9°30'N 82°35'W
alajara 150 C4 Mexico 20°43'N 103°24'W
alajara 75 I6 Spain 40°37'N 3°10'W
alquivir 74 G4 ≈ W Spain
alupe Peak 147 H4 ▲ Texas, SW USA
arrama, Sierra de 75 I7 ▲▲ C Spain
eloupe 151 M4 *French* ◇ West Indies
iana 74 F4 ≈ Portugal/Spain
ix 75 I4 Spain 37°19'N 3°8'W
rá-Mirim 162 E6 Brazil 10°50'S 65°21'W
128 *US* ◇ Pacific Ocean
úchil 150 C5 Mexico 25°23'N 108°1'W
abacoa 151 H5 Cuba 23°2'N 82°12'W
ajuato 150 D4 Mexico 21°N 101°19'W
are 160 C12 Venezuela 9°4'N 69°45'W
gdong 123 J2 ⬖ *Province* China
gyuan 123 H4 China 32°27'N 105°49'E
ánamo 151 J4 Cuba 20°6'N 75°16'W
oré, Rio 160 D8 ≈ Bolivia/Brazil
apuava 163 H2 Brazil 25°22'S 51°28'W
da 74 F6 Portugal 40°32'N 7°17'W
ave 150 B6 Mexico 25°33'N 108°29'W
emala 150 F2 ◆ *Republic* Central America
emala Basin 24 *Undersea feature*
acific Ocean
emala City 150 F2 ● Guatemala
38'N 90°29'W

Guaviare, Río 160 C11 ≈ E Colombia
Guayaquil 160 A10 Ecuador 2°13'S 79°54'W
Guaymas 150 B6 Mexico 27°56'N 110°54'W
Gubadag 116 G8 Turkmenistan 42°7'N 59°55'E
Guben 82 H9 Germany 51°59'N 14°42'E
Gubkin 89 D5 Russian Fed. 51°16'N 37°32'E
Gudaut'a 111 H8 Georgia 43°7'N 40°35'E
Guéret 72 G5 France 46°10'N 1°52'E
Guernsey 72 E8 *UK* ◇ Channel Islands
Guerrero Negro 150 A6 Mexico 27°56'N 114°4'W
Guiana Basin 24 *Undersea feature* W Atlantic Ocean
Guiana Highlands 160 E11 ▲▲ N South America
Guildford 50 F4 England, UK 51°14'N 0°35'W
Guildtown 57 G7 Scotland, UK 56°29'N 3°23'W
Guilin 123 I2 China 25°15'N 110°16'E
Guimarães 74 F7 Portugal 41°26'N 8°19'W
Guinea 96 D4 ◆ *Republic* W Africa
Guinea-Bissau 96 D4 ◆ *Republic* W Africa
Guinea, Gulf of 96 F3 *Gulf* E Atlantic Ocean
Guiyang 123 H3 China 26°33'N 106°45'E
Guizhou 123 I3 ⬖ *Province* China
Gujarāt 118 F6 ⬖ *State* India
Gujranwala 118 G8 Pakistan 32°11'N 74°9'E
Gujrat 118 G8 Pakistan 32°34'N 74°4'E
Gulbarga 118 G4 India 17°22'N 76°47'E
Gulbene 69 H5 Latvia 57°10'N 26°44'E
Gulfport 147 K3 Mississippi, USA 30°22'N 89°6'W
Gulf, The 115 I7 *Gulf* SW Asia
Guliston 117 J7 Uzbekistan 40°29'N 68°46'E
Gulu 99 I8 Uganda 2°46'N 32°21'E
Gümüşhane 111 H7 Turkey 40°31'N 39°27'E
Gunnbjørn Fjeld 145 K8 ▲ C Greenland
Gunnedah 135 K3 New South Wales, Australia 30°59'S 150°15'E
Gurktaler Alpen 83 H5 ▲▲ S Austria
Gürün 110 G6 Turkey 38°44'N 37°15'E
Gurupi 163 I5 Brazil 11°44'S 49°1'W
Gusau 96 G4 Nigeria 12°18'N 6°27'E
Gusev 69 G3 Russian Fed. 54°36'N 22°14'E
Güstrow 82 G11 Germany 53°48'N 12°12'E
Gütersloh 82 D9 Germany 51°54'N 8°23'E
Guwahati 119 J7 India 26°9'N 91°42'E
Guyana 160 E11 ◆ *Republic* N South America
Guyhirn 53 J5 England, UK 52°37'N 0°1'E
Güzelyurt *see* Morfou
Gwadar 118 D7 Pakistan 25°9'N 62°21'E
Gwalior 118 G7 India 26°16'N 78°12'E
Gwanda 99 H4 Zimbabwe 20°56'S 29°E
Gweedore 58 E12 Ireland 55°3'N 8°14'W
Gwynedd 48 E11 ⬖ *Unitary authority* Wales, UK
Gyangzê 122 E3 China 28°50'N 89°38'E
Gympie 135 L5 Queensland, Australia 26°5'S 152°40'E
Gyomaendrőd 85 G4 Hungary 46°56'N 20°50'E
Gyöngyös 85 F5 Hungary 47°44'N 19°49'E
Győr 85 E5 Hungary 47°41'N 17°40'E
Gyumri 111 I7 Armenia 40°48'N 43°51'E

H

Haacht 71 E6 Belgium 50°58'N 4°38'E
Haaksbergen 70 H10 Netherlands 52°9'N 6°45'E
Haapavesi 68 G9 Finland 64°9'N 25°25'E
Haapsalu 69 G6 Estonia 58°58'N 23°32'E
Haarlem 70 E10 Netherlands 52°23'N 4°39'E
Haast 136 B3 New Zealand 43°53'S 169°2'E
Haba 115 K6 United Arab Emirates 25°1'N 55°37'E
Ḩabarūt 115 J3 Oman 17°19'N 52°45'E
Habrough 53 J9 England, UK 53°36'N 0°17'W
Ḩabshān 115 K6 United Arab Emirates 23°51'N 53°34'E
Hachinohe 125 K7 Japan 40°30'N 141°29'E
Hackney 37 ⬖ *London Borough* England, UK
Haddenham 53 I5 England, UK 52°21'N 0°1'E
Haddington 57 H5 Scotland, UK 55°59'N 2°46'W
Haddiscoe 53 M5 England, UK 52°30'N 1°34'E
Ḩadd, Ra's al 115 M6 *Headland* NE Oman
Hadejia 97 H4 ≈ N Nigeria
Hadiboh 115 K1 Yemen 12°38'N 54°5'E
Hadīyah 114 E7 Saudi Arabia 25°36'N 38°31'E
Hadleigh 53 L6 England, UK 51°33'N 0°32'E
Ha Dong 126 G7 Vietnam 20°58'N 105°46'E
Hadrian's Wall 54 F7 *Ancient monument* N England, UK
Haeju 124 D5 North Korea 38°4'N 125°40'E
Ḩafar al Bāṭin 115 H8 Saudi Arabia 28°25'N 45°59'E
Hagondange 73 I7 France 49°16'N 6°6'E
Hag's Head 59 C7 *Headland* W Ireland
Haguenau 73 J7 France 48°49'N 7°47'E
Haicheng 123 K6 China 40°53'N 122°45'E
Haikou 123 I1 China 20°N 110°17'E
Ha'il 114 F7 Saudi Arabia 27°N 42°50'E
Hailar 123 J8 China 49°15'N 119°41'E
Hailsham 51 H3 England, UK 50°51'N 0°14'E
Hailuoto 68 G10 *Island* W Finland
Hainan 123 I1 ⬖ *Province* China
Hainan Dao 123 I1 *Island* S China
Hainichen 82 G8 Germany 50°58'N 13°8'E
Hai Phong 126 G7 Vietnam 20°50'N 106°41'E
Haiti 151 J4 ◆ *Republic* C West Indies
Haiya 97 L5 Sudan 18°17'N 36°21'E
Hajdúböszörmény 85 G5 Hungary 47°39'N 21°32'E
Hajdúhadház 85 H5 Hungary 47°40'N 21°40'E
Hajdúszoboszló 85 G4 Hungary 47°27'N 21°24'E
Hakkas 68 F11 Sweden 66°53'N 21°36'E
Hakodate 125 K7 Japan 41°46'N 140°43'E
Ḩalabān 114 G6 Saudi Arabia 23°29'N 44°20'E
Halberstadt 82 F9 Germany 51°54'N 11°4'E
Halden 69 C6 Norway 59°8'N 11°20'E
Halesowen 52 F5 England, UK 52°26'N 2°13'W
Halesworth 53 M5 England, UK 52°20'N 1°22'E
Halfmoon Bay 136 B1 New Zealand 46°53'S 168°8'E
Halford 52 G4 England, UK 52°6'N 1°36'W
Halifax 145 K2 Nova Scotia, Canada 44°38'N 63°35'W
Halifax 54 G2 England, UK 53°44'N 1°52'W
Halīl Rūd 116 G2 ≈ SE Iran

Halkirk 56 G12 Scotland, UK 58°30'N 3°29'W
Hälla 68 E9 Sweden 63°56'N 17°20'E
Halladale 56 F12 ≈ N Scotland, UK
Halle 71 D6 Belgium 50°44'N 4°14'E
Halle 82 F9 Germany 51°28'N 11°58'E
Halle-Neustadt 82 F9 Germany 51°29'N 11°54'E
Hällnäs 68 E9 Sweden 64°20'N 19°41'E
Halls Creek 134 F7 Western Australia 18°17'S 127°39'E
Hallworthy 49 D5 England, UK 50°40'N 4°37'W
Halmahera, Pulau 127 K3 *Island* E Indonesia
Halmahera Sea 127 K3 *Sea* E Indonesia
Halmstad 69 C4 Sweden 56°41'N 12°49'E
Halstead 51 I7 England, UK 51°57'N 0°32'E
Halton 37 ⬖ *Unitary authority* England, UK
Haltwhistle 54 F7 England, UK 54°59'N 2°30'W
Hamada 124 G3 Japan 34°54'N 132°7'E
Hamadan 116 D5 Iran 34°51'N 48°31'E
Hamah 110 G4 Syria 35°9'N 36°44'E
Hamamatsu 125 I3 Japan 34°43'N 137°46'E
Hamburg 82 E11 Germany 53°33'N 10°3'E
Hamd, Wadi al 114 E6 *Dry watercourse* W Saudi Arabia
Hämeenlinna 69 G7 Finland 61°N 24°25'E
Hamersley Range 134 D6 ▲▲ Western Australia
Hamgyŏng-sanmaek 124 F7 ▲▲ N North Korea
Hamhung 124 E6 North Korea 39°53'N 127°31'E
Hami 122 F7 China 42°48'N 93°27'E
Hamilton 145 I1 Ontario, Canada 43°15'N 79°50'W
Hamilton 136 E6 New Zealand 37°49'S 175°16'E
Hamilton 57 F5 Scotland, UK 55°47'N 4°3'W
Hamim, Wadi al 97 I7 ≈ NE Libya
Hamm 82 D9 Germany 51°39'N 7°49'E
Hammaslahti 68 H8 Finland 62°26'N 29°58'E
Hammersmith and Fulham 37 ⬖ *London Borough* England, UK
Hampden 136 C2 New Zealand 45°18'S 170°49'E
Hampshire 50 E4 ⬖ *County* England, UK
Handan 123 J5 China 36°35'N 114°28'E
Handlová 85 E6 Slovakia 48°45'N 18°45'E
Hangayn Nuruu 122 G8 ▲▲ C Mongolia
Hangzhou 123 K4 China 30°18'N 120°7'E
Hanko 69 G6 Finland 59°50'N 23°E
Hanley 52 F7 England, UK 53°2'N 2°14'W
Hanmer Springs 136 D4 New Zealand 42°31'S 172°49'E
Hanöbukten 69 D4 *Bay* S Sweden
Hanoi 126 G7 ● Vietnam 21°1'N 105°52'E
Hanover 82 E10 Germany 52°23'N 9°43'E
Han Shui 123 I4 ≈ C China
Hanzhong 123 H4 China 33°12'N 107°E
Haora 119 I6 India 22°35'N 88°20'E
Haparanda 68 F10 Sweden 65°49'N 24°5'E
Ḩaql 114 D8 Saudi Arabia 29°18'N 34°58'E
Ḩaraḑ 115 I6 Saudi Arabia 24°8'N 49°2'E
Haradok 89 C6 Belarus 55°28'N 30°0'E
Haramachi 125 K5 Japan 37°40'N 140°55'E
Harare 99 I4 ● Zimbabwe 17°47'S 31°4'E
Harbel 96 D3 Liberia 6°19'N 10°20'W
Harbin 123 K8 China 45°45'N 126°41'E
Harby 53 H6 England, UK 52°53'N 0°58'W
Hardangerfjorden 69 A7 *Fjord* S Norway
Hardangervidda 69 B7 ▲▲ S Norway
Hardenberg 70 H11 Netherlands 52°34'N 6°38'E
Harelbeke 71 B6 Belgium 50°51'N 3°19'E
Haren 70 H12 Netherlands 53°10'N 6°37'E
Harer 97 M4 Ethiopia 9°17'N 42°19'E
Harewood 55 H3 England, UK 53°53'N 1°32'W
Hargeysa 97 M4 Somalia 9°32'N 44°7'E
Ḩarīb 115 H2 Yemen 15°8'N 45°35'E
Haringey 37 ⬖ *London Borough* England, UK
Harirud 117 I5 ≈ Afghanistan/Iran
Harlech 48 E11 Wales, UK 52°51'N 4°12'W
Harleston 53 M5 England, UK 52°24'N 1°16'E
Harlingen 70 F12 Netherlands 53°10'N 5°25'E
Harlow 51 H6 England, UK 51°47'N 0°7'E
Harney Basin 146 E7 *Basin* Oregon, NW USA
Härnösand 68 E8 Sweden 62°37'N 17°55'E
Har Nuur 122 F8 ◎ NW Mongolia
Harpenden 50 G7 England, UK 51°49'N 0°22'W
Harper 96 E3 Liberia 4°25'N 7°43'W
Harpley 53 K6 England, UK 52°47'N 0°38'E
Ḩarrah 115 J2 Yemen 15°2'N 50°23'E
Harricana 145 I2 ≈ Québec, SE Canada
Harrietsham 51 I4 England, UK 51°14'N 0°40'E
Harris 56 C8 Scotland, UK 56°59'N 6°20'W
Harrisburg 147 M6 Pennsylvania, USA 40°16'N 76°53'W
Harrison, Cape 145 K4 *Headland* Newfoundland and Labrador, E Canada
Harris, Sound of 56 B10 *Strait* NW Scotland, UK
Harrogate 55 H3 England, UK 54°N 1°33'W
Harrow 50 G6 England, UK 51°36'N 0°22'W
Harrow 37 ⬖ *London Borough* England, UK
Harstad 68 D12 Norway 68°48'N 16°31'E
Harston 53 J4 England, UK 52°8'N 0°5'W
Hartford 147 N7 Connecticut, USA 41°46'N 72°41'W
Hartington 52 G7 England, UK 53°8'N 1°57'W
Hartland 49 D6 England, UK 51°0'N 4°35'W
Hartland Point 49 D6 *Headland* SW England, UK
Hartlepool 55 I6 England, UK 54°41'N 1°13'W
Hartlepool 36 ⬖ *Unitary authority* England, UK
Harwich 51 K7 England, UK 51°56'N 1°16'E
Harwood Dale 55 J5 England, UK 54°22'N 0°43'W
Haryana 118 G7 ⬖ *State* India
Harz 82 F9 ▲▲ C Germany
Ḩāsik 115 L3 Oman 17°22'N 55°18'E
Haslemere 50 F4 England, UK 51°6'N 0°45'W
Hassela 68 D8 Sweden 62°6'N 16°45'E
Hasselt 71 F6 Belgium 50°56'N 5°20'E
Hässleholm 69 C4 Sweden 56°9'N 13°45'E
Hastings 136 F5 New Zealand 39°39'S 176°51'E
Hastings 51 I3 England, UK 50°51'N 0°36'E
Hatfield 50 G6 England, UK 51°46'N 0°13'W
Hatfield 53 H9 England, UK 53°34'N 1°2'W
Hathersage 52 G8 England, UK 53°20'N 1°41'W
Hattem 70 G10 Netherlands 52°29'N 6°4'E
Hatteras, Cape 147 N5 *Headland* North Carolina, SE USA
Hattiesburg 147 K4 Mississippi, USA 31°20'N 89°17'W
Hatvan 85 F5 Hungary 47°40'N 19°39'E

Hat Yai 126 F4 Thailand 7°1'N 100°27'E
Haugesund 69 A6 Norway 59°24'N 5°17'E
Haughley 53 L4 England, UK 52°12'N 0°57'E
Haughton 52 F6 England, UK 52°46'N 2°12'W
Haukeligrend 69 B6 Norway 59°45'N 7°33'E
Haukivesi 68 H8 ◎ SE Finland
Hauraki Gulf 136 E7 *Gulf* North Island, N New Zealand
Hauroko, Lake 136 B1 ◎ South Island, New Zealand
Hautes Fagnes 71 G5 ▲▲ E Belgium
Hauts Plateaux 96 F8 *Plateau* Algeria/Morocco
Hauzenberg 83 G6 Germany 48°39'N 13°37'E
Havana 151 H5 ● Cuba 23°7'N 82°25'W
Havant 50 E3 England, UK 50°51'N 0°59'W
Havelock North 136 F5 New Zealand 39°40'S 176°53'E
Haverfordwest 48 C8 Wales, UK 51°50'N 4°58'W
Haverhill 53 K4 England, UK 52°5'N 0°26'E
Havering 37 ⬖ *London Borough* England, UK
Havířov 85 E7 Czech Republic 49°47'N 18°30'E
Havre 146 G8 Montana, USA 48°33'N 109°41'W
Havre-St-Pierre 145 J3 Québec, Canada 50°16'N 63°36'W
Hawai'i 146 F2 ⬖ *State* USA
Hawai'i 146 G1 *Island* Hawaiian Islands, USA, C Pacific Ocean
Hawaiian Islands 24 *Island group* Hawai'i, USA
Hawea, Lake 136 B2 ◎ South Island, New Zealand
Hawera 136 D5 New Zealand 39°36'S 174°16'E
Hawes 54 G4 England, UK 54°17'N 2°19'W
Hawick 57 H4 Scotland, UK 55°24'N 2°49'W
Hawke Bay 136 F5 *Bay* North Island, New Zealand
Hawkhurst 51 I4 England, UK 51°1'N 0°29'E
Ḩawrā' 115 I2 Yemen 15°39'N 48°21'E
Hawthorne 146 E6 Nevada, USA 38°30'N 118°38'W
Haxby 55 I3 England, UK 54°1'N 1°4'W
Hay 135 J3 New South Wales, Australia 34°31'S 144°51'E
Haydon Bridge 54 G7 England, UK 54°58'N 2°19'W
Hayes 144 G3 ≈ Manitoba, C Canada
Hayle 49 B3 England, UK 50°12'N 5°23'W
Haymā' 115 L4 Oman 19°59'N 56°20'E
Hay-on-Wye 48 G9 Wales, UK 52°3'N 3°7'W
Hay River 144 E4 Northwest Territories, Canada 60°51'N 115°42'W
Hays 147 I5 Kansas, USA 38°53'N 99°20'W
Hayton 55 J3 England, UK 53°54'N 0°50'W
Haywards Heath 50 G3 England, UK 51°N 0°6'W
Hazar 116 E7 Turkmenistan 39°26'N 53°7'E
Hazel Grove 54 G1 England, UK 53°22'N 2°7'W
Headcorn 51 I4 England, UK 51°10'N 0°36'E
Headford 58 D8 Ireland 53°28'N 9°15'W
Headley 50 E5 England, UK 51°7'N 0°17'W
Heard and McDonald Islands 13 *Australian* ◇ Indian Ocean
Hearst 145 H2 Ontario, Canada 49°42'N 83°40'W
Herat 117 H5 Afghanistan 34°23'N 62°11'E
Hebburn 55 H7 England, UK 54°58'N 1°28'W
Hebden Bridge 54 G2 England, UK 53°46'N 2°5'W
Hebei 123 J6 ⬖ *Province* China
Hebrides, Sea of the 56 B9 *Sea* NW Scotland, UK
Hebron 110 B3 West Bank 31°30'N 35°E
Heemskerk 70 E11 Netherlands 52°31'N 4°40'E
Heerde 70 G10 Netherlands 52°24'N 6°2'E
Heerenveen 70 G12 Netherlands 52°57'N 5°55'E
Heerhugowaard 70 E11 Netherlands 52°40'N 4°50'E
Heerlen 71 G6 Netherlands 50°55'N 6°E
Hefa 110 A4 Israel 32°49'N 34°59'E
Hefei 123 J4 China 31°51'N 117°20'E
Hegang 123 L8 China 47°18'N 130°16'E
Heide 82 E11 Germany 54°12'N 9°6'E
Heidelberg 83 D7 Germany 49°24'N 8°41'E
Heidenheim an der Brenz 83 E6 Germany 48°41'N 10°9'E
Heilbronn 83 E7 Germany 49°9'N 9°13'E
Heilongjiang 123 K8 ⬖ *Province* China
Heiloo 70 E11 Netherlands 52°36'N 4°43'E
Heimaey 68 A10 *Island* S Iceland
Heimdal 68 C8 Norway 63°21'N 10°23'E
Hekimhan 110 G6 Turkey 38°50'N 37°56'E
Helena 146 F8 Montana, USA 46°36'N 112°2'W
Helensburgh 57 E6 Scotland, UK 56°0'N 4°45'W
Helensville 136 D7 New Zealand 36°42'S 174°26'E
Helgoländer Bucht 82 D11 *Bay* NW Germany
Hellevoetsluis 70 D9 Netherlands 51°49'N 4°8'E
Hellifield 54 G3 England, UK 54°1'N 2°15'W
Hellin 75 J5 Spain 38°31'N 1°43'W
Hellingly 51 H3 England, UK 50°53'N 0°8'E
Helmand, Darya-ye 117 H3 ≈ Afghanistan/Iran
Helmond 70 F8 Netherlands 51°29'N 5°41'E
Helmsdale 56 G11 Scotland, UK 58°6'N 3°36'W
Helmsdale 56 F11 ≈ N Scotland, UK
Helmsley 55 I4 England, UK 54°14'N 1°8'W
Helsingborg 69 C4 Sweden 56°N 12°48'E
Helsingør 69 C4 Denmark 56°3'N 12°38'E
Helsinki 69 G7 ● Finland 60°18'N 24°58'E
Helston 49 C3 England, UK 50°4'N 5°17'W
Helvellyn 54 E5 ▲ NW England, UK
Hemel Hempstead 50 G6 England, UK 51°46'N 0°28'W
Hemsworth 55 H2 England, UK 53°37'N 1°30'W
Henan 123 J4 ⬖ *Province* China
Hendon 50 G6 England, UK 51°35'N 0°14'W
Hengelo 70 H10 Netherlands 52°3'N 6°19'E
Hengyang 123 J3 China 26°55'N 112°34'E
Heniches'k 89 D3 Ukraine 46°10'N 34°49'E
Henley-on-Thames 50 F5 England, UK 51°33'N 0°54'W
Hennebont 72 D6 France 47°48'N 3°17'W
Henzada 126 E6 Burma 17°36'N 95°26'E
Heredia 151 H1 Costa Rica 10°N 84°6'W
Hereford 52 E4 England, UK 52°4'N 2°43'W
Herefordshire 52 E4 ⬖ *Unitary authority* England, UK
Herford 82 E9 Germany 52°7'N 8°41'E
Herk-de-Stad 71 E6 Belgium 50°57'N 5°12'E

Herma Ness 56 I12 *Headland* NE Scotland, UK
Hermansverk 69 A7 Norway 61°11'N 6°52'E
Hermosillo 150 B6 Mexico 28°59'N 110°53'W
Herne Bay 51 J5 England, UK 51°24'N 1°6'E
Herrera del Duque 75 H5 Spain 39°10'N 5°3'W
Herselt 71 E7 Belgium 51°4'N 4°53'E
Herstal 71 F6 Belgium 50°40'N 5°38'E
Hertfordshire 51 H7 ⬖ *County* England, UK
Hessle 55 J2 England, UK 53°43'N 0°23'W
Heswall 52 D8 England, UK 53°20'N 3°6'W
Hethersett 53 M5 England, UK 52°36'N 1°10'E
Hexham 54 G7 England, UK 54°58'N 2°12'W
Heysham 54 E3 England, UK 54°2'N 2°54'W
Heywood 54 G2 England, UK 53°36'N 2°16'W
Heze 123 J5 China 35°16'N 115°27'E
Hidalgo del Parral 150 C6 Mexico 26°58'N 105°40'W
Hida-sanmyaku 125 I4 ▲▲ Honshū, S Japan
Highbridge 49 G6 England, UK 51°13'N 3°7'W
Higher Town 49 A3 England, UK 50°13'N 5°59'W
Highland 56 E9 ⬖ *Unitary authority* Scotland, UK
High Willhays 49 E5 ▲ SW England, UK
High Wycombe 50 F6 England, UK 51°38'N 0°46'W
Hiiumaa 69 F6 *Island* W Estonia
Hikurangi 136 D8 New Zealand 35°37'S 174°16'E
Hilborough 53 L5 England, UK 52°34'N 0°34'E
Hildesheim 82 E9 Germany 52°9'N 9°57'E
Hillegom 70 E10 Netherlands 52°18'N 4°35'E
Hillingdon 37 ⬖ *London Borough* England, UK
Hillsborough 58 H11 Northern Ireland, UK 54°27'N 6°6'W
Hilo 146 G2 Hawai'i, USA 19°42'N 155°4'W
Hilversum 70 E10 Netherlands 52°14'N 5°10'E
Himāchal Pradesh 118 G8 ⬖ *State* India
Himalayas 103 ▲▲ S Asia
Himeji 125 H3 Japan 34°47'N 134°32'E
Hims 110 G4 Syria 34°44'N 36°43'E
Hinchinbrook Island 135 K7 *Island* Queensland, NE Australia
Hinckley 52 G5 England, UK 52°33'N 1°21'W
Hinderwell 55 J5 England, UK 54°32'N 0°46'W
Hindhead 50 F4 England, UK 51°7'N 0°46'W
Hindley 54 F2 England, UK 53°31'N 2°34'W
Hinds 136 C3 New Zealand 44°1'S 171°33'E
Hindu Kush 103 ▲▲ Afghanistan/Pakistan
Hingham 53 L5 England, UK 52°35'N 0°52'E
Hinnøya 68 D12 *Island* C Norway
Hiratsuka 125 J4 Japan 35°20'N 139°20'E
Hirosaki 125 J7 Japan 40°34'N 140°28'E
Hiroshima 124 G3 Japan 34°23'N 132°26'E
Hirson 73 H8 France 49°56'N 4°5'E
Hispaniola 151 J3 *Island* Dominican Republic/Haiti
Hit 111 I3 Iraq 33°38'N 42°50'E
Hitachi 125 K4 Japan 36°40'N 140°42'E
Hitchin 50 G7 England, UK 51°57'N 0°17'W
Hitra 68 B9 *Island* S Norway
Hjälmaren 69 D6 ◎ C Sweden
Hjelmeland 69 A6 Norway 59°12'N 6°7'E
Hjørring 69 B5 Denmark 57°28'N 9°59'E
Hkakabo Razi 126 E9 ▲ Burma/China
Hlukhiv 89 C5 Ukraine 51°40'N 33°53'E
Hoang Liên Son 126 F7 ▲▲ N Vietnam
Hobart 135 J1 Tasmania, Australia 42°54'S 147°18'E
Hobro 69 B4 Denmark 56°39'N 9°51'E
Ho Chi Minh 126 G5 Vietnam 10°46'N 106°43'E
Hodeida 114 G2 Yemen 15°N 42°50'E
Hódmezővásárhely 85 G3 Hungary 46°27'N 20°18'E
Hodnet 52 E6 England, UK 52°51'N 2°37'W
Hodonín 85 D6 Czech Republic 48°52'N 17°7'E
Hoeryong 124 F7 North Korea 42°23'N 129°46'E
Hoeselt 71 F6 Belgium 50°50'N 5°30'E
Hof 82 F8 Germany 50°19'N 11°55'E
Hofsjökull 68 B11 *Glacier* C Iceland
Hofu 124 G3 Japan 34°1'N 131°34'E
Hohenems 83 E5 Austria 47°23'N 9°43'E
Hohe Tauern 83 G5 ▲▲ W Austria
Hohhot 123 I6 China 40°49'N 111°37'E
Hokianga Harbour 136 D8 *Inlet* SE Tasman Sea
Hokitika 136 C3 New Zealand 42°44'S 170°58'E
Hokkaido 125 K8 *Island* NE Japan
Holbeach 53 J6 England, UK 52°47'N 0°3'E
Holbrook 53 M3 England, UK 51°58'N 1°9'E
Holguín 151 I4 Cuba 20°51'N 76°16'W
Hollabrunn 83 I6 Austria 48°33'N 16°6'E
Hollingworth 52 F8 England, UK 53°28'N 2°0'W
Hollola 69 G7 Finland 61°N 25°32'E
Holman 144 E6 Northwest Territories, Canada 70°42'N 117°45'W
Holme on Spalding Moor 55 J3 England, UK 53°50'N 0°47'W
Holmsund 68 F9 Sweden 63°42'N 20°26'E
Holon 110 A4 Israel 32°1'N 34°46'E
Holstebro 69 B4 Denmark 56°22'N 8°38'E
Holsworthy 49 D5 England, UK 50°49'N 4°21'W
Holt 53 L6 England, UK 52°53'N 1°2'E
Holycross 59 E6 Ireland 52°38'N 7°52'W
Holyhead 48 D12 Wales, UK 53°19'N 4°38'W
Holyhead Bay 48 D13 *Bay* NW Wales, UK
Hombori 96 F5 Mali 15°13'N 1°39'W
Homyel' 89 C5 Belarus 52°25'N 31°E
Hondo 150 G3 ≈ Central America
Honduras 150 G3 ◆ *Republic* Central America
Honduras, Gulf of 150 G3 *Gulf* W Caribbean Sea
Hønefoss 69 B6 Norway 60°10'N 10°15'E
Hong Gai 126 G7 Vietnam 20°57'N 107°6'E
Hong Kong 123 J2 China 22°17'N 114°9'E
Honiara 128 ● Solomon Islands 9°27'S 159°56'E
Honiton 49 F5 England, UK 50°48'N 3°12'W
Honjo 125 J6 Japan 39°23'N 140°3'E
Honolulu 146 F2 Hawai'i, USA 21°18'N 157°52'W
Honshu 125 J4 *Island* SW Japan
Hoogeveen 70 H11 Netherlands 52°44'N 6°30'E
Hoogezand-Sappemeer 70 H12 Netherlands 53°10'N 6°47'E
Hook Head 59 G5 *Headland* SE Ireland
Hoorn 70 E11 Netherlands 52°38'N 5°4'E
Hopa 111 H7 Turkey 41°23'N 41°28'E
Hope 146 B6 Alaska, USA 60°55'N 149°38'W

◆ Country ● Country capital ◇ Dependent territory ○ Dependent territory capital ⬖ Administrative region ▲ Mountain ▲▲ Mountain range Volcano ≈ River ◎ Lake Reservoir

Kaipara Harbour - Kong Christian IX Land 179

Harbour 136 D7 *Harbour* North Island, ealand
n 97 H8 Tunisia *35°46'N 10°11'E*
autern 83 D7 Germany *49°27'N 7°46'E*
136 D8 New Zealand *35°7'S 173°13'E*
123 H2 China *23°42'N 103°14'E*
68 H9 Finland *64°17'N 27°46'E*
16 G6 Turkmenistan *37°20'N 59°37'E*
a 119 H4 India *16°56'N 82°13'E*
k 146 C7 Alaska, USA *70°8'N 143°37'W*
Desert 98 G3 *Desert* Southern Africa
68 F9 Finland *64°15'N 24°E*
iá 87 H4 Greece *40°37'N 22°58'E*
a 86 G2 Greece *37°2'N 22°7'E*
17 I4 Afghanistan *32°10'N 66°54'E*
134 C4 Western Australia
'S 114°8'E
110 F6 Turkey *40°8'N 33°27'E*
99 H7 Dem. Rep. Congo *5°55'S 29°9'E*
lie 134 E4 Western Australia
'S 121°27'E
99 H7 Dem. Rep. Congo *2°34'S 26°27'E*
tan 127 H3 Region, Indonesia
grad 69 F3 Russian Fed. *54°48'N 21°33'E*
34 E9 Poland *51°46'N 18°4'E*
8 F10 Sweden *65°51'N 23°14'E*
en 68 F10 ≈ N Sweden
ndji 134 G7 Northern Territory, Australia
'S 130°40'E
C8 Sweden *63°31'N 13°16'E*
si 68 H8 ◎ SE Finland
87 I3 Greece *39°14'N 26°16'E*
69 D4 Sweden *56°40'N 16°22'E*
out 70 D8 Belgium *51°24'N 4°27'E*
89 D6 Russian Fed. *54°31'N 36°16'E*
118 F5 India *19°17'N 73°11'E*
os 87 J2 *Island* Dodecanese, Greece, an Sea
88 G8 ≈ NW Russian Fed.
99 H6 Dem. Rep. Congo *8°42'S 25°1'E*
ps 144 D2 British Columbia, Canada
'N 120°24'W
a 99 I8 ● Uganda *0°20'N 32°28'E*
ng Cham 126 G5 Cambodia
105°27'E
ng Saom 126 F5 Cambodia
'N 103°30'E
anets'-Podil's'kyy 89 B4 Ukraine
'N 26°36'E
nin 89 F5 Russian Fed. *50°7'N 45°20'E*
ga 98 G7 Dem. Rep. Congo
S 22°22'E
89 F6 Russian Fed. *55°30'N 47°27'E*
wa 125 I4 Japan *36°35'N 136°40'E*
puram 119 H3 India *12°50'N 79°44'E*
har 117 I4 Afghanistan *31°36'N 65°48'E*
aksha 88 D10 Russian Fed.
'N 32°14'E
ngan 127 H2 Indonesia *2°50'S 115°15'E*
96 F4 Benin *11°5'N 2°59'E*
119 H1 Sri Lanka *7°17'N 80°40'E*
he 146 F2 Hawai'i, USA
'N 157°48'W
116 E2 Iran *27°51'N 52°7'E*
oo Island 135 H2 *Island* South Australia
sniemi 68 G8 Finland *61°58'N 26°37'E*
ye 124 E7 North Korea *40°58'N 126°37'E*
ing 124 F5 South Korea
'N 128°51'E
Nos 88 E11 Russian Fed. *68°38'N 43°19'E*
96 E4 Guinea *10°25'N 9°19'W*
nkoski 68 G8 Finland *62°59'N 25°20'E*
96 G4 Nigeria *11°56'N 8°31'E*
119 H7 India *26°28'N 80°21'E*
147 I5 ⬖ *State* USA
City 147 J6 Kansas, USA
'N 94°38'W
City 147 J6 Missouri, USA
'N 94°35'W
109 H4 Russian Fed. *56°11'N 95°32'E*
nirovka 89 E4 Russian Fed.
'N 39°53'E
Plain 125 J4 *Plain* Honshū, C Japan
99 H3 Botswana *24°55'S 25°14'E*
ung 123 K2 Taiwan *22°36'N 120°17'E*
k 96 D5 Senegal *14°9'N 16°8'W*
e 70 C8 Netherlands *51°29'N 3°58'E*
en 71 D7 Belgium *51°19'N 4°25'E*
gky, Plato 116 F7 *Ridge* Turkmenistan/ ekistan
ta 97 K3 Sudan *4°50'N 33°35'E*
vár 85 E3 Hungary *46°23'N 17°54'E*
ln 82 E12 Germany *54°41'N 9°56'E*
s, Sungai 127 H3 ≈ Borneo, C Indonesia
kasing 145 I2 Ontario, Canada
5'N 82°26'W
alta 117 K8 Kyrgyzstan *42°51'N 73°51'E*
l', Vozvyshennost' 117 H6 ▲▲ rkmenistan
ogaz-Gol, Zaliv 116 E7 ◎ Turkmenistan
ik 110 E7 Turkey *41°12'N 32°36'E*
i 118 E6 Pakistan *24°51'N 67°2'E*
anda 108 F3 Kazakhstan *49°53'N 73°7'E*
nskiy, Ostrov 109 L7 *Island* E Russian Fed.
116 D5 Iran *35°44'N 51°26'E*
ol 117 L8 Kyrgyzstan *41°30'N 77°18'E*
ol 117 L8 Kyrgyzstan *42°32'N 78°21'E*
oram Range 118 G9 ▲▲ C Asia
um 116 G6 *Desert* C Turkmenistan
an 110 E5 Turkey *37°11'N 33°13'E*
ay 122 E7 China *45°33'N 84°45'E*
ea Bight 136 C4 *Gulf* South Island, Zealand
ay 117 L8 Kyrgyzstan *41°34'N 77°56'E*
urg 98 F2 Namibia *27°59'S 18°46'E*
ea 25 *Sea* Arctic Ocean
ok 68 F12 Norway *69°27'N 25°28'E*
au 108 F2 Kazakhstan *43°9'N 70°28'E*
ä' 111 J3 Iraq *32°37'N 44°3'E*
g 85 G4 Hungary *47°22'N 20°51'E*
sa 86 G3 Greece *39°22'N 21°56'E*
110 F7 Turkey *41°9'N 34°32'E*
a 99 H5 Zimbabwe *16°29'S 28°48'E*
, Lake 99 H4 ⊠ Zambia/Zimbabwe
b 98 F4 Namibia *21°56'S 15°51'E*
asniemi 68 G12 Finland *69°24'N 25°52'E*
nagar 119 H4 India *18°28'N 79°9'E*

Karkinits'ka Zatoka 89 C3 *Gulf* S Ukraine
Karlino 84 D11 Poland *54°2'N 15°52'E*
Karlovac 86 D7 Croatia *45°29'N 15°31'E*
Karlovy Vary 85 A7 Czech Republic *50°13'N 12°51'E*
Karlskrona 69 D4 Sweden *56°11'N 15°39'E*
Karlsruhe 83 D7 Germany *49°1'N 8°24'E*
Karlstad 69 D6 Sweden *59°22'N 13°36'E*
Karnal 118 G7 India *29°41'N 76°58'E*
Karnātaka 118 G4 ⬖ *State* India
Kárpathos 87 J1 Greece *35°30'N 27°13'E*
Karpathos 87 J1 *Island* SE Greece
Karpenísi 86 G3 Greece *38°55'N 21°46'E*
Kars 111 I7 Turkey *40°35'N 43°5'E*
Karst 83 H4 *Physical region* Croatia/Slovenia
Kārūn 116 D4 ≈ SW Iran
Karunki 68 F10 Finland *66°1'N 24°6'E*
Karyés 87 H4 Greece *40°15'N 24°15'E*
Kaş 110 D4 Turkey *36°12'N 29°38'E*
Kasai 98 G6 ≈ Angola/Dem. Rep. Congo
Kasaji 98 G6 Dem. Rep. Congo *10°23'S 23°29'E*
Kasama 99 I6 Zambia *10°14'S 31°12'E*
Kasese 99 I8 Uganda *0°10'N 30°6'E*
Kashan 116 E5 Iran *33°57'N 51°31'E*
Kashi 122 C7 China *39°32'N 75°58'E*
Kasongo 99 H7 Dem. Rep. Congo *4°22'S 26°42'E*
Kasongo-Lunda 98 F6 Dem. Rep. Congo *6°30'S 16°51'E*
Kasos 87 J1 *Island* S Greece
Kassala 97 L5 Sudan *15°24'N 36°25'E*
Kassel 82 E9 Germany *51°19'N 9°30'E*
Kastamonu 110 F7 Turkey *41°22'N 33°47'E*
Kastsyukovichy 89 C6 Belarus *53°20'N 32°3'E*
Kasumiga-ura 125 K4 ◎ Honshū, S Japan
Katahdin, Mount 147 N8 ▲ Maine, NE USA
Katalla 146 C6 Alaska, USA *60°12'N 144°31'W*
Katanning 134 D3 Western Australia *33°45'S 117°33'E*
Katchall Island 119 L2 *Island* Nicobar Islands, India, NE Indian Ocean
Katherine 134 G8 Northern Territory, Australia *14°29'S 132°20'E*
Kathmandu 119 I7 ● Nepal *27°46'N 85°17'E*
Katikati 136 E6 New Zealand *37°34'S 175°55'E*
Katima Mulilo 98 G4 Namibia *17°31'S 24°20'E*
Katowice 85 F7 Poland *50°15'N 19°1'E*
Katrineholm 68 D6 Sweden *58°59'N 16°15'E*
Katsina 96 G4 Nigeria *12°59'N 7°33'E*
Kattaqo'rg'on 117 I7 Uzbekistan *39°56'N 66°11'E*
Kattegat 69 C4 *Strait* N Europe
Kaua'i 146 E2 *Island* Hawaiian Islands, Hawai'i, USA
Kaufbeuren 83 F5 Germany *47°53'N 10°37'E*
Kauhava 68 F8 Finland *63°6'N 23°8'E*
Kaunas 69 G3 Lithuania *54°54'N 23°57'E*
Kautokeino 68 F12 Norway *69°N 23°1'E*
Kavála 87 H4 Greece *40°57'N 24°26'E*
Kavali 119 H4 India *15°5'N 80°2'E*
Kavaratti 118 F2 India *10°33'N 72°38'E*
Kavarna 87 J6 Bulgaria *43°27'N 28°21'E*
Kavir, Dasht-e 116 F5 *Salt lake* N Iran
Kawerau 136 F6 New Zealand *38°6'S 176°43'E*
Kayan, Sungai 127 I3 ≈ Borneo, C Indonesia
Kayes 96 D5 Mali *14°26'N 11°22'W*
Kayseri 110 F6 Turkey *38°42'N 35°28'E*
Kazach'ye 109 J7 Russian Fed. *70°38'N 135°54'E*
Kazakhstan 108 E3 ◆ *Republic* C Asia
Kazan' 89 F7 Russian Fed. *55°43'N 49°7'E*
Kazanlŭk 87 I6 Bulgaria *42°38'N 25°24'E*
Kazerun 116 D3 Iran *29°41'N 51°38'E*
Kea 87 H2 *Island* Cyclades, Greece, Aegean Sea
Keady 58 G10 Northern Ireland, UK *54°15'N 6°41'W*
Kea, Mauna 146 G2 ▲ Hawai'i, USA
Kebnekaise 68 E11 ▲ N Sweden
Kecskemét 85 F4 Hungary *46°54'N 19°42'E*
Kediri 127 H1 Indonesia *7°45'S 112°1'E*
Kędzierzyn-Kozle 85 E7 Poland *50°20'N 18°12'E*
Keetmanshoop 98 F3 Namibia *26°36'S 18°8'E*
Kefallonia 86 G3 *Island* Ionian Islands, Greece, C Mediterranean Sea
Keflavík 68 A11 Iceland *64°1'N 22°35'W*
Kehl 83 D6 Germany *48°34'N 7°49'E*
Keighley 54 G3 England, UK *53°51'N 1°58'W*
Keith 135 I2 South Australia *36°1'S 140°22'E*
Keith 56 G9 Scotland, UK *57°33'N 2°57'W*
Kek-Art 117 K7 Kyrgyzstan *40°16'N 74°21'E*
Kékes 85 F5 ▲ N Hungary
Keld 54 G5 England, UK *54°24'N 2°11'W*
Kelloselkä 68 H11 Finland *66°56'N 28°52'E*
Kells 58 G9 Ireland *53°44'N 6°53'W*
Kelowna 144 D2 British Columbia, Canada *49°50'N 119°29'W*
Kelso 57 H5 Scotland, UK *55°36'N 2°27'W*
Keluang 126 F3 Malaysia *2°1'N 103°18'E*
Kelvedon 51 I7 England, UK *51°50'N 0°41'E*
Kem' 88 D10 Russian Fed. *64°55'N 34°18'E*
Kemah 111 H6 Turkey *39°35'N 39°2'E*
Kemerovo 108 G4 Russian Fed. *55°25'N 86°5'E*
Kemi 68 G10 Finland *65°46'N 24°34'E*
Kemijärvi 68 G11 Finland *66°41'N 27°24'E*
Kemijoki 68 G10 ≈ NW Finland
Kempele 68 G10 Finland *64°56'N 25°26'E*
Kemp Land 166 F6 *Physical region* Antarctica
Kempsey 52 F4 England, UK *52°8'N 2°13'W*
Kempston 50 G8 England, UK *52°7'N 0°30'W*
Kempten 83 E5 Germany *47°44'N 10°19'E*
Kendal 54 F4 England, UK *54°20'N 2°45'W*
Kendari 127 J2 Indonesia *3°57'S 122°36'E*
Keng Tung 126 E7 Burma *21°18'N 99°36'E*
Kenilworth 52 G4 England, UK *52°20'N 1°41'W*
Kénitra 96 E8 Morocco *34°20'N 6°29'W*
Kenmare 59 C4 Ireland *51°53'N 9°35'W*
Kensington and Chelsea 37 ⬖ *London Borough* England, UK
Kent 51 J4 ⬖ *County* England, UK
Kentau 108 F2 Kazakhstan *43°28'N 68°41'E*
Kentford 53 K4 England, UK *52°16'N 0°24'E*
Kentucky 147 L5 ⬖ *State* USA
Kentucky Lake 147 K5 ⊠ Kentucky/Tennessee, S USA
Kenya 99 J8 ◆ *Republic* E Africa
Kępno 84 E8 Poland *51°17'N 17°57'E*
Kerala 118 G2 ⬖ *State* India
Kerch 89 D3 Ukraine *45°22'N 36°30'E*

Kerguelen 25 *Island* C French Southern and Antarctic Territories
Kerí 86 G2 Greece *37°40'N 20°48'E*
Kerikeri 136 D8 New Zealand *35°14'S 173°58'E*
Kerkenah, Îles de 78 G4 *Island group* E Tunisia
Kerkrade 71 G6 Netherlands *50°53'N 6°4'E*
Kérkyra *see* Corfu
Kermadec Trench 24 *Undersea feature* SW Pacific Ocean
Kerman 116 F3 Iran *30°18'N 57°5'E*
Kermānshāh 116 C5 Iran *34°19'N 47°4'E*
Kerry 59 C5 ⬖ *County* Ireland
Kerry Head 59 B6 *Headland* SW Ireland
Kerulen 123 I8 ≈ China/Mongolia
Kesennuma 125 K6 Japan *38°55'N 141°35'E*
Kessingland 53 N5 England, UK *52°24'N 1°43'E*
Keswick 54 E5 England, UK *54°30'N 3°4'W*
Keszthely 85 D4 Hungary *46°47'N 17°16'E*
Ketchikan 146 C6 Alaska, USA *55°21'N 131°39'W*
Kettering 53 I5 England, UK *52°24'N 0°44'W*
Kettlewell 54 G4 England, UK *54°9'N 2°5'W*
Keuruu 68 G8 Finland *62°15'N 24°34'E*
Kevo 68 G13 Finland *69°42'N 27°8'E*
Key Largo 147 M2 Florida, USA *25°6'N 80°25'W*
Keynsham 49 H7 England, UK *51°24'N 2°31'W*
Key West 147 M2 Florida, USA *24°34'N 81°48'W*
Khabarovsk 109 L4 Russian Fed. *48°32'N 135°8'E*
Khādhil 115 L4 Oman *18°48'N 56°48'E*
Khairpur 118 E7 Pakistan *27°30'N 68°50'E*
Khalūf 115 L5 Oman *20°27'N 57°59'E*
Khambhat, Gulf of 118 F5 *Coastal sea feature* W India
Khamir 114 G2 Yemen *16°N 43°56'E*
Khānaqīn 111 J4 Iraq *34°22'N 45°22'E*
Khandwa 118 G5 India *21°49'N 76°23'E*
Khanka, Lake 109 L3 ◎ China/Russian Fed.
Khanthabouli 126 F6 Laos *16°38'N 104°49'E*
Khanty-Mansiysk 108 F5 Russian Fed. *61°1'N 69°E*
Khao Laem Reservoir 126 E6 ⊠ W Thailand
Kharagpur 119 J6 India *22°30'N 87°19'E*
Kharkiv 89 D5 Ukraine *50°N 36°14'E*
Khartoum 97 K5 ● Sudan *15°33'N 32°32'E*
Khartoum North 97 K5 Sudan *15°38'N 32°33'E*
Khasavyurt 89 F2 Russian Fed. *43°16'N 46°33'E*
Khāsh 117 H2 Iran *28°15'N 61°11'E*
Khash, Dasht-e 117 H4 *Desert* SW Afghanistan
Khaskovo 87 I5 Bulgaria *41°56'N 25°35'E*
Khatyrka 109 M7 Russian Fed. *62°3'N 175°9'E*
Khawr Fakkān 115 L7 United Arab Emirates *25°22'N 56°19'E*
Khaybar 114 E7 Saudi Arabia *25°53'N 39°16'E*
Khaydarkan 117 J7 Kyrgyzstan *39°56'N 71°17'E*
Kherson 89 C4 Ukraine *46°39'N 32°38'E*
Kheta 109 H6 ≈ N Russian Fed.
Khmel'nyts'kyy 89 B5 Ukraine *49°24'N 26°59'E*
Kholm 117 J6 Afghanistan *36°42'N 67°41'E*
Khon Kaen 126 F6 Thailand *16°25'N 102°50'E*
Khor 109 L4 Russian Fed. *47°44'N 134°48'E*
Khorramābād 116 D5 Iran *33°29'N 48°21'E*
Khorramshahr 116 C3 Iran *30°30'N 48°9'E*
Khorugh 117 K6 Tajikistan *37°30'N 71°31'E*
Khouribga 96 E8 Morocco *32°55'N 6°51'W*
Khowst 117 J4 Afghanistan *33°22'N 69°57'E*
Khŭjand 117 J7 Tajikistan *40°17'N 69°37'E*
Khulna 119 J6 Bangladesh *22°48'N 89°32'E*
Khurayṣ 115 H6 Saudi Arabia *25°6'N 48°3'E*
Khvormūj 116 D3 Iran *28°32'N 51°22'E*
Khvoy 116 C7 Iran *38°36'N 45°4'E*
Khyber Pass 118 F9 *Pass* Afghanistan/Pakistan
Kibombo 99 H7 Dem. Rep. Congo *3°52'S 25°59'E*
Kibworth Harcourt 53 H5 England, UK *52°32'N 1°4'W*
Kidderminster 52 F5 England, UK *52°23'N 2°14'W*
Kidlington 50 E7 England, UK *51°48'N 1°26'W*
Kidsgrove 52 F7 England, UK *53°5'N 2°13'W*
Kidwelly 48 D8 Wales, UK *51°44'N 4°24'W*
Kiel 82 E11 Germany *54°21'N 10°5'E*
Kielce 84 G8 Poland *50°53'N 20°39'E*
Kielder 54 F8 England, UK *55°14'N 2°36'W*
Kielder Water 54 F8 ◎ N England, UK
Kieler Bucht 82 F12 *Bay* N Germany
Kiev 89 C5 ● Ukraine *50°26'N 30°32'E*
Kiffa 96 D5 Mauritania *16°38'N 11°23'W*
Kigali 99 I7 ● Rwanda *1°59'S 30°2'E*
Kigoma 99 H7 Tanzania *4°52'S 29°36'E*
Kihniö 68 F8 Finland *62°11'N 23°10'E*
Kiiminki 68 G10 Finland *65°5'N 25°47'E*
Kii-suido 125 H3 *Strait* S Japan
Kikinda 86 G8 Serbia and Montenegro *45°48'N 20°29'E*
Kikwit 98 F7 Dem. Rep. Congo *5°S 18°53'E*
Kilbaha 59 B6 Ireland *52°33'N 9°52'W*
Kilbeggan 58 F8 Ireland *53°21'N 7°30'W*
Kilchoan 57 C7 Scotland, UK *56°43'N 6°2'W*
Kilchu 124 F7 North Korea *40°58'N 129°22'E*
Kilcock 58 G8 Ireland *53°25'N 6°40'W*
Kilcogy 58 F9 Ireland *53°49'N 7°26'W*
Kilcolgan 58 D8 Ireland *53°12'N 9°2'W*
Kilcommon 59 E6 Ireland *52°21'N 7°56'W*
Kilconnell 58 E8 Ireland *53°20'N 8°24'W*
Kilcormac 58 F8 Ireland *53°10'N 7°43'W*
Kildare 58 G8 Ireland *53°10'N 6°55'W*
Kildare 58 G8 ⬖ *County* Ireland
Kildorrery 59 E5 Ireland *52°13'N 8°25'W*
Kilimanjaro 99 J7 ✳ NE Tanzania
Kilis 110 G5 Turkey *36°43'N 37°7'E*
Kilkee 59 C6 Ireland *52°41'N 9°38'W*
Kilkeel 58 H10 Northern Ireland, UK *54°5'N 6°3'W*
Kilkelly 58 D9 Ireland *53°53'N 8°58'W*
Kilkenny 59 F6 Ireland *52°39'N 7°15'W*
Kilkenny 59 F6 ⬖ *County* Ireland
Kilkhampton 49 D5 England, UK *50°53'N 4°32'W*
Kilkinlea 59 C6 Ireland *52°20'N 9°27'W*
Kilkis 87 H4 Greece *40°59'N 22°55'E*
Killagan 58 G12 Northern Ireland, UK *55°2'N 6°20'W*
Killala 58 C10 Ireland *54°13'N 9°21'W*
Killala Bay 58 D10 *Inlet* NW Ireland
Killaloe 59 E7 Ireland *52°47'N 8°34'W*
Killarney 59 C5 Ireland *52°3'N 9°30'W*

Killeany 59 C7 Ireland *53°6'N 9°39'W*
Killeen 58 H10 Northern Ireland, UK *54°6'N 6°29'W*
Killeen 147 I3 Texas, USA *31°7'N 97°44'W*
Killimer 59 C6 Ireland *52°37'N 9°24'W*
Killimor 58 E8 Ireland *53°9'N 8°25'W*
Killin 57 F7 Scotland, UK *56°27'N 4°17'W*
Killmallock 59 D6 Ireland *52°23'N 8°33'W*
Killorglin 59 C5 Ireland *52°6'N 9°54'W*
Killybegs 58 E11 Ireland *54°38'N 8°27'W*
Killyleagh 58 I11 Northern Ireland, UK *54°23'N 5°41'W*
Kilmaine 58 D9 Ireland *53°36'N 9°8'W*
Kilmarnock 57 E5 Scotland, UK *55°37'N 4°30'W*
Kilmartin 57 D6 Scotland, UK *56°9'N 5°32'W*
Kilmona 59 D5 Ireland *51°59'N 8°34'E*
Kilmurvy 59 C7 Ireland *53°8'N 9°55'W*
Kilpisjarvi 68 E12 Finland *69°3'N 20°50'E*
Kilrea 58 G12 Northern Ireland, UK *54°57'N 6°36'W*
Kilrush 59 C6 Ireland *52°39'N 9°29'W*
Kiltealy 59 G6 Ireland *52°33'N 6°44'W*
Kilwa Kivinje 99 J6 Tanzania *8°45'S 39°21'E*
Kilwinning 57 E5 Scotland, UK *55°40'N 4°40'W*
Kimberley 99 H2 South Africa *28°45'S 24°46'E*
Kimberley Plateau 134 F8 *Plateau* Western Australia
Kimch'aek 124 F7 North Korea *40°42'N 129°13'E*
Kimito 69 F6 Finland *60°10'N 22°45'E*
Kinabalu, Gunung 127 I4 ▲ East Malaysia
Kinbrace 56 F11 Scotland, UK *58°16'N 3°53'W*
Kincardine 57 F6 Scotland, UK *56°5'N 3°39'W* .
Kincaslough 58 E12 Ireland *55°1'N 8°24'W*
Kinder Scout 52 G8 ▲ C England, UK
Kindersley 144 F2 Saskatchewan, Canada *51°29'N 109°8'W*
Kindia 96 D4 Guinea *10°12'N 12°26'W*
Kindu 99 H7 Dem. Rep. Congo *2°57'S 25°54'E*
Kineshma 89 E7 Russian Fed. *57°28'N 42°8'E*
King Island 135 J1 *Island* Tasmania, SE Australia
Kingman Reef 128 *US* ◇ Pacific Ocean
Kingsclere 50 E5 England, UK *51°19'N 1°22'W*
Kingscourt 58 G9 Ireland *53°55'N 6°57'W*
King's Lynn 53 K6 England, UK *52°45'N 0°24'E*
King's Nympton 49 E6 England, UK *50°57'N 3°53'W*
King Sound 134 E7 *Sound* Western Australia
King's Sutton 53 H3 England, UK *52°1'N 1°17'W*
Kingston 151 I3 ● Jamaica *17°58'N 76°48'W*
Kingston Bagpuize 50 D6 England, UK *51°40'N 1°28'W*
Kingstone 52 E3 England, UK *52°1'N 2°47'W*
Kingston upon Hull 55 J2 England, UK *53°45'N 0°20'W*
Kingston upon Hull, City of 37 ⬖ *Unitary authority* England, UK
Kingston upon Thames 50 G5 England, UK *51°26'N 0°18'W*
Kingston upon Thames 37 ⬖ *London Borough* England, UK
Kingstown 151 M3 ● Saint Vincent and the Grenadines *13°9'N 61°14'W*
Kingswood 49 H7 England, UK *51°28'N 2°30'W*
Kings Worthy 50 E4 England, UK *51°5'N 1°19'W*
Kington 52 D4 England, UK *52°12'N 3°W*
Kingussie 56 F8 Scotland, UK *57°5'N 4°11'W*
King William Island 144 G5 *Island* Northwest Territories, N Canada Arctic Ocean
Kinlochbervie 56 E12 Scotland, UK *58°28'N 4°58'W*
Kinlocheil 56 D8 Scotland, UK *56°52'N 5°15'W*
Kinnegad 58 G8 Ireland *53°26'N 7°13'W*
Kinnula 68 G9 Finland *63°24'N 25°E*
Kinrooi 71 G7 Belgium *51°9'N 5°48'E*
Kinross 57 G6 Scotland, UK *56°14'N 3°27'W*
Kinsale 59 D4 Ireland *51°42'N 8°32'W*
Kinsalebeg 59 E5 Ireland *51°58'N 7°47'W*
Kinshasa 98 F7 ● Dem. Rep. Congo *4°21'S 15°16'E*
Kintour 57 C5 Scotland, UK *55°41'N 6°3'W*
Kintyre 57 D4 *Coastal feature* W Scotland, UK
Kintyre, Mull of 57 C4 *Headland* W Scotland, UK
Kinvara 59 D7 Ireland *53°7'N 8°55'W*
Kipili 99 I6 Tanzania *7°30'S 30°39'E*
Kippure 58 H8 ▲ E Ireland
Kipushi 99 H5 Dem. Rep. Congo *11°45'S 27°20'E*
Kirghiz Range 117 K8 ▲▲ Kazakhstan/Kyrgyzstan
Kiribati 128 ◆ *Republic* C Pacific Ocean
Kırıkhan 110 G4 Turkey *36°30'N 36°20'E*
Kırıkkale 110 F6 Turkey *39°50'N 33°31'E*
Kirinyaga 99 J8 ✳ C Kenya
Kirishi 88 C8 Russian Fed. *59°28'N 32°2'E*
Kirkbean 57 D3 Scotland, UK *54°55'N 3°36'W*
Kirkbride 54 E6 England, UK *54°54'N 3°19'W*
Kirkburton 55 H2 England, UK *53°37'N 1°43'W*
Kirkby 54 E1 England, UK *53°29'N 2°54'W*
Kirkby in Ashfield 53 H7 England, UK *53°5'N 1°19'W*
Kirkby Lonsdale 54 F4 England, UK *54°12'N 2°38'W*
Kirkby Malham 54 G3 England, UK *54°3'N 2°21'W*
Kirkbymoorside 55 I4 England, UK *54°16'N 1°2'W*
Kirkby Stephen 54 F5 England, UK *54°28'N 2°26'W*
Kirkcaldy 57 G6 Scotland, UK *56°7'N 3°10'W*
Kirkcambeck 54 F7 England, UK *55°1'N 2°44'W*
Kirkconnel 57 F4 Scotland, UK *55°24'N 4°1'W*
Kirkcudbright 57 F3 Scotland, UK *54°50'N 4°3'W*
Kirkenes 68 G13 Norway *69°43'N 30°2'E*
Kirkintilloch 57 F5 Scotland, UK *55°56'N 4°5'W*
Kirkland Lake 145 I2 Ontario, Canada *48°10'N 80°2'W*
Kırklareli 110 C7 Turkey *41°45'N 27°12'E*
Kirklees 55 H2 ⬖ *Unitary authority* England, UK
Kirkmuirhill 57 F5 Scotland, UK *55°41'N 3°53'W*
Kirkpatrick, Mount 166 D4 ▲ Antarctica
Kirksville 147 J6 Missouri, USA *40°12'N 92°35'W*
Kirkūk 111 J4 Iraq *35°28'N 44°26'E*

Kirkwall 56 G13 Scotland, UK *58°59'N 2°58'W*
Kirov 89 F7 Russian Fed. *58°35'N 49°39'E*
Kirov 89 D6 Russian Fed. *54°2'N 34°17'E*
Kirovohrad 89 C4 Ukraine *48°30'N 31°17'E*
Kirriemuir 57 G7 Scotland, UK *56°38'N 3°1'W*
Kirton 53 J6 England, UK *52°56'N 0°8'W*
Kirton in Lindsey 53 I8 England, UK *53°28'N 0°41'W*
Kiruna 68 E11 Sweden *67°50'N 20°16'E*
Kisa 68 D5 Sweden *58°N 15°39'E*
Kisangani 99 H8 Dem. Rep. Congo *0°30'N 25°14'E*
Kiskunfélegyháza 85 F3 Hungary *46°42'N 19°52'E*
Kislovodsk 89 E3 Russian Fed. *43°55'N 42°45'E*
Kismaayo 97 M2 Somalia *0°5'S 42°35'E*
Kissidougou 96 D4 Guinea *9°15'N 10°8'W*
Kissimmee, Lake 147 M3 ◎ Florida, SE USA
Kisumu 99 I8 Kenya *0°2'N 34°42'E*
Kisvárda 85 H5 Hungary *48°13'N 22°3'E*
Kita 96 E5 Mali *13°0'N 9°28'W*
Kitakyushu 125 F3 Japan *33°51'N 130°49'E*
Kitami 125 L8 Japan *43°52'N 143°51'E*
Kitchener 145 I1 Ontario, Canada *43°28'N 80°27'W*
Kitimat 144 D3 British Columbia, Canada *54°5'N 128°38'W*
Kitinen 68 G11 ≈ N Finland
Kitob 117 I7 Uzbekistan *39°6'N 66°47'E*
Kittilä 68 F11 Finland *67°39'N 24°53'E*
Kitwe 99 H5 Zambia *12°48'S 28°13'E*
Kitzbüheler Alpen 83 G5 ▲▲ W Austria
Kivalina 146 B7 Alaska, USA *67°44'N 164°32'W*
Kivalo 68 G10 *Ridge* C Finland
Kivu, Lake 99 H7 ◎ Rwanda/Dem. Rep. Congo
Kladno 85 B7 Czech Republic *50°10'N 14°5'E*
Klagenfurt 83 H4 Austria *46°38'N 14°20'E*
Klaipėda 69 F4 Lithuania *55°42'N 21°9'E*
Klang 126 F4 Malaysia *3°2'N 101°27'E*
Klarälven 69 C7 ≈ Norway/Sweden
Klatovy 85 A6 Czech Republic *49°24'N 13°16'E*
Klazienaveen 70 H11 Netherlands *52°43'N 7°E*
Klimpfjäll 68 D10 Sweden *65°5'N 14°50'E*
Klintsy 89 C6 Russian Fed. *52°46'N 32°21'E*
Kłobuck 84 E8 Poland *50°56'N 18°55'E*
Kłodzko 84 D8 Poland *50°27'N 16°37'E*
Klosters 83 E5 Switzerland *46°54'N 9°52'E*
Kluczbork 84 E8 Poland *50°59'N 18°13'E*
Klyuchevka 117 J8 Kyrgyzstan *42°34'N 71°45'E*
Klyuchevskaya Sopka, Vulkan 109 M6 ✳ E Russian Fed.
Knaresborough 55 H3 England, UK *54°1'N 1°35'W*
Knayton 55 I4 England, UK *54°18'N 1°21'W*
Kneesall 53 H7 England, UK *53°10'N 1°1'W*
Knighton 48 G10 Wales, UK *52°20'N 3°1'W*
Knock 58 D9 Ireland *53°48'N 8°55'W*
Knockadoon Head 59 E4 *Headland* S Ireland
Knockalough 59 C6 Ireland *52°43'N 9°16'W*
Knocktopher 59 F6 Ireland *52°27'N 7°12'W*
Knokke-Heist 70 B8 Belgium *51°21'N 3°19'E*
Knottingley 55 I2 England, UK *53°43'N 1°16'W*
Knowle 52 G5 England, UK *52°22'N 1°43'W*
Knowsley 36 ⬖ *Unitary authority* England, UK
Knoxville 147 L5 Tennessee, USA *35°58'N 83°55'W*
Knud Rasmussen Land 145 H9 *Physical region* N Greenland
Knutsford 52 E8 England, UK *53°18'N 2°21'W*
Kobe 125 H3 Japan *34°40'N 135°10'E*
København *see* Copenhagen
Koblenz 82 D8 Germany *50°21'N 7°36'E*
K'obulet'i 111 I7 Georgia *41°47'N 41°47'E*
Kočevje 83 H4 Slovenia *45°41'N 14°48'E*
Koch Bihar 119 J7 India *26°19'N 89°26'E*
Kochi 125 H3 Japan *33°31'N 133°30'E*
Kodiak 146 B6 Alaska, USA *57°47'N 152°24'W*
Kodiak Island 146 B6 *Island* Alaska, USA
Kofu 125 J4 Japan *35°41'N 138°33'E*
Kogon 117 I7 Uzbekistan *39°47'N 64°29'E*
Kogum-do 124 E3 *Island* S South Korea
Kohima 119 K7 India *25°40'N 94°8'E*
Kohtla-Järve 69 H6 Estonia *59°22'N 27°21'E*
Koidu 96 D4 Sierra Leone *8°40'N 11°1'W*
Koje-do 124 F3 *Island* S South Korea
Kokkola 68 F9 Finland *63°50'N 23°10'E*
Kokrines 146 B7 Alaska, USA *64°58'N 154°42'W*
Kokshaal-Tau 117 L8 ▲▲ China/Kyrgyzstan
Kokshetau 108 F4 Kazakhstan *53°18'N 69°25'E*
Koksijde 71 A7 Belgium *51°7'N 2°40'E*
Koksoak 145 I4 ≈ Québec, E Canada
Kokstad 99 H2 South Africa *30°23'S 29°23'E*
Kolari 68 F11 Finland *67°20'N 23°51'E*
Kolárovo 85 E5 Slovakia *47°54'N 18°1'E*
Kolda 96 D5 Senegal *12°58'N 14°58'W*
Kolding 69 B3 Denmark *55°29'N 9°30'E*
Kolguyev, Ostrov 88 F11 *Island* NW Russian Fed.
Kolhapur 118 F4 India *16°42'N 74°13'E*
Koli 68 H9 Finland *63°6'N 29°46'E*
Kolín 85 C7 Czech Republic *50°2'N 15°10'E*
Kolka 69 G5 Latvia *57°44'N 22°34'E*
Kolkata 119 J6 India *22°30'N 88°20'E*
Köln *see* Cologne
Koło 84 E9 Poland *52°11'N 18°39'E*
Kołobrzeg 84 C12 Poland *54°11'N 15°34'E*
Kolokani 96 E5 Mali *13°35'N 8°1'W*
Kolomna 89 D6 Russian Fed. *55°3'N 38°52'E*
Kolpa 86 D8 ≈ Croatia/Slovenia
Kolpino 88 C8 Russian Fed. *59°44'N 30°39'E*
Kolwezi 99 H6 Dem. Rep. Congo *10°43'S 25°29'E*
Kolyma 109 K7 ≈ NE Russian Fed.
Komárno 85 E5 Slovakia *47°46'N 18°7'E*
Komatsu 125 I4 Japan *36°25'N 136°27'E*
Komoé 96 E4 ≈ E Ivory Coast
Komotiní 87 I5 Greece *41°7'N 25°27'E*
Komsomolets, Ostrov 109 H8 *Island* Severnaya Zemlya, N Russian Fed.
Komsomol'sk-na-Amure 109 L4 Russian Fed. *50°32'N 136°59'E*
Konārak 116 G1 Iran *25°26'N 60°23'E*
Kondopoga 88 D9 Russian Fed. *62°13'N 34°17'E*
Köneürgenç 116 G8 Turkmenistan *42°21'N 59°9'E*
Kong Christian IX Land 145 K7 *Physical region* SE Greenland

◆ Country ● Country capital ◇ Dependent territory ○ Dependent territory capital ⬖ Administrative region ▲ Mountain ▲▲ Mountain range ✳ Volcano ≈ River ◎ Lake ⊠ Reservoir

e 50 F7 England, UK 51°54'N 0°47'W
53 K4 England, UK 52°6'N 0°16'E
123 H5 China 35°34'N 103°8'E
23 J5 China 34°53'N 117°38'E
3 H6 Austria 48°19'N 14°18'E
77 J2 Island Isole Eolie, S Italy
89 E5 Russian Fed. 52°37'N 39°38'E
k 50 F4 England, UK 51°4'N 0°54'W
84 F10 Poland 52°52'N 19°11'E
ký Mikuláš 85 F6 Slovakia
N 19°36'E
I8 Uganda 2°15'N 32°55'E
98 G8 Dem. Rep. Congo 2°10'N 21°29'E
see Lisbon
74 E5 ● Portugal 38°44'N 9°8'W
58 H11 Northern Ireland, UK
'N 6°3'W
58 H11 ⬖ District Northern Ireland, UK
nvarna 59 C7 Ireland 53°1'N 9°17'W
72 F7 France 49°9'N 0°13'E
E5 Russian Fed. 51°0'N 39°36'E
e 59 E5 Ireland 52°10'N 7°10'W
ea 58 F10 Northern Ireland, UK
5'N 7°23'W
'0 D10 Netherlands 52°15'N 4°33'E
el 59 C6 Ireland 52°27'N 9°29'W
122 G4 China 30°3'N 100°12'E
n 53 L6 England, UK 52°44'N 0°47'E
w 135 K3 New South Wales, Australia
0'S 150°9'E
nia 69 G3 ◆ Republic NE Europe
ndaman 119 K3 Island Andaman Islands,
, NE Indian Ocean
arrier Island 136 E7 Island
w Zealand
orough 54 G2 England, UK
9'N 1°59'W
Cayman 151 I4 Island E Cayman Islands
ampton 50 F3 England, UK
8'N 0°33'W
nagua 151 J4 Island S Bahamas
ondon 50 E6 Jamaica 18°15'N 78°13'W
Minch, The 56 B10 Strait NW Scotland, UK
Nicobar 119 L2 Island Nicobar Islands,
, NE Indian Ocean
Ouse 53 K5 ≈ E England, UK
ort 53 K5 England, UK 52°28'N 0°12'E
Rock 147 J4 Arkansas, USA
5'N 92°17'W
Saint Bernard Pass 73 J4 Pass France/Italy
Sandy Desert 134 E5 Desert
tern Australia
u 123 I2 China 24°9'N 108°55'E
ool 145 K2 Nova Scotia, Canada
'N 64°43'W
ool 54 E1 England, UK 53°25'N 2°55'W
ool 36 ⬖ Unitary authority England, UK
ool Bay 52 D8 Bay England/Wales, UK
ston 57 G5 Scotland, UK 55°51'N 3°31'W
stone 99 H4 Zambia 17°51'S 25°48'E
stone Mountains 136 B2 ▲▲ South Island,
Zealand
ki 68 G10 ≈ C Finland
o 76 G6 Italy 43°32'N 10°18'E
49 C3 England, UK 49°58'N 5°14'W
Point 49 C3 Headland SW England, UK
ana 83 H4 ● Slovenia 46°3'N 14°29'E
oy 69 C4 Sweden 56°49'N 13°55'E
l 69 D7 Sweden 61°50'N 16°10'E
n 68 D8 ≈ C Sweden
lhaearn 48 D11 Wales, UK
59'N 4°24'W
th 48 D9 Wales, UK 52°12'N 4°17'W
edr 48 E11 Wales, UK 52°49'N 4°6'W
edrog 48 D11 Wales, UK 52°51'N 4°26'W
eris 48 E12 Wales, UK 53°8'N 4°6'W
ster 48 F10 Wales, UK 52°21'N 3°19'W
rynmair 48 F10 Wales, UK
36'N 3°42'W
eilo 48 E8 Wales, UK 51°52'N 4°W
overy 48 E9 Wales, UK 52°N 3°55'W
rindod Wells 48 F9 Wales, UK
15'N 3°23'W
udno 48 E12 Wales, UK 53°19'N 3°49'W
lli 48 E8 Wales, UK 51°41'N 4°12'W
rchymedd 48 D12 Wales, UK
20'N 4°25'W
s 75 H9 Spain 43°25'N 4°46'W
ir Caereinion 48 F10 Wales, UK
38'N 3°24'W
ir Talhaiarn 48 F12 Wales, UK
14'N 3°38'W
hangel-nant-Melan 48 F9 Wales, UK
12'N 3°14'W
ellin 48 F11 Wales, UK 52°46'N 3°20'W
adfan 48 F11 Wales, UK 52°40'N 3°31'W
adog 48 E8 Wales, UK 51°56'N 3°53'W
efni 48 D12 Wales, UK 53°15'N 4°17'W
ollen 48 F11 Wales, UK 52°58'N 3°10'W
urig 48 F10 Wales, UK 52°24'N 3°36'W
ar 48 E10 Wales, UK 52°22'N 4°1'W
s 160 C11 Physical region Colombia/
ezuela
haeadr-ym-Mochnant 48 F11 Wales, UK
49'N 3°18'W
nystud 48 E9 Wales, UK 52°18'N 4°14'W
wst 48 E12 Wales, UK 53°8'N 3°54'W
teffan 48 D8 Wales, UK 51°46'N 4°23'W
risant 49 F7 Wales, UK 51°33'N 3°21'W
wit Major 49 F7 Wales, UK
24'N 3°29'W
wchllyn 48 F11 Wales, UK
53'N 3°44'W
rtyd Wells 48 F9 Wales, UK
5'N 3°39'W
bydder 48 E9 Wales, UK 52°4'N 4°15'W
a 75 K7 Spain 41°38'N 0°35'E
Peninsula 48 D11 Coastal feature
Wales, UK
ajor 75 M6 Spain 39°29'N 2°53'E
ngwril 48 E11 Wales, UK 52°40'N 4°10'W
Mauna 146 G2 ▲ Hawai'i, USA
tse 99 H3 Botswana 25°11'S 25°40'E
u 82 H8 Germany 51°7'N 14°40'E
o 98 E5 Angola 12°20'S 13°34'E
no 83 D4 Switzerland 46°11'N 8°48'E
albot 56 D8 Scotland, UK 56°52'N 5°37'W
aline 57 D7 Scotland, UK 56°33'N 5°44'W
Lochboisdale 56 A8 Scotland, UK
57°8'N 7°17'W
Lochdon 57 D7 Scotland, UK 56°27'N 5°38'W
Lochearnhead 57 F6 Scotland, UK
56°24'N 4°21'W
Lochem 70 H10 Netherlands 52°10'N 6°25'E
Lochgilphead 57 D6 Scotland, UK
56°2'N 5°27'W
Lochinver 56 D11 Scotland, UK 58°10'N 5°15'W
Lochmaddy 56 B10 Scotland, UK 57°37'N 7°7'W
Lochnagar 56 G8 ▲ C Scotland, UK
Lochranza 57 D5 Scotland, UK 55°43'N 5°18'W
Lochy, Loch 56 E8 ◎ N Scotland, UK
Lockerbie 57 G3 Scotland, UK 55°11'N 3°27'W
Loddon 53 M5 England, UK 52°32'N 1°28'E
Lodja 98 G7 Dem. Rep. Congo 3°29'S 23°25'E
Lodwar 99 J8 Kenya 3°6'N 35°38'E
Łódź 84 F9 Poland 51°51'N 19°26'E
Lofoten 68 D11 Island group C Norway
Logan, Mount 144 C4 ▲ Yukon Territory,
W Canada
Logroño 75 I8 Spain 42°28'N 2°26'W
Loibl Pass 83 H4 Pass Austria/Slovenia
Loimaa 69 F7 Finland 60°51'N 23°3'E
Loire 72 F6 ≈ C France
Loja 160 B9 Ecuador 3°59'S 79°16'W
Lokan Tekojarvi 68 G12 Finland
67°49'N 27°45'E
Lokitaung 99 J9 Kenya 4°15'N 35°45'E
Lokka 68 G11 Finland 67°48'N 27°41'E
Lokoja 96 G4 Nigeria 7°48'N 6°45'E
Lolland 69 B3 Island S Denmark
Lom 87 H6 Bulgaria 43°49'N 23°16'E
Lomami 99 H7 ≈ C Dem. Rep. Congo
Lomas de Zamora 161 E4 Argentina
34°53'S 58°26'W
Lombok, Pulau 127 I1 Island Lesser Sunda
Islands, C Indonesia
Lomé 96 F3 ● Togo 6°8'N 1°13'E
Lomela 98 G7 Dem. Rep. Congo 2°19'S 23°15'E
Lommel 71 F7 Belgium 51°14'N 5°19'E
Lomond, Loch 57 E6 ◎ C Scotland, UK
Łomża 84 H11 Poland 53°11'N 22°04'E
Loncoche 161 C4 Chile 39°22'S 72°34'W
London 145 I1 Ontario, Canada
42°59'N 81°13'W
London 51 H5 ● UK 51°30'N 0°10'W
London, City of 37 ⬖ London Borough
England, UK
Londonderry 58 F12 Northern Ireland, UK
55°N 7°19'W
Londonderry 58 F12 ⬖ District
Northern Ireland, UK
Londonderry, Cape 134 F8 Headland
Western Australia
Londrina 163 H3 Brazil 23°18'S 51°13'W
Long Bay 147 M5 Bay North Carolina/
South Carolina, E USA
Long Beach 146 E4 California, USA
33°46'N 118°11'W
Longbridge 52 F5 England, UK 52°24'N 2°E
Longbridge Deverill 49 H6 England, UK
51°11'N 2°13'W
Long Buckby 53 H4 England, UK 52°17'N 1°9'W
Long Eaton 53 H6 England, UK 52°54'N 1°16'W
Longford 58 F9 Ireland 53°45'N 7°50'W
Longford 58 F9 ⬖ County Ireland
Longframlington 55 H8 England, UK
55°19'N 1°47'W
Longhorsley 55 H8 England, UK
55°14'N 1°54'W
Long Island 151 J5 Island C Bahamas
Long Island 147 N7 Island New York, NE USA
Long Island Sound 147 N7 Sound NE USA
Longlac 145 H2 Ontario, Canada
49°47'N 86°34'W
Long Melford 53 L4 England, UK 52°4'N 0°42'E
Long Preston 54 G3 England, UK
54°1'N 2°25'W
Longreach 135 J6 Queensland, Australia
23°31'S 144°18'E
Longridge 54 F3 England, UK 53°49'N 2°42'W
Long Stratton 53 M5 England, UK
52°29'N 1°13'E
Longton 54 F2 England, UK 53°44'N 2°55'W
Longtown 52 D3 England, UK 51°57'N 2°57'W
Longtown 54 E7 England, UK 55°1'N 2°59'W
Longview 146 D8 Washington, USA
46°8'N 122°56'W
Longyan 123 K3 China 25°6'N 117°2'E
Lons-le-Saunier 73 I5 France 46°41'N 5°32'E
Loop Head 59 B6 Headland W Ireland
Lop Nur 122 F6 ◎ NW China
Loppersum 70 H13 Netherlands
53°20'N 6°45'E
Lorca 75 J4 Spain 37°40'N 1°41'W
Loreto 150 B6 Mexico 25°59'N 111°22'W
Lorient 72 D6 France 47°45'N 3°22'W
Lorn, Firth of 57 C6 Inlet W Scotland, UK
Lörrach 83 D5 Germany 47°38'N 7°40'E
Los 68 D7 Sweden 61°43'N 15°15'E
Los Ángeles 161 C4 Chile 37°30'S 72°18'W
Los Angeles 146 E5 California, USA
34°3'N 118°15'W
Lošinj 86 D7 Island W Croatia
Los Mochis 150 B6 Mexico 25°48'N 108°58'W
Lossiemouth 56 G10 Scotland, UK
57°43'N 3°18'W
Lot 72 G3 Cultural region France
Lot 72 G3 ≈ S France
Lotagipi Swamp 99 I9 Wetland Kenya/Sudan
Louangphabang 126 F7 Laos 19°51'N 102°8'E
Loudéac 72 D6 France 48°11'N 2°45'W
Loudi 123 I3 China 27°51'N 111°59'E
Louga 96 D5 Senegal 15°36'N 16°15'W
Loughborough 53 H6 England, UK
52°47'N 1°11'W
Loughrea 58 D8 Ireland 53°12'N 8°34'W
Louisburgh 58 C9 Ireland 53°45'N 10°W
Louisiana 147 J4 ⬖ State USA
Louisville 147 K6 Kentucky, USA
38°15'N 85°46'W
Louisville Ridge 24 Undersea feature
S Pacific Ocean
Lourdes 72 F2 France 43°6'N 0°3'W
Louth 58 G9 Ireland 53°37'N 6°53'W
Louth 53 J8 England, UK 53°19'N 0°0'E
Louth 58 G9 ⬖ County Ireland
Loutrá 87 H4 Greece 39°55'N 23°37'E
Louvain-la Neuve 71 E6 Belgium
50°39'N 4°36'E
Louviers 72 G7 France 49°13'N 1°11'E
Lövånger 68 F9 Sweden 64°22'N 21°19'E
Lovosice 84 B8 Czech Republic 50°30'N 14°2'E
Lóvua 98 G6 Angola 7°21'S 20°9'E
Lowdham 53 H7 England, UK 53°1'N 1°7'W
Lower California 150 B6 Coastal feature
NW Mexico
Lower Hutt 136 E4 New Zealand
41°13'S 174°51'E
Lower Lough Erne 58 E11 ◎
SW Northern Ireland, UK
Lower Red Lake 147 J8 ◎ Minnesota, N USA
Lowestoft 53 N5 England, UK 52°29'N 1°45'E
Lualaba 99 H7 ≈ SE Dem. Rep. Congo
Luanda 98 E6 ● Angola 8°48'S 13°17'E
Luangwa 99 I5 ≈ Mozambique/Zambia
Luanshya 99 H5 Zambia 13°9'S 28°24'E
Luarca 74 G9 Spain 43°33'N 6°31'W
Lubaczów 85 I7 Poland 50°10'N 23°8'E
Lubań 84 C8 Poland 51°7'N 15°17'E
Lubango 98 E5 Angola 14°55'S 13°33'E
Lübben 82 H9 Germany 51°56'N 13°52'E
Lübbenau 82 H9 Germany 51°52'N 13°57'E
Lubbock 147 H4 Texas, USA 33°35'N 101°51'W
Lübeck 82 F11 Germany 53°52'N 10°41'E
Lubelska, Wyżyna 84 H8 Plateau SE Poland
Lubin 84 D9 Poland 51°23'N 16°12'E
Lublin 84 H8 Poland 51°15'N 22°33'E
Lubliniec 84 E8 Poland 50°41'N 18°41'E
Lubsko 84 C9 Poland 51°47'N 14°57'E
Lubumbashi 99 H5 Dem. Rep. Congo
11°40'S 27°31'E
Lucan 58 G8 Ireland 53°22'N 6°27'W
Lucano, Appennino 77 J4 ▲▲ S Italy
Lucapa 98 G6 Angola 8°24'S 20°42'E
Lucca 76 G7 Italy 43°50'N 10°30'E
Luce Bay 57 E2 Inlet SW Scotland, UK
Lucena 127 J6 Philippines 13°57'N 121°38'E
Lucena 75 H4 Spain 37°25'N 4°29'W
Lučenec 85 F5 Slovakia 48°21'N 19°37'E
Lucknow 119 H7 India 26°50'N 80°54'E
Luda Kamchiya 87 J6 ≈ E Bulgaria
Ludborough 53 J8 England, UK 53°26'N 0°4'W
Lüderitz 98 F3 Namibia 26°38'S 15°10'E
Ludhiana 118 G8 India 30°56'N 75°52'E
Ludlow 52 E5 England, UK 52°20'N 2°28'W
Ludvika 69 D6 Sweden 60°8'N 15°14'E
Ludwigsburg 83 E6 Germany 48°54'N 9°12'E
Ludwigsfelde 82 G9 Germany
52°17'N 13°15'E
Ludwigshafen 83 D7 Germany 49°29'N 8°24'E
Ludwigslust 82 F10 Germany 53°19'N 11°29'E
Ludza 69 H4 Latvia 56°32'N 27°41'E
Luena 98 G5 Angola 11°47'S 19°52'E
Lufira 99 H6 ≈ SE Dem. Rep. Congo
Luga 88 C8 Russian Fed. 58°43'N 29°46'E
Lugano 83 D4 Switzerland 46°1'N 8°57'E
Lugenda, Rio 99 J5 ≈ N Mozambique
Lugnaquillia Mountain 59 G7 ▲ E Ireland
Lugo 74 F9 Spain 43°N 7°33'W
Lugoj 86 G7 Romania 45°41'N 21°56'E
Luhans'k 89 E4 Ukraine 48°32'N 39°21'E
Lukenie 98 G7 ≈ C Dem. Rep. Congo
Łuków 84 H9 Poland 51°57'N 22°22'E
Luleå 68 F10 Sweden 65°35'N 22°10'E
Luleälven 68 F10 ≈ N Sweden
Lulimba 99 H7 Dem. Rep. Congo
4°42'S 28°38'E
Lulonga 98 G8 ≈ NW Dem. Rep. Congo
Lumbo 99 J5 Mozambique 15°S 40°40'E
Lumsden 136 B2 New Zealand
45°43'S 168°26'E
Lund 69 C4 Sweden 55°42'N 13°10'E
Lundy 49 D6 Island SW England, UK
Lune 54 F4 ≈ NW England, UK
Lüneburg 82 F10 Germany 53°15'N 10°25'E
Lungué-Bungo 98 G5 ≈ Angola/Zambia
Lunteren 70 F9 Netherlands 52°5'N 5°38'E
Luoyang 123 I5 China 34°41'N 112°25'E
Lupanshui 123 H3 China 26°38'N 104°49'E
Lurgan 58 H11 Northern Ireland, UK
54°28'N 6°20'W
Lúrio 99 J5 Mozambique 13°32'S 40°34'E
Lúrio, Rio 99 J5 ≈ NE Mozambique
Lusaka 99 H5 ● Zambia 15°24'S 28°17'E
Lut, Dasht-e 116 G3 Desert E Iran
Luton 50 G7 England, UK 51°53'N 0°25'W
Luton 37 ⬖ Unitary authority England, UK
Łutselk'e 144 F4 Northwest Territories, Canada
62°24'N 110°42'W
Luts'k 89 B5 Ukraine 50°45'N 25°23'E
Lutterworth 53 H5 England, UK
52°28'N 1°16'W
Lutzow-Holm Bay 166 E7 Bay Antarctica
Luwego 99 J6 ≈ S Tanzania
Luxborough 49 F6 England, UK
51°7'N 3°29'W
Luxembourg 71 G3 ● Luxembourg
49°37'N 6°8'E
Luxembourg 71 G3 ◆ Monarchy NW Europe
Luxor 97 K7 Egypt 25°39'N 32°39'E
Luza 88 F8 Russian Fed. 60°38'N 47°13'E
Luzern 83 D5 Switzerland 47°3'N 8°17'E
Luzon 127 J6 Island N Philippines
Luzon Strait 123 L1 Strait Philippines/Taiwan
L'viv 89 A5 Ukraine 49°49'N 24°5'E
Lycksele 68 E9 Sweden 64°34'N 18°40'E
Lydd 51 J3 England, UK 50°56'N 0°51'E
Lydford 49 E5 England, UK 50°39'N 4°4'W
Lydham 52 D5 England, UK 52°31'N 3°5'W
Lyepyel' 89 C6 Belarus 54°54'N 28°44'E
Lyme Bay 49 G5 Bay S England, UK
Lyme Regis 49 G5 England, UK
50°44'N 2°56'W
Lymington 50 D2 England, UK 50°45'N 1°34'W
Lympne 51 J4 England, UK 51°3'N 0°55'E
Lyndhurst 50 D3 England, UK 50°51'N 1°35'W
Lyness 56 G13 Scotland, UK 58°50'N 3°16'W
Lynmouth 49 E6 England, UK 51°13'N 3°49'W
Lynton 49 E6 England, UK 51°14'N 3°55'W
Lyon 73 I4 France 45°46'N 4°50'E
Lytham St Anne's 54 E2 England, UK
53°45'N 3°1'W
Lyttelton 136 D3 New Zealand
43°35'S 172°44'E

M

Maamturk Mountains 58 C8 ▲▲ W Ireland
Maanselkä 68 H9 Finland 63°54'N 28°28'E
Maas 58 E11 Ireland 54°50'N 8°22'W
Maaseik 71 G7 Belgium 51°5'N 5°48'E
Maastricht 71 F6 Netherlands 50°51'N 5°42'E
Mablethorpe 53 K8 England, UK
53°21'N 0°14'E
Macaé 163 J3 Brazil 22°21'S 41°48'W
Macapá 163 H8 Brazil 0°4'N 51°4'W
Macclesfield 52 F8 England, UK 53°16'N 2°7'W
Macdonnell Ranges 134 G6 ▲▲ Northern
Territory, C Australia
Macduff 56 H10 Scotland, UK 57°40'N 2°29'W
Macedonia 86 G5 ◆ Republic SE Europe
Maceió 163 L6 Brazil 9°40'S 35°44'W
Macgillycuddy's Reeks 59 B5 ▲▲ SW Ireland
Machala 160 A10 Ecuador 3°20'S 79°57'W
Machanga 99 I4 Mozambique 20°56'S 35°4'E
Machilipatnam 119 H4 India 16°12'N 81°11'E
Machynlleth 48 E10 Wales, UK 52°35'N 3°49'W
Mackay 135 K6 Queensland, Australia
21°10'S 149°10'E
Mackay, Lake 134 F6 Salt lake Northern
Territory/Western Australia
Mackenzie 144 D5 ≈ Northwest Territories,
NW Canada
Mackenzie Bay 166 F6 Bay Antarctica
Mackenzie Mountains 145 D5 ▲▲ Northwest
Territories, NW Canada
Macleod, Lake 134 C5 ◎ Western Australia
Macomer 76 F4 Italy 40°15'N 8°47'E
Mâcon 73 I5 France 46°19'N 4°49'E
Macon 147 L4 Georgia, USA 32°49'N 83°41'W
Macroom 59 D5 Ireland 51°54'N 8°57'W
Macuspana 150 F3 Mexico 17°43'N 92°36'W
Ma'dabā 110 F2 Jordan 31°44'N 35°48'E
Madagascar 99 L4 ◆ Republic W Indian Ocean
Made 70 E8 Netherlands 51°41'N 4°48'E
Madeira, Rio 162 F7 ≈ Bolivia/Brazil
Madeleine, Îles de la 145 K3 Island group
Québec, E Canada
Madhya Pradesh 119 H6 ⬖ State India
Madison 147 K7 Wisconsin, USA
43°4'N 89°22'W
Madiun 127 H1 Indonesia 7°37'S 111°33'E
Madras see Chennai
Madre de Dios, Río 155 ≈ Bolivia/Peru
Madre del Sur, Sierra 150 D3 ▲▲ S Mexico
Madre, Laguna 150 E5 Lagoon NE Mexico
Madre Occidental, Sierra 150 C6 ▲▲ C Mexico
Madre Oriental, Sierra 150 D5 ▲▲ C Mexico
Madrid 75 I6 ● Spain 40°25'N 3°43'W
Madurai 118 G2 India 9°55'N 78°7'E
Madura, Pulau 127 H2 Island C Indonesia
Maebashi 125 J4 Japan 36°24'N 139°2'E
Mae Nam Nan 126 E6 ≈ NW Thailand
Maesteg 49 F7 Wales, UK 51°35'N 3°39'W
Mafa 127 K3 Indonesia 0°1'N 127°50'E
Magadan 109 L6 Russian Fed. 59°38'N 150°50'E
Magdalena 160 D8 Bolivia 13°22'S 64°7'W
Magdalena 150 B7 Mexico 30°38'N 110°59'W
Magdalena, Isla 150 B6 Island W Mexico
Magdalena, Río 155 ≈ C Colombia
Magdeburg 82 F9 Germany 52°8'N 11°39'E
Magee, Island 58 H12 Island
E Northern Ireland, UK
Magelang 126 G1 Indonesia 7°28'S 110°11'E
Magellan, Strait of 161 D1 Strait
Argentina/Chile
Magerøya 68 F14 Island N Norway
Maggiore, Lake 76 F9 ◎ Italy/Switzerland
Maghera 58 G12 Northern Ireland, UK
54°51'N 6°40'W
Magherafelt 58 G11 ⬖ District
Northern Ireland, UK
Maglie 77 L4 Italy 40°7'N 18°18'E
Magnitogorsk 108 E4 Russian Fed.
53°28'N 59°6'E
Magta' Lahjar 96 D5 Mauritania
17°27'N 13°7'W
Mahajanga 99 L5 Madagascar 15°40'S 46°20'E
Mahakam, Sungai 127 I3 ≈ Borneo,
C Indonesia
Mahalapye 99 H3 Botswana 23°2'S 26°53'E
Mahanadi 119 I5 ≈ E India
Maharashtra 118 G5 ⬖ State India
Mahbubnagar 118 G4 India 16°46'N 78°1'E
Mahd adh Dhahab 114 F6 Saudi Arabia
23°33'N 40°56'E
Mahia Peninsula 136 F5 Coastal feature
North Island, New Zealand
Mahilyow 89 C6 Belarus 53°55'N 30°23'E
Mahmud-e Raqi 117 J5 Afghanistan
35°1'N 69°20'E
Mahón 75 N6 Spain 39°54'N 4°15'E
Maidenhead 50 F5 England, UK
51°32'N 0°44'W
Maidens, The 58 H12 Island group E Northern
Ireland, UK
Maidstone 51 I4 England, UK 51°17'N 0°31'E
Maiduguri 97 H4 Nigeria 11°51'N 13°10'E
Main 83 E7 ≈ C Germany
Mai-Ndombe, Lac 98 F7 ◎ W Dem. Rep. Congo
Maine 147 N8 ⬖ State USA
Maine 72 F6 Cultural region France
Maine, Gulf of 147 N8 Gulf NE USA
Mainz 83 D7 Germany 50°0'N 8°16'E
Maizhokunggar 122 E4 China
29°50'N 91°40'E
Majorca 75 M6 Island Islas Baleares, Spain,
W Mediterranean Sea
Majuro 128 ● Marshall Islands 7°6'N 171°23'E
Makassar Strait 127 I2 Strait C Indonesia
Makay 99 K4 ▲▲ SW Madagascar
Makeni 96 D4 Sierra Leone 8°57'N 12°2'W
Makhachkala 89 F2 Russian Fed.
42°58'N 47°30'E
Makkovik 145 J4 Newfoundland and Labrador,
Canada 55°6'N 59°7'W
Makó 85 G3 Hungary 46°14'N 20°28'E
Makoua 98 F8 Congo 0°1'S 15°40'E
Makran Coast 116 G1 Physical region SE Iran
Makrany 89 A5 Belarus 51°50'N 24°15'E
Makurdi 96 G4 Nigeria 7°42'N 8°36'E
Malabo 96 G3 ● Equatorial Guinea
3°43'N 8°52'E
Malacca, Strait of 126 F4 Strait
Indonesia/Malaysia
Malacky 85 D5 Slovakia 48°26'N 17°1'E
Maladyechna 89 B6 Belarus 54°19'N 26°51'E
Málaga 75 H3 Spain 36°43'N 4°25'W
Malahide 58 H8 Ireland 53°27'N 6°9'W
Malakal 97 K4 Sudan 9°31'N 31°40'E
Malang 127 H1 Indonesia 7°59'S 112°45'E
Malanje 98 F6 Angola 9°34'S 16°25'E
Mälaren 69 E6 ◎ C Sweden
Malatya 110 G5 Turkey 38°22'N 38°18'E
Malawi 99 I5 ◆ Republic S Africa
Malāyer 116 D5 Iran 34°20'N 48°47'E
Malay Peninsula 126 F4 Coastal feature
Malaysia/Thailand
Malaysia 126 F4 ◆ Monarchy SE Asia
Malbork 84 F11 Poland 54°1'N 19°3'E
Malchin 82 G11 Germany 53°43'N 12°46'E
Maldives 118 F1 ◆ Republic N Indian Ocean
Maldon 51 I6 England, UK 51°44'N 0°40'E
Male' 118 F1 ● Maldives 4°10'N 73°29'E
Malheur Lake 146 E7 ◎ Oregon, NW USA
Mali 96 F6 ◆ Republic W Africa
Mali Kyun 126 E5 Island Mergui Archipelago,
S Burma
Malin 58 F13 Ireland 55°18'N 7°15'W
Malindi 99 J7 Kenya 3°14'S 40°5'E
Malin Head 58 F13 Headland NW Ireland
Malin More 58 D11 Ireland 54°41'N 9°W
Mallaig 56 D8 Scotland, UK 57°4'N 5°48'W
Mallow 59 D5 Ireland 52°8'N 8°39'W
Mallwyd 48 F11 Wales, UK 52°41'N 3°41'W
Malmberget 68 E11 Sweden 67°9'N 20°39'E
Malmédy 71 G5 Belgium 50°26'N 6°2'E
Malmö 69 C3 Sweden 55°36'N 13°E
Małopolska 84 G8 Plateau S Poland
Malozemel'skaya Tundra 88 F11 Physical region
NW Russian Fed.
Malpas 52 E7 England, UK 53°1'N 2°51'W
Malta 79 H4 ◆ Republic C Mediterranean Sea
Malta Channel 77 J1 Strait Italy/Malta
Maltby le Marsh 53 K8 England, UK
53°18'N 0°7'E
Malton 55 J4 England, UK 54°7'N 0°50'W
Malung 69 D7 Sweden 60°40'N 13°45'E
Malvern Hills 52 E4 Hill range W England, UK
Mamberamo, Sungai 127 M2 ≈ Irian Jaya,
E Indonesia
Mamonovo 69 F3 Russian Fed. 54°28'N 19°57'E
Mamoré, Rio 160 D8 ≈ Bolivia/Brazil
Mamoudzou 99 K5 ○ Mayotte 12°48'S 45°E
Mamuno 98 G3 Botswana 22°15'S 20°2'E
Manacor 75 M6 Spain 39°35'N 3°12'E
Manado 127 J3 Indonesia 1°32'N 124°55'E
Managua 150 G2 ● Nicaragua 12°8'N 86°15'W
Managua, Lake 150 G2 ◎ W Nicaragua
Manakara 99 L3 Madagascar 22°9'S 48°E
Manama 115 I7 ● Bahrain 26°13'N 50°33'E
Mananjary 99 L4 Madagascar 21°13'S 48°20'E
Manapouri, Lake 136 B2 ◎ South Island,
New Zealand
Manas, Gora 117 J8 ▲ Kyrgyzstan/Uzbekistan
Manaus 162 F7 Brazil 3°6'S 60°W
Manavgat 110 E5 Turkey 36°47'N 31°28'E
Manbij 110 G5 Syria 36°32'N 37°55'E
Manchester 54 G1 England, UK 53°30'N 2°15'W
Manchester 147 N7 New Hampshire, USA
42°59'N 71°26'W
Manchester 36 ⬖ Unitary authority England, UK
Mandalay 126 E7 Burma 21°57'N 96°4'E
Mandalī 111 J3 Iraq 33°43'N 45°33'E
Mand, Rud-e 116 E2 ≈ S Iran
Mandurah 134 D3 Western Australia
32°31'S 115°41'E
Manduria 77 K4 Italy 40°24'N 17°38'E
Mandya 118 G3 India 12°34'N 76°55'E
Manfredonia 77 J5 Italy 41°38'N 15°54'E
Mangai 98 F7 Dem. Rep. Congo 3°58'S 19°32'E
Mangalore 118 F3 India 12°54'N 74°51'E
Mangerton Mountain 59 C5 ▲ SW Ireland
Mangoky 99 K3 ≈ W Madagascar
Mangotsfield 49 H7 England, UK
51°29'N 2°38'W
Manicoré 162 F7 Brazil 5°48'S 61°16'W
Manicouagan, Réservoir 145 J3 ◎ Québec,
E Canada
Manila 127 J6 ● Philippines 14°34'N 120°59'E
Manipur 119 K7 ⬖ State India
Manisa 110 C6 Turkey 38°36'N 27°29'E
Manitoba 144 G3 ⬖ Province Canada
Manitoba, Lake 144 G2 ◎ Manitoba, S Canada
Manizales 160 B11 Colombia 5°3'N 73°52'W
Manjimup 134 D2 Western Australia
34°18'S 116°14'E
Manlleu 75 L8 Spain 41°59'N 2°17'E
Manmad 118 F5 India 20°15'N 74°29'E
Mannar 119 H2 Sri Lanka 9°1'N 79°53'E
Mannar, Gulf of 119 H2 Gulf India/Sri Lanka
Mannheim 83 D7 Germany 49°29'N 8°29'E
Manningtree 51 J7 England, UK 51°55'N 1°1'E
Manono 99 H6 Dem. Rep. Congo
7°18'S 27°25'E
Manorhamilton 58 E10 Ireland 54°18'N 8°10'W
Manosque 73 I3 France 43°50'N 5°47'E
Mansa 99 H6 Zambia 11°14'S 28°55'E
Mansel Island 145 H4 Island Northwest
Territories, NE Canada
Mansfield 53 H7 England, UK 53°9'N 1°11'W
Mansidão 163 J5 Brazil 10°46'S 44°4'W
Mantiqueira, Serra da 163 J3 ▲▲ S Brazil
Mantova 76 G8 Italy 45°10'N 10°47'E
Mäntsälä 69 G7 Finland 60°38'N 25°21'E
Mäntyharju 69 H7 Finland 61°25'N 26°53'E
Manuel Zinho 162 H6 Brazil 7°21'S 54°47'W
Manurewa 136 E7 New Zealand
37°1'S 174°55'E
Manzanares 75 I5 Spain 39°N 3°23'W
Manzanillo 151 I4 Cuba 20°21'N 77°7'W
Manzanillo 150 C4 Mexico 19°0'N 104°19'W
Manzhouli 123 J8 China 49°36'N 117°28'E
Mao 97 H5 Chad 14°6'N 15°17'E
Maoke, Pegunungan 127 M2 ▲▲ Irian Jaya,
E Indonesia
Maoming 123 I2 China 21°46'N 110°51'E
Maputo 99 I3 ● Mozambique 25°58'S 32°35'E

◆ Country ● Country capital ◇ Dependent territory ○ Dependent territory capital ⬖ Administrative region ▲ Mountain ▲▲ Mountain range Volcano ≈ River ◎ Lake Reservoir

182 Marabá - Mopti

Marabá 163 I7 Brazil 5°23'S 49°10'W
Maracaibo 160 C12 Venezuela 10°40'N 71°39'W
Maracá, Ilha de 163 I8 Island NE Brazil
Maracaju, Serra de 162 G3 ▲▲ S Brazil
Maracanaquará, Planalto 163 H8 ▲▲ NE Brazil
Maradah 97 I7 Libya 29°16'N 19°29'E
Maradi 96 G5 Niger 13°30'N 7°5'E
Marāgheh 116 C6 Iran 37°21'N 46°14'E
Marajó, Baía de 163 I8 Bay N Brazil
Marajó, Ilha de 163 I8 Island N Brazil
Maranhão 163 J7 ⬖ State Brazil
Marañón, Río 160 B9 ≈ N Peru
Marathon 145 H2 Ontario, Canada 48°44'N 86°23'W
Maraza 111 K7 Azerbaijan 40°31'N 48°55'E
Marazion 49 B3 England, UK 50°7'N 5°25'W
Marbella 75 H3 Spain 36°31'N 4°50'W
Marble Bar 134 D6 Western Australia 21°13'S 119°48'E
Marburg an der Lahn 82 E8 Germany 50°49'N 8°46'E
March 53 J5 England, UK 52°37'N 0°13'E
Marche 72 G5 Cultural region France
Marche 77 I6 Cultural region Italy
Marche-en-Famenne 71 F4 Belgium 50°13'N 5°21'E
Mar Chiquita, Laguna 161 D5 ◎ C Argentina
Mardan 118 F9 Pakistan 34°14'N 71°59'E
Mar del Plata 161 E4 Argentina 38°S 57°32'W
Mardin 111 H5 Turkey 37°19'N 40°43'E
Mareeba 135 K7 Queensland, Australia 17°3'S 145°30'E
Maree, Loch 56 D10 ◎ N Scotland, UK
Margarita, Isla de 160 D12 Island N Venezuela
Margate 51 K5 England, UK 51°24'N 1°24'E
Margow, Dasht-e 117 H3 Desert SW Afghanistan
Maria Island 135 J1 Island Tasmania, SE Australia
Mariana Islands 25 Island group Guam/Northern Mariana Islands
Mariana Trench 25 Undersea feature W Pacific Ocean
Mariánské Lázně 85 A7 Czech Republic 49°57'N 12°43'E
Mar'ib 115 H2 Yemen 15°28'N 45°25'E
Maribor 83 I4 Slovenia 46°34'N 15°40'E
Marie Byrd Land 166 C4 Physical region Antarctica
Mariental 98 F3 Namibia 24°35'S 17°56'E
Mariestad 69 D5 Sweden 58°42'N 13°50'E
Marijampolė 69 G3 Lithuania 54°33'N 23°21'E
Marília 163 I3 Brazil 22°13'S 49°58'W
Marín 74 E8 Spain 42°23'N 8°43'W
Maringá 163 H3 Brazil 23°26'S 51°55'W
Mariscal Estigarribia 161 E6 Paraguay 22°3'S 60°39'W
Maritsa 87 I5 ≈ SW Europe
Mariupol' 89 D4 Ukraine 47°6'N 37°34'E
Marka 97 M3 Somalia 1°43'N 44°45'E
Market Deeping 53 J6 England, UK 52°41'N 0°19'W
Market Drayton 52 E6 England, UK 52°55'N 2°34'W
Market Harborough 53 H5 England, UK 52°30'N 0°57'W
Market Rasen 53 I8 England, UK 53°23'N 0°21'W
Market Weighton 55 J3 England, UK 53°51'N 0°41'W
Markham, Mount 166 D4 ▲ Antarctica
Markounda 97 I4 Central African Republic 7°38'N 17°0'E
Marktredwitz 83 F7 Germany 50°N 12°4'E
Marlborough 49 I7 England, UK 51°25'N 1°45'W
Marlow 50 F6 England, UK 51°34'N 0°53'W
Marmande 72 F3 France 44°30'N 0°10'E
Marmaris 110 C5 Turkey 36°52'N 28°17'E
Marne 73 H7 Cultural region France
Marne 73 I7 ≈ N France
Maroantsetra 99 L5 Madagascar 15°23'S 49°44'E
Maromokotro 99 L5 ▲ N Madagascar
Maroua 97 H4 Cameroon 10°35'N 14°20'E
Marquesas Islands 24 Island group N French Polynesia
Marrakech 96 E8 Morocco 31°39'N 7°58'W
Marrawah 135 J1 Tasmania, Australia 40°56'S 144°41'E
Marree 135 I4 South Australia 29°40'S 138°6'E
Marsabit 99 J8 Kenya 2°20'N 37°59'E
Marsala 77 H2 Italy 37°48'N 12°26'E
Marsberg 82 E9 Germany 51°28'N 8°51'E
Marsden 54 G2 England, UK 53°36'N 1°57'W
Marseille 73 I2 France 43°19'N 5°22'E
Mar, Serra do 163 I2 ▲▲ S Brazil
Marshall Islands 128 ◆ Republic W Pacific Ocean
Marshchapel 53 J8 England, UK 53°29'N 0°1'E
Marsh Harbour 151 I5 Bahamas 26°31'N 77°3'W
Marston Magna 49 H6 England, UK 51°1'N 2°36'W
Martigues 73 I2 France 43°24'N 5°3'E
Martin 85 F6 Slovakia 49°3'N 18°54'E
Martinique 151 M4 French ◇ West Indies
Martinique Passage 151 M4 Channel Dominica/Martinique
Marton 136 E5 New Zealand 40°5'S 175°22'E
Marton 53 I8 England, UK 53°20'N 0°46'W
Marton 55 H4 England, UK 54°4'N 1°24'W
Martos 75 I4 Spain 37°44'N 3°58'W
Martti 68 G11 Finland 67°28'N 28°20'E
Mary 117 H6 Turkmenistan 37°25'N 61°48'E
Maryborough 135 L5 Queensland, Australia 25°32'S 152°36'E
Maryland 147 M6 ⬖ State USA
Maryport 54 D6 England, UK 54°45'N 3°28'W
Masan 124 F4 South Korea 35°11'N 128°36'E
Masasi 99 J6 Tanzania 10°43'S 38°48'E
Masaya 150 G2 Nicaragua 11°59'N 86°6'W
Maseru 99 H2 ● Lesotho 29°21'S 27°35'E
Masham 55 H4 England, UK 54°13'N 1°41'W
Mashhad 116 G5 Iran 36°16'N 59°34'E
Masindi 99 I8 Uganda 1°41'N 31°45'E
Mask, Lough 58 C9 ◎ W Ireland
Masqat see Muscat
Massa 76 G7 Italy 44°2'N 10°7'E
Massachusetts 147 N7 ⬖ State USA
Massawa 97 L5 Eritrea 15°37'N 39°27'E
Massif Central 73 H4 Plateau C France
Masterton 136 E4 New Zealand 40°56'S 175°40'E
Masuda 124 G3 Japan 34°40'N 131°50'E
Masvingo 99 I4 Zimbabwe 20°5'S 30°50'E
Matadi 98 E7 Dem. Rep. Congo 5°49'S 13°31'E
Matagalpa 150 G2 Nicaragua 12°53'N 85°56'W
Matale 119 H1 Sri Lanka 7°29'N 80°38'E
Matamata 136 E6 New Zealand 37°49'S 175°45'E
Matamoros 150 D5 Mexico 25°34'N 103°13'W
Matanzas 151 H5 Cuba 23°N 81°32'W
Matara 119 H1 Sri Lanka 5°58'N 80°33'E
Mataram 127 I1 Indonesia 8°36'S 116°7'E
Mataró 75 M8 Spain 41°32'N 2°27'E
Mataura 136 B1 New Zealand 46°12'S 168°53'E
Matera 77 K4 Italy 40°39'N 16°35'E
Mátészalka 85 H5 Hungary 47°58'N 22°17'E
Matlock 52 G7 England, UK 53°8'N 1°32'W
Mato Grosso 162 F5 Brazil 14°53'S 59°58'W
Mato Grosso 162 G5 ⬖ State Brazil
Mato Grosso do Sul 163 H3 ⬖ State Brazil
Matosinhos 74 E7 Portugal 41°11'N 8°42'W
Maţraḩ 115 L6 Oman 23°35'N 58°31'E
Matsue 124 G4 Japan 35°27'N 133°4'E
Matsumoto 125 J4 Japan 36°18'N 137°58'E
Matsuyama 124 G3 Japan 33°50'N 132°47'E
Matterhorn 83 D4 ▲ Italy/Switzerland
Matthew Town 151 J4 Bahamas 20°56'N 73°41'W
Maturín 160 D12 Venezuela 9°45'N 63°10'W
Mau 119 I7 India 25°57'N 83°33'E
Maui 146 G2 Island Hawai'i, USA, C Pacific Ocean
Maun 98 G4 Botswana 20°1'S 23°28'E
Mauritania 96 D6 ◆ Republic W Africa
Mauritius 99 M4 ◆ Republic W Indian Ocean
Mayaguana Passage 151 J5 Passage SE Bahamas
Mayagüez 151 K4 Puerto Rico 18°12'N 67°8'W
Maybole 57 E4 Scotland, UK 55°22'N 4°40'W
Maydan Shahr 117 J5 Afghanistan 34°27'N 68°48'E
Mayfield 136 C3 New Zealand 43°50'S 171°24'E
May, Isle of 57 H6 Island E Scotland, UK
Maykop 89 E3 Russian Fed. 44°36'N 40°7'E
Maymyo 126 E7 Burma 22°3'N 96°30'E
Mayo 58 C9 ⬖ County Ireland
Mayor Island 136 E7 Island NE New Zealand
Mayotte 99 K5 French ◇ Africa
Mazabuka 99 H5 Zambia 15°52'S 27°46'E
Mazar-e Sharif 117 I6 Afghanistan 36°44'N 67°6'E
Mazatlán 150 C5 Mexico 23°15'N 106°24'W
Mažeikiai 69 G4 Lithuania 56°19'N 22°22'E
Mazury 84 G11 Physical region NE Poland
Mazyr 89 B5 Belarus 52°4'N 29°15'E
Mbabane 99 I3 ● Swaziland 26°24'S 31°13'E
Mbala 99 I6 Zambia 8°50'S 31°23'E
Mbale 99 I8 Uganda 1°4'N 34°12'E
Mbandaka 98 F8 Dem. Rep. Congo 0°7'N 18°12'E
M'Banza Congo 98 E7 Angola 6°11'S 14°16'E
Mbanza-Ngungu 98 F7 Dem. Rep. Congo 5°19'S 14°45'E
Mbarara 99 I8 Uganda 0°36'S 30°40'E
Mbeya 99 I6 Tanzania 8°54'S 33°29'E
Mbuji-Mayi 98 G7 Dem. Rep. Congo 6°5'S 23°30'E
McAllen 147 I2 Texas, USA 26°12'N 98°14'W
McClintock Channel 144 F6 Channel Northwest Territories, N Canada
McCook 147 H6 Nebraska, USA 40°12'N 100°38'W
McKinley, Mount 146 B7 ▲ Alaska, USA
McKinley Park 146 B7 Alaska, USA 63°42'N 149°1'W
Mdantsane 99 H1 South Africa 32°55'S 27°39'E
Meath 58 G9 ⬖ County Ireland
Mecca 114 E5 Saudi Arabia 21°28'N 39°50'E
Mechelen 71 D7 Belgium 51°2'N 4°29'E
Mecklenburger Bucht 82 F11 Bay N Germany
Mecsek 85 E3 ▲▲ SW Hungary
Medan 126 E4 Indonesia 3°35'N 98°39'E
Medellín 160 B11 Colombia 6°15'N 75°36'W
Mediaş 87 H8 Romania 46°10'N 24°20'E
Medicine Hat 144 E2 Alberta, Canada 50°3'N 110°41'W
Medina 114 E6 Saudi Arabia 24°25'N 39°29'E
Medinaceli 75 I7 Spain 41°10'N 2°26'W
Medina del Campo 75 H7 Spain 41°18'N 4°55'W
Medininkai 68 H3 Lithuania 54°32'N 25°40'E
Mediterranean Sea 78 F5 Sea Africa/Asia/Europe
Médoc 72 E4 Cultural region France
Medvezh'yegorsk 88 D9 Russian Fed. 62°56'N 34°26'E
Medway 37 ⬖ Unitary authority England, UK
Medway 51 I4 ≈ SE England, UK
Meekatharra 134 D5 Western Australia 26°37'S 118°35'E
Meerssen 71 G6 Netherlands 50°53'N 5°45'E
Meerut 118 G7 India 29°1'N 77°41'E
Meghālaya 119 J7 ⬖ State India
Meharry, Mount 134 D5 ▲ Western Australia
Mehtarlam 117 J5 Afghanistan 34°39'N 70°10'E
Mejillones 161 C6 Chile 23°3'S 70°25'W
Mek'ele 97 L5 Ethiopia 13°36'N 39°29'E
Mekong 126 G6 ≈ SE Asia
Mekong, Mouths of the 126 G5 Delta S Vietnam
Melaka 126 F3 Malaysia 2°14'N 102°14'E
Melbourne 135 J2 Victoria, Australia 37°51'S 144°56'E
Melbourne 52 G6 England, UK 52°49'N 1°23'W
Meldreth 53 J4 England, UK 52°5'N 0°5'W
Melghir, Chott 96 G8 Salt lake E Algeria
Melilla 96 F8 Spain 35°18'N 2°56'W
Melita 144 G2 Manitoba, Canada 49°16'N 100°59'W
Melitopol' 89 D4 Ukraine 46°49'N 35°23'E
Melle 71 C7 Belgium 51°N 3°48'E
Melleray, Mount 59 E5 ▲ S Ireland
Mellerud 69 C5 Sweden 58°42'N 12°27'E
Melling 54 F4 England, UK 54°8'N 2°38'W
Mellizo Sur, Cerro 161 C2 ▲ S Chile
Melmerby 54 F6 England, UK 54°43'N 2°33'W
Melo 161 F5 Uruguay 32°22'S 54°10'W
Melsungen 82 E8 Germany 51°8'N 9°33'E
Meltaus 68 G11 Finland 66°54'N 25°18'E
Melton Mowbray 53 H6 England, UK 52°46'N 1°4'W
Melun 72 G7 France 48°32'N 2°40'E
Melville Island 134 G9 Island Northern Territory, N Australia
Melville Island 144 F7 Island Parry Islands, Northwest Territories, NW Canada
Melville, Lake 145 K4 ◎ Newfoundland and Labrador, E Canada
Melville Peninsula 145 H5 Coastal feature Northwest Territories, NE Canada
Memmingen 83 E6 Germany 47°59'N 10°11'E
Memphis 147 K5 Tennessee, USA 35°9'N 90°3'W
Menai Bridge 48 E12 Wales, UK 53°14'N 4°17'W
Menai Strait 48 E12 Strait NW Wales, UK
Ménaka 96 F5 Mali 15°55'N 2°25'E
Menaldum 70 F12 Netherlands 53°14'N 5°38'E
Mende 73 H3 France 44°32'N 3°30'E
Mendip Hills 49 G7 Hill range S England, UK
Mendocino, Cape 146 D7 Headland California, W USA
Mendocino Fracture Zone 24 Undersea feature NE Pacific Ocean
Mendoza 161 C5 Argentina 33°0'S 68°47'W
Menemen 110 C6 Turkey 38°34'N 27°3'E
Menengiyn Tal 123 J8 Plain E Mongolia
Menongue 98 F5 Angola 14°38'S 17°39'E
Mentawai, Kepulauan 126 E2 Island group W Indonesia
Menzies, Mount 166 F6 ▲ Antarctica
Meophan 51 I5 England, UK 51°21'N 0°21'E
Meppel 70 G11 Netherlands 52°42'N 6°12'E
Merano 76 G9 Italy 46°40'N 11°10'E
Mercedes 161 E5 Argentina 29°9'S 58°5'W
Mere 49 H6 England, UK 51°5'N 2°18'W
Mergui 126 E5 Burma 12°26'N 98°34'E
Mérida 150 F4 Mexico 20°58'N 89°35'W
Mérida 74 G5 Spain 38°55'N 6°20'W
Mérida 160 C12 Venezuela 8°36'N 71°8'W
Mérignac 72 F4 France 44°50'N 0°40'W
Merikarvia 69 F7 Finland 61°51'N 21°30'E
Merredin 134 D3 Western Australia 31°31'S 118°18'E
Merrick 57 E3 ▲ S Scotland, UK
Mersey 52 D8 ≈ NW England, UK
Mersin 110 F5 Turkey 36°50'N 34°39'E
Merthyr Tydfil 48 F8 Wales, UK 51°46'N 3°23'W
Merthyr Tydfil 37 ⬖ Unitary authority Wales, UK
Merton 49 E5 England, UK 50°53'N 4°10'W
Merton 50 G5 England, UK 51°23'N 0°14'W
Merton 37 ⬖ London Borough England, UK
Meru 99 J8 Kenya 0°3'N 37°38'E
Merzifon 110 F7 Turkey 40°52'N 35°28'E
Merzig 83 C7 Germany 49°27'N 6°39'E
Mesa 146 F4 Arizona, USA 33°25'N 111°49'W
Messalo, Rio 99 J5 ≈ NE Mozambique
Messina 77 J2 Italy 38°12'N 15°33'E
Messina 99 I3 South Africa 22°18'S 30°2'E
Messingham 53 I8 England, UK 53°32'N 0°49'W
Mestia 111 I8 Georgia 43°3'N 42°50'E
Mestre 77 H8 Italy 45°30'N 12°14'E
Mestre, Espig˜ao 163 J5 ▲▲ E Brazil
Metairie 147 K3 Louisiana, USA 29°58'N 90°9'W
Meta, Río 160 C11 ≈ Colombia/Venezuela
Methven 57 G7 Scotland, UK 56°25'N 3°38'W
Metsovo 86 G4 Greece 39°47'N 21°12'E
Metz 73 I7 France 49°7'N 6°9'E
Meulaboh 126 E4 Indonesia 4°10'N 96°9'E
Mevagissey 49 D4 England, UK 50°17'N 4°43'W
Mexborough 53 H8 England, UK 53°29'N 1°25'W
Mexicali 150 A7 Mexico 32°34'N 115°26'W
Mexico 150 C5 ◆ Federal republic N Central America
Mexico City 150 D4 ● Mexico 19°26'N 99°8'W
Mexico, Gulf of 150 F5 Gulf W Atlantic Ocean
Meymaneh 117 I5 Afghanistan 35°57'N 64°48'E
Meymeh 116 D4 Iran 33°29'N 51°9'E
Mezen' 88 F10 ≈ NW Russian Fed.
Mezőtúr 85 G4 Hungary 47°N 20°37'E
Miami 147 M2 Florida, USA 25°46'N 80°12'W
Miami Beach 147 M2 Florida, USA 25°47'N 80°8'W
Mianyang 123 H4 China 31°29'N 104°43'E
Miastko 84 D11 Poland 54°N 16°58'E
Michalovce 85 H6 Slovakia 48°46'N 21°55'E
Michelderver 50 E4 England, UK 51°9'N 1°17'W
Michigan 147 K7 ⬖ State USA
Michigan, Lake 147 K7 ◎ N USA
Michurinsk 89 E6 Russian Fed. 52°56'N 40°31'E
Micronesia 128 ◆ Federation W Pacific Ocean
Mid-Atlantic Ridge 24 Undersea feature Atlantic Ocean
Middelburg 70 C8 Netherlands 51°30'N 3°36'E
Middelharnis 70 D9 Netherlands 51°45'N 4°10'E
Middelkerke 71 B7 Belgium 51°12'N 2°51'E
Middle America Trench 24 Undersea feature E Pacific Ocean
Middle Andaman 119 K3 Island Andaman Islands, India, NE Indian Ocean
Middleham 54 G4 England, UK 54°17'N 1°58'W
Middlesbrough 55 I5 England, UK 54°35'N 1°14'W
Middlesbrough 37 ⬖ Unitary authority England, UK
Middleton 53 K6 England, UK 52°43'N 0°27'E
Middleton 54 G2 England, UK 53°33'N 2°13'W
Middleton in Teesdale 54 G5 England, UK 54°37'N 2°11'W
Middleton-on-the-Wolds 55 J3 England, UK 53°55'N 0°38'W
Middletown 48 G11 Wales, UK 52°43'N 2°58'W
Middle Wallop 50 D4 England, UK 51°7'N 1°36'W
Middlewich 52 E7 England, UK 53°10'N 2°29'W
Midhurst 50 F3 England, UK 50°58'N 0°50'W
Mid-Indian Ridge 25 Undersea feature C Indian Ocean
Midland 147 H4 Texas, USA 32°N 102°5'W
Midleton 59 E5 Ireland 51°55'N 8°10'W
Midlothian 36 ⬖ Unitary authority Scotland, UK
Mid-Pacific Mountains 25 Undersea feature NW Pacific Ocean
Midsomer Norton 49 H7 England, UK 51°16'N 2°32'W
Midway Islands 12 US ◇ Pacific Ocean
Miechów 85 F7 Poland 50°21'N 20°1'E
Międzyrzec Podlaski 84 H9 Poland 52°N 22°47'E
Międzyrzecz 84 C10 Poland 52°26'N 15°33'E
Mielec 85 G7 Poland 50°18'N 21°27'E
Miercurea-Ciuc 87 I8 Romania 46°24'N 25°48'E
Mieres del Camino 74 G9 Spain 43°15'N 5°46'W
Miguel Asua 150 C5 Mexico 24°17'N 103°29'W
Mijdrecht 70 E10 Netherlands 52°12'N 4°52'E
Mikhaylovka 89 E5 Russian Fed. 50°6'N 43°17'E
Mikun' 88 F9 Russian Fed. 62°20'N 50°2'E
Mikura-jima 125 J3 Island E Japan
Milan 76 F8 Italy 45°28'N 9°10'E
Milano see Milan
Milas 110 C5 Turkey 37°17'N 27°46'E
Mildenhall 53 K4 England, UK 52°20'N 0°30'E
Mildura 135 I3 Victoria, Australia 34°13'S 142°9'E
Miles 135 K4 Queensland, Australia 26°41'S 150°15'E
Milestone 59 E6 Ireland 52°39'N 8°10'W
Milford 50 F4 England, UK 51°10'N 0°39'W
Milford Haven 48 C8 Wales, UK 51°44'N 5°2'W
Milford Haven 48 C8 Inlet SW Wales, UK
Milford Sound 136 B2 New Zealand 44°41'S 167°57'E
Mil'kovo 109 M6 Russian Fed. 54°40'N 158°35'E
Milk River 146 G8 ≈ Montana, NW USA
Milk, Wadi el 97 K5 ≈ C Sudan
Mille Lacs Lake 147 J7 ◎ Minnesota, N USA
Millerovo 89 E4 Russian Fed. 48°57'N 40°26'E
Millford 58 F12 Ireland 55°7'N 7°43'W
Milos 87 H2 Island Cyclades, Greece, Aegean Sea
Milovaig 56 B9 Scotland, UK 57°26'N 6°42'W
Milton 136 C1 New Zealand 46°8'S 169°59'E
Milton Ernest 50 G8 England, UK 52°11'N 0°30'W
Milton Keynes 50 F7 England, UK 52°N 0°43'W
Milton Keynes 37 ⬖ Unitary authority England, UK
Milwaukee 147 K7 Wisconsin, USA 43°3'N 87°56'W
Minas Gerais 163 J4 ⬖ State Brazil
Minatitlán 150 E3 Mexico 17°59'N 94°32'W
Minbu 126 E7 Burma 20°9'N 94°52'E
Minch, The 56 D11 Strait NW Scotland, UK
Mindanao 127 K4 Island S Philippines
Mindelheim 83 F6 Germany 48°3'N 10°30'E
Minden 82 E10 Germany 52°18'N 8°55'E
Mindoro Strait 127 I5 Strait W Philippines
Minehead 49 F6 England, UK 51°13'N 3°29'W
Mingacevir 111 K7 Azerbaijan 40°46'N 47°2'E
Mingaora 118 F9 Pakistan 34°47'N 72°22'E
Mingulay 56 A8 Island NW Scotland, UK
Minicoy Island 118 F2 Island SW India
Minna 96 G4 Nigeria 9°33'N 6°33'E
Minneapolis 147 J7 Minnesota, USA 44°59'N 93°16'W
Minnesota 147 J7 ⬖ State USA
Minorca 75 N6 Island Islas Baleares, Spain, W Mediterranean Sea
Minsk 89 B6 ● Belarus 53°52'N 27°34'E
Minster 51 J5 England, UK 51°25'N 0°48'E
Minsterley 52 D5 England, UK 52°38'N 2°59'W
Mintlaw 56 I9 Scotland, UK 57°32'N 1°57'W
Minto, Lac 145 I3 ◎ Québec, C Canada
Minto, Mount 166 D3 ▲ Antarctica
Minwakh 115 I3 Yemen 16°55'N 48°4'E
Miraflores 150 B5 Mexico 23°24'N 109°45'W
Miranda de Ebro 75 I8 Spain 42°41'N 2°57'W
Mirbāţ 115 K3 Oman 17°3'N 54°44'E
Miri 127 H4 Malaysia 4°23'N 113°59'E
Mirim Lagoon 163 H1 Lagoon Brazil/Uruguay
Mirjaveh 117 H3 Iran 29°1'N 61°24'E
Mirnyy 109 I5 Russian Fed. 62°30'N 113°58'E
Mirpur Khas 118 E6 Pakistan 25°31'N 69°1'E
Miskitos, Cayos 151 H2 Island group NE Nicaragua
Miskolc 85 G5 Hungary 48°5'N 20°46'E
Misratah 97 H8 Libya 32°23'N 15°6'E
Missão Catrimani 162 F8 Brazil 1°26'N 62°5'W
Mississippi 147 K4 ⬖ State USA
Mississippi River 147 K5 ≈ C USA
Mississippi Delta 147 K3 Delta Louisiana, S USA
Missoula 146 F8 Montana, USA 46°54'N 114°3'W
Missouri 147 J5 ⬖ State USA
Missouri River 146 G8 ≈ C USA
Mistassini, Lac 145 I2 ◎ Québec, SE Canada
Mistelbach an der Zaya 83 I6 Austria 48°34'N 16°33'E
Misterton 53 H8 England, UK 53°26'N 0°59'W
Misti, Volcán 161 C7 ⅄ S Peru
Mitcheldean 48 H8 England, UK 51°51'N 2°38'W
Mitchell 135 K5 Queensland, Australia 26°29'S 148°0'E
Mitchell 135 J8 ≈ Queensland, NE Australia
Mitchell, Mount 147 L5 ▲ North Carolina, SE USA
Mitchell River 135 J8 ≈ Queensland, NE Australia
Mitchelstown 59 E5 Ireland 52°20'N 8°16'W
Mito 125 K4 Japan 36°21'N 140°26'E
Mitú 160 C10 Colombia 1°7'N 70°5'W
Miyako 125 K6 Japan 39°39'N 141°57'E
Miyakonojo 124 G2 Japan 31°42'N 131°4'E
Miyazaki 124 G2 Japan 31°55'N 131°24'E
Mizen Head 59 B3 Headland SW Ireland
Mizoram 119 K6 ⬖ State India
Mizpe Ramon 110 A2 Israel 30°38'N 34°47'E
Mjøsa 69 C7 ◎ S Norway
Mława 84 F10 Poland 53°7'N 20°23'E
Mljet 86 E6 Island S Croatia
Moa Island 135 J9 Island Queensland, NE Australia
Moanda 98 E7 Gabon 1°31'S 13°7'E
Moate 58 F8 Ireland 53°23'N 7°48'W
Moba 99 H6 Dem. Rep. Congo 7°3'S 29°52'E
Mobile 147 K3 Alabama, USA 30°42'N 88°3'W
Mochudi 99 H3 Botswana 24°25'S 26°7'E
Mocímboa da Praia 99 J6 Mozambique 11°17'S 40°21'E
Môco 98 F5 ▲ W Angola
Mocuba 99 J4 Mozambique 16°50'S 37°2
Modbury 49 E4 England, UK 50°22'N 3°
Modena 76 G7 Italy 44°39'N 10°55'E
Modesto 146 D6 California, USA 37°38'N 121°2'W
Modica 77 J1 Italy 36°52'N 14°45'E
Moe 135 J2 Victoria, Australia 38°11'S 14
Moelfre 48 E12 Wales, UK 53°21'N 4°14'
Moelfre 48 F10 Hill E Wales, UK
Moffat 57 G4 Scotland, UK 55°29'N 3°36
Mogadishu 97 M3 ● Somalia 2°6'N 45°2
Mogilno 84 E10 Poland 52°39'N 17°58'E
Mohács 85 E3 Hungary 46°N 18°40'E
Mohe 123 J9 China 53°0'N 122°34'E
Mohoro 99 J6 Tanzania 8°9'S 39°10'E
Moi 69 A5 Norway 58°27'N 6°32'E
Mo i Rana 68 D10 Norway 66°19'N 14°1
Mõisaküla 69 G5 Estonia 58°5'N 25°12'E
Moissac 72 G3 France 44°7'N 1°5'E
Mojácar 75 J3 Spain 37°9'N 1°50'W
Mojave Desert 146 E5 Plain California, W
Mokp'o 124 E4 South Korea 34°50'N 126
Mol 71 E7 Belgium 51°11'N 5°7'E
Mold 48 F12 Wales, UK 53°10'N 3°8'W
Molde 68 B8 Norway 62°44'N 7°8'E
Moldo-Too, Khrebet 117 K8 ▲▲ C Kyrgyz
Moldova 89 B4 ◆ Republic SE Europe
Molfetta 77 K5 Italy 41°12'N 16°35'E
Mölndal 69 C5 Sweden 57°39'N 12°5'E
Moloka'i 146 F2 Island Hawaiian Islands, Hawai'i, USA
Molopo 98 G3 ≈ Botswana/South Africa
Moluccas 127 J2 Island group E Indonesia
Molucca Sea 127 J3 Sea E Indonesia
Mombasa 99 J7 Kenya 4°4'N 39°40'E
Møn 69 C3 Island SE Denmark
Monach Islands 56 A9 Island group NW Scotland, UK
Monaco 73 J3 ● Monaco 43°46'N 7°23'E
Monaco 73 J3 ◆ Monarchy W Europe
Monadhliath Mountains 56 F9 ▲▲ N Scotland, UK
Monaghan 58 G10 Ireland 54°15'N 6°58'
Monaghan 58 G10 ⬖ County Ireland
Monasterevin 59 G7 Ireland 53°8'N 7°3'
Monbetsu 125 K9 Japan 44°23'N 143°22'
Moncalieri 76 E8 Italy 45°N 7°41'E
Monchegorsk 88 D11 Russian Fed. 67°56'N 32°47'E
Monclova 150 D6 Mexico 26°55'N 101°2
Moncton 145 K2 New Brunswick, Canada 46°4'N 64°50'W
Mondovi 76 E7 Italy 44°23'N 7°56'E
Moneygall 59 E7 Ireland 52°52'N 7°57'W
Moneymore 58 G11 Northern Ireland, UK 54°43'N 6°45'W
Monfalcone 77 I8 Italy 45°49'N 13°32'E
Monforte 74 F8 Spain 42°32'N 7°30'W
Mongo 97 I4 Chad 12°12'N 18°40'E
Mongolia 123 H7 ◆ Republic E Asia
Mongu 98 G5 Zambia 15°13'S 23°9'E
Monkey Bay 99 I5 Malawi 14°9'S 34°53'E
Monmouth 48 G8 Wales, UK 51°50'N 2°4
Monmouthshire 48 G8 ⬖ Unitary authorit Wales, UK
Monóvar 75 K5 Spain 38°26'N 0°50'W
Monroe 147 J4 Louisiana, USA 32°32'N 92
Monrovia 96 D3 ● Liberia 6°18'N 10°48'W
Mons 71 C5 Belgium 50°28'N 3°58'E
Monselice 77 H8 Italy 45°15'N 11°47'E
Montana 87 H6 Bulgaria 43°25'N 23°14'E
Montana 146 G8 ⬖ State USA
Montargis 72 G6 France 48°N 2°44'E
Montauban 72 G3 France 44°1'N 1°20'E
Montbéliard 73 J6 France 47°31'N 6°49'E
Mont Cenis, Col du 73 J4 Pass E France
Mont-de-Marsan 72 F3 France 43°54'N 0°
Monteagudo 161 D7 Bolivia 19°48'S 63°5
Monte Caseros 161 E5 Argentina 30°15'S 57°39'W
Monte Cristi 151 J4 Dominican Republic 19°52'N 71°39'W
Monte Cristo 162 E7 Brazil 3°14'S 68°0'W
Montego Bay 151 I4 Jamaica 18°28'N 77°
Montélimar 73 I3 France 44°33'N 4°45'E
Montemorelos 150 D5 Mexico 25°10'N 99°52'W
Montenegro 86 F6 ⬖ Republic Serbia and Montenegro
Monterey Bay 146 D6 Bay California, W U
Montería 160 B12 Colombia 8°45'N 75°54
Montero 161 D7 Bolivia 17°20'S 63°15'W
Monterrey 150 D5 Mexico 25°41'N 100°1
Monte Santo 163 K6 Brazil 10°25'S 39°18
Montes Claros 163 J4 Brazil 16°45'S 43°52
Montevideo 161 E4 ● Uruguay 34°55'S 56°10'W
Montgenèvre, Col de 73 J4 Pass France/It
Montgomery 48 F10 Wales, UK 52°38'N 3
Montgomery 147 L4 Alabama, USA 32°22'N 86°18'W
Monthey 83 C4 Switzerland 46°15'N 6°56'
Montluçon 72 G5 France 46°21'N 2°37'E
Montoro 75 H4 Spain 38°0'N 4°21'W
Montpelier 147 N8 Vermont, USA 44°16'N 72°32'W
Montpellier 73 H3 France 43°37'N 3°52'E
Montréal 145 J2 Québec, Canada 45°30'N 73°36'W
Montrose 57 H7 Scotland, UK 56°43'N 2°2
Montserrat 151 M4 UK ◇ West Indies
Monywa 126 E7 Burma 22°5'N 95°12'E
Monza 76 F8 Italy 45°35'N 9°16'E
Monze 99 H5 Zambia 16°20'S 27°29'E
Monzón 75 K8 Spain 41°54'N 0°12'E
Moonie 135 K4 Queensland, Australia 27°46'S 150°22'E
Moora 134 D3 Western Australia 30°23'S 116°5'E
Moore, Lake 134 C5 ◎ Western Australia
Moose 145 I2 ≈ Ontario, S Canada
Moosehead Lake 147 N8 ◎ Maine, NE US
Moosonee 145 I2 Ontario, Canada 51°18'N 80°40'W
Mopti 96 E5 Mali 14°30'N 4°15'W

◆ Country ● Country capital ◇ Dependent territory ○ Dependent territory capital ⬖ Administrative region ▲ Mountain ▲▲ Mountain range ⅄ Volcano ≈ River ◎ Lake ⊠ Reservoir

184 Nola - Pančevo

Nola 97 I3 Central African Republic 3°29'N 16°5'E
Nolinsk 89 F7 Russian Fed. 57°35'N 49°54'E
Noord-Beveland 70 C8 *Island* SW Netherlands
Noordwijk aan Zee 70 D10 Netherlands 52°15'N 4°25'E
Noormarkku 69 F7 Finland 61°35'N 21°54'E
Nora 69 D6 Sweden 59°31'N 15°2'E
Norak 117 J6 Tajikistan 38°23'N 69°14'E
Norden 82 D11 Germany 53°36'N 7°12'E
Norderstedt 82 E11 Germany 53°42'N 9°59'E
Nordfjordeid 68 A8 Norway 61°54'N 6°E
Nordhausen 82 F9 Germany 51°31'N 10°48'E
Nordhorn 82 D10 Germany 52°26'N 7°4'E
Nore 59 F6 ≈ S Ireland
Norfolk 147 M6 Virginia, USA 36°51'N 76°17'W
Norfolk 53 L6 ◈ *County* England, UK
Norfolk Island 128 *Australian* ◇ Pacific Ocean
Norham 54 G9 England, UK 55°43'N 2°7'W
Noril'sk 109 H6 Russian Fed. 69°21'N 88°2'E
Norman 147 I4 Oklahoma, USA 35°13'N 97°27'W
Normandy 72 F7 *Cultural region* France
Normanton 135 J7 Queensland, Australia 17°49'S 141°8'E
Normanton 55 H2 England, UK 53°42'N 1°34'W
Norrköping 69 D5 Sweden 58°35'N 16°10'E
Norrtälje 69 E6 Sweden 59°46'N 18°42'E
Norseman 134 E3 Western Australia 32°16'S 121°46'E
Northallerton 55 H5 England, UK 54°20'N 1°26'W
Northam 134 D3 Western Australia 31°40'S 116°40'E
North America 139 *Continent*
North American Basin 24 *Undersea feature* W Sargasso Sea
Northampton 53 H4 England, UK 52°14'N 0°54'W
Northamptonshire 53 I5 ◈ *County* England, UK
North Andaman 119 K3 *Island* Andaman Islands, India, NE Indian Ocean
North Ayrshire 57 D4 ◈ *Unitary authority* Scotland, UK
North Bay 145 I2 Ontario, Canada 46°20'N 79°28'W
North Berwick 57 H6 Scotland, UK 56°4'N 2°44'W
North Cape 136 D8 *Headland* North Island, New Zealand
North Cape 68 G14 *Headland* N Norway
North Carolina 147 M5 ◈ *State* USA
North Channel 57 C4 *Strait* Northern Ireland/ Scotland, UK
North Dakota 147 H8 ◈ *State* USA
North Down 51 H5 ◈ *District* Northern Ireland, UK
North East Lincolnshire 37 ◈ *Unitary authority* England, UK
Northeim 82 E9 Germany 51°42'N 10°E
Northern Ireland 58 G11 ◈ *Political division* UK
Northern Mariana Islands 128 *US* ◇ Pacific Ocean
Northern Territory 135 H7 ◈ *Territory* Australia
North Esk 56 H8 ≈ E Scotland, UK
North Foreland 51 K5 *Headland* SE England, UK
North Frisian Islands 82 E12 *Island group* N Germany
North Grimston 55 J4 England, UK 54°5'N 0°44'W
North Hill 49 D4 England, UK 50°33'N 4°29'W
North Island 136 E7 *Island* N New Zealand
North Korea 124 E6 ◆ *Republic* E Asia
North Lanarkshire 36 ◈ *Unitary authority* Scotland, UK
Northleach 48 I8 England, UK 51°48'N 1°49'W
North Lincolnshire 53 I9 ◈ *Unitary authority* England, UK
North Little Rock 147 J4 Arkansas, USA 34°46'N 92°15'W
North Platte River 147 H6 ≈ C USA
North Pole 168 D5 Arctic Ocean
North Ronaldsay 56 H14 *Island* NE Scotland, UK
North Saskatchewan 144 F2 ≈ Alberta/ Saskatchewan, S Canada
North Sea 61 *Sea* NW Europe
North Somerset 49 G7 ◈ *Unitary authority* England, UK
North Sound 58 C8 *Sound* W Ireland
North Sound, The 56 H14 *Sound* N Scotland, UK
North Sunderland 55 H9 England, UK 55°34'N 1°36'W
North Taranaki Bight 136 D6 *Gulf* North Island, New Zealand
North Tidworth 50 D4 England, UK 51°14'N 1°45'W
North Tyne 54 F7 ≈ N England, UK
North Tyneside 36 ◈ *Unitary authority* England, UK
North Uist 56 A10 *Island* NW Scotland, UK
Northumberland 54 G7 ◈ *County* England, UK
Northwest Cape 134 C6 *Headland* Saint Lawrence Island, Alaska, USA
North West Highlands 56 D9 ▲▲ N Scotland, UK
Northwest Pacific Basin 25 *Undersea feature* NW Pacific Ocean
Northwest Territories 144 E4 ◈ *Territory* Canada
Northwich 52 E8 England, UK 53°16'N 2°32'W
Northwold 53 K5 England, UK 52°32'N 0°35'E
North York Moors 55 I5 *Heathland* N England, UK
North Yorkshire 55 H4 ◈ *County* England, UK
Norton Fitzwarren 49 G6 England, UK 51°2'N 3°9'W
Norway 68 B8 ◆ *Monarchy* N Europe
Norwegian Sea 61 *Sea* NE Atlantic Ocean
Norwich 53 M5 England, UK 52°38'N 1°18'E
Noshiro 125 J6 Japan 40°11'N 140°2'E
Noşratābād 116 G3 Iran 29°53'N 59°57'E
Nossob 98 G3 ≈ E Namibia
Noteć 84 D10 ≈ NW Poland
Nottingham 53 H7 England, UK 52°58'N 1°10'W
Nottingham, City of 37 ◈ *Unitary authority* England, UK
Nottinghamshire 53 H7 ◈ *County* England, UK
Nouâdhibou 96 D6 Mauritania 20°54'N 17°1'W
Nouakchott 96 D5 ● Mauritania 18°9'N 15°58'W
Nová Bystřice 85 C6 Czech Republic 49°N 15°5'E
Nova Gorica 83 G4 Slovenia 45°57'N 13°40'E
Nova Iguaçu 163 J3 Brazil 22°31'S 44°5'W
Novara 76 F8 Italy 45°27'N 8°36'E
Nova Scotia 145 K2 ◈ *Province* Canada
Novaya Sibir', Ostrov 109 J8 *Island* Novosibirskiye Ostrova, NE Russian Fed.
Novaya Zemlya 88 G13 *Island group* N Russian Fed.
Novgorod 89 C7 Russian Fed. 58°32'N 31°15'E
Novi Sad 86 F7 Serbia and Montenegro 45°16'N 19°49'E
Novo Airão 162 F8 Brazil 2°6'S 61°20'W
Novocheboksarsk 89 F7 Russian Fed. 56°7'N 47°33'E
Novocherkassk 89 E4 Russian Fed. 47°23'N 40°E
Novodvinsk 88 E9 Russian Fed. 64°22'N 40°49'E
Novo Hamburgo 163 H1 Brazil 29°42'S 51°7'W
Novokazalinsk 108 E3 Kazakhstan 45°53'N 62°10'E
Novokuznetsk 108 G4 Russian Fed. 53°45'N 87°12'E
Novo Mesto 83 H4 Slovenia 45°49'N 15°9'E
Novomoskovsk 89 D6 Russian Fed. 54°5'N 38°23'E
Novorossiysk 89 D3 Russian Fed. 44°50'N 37°38'E
Novoshakhtinsk 89 E4 Russian Fed. 47°48'N 39°51'E
Novosibirsk 108 G4 Russian Fed. 55°4'N 83°5'E
Novotroitsk 89 H5 Russian Fed. 51°10'N 58°18'E
Nowa Sól 84 C9 Poland 51°47'N 15°43'E
Nowe 84 E11 Poland 53°40'N 18°44'E
Nowogard 84 C11 Poland 53°41'N 15°9'E
Nowy Dwór Gdański 84 F12 Poland 54°12'N 19°3'E
Nowy Dwór Mazowiecki 84 G10 Poland 52°26'N 20°43'E
Nowy Sącz 85 G7 Poland 49°36'N 20°42'E
Nowy Tomyśl 84 D10 Poland 52°18'N 16°7'E
Noyon 73 H8 France 49°35'N 3°E
Ntomba, Lac 98 F8 ◎ NW Dem. Rep. Congo
Nubian Desert 97 K6 *Desert* NE Sudan
Nueva Gerona 151 H4 Cuba 21°49'N 82°49'W
Nueva Rosita 150 D6 Mexico 27°58'N 101°11'W
Nuevo Casas Grandes 150 C7 Mexico 30°23'N 107°54'W
Nuevo, Golfo 161 D3 *Gulf* S Argentina
Nuevo Laredo 150 D6 Mexico 27°28'N 99°32'W
Nuku'alofa 128 ● Tonga 21°8'S 175°13'W
Nukus 116 G8 Uzbekistan 42°29'N 59°32'E
Nullarbor Plain 134 F3 *Plateau* South Australia/ Western Australia
Nunavut 144 F5 ◈ *Territory* Canada
Nuneaton 52 G5 England, UK 52°32'N 1°28'W
Nunivak Island 146 B6 *Island* Alaska, USA
Nunspeet 70 F10 Netherlands 52°21'N 5°45'E
Nuoro 76 F4 Italy 40°20'N 9°20'E
Nūrābād 116 D3 Iran 30°8'N 51°30'E
Nuremberg 83 F7 Germany 49°27'N 11°5'E
Nurmes 68 H9 Finland 63°31'N 29°10'E
Nürnberg *see* Nuremberg
Nurota 117 I7 Uzbekistan 40°41'N 65°43'E
Nusaybin 111 I5 Turkey 37°8'N 41°11'E
Nuuk 145 I6 ○ Greenland 64°15'N 51°35'W
Nyagan' 108 F5 Russian Fed. 62°10'N 65°32'E
Nyainqêntanglha Shan 122 F4 ▲▲ W China
Nyala 97 J4 Sudan 12°1'N 24°50'E
Nyamtumbo 99 J6 Tanzania 10°33'S 36°8'E
Nyandoma 88 E8 Russian Fed. 61°39'N 40°10'E
Nyantakara 99 I7 Tanzania 3°5'S 31°23'E
Nyasa, Lake 99 I5 ◎ E Africa
Nybro 68 D4 Sweden 56°45'N 15°54'E
Nyeri 99 J8 Kenya 0°25'S 36°56'E
Nyima 122 E4 China 31°53'N 87°51'E
Nyíregyháza 85 H5 Hungary 47°57'N 21°43'E
Nykarleby 68 F9 Finland 63°22'N 22°30'E
Nykøbing 69 C3 Denmark 54°47'N 11°53'E
Nyköping 69 E5 Sweden 58°45'N 17°3'E
Nylstroom 99 H3 South Africa 24°39'S 28°24'E
Nyngan 135 K3 New South Wales, Australia 31°36'S 147°7'E
Nysa 84 D8 Poland 50°28'N 17°20'E
Nyurba 109 I5 Russian Fed. 63°17'N 118°15'E
Nzega 99 I7 Tanzania 4°13'S 33°11'E
Nzérékoré 96 E4 Guinea 7°45'N 8°49'W
N'Zeto 98 E6 Angola 7°14'S 12°52'E

O

O'ahu 146 F2 *Island* Hawaiian Islands, Hawai'i, USA
Oakengates 52 E6 England, UK 52°41'N 2°20'W
Oakford 49 F6 England, UK 50°59'N 3°39'W
Oakham 53 I5 England, UK 52°41'N 0°45'W
Oakland 146 D6 California, USA 37°48'N 122°16'W
Oamaru 136 C2 New Zealand 45°10'S 170°51'E
Oa, Mull of 57 C4 *Headland* W Scotland, UK
Oaxaca 150 E3 Mexico 17°4'N 96°41'W
Ob' 108 F5 ≈ C Russian Fed.
Oban 57 D7 Scotland, UK 56°25'N 5°29'W
Óbidos 162 G8 Brazil 1°52'S 55°30'W
Obihiro 125 K8 Japan 42°56'N 143°10'E
Obo 97 J3 Central African Republic 5°20'N 26°29'E
Oborniki 84 D10 Poland 52°38'N 16°48'E
Ocaña 75 I6 Spain 39°57'N 3°30'W
O Carballiño 74 F8 Spain 42°26'N 8°5'W
Occidental, Cordillera 155 ▲▲ Bolivia/Chile
Ocean Falls 144 D3 British Columbia, Canada 52°24'N 127°42'W
Oceanside 146 E4 California, USA 33°12'N 117°23'W
Och'amch'ire 111 H8 Georgia 42°45'N 41°30'E
Ochil Hills 57 G6 ▲▲ C Scotland, UK
Ochiltree 57 E4 Scotland, UK 55°28'N 4°26'W
Ocotal 150 G2 Nicaragua 13°38'N 86°28'W
Odate 125 K6 Japan 40°18'N 140°34'E
Odda 69 A7 Norway 60°3'N 6°34'E
Ödemiş 110 C5 Turkey 38°11'N 27°58'E
Odense 69 B3 Denmark 55°24'N 10°23'E
Oder 84 E8 ≈ C Europe
Odesa 89 C4 Ukraine 46°29'N 30°44'E
Odessa 147 H4 Texas, USA 31°51'N 102°22'W
Odienné 96 E4 Ivory Coast 9°32'N 7°35'W
Odiham 50 F4 England, UK 51°14'N 1°2'W
Odoorn 70 H12 Netherlands 52°52'N 6°49'E
Of 111 H7 Turkey 40°57'N 40°17'E
Ofanto 77 J4 ≈ S Italy
Offaly 58 F8 ◈ *County* Ireland
Offenbach 82 E8 Germany 50°6'N 8°46'E
Offenburg 83 D6 Germany 48°28'N 7°57'E
Ogaden 97 M4 *Plateau* Ethiopia/Somalia
Ogaki 125 I4 Japan 35°22'N 136°35'E
Ogden 146 F6 Utah, USA 41°9'N 111°58'W
Ohio 147 L6 ◈ *State* USA
Ohio River 147 K5 ≈ N USA
Ohrid, Lake 86 G4 ◎ Albania/Macedonia
Ohura 136 E6 New Zealand 38°51'S 174°58'E
Oiapoque 163 H9 Brazil 3°54'N 51°46'W
Oijärvi 68 G10 Finland 65°38'N 26°5'E
Oirschot 70 F8 Netherlands 51°30'N 5°18'E
Oise 73 H8 ≈ N France
Oita 124 G3 Japan 33°15'N 131°35'E
Ojinaga 150 C6 Mexico 29°31'N 104°26'W
Ojos del Salado, Cerro 161 C5 ▲ W Argentina
Okaihau 136 D8 New Zealand 35°19'S 173°45'E
Okara 118 F8 Pakistan 30°49'N 73°31'E
Okavango 98 G4 ≈ S Africa *see also* Cubango
Okavango Delta 98 G4 *Wetland* N Botswana
Okayama 125 H3 Japan 34°40'N 133°54'E
Okazaki 125 I4 Japan 34°58'N 137°10'E
Okeechobee, Lake 147 M3 ◎ Florida, SE USA
Okehampton 49 E5 England, UK 50°44'N 4°W
Okhotsk 109 K6 Russian Fed. 59°21'N 143°15'E
Okhotsk, Sea of 109 L5 *Sea* NW Pacific Ocean
Okhtyrka 89 D5 Ukraine 50°19'N 34°54'E
Oki-shoto 124 G4 *Island group* SW Japan
Oklahoma 147 I4 ◈ *State* USA
Oklahoma City 147 I5 Oklahoma, USA 35°28'N 97°31'W
Oko, Wadi 97 L6 ≈ NE Sudan
Okushiri-to 125 J7 *Island* NE Japan
Öland 69 D4 *Island* S Sweden
Olavarría 161 E4 Argentina 36°57'S 60°20'W
Oława 84 D8 Poland 50°57'N 17°18'E
Olbia 76 F4 Italy 40°55'N 9°30'E
Oldbury 52 F5 England, UK 52°30'N 2°E
Oldcastle 58 F9 Ireland 53°45'N 7°10'W
Oldebroek 70 G10 Netherlands 52°27'N 5°54'E
Oldenburg 82 D10 Germany 53°9'N 8°13'E
Oldenburg 82 F11 Germany 54°17'N 10°55'E
Oldenzaal 70 H10 Netherlands 52°19'N 6°53'E
Oldham 54 G2 England, UK 53°36'N 2°W
Oldham 36 ◈ *Unitary authority* England, UK
Old Head of Kinsale 59 D4 *Headland* SW Ireland
Olëkminsk 109 J5 Russian Fed. 60°25'N 120°25'E
Olenegorsk 88 D11 Russian Fed. 68°6'N 33°15'E
Olenek 109 I6 Russian Fed. 68°28'N 112°18'E
Oléron, Île d' 72 E5 *Island* W France
Oleśnica 84 D8 Poland 51°13'N 17°20'E
Olgiy 122 F8 Mongolia 48°57'N 89°59'E
Olhão 74 F3 Portugal 37°1'N 7°50'W
Olhava 68 G10 Finland 65°28'N 25°25'E
Olifa 98 F4 Namibia 17°25'S 14°27'E
Olinda 163 L6 Brazil 8°S 34°51'W
Oliva 75 K5 Spain 38°55'N 0°9'W
Olivet 72 G6 France 47°53'N 1°53'E
Ollerton 53 H7 England, UK 53°12'N 1°4'W
Olmaliq 117 J7 Uzbekistan 40°51'N 69°39'E
Olofström 68 D4 Sweden 56°16'N 14°33'E
Olomouc 85 D7 Czech Republic 49°36'N 17°13'E
Olonets 88 D8 Russian Fed. 60°58'N 33°1'E
Olovyannaya 109 J4 Russian Fed. 50°59'N 115°24'E
Olpe 82 D8 Germany 51°2'N 7°51'E
Olsztyn 84 G11 Poland 53°46'N 20°28'E
Olsztynek 84 F11 Poland 53°35'N 20°17'E
Olt 87 H6 ≈ S Romania
Olvera 75 H3 Spain 36°56'N 5°15'W
Olympia 146 E8 Washington, USA 47°2'N 122°54'W
Omagh 58 F11 Northern Ireland, UK 54°36'N 7°18'W
Omagh 58 F11 ◈ *District* Northern Ireland, UK
Omaha 147 I6 Nebraska, USA 41°14'N 95°57'W
Oman 115 L4 ◆ *Monarchy* SW Asia
Oman, Gulf of 115 M6 *Gulf* N Arabian Sea
Omboué 98 E7 Gabon 1°38'S 9°20'E
Omdurman 97 K5 Sudan 15°37'N 32°29'E
Ometepe, Isla de 150 G2 *Island* S Nicaragua
Ommen 70 H11 Netherlands 52°31'N 6°25'E
Omsk 108 F4 Russian Fed. 55°N 73°22'E
Omuta 124 F2 Japan 33°1'N 130°27'E
Onda 75 K6 Spain 39°58'N 0°17'W
Ondorhaan 123 I8 Mongolia 47°21'N 110°42'E
Onega 88 D9 Russian Fed. 63°54'N 37°59'E
Onega 88 E9 ≈ NW Russian Fed.
Onex 83 C4 Switzerland 46°12'N 6°4'E
Ongjin 124 D5 North Korea 37°56'N 125°22'E
Onon Gol 123 I8 ≈ N Mongolia
Onslow 134 C6 Western Australia 21°42'S 115°8'E
Onslow Bay 147 M5 *Bay* North Carolina, E USA
Ontario 145 H2 ◈ *Province* Canada
Ontario, Lake 145 I1 ◎ Canada/USA
Ontario Peninsula 145 H2 *Coastal feature* Canada/USA
Ontinyent 75 K5 Spain 38°49'N 0°37'W
Oostakker 71 C7 Belgium 51°6'N 3°46'E
Oostburg 71 C7 Netherlands 51°20'N 3°30'E
Oostende *see* Ostend
Oosterbeek 70 G9 Netherlands 51°59'N 5°51'E
Oosterhout 70 E8 Netherlands 51°38'N 4°51'E
Oosterwolde 70 G12 Netherlands 53°1'N 6°15'E
Opatów 84 G8 Poland 50°45'N 21°27'E
Opava 85 E7 Czech Republic 49°56'N 17°53'E
Opmeer 70 E11 Netherlands 52°43'N 4°56'E
Opochka 89 C7 Russian Fed. 56°42'N 28°40'E
Opoczno 84 G9 Poland 51°24'N 20°18'E
Opole 84 E8 Poland 50°40'N 17°56'E
Oporto 74 E7 Portugal 41°9'N 8°37'W
Opotiki 136 F6 New Zealand 38°2'S 177°18'E
Oppdal 68 B8 Norway 62°36'N 9°41'E
Oqtosh 117 I7 Uzbekistan 39°23'N 65°46'E
Oradea 86 G8 Romania 47°3'N 21°56'E
Oran 96 F8 Algeria 35°42'N 0°37'W
Orange 135 K3 New South Wales, Australia 33°16'S 149°6'E
Orange 73 I3 France 44°6'N 4°52'E
Orange River 98 F2 ≈ S Africa
Orange Walk 150 G3 Belize 18°6'N 88°30'W
Oranienburg 82 G10 Germany 52°46'N 13°15'E
Oranjemund 98 F2 Namibia 28°33'S 16°28'E
Oranjestad 151 K2 ○ Aruba 12°31'N 70°W
Oranmore 58 D8 Ireland 53°17'N 8°58'W
Oravais 68 F8 Finland 63°18'N 22°25'E
Orbetello 76 G5 Italy 42°28'N 11°15'E
Ord River 134 F7 ≈ N Australia Oceania
Ordu 110 G7 Turkey 41°N 37°52'E
Örebro 69 D6 Sweden 59°18'N 15°12'E
Oregon 146 E7 ◈ *State* USA
Orël 89 D6 Russian Fed. 52°57'N 36°6'E
Orem 146 F6 Utah, USA 40°18'N 111°42'W
Orenburg 89 H5 Russian Fed. 51°46'N 55°12'E
Orense *see* Ourense
Orford 53 M4 England, UK 52°5'N 1°31'E
Orford Ness 53 M4 *Headland* E England, UK
Oriental, Cordillera 155 ▲▲ Bolivia/Peru
Orihuela 75 K4 Spain 38°5'N 0°56'W
Orinoco, Río 160 D11 ≈ Colombia/Venezuela
Orissa 119 I5 ◈ *State* India
Oristano 76 F3 Italy 39°54'N 8°35'E
Orkney Islands 36 ◈ *Unitary authority* Scotland, UK
Orlando 147 M3 Florida, USA 28°32'N 81°23'W
Orléanais 72 G6 *Cultural region* France
Orléans 72 G6 France 47°54'N 1°53'E
Ormesby St Margaret 53 N6 England, UK 52°41'N 1°41'E
Ormskirk 54 E2 England, UK 53°35'N 2°54'W
Ørnes 68 D11 Norway 66°51'N 13°43'E
Örnsköldsvik 68 E8 Sweden 63°16'N 18°45'E
Orosháza 85 G3 Hungary 46°33'N 20°40'E
Orpington 51 H5 England, UK 51°21'N 0°5'E
Orsha 89 C6 Belarus 54°30'N 30°26'E
Orsk 89 H5 Russian Fed. 51°13'N 58°35'E
Orthez 72 E3 France 43°29'N 0°46'W
Orton 54 F5 England, UK 54°28'N 2°36'W
Ortona 77 I5 Italy 42°21'N 14°24'E
Orūmīyeh 116 C6 Iran 37°33'N 45°6'E
Oruro 161 D7 Bolivia 17°58'S 67°6'W
Orwell 53 J4 England, UK 52°7'N 0°0'W
Orwell 53 L4 ≈ E England, UK
Orzysz 84 H11 Poland 53°49'N 21°54'E
Osaka 125 H3 Japan 34°38'N 135°28'E
Osa, Península de 151 H1 *Coastal feature* S Costa Rica
Osbournby 53 I6 England, UK 52°55'N 0°28'W
Osh 117 K7 Kyrgyzstan 40°34'N 72°46'E
Oshakati 98 F4 Namibia 17°46'S 15°43'E
Oshawa 145 I1 Ontario, Canada 43°54'N 78°50'W
Oshikango 98 F4 Namibia 17°29'S 15°54'E
O-shima 125 J3 *Island* S Japan
Oshkosh 147 K7 Wisconsin, USA 44°1'N 88°32'W
Osijek 86 F7 Croatia 45°33'N 18°41'E
Oskarshamn 69 D4 Sweden 57°16'N 16°25'E
Oslo 69 C6 ● Norway 59°54'N 10°44'E
Osmaniye 110 G5 Turkey 37°4'N 36°15'E
Osnabrück 82 D10 Germany 52°9'N 7°42'E
Osorno 161 C3 Chile 40°39'S 73°5'W
Oss 70 F9 Netherlands 51°46'N 5°32'E
Ossa, Mount 135 J1 ▲ Tasmania, SE Australia
Ossa, Serra d' 74 F5 ▲▲ SE Portugal
Ossora 109 L7 Russian Fed. 59°16'N 163°2'E
Ostend 71 B7 Belgium 51°13'N 2°55'E
Östersund 68 D8 Sweden 63°10'N 14°44'E
Ostiglia 76 G8 Italy 45°4'N 11°9'E
Ostrava 85 E7 Czech Republic 49°50'N 18°15'E
Ostróda 84 F11 Poland 53°42'N 19°59'E
Ostrołęka 84 G10 Poland 53°6'N 21°34'E
Ostrov 89 C7 Russian Fed. 57°21'N 28°18'E
Ostrowiec Świętokrzyski 84 G8 Poland 50°55'N 21°23'E
Ostrów Mazowiecka 84 H10 Poland 52°49'N 21°53'E
Ostrów Wielkopolski 84 E9 Poland 51°40'N 17°47'E
Osumit, Lumi i 86 F4 ≈ SE Albania
Osuna 75 H3 Spain 37°14'N 5°6'W
Oswaldkirk 55 I4 England, UK 54°13'N 1°7'W
Oswestry 52 D6 England, UK 52°51'N 3°6'W
Otaki 136 E5 New Zealand 40°46'S 175°8'E
Otaru 125 K8 Japan 43°14'N 140°59'E
Otavi 98 F4 Namibia 19°35'S 17°25'E
Otira 136 C3 New Zealand 42°52'S 171°33'E
Otjiwarongo 98 F4 Namibia 20°29'S 16°36'E
Otley 55 H3 England, UK 53°53'N 1°42'W
Otorohanga 136 E6 New Zealand 38°10'S 175°14'E
Otranto, Strait of 77 L4 *Strait* Albania/Italy
Otrokovice 85 E6 Czech Republic 49°13'N 17°33'E
Otsu 125 I4 Japan 35°3'N 135°49'E
Ottawa 145 I2 ● Canada 45°24'N 75°41'W
Ottawa Islands 145 H4 *Island group* Northwest Territories, C Canada
Otterburn 54 G8 England, UK 55°14'N 2°14'W
Ottery St Mary 49 F5 England, UK 50°46'N 3°17'W
Ottignies 71 D6 Belgium 50°40'N 4°34'E
Otway, Cape 135 J2 *Headland* Victoria, SE Australia
Ouachita Mountains 147 J4 ▲▲ Arkansas/ Oklahoma, C USA
Ouachita River 147 J4 ≈ Arkansas/ Louisiana, C USA
Ouagadougou 96 F4 ● Burkina 12°20'N 1°32'W
Ouahigouya 96 F5 Burkina 13°31'N 2°20'W
Ouarâne 96 D6 *Desert* C Mauritania
Ouargla 96 G8 Algeria 32°N 5°16'E
Oubangui 98 G9 ≈ C Africa
Ouessant, Île d' 72 C7 *Island* NW France
Ouésso 98 F8 Congo 1°38'N 16°3'E
Oughterard 58 C8 Ireland 53°24'N 9°29'W
Oujda 96 F8 Morocco 34°45'N 1°53'W
Oulu 68 G10 Finland 65°1'N 25°28'E
Oulujärvi 68 G9 ◎ C Finland
Oulujoki 68 G9 ≈ C Finland
Ounasjoki 68 G11 ≈ N Finland
Oundle 53 I5 England, UK 52°28'N 0°32'W
Ounianga Kébir 97 I5 Chad 19°6'N 20°2
Oupeye 71 F6 Belgium 50°42'N 5°38'E
Our 71 G4 ≈ NW Europe
Ourense 74 F8 Spain 42°20'N 7°52'W
Ourique 74 E4 Portugal 37°38'N 8°13'W
Ourthe 71 F4 ≈ E Belgium
Ōu-sanmyaku 125 K6 ▲▲ Honshū, C Japa
Ouse 55 I4 ≈ N England, UK
Ouse 51 H3 ≈ SE England, UK
Outer Hebrides 56 A11 *Island group* NW Scotland, UK
Outes 74 E9 Spain 42°50'N 8°54'W
Out Skerries 56 I12 *Island group* NE Scotland, UK
Outwell 53 K5 England, UK 52°37'N 0°1
Ouyen 135 I3 Victoria, Australia 35°7'S 1
Ovalle 161 C5 Chile 30°33'S 71°16'W
Ovar 74 E7 Portugal 40°52'N 8°38'W
Overflakkee 70 D8 *Island* SW Netherland
Overijse 71 E6 Belgium 50°46'N 4°32'E
Overton 50 E4 England, UK 51°14'N 1°1
Overton 54 E3 England, UK 54°1'N 2°59'
Overton 48 G11 Wales, UK 52°58'N 2°54
Oviedo 74 G9 Spain 43°21'N 5°50'W
Övre Soppero 68 F11 Sweden 68°7'N 21
Owando 98 F8 Congo 0°29'S 15°55'E
Owase 125 I3 Japan 34°4'N 136°11'E
Owen, Mount 136 D4 ▲ South Island, New Zealand
Owensboro 147 K5 Kentucky, USA 37°46'N 87°7'W
Oxford 136 D3 New Zealand 43°18'S 172
Oxford 50 E6 England, UK 51°46'N 1°15'
Oxford Canal 53 H4 *Canal* S England, UK
Oxfordshire 50 E6 ◈ *County* England, UK
Oxted 51 H4 England, UK 51°14'N 0°1'W
Oyama 125 J4 Japan 36°19'N 139°46'E
Oyem 98 E8 Gabon 1°34'N 11°31'E
Oykel 56 E10 ≈ N Scotland, UK
Ozark Plateau 147 J5 *Plain* Arkansas/ Missouri, C USA
Ozarks, Lake of the 147 J5 ⊠ Missouri, C
Ózd 85 G5 Hungary 48°15'N 20°18'E
Ozieri 76 F4 Italy 40°35'N 9°1'E

P

Pabbay 56 A8 *Island* NW Scotland, UK
Pabbay 56 B10 *Island* Western Isles, NW Scotland, UK
Pabna 119 J6 Bangladesh 24°2'N 89°15'E
Pachuca 150 D4 Mexico 20°5'N 98°46'W
Pacific Ocean 24 *Ocean*
Padang 126 F3 Indonesia 1°S 100°21'E
Padasjoki 69 G7 Finland 61°20'N 25°21'E
Paddock Wood 51 I4 England, UK 51°10'N 0°22'E
Paderborn 82 E9 Germany 51°43'N 8°45'E
Padiham 54 G3 England, UK 53°48'N 2°17
Padova *see* Padua
Padre Island 147 I2 *Island* Texas, SW USA
Padstow 49 C4 England, UK 50°33'N 5°W
Padua 77 H8 Italy 45°24'N 11°52'E
Paektu-san 124 F7 ▲ China/North Korea
Paeroa 136 E6 New Zealand 37°23'S 175°
Pafos 79 L8 Cyprus 34°46'N 32°26'E
Pag 86 D7 *Island* C Croatia
Pahiatua 136 E5 New Zealand 40°30'S 175
Paide 69 G6 Estonia 58°55'N 25°36'E
Paignton 49 F4 England, UK 50°26'N 3°34
Paihia 136 D8 New Zealand 35°18'S 174°6
Päijänne 69 G7 ◎ S Finland
Paine, Cerro 161 C2 ▲ S Chile
Painswick 48 H8 England, UK 51°48'N 2°1
Painted Desert 146 F5 *Desert* Arizona, SW
Paisley 57 E5 Scotland, UK 55°50'N 4°26'V
Pakistan 118 E7 ◆ *Republic* S Asia
Pakokku 126 E7 Burma 21°20'N 95°5'E
Pakruojis 69 G4 Lithuania 56°N 23°51'E
Paks 85 E3 Hungary 46°38'N 18°51'E
Pakwach 99 I8 Uganda 2°28'N 31°28'E
Pakxe 126 G6 Laos 15°9'N 105°49'E
Palafrugell 75 M8 Spain 41°55'N 3°10'E
Palagruža 86 D5 *Island* SW Croatia
Palamós 75 M8 Spain 41°51'N 3°6'E
Palapye 99 H3 Botswana 22°37'S 27°6'E
Palau 128 ◆ *Republic* W Pacific Ocean
Palawan 127 I5 *Island* W Philippines
Palawan Passage 127 I5 *Passage* W Philipp
Palembang 126 F2 Indonesia 2°59'S 104°4
Palencia 75 H8 Spain 42°23'N 4°32'W
Palermo 77 I2 Italy 38°8'N 13°23'E
Pali 118 F6 India 25°48'N 73°21'E
Palikir 128 ● Micronesia 6°58'N 158°13'E
Pälkäne 69 G7 Finland 61°22'N 24°16'E
Palk Strait 119 H2 *Strait* India/Sri Lanka
Pallas Grean 59 E6 Ireland 52°34'N 8°20'W
Palliser, Cape 136 E4 *Headland* North Island, New Zealand
Palma del Río 75 H4 Spain 37°42'N 5°16'V
Palma de Mallorca 75 M6 Spain 39°35'N 2
Palmas do Tocantins 163 I6 Brazil 10°24'S 48°19'W
Palmerston North 136 E5 New Zealand 40°20'S 175°52'E
Palmi 77 J2 Italy 38°21'N 15°51'E
Palmyra Atoll 128 *US* ◇ C Pacific Ocean
Palu 127 I3 Indonesia 0°54'S 119°52'E
Pamiers 72 G2 France 43°7'N 1°37'E
Pamir 117 K6 ≈ Afghanistan/Tajikistan
Pamirs 117 K6 ▲▲ C Asia
Pamlico Sound 147 N5 *Sound* North Carolir SE USA
Pampas 161 D4 *Plain* C Argentina
Pamplona 75 J8 Spain 42°49'N 1°39'W
Panaji 118 F4 India 15°31'N 73°52'E
Panama 151 I1 ◆ *Republic* Central America
Panama Canal 151 I1 *Canal* E Panama
Panama City 151 I1 ● Panama 8°57'N 79°3
Panama, Gulf of 151 I1 *Coastal sea feature* S Panama
Panama, Isthmus of 151 I1 *Coastal feature* E Panama
Panay Island 127 J5 *Island* C Philippines
Pančevo 86 G7 Serbia and Montenegro 44°53'N 20°40'E

◆ Country ● Country capital ◇ Dependent territory ○ Dependent territory capital ◈ Administrative region ▲ Mountain ▲▲ Mountain range ♨ Volcano ≈ River ◎ Lake ⊠ Reservoir

186 Pukekohe - St Abb's Head

Pukekohe 136 E7 New Zealand 37°12'S 174°54'E
Pula 86 D7 Croatia 44°53'N 13°51'E
Puławy 84 H9 Poland 51°25'N 21°57'E
Pulkkila 68 G9 Finland 64°15'N 25°53'E
Pułtusk 84 G10 Poland 52°41'N 21°4'E
Pune 118 F5 India 18°32'N 73°52'E
Punjab 118 G8 ⬖ State India
Puno 161 C7 Peru 15°53'S 70°3'W
Punta Alta 161 E4 Argentina 38°54'S 62°1'W
Punta Arenas 161 D1 Chile 53°10'S 70°56'W
Punta Gorda 153 G3 Belize 16°7'N 88°47'W
Puntarenas 151 H1 Costa Rica 9°58'N 84°50'W
Pupuya, Nevado 160 C8 ▲ W Bolivia
Purfleet 51 H5 England, UK 51°29'N 0°9'E
Puri 119 I5 India 19°52'N 85°49'E
Puriton 49 G6 England, UK 51°10'N 2°58'W
Purley 50 G5 England, UK 51°20'N 0°7'W
Purmerend 70 E11 Netherlands 52°30'N 4°56'E
Purus, Rio 162 E6 〜 Brazil/Peru
Pusan 124 F4 South Korea 35°11'N 129°4'E
Püspökladány 85 G4 Hungary 47°20'N 21°5'E
Putrajaya 126 F3 ● Malaysia 3°7'N 101°42'E
Puttalam 119 H2 Sri Lanka 8°2'N 79°55'E
Puttgarden 82 F11 Germany 54°30'N 11°13'E
Putumayo, Río 160 C10 〜 NW South America
Puurmani 69 H5 Estonia 58°36'N 26°17'E
Pwllheli 48 D11 Wales, UK 52°54'N 4°23'W
Pyalitsa 88 E10 Russian Fed. 66°17'N 39°56'E
Pyatigorsk 89 E3 Russian Fed. 44°1'N 43°6'E
Pyhäsalmi 68 G9 Finland 63°38'N 26°E
Pyle 49 F7 Wales, UK 51°32'N 3°43'W
Pyongyang 124 E6 ● North Korea 39°4'N 125°46'E
Pyramid Lake 146 E6 ◎ Nevada, W USA
Pyrenees 61 ▲▲ SW Europe
Pyrgos 86 G2 Greece 37°40'N 21°27'E
Pyrzyce 84 C10 Poland 53°9'N 14°53'E

Q

Qā'emshahr 116 E6 Iran 36°31'N 52°49'E
Qaidam Pendi 122 F5 Basin C China
Qal'aikhum 117 J6 Tajikistan 38°28'N 70°49'E
Qal'at Bishah 114 F4 Saudi Arabia 19°59'N 42°38'E
Qal'at Şāliḩ 111 K2 Iraq 31°30'N 47°24'E
Qal'eh-ye Now 117 H5 Afghanistan 35°N 63°8'E
Qamdo 122 F4 China 31°11'N 97°7'E
Qarokŭl 117 K7 Tajikistan 39°7'N 73°33'E
Qarokŭl 117 K7 ◎ E Tajikistan
Qarshi 117 I6 Uzbekistan 38°54'N 65°48'E
Qasr Farafra 97 J7 Egypt 27°0'N 27°59'E
Qatar 115 J6 ◆ Monarchy SW Asia
Qaţrūyeh 116 E3 Iran 29°8'N 54°42'E
Qazimammad 111 K7 Azerbaijan 40°3'N 48°56'E
Qazvin 116 D6 Iran 36°16'N 50°E
Qena 97 K7 Egypt 26°12'N 32°49'E
Qezel Owzan 116 D6 〜 NW Iran
Qilian Shan 122 F6 ▲▲ N China
Qingdao 123 K5 China 36°31'N 120°55'E
Qinghai 122 F5 ⬖ Province China
Qinghai Hu 122 G5 ◎ C China
Qinhuangdao 123 J6 China 39°57'N 119°31'E
Qinzhou 123 I2 China 22°9'N 108°36'E
Qiqihar 123 K8 China 47°23'N 124°E
Qira 122 D6 China 37°5'N 80°45'E
Qitai 122 F7 China 44°N 89°34'E
Qizilrabot 117 L6 Tajikistan 37°29'N 74°44'E
Qom 116 D5 Iran 34°43'N 50°54'E
Qo'ng'irot 116 G8 Uzbekistan 43°1'N 58°49'E
Qo'qon 117 J7 Uzbekistan 40°34'N 70°55'E
Quang Ngai 126 G6 Vietnam 15°9'N 108°50'E
Quanzhou 123 I3 China 25°59'N 111°2'E
Quanzhou 123 K3 China 24°56'N 118°31'E
Qu'Appelle 144 F2 〜 Saskatchewan, S Canada
Quarles, Pegunungan 127 I2 ▲▲ Celebes, C Indonesia
Quartu Sant' Elena 76 F3 Italy 39°15'N 9°12'E
Quba 111 K7 Azerbaijan 41°22'N 48°30'E
Qūchān 116 G6 Iran 37°12'N 58°28'E
Québec 145 J2 Québec, Canada 46°50'N 71°15'W
Québec 145 I3 ⬖ Province Canada
Queen Charlotte Islands 144 C3 Island group British Columbia, SW Canada
Queen Charlotte Sound 144 D2 Sea area British Columbia, W Canada
Queen Elizabeth Islands 144 F7 Island group Northwest Territories, N Canada
Queensland 135 J6 ⬖ State Australia
Queenstown 136 B2 New Zealand 45°1'S 168°44'E
Queenstown 99 H2 South Africa 31°52'S 26°50'E
Quelimane 99 J4 Mozambique 17°53'S 36°51'E
Querétaro 150 D4 Mexico 20°36'N 100°24'W
Quetta 118 E8 Pakistan 30°15'N 67°E
Quilon 118 G2 India 8°57'N 76°37'E
Quilty 59 C7 Ireland 52°48'N 9°26'W
Quimper 72 D6 France 48°0'N 4°5'W
Quimperlé 72 D6 France 47°52'N 3°33'W
Quito 160 B10 ● Ecuador 0°14'S 78°30'W
Quixadá 163 K7 Brazil 4°57'S 39°4'W
Qujing 123 H2 China 25°39'N 103°52'E
Qŭrghonteppa 117 J6 Tajikistan 37°51'N 68°42'E
Quy Nhon 126 G6 Vietnam 13°47'N 109°11'E

R

Raahe 68 G9 Finland 64°42'N 24°31'E
Raalte 70 G10 Netherlands 52°23'N 6°16'E
Raamsdonksveer 70 E8 Netherlands 51°42'N 4°54'E
Raanujärvi 68 G11 Finland 66°39'N 24°40'E
Raasay 56 C9 Island NW Scotland, UK
Rába 85 D4 〜 Austria/Hungary
Rabat 96 E8 ● Morocco 34°2'N 6°51'W
Rābigh 114 E5 Saudi Arabia 22°51'N 39°E
Rabka 85 F7 Poland 49°38'N 20°E
Race, Cape 145 L3 Headland Newfoundland, Newfoundland and Labrador, E Canada
Rach Gia 126 F5 Vietnam 10°1'N 105°5'E
Rackwick 56 G14 Scotland, UK 59°20'N 3°3'W
Radom 84 G9 Poland 51°23'N 21°8'E
Radomsko 84 F8 Poland 51°4'N 19°25'E
Radzyń Podlaski 84 H9 Poland 51°48'N 22°37'E
Raetihi 136 E5 New Zealand 39°29'S 175°16'E
Rafaela 161 E5 Argentina 31°16'S 61°25'W
Rafḩah 114 G8 Saudi Arabia 29°41'N 43°29'E
Rafsanjān 116 F3 Iran 30°25'N 56°E
Raglan 48 G8 Wales, UK 51°46'N 2°50'W
Ragusa 77 J1 Italy 36°56'N 14°42'E
Rahimyar Khan 118 F7 Pakistan 28°27'N 70°21'E
Raichur 118 G4 India 16°15'N 77°20'E
Rainford 54 F2 England, UK 53°30'N 2°53'W
Rainham 51 H5 England, UK 51°30'N 0°6'E
Rainier, Mount 146 E8 ⛰ Washington, NW USA
Rainy Lake 145 H2 ◎ Canada/USA
Raipur 119 H5 India 21°16'N 81°42'E
Rajahmundry 119 H4 India 17°5'N 81°42'E
Rajang, Batang 127 H3 〜 East Malaysia
Rajapalaiyam 118 G2 India 9°26'N 77°36'E
Rajasthan 118 F7 ⬖ State India
Rajkot 118 F6 India 22°18'N 70°47'E
Rajshahi 119 J6 Bangladesh 24°24'N 88°40'E
Rakaia 136 C3 〜 South Island, New Zealand
Rakvere 69 H6 Estonia 59°21'N 26°20'E
Raleigh 147 M5 North Carolina, USA 35°46'N 78°38'W
Rame 49 E4 England, UK 50°19'N 4°17'W
Râmnicu Vâlcea 87 H7 Romania 45°4'N 24°32'E
Ramree Island 126 D7 Island W Burma
Ramsbottom 54 F2 England, UK 53°39'N 2°21'W
Ramsey 54 B4 Isle of Man 54°19'N 4°24'W
Ramsey Bay 54 G5 Bay NE Isle of Man
Ramsey Island 48 C8 Island SW Wales, UK
Ramsgate 51 K5 England, UK 51°20'N 1°25'E
Rancagua 161 C4 Chile 34°10'S 70°45'W
Ranchi 119 I6 India 23°22'N 85°20'E
Randers 69 B4 Denmark 56°28'N 10°3'E
Rangiora 136 D3 New Zealand 43°19'S 172°34'E
Rangitikei 136 E5 〜 North Island, New Zealand
Rangoon 126 E6 ● Burma 16°50'N 96°11'E
Rangpur 119 J7 Bangladesh 25°46'N 89°20'E
Rankin Inlet 144 G4 Northwest Territories, Canada 62°52'N 92°14'W
Rannoch Moor 57 F7 Heathland C Scotland, UK
Rapid City 147 H7 South Dakota, USA 44°5'N 103°14'W
Räpina 69 H5 Estonia 58°6'N 27°27'E
Ra's al Khafjī 115 I8 Saudi Arabia 28°22'N 48°30'E
Ra's al Khaymah 115 K7 United Arab Emirates 25°44'N 55°55'E
Rasht 116 D6 Iran 37°18'N 49°38'E
Ra's Tannūrah 115 I7 Saudi Arabia 26°44'N 50°4'E
Rätan 68 D8 Sweden 62°28'N 14°35'E
Rathdowney 59 F7 Ireland 52°51'N 7°36'W
Rathdrum 59 H7 Ireland 52°55'N 6°24'W
Rathfriland 58 H10 Northern Ireland, UK 54°16'N 6°15'W
Rathkeale 59 D6 Ireland 52°32'N 8°56'W
Rathlin Island 58 H13 Island N Northern Ireland, UK
Ráth Luirc 59 D6 Ireland 52°20'N 8°40'W
Rathmelton 58 F12 Ireland 55°2'N 7°39'W
Rathmore 59 C5 Ireland 52°5'N 9°21'W
Rathmullan 58 F12 Ireland 55°6'N 7°32'W
Rathnew 59 H7 Ireland 52°59'N 6°14'W
Rat Islands 146 A6 Island group Aleutian Islands, Alaska, USA
Ratlam 118 G6 India 23°23'N 75°4'E
Ratnapura 119 H1 Sri Lanka 6°41'N 80°25'E
Rattray Head 56 I10 Headland NE Scotland, UK
Rättvik 69 D7 Sweden 60°53'N 15°12'E
Raufarhöfn 68 B12 Iceland 66°27'N 15°58'W
Raukumara Range 136 F6 ▲▲ North Island, New Zealand
Rauma 69 F7 Finland 61°9'N 21°30'E
Raunds 53 I4 England, UK 52°20'N 0°33'W
Raurkela 119 I6 India 22°13'N 84°53'E
Rāvar 116 F4 Iran 31°15'N 56°51'E
Ravenglass 54 D5 England, UK 54°21'N 3°32'W
Ravenna 77 H7 Italy 44°28'N 12°15'E
Ravi 118 F8 〜 India/Pakistan
Rawalpindi 118 F8 Pakistan 33°38'N 73°6'E
Rawa Mazowiecka 84 F9 Poland 51°47'N 20°16'E
Rawāndiz 111 J5 Iraq 36°38'N 44°32'E
Rawicz 84 D9 Poland 51°37'N 16°51'E
Rawlinna 134 F4 Western Australia 31°1'S 125°36'E
Rawson 161 D3 Argentina 43°22'S 65°1'W
Rawtenstall 54 G2 England, UK 53°42'N 2°11'W
Rayleigh 51 I6 England, UK 51°35'N 0°36'E
Rayong 126 F5 Thailand 12°42'N 101°17'E
Raysūt 115 K3 Oman 16°58'N 54°2'E
Razgrad 87 I6 Bulgaria 43°33'N 26°31'E
Razim, Lacul 87 J7 Lagoon NW Black Sea
Reading 50 E5 England, UK 51°28'N 0°59'W
Reading 37 ⬖ Unitary authority England, UK
Real, Cordillera 155 ▲▲ C Ecuador
Realicó 161 D4 Argentina 35°2'S 64°14'W
Rebecca, Lake 134 E4 ◎ Western Australia
Rebun-to 125 K9 Island NE Japan
Recess 58 C8 Ireland 53°29'N 9°47'W
Recife 163 L6 Brazil 8°6'S 34°53'W
Recklinghausen 82 D9 Germany 51°37'N 7°12'E
Recogne 71 F4 Belgium 49°56'N 5°20'E
Redbridge 37 ⬖ London Borough England, UK
Redcar 55 I5 England, UK 54°36'N 0°57'W
Redcar and Cleveland 36 ⬖ Unitary authority England, UK
Red Deer 144 E2 Alberta, Canada 52°15'N 113°48'W
Redditch 52 F4 England, UK 52°19'N 1°56'W
Rede 54 G8 〜 N England, UK
Redhill 50 G4 England, UK 51°13'N 0°11'W
Redon 72 E6 France 47°39'N 2°5'W
Red River 147 J4 〜 Canada/USA
Red River 123 H2 〜 China/Vietnam
Redruth 49 C4 England, UK 50°14'N 5°11'W
Red Sea 114 E5 Sea Africa/Asia
Red Wharf Bay 48 E13 Bay N Wales, UK
Reefton 136 C4 New Zealand 42°7'S 171°53'E
Ree, Lough 58 E9 ◎ C Ireland
Reeth 54 G5 England, UK 54°23'N 1°57'W
Refahiye 111 H6 Turkey 39°54'N 38°45'E
Regensburg 83 G6 Germany 49°1'N 12°6'E
Regenstauf 83 G7 Germany 49°6'N 12°7'E
Reggane 96 F7 Algeria 26°46'N 0°9'E
Reggio di Calabria 77 J2 Italy 38°6'N 15°39'E
Reggio nell' Emilia 76 G7 Italy 44°42'N 10°37'E
Regina 144 F2 Saskatchewan, Canada 50°25'N 104°39'W
Rehoboth 98 F3 Namibia 23°18'S 17°3'E
Reid 134 F4 Western Australia 30°49'S 128°24'E
Reiff 56 D11 Scotland, UK 58°4'N 5°27'W
Ré, Île de 72 E5 Island W France
Reims 73 H7 France 49°16'N 4°1'E
Reindeer Lake 144 F3 ◎ Manitoba/Saskatchewan, C Canada
Reinga, Cape 136 D8 Headland North Island, New Zealand
Reinosa 75 H9 Spain 43°1'N 4°9'W
Reliance 144 F4 Northwest Territories, Canada 62°45'N 109°8'W
Rena 68 C7 Norway 61°8'N 11°21'E
Rendsburg 82 E11 Germany 54°18'N 9°40'E
Renfrewshire 36 ⬖ Unitary authority Scotland, UK
Rengat 126 F3 Indonesia 0°26'S 102°38'E
Rennes 72 E6 France 48°8'N 1°40'W
Reno 146 E6 Nevada, USA 39°32'N 119°49'W
Repulse Bay 144 G5 Northwest Territories, Canada 66°35'N 86°20'W
Resistencia 161 E5 Argentina 27°27'S 58°56'W
Reşiţa 86 G7 Romania 45°14'N 21°58'E
Resolute 144 G6 Northwest Territories, Canada 74°41'N 94°54'W
Resolution Island 145 I5 Island Northwest Territories, NE Canada
Retford 53 H8 England, UK 53°18'N 0°52'W
Rethymno 87 H1 Greece 35°21'N 24°29'E
Rétság 85 F5 Hungary 47°57'N 19°8'E
Réunion 99 M4 French ◇ Indian Ocean
Reus 75 L7 Spain 41°10'N 1°6'E
Reutlingen 83 E6 Germany 48°30'N 9°13'E
Reuver 71 G7 Netherlands 51°17'N 6°5'E
Reyes 160 D8 Bolivia 14°17'S 67°18'W
Reykjavík 68 A11 ● Iceland 64°8'N 21°54'W
Reynosa 150 E5 Mexico 26°3'N 98°19'W
Rezé 72 E6 France 47°10'N 1°36'W
Rheidol 48 E10 〜 W Wales, UK
Rheine 82 D10 Germany 52°17'N 7°27'E
Rheinisches Schiefergebirge 82 D8 ▲▲ W Germany
Rhine 61 〜 W Europe
Rho 76 F8 Italy 45°32'N 9°2'E
Rhode Island 147 N7 ⬖ State USA
Rhodes 87 J1 Island Dodecanese, Greece, Aegean Sea
Rhodope Mountains 87 H5 ▲▲ Bulgaria/Greece
Rhondda Cynon Taff 37 ⬖ Unitary authority Wales, UK
Rhoose 49 F7 Wales, UK 51°23'N 3°25'W
Rhos 48 D9 Wales, UK 52°0'N 4°22'W
Rhosneigr 48 D12 Wales, UK 53°13'N 4°36'W
Rhossili 49 D7 Wales, UK 51°33'N 4°19'W
Rhum 56 C8 Island W Scotland, UK
Rhyl 48 F12 Wales, UK 53°19'N 3°28'W
Rhymney 48 F8 Wales, UK 51°46'N 3°24'W
Ribble 54 F3 〜 NW England, UK
Ribeira 74 E8 Spain 42°33'N 9°0'W
Ribeirão Preto 163 I3 Brazil 21°9'S 47°48'W
Riberalta 160 D8 Bolivia 11°1'S 66°4'W
Riccall 55 I3 England, UK 53°50'N 1°5'W
Richard Toll 96 D5 Senegal 16°28'N 15°44'W
Richmond 136 D4 New Zealand 41°25'S 173°4'E
Richmond 55 H5 England, UK 54°24'N 1°50'W
Richmond 147 M6 Virginia, USA 37°33'N 77°28'W
Richmond Range 136 D4 ▲▲ South Island, New Zealand
Richmond upon Thames 37 ⬖ London Borough England, UK
Rickmansworth 50 G6 England, UK 51°37'N 0°23'W
Ricobayo, Embalse de 74 G7 ▣ NW Spain
Ridsdale 54 G7 England, UK 55°9'N 2°15'W
Ried im Innkreis 83 G6 Austria 48°13'N 13°29'E
Riemst 71 F6 Belgium 50°49'N 5°36'E
Riesa 82 G9 Germany 51°18'N 13°18'E
Rīga 69 G4 ● Latvia 56°57'N 24°8'E
Riga, Gulf of 69 G5 Gulf Estonia/Latvia
Rīgān 116 G2 Iran 28°39'N 59°1'E
Rigestan 117 I3 Physical region S Afghanistan
Riihimäki 69 G7 Finland 60°45'N 24°45'E
Rijeka 86 D7 Croatia 45°20'N 14°26'E
Rijssen 70 H10 Netherlands 52°19'N 6°30'E
Rillington 55 J4 England, UK 54°9'N 0°44'W
Rimah, Wadi ar 114 G6 Dry watercourse C Saudi Arabia
Rimavská Sobota 85 F5 Slovakia 48°24'N 20°1'E
Rimini 77 H7 Italy 44°3'N 12°33'E
Rimouski 145 J2 Québec, Canada 48°26'N 68°32'W
Ringebu 69 C7 Norway 61°31'N 10°9'E
Ringkøbing Fjord 69 A4 Fjord W Denmark
Ringvassøya 68 E13 Island N Norway
Ringwood 50 C3 England, UK 50°50'N 1°58'W
Rio Branco 162 E6 Brazil 9°59'S 67°49'W
Río Bravo 150 E5 Mexico 25°57'N 98°3'W
Río Cuarto 161 D5 Argentina 33°6'S 64°20'W
Rio de Janeiro 163 J3 Brazil 22°53'S 43°17'W
Rio de Janeiro 163 J3 ⬖ State Brazil
Río Gallegos 161 D2 Argentina 51°40'S 69°21'W
Rio Grande 163 H1 Brazil 32°3'S 52°8'W
Río Grande 161 D1 Argentina 53°45'S 67°46'W
Rio Grande do Norte 163 L7 ⬖ State Brazil
Rio Grande do Sul 163 H1 ⬖ State Brazil
Ríohacha 160 C12 Colombia 11°23'N 72°47'W
Río Lagartos 150 G4 Mexico 21°35'N 88°8'W
Riom 73 H5 France 45°54'N 3°6'E
Rio Verde 163 H4 Brazil 17°50'S 50°55'W
Río Verde 150 D4 Mexico 21°58'N 100°W
Ripley 55 H3 England, UK 54°3'N 1°35'W
Ripoll 75 L8 Spain 42°12'N 2°12'E
Ripon 55 H4 England, UK 54°7'N 1°31'W
Rishiri-to 125 K9 Island NE Japan
Ristijärvi 68 H9 Finland 64°30'N 28°15'E
Rivas 151 G2 Nicaragua 11°26'N 85°50'W
Rivera 161 F5 Uruguay 30°54'S 55°31'W
Riverside 146 E5 California, USA 33°58'N 117°25'W
Riverstown 59 E5 Ireland 51°56'N 8°22'W
Riverton 136 B1 New Zealand 46°20'S 168°2'E
Rivière-du-Loup 145 J2 Québec, Canada 47°49'N 69°32'W
Rivne 89 B5 Ukraine 50°37'N 26°16'E
Rivoli 76 E8 Italy 45°4'N 7°31'E
Riyadh 115 H6 ● Saudi Arabia 24°50'N 46°50'E
Rize 111 H7 Turkey 41°3'N 40°33'E
Roag, Loch 56 B11 Inlet NW Scotland, UK
Roanne 73 H5 France 46°3'N 4°4'E
Roanoke 147 M5 Virginia, USA 37°16'N 79°57'W
Roanoke River 147 M5 〜 North Carolina/Virginia, SE USA
Roatán 150 G3 Honduras 16°19'N 86°33'W
Robāţ-e Chāh Gonbad 116 F4 Iran 33°24'N 57°43'E
Robertsbridge 51 I3 England, UK 50°58'N 0°19'E
Robertstown 58 G8 Ireland 53°14'N 6°54'W
Robin Hood's Bay 55 J5 England, UK 54°26'N 0°32'W
Robson, Mount 144 E2 ▲ British Columbia, SW Canada
Rochdale 54 G2 England, UK 53°38'N 2°9'W
Rochdale 36 ⬖ Unitary authority England, UK
Rochefort 71 F4 Belgium 50°10'N 5°13'E
Rochefort 72 E5 France 45°57'N 0°58'W
Rochester 51 I5 England, UK 51°24'N 0°30'E
Rochester 54 G8 England, UK 55°17'N 2°12'W
Rochester 147 J7 Minnesota, USA 44°1'N 92°28'W
Rochester 147 M7 New York, USA 43°9'N 77°37'W
Rochford 51 I6 England, UK 51°33'N 0°42'E
Rochfortbridge 58 F8 Ireland 53°24'N 7°18'W
Rockchapel 59 C5 Ireland 52°17'N 9°12'W
Rockcliffe 54 E7 England, UK 54°56'N 3°11'W
Rockford 147 K6 Illinois, USA 42°16'N 89°6'W
Rockhampton 135 L5 Queensland, Australia 23°31'S 150°31'E
Rock Sound 151 I5 Bahamas 24°52'N 76°10'W
Rocky Mountains 139 ▲▲ Canada/USA
Rodel 56 B10 Scotland, UK 57°45'N 6°56'W
Roden 70 H12 Netherlands 53°8'N 6°26'E
Rodez 72 G3 France 44°21'N 2°34'E
Roermond 71 G7 Netherlands 51°12'N 6°E
Roeselare 71 B6 Belgium 50°57'N 3°8'E
Rogoźno 84 D10 Poland 52°46'N 16°58'E
Roi Et 126 F6 Thailand 16°5'N 103°38'E
Rokiškis 69 H4 Lithuania 55°58'N 25°35'E
Rokycany 85 B7 Czech Republic 49°45'N 13°36'E
Roma 135 K5 Queensland, Australia 26°37'S 148°54'E
Roma see Rome
Romaldkirk 54 G5 England, UK 54°35'N 1°57'W
Roman 87 I8 Romania 46°46'N 26°56'E
Romania 87 H8 ◆ Republic SE Europe
Rome 77 H5 ● Italy 41°53'N 12°30'E
Romford 51 H6 England, UK 51°35'N 0°6'E
Romney Marsh 51 J3 Physical region SE England, UK
Romny 89 C5 Ukraine 50°45'N 33°30'E
Rømø 69 A3 Island SW Denmark
Romsey 50 D3 England, UK 50°59'N 1°31'W
Ronda 75 H3 Spain 36°45'N 5°10'W
Rondônia 162 F5 ⬖ State Brazil
Rondonópolis 163 H4 Brazil 16°29'S 54°37'W
Rønne 69 D3 Denmark 55°7'N 14°43'E
Ronne Ice Shelf 166 C6 Ice feature Antarctica
Roos 55 K3 England, UK 53°45'N 0°4'W
Roosendaal 70 D8 Netherlands 51°32'N 4°29'E
Roosevelt Island 166 C4 Island Antarctica
Roosky 58 E9 Ireland 53°49'N 7°55'W
Roraima 162 F9 ⬖ State Brazil
Roraima, Mount 162 F9 ▲▲ N South America
Røros 68 C8 Norway 62°37'N 11°25'E
Rosario 161 E5 Argentina 32°56'S 60°39'W
Rosario 161 E6 Paraguay 24°26'S 57°6'W
Rosarito 150 A7 Mexico 32°25'N 117°4'W
Roscommon 58 E9 Ireland 53°38'N 8°11'W
Roscommon 147 K7 Michigan, USA 44°30'N 84°35'W
Roscommon 58 E9 ⬖ County Ireland
Roscrea 59 F7 Ireland 52°57'N 7°47'W
Roseau 151 M4 ● Dominica 15°17'N 61°23'W
Rosengarten 82 E11 Germany 53°24'N 9°54'E
Rosenheim 83 G5 Germany 47°51'N 12°8'E
Roslavl' 89 C6 Russian Fed. 54°N 32°57'E
Rosmalen 70 F8 Netherlands 51°43'N 5°21'E
Ross 136 C3 New Zealand 42°54'S 170°52'E
Rossano 77 K3 Italy 39°35'N 16°38'E
Ross Carbery 59 D4 Ireland 51°35'N 9°1'W
Ross Ice Shelf 166 D4 Ice feature Antarctica
Rosslare 59 H5 Ireland 52°16'N 6°23'W
Rosslare Harbour 59 H5 Ireland 52°15'N 6°20'W
Rosso 96 D5 Mauritania 16°36'N 15°50'W
Ross-on-Wye 52 E3 England, UK 51°55'N 2°34'W
Rossosh' 89 E5 Russian Fed. 50°10'N 39°34'E
Ross Sea 166 D3 Sea Antarctica
Rostock 82 G11 Germany 54°5'N 12°8'E
Rostov-na-Donu 89 E4 Russian Fed. 47°16'N 39°45'E
Rosyth 57 G6 Scotland, UK 56°3'N 3°28'W
Rothbury 54 G8 England, UK 55°18'N 1°54'W
Rother 51 I3 〜 S England, UK
Rotherham 52 G8 England, UK 53°26'N 1°20'W
Rotherham 37 ⬖ Unitary authority England, UK
Rothes 56 G9 Scotland, UK 57°32'N 3°10'W
Rothesay 57 E5 Scotland, UK 55°50'N 5°10'W
Rothwell 53 I5 England, UK 52°25'N 0°53'W
Rothwell 55 H2 England, UK 53°45'N 1°25'W
Rotorua 136 E6 New Zealand 38°10'S 176°14'E
Rotorua, Lake 136 E6 ◎ North Island, New Zealand
Rotterdam 70 D9 Netherlands 51°55'N 4°30'E
Rottweil 83 D6 Germany 48°10'N 8°38'E
Roubaix 73 H8 France 50°42'N 3°10'E
Roudnice nad Labem 84 B8 Czech Repub 50°25'N 14°14'E
Rouen 72 G7 France 49°26'N 1°5'E
Roughton 53 M6 England, UK 52°54'N 1°
Roundstone 58 B8 Ireland 53°23'N 10°7'W
Roundwood 59 H7 Ireland 53°4'N 6°17'W
Rousay 56 G14 Island N Scotland, UK
Roussillon 72 G2 Cultural region France
Rovaniemi 68 G11 Finland 66°29'N 25°40
Rovigo 77 H8 Italy 45°4'N 11°48'E
Rovuma, Rio 99 J6 〜 Mozambique/Tanza
Roxas City 127 J5 Philippines 11°33'N 122
Royale, Isle 147 K8 Island Michigan, N US
Royal Leamington Spa 52 G4 England, UK 52°18'N 1°31'W
Royal Tunbridge Wells 51 H4 England, UK 51°8'N 0°16'E
Royan 72 E4 France 45°37'N 1°1'W
Rožňava 85 G6 Slovakia 48°41'N 20°32'E
Rožnov pod Radhoštěm 85 E6 Czech Rep 49°28'N 18°9'E
Ruabon 48 G11 Wales, UK 52°59'N 3°5'W
Ruapehu, Mount 136 E5 ⛰ North Island, New Zealand
Ruapuke Island 136 B1 Island SW New Zea
Ruatoria 136 F6 New Zealand 37°54'S 178
Ruawai 136 D7 New Zealand 36°8'S 174°4
Rudnyy 108 E4 Kazakhstan 53°N 63°5'E
Rue Point 54 B5 Headland N Isle of Man
Rufford 54 E2 England, UK 53°38'N 2°55'W
Rufiji 99 J6 〜 E Tanzania
Rugby 53 H5 England, UK 52°22'N 1°18'W
Rugeley 52 F6 England, UK 52°46'N 1°56'
Rügen 82 G11 Headland NE Germany
Rumāh 115 H6 Saudi Arabia 25°35'N 47°9
Rumbek 97 K4 Sudan 6°50'N 29°42'E
Rumia 84 E12 Poland 54°36'N 18°21'E
Rumney 49 G7 Wales, UK 51°30'N 3°7'W
Runanga 136 C4 New Zealand 42°25'S 17
Runcorn 54 F1 England, UK 53°20'N 2°44'W
Rundu 98 G4 Namibia 17°55'S 19°45'E
Ruoqiang 122 E6 China 38°59'N 88°8'E
Rupel 71 D7 〜 N Belgium
Rupert, Rivière de 145 I3 〜 Québec, C C
Ruse 87 I6 Bulgaria 43°50'N 25°59'E
Rushden 53 I4 England, UK 52°17'N 0°36'W
Russian Federation 109 I5 ◆ Republic Asia/Europe
Rust'avi 111 J7 Georgia 41°36'N 45°0'E
Rutland 37 ⬖ Unitary authority England, UK
Rutland Water 53 I6 ◎ C England, UK
Rutog 122 C5 China 33°27'N 79°43'E
Ružomberok 85 F6 Slovakia 49°4'N 19°19'
Rwanda 99 I7 ◆ Republic C Africa
Ryazan' 89 E6 Russian Fed. 54°37'N 39°37
Rybinsk 89 D7 Russian Fed. 58°3'N 38°53'E
Rybnik 85 E7 Poland 50°5'N 18°31'E
Rychwał 84 E9 Poland 52°4'N 18°10'E
Ryde 50 E2 England, UK 50°43'N 1°10'W
Rye 51 I3 England, UK 50°57'N 0°42'E
Rye 55 I4 〜 N England, UK
Ryki 84 H9 Poland 51°38'N 21°57'E
Rylstone 54 G3 England, UK 54°1'N 2°4'W
Rypin 84 F10 Poland 53°3'N 19°25'E
Rzeszów 85 H7 Poland 50°3'N 22°1'E
Rzhev 89 D7 Russian Fed. 56°17'N 34°22'E

S

Saale 82 F8 〜 C Germany
Saalfeld 82 F8 Germany 50°39'N 11°22'E
Saarbrücken 83 C7 Germany 49°13'N 7°1'
Saaremaa 69 F5 Island W Estonia
Saariselkä 68 G12 Finland 68°27'N 27°29'E
Šabac 86 F7 Serbia and Montenegro 44°45'N 19°42'E
Sabadell 75 L7 Spain 41°33'N 2°7'E
Sabah 127 I4 Cultural region Malaysia
Sabalān, Kuhhā-ye 116 D6 ▲▲ NW Iran
Sab'atayn, Ramlat as 115 H2 Desert C Yem
Sabaya 161 C7 Bolivia 19°9'S 68°21'W
Saberi, Hamun-e 117 H4 ◎ Afghanistan/Ira
Sabha 97 H7 Libya 27°2'N 14°26'E
Sabinas 150 D6 Mexico 27°52'N 101°4'W
Sabinas Hidalgo 150 D5 Mexico 26°29'N 100°9'W
Sable Island 145 K2 Island Nova Scotia, SE Canada
Sabzevar 116 G5 Iran 36°13'N 57°38'E
Sabzvārān 116 F2 Iran 28°40'N 57°40'E
Sachs Harbour 144 E6 Northwest Territories Canada 72°N 125°14'W
Sacramento 146 D6 California, USA 38°35'N 121°30'W
Sacramento Mountains 146 G4 ▲▲ New Mexico, SW USA
Sacramento River 146 D6 〜 California, W
Sacramento Valley 146 D6 Valley California W USA
Sa'dah 114 G3 Yemen 16°59'N 43°45'E
Sado 125 J5 Island C Japan
Säffle 69 C6 Sweden 59°8'N 12°55'E
Saffron Walden 51 H7 England, UK 52°1'N 0°14'E
Safidābeh 116 G3 Iran 31°5'N 60°30'E
Safid Kūh, Selseleh-ye 117 H5 ▲▲ W Afghanistan
Safwān 111 L2 Iraq 30°6'N 47°44'E
Saga 122 D4 China 29°22'N 85°19'E
Saga 124 F3 Japan 33°14'N 130°16'E
Sagaing 126 E7 Burma 21°55'N 95°56'E
Sagami-nada 125 J4 Inlet SW Japan
Sagar 118 G6 India 23°53'N 78°46'E
Sāghand 116 F4 Iran 32°33'N 55°12'E
Saginaw 147 L7 Michigan, USA 43°25'N 83°57'W
Saginaw Bay 147 L7 Lake bay Michigan, N
Sagunt see Sagunto
Sagunto 75 K6 Spain 39°40'N 0°17'W
Sahara 97 H6 Desert Libya/Algeria
Sahel 96 G5 Physical region C Africa
Sahiwal 118 F8 Pakistan 30°40'N 73°5'E
Saidpur 119 J7 Bangladesh 25°48'N 89°E
Saimaa 68 H8 ◎ SE Finland
St Abb's Head 57 I5 Headland SE Scotland,

◆ Country ● Country capital ◇ Dependent territory ○ Dependent territory capital ⬖ Administrative region ▲ Mountain ▲▲ Mountain range ⛰ Volcano 〜 River ◎ Lake ▣ Reservoir

◆ Country   ● Country capital   ◇ Dependent territory   O Dependent territory capital   ◆ Administrative region   ▲ Mountain   ▲ Mountain range   ♒ Volcano   ♒ River   ⊠ Lake   ⊠ Reservoir

188 Sharūrah - Suck

Sharūrah 115 H3 Saudi Arabia *17°29'N 47°5'E*
Shashe 99 H4 ≈ Botswana/Zimbabwe
Shawbury 52 E6 England, UK *52°48'N 2°37'W*
Shaykh Ḥātim 111 J3 Iraq *33°29'N 44°15'E*
Shchuchinsk 108 F4 Kazakhstan *52°57'N 70°10'E*
Shebekino 89 D5 Russian Fed. *50°25'N 36°55'E*
Shebeli 97 M3 ≈ Ethiopia/Somalia
Sheberghan 117 I6 Afghanistan *36°41'N 65°45'E*
Shebshi Mountains 97 H4 ⛰ E Nigeria
Sheelin, Lough 58 F9 ◎ C Ireland
Sheerness 51 J5 England, UK *51°27'N 0°45'E*
Sheffield 52 G8 England, UK *53°23'N 1°30'W*
Sheffield 37 ◈ *Unitary authority* England, UK
Shendi 97 K5 Sudan *16°41'N 33°22'E*
Shenyang 123 K7 China *41°50'N 123°26'E*
Shenzhen 123 J2 China *22°39'N 114°2'E*
Shepparton 135 J2 Victoria, Australia *36°25'S 145°26'E*
Sheppey, Isle of 51 J5 *Island* SE England, UK
Shepton Mallet 49 H6 England, UK *51°12'N 2°33'W*
Sherborne 49 H6 England, UK *50°58'N 2°30'W*
Sherbrooke 145 J2 Québec, Canada *45°23'N 71°55'W*
Sherburn 55 J4 England, UK *54°10'N 0°34'W*
Shereik 97 K5 Sudan *18°44'N 33°37'E*
's-Hertogenbosch 70 F8 Netherlands *51°41'N 5°19'E*
Shetland Islands 36 ◈ *Unitary authority* Scotland, UK
Shetland Islands 56 I12 *Island group* NE Scotland, UK
Shiant Islands 56 C10 *Island group* NW Scotland, UK
Shibām 115 I2 Yemen *15°49'N 48°24'E*
Shibetsu 125 K9 Japan *43°57'N 142°13'E*
Shīb, Kūh-e 116 E2 ⛰ S Iran
Shibushi-wan 124 G1 *Bay* SW Japan
Shiel Bridge 56 D9 Scotland, UK *57°12'N 5°29'W*
Shihezi 122 E7 China *44°21'N 85°59'E*
Shijiazhuang 123 J5 China *38°4'N 114°28'E*
Shikarpur 118 E7 Pakistan *27°59'N 68°39'E*
Shikoku 125 H3 *Island* SW Japan
Shilabo 97 M3 Ethiopia *6°5'N 44°48'E*
Shilbottle 55 H8 England, UK *55°23'N 1°38'W*
Shildon 55 H6 England, UK *54°38'N 1°38'W*
Shiliguri 119 J7 India *26°46'N 88°24'E*
Shilka 109 J4 ≈ S Russian Fed.
Shillong 119 J7 India *25°37'N 91°54'E*
Shimbiris 97 M4 ▲ N Somalia
Shimla 118 G8 India *31°7'N 77°9'E*
Shimoga 118 G3 India *13°56'N 75°31'E*
Shimonoseki 124 G3 Japan *33°57'N 130°54'E*
Shinano-gawa 125 J5 ≈ Honshū, C Japan
Shināş 115 L6 Oman *24°45'N 56°24'E*
Shindand 117 H4 Afghanistan *33°19'N 62°9'E*
Shingu 125 I3 Japan *33°41'N 135°57'E*
Shinjo 125 J6 Japan *38°47'N 140°17'E*
Shin, Loch 56 E11 ◎ N Scotland, UK
Shinyanga 99 I7 Tanzania *3°40'S 33°25'E*
Shipdham 53 L5 England, UK *52°37'N 0°52'E*
Shipley 55 H3 England, UK *53°50'N 1°44'W*
Shipston on Stour 52 G4 England, UK *52°4'N 1°37'W*
Shipton 55 I3 England, UK *54°2'N 1°8'W*
Shiraz 116 E3 Iran *29°38'N 52°34'E*
Shivpuri 118 G6 India *25°28'N 77°41'E*
Shizugawa 125 K6 Japan *38°40'N 141°26'E*
Shizuoka 125 J4 Japan *34°59'N 138°20'E*
Shkodër 86 F5 Albania *42°3'N 19°31'E*
Shoreham-by-Sea 50 G3 England, UK *50°51'N 0°18'W*
Shostka 89 C5 Ukraine *51°52'N 33°30'E*
Shouldham 53 K6 England, UK *52°38'N 0°22'E*
Shreveport 147 J4 Louisiana, USA *32°32'N 93°45'W*
Shrewsbury 52 E6 England, UK *52°43'N 2°45'W*
Shrivenham 50 D6 England, UK *51°35'N 1°38'W*
Shropshire 52 E5 ◈ *County* England, UK
Shu 108 F2 Kazakhstan *43°34'N 73°41'E*
Shumagin Islands 146 B6 *Island group* Alaska, USA
Shumen 87 J6 Bulgaria *43°17'N 26°57'E*
Shuqrah 115 H1 Yemen *13°26'N 45°44'E*
Shymkent 108 F2 Kazakhstan *42°19'N 69°36'E*
Šiauliai 69 G4 Lithuania *55°55'N 23°21'E*
Sibay 89 H6 Russian Fed. *52°40'N 58°39'E*
Siberut, Pulau 126 E3 *Island* Kepulauan Mentawai, W Indonesia
Sibi 118 E8 Pakistan *29°31'N 67°54'E*
Sibiti 98 E7 Congo *3°41'S 13°20'E*
Sibiu 87 H8 Romania *45°48'N 24°9'E*
Sibolga 126 E3 Indonesia *1°42'N 98°48'E*
Sibsey 53 J7 England, UK *53°2'N 0°5'W*
Sibu 127 H3 Malaysia *2°18'N 111°49'E*
Sibut 97 I3 Central African Republic *5°44'N 19°7'E*
Sibuyan Sea 127 J5 *Sea* W Pacific Ocean
Sichon 126 E5 Thailand *9°3'N 99°51'E*
Sichuan 122 G4 ◈ *Province* China
Sichuan Pendi 123 H4 *Basin* C China
Sicily 77 J2 *Island* Italy, C Mediterranean Sea
Sicily, Strait of 77 H1 *Strait* C Mediterranean Sea
Sidcup 51 H5 England, UK *51°25'N 0°6'E*
Siderno 77 K2 Italy *38°18'N 16°19'E*
Sidi Bel Abbès 96 F8 Algeria *35°12'N 0°43'W*
Sidlaw Hills 57 G7 ⛰ E Scotland, UK
Sidley, Mount 166 C4 ▲ Antarctica
Sidmouth 49 F5 England, UK *50°40'N 3°15'W*
Siedlce 84 H9 Poland *52°10'N 22°18'E*
Siegen 82 D8 Germany *50°53'N 8°2'E*
Siemiatycze 84 H10 Poland *52°27'N 22°52'E*
Siena 77 H6 Italy *43°20'N 11°20'E*
Sieradz 84 E9 Poland *51°36'N 18°42'E*
Sierpc 84 F10 Poland *52°51'N 19°44'E*
Sierra Leone 96 D4 ◆ *Republic* W Africa
Sierra Madre 150 F3 ⛰ Guatemala/Mexico
Sierra Nevada 75 I3 ⛰ S Spain
Sierra Nevada 146 E5 ⛰ W USA
Sifnos 87 I2 *Island* Cyclades, Greece, Aegean Sea
Sigli 126 E4 Indonesia *5°30'N 96°E*
Siglufjördhur 68 B11 Iceland *66°9'N 18°56'W*
Siguiri 96 E4 Guinea *11°26'N 9°8'W*
Siilinjärvi 68 H8 Finland *63°5'N 27°40'E*
Siirt 111 I5 Turkey *37°56'N 41°56'E*
Sikasso 96 E4 Mali *11°21'N 5°43'W*
Sikkim 119 J7 ◈ *State* India
Siklós 85 E3 Hungary *45°51'N 18°18'E*
Silchar 119 K6 India *24°49'N 92°48'E*
Silesia 84 D8 *Physical region* SW Poland
Silifke 110 F4 Turkey *36°22'N 33°57'E*
Silloth 54 D6 England, UK *54°53'N 3°28'W*
Šilutė 69 F3 Lithuania *55°20'N 21°30'E*
Silvan 111 H5 Turkey *38°8'N 41°E*
Silvassa 118 F5 India *20°13'N 73°3'E*
Silverstone 53 H4 England, UK *52°6'N 1°3'W*
Simav 110 D6 Turkey *39°5'N 28°59'E*
Simav Çayi 110 D6 ≈ NW Turkey
Simeto 77 J2 ≈ Sicilia, Italy, C Mediterranean Sea
Simeulue, Pulau 126 E3 *Island* NW Indonesia
Simferopol' 89 C3 Ukraine *44°55'N 33°6'E*
Simpelveld 71 G6 Netherlands *50°50'N 5°59'E*
Simplon Pass 83 D4 *Pass* S Switzerland
Simpson Desert 135 H5 *Desert* Northern Territory/South Australia
Sinai 97 K7 *Physical region* NE Egypt
Sincelejo 160 B12 Colombia *9°17'N 75°23'W*
Sindelfingen 83 E6 Germany *48°43'N 9°E*
Sines 74 E4 Portugal *37°58'N 8°52'W*
Singapore 126 F3 ● Singapore *1°17'N 103°48'E*
Singapore 126 F3 ◆ *Republic* SE Asia
Singen 83 D5 Germany *47°46'N 8°50'E*
Singida 99 I7 Tanzania *4°45'S 34°48'E*
Singkawang 126 G3 Indonesia *0°57'N 108°57'E*
Siniscola 76 G4 Italy *40°34'N 9°42'E*
Sinjār 111 I5 Iraq *36°20'N 41°51'E*
Sinmi-do 124 D6 *Island* NW North Korea
Sinoie, Lacul 87 J7 *Lagoon* SE Romania
Sinop 162 G5 Brazil *11°38'S 55°27'W*
Sinop 110 F7 Turkey *42°2'N 35°9'E*
Sinp'o 124 F6 North Korea *40°1'N 128°10'E*
Sinsheim 83 E7 Germany *49°15'N 8°53'E*
Sint-Michielsgestel 70 F8 Netherlands *51°38'N 5°21'E*
Sint-Niklaas 71 D7 Belgium *51°10'N 4°9'E*
Sint-Pieters-Leeuw 71 D6 Belgium *50°47'N 4°16'E*
Sintra 74 E5 Portugal *38°48'N 9°22'W*
Sinuiju 124 D6 North Korea *40°8'N 124°33'E*
Siófok 85 E4 Hungary *46°54'N 18°3'E*
Sion 83 D4 Switzerland *46°15'N 7°23'E*
Sion Mills 58 F11 Northern Ireland, UK *54°47'N 7°31'W*
Sioux City 147 I6 Iowa, USA *42°30'N 96°24'W*
Sioux Falls 147 I7 South Dakota, USA *43°33'N 96°45'W*
Siping 123 K7 China *43°9'N 124°22'E*
Siple, Mount 166 B4 ▲ Siple Island, Antarctica
Siracusa 77 J1 Italy *37°4'N 15°17'E*
Sir Edward Pellew Group 135 I8 *Island group* Northern Territory, NE Australia
Sīrīk 116 F2 Iran *26°32'N 57°7'E*
Sirikit Reservoir 126 F6 ◎ N Thailand
Sirjan 116 F3 Iran *29°29'N 55°39'E*
Şirnak 111 I5 Turkey *37°33'N 42°27'E*
Sitges 75 L7 Spain *41°14'N 1°49'E*
Sittang 126 E7 ≈ S Burma
Sittard 71 G7 Netherlands *51°N 5°52'E*
Sittingbourne 51 I5 England, UK *51°20'N 0°43'E*
Sittwe 126 D7 Burma *22°9'N 92°51'E*
Sivas 110 G6 Turkey *39°44'N 37°1'E*
Six-Fours-les-Plages 73 I2 France *43°5'N 5°50'E*
Siyazan 111 K7 Azerbaijan *41°5'N 49°5'E*
Skagerrak 69 B5 *Channel* N Europe
Skaidi 68 F13 Norway *70°26'N 24°31'E*
Skarżysko-Kamienna 84 G8 Poland *51°7'N 20°52'E*
Skegness 53 K7 England, UK *53°10'N 0°21'E*
Skellefteå 68 F9 Sweden *64°45'N 20°58'E*
Skelleftealven 68 E10 ≈ N Sweden
Skelmersdale 54 F2 England, UK *53°33'N 2°52'W*
Skelton 54 E6 England, UK *54°42'N 2°58'W*
Skerries 58 H9 Ireland *53°35'N 6°7'W*
Ski 69 C6 Norway *59°43'N 10°50'E*
Skibbereen 59 C4 Ireland *51°33'N 9°15'W*
Skibotn 68 E12 Norway *69°22'N 20°18'E*
Skiddaw 54 E6 ▲ NW England, UK
Skikda 96 G8 Algeria *36°51'N 7°E*
Skipsea 55 K3 England, UK *53°59'N 0°15'W*
Skipton 54 G3 England, UK *53°57'N 2°W*
Skipton-on-Swale 55 H4 England, UK *54°13'N 1°28'W*
Skokholm Island 48 C8 *Island* SW Wales, UK
Skomer Island 48 C8 *Island* SW Wales, UK
Skopje 86 G5 ● Macedonia *42°N 21°28'E*
Skorped 68 E8 Sweden *63°23'N 17°55'E*
Skovorodino 109 J4 Russian Fed. *54°3'N 123°47'E*
Skr̄iveri 69 G4 Latvia *56°39'N 25°8'E*
Skrunda 69 F4 Latvia *56°39'N 22°1'E*
Skull 59 C4 Ireland *51°32'N 9°34'W*
Skwierzyna 84 C10 Poland *52°37'N 15°27'E*
Skye, Isle of 56 C9 *Island* NW Scotland, UK
Skyros 87 H3 *Island* Northern Sporades, Greece, Aegean Sea
Slagelse 69 B3 Denmark *55°25'N 11°22'E*
Slagnäs 68 E10 Sweden *65°36'N 18°10'E*
Slaidburn 54 F3 England, UK *53°58'N 2°29'W*
Slane 58 G9 Ireland *53°43'N 6°37'W*
Slaney 59 G6 ≈ SE Ireland
Slatina 87 H7 Romania *45°27'N 24°21'E*
Slavonski Brod 86 E7 Croatia *45°9'N 18°0'E*
Sławno 84 D12 Poland *54°23'N 16°43'E*
Sleaford 53 I7 England, UK *52°59'N 0°28'W*
Sleat, Sound of 56 D8 *Strait* NW Scotland, UK
Sleights 55 J5 England, UK *54°26'N 0°39'W*
Slieve Gamph 58 D10 ⛰ N Ireland
Slieve Mish Mountains 59 B5 ⛰ SW Ireland
Slievenamon 59 F6 ▲ S Ireland
Sligo 58 E10 Ireland *54°17'N 8°28'W*
Sligo 58 D10 ◈ *County* Ireland
Sligo Bay 58 D10 *Inlet* NW Ireland
Sliven 87 I6 Bulgaria *42°42'N 26°21'E*
Slough 50 F5 England, UK *51°31'N 0°36'W*
Slough 37 ◈ *Unitary authority* England, UK
Slovakia 85 F6 ◆ *Republic* C Europe
Slovenia 83 H4 ◆ *Republic* SE Europe
Slovenské rudohorie 85 F5 ⛰ C Slovakia
Slov"yans'k 89 D4 Ukraine *48°51'N 37°38'E*
Słubice 84 C10 Poland *52°20'N 14°35'E*
Sluch 89 B5 ≈ NW Ukraine
Słupsk 84 D12 Poland *54°28'N 17°1'E*
Slutsk 89 B6 Belarus *53°2'N 27°32'E*
Slyne Head 58 B8 *Headland* W Ireland
Smallwood Reservoir 145 J3 ◎ Newfoundland and Labrador, S Canada
Smara 96 E7 Western Sahara *26°45'N 11°44'W*
Smederevo 86 G7 Serbia and Montenegro *44°41'N 20°56'E*
Smederevska Palanka 86 G7 Serbia and Montenegro *44°24'N 20°56'E*
Smøla 68 B9 *Island* W Norway
Smolensk 89 C6 Russian Fed. *54°48'N 32°8'E*
Snaefell 54 B4 ▲ C Isle of Man
Snaith 55 I2 England, UK *53°42'N 1°8'W*
Snake River 146 E7 ≈ NW USA
Snake River Plain 146 F7 *Plain* Idaho, NW USA
Sneek 70 F12 Netherlands *53°2'N 5°40'E*
Sneem 59 B4 Ireland *51°50'N 10°W*
Sněžka 84 C8 ▲ N Czech Republic
Snina 85 H6 Slovakia *49°N 22°10'E*
Snodland 51 I5 England, UK *51°19'N 0°19'E*
Snowdon 48 E12 ▲ NW Wales, UK
Snowdonia 48 E12 ⛰ NW Wales, UK
Sobradinho, Represa de 163 J6 ⊠ E Brazil
Sobral 163 K7 Brazil *3°45'S 40°20'W*
Sochaczew 84 F9 Poland *52°15'N 20°15'E*
Sochi 89 E3 Russian Fed. *43°35'N 39°46'E*
Society Islands 24 *Island group* W French Polynesia
Socuéllamos 75 I5 Spain *39°18'N 2°48'W*
Sodankylä 68 G11 Finland *67°26'N 26°35'E*
Söderhamn 69 E7 Sweden *61°19'N 17°10'E*
Södertälje 69 E6 Sweden *59°11'N 17°39'E*
Sofia 87 H6 ● Bulgaria *42°42'N 23°20'E*
Sofiya *see* Sofia
Sogamoso 160 C11 Colombia *5°43'N 72°56'W*
Sognefjorden 69 A7 *Fjord* NE North Sea
Sohag 97 K7 Egypt *26°28'N 31°44'E*
Soham 53 K4 England, UK *52°19'N 0°16'E*
Sokch'o 124 F5 South Korea *38°7'N 128°34'E*
Söke 110 C5 Turkey *37°46'N 27°24'E*
Sokhumi 111 H8 Georgia *43°2'N 41°1'E*
Sokol 88 E8 Russian Fed. *59°26'N 40°9'E*
Sokółka 84 I11 Poland *53°24'N 23°31'E*
Sokolov 85 A7 Czech Republic *50°10'N 12°38'E*
Sokołów Podlaski 84 H10 Poland *52°26'N 22°14'E*
Sokone 96 D5 Senegal *13°53'N 16°22'W*
Sokoto 96 G5 Nigeria *13°5'N 5°16'E*
Solapur 118 G4 India *17°43'N 75°54'E*
Sol, Costa del 75 I3 *Physical region* S Spain
Solec Kujawski 84 E10 Poland *53°4'N 18°9'E*
Solent, The 50 E3 *Channel* S England, UK
Solihull 52 G5 England, UK *52°25'N 1°45'W*
Solihull 37 ◈ *Unitary authority* England, UK
Solikamsk 88 H8 Russian Fed. *59°37'N 56°46'E*
Sol'-Iletsk 89 H5 Russian Fed. *51°9'N 55°5'E*
Solimões, Rio 162 E7 ≈ C Brazil
Solingen 82 D9 Germany *51°10'N 7°5'E*
Sollefteå 68 E8 Sweden *63°9'N 17°15'E*
Sollentuna 69 E6 Sweden *59°26'N 17°56'E*
Solomon Islands 128 ◆ *Commonwealth republic* W Pacific Ocean
Soltau 82 E10 Germany *52°59'N 9°50'E*
Sol'tsy 89 C7 Russian Fed. *58°9'N 30°23'E*
Solva 48 C8 Wales, UK *51°53'N 5°9'W*
Solway Firth 54 D6 *Inlet* England/Scotland, UK
Solwezi 99 H5 Zambia *12°11'S 26°23'E*
Soma 125 K5 Japan *37°50'N 140°52'E*
Somalia 97 N4 ◆ *Republic* E Africa
Somali Plain 25 *Undersea feature* W Indian Ocean
Someren 70 F8 Netherlands *51°23'N 5°42'E*
Somerset 49 G6 ◈ *County* England, UK
Somerset Island 144 G6 *Island* Queen Elizabeth Islands, Northwest Territories, NW Canada
Somme 72 G8 ≈ N France
Somoto 150 G2 Nicaragua *13°29'N 86°36'W*
Songea 99 J6 Tanzania *10°42'S 35°39'E*
Songkhla 126 F4 Thailand *7°12'N 100°35'E*
Sonoran Desert 146 E4 *Desert* Mexico/USA *see also* Altar, Desierto de
Sonsonate 150 F2 El Salvador *13°44'N 89°43'W*
Sopot 84 E12 Poland *54°26'N 18°33'E*
Sopron 85 D5 Hungary *47°40'N 16°35'E*
Sorgues 73 I3 France *44°N 4°52'E*
Sorgun 110 F6 Turkey *39°49'N 35°10'E*
Soria 75 I8 Spain *41°47'N 2°26'W*
Sorong 127 L3 Indonesia *0°50'S 131°17'E*
Sørøya 68 F13 *Island* N Norway
Sortavala 88 C9 Russian Fed. *61°45'N 30°37'E*
Sotkamo 68 H9 Finland *64°6'N 28°30'E*
Sŭul *see* Seoul
Soúrpi 87 H3 Greece *39°7'N 22°55'E*
Sousse 97 H8 Tunisia *35°46'N 10°38'E*
South Africa 98 G2 ◆ *Republic* S Africa
Southall 50 G5 England, UK *54°35'N 1°8'W*
South America 161 *Continent*
Southampton 50 D3 England, UK *50°54'N 1°23'W*
Southampton, City of 37 ◈ *Unitary authority* England, UK
Southampton Island 145 H5 *Island* Northwest Territories, NE Canada
South Andaman 119 K3 *Island* Andaman Islands, India, NE Indian Ocean
South Australia 135 H5 ◈ *State* Australia
South Ayrshire 57 E4 ◈ *Unitary authority* Scotland, UK
South Bank 55 I5 England, UK *54°35'N 1°10'W*
South Bend 147 K6 Indiana, USA *41°40'N 86°15'W*
Southborough 51 H4 England, UK *51°9'N 0°15'E*
South Bruny Island 135 J1 *Island* Tasmania, SE Australia
South Carolina 147 M5 ◈ *State* USA
South Cave 55 J3 England, UK *53°45'N 0°44'W*
South Cerney 48 I8 England, UK *51°42'N 1°58'W*
South China Sea 123 K1 *Sea* SE Asia
South Dakota 147 H7 ◈ *State* USA
South Downs 50 F3 *Hill range* SE England, UK
Southeast Indian Ridge 25 *Undersea feature* Indian Ocean/Pacific Ocean
South East Point 135 J1 *Headland* Victoria, S Australia
Southend-on-Sea 51 I5 England, UK *51°33'N 0°43'E*
Southend-on-Sea 37 ◈ *Unitary authority* England, UK
Southern Alps 136 C3 ⛰ South Island, New Zealand
Southern Cross 134 D3 Western Australia *31°17'S 119°15'E*
Southern Indian Lake 144 G3 ◎ Manitoba, C Canada
Southern Ocean 24 *Ocean* Atlantic Ocean/Indian Ocean/Pacific Ocean
Southery 53 K5 England, UK *52°31'N 0°23'E*
South Esk 57 H7 ≈ E Scotland, UK
South Foreland 51 K4 *Headland* SE England, UK
South Georgia 24 *Island* South Georgia and the South Sandwich Islands, SW Atlantic Ocean
South Georgia and the South Sandwich Islands 12 *UK* ◇ Atlantic Ocean
South Gloucestershire 49 H7 ◈ *Unitary authority* England, UK
South Goulburn Island 135 H9 *Island* Northern Territory, N Australia
South Hayling 50 E3 England, UK *50°47'N 1°0'W*
South Indian Basin 25 *Undersea feature* Indian Ocean/Pacific Ocean
South Island 136 C3 *Island* S New Zealand
South Korea 124 F5 ◆ *Republic* E Asia
South Lanarkshire 57 F4 ◈ *Unitary authority* Scotland, UK
South Molton 49 E6 England, UK *51°0'N 3°52'W*
South Orkney Islands 166 A7 *Island group* Antarctica
South Pole 166 D5 Antarctica
Southport 54 E2 England, UK *53°39'N 3°1'W*
South Ronaldsay 56 G13 *Island* NE Scotland, UK
South Shetland Islands 166 A6 *Island group* Antarctica
South Shields 55 H7 England, UK *55°N 1°25'W*
South Sound 59 C7 *Sound* W Ireland
South Taranaki Bight 136 D5 *Bight* SE Tasman Sea
South Tyne 54 F6 ≈ N England, UK
South Tyneside 36 ◈ *Unitary authority* England, UK
South Uist 56 A9 *Island* NW Scotland, UK
Southwark 37 ◈ *London Borough* England, UK
Southwell 53 H7 England, UK *53°4'N 0°55'W*
South West Cape 136 B1 *Headland* Stewart Island, New Zealand
Southwest Indian Ridge 25 *Undersea feature* SW Indian Ocean
Southwest Pacific Basin 24 *Undersea feature* SE Pacific Ocean
Southwold 53 N4 England, UK *52°15'N 1°36'E*
South Woodham Ferrers 51 I6 England, UK *51°39'N 0°37'E*
Sovetsk 69 F3 Russian Fed. *53°4'N 21°52'E*
Sowerby 55 H4 England, UK *54°13'N 1°22'W*
Soweto 99 H3 South Africa *26°8'S 27°54'E*
Spain 75 I7 ◆ *Monarchy* SW Europe
Spalding 53 J6 England, UK *52°49'N 0°6'W*
Spaldwick 53 I4 England, UK *52°21'N 0°24'W*
Spanish Town 151 I3 Jamaica *18°N 76°57'W*
Sparti 86 G2 Greece *37°5'N 22°25'E*
Spean Bridge 56 E8 Scotland, UK *56°53'N 4°56'W*
Spencer Gulf 135 H3 *Gulf* South Australia
Spennymoor 55 H6 England, UK *54°41'N 1°43'W*
Spey 56 G9 ≈ NE Scotland, UK
Spiddle 58 C8 Ireland *53°16'N 9°18'W*
Spijkenisse 70 D9 Netherlands *51°52'N 4°19'E*
Spilsby 53 J7 England, UK *53°11'N 0°5'E*
Spin Buldak 117 I3 Afghanistan *31°1'N 66°23'E*
Spittal of Glenshee 56 G8 Scotland, UK *56°49'N 3°23'W*
Split 86 E6 Croatia *43°31'N 16°27'E*
Spofforth 55 H3 England, UK *53°58'N 1°31'W*
Spokane 146 F8 Washington, USA *47°40'N 117°26'W*
Spratly Islands 127 H5 *Disputed* ◇ Asia
Spree 82 H9 ≈ E Germany
Springfield 146 K6 Illinois, USA *39°48'N 89°39'W*
Springfield 147 J5 Missouri, USA *37°13'N 93°18'W*
Springfield 147 L6 Ohio, USA *39°55'N 83°49'W*
Springs Junction 136 D4 New Zealand *42°21'S 172°11'E*
Springsure 135 K5 Queensland, Australia *24°9'S 148°6'E*
Spruce Knob 147 M6 ▲ West Virginia, NE USA
Spurn Head 53 J9 *Headland* E England, UK
Sri Aman 127 H3 Malaysia *1°15'N 111°26'E*
Sri Jayawardanapura 119 H1 Sri Lanka *6°54'N 79°58'E*
Srikakulam 119 I4 India *18°18'N 83°54'E*
Sri Lanka 119 H1 ◆ *Republic* S Asia
Srinagar 118 G9 India *34°7'N 74°50'E*
Środa Wielkopolska 84 D9 Poland *52°13'N 17°17'E*
Stack Skerry 56 E13 *Island* N Scotland, UK
Stade 82 E11 Germany *53°36'N 9°29'E*
Stadskanaal 70 H12 Netherlands *53°N 6°55'E*
Stafford 52 F6 England, UK *52°48'N 2°7'W*
Staffordshire 52 F6 ◈ *County* England, UK
Staindrop 55 H5 England, UK *54°36'N 1°48'W*
Staines 50 G5 England, UK *51°25'N 0°29'W*
Stainforth 54 G4 England, UK *54°6'N 2°18'W*
Stalowa Wola 84 H8 Poland *50°35'N 22°2'E*
Stamford 53 I6 England, UK *52°39'N 0°32'W*
Stamford 147 N7 Connecticut, USA *41°3'N 73°32'W*
Stamford Bridge 55 I3 England, UK *53°59'N 0°49'W*
Standish 54 F2 England, UK *53°34'N 2°38'W*
Stanhope 54 G6 England, UK *54°45'N 2°4'W*
Stanley 161 E2 ○ Falkland Islands *51°45'S 57°56'W*
Stanley 55 H6 England, UK *54°52'N 1°47'W*
Stannington 55 H7 England, UK *55°7'N 1°44'W*
Stansted Mountfitchet 51 H7 England, U *51°54'N 0°12'E*
Stanthorpe 135 L4 Queensland, Australia *28°35'S 151°52'E*
Stanton 53 L4 England, UK *52°19'N 0°47*
Staphorst 70 G11 Netherlands *52°38'N 6°*
Staplehurst 51 I4 England, UK *51°9'N 0°3*
Starachowice 84 G8 Poland *51°4'N 21°2'*
Stará L'ubovňa 85 G6 Slovakia *49°19'N 2*
Stara Zagora 87 I5 Bulgaria *42°26'N 25°3*
Stargard Szczeciński 84 C11 Poland *53°20'N 15°2'E*
Starogard Gdański 84 E11 Poland *53°57'N 18°29'E*
Starominskaya 89 D3 Russian Fed. *46°31'N 39°3'E*
Start Bay 49 F4 *Bay* SW England, UK
Start Point 49 F3 *Headland* SW England, U
Staryy Oskol 89 D5 Russian Fed. *51°21'N 37°52'E*
Stavanger 69 A6 Norway *58°58'N 5°43'E*
Stavropol' 89 E3 Russian Fed. *45°2'N 41°5*
Staxton 55 J4 England, UK *54°12'N 0°33'*
Steenwijk 70 G11 Netherlands *52°47'N 6°*
Steinkjer 68 C9 Norway *64°1'N 11°29'E*
Stendal 82 F10 Germany *52°36'N 11°52'E*
Sterlitamak 89 H6 Russian Fed. *53°39'N 5*
Šternberk 85 D7 Czech Republic *49°45'N 17°20'E*
Steroh 115 K1 Yemen *12°21'N 53°50'E*
Stevenage 50 G7 England, UK *51°55'N 0°*
Stewart Island 136 B1 *Island* S New Zeala
Steyr 83 H6 Austria *48°2'N 14°26'E*
Stickford 53 J7 England, UK *53°7'N 0°0'E*
Stickney 53 J7 England, UK *53°5'N 0°6'W*
Stillington 55 I4 England, UK *54°7'N 1°4'*
Stilton 53 J5 England, UK *52°29'N 0°18'W*
Stirling 57 F6 Scotland, UK *56°7'N 3°57'W*
Stirling 57 F6 ◈ *Unitary authority* Scotland
Stjørdalshalsen 68 C8 Norway *63°27'N 10*
Stockach 83 E5 Germany *47°51'N 9°1'E*
Stockbridge 50 D4 England, UK *51°7'N 1°*
Stockholm 69 E6 ● Sweden *59°17'N 18°3*
Stockport 54 G1 England, UK *53°25'N 2°1*
Stockport 36 ◈ *Unitary authority* England,
Stocksbridge 52 G8 England, UK *53°28'N 1°43'W*
Stockton 146 D6 California, USA *37°56'N 121°19'W*
Stockton-on-Tees 55 I5 England, UK *54°34'N 1°19'W*
Stockton-on-Tees 36 ◈ *Unitary authority* England, UK
Stokenchurch 50 F6 England, UK *51°39'N 0°49'W*
Stoke-on-Trent 52 F7 England, UK *53°N 2°*
Stoke-on-Trent, City of 37 ◈ *Unitary auth* England, UK
Stokesley 55 I5 England, UK *54°28'N 1°18*
Stone 48 H8 England, UK *51°40'N 2°29'W*
Stone 50 F6 England, UK *51°47'N 0°52'W*
Stone 52 F6 England, UK *52°53'N 2°13'W*
Stonehaven 56 I8 Scotland, UK *56°59'N 2°*
Støren 68 C8 Norway *63°2'N 10°16'E*
Stornoway 56 C11 Scotland, UK *58°13'N 6°23'W*
Storrington 50 G3 England, UK *50°54'N 0°*
Storsjön 68 D8 ◎ C Sweden
Storuman 68 E9 Sweden *65°5'N 17°10'E*
Storuman 68 D10 ◎ N Sweden
Stour 53 L3 ≈ E England, UK
Stourbridge 52 F5 England, UK *52°27'N 2°*
Stourport-on-Severn 52 F4 England, UK *52°19'N 2°18'W*
Stow 57 H5 Scotland, UK *55°41'N 2°55'W*
Stowmarket 53 L4 England, UK *52°5'N 0°5*
Stow-on-the-Wold 48 I8 England, UK *51°56'N 1°50'W*
Strabane 58 F12 Northern Ireland, UK *54°49'N 7°27'W*
Strabane 58 F11 ◈ *District* Northern Ireland
Stradbally 59 F7 Ireland *52°59'N 7°13'W*
Strakonice 85 B6 Czech Republic *49°14'N 13°55'E*
Stralsund 82 G11 Germany *54°18'N 13°6'E*
Strangford Lough 58 I11 *Inlet* E Northern Ireland, UK
Stranraer 57 E3 Scotland, UK *54°54'N 5°2'*
Strasbourg 73 J7 France *48°35'N 7°45'E*
Stratford 136 D5 New Zealand *39°20'S 174°16'E*
Stratford-upon-Avon 52 G4 England, UK *52°12'N 1°41'W*
Strathy Point 56 F12 *Headland* N Scotland,
Straubing 83 G6 Germany *48°53'N 12°35'E*
Streatham 50 G5 England, UK *51°25'N 0°8*
Street 49 G6 England, UK *51°7'N 2°44'W*
Strehaia 87 H7 Romania *44°37'N 23°10'E*
Strelka 109 H4 Russian Fed. *58°5'N 92°54'E*
Strensall 55 I4 England, UK *54°3'N 1°7'W*
Stretford 54 G1 England, UK *53°26'N 2°13*
Stretton 53 I6 England, UK *52°43'N 0°36'W*
Strokestown 58 E9 Ireland *53°47'N 8°6'W*
Stromboli 77 J3 🌋 Isola Stromboli, SW Italy
Stromeferry 56 D9 Scotland, UK *57°20'N 5°35'W*
Stromness 56 G13 Scotland, UK *58°57'N 3°18'W*
Strömstad 69 C6 Sweden *58°56'N 11°11'E*
Strömsund 68 D9 Sweden *63°51'N 15°35'E*
Stronsay 56 H13 *Island* NE Scotland, UK
Strontian 57 D7 Scotland, UK *56°42'N 5°30*
Stroud 48 H8 England, UK *51°46'N 2°15'W*
Strumble Head 48 C9 *Headland* SW Wales,
Strymonas 87 H4 ≈ Bulgaria/Greece
Stryy 89 A5 Ukraine *49°16'N 23°51'E*
Strzelce Opolskie 84 E8 Poland *50°31'N 18°19'E*
Studholme 136 C2 New Zealand *44°45'S 171°8'E*
Sturry 51 J5 England, UK *51°18'N 1°3'E*
Stuttgart 83 E6 Germany *48°47'N 9°12'E*
Stykkishólmur 68 A11 Iceland *65°4'N 22°4*
Styr 89 B5 ≈ Belarus/Ukraine
Subotica 86 F8 Serbia and Montenegro *46°6'N 19°41'E*
Suceava 87 I9 Romania *47°41'N 26°16'E*
Suck 58 E8 ≈ C Ireland

◆ Country ● Country capital ◇ Dependent territory ○ Dependent territory capital ◈ Administrative region ▲ Mountain ⛰ Mountain range 🌋 Volcano ≈ River ◎ Lake ⊠ Reservoir

161 D7 ● Bolivia 18°53'S 65°25'W
163 I8 Brazil 1°31'N 50°W
97 K5 ◆ Republic N Africa
y 145 I2 Ontario, Canada 46°29'N 81°W
y 52 G6 England, UK 52°52'N 1°53'W
y 53 L3 England, UK 52°4'N 0°43'E
7 K4 Wetland S Sudan
n 85 D7 ⛰ Czech Republic/Poland
K3 〰 S Sudan
75 K5 Spain 39°13'N 0°19'W
7 K7 Egypt 29°59'N 32°33'E
anal 97 K7 Canal NE Egypt
'ulf of 114 C8 Gulf NE Egypt
53 L4 ◈ County England, UK
Gölü 110 E5 ◎ SW Turkey
115 L6 Oman 24°20'N 56°43'E
tar 123 H8 Mongolia 50°12'N 106°14'E
2 F8 Germany 50°37'N 10°43'E
E5 〰 S Ireland
l 118 E6 Pakistan 24°36'N 68°6'E
mi 126 G1 Indonesia 6°55'S 106°56'E
wa 125 K5 Japan 37°16'N 140°20'E
a 88 E8 〰 NW Russian Fed.
118 E7 Pakistan 27°45'N 68°46'E
o 124 G2 Japan 32°55'N 132°42'E
ān Range 118 F8 ⛰ C Pakistan
epulauan 127 J3 Island group lonesia
v 84 F8 Poland 51°21'N 19°57'E
kerry 56 E13 Island N Scotland, UK
a 160 A9 Peru 4°54'S 80°42'W
rchipelago 127 I4 Island group hilippines
ea 127 J5 Sea SW Philippines
ta 117 J7 Kyrgyzstan 39°57'N 69°31'E
, Pulau 127 I1 Island Lesser Sunda Islands, lonesia
, Selat 127 I1 Strait Lesser Sunda Islands, lonesia
wanga 99 I6 Tanzania 7°57'S 31°37'E
98 E6 Angola 11°13'S 13°53'E
rgh 56 I11 Scotland, UK 59°52'N 1°12'W
rgh Head 56 I11 Headland cotland, UK
85 D4 Hungary 47°1'N 17°13'E
h 97 J4 Sudan 9°50'N 27°39'E
er Bridge 55 H4 England, UK 'N 1°44'W
er Isles 56 D11 Island group Scotland, UK
ayit 111 L7 Azerbaijan 40°33'N 49°41'E
89 D5 Ukraine 50°54'N 34°49'E
on 124 E4 South Korea 34°56'N 127°29'E
Selat 126 F2 Strait Java/Sumatra, ndonesia
rland 55 H7 England, UK 54°55'N 1°23'W
rland 36 ◈ Unitary authority England, UK
vall 68 E8 Sweden 62°22'N 17°20'E
ipenuh 126 F2 Indonesia 2°S 101°28'E
r 109 I5 Russian Fed. 62°10'N 117°34'E
ussalmi 68 H10 Finland 64°54'N 29°5'E
njoki 68 H8 Finland 62°36'N 27°7'E
rvi 88 C9 Russian Fed. 62°2'N 32°24'E
ior 147 J8 Wisconsin, USA 42'N 92°4'W
ior, Lake 147 K8 ◎ Canada/USA
15 M6 Oman 22°32'N 59°33'E
aya 127 H1 Indonesia 7°14'S 112°45'E
arta 127 H1 Indonesia 7°32'S 110°50'E
y 85 E5 Slovakia 48°5'N 18°10'E
118 F5 India 21°10'N 72°54'E
r 115 L4 Oman 19°56'N 57°47'E
71 G4 〰 W Europe
dranagar 118 F6 India 22°44'N 71°43'E
's Paradise 135 L4 Queensland, Australia 54'S 153°18'E
t 108 F5 Russian Fed. 61°13'N 73°28'E
am 160 E11 ◆ Republic N South America
ob 117 K7 〰 C Tajikistan
y 37 ◈ County England, UK
ey 68 A10 Island S Iceland
a-wan 125 J3 Bay SE Japan
76 E8 Italy 45°10'N 7°1'E
ren 71 G7 Netherlands 51°4'N 5°50'E
nan 109 K6 Russian Fed. 62°46'N 148°8'E
118 F7 〰 India/Pakistan
n 50 G5 England, UK 51°20'N 0°13'W
n 37 ◈ London Borough England, UK
n Bridge 53 K6 England, UK 47'N 0°11'E
n Coldfield 52 G5 England, UK 34'N 1°48'W
n in Ashfield 53 H7 England, UK 7'N 1°16'W
n-on-Trent 53 I7 England, UK 10'N 0°54'W
n Scotney 50 E4 England, UK 10'N 1°23'W
128 ● Fiji 18°8'S 178°27'E
łki 84 H12 Poland 54°6'N 22°56'E
ydān 115 K6 United Arab Emirates 30'N 55°19'E
on 124 E5 South Korea 37°17'N 127°3'E
ou 123 K4 China 31°23'N 120°34'E
125 I5 Japan 37°24'N 137°13'E
ard 108 E8 Norwegian ◇ Arctic Ocean
isen 68 D11 Glacier C Norway
68 D8 Sweden 62°2'N 14°20'E
stavik 68 D8 Sweden 62°40'N 14°24'E
ograd 89 E3 Russian Fed. 45°20'N 42°53'E
vy 85 D7 Czech Republic 49°45'N 16°27'E
odnyy 109 K4 Russian Fed. 24'N 128°5'E
fham 53 L5 England, UK 52°39'N 0°40'E
nby 55 I5 England, UK 54°24'N 1°16'W
kopmund 98 F3 Namibia 22°40'S 14°34'E
e 55 H4 〰 N England, UK
nage 49 I5 England, UK 50°37'N 1°59'W
n Island 151 H3 Island C Falkland Islands
nsea 49 E7 Wales, UK 51°38'N 3°57'W
nsea 49 E7 ◈ Unitary authority Wales, UK
nsea Bay 49 E7 Bay S Wales, UK
rzędz 84 D10 Poland 52°24'N 17°5'E
ziland 99 I3 ◆ Monarchy S Africa
den 68 D8 ◆ Monarchy N Europe
nica 84 D8 Poland 50°51'N 16°29'E
win 84 C11 Poland 53°47'N 15°44'E
bodzice 84 D8 Poland 50°54'N 16°23'E
Świebodzin 84 C9 Poland 52°15'N 15°31'E
Świecie 84 E11 Poland 53°24'N 18°24'E
Swilly, Lough 58 F12 Inlet N Ireland
Swindon 49 I7 England, UK 51°34'N 1°47'W
Swindon 49 I7 ◈ Unitary authority England, UK
Swinford 58 D9 Ireland 53°57'N 9°7'W
Swinford 53 H5 England, UK 52°25'N 1°14'W
Świnoujście 84 B11 Poland 53°54'N 14°13'E
Switzerland 83 D5 ◆ Federal republic C Europe
Swords 58 H8 Ireland 53°28'N 6°13'W
Sydney 135 K3 New South Wales, Australia 33°55'S 151°10'E
Sydney 145 K2 Nova Scotia, Canada 46°10'N 60°10'W
Syeverodonets'k 89 D4 Ukraine 48°59'N 38°28'E
Syktyvkar 88 G9 Russian Fed. 61°42'N 50°45'E
Sylhet 119 K6 Bangladesh 24°53'N 91°51'E
Syracuse 147 M7 New York, USA 43°3'N 76°9'W
Syr Darya 108 E3 〰 C Asia
Syria 111 H4 ◆ Republic SW Asia
Syrian Desert 111 H3 Desert SW Asia
Syros 87 I2 Island Cyclades, Greece, Aegean Sea
Syston 53 H6 England, UK 52°41'N 1°6'W
Syzran' 89 F6 Russian Fed. 53°10'N 48°23'E
Szamotuły 84 D10 Poland 52°35'N 16°36'E
Szczecin 84 C11 Poland 53°25'N 14°32'E
Szczecinek 84 D11 Poland 53°43'N 16°40'E
Szczytno 84 G11 Poland 53°34'N 21°E
Szeged 85 F3 Hungary 46°17'N 20°6'E
Székesfehérvár 85 E4 Hungary 47°13'N 18°24'E
Szekszárd 85 E3 Hungary 46°21'N 18°41'E
Szolnok 85 F4 Hungary 47°11'N 20°12'E
Szombathely 85 D4 Hungary 47°14'N 16°38'E
Szprotawa 84 C9 Poland 51°33'N 15°32'E

T

Taagan 56 D10 Scotland, UK 57°38'N 5°17'W
Tábor 85 C6 Czech Republic 49°25'N 14°41'E
Tabor 109 K7 Russian Fed. 71°14'N 150°23'E
Tabora 99 I7 Tanzania 5°4'S 32°49'E
Tabrīz 116 C6 Iran 38°5'N 46°18'E
Tabūk 114 D8 Saudi Arabia 28°25'N 36°34'E
Täby 69 E6 Sweden 59°29'N 18°4'E
Tacaná, Volcán 150 F3 🌋 Guatemala/Mexico
Tacheng 122 E8 China 46°45'N 82°55'E
Tachov 85 A7 Czech Republic 49°48'N 12°38'E
Tacloban 127 J5 Philippines 11°15'N 125°E
Tacna 161 C7 Peru 18°S 70°15'W
Tacoma 146 E8 Washington, USA 47°15'N 122°27'W
Tacuarembó 161 E5 Uruguay 31°42'S 56°W
Tadcaster 55 I3 England, UK 53°53'N 1°18'W
Tademaït, Plateau du 96 F7 Plateau C Algeria
Tadley 50 E5 England, UK 51°20'N 1°13'W
T'aebaek-sanmaek 124 F5 ⛰ E South Korea
Taedong-gang 124 E6 〰 C North Korea
Taegu 124 F4 South Korea 35°55'N 128°33'E
Taejon 124 E4 South Korea 36°20'N 127°28'E
Taff 49 F7 〰 SE Wales, UK
Taganrog 89 D4 Russian Fed. 47°10'N 38°55'E
Taganrog, Gulf of 89 D4 Gulf Russian Fed./Ukraine
Taghmon 59 G6 Ireland 52°17'N 6°45'W
Taguatinga 163 I5 Brazil 12°16'S 46°25'W
Tagus 75 I6 〰 Portugal/Spain
Tahat 96 G6 ▲ SE Algeria
Tahoe, Lake 146 E6 ◎ California/Nevada, W USA
Tahoua 96 G5 Niger 14°53'N 5°18'E
T'aichung 123 K2 Taiwan 24°9'N 120°40'E
Taihape 136 E5 New Zealand 39°41'S 175°47'E
Tailem Bend 135 I3 South Australia 35°20'S 139°34'E
Tain 56 F10 Scotland, UK 57°49'N 4°4'W
T'ainan 123 K2 Taiwan 23°1'N 120°5'E
T'aipei 123 K3 ● Taiwan 25°2'N 121°28'E
Taiping 126 F4 Malaysia 4°54'N 100°42'E
Taiwan 123 K2 ◆ Republic E Asia
Taiwan 123 K2 Island E Asia
Taiwan Strait 123 K2 Strait China/Taiwan
Taiyuan 123 I5 China 37°48'N 112°33'E
Ta'izz 114 G1 Yemen 13°36'N 44°4'E
Tajikistan 117 J7 ◆ Republic C Asia
Takamatsu 125 H3 Japan 34°19'N 133°59'E
Takaoka 125 I4 Japan 36°44'N 137°2'E
Takapuna 136 E7 New Zealand 36°48'S 174°46'E
Takikawa 125 K8 Japan 43°35'N 141°54'E
Takla Makan Desert 122 D6 Desert NW China
Talara 160 A9 Peru 4°31'S 81°17'W
Talas 117 K8 Kyrgyzstan 42°29'N 72°21'E
Talaud, Kepulauan 127 K4 Island group E Indonesia
Talavera de la Reina 75 H6 Spain 39°58'N 4°50'W
Talca 161 C4 Chile 35°28'S 71°42'W
Talcahuano 161 C4 Chile 36°43'S 73°7'W
Taldykorgan 108 G2 Kazakhstan 45°N 78°23'E
Talgarth 48 F9 Wales, UK 52°0'N 3°14'W
Tall 'Afar 111 I5 Iraq 36°22'N 42°27'E
Tallahassee 147 L4 Florida, USA 30°26'N 84°17'W
Tallinn 69 G6 ● Estonia 59°26'N 24°42'E
Tallow 59 E5 Ireland 52°4'N 8°W
Tall Ẓāhir 111 I5 Iraq 36°51'N 42°29'E
Talnakh 109 H6 Russian Fed. 69°26'N 88°27'E
Taloqan 117 J6 Afghanistan 36°44'N 69°33'E
Talsi 69 G5 Latvia 57°14'N 22°35'E
Taltal 161 C6 Chile 25°22'S 70°27'W
Talvik 68 F13 Norway 70°2'N 22°59'E
Tamabo, Banjaran 127 H4 ⛰ East Malaysia
Tamale 96 F4 Ghana 9°21'N 0°54'W
Tamanrasset 96 G6 Algeria 22°49'N 5°32'E
Tamar 49 D5 〰 SW England, UK
Tamazunchale 150 D4 Mexico 21°17'N 98°46'W
Tambacounda 96 D5 Senegal 13°44'N 13°43'W
Tambov 89 E5 Russian Fed. 52°43'N 41°28'E
Tameside 36 ◈ Unitary authority England, UK
Tamiahua, Laguna de 150 E4 Lagoon E Mexico
Tamil Nādu 118 G2 ◈ State India
Tampa 147 M3 Florida, USA 27°57'N 82°27'W
Tampere 69 G7 Finland 61°30'N 23°45'E
Tampico 150 E4 Mexico 22°18'N 97°52'W
Tamworth 135 K3 New South Wales, Australia 31°7'S 150°54'E
Tamworth 52 G5 England, UK 52°39'N 1°40'W
Tana 99 J7 〰 SE Kenya
Tanabe 125 H3 Japan 33°43'N 135°22'E
Tana Bru 68 G13 Norway 70°11'N 28°6'E
Tanami Desert 134 G7 Desert Northern Territory, N Australia
Tanat 48 F11 〰 E Wales, UK
Tandil 161 E4 Argentina 37°18'S 59°10'W
Tane Range 126 E6 ⛰ W Thailand
Tanga 99 J7 Tanzania 5°7'S 39°5'E
Tanganyika, Lake 99 H7 ◎ E Africa
Tanggula Shan 122 E4 ⛰ W China
Tangier 96 F8 Morocco 35°49'N 5°49'W
Tangshan 123 J6 China 39°39'N 118°15'E
Tanimbar, Kepulauan 127 L1 Island group Moluccas, E Indonesia
Tännäs 68 C8 Sweden 62°27'N 12°40'E
Tan-Tan 96 E7 Morocco 28°30'N 11°11'W
Tanzania 99 I6 ◆ Republic E Africa
Taoudenni 96 F6 Mali 22°46'N 3°54'W
Taoudenni Basin 91 Basin Mali/Mauritania
Tapa 69 H6 Estonia 59°15'N 26°E
Tapachula 150 F2 Mexico 14°53'N 92°18'W
Tapajós, Rio 162 G7 〰 NW Brazil
Tapauá 162 E7 Brazil 5°42'S 64°15'W
Tapauá, Rio 162 E7 〰 W Brazil
Taranaki, Mount 136 D5 🌋 North Island, New Zealand
Tarancón 75 I6 Spain 40°1'N 3°1'W
Taransay 56 B10 Island NW Scotland, UK
Taranto 77 K4 Italy 40°30'N 17°11'E
Taranto, Gulf of 77 K4 Coastal sea feature S Italy
Tarare 73 I5 France 45°54'N 4°26'E
Tarascon 73 I3 France 43°48'N 4°39'E
Tarazona 75 J8 Spain 41°54'N 1°44'W
Tarbat Ness 56 F10 Headland N Scotland, UK
Tarbert 59 C6 Ireland 52°34'N 9°29'W
Tarbert 56 B10 Scotland, UK 57°54'N 6°48'W
Tarbert 57 D5 Scotland, UK 55°52'N 5°26'W
Tarbes 72 F2 France 43°14'N 0°4'E
Tarbet 57 E6 Scotland, UK 56°13'N 4°45'W
Tarcoola 135 H4 South Australia 30°44'S 134°34'E
Taree 135 L3 New South Wales, Australia 31°56'S 152°29'E
Târgovişte 87 I7 Romania 44°54'N 25°29'E
Târgu Jiu 87 H7 Romania 45°3'N 23°20'E
Târgu Mureş 87 H8 Romania 46°33'N 24°36'E
Ţarīf 115 K6 United Arab Emirates 24°2'N 53°47'E
Tarija 161 D6 Bolivia 21°33'S 64°42'W
Tarim 115 I2 Yemen 16°N 48°50'E
Tarim He 122 D6 〰 NW China
Tarn 72 G3 Cultural region France
Tarn 73 H3 〰 S France
Tärnaby 68 D10 Sweden 65°44'N 15°20'E
Tarnobrzeg 84 G8 Poland 50°35'N 21°40'E
Tarnów 85 G7 Poland 50°1'N 20°59'E
Tarporley 52 E7 England, UK 53°10'N 2°42'W
Tarragona 75 L7 Spain 41°7'N 1°15'E
Tàrrega 75 L8 Spain 41°39'N 1°9'E
Tarsus 110 F5 Turkey 36°52'N 34°52'E
Tartu 69 H5 Estonia 58°20'N 26°44'E
Tartus 110 F4 Syria 34°55'N 35°52'E
Tarvin 52 F7 England, UK 53°13'N 2°50'W
Tarvisio 77 I9 Italy 46°31'N 13°33'E
Ţashk, Daryācheh-ye 116 E3 ◎ C Iran
Tashkent 117 J7 ● Uzbekistan 41°19'N 69°17'E
Tash-Kumyr 117 K8 Kyrgyzstan 41°22'N 72°9'E
Tasikmalaya 126 G1 Indonesia 7°20'S 108°16'E
Tasman Bay 136 D4 Inlet South Island, New Zealand
Tasmania 135 J1 ◈ State Australia
Tasman Sea 135 L2 Sea SW Pacific Ocean
Tassili-n-Ajjer 96 G7 Plateau E Algeria
Tatabánya 85 E4 Hungary 47°33'N 18°23'E
Tathlith 114 G4 Saudi Arabia 19°38'N 43°32'E
Tatra Mountains 85 F6 ⛰ Poland/Slovakia
Tatvan 111 I6 Turkey 38°31'N 42°15'E
Tauá 163 K7 Brazil 6°4'S 40°26'W
Taubaté 163 I3 Brazil 23°S 45°36'W
Taumarunui 136 E6 New Zealand 38°52'S 175°14'E
Taunggyi 126 E7 Burma 20°47'N 97°0'E
Taunton 49 G6 England, UK 51°1'N 3°6'W
Taupo 136 E6 New Zealand 38°42'S 176°5'E
Taupo, Lake 136 E6 ◎ North Island, New Zealand
Tauragė 69 F3 Lithuania 55°16'N 22°17'E
Tauranga 136 E6 New Zealand 37°42'S 176°9'E
Tavas 110 D5 Turkey 37°33'N 29°4'E
Tavira 74 F3 Portugal 37°7'N 7°39'W
Tavoy 126 E6 Burma 14°2'N 98°12'E
Tavy 49 E4 〰 SW England, UK
Taw 49 E5 〰 SW England, UK
Tawau 127 I4 Malaysia 4°16'N 117°54'E
Tawnyinah 58 D9 Ireland 53°54'N 8°47'W
Taxco 150 D4 Mexico 18°32'N 99°37'W
Taxiatosh 116 G8 Uzbekistan 42°27'N 59°27'E
Taxtako'pir 116 G8 Uzbekistan 43°4'N 60°23'E
Tay 57 F7 〰 C Scotland, UK
Tāybād 116 G5 Iran 34°48'N 60°46'E
Tay, Firth of 57 H7 Inlet E Scotland, UK
Tay, Loch 57 F7 ◎ C Scotland, UK
Taymā' 114 E7 Saudi Arabia 27°39'N 38°32'E
Taymyr, Ozero 109 H7 ◎ N Russian Fed.
Taymyr, Poluostrov 109 H7 Coastal feature N Russian Fed.
Taz 108 G5 〰 N Russian Fed.
Tāza Khurmātū 111 J4 Iraq 35°18'N 44°22'E
T'bilisi 111 J7 ● Georgia 41°41'N 44°55'E
Tczew 84 E11 Poland 54°5'N 18°46'E
Te Anau 136 B2 New Zealand 45°25'S 167°45'E
Te Anau, Lake 136 B2 ◎ South Island, New Zealand
Tebay 54 F5 England, UK 54°25'N 2°36'W
Tecomán 150 C4 Mexico 18°53'N 103°54'W
Tecpan 150 D3 Mexico 17°12'N 100°39'W
Tedburn St Mary 49 F5 England, UK 50°44'N 3°44'W
Tees 55 H5 〰 N England, UK
Tefé 162 E7 Brazil 3°24'S 64°45'W
Tefé, Rio 162 E7 〰 NW Brazil
Tegal 126 G1 Indonesia 6°52'S 109°7'E
Tegelen 71 G7 Netherlands 51°20'N 6°9'E
Tegucigalpa 150 G2 ● Honduras 14°4'N 87°11'W
Tehrān 116 E5 ● Iran 35°44'N 51°27'E
Tehuacán 150 E3 Mexico 18°29'N 97°24'W
Tehuantepec 150 E3 Mexico 16°18'N 95°14'W
Tehuantepec, Gulf of 150 E3 Coastal sea feature S Mexico
Tehuantepec, Isthmus of 150 E3 Coastal feature SE Mexico
Teifi 48 D9 〰 SW Wales, UK
Teignmouth 49 F4 England, UK 50°34'N 3°29'W
Tejen 116 G6 Turkmenistan 37°24'N 60°29'E
Te Kao 136 D8 New Zealand 34°40'S 172°57'E
Tekax 150 F4 Mexico 20°7'N 89°10'W
Tekeli 108 G2 Kazakhstan 44°50'N 78°47'E
Tekirdağ 110 C7 Turkey 40°59'N 27°31'E
Te Kuiti 136 E6 New Zealand 38°21'S 175°10'E
Telford 52 E6 England, UK 52°42'N 2°28'W
Telford and the Wrekin 37 ◈ Unitary authority England, UK
Tembagapura 127 M2 Indonesia 4°10'S 137°19'E
Teme 52 E4 〰 England/Wales, UK
Temirtau 108 F3 Kazakhstan 50°5'N 72°55'E
Tempio Pausania 76 F4 Italy 40°55'N 9°7'E
Templemore 59 E7 Ireland 52°48'N 7°50'W
Temple Sowerby 54 F6 England, UK 54°38'N 2°31'W
Temuco 161 C4 Chile 38°45'S 72°37'W
Temuka 136 C3 New Zealand 44°14'S 171°17'E
Tenby 48 D8 Wales, UK 51°41'N 4°43'W
Ten Degree Channel 119 K2 Strait Andaman and Nicobar Islands, India, E Indian Ocean
Ténenkou 96 E5 Mali 14°28'N 4°55'W
Ténéré 97 H5 Physical region C Niger
Tengger Shamo 123 H5 Desert N China
Tennant Creek 135 H7 Northern Territory, Australia 19°40'S 134°16'E
Tennessee 147 K5 ◈ State USA
Tennessee River 147 K5 〰 S USA
Tenojoki 68 G13 〰 Finland/Norway
Tenterden 51 I4 England, UK 51°3'N 0°41'E
Teófilo Otoni 163 J4 Brazil 17°52'S 41°31'W
Tepic 150 C4 Mexico 21°30'N 104°55'W
Teplice 84 B8 Czech Republic 50°38'N 13°49'E
Teramo 77 I6 Italy 42°40'N 13°43'E
Tercan 111 H6 Turkey 39°47'N 40°23'E
Teresina 163 J7 Brazil 5°9'S 42°46'W
Termiz 117 I6 Uzbekistan 37°17'N 67°12'E
Termoli 77 J5 Italy 42°0'N 14°58'E
Termon 58 E12 Ireland 55°3'N 7°49'W
Terneuzen 71 C7 Netherlands 51°20'N 3°50'E
Terni 77 H6 Italy 42°34'N 12°38'E
Ternopil' 89 B5 Ukraine 49°32'N 25°38'E
Terracina 77 I5 Italy 41°18'N 13°13'E
Terrassa 75 L7 Spain 41°34'N 2°1'E
Terre Adélie 166 F3 Physical region Antarctica
Terre Haute 147 K6 Indiana, USA 39°27'N 87°24'W
Terschelling 70 F13 Island Waddeneilanden, N Netherlands
Teruel 75 J6 Spain 40°21'N 1°6'W
Tervuren 71 D6 Belgium 50°48'N 4°28'E
Tessalit 96 F6 Mali 20°12'N 0°58'E
Tessenderlo 71 E7 Belgium 51°5'N 5°4'E
Test 50 D4 〰 S England, UK
Tetbury 48 H8 England, UK 51°39'N 2°11'W
Tete 99 I5 Mozambique 16°14'S 33°34'E
Teterow 82 G11 Germany 53°47'N 12°34'E
Tetouan 96 F8 Morocco 35°33'N 5°22'W
Teuva 68 F8 Finland 62°29'N 21°45'E
Teviot 57 H4 〰 SE Scotland, UK
Teviothead 57 H4 Scotland, UK 55°20'N 3°4'W
Te Waewae Bay 136 B1 Bay South Island, New Zealand
Tewkesbury 48 H9 England, UK 51°59'N 2°9'W
Texas 147 I4 ◈ State USA
Texel 70 E12 Island Waddeneilanden, NW Netherlands
Thailand 126 F6 ◆ Monarchy SE Asia
Thailand, Gulf of 126 F5 Gulf SE Asia
Thai Nguyen 126 G7 Vietnam 21°36'N 105°50'E
Thakhèk 126 F6 Laos 17°25'N 104°51'E
Thamarīt 115 K3 Oman 17°39'N 54°2'E
Thamar, Jabal 115 H1 ▲ SW Yemen
Thame 50 E6 England, UK 51°43'N 1°2'W
Thames 136 E7 New Zealand 37°10'S 175°33'E
Thamūd 115 I3 Yemen 17°18'N 49°57'E
Thar Desert 118 F7 Desert India/Pakistan
Thasos 87 I4 Greece 40°47'N 24°43'E
Thasos 87 H4 Island E Greece
Thatcham 50 E5 England, UK 51°24'N 1°17'W
Thaton 126 E6 Burma 16°56'N 97°20'E
Thaxted 51 I7 England, UK 51°57'N 0°15'E
Thayetmyo 126 E7 Burma 19°20'N 95°10'E
The Hague 70 D9 ● Netherlands 52°7'N 4°17'E
The Mumbles 49 E7 Wales, UK 51°34'N 3°55'W
The Pas 144 F2 Manitoba, Canada 53°49'N 101°9'W
Therfield 51 H7 England, UK 52°0'N 0°9'W
Thessaloníki see Salonica
Thetford 53 L5 England, UK 52°25'N 0°45'E
The Valley 151 L4 ○ Anguilla 18°13'N 63°0'W
Thiers 73 H4 France 45°51'N 3°33'E
Thimphu 119 J7 ● Bhutan 27°28'N 89°37'E
Thionville 73 I7 France 49°22'N 6°11'E
Thira 87 I1 Island Cyclades, Greece, Aegean Sea
Thirsk 55 H4 England, UK 54°7'N 1°17'W
Thisted 69 B4 Denmark 56°58'N 8°42'E
Thjórsá 68 B11 〰 C Iceland
Tholen 70 D8 Island SW Netherlands
Thompson 144 G3 Manitoba, Canada 55°45'N 97°54'W
Thonon-les-Bains 73 J5 France 46°22'N 6°30'E
Thorlákshöfn 68 A10 Iceland 63°52'N 21°24'W
Thornbury 49 H7 England, UK 51°37'N 2°36'W
Thorndon 53 L4 England, UK 52°17'N 1°7'E
Thorne 53 H9 England, UK 53°36'N 1°W
Thornhill 57 F4 Scotland, UK 55°13'N 3°46'W
Thornton 54 E3 England, UK 53°52'N 3°1'W
Thornton-le-Street 55 H4 England, UK 54°19'N 1°26'W
Thouars 72 F5 France 46°59'N 0°13'W
Thracian Sea 87 I4 Sea Greece/Turkey
Thrapston 53 I5 England, UK 52°24'N 0°31'W
Threshfield 54 G4 England, UK 54°4'N 2°10'W
Thruxton 50 D4 England, UK 51°12'N 1°43'W
Thuin 71 D5 Belgium 50°21'N 4°18'E
Thun 83 D5 Switzerland 46°46'N 7°38'E
Thunder Bay 145 H2 Ontario, Canada 48°27'N 89°12'W
Thuner See 83 D4 ◎ C Switzerland
Thung Song 126 E4 Thailand 8°10'N 99°41'E
Thurcroft 53 H8 England, UK 53°24'N 1°16'W
Thurles 59 E6 Ireland 52°41'N 7°49'W
Thurlestone 49 E4 England, UK 50°16'N 3°55'W
Thurlow 53 K4 England, UK 52°7'N 0°26'E
Thurrock 37 ◈ Unitary authority England, UK
Thursby 54 E6 England, UK 54°50'N 3°9'W
Thurso 56 G12 Scotland, UK 58°35'N 3°32'W
Thurston Island 166 B5 Island Antarctica
Thyamis 86 G4 〰 W Greece
Tianjin 123 J6 China 39°13'N 117°6'E
Tianshui 123 H5 China 34°33'N 105°51'E
Tiber 77 H6 〰 C Italy
Tibesti 97 I6 ⛰ N Africa
Tiburón, Isla 150 B6 Island NW Mexico
Ticehurst 51 I4 England, UK 51°1'N 0°24'E
Tîchît 96 E5 Mauritania 18°26'N 9°31'W
Ticul 150 F4 Mexico 20°22'N 89°30'W
Tideswell 52 G8 England, UK 53°16'N 1°47'W
Tidjikja 96 D5 Mauritania 18°31'N 11°24'W
Tienen 71 E6 Belgium 50°48'N 4°56'E
Tien Shan 103 ⛰ C Asia
Tierp 69 E6 Sweden 60°20'N 17°30'E
Tierra del Fuego 161 D1 Island Argentina/Chile
Tighina 89 B4 Moldova 46°51'N 29°28'E
Tigris 111 I4 〰 Iraq/Turkey
Tijuana 150 A8 Mexico 32°32'N 117°1'W
Tikhoretsk 89 E3 Russian Fed. 45°51'N 40°7'E
Tikhvin 88 D8 Russian Fed. 59°37'N 33°30'E
Tikrīt 111 J4 Iraq 34°36'N 43°42'E
Tiksi 109 J7 Russian Fed. 71°40'N 128°47'E
Tilburg 70 E8 Netherlands 51°34'N 5°5'E
Tilbury 51 I5 England, UK 51°27'N 0°22'E
Tilehurst 50 E5 England, UK 51°28'N 1°6'W
Tillingham 51 J6 England, UK 51°42'N 0°51'E
Tilos 87 J2 Island Dodecanese, Greece, Aegean Sea
Timan Ridge 88 F10 Ridge NW Russian Fed.
Timaru 136 C2 New Zealand 44°23'S 171°15'E
Timbedgha 96 E5 Mauritania 16°17'N 8°14'W
Timbuktu 96 F5 Mali 16°47'N 3°3'W
Timişoara 86 G8 Romania 45°46'N 21°17'E
Timmins 145 I2 Ontario, Canada 48°9'N 80°1'W
Timon 163 J7 Brazil 5°8'S 42°52'W
Timor 127 J1 Island Lesser Sunda Islands, C Indonesia
Timor Sea 134 F9 Sea E Indian Ocean
Timrå 68 E8 Sweden 62°29'N 17°20'E
Timsgarry 56 B11 Scotland, UK 58°12'N 7°4'W
Tindouf 96 E7 Algeria 27°43'N 8°9'W
Tineo 74 G9 Spain 43°20'N 6°25'W
Tingewick 50 E7 England, UK 51°58'N 1°7'W
Tingsryd 68 D4 Sweden 56°30'N 15°E
Tinos 87 I2 Island Cyclades, Greece, Aegean Sea
Tipperary 59 E6 Ireland 52°29'N 8°10'W
Tipperary 59 E6 ◈ County Ireland
Tip Top Mountain 145 H2 ▲ Ontario, S Canada
Tiracambu, Serra do 163 I7 ⛰ E Brazil
Tirana 86 F4 ● Albania 41°20'N 19°50'E
Tiraspol 89 B4 Moldova 46°50'N 29°35'E
Tiree 57 B7 Island W Scotland, UK
Tiruchchirappalli 118 G2 India 10°50'N 78°43'E
Tisza 85 G5 〰 SE Europe
Tiszakécske 85 F4 Hungary 46°56'N 20°4'E
Tiszaújváros 85 G5 Hungary 47°56'N 21°3'E
Titicaca, Lake 161 C7 ◎ Bolivia/Peru
Titule 99 H8 Dem. Rep. Congo 3°20'N 25°23'E
Tiverton 49 F5 England, UK 50°54'N 3°30'W
Tivoli 77 H5 Italy 41°58'N 12°45'E
Tizimín 150 G4 Mexico 21°10'N 88°9'W
Tizi Ouzou 96 G8 Algeria 36°44'N 4°6'E
Tlaxcala 150 D4 Mexico 19°17'N 98°16'W
Toamasina 99 L4 Madagascar 18°10'S 49°23'E
Toba, Danau 126 E3 ◎ Sumatra, W Indonesia
Tobago 151 N3 Island NE Trinidad and Tobago
Toba Kākar Range 118 E8 ⛰ NW Pakistan
Tobercurry 58 D10 Ireland 54°4'N 8°44'W
Tobermory 57 C7 Scotland, UK 56°37'N 6°12'W
Tobol'sk 108 F4 Russian Fed. 58°15'N 68°12'E
Tobruk 97 J8 Libya 32°5'N 23°59'E
Tocantins 163 I6 ◈ State Brazil
Tocantins, Rio 163 I7 〰 N Brazil
Tocopilla 161 C6 Chile 22°6'S 70°8'W
Todi 77 H6 Italy 42°47'N 12°25'E
Todmorden 52 G2 England, UK 53°44'N 2°8'W
Todos os Santos, Baía de 163 K5 Bay E Brazil
Togi 125 I5 Japan 37°6'N 136°44'E
Togo 96 F4 ◆ Republic W Africa
Tokaj 85 G5 Hungary 48°8'N 21°25'E
Tokanui 136 B1 New Zealand 46°33'S 169°2'E
Tokar 97 L5 Sudan 18°27'N 37°41'E
Tokat 110 G6 Turkey 40°20'N 36°35'E
Tokelau 128 NZ ◇ Polynesia
Tokmak 117 K8 Kyrgyzstan 42°50'N 75°18'E
Tokoroa 136 E6 New Zealand 38°14'S 175°52'E
Tokushima 125 H3 Japan 34°4'N 134°28'E
Tokyo 125 J4 ● Japan 35°40'N 139°45'E
Toledo 75 H6 Spain 39°52'N 4°2'W
Toledo 147 L6 Ohio, USA 41°40'N 83°33'W
Toledo Bend Reservoir 147 J3 ▣ Louisiana/Texas, SW USA
Toliara 99 K3 Madagascar 23°20'S 43°41'E
Tollerton 55 I4 England, UK 54°5'N 1°20'W
Tollesbury 51 J6 England, UK 51°45'N 0°49'E
Tolmin 83 G4 Slovenia 46°12'N 13°39'E
Tolna 85 E3 Hungary 46°26'N 18°47'E
Tolosa 75 J9 Spain 43°9'N 2°4'W
Toluca 150 D4 Mexico 19°20'N 99°40'W
Tol'yatti 89 G6 Russian Fed. 53°32'N 49°27'E
Tomakomai 125 K8 Japan 42°38'N 141°32'E
Tomar 74 E6 Portugal 39°36'N 8°25'W
Tomaszów Lubelski 84 I8 Poland 50°29'N 23°23'E
Tomaszów Mazowiecki 84 F9 Poland 51°33'N 20°E
Tombigbee River 147 K4 〰 Alabama/Mississippi, S USA
Tombua 98 E5 Angola 15°49'S 11°53'E
Tomé-Açu 163 I7 Brazil 2°25'S 48°9'W
Tomelloso 75 I5 Spain 39°9'N 3°1'W
Tomini, Gulf of 127 I3 Bay Celebes, C Indonesia
Tomintoul 56 G9 Scotland, UK 57°16'N 3°23'W
Tommot 109 J5 Russian Fed. 58°57'N 126°24'E

◆ Country ● Country capital ◇ Dependent territory ○ Dependent territory capital ◈ Administrative region ▲ Mountain ⛰ Mountain range 🌋 Volcano 〰 River ◎ Lake ▣ Reservoir

U

V

Vilhelmina - Xiva 191

na 68 D9 Sweden 64°38'N 16°40'E
162 F5 Brazil 12°40'S 60°8'W
uña 150 D6 Mexico 29°18'N 100°58'W
lla 160 D8 Bolivia 10°21'S 65°25'W
illo 75 I4 Spain 38°7'N 3°5'W
83 H4 Austria 46°36'N 13°49'E
o 76 F3 Italy 39°28'N 8°43'E
ca de los Barros 74 G5 Spain
'N 6°20'W
mosa 150 F3 Mexico 17°56'N 92°50'W
osa 75 K5 Spain 38°31'N 0°14'W
ría 161 D5 Argentina 32°23'S 63°15'W
va de la Serena 74 G5 Spain
'N 5°48'W
va de los Infantes 75 I5 Spain
'N 3°1'W
a 161 E6 Paraguay 25°45'S 56°28'W
encio 160 B11 Colombia 4°9'N 73°38'W
osa 75 G9 Spain 43°29'N 5°26'W
75 K5 Spain 38°39'N 0°52'W
anne 73 I4 France 45°46'N 4°54'E
n-Schwenningen 83 D6 Germany
N 8°27'E
69 H3 ● Lithuania 54°41'N 25°20'E
a 68 G8 Finland 62°2'N 24°30'E
de 71 D6 Belgium 50°56'N 4°25'E
109 J6 NE Russian Fed.
by 68 D5 Sweden 57°40'N 15°50'E
l Mar 161 C5 Chile 33°2'S 71°35'W
75 K6 Spain 40°29'N 0°28'E
es Bay 166 F4 Bay Antarctica
a Range 118 G6 N India
26 G7 Vietnam 18°42'N 105°41'E
ya 89 B4 Ukraine 49°14'N 28°30'E
Massif 166 C5 ▲ Antarctica
hir 111 H5 Turkey 37°13'N 39°32'E
a 58 G9 Ireland 53°50'N 7°5'W
a 147 J8 Minnesota, USA
'N 92°32'W
a 147 M6 ◆ State USA
a Beach 147 M6 Virginia, USA
'N 75°59'W
Islands (US) 151 L4 US ◇ West Indies
ca 86 E8 Croatia 45°49'N 17°25'E
71 F3 Belgium 49°34'N 5°32'E
69 G5 Estonia 58°35'N 23°33'E
D6 Island S Croatia
apatnam 119 I4 India 17°45'N 83°19'E
69 E5 Sweden 57°37'N 18°20'E
nt Melville Sound 144 F6 Sound
west Territories, N Canada
1 F6 Belgium 50°44'N 5°42'E
74 F7 Portugal 40°40'N 7°55'W
Lagoon 84 F12 Lagoon
nd/Russian Fed.
o 77 H5 Italy 42°25'N 12°8'E
109 J4 C Russian Fed.
163 K3 Brazil 20°19'S 40°21'W
da Conquista 163 K5 Brazil
3'S 40°52'W
-Gasteiz 75 I8 Spain 42°51'N 2°40'W
72 E6 France 48°7'N 1°12'W
bsk 89 C6 Belarus 55°11'N 30°10'E
a 77 J1 Italy 36°56'N 14°30'E
agaram 119 I4 India 18°7'N 83°25'E
ingen 70 D9 Netherlands 51°55'N 4°21'E
avkaz 89 F2 Russian Fed. 42°58'N 44°41'E
nir 89 E7 Russian Fed. 56°9'N 40°21'E
ostok 109 L3 Russian Fed.
'N 131°53'E
vedde 70 I12 Netherlands 53°2'N 7°7'E
nd 70 E13 Island Waddeneilanden,
etherlands
n 70 F8 Netherlands 51°42'N 5°14'E
gen 70 C8 Netherlands 51°26'N 3°34'E
86 F4 Albania 40°28'N 19°31'E
bruck 83 G6 Austria 48°1'N 13°38'E
ena, Tanjona 99 K3 Headland
adagascar
73 I4 France 45°22'N 5°35'E
dina 86 F8 Cultural region Serbia and
ntenegro
108 D4 NW Russian Fed.
donsk 89 E4 Russian Fed. 47°35'N 42°3'E
grad 89 F4 Russian Fed. 48°42'N 44°29'E
da 88 E8 Russian Fed. 59°10'N 39°55'E
87 H3 Greece 39°21'N 22°58'E
89 F5 Russian Fed. 52°4'N 47°20'E
Lake 96 F4 SE Ghana
Redonda 163 J3 Brazil 22°31'S 44°5'W
no 77 I5 S Italy
skiy 89 F4 Russian Fed. 48°49'N 44°40'E
70 G10 Netherlands 52°10'N 6°10'E
rrhein 83 E4 SE Switzerland
ta 88 H11 Russian Fed. 67°27'N 64°E
ezh 89 E5 Russian Fed. 51°40'N 39°13'E
ärv 69 H5 SE Estonia
69 H5 Estonia 57°51'N 27°1'E
es 73 J6 NE France
69 A7 Norway 60°38'N 6°25'E
a 68 D7 Sweden 61°21'N 15°35'E
v nad Topl'ou 85 H6 Slovakia
54'N 21°41'E
a 87 H6 Bulgaria 43°13'N 23°34'E
86 F7 Serbia and Montenegro
34'N 19°39'E
86 E7 N Bosnia and Herzegovina
86 G7 Serbia and Montenegro
8'N 21°18'E
n 85 E6 Czech Republic 49°21'N 17°57'E
var 86 F7 Croatia 45°18'N 18°45'E
Tau 126 G5 Vietnam 10°21'N 107°4'E
ka 88 G8 NW Russian Fed.
rg 88 C8 Russian Fed. 60°44'N 28°47'E
wy 48 F11 E Wales, UK

W

96 F4 Ghana 10°7'N 2°28'W
70 F9 S Netherlands
lan 97 I7 Libya 29°10'N 16°8'E
denzee 70 E12 Sea SE North Sea
desdon 50 F7 England, UK 51°50'N 0°58'W
dington 53 I7 England, UK 53°11'N 0°38'W
dington, Mount 144 D2 ▲
tish Columbia, SW Canada
Wadebridge 49 C4 England, UK
50°32'N 4°48'W
Wad Medani 97 K5 Sudan 14°24'N 33°30'E
Wadworth 53 H8 England, UK 53°27'N 1°10'W
Waflia 127 K2 Indonesia 3°10'S 126°5'E
Wagga Wagga 135 J2 New South Wales, Australia 35°11'S 147°22'E
Wagin 134 D3 Western Australia
33°16'S 117°26'E
Wah 118 F9 Pakistan 33°50'N 72°44'E
Wahai 127 K2 Indonesia 2°48'S 129°29'E
Wahiawā 146 F2 Hawai'i, USA 21°30'N 158°1'W
Waiau 136 B2 South Island, New Zealand
Waikabubak 127 I1 Indonesia 9°40'S 119°25'E
Waikaremoana, Lake 136 F6 North Island, New Zealand
Wailuku 146 F2 Hawai'i, USA 20°53'N 156°30'W
Waimate 136 C2 New Zealand 44°44'S 171°3'E
Wainfleet All Saints 53 K7 England, UK
53°6'N 0°13'E
Waiouru 136 E5 New Zealand 39°28'S 175°41'E
Waipara 136 D3 New Zealand 43°4'S 172°45'E
Waipawa 136 E5 New Zealand 39°57'S 176°36'E
Waipukurau 136 E5 New Zealand
40°1'S 176°34'E
Wairoa 136 F5 New Zealand 39°3'S 177°26'E
Wairoa 136 D7 North Island, New Zealand
Waitaki 136 C2 South Island, New Zealand
Waitara 136 D6 New Zealand 39°1'S 174°14'E
Waiuku 136 E7 New Zealand 37°15'S 174°45'E
Wakasa-wan 125 I4 Bay C Japan
Wakatipu, Lake 136 B2 South Island, New Zealand
Wakayama 125 H3 Japan 34°12'N 135°9'E
Wakefield 55 H2 England, UK 53°42'N 1°29'W
Wakefield 55 H2 ◆ Unitary authority England, UK
Wake Island 128 US ◇ Pacific Ocean
Wakkanai 125 K9 Japan 45°25'N 141°39'E
Wałbrzych 84 D8 Poland 50°45'N 16°20'E
Walcourt 71 D5 Belgium 50°16'N 4°26'E
Wałcz 84 D11 Poland 53°17'N 16°29'E
Wales 146 B7 Alaska, USA 65°36'N 168°3'W
Wales 48 F10 ◆ National region, UK
Walgett 135 K4 New South Wales, Australia
30°2'S 148°14'E
Wallasey 52 D8 England, UK 53°26'N 3°9'W
Wallingford 50 E6 England, UK 51°36'N 1°4'W
Wallis and Futuna 128 French ◇ Pacific Ocean
Wallsend 55 H7 England, UK 55°N 1°31'W
Walney, Isle of 54 E4 Island NW England, UK
Walsall 52 F5 England, UK 52°35'N 1°58'W
Walsall 37 ◆ Unitary authority England, UK
Waltham Abbey 51 H6 England, UK
51°42'N 0°0'W
Waltham Forest 37 ◆ London Borough England, UK
Waltham on the Wolds 53 I6 England, UK
52°50'N 0°53'W
Walton-on-the-Naze 51 K7 England, UK
51°51'N 1°15'E
Walvis Bay 98 F3 Namibia 22°59'S 14°34'E
Wanaka 136 B2 New Zealand 44°42'S 169°9'E
Wanaka, Lake 136 B2 South Island, New Zealand
Wandsworth 37 ◆ London Borough England, UK
Wanganui 136 E5 New Zealand 39°56'S 175°2'E
Wangaratta 135 J2 Victoria, Australia
36°22'S 146°17'E
Wanlaweyn 97 M3 Somalia 2°36'N 44°47'E
Wantage 50 D6 England, UK 51°34'N 1°23'W
Wanxian 123 I4 China 30°48'N 108°21'E
Warangal 119 H4 India 18°N 79°35'E
Warboys 53 J5 England, UK 52°25'N 0°11'W
Warburg 82 E9 Germany 51°30'N 9°11'E
Ware 144 D3 British Columbia, Canada
57°26'N 125°41'W
Ware 51 H6 England, UK 51°47'N 0°1'W
Wareham 49 H5 England, UK 50°40'N 2°4'W
Waremme 71 F6 Belgium 50°41'N 5°15'E
Waren 82 G11 Germany 53°32'N 12°42'E
Wark 54 G9 England, UK 55°38'N 2°15'W
Warminster 49 H6 England, UK 51°13'N 2°12'W
Warnemünde 82 G11 Germany 54°10'N 12°3'E
Warrego River 135 J4 New South Wales/Queensland, E Australia
Warren 147 L7 Michigan, USA 42°29'N 83°2'W
Warren 147 L6 Ohio, USA 41°14'N 80°49'W
Warrenpoint 58 H10 Northern Ireland, UK
54°7'N 6°16'W
Warrington 54 F1 England, UK 53°24'N 2°37'W
Warrington 36 ◆ Unitary authority England, UK
Warrnambool 135 I2 Victoria, Australia
38°23'S 142°30'E
Warsaw 84 G9 ● Poland 52°15'N 21°E
Warszawa see Warsaw
Warta 84 F8 W Poland
Warwick 135 L4 Queensland, Australia
28°12'S 152°E
Warwick 52 G4 England, UK 52°17'N 1°34'W
Warwickshire 52 G4 ◆ County England, UK
Washington 55 H6 England, UK
54°54'N 1°31'W
Washington 146 E8 ◆ State USA
Washington DC 147 M6 ● USA
38°54'N 77°2'W
Washington, Mount 147 N8 ▲ New Hampshire, NE USA
Wash, The 53 K6 Inlet E England, UK
Waspam 151 H2 Nicaragua 14°41'N 84°4'W
Waterbeach 53 K4 England, UK 52°15'N 0°11'E
Waterford 59 G5 Ireland 52°15'N 7°8'W
Waterford 59 F5 ◆ County Ireland
Watergrasshill 59 E5 Ireland 52°1'N 8°21'W
Waterlooville 50 E3 England, UK
50°52'N 1°10'W
Watertown 147 I7 South Dakota, USA
44°54'N 97°7'W
Waterville 59 B4 Ireland 51°50'N 10°14'W
Watford 50 G6 England, UK 51°39'N 0°24'W
Wāṭif 115 L4 Oman 18°34'N 56°31'E
Watlington 50 E6 England, UK 51°38'N 1°0'W
Watson 134 G4 South Australia
30°32'S 131°29'E
Watson Lake 144 D4 Yukon Territory, Canada
60°5'N 128°47'W
Watton 53 L5 England, UK 52°34'N 0°44'E
Watts Bar Lake 147 L5 Tennessee, S USA
Wau 97 J4 Sudan 7°43'N 28°1'E
Waukesha 147 K7 Wisconsin, USA
43°1'N 88°14'W
Waveney 53 M5 E England, UK
Wavre 71 E6 Belgium 50°43'N 4°37'E
Wawa 145 H2 Ontario, Canada
47°59'N 84°43'W
Waycross 147 M4 Georgia, USA
31°13'N 82°21'W
Weald, The 51 H4 Plain SE England, UK
Wear 54 G6 N England, UK
Weaverham 52 E8 England, UK 53°15'N 2°36'W
Weddell Sea 166 B6 Sea SW Atlantic Ocean
Weedon Bec 53 H4 England, UK 52°13'N 1°7'W
Week St Mary 49 D5 England, UK
50°44'N 4°30'W
Weener 82 D10 Germany 53°9'N 7°19'E
Weert 71 F7 Netherlands 51°15'N 5°43'E
Weesp 70 E10 Netherlands 52°18'N 5°3'E
Węgorzewo 84 G12 Poland 54°12'N 21°49'E
Weifang 123 K5 China 36°44'N 119°10'E
Weimar 82 F8 Germany 50°59'N 11°20'E
Weissenburg 83 F6 Germany 49°2'N 10°59'E
Weiswampach 71 G4 Luxembourg 50°8'N 6°5'E
Wejherowo 84 E12 Poland 54°36'N 18°12'E
Weldiya 97 L4 Ethiopia 11°45'N 39°39'E
Welkom 99 H2 South Africa 27°59'S 26°44'E
Welland 53 J6 C England, UK
Wellesley Islands 135 I8 Island group Queensland, N Australia
Wellingborough 53 I4 England, UK
52°19'N 0°42'W
Wellington 136 E4 ● New Zealand
41°17'S 174°47'E
Wellington 49 F6 England, UK 50°57'N 3°18'W
Wellingtonbridge 59 G5 Ireland
52°15'N 6°44'W
Wellington, Isla 161 C2 Island S Chile
Wells 49 H6 England, UK 51°13'N 2°39'W
Wells 146 F6 Nevada, USA 41°7'N 114°58'W
Wellsford 136 E7 New Zealand
36°17'S 174°30'E
Wells, Lake 134 E5 Western Australia
Wells-next-the-Sea 53 L7 England, UK
52°58'N 0°48'E
Wels 83 H6 Austria 48°10'N 14°2'E
Welshampton 52 E6 England, UK
52°55'N 2°46'W
Welshpool 48 G10 Wales, UK 52°38'N 3°6'W
Welwyn Garden City 50 G6 England, UK
51°48'N 0°13'W
Wem 52 E6 England, UK 52°52'N 2°43'W
Wemmel 71 D6 Belgium 50°54'N 4°18'E
Wemyss Bay 57 E5 Scotland, UK
55°54'N 4°50'W
Wendover 50 F6 England, UK 51°46'N 0°42'W
Wenquan 122 F4 China 33°16'N 91°44'E
Wenzhou 123 K3 China 28°2'N 120°36'E
Weobley 52 D4 England, UK 52°9'N 2°50'W
Werkendam 70 E9 Netherlands 51°48'N 4°54'E
Weser 82 E10 NW Germany
Wessel Islands 135 I9 Island group Northern Territory, N Australia
West Bank 110 B4 Disputed region West Bank
West Bengal 119 J6 ◆ State India
West Berkshire 50 E5 ◆ Unitary authority England, UK
West Bromwich 52 F5 England, UK
52°29'N 1°59'W
West Burra 56 I11 Island NE Scotland, UK
Westbury 52 D6 England, UK 52°41'N 3°W
West Dean 49 I6 England, UK 51°3'N 1°42'W
West Dunbartonshire 36 ◆ Unitary authority Scotland, UK
Westerland 82 E12 Germany 54°54'N 8°19'E
Western Australia 134 D4 ◆ State Australia
Western Desert 91 Desert C Egypt
Western Dvina 69 H4 W Europe
Western Ghats 118 F4 SW India
Western Isles 36 ◆ Unitary authority Scotland, UK
Western Sahara 96 D6 Disputed ◇ Africa
West Falkland 161 E2 Island W Falkland Islands
West Felton 52 D6 England, UK
52°51'N 2°59'W
West Frisian Islands 70 F13 Island group N Netherlands
West Hoathly 51 H4 England, UK 51°5'N 0°5'W
West Kirby 52 D8 England, UK 53°23'N 3°19'W
West Linton 57 G5 Scotland, UK
55°45'N 3°20'W
West Looe 49 D4 England, UK 50°21'N 4°27'W
West Lothian 36 ◆ Unitary authority Scotland, UK
West Lulworth 49 H5 England, UK
50°38'N 2°11'W
Westmeath 58 F9 ◆ County Ireland
West Mersea 51 J6 England, UK 51°46'N 0°53'E
Westminster, City of 37 ◆ London Borough England, UK
Weston-super-Mare 49 G7 England, UK
51°21'N 2°59'W
West Palm Beach 147 M3 Florida, USA
26°43'N 80°3'W
Westport 58 C9 Ireland 53°48'N 9°32'W
Westport 136 C4 New Zealand
41°46'S 171°37'E
Westray 56 G14 Island NE Scotland, UK
West Sussex 50 F3 ◆ County England, UK
West-Terschelling 70 F13 Netherlands
53°23'N 5°15'E
West Virginia 147 L6 ◆ State USA
Wetar, Pulau 127 K1 Island Kepulauan Damar, E Indonesia
Wetherby 55 H3 England, UK 53°55'N 1°22'W
Wetzlar 82 D8 Germany 50°33'N 8°30'E
Wevok 146 B7 Alaska, USA 68°52'N 166°5'W
Wexford 59 G6 Ireland 52°21'N 6°31'W
Wexford 59 G6 ◆ County Ireland
Wexford Bay 59 H6 Bay SE Ireland
Weyburn 144 F2 Saskatchewan, Canada
49°39'N 103°51'W
Weymouth 49 H5 England, UK 50°36'N 2°28'W
Wezep 70 G10 Netherlands 52°28'N 6°E
Whakatane 136 F6 New Zealand 37°58'S 177°E
Whale Cove 144 G4 Northwest Territories, Canada 62°14'N 92°10'W
Whalsay 56 I12 Island NE Scotland, UK
Whangarei 136 D7 New Zealand
35°44'S 174°18'E
Wharfe 54 G4 N England, UK
Whataroa 136 C3 New Zealand
43°17'S 170°20'E
Wheatley 50 E6 England, UK 51°43'N 1°11'W
Wheatley Hill 55 H6 England, UK
54°45'N 1°25'W
Whernside 54 F4 ▲ N England, UK
Whiddon Down 49 E5 England, UK
50°42'N 3°54'W
Whitby 55 J5 England, UK 54°29'N 0°37'W
Whitchurch 50 F7 England, UK 51°52'N 0°56'W
Whitchurch 50 E4 England, UK 51°14'N 1°28'W
Whitchurch 52 E7 England, UK 52°58'N 2°45'W
Whitchurch 52 E3 England, UK 51°52'N 2°44'W
Whitehaven 54 D5 England, UK
54°33'N 3°35'W
Whitehead 58 H11 Northern Ireland, UK
54°46'N 5°42'W
Whitehorse 144 C4 Yukon Territory, Canada
60°41'N 135°8'W
White Nile 97 K4 SE Sudan
Whites Town 58 H10 Ireland 53°58'N 6°9'W
White Volta 96 F4 Burkina/Ghana
Whitfield 51 K4 England, UK 51°8'N 1°11'E
Whithorn 57 E2 Scotland, UK 54°44'N 4°26'W
Whitianga 136 E7 New Zealand
36°50'S 175°42'E
Whitland 48 D8 Wales, UK 51°49'N 4°42'W
Whitley Bay 55 H7 England, UK 55°3'N 1°22'W
Whitstable 51 J5 England, UK 51°21'N 0°52'E
Whitsunday Group 135 K6 Island group Queensland, E Australia
Whittington 52 D6 England, UK
52°53'N 2°57'W
Whittlesey 53 J5 England, UK 52°33'N 0°5'W
Whyalla 135 H3 South Australia 33°4'S 137°34'E
Wichita 147 I5 Kansas, USA 37°42'N 97°20'W
Wichita Falls 147 I4 Texas, USA
33°55'N 98°30'W
Wick 56 G12 Scotland, UK 58°26'N 3°6'W
Wickford 51 J6 England, UK 51°36'N 0°30'E
Wickhambrook 53 K4 England, UK
52°10'N 0°32'E
Wickham Market 53 M4 England, UK
52°10'N 1°19'E
Wicklow 59 H7 Ireland 52°59'N 6°3'W
Wicklow 59 H7 ◆ County Ireland
Wicklow Mountains 59 H7 E Ireland
Widdrington 55 H8 England, UK
55°15'N 1°36'W
Widnes 54 F1 England, UK 53°22'N 2°44'W
Wieliczka 85 F7 Poland 50°N 20°2'E
Wieluń 84 E8 Poland 51°14'N 18°33'E
Wien see Vienna
Wiener Neustadt 83 I5 Austria 47°49'N 16°8'E
Wierden 70 H10 Netherlands 52°22'N 6°35'E
Wiesbaden 82 D8 Germany 50°6'N 8°14'E
Wigan 54 F2 England, UK 53°33'N 2°38'W
Wigan 36 ◆ Unitary authority England, UK
Wigmore 52 D4 England, UK 52°19'N 2°53'W
Wigston 53 H5 England, UK 52°34'N 1°4'W
Wigton 54 E6 England, UK 54°50'N 3°15'W
Wigtown 57 E3 Scotland, UK 54°53'N 4°27'W
Wigtown Bay 57 F2 Bay SW Scotland, UK
Wijchen 70 F9 Netherlands 51°48'N 5°44'E
Wijk bij Duurstede 70 F9 Netherlands
51°58'N 5°21'E
Wilberfoss 55 I3 England, UK 53°58'N 0°57'W
Wilcannia 135 J3 New South Wales, Australia
31°34'S 143°23'E
Wilhelmshaven 82 D11 Germany
53°31'N 8°7'E
Wilkes Land 166 F4 Physical region Antarctica
Willebroek 71 D7 Belgium 51°4'N 4°22'E
Willemstad 151 K2 ○ Netherlands Antilles
12°7'N 68°54'W
Willington 55 H6 England, UK 54°44'N 1°44'W
Williton 49 F6 England, UK 51°8'N 3°20'W
Wilmington 147 M6 Delaware, USA
39°45'N 75°33'W
Wilmslow 52 F8 England, UK 53°19'N 2°12'W
Wilrijk 71 D7 Belgium 51°11'N 4°25'E
Wilton 49 I6 England, UK 51°5'N 1°53'W
Wiltshire 49 I7 ◆ County England, UK
Wimborne Minster 49 I5 England, UK
50°48'N 2°W
Wincanton 49 H6 England, UK 51°2'N 2°26'W
Winchelsea 51 I3 England, UK 50°54'N 0°41'E
Winchester 50 E4 England, UK 51°4'N 1°19'W
Windermere 54 E5 England, UK
54°24'N 2°54'W
Windermere 54 E5 NW England, UK
Windhoek 98 F3 ● Namibia 22°34'S 17°6'E
Windorah 135 J5 Queensland, Australia
25°25'S 142°41'E
Windsor 145 I1 Ontario, Canada 42°18'N 83°W
Windsor 50 F5 England, UK 51°29'N 0°39'W
Windsor and Maidenhead 37 ◆ Unitary authority England, UK
Windward Islands 151 N3 Island group E West Indies
Windward Passage 151 J4 Channel Cuba/Haiti
Winisk 145 H3 Ontario, S Canada
Winnebago, Lake 147 K7 Wisconsin, N USA
Winnemucca 146 E6 Nevada, USA
40°59'N 117°44'W
Winnipeg 144 G2 Manitoba, Canada
49°53'N 97°10'W
Winschoten 70 I12 Netherlands 53°9'N 7°3'E
Winsen 82 F10 Germany 53°22'N 10°13'E
Winsham 49 G5 England, UK 50°51'N 2°54'W
Winslow 50 F7 England, UK 51°56'N 0°54'W
Winston Salem 147 M5 North Carolina, USA
36°6'N 80°15'W
Winterbourne Abbas 49 H5 England, UK
50°42'N 2°33'W
Winteringham 53 I9 England, UK
53°41'N 0°46'W
Winterswijk 70 H9 Netherlands 51°58'N 6°44'E
Winterthur 83 D5 Switzerland 47°30'N 8°43'E
Winterton-on-Sea 53 N6 England, UK
52°43'N 1°41'E
Winton 135 J6 Queensland, Australia
22°22'S 143°4'E
Winton 136 B1 New Zealand 46°8'S 168°20'E
Wirksworth 52 G7 England, UK 53°4'N 1°42'W
Wirral 36 ◆ Unitary authority England, UK
Wisbech 53 K6 England, UK 52°39'N 0°8'E
Wisconsin 147 J7 ◆ State USA
Wismar 82 F11 Germany 53°54'N 11°28'E
Wissey 53 K5 E England, UK
Witham 51 I6 England, UK 51°47'N 0°38'E
Witham 53 J7 E England, UK
Withernsea 55 K2 England, UK 53°46'N 0°1'W
Withington 48 I8 England, UK 51°50'N 2°3'W
Witney 50 D6 England, UK 51°47'N 1°30'W
Wittenberge 82 F10 Germany 52°59'N 11°45'E
Wittlich 83 C7 Germany 49°59'N 6°54'E
Wittstock 82 G10 Germany 53°10'N 12°29'E
Wivenhoe 51 J7 England, UK 51°51'N 0°50'E
Wiżajny 84 H12 Poland 54°22'N 22°51'E
Władysławowo 84 E12 Poland 54°48'N 18°25'E
Włocławek 84 F10 Poland 52°39'N 19°3'E
Włodawa 84 I9 Poland 51°33'N 23°31'E
Wlotzkasbaken 98 F3 Namibia 22°26'S 14°30'E
Wodonga 135 J2 Victoria, Australia
36°11'S 146°55'E
Wodzisław Śląski 85 E7 Poland
49°59'N 18°27'E
Woking 50 F5 England, UK 51°20'N 0°34'W
Wokingham 50 F5 England, UK 51°24'N 1°0'W
Wokingham 37 ◆ Unitary authority England, UK
Wolds, The 53 J8 Hill range E England, UK
Wolfsberg 83 H5 Austria 46°50'N 14°50'E
Wolfsburg 82 F10 Germany 52°25'N 10°47'E
Wolgast 82 G11 Germany 54°4'N 13°47'E
Wolin 84 C11 Poland 53°52'N 14°35'E
Wollaston Lake 144 F3 Saskatchewan, Canada
58°5'N 103°38'W
Wollongong 135 K2 New South Wales, Australia
34°25'S 150°52'E
Wolsingham 54 G6 England, UK
54°43'N 1°55'W
Wolsztyn 84 D9 Poland 52°7'N 16°7'E
Wolvega 70 G12 Netherlands 52°53'N 6°E
Wolverhampton 52 F5 England, UK
52°36'N 2°8'W
Wolverhampton 37 ◆ Unitary authority England, UK
Wolviston 55 I5 England, UK 54°37'N 1°25'W
Wonju 124 E5 South Korea 37°21'N 127°57'E
Wonsan 124 E6 North Korea 39°11'N 127°21'E
Woodbridge 53 M4 England, UK 52°4'N 1°19'E
Woodenbridge 59 H7 Ireland 52°49'N 6°13'W
Woods, Lake of the 144 G2 Canada/USA
Woodstock 50 E7 England, UK 51°51'N 1°27'W
Woodville 136 E5 New Zealand
40°22'S 175°59'E
Woofferton 52 E4 England, UK
52°19'N 2°43'W
Wookey 49 G6 England, UK 51°12'N 2°48'W
Woolacombe 49 E6 England, UK
51°10'N 4°20'W
Wooler 54 G9 England, UK 55°33'N 2°W
Wootton 50 E7 England, UK 51°52'N 1°21'W
Wootton Bassett 49 I7 England, UK
51°31'N 1°58'W
Worcester 52 F4 England, UK 52°11'N 2°13'W
Worcester 98 G1 South Africa 33°41'S 19°22'E
Worcestershire 52 F4 ◆ County England, UK
Workington 54 D6 England, UK
54°39'N 3°33'W
Worksop 53 H8 England, UK 53°18'N 1°4'W
Worms 83 D7 Germany 49°38'N 8°22'E
Worthing 50 G3 England, UK 50°48'N 0°23'W
Worthington 147 I7 Minnesota, USA
43°37'N 95°37'W
Woudrichem 70 E9 Netherlands 51°49'N 5°E
Wragby 53 J8 England, UK 53°18'N 0°23'W
Wrangle 53 J7 England, UK 53°2'N 0°1'E
Wrath, Cape 56 E12 Headland N Scotland, UK
Wrentham 53 M5 England, UK 52°23'N 1°33'E
Wrexham 48 G12 Wales, UK 53°3'N 3°W
Wrexham 48 G12 ◆ Unitary authority Wales, UK
Wrocław 84 D8 Poland 51°7'N 17°1'E
Wroxham 53 M6 England, UK 52°41'N 1°23'E
Września 84 E10 Poland 52°19'N 17°34'E
Wuhai 123 H6 China 39°40'N 106°48'E
Wuhan 123 J4 China 30°35'N 114°19'E
Wuhu 123 K4 China 31°23'N 118°25'E
Wuliang Shan 122 G2 SW China
Wuppertal 82 D9 Germany 51°16'N 7°12'E
Würzburg 83 E7 Germany 49°48'N 9°56'E
Wuxi 123 K4 China 31°35'N 120°19'E
Wye 51 J4 England, UK 51°11'N 0°55'E
Wye 48 F10 England/Wales, UK
Wymondham 53 L5 England, UK
52°29'N 1°10'E
Wyndham 134 F8 Western Australia
15°28'S 128°8'E
Wyoming 146 G7 ◆ State USA
Wyre 54 E3 NW England, UK
Wyszków 84 G10 Poland 52°36'N 21°28'E

X

Xaafuun, Raas 97 N4 Headland NE Somalia
Xacmaz 111 K7 Azerbaijan 41°26'N 48°47'E
Xai-Xai 99 I3 Mozambique 25°1'S 33°37'E
Xalapa 150 E4 Mexico 19°32'N 92°58'W
Xankandi 111 K6 Azerbaijan 39°50'N 46°44'E
Xanthi 87 I5 Greece 41°9'N 24°54'E
Xátiva 75 K5 Spain 39°N 0°32'W
Xiamen 123 K2 China 24°28'N 118°5'E
Xi'an 123 I5 China 34°16'N 108°54'E
Xiangkhoang, Plateau de 126 F7 Plateau N Laos
Xiangtan 123 J3 China 27°53'N 112°55'E
Xiao Hinggan Ling 123 K8 NE China
Xichang 122 G3 China 27°52'N 102°16'E
Xigazê 122 E4 China 29°18'N 88°50'E
Xi Jiang 103 S China
Xilinhot 123 J7 China 43°58'N 116°7'E
Xingu, Rio 163 H6 C Brazil
Xining 122 G5 China 36°37'N 101°46'E
Xinxiang 123 J5 China 35°13'N 113°48'E
Xinyang 123 J4 China 32°9'N 114°4'E
Xinzo de Limia 74 F8 Spain 42°5'N 7°45'W
Xique-Xique 163 J5 Brazil 10°47'S 42°44'W
Xiva 116 G7 Uzbekistan 41°22'N 60°22'E

◆ Country ● Country capital ◇ Dependent territory ○ Dependent territory capital ◆ Administrative region ▲ Mountain ▲ Mountain range Volcano River Lake Reservoir

◆ Country ● Country capital ◇ Dependent territory ○ Dependent territory capital ◆ Administrative region ▲ Mountain ▲▲ Mountain range ⊻ Volcano ↓ River ⊘ Lake ▨ Reservoir